THE WORLD OF
Business

A SELECTED LIBRARY OF THE LITERATURE OF BUSINESS FROM THE ACCOUNTING CODE OF HAMMURABI TO THE 20TH-CENTURY "ADMINISTRATOR'S PRAYER"

EDITED WITH COMMENTARIES AND NOTES BY THREE MEMBERS OF THE FACULTY OF THE

HARVARD
BUSINESS SCHOOL

EDWARD C. BURSK
Editor of the *Harvard Business Review*

DONALD T. CLARK
Librarian of the Baker Library

RALPH W. HIDY
Isidor Straus Professor of Business History

VOLUME IV

SIMON AND SCHUSTER · NEW YORK · 1962

LIBRARY OF CONGRESS CATALOG CARD NUMBER: 62-14278
MANUFACTURED IN THE UNITED STATES OF AMERICA
BY THE RAND McNALLY COMPANY, CHICAGO, ILL.

CONTENTS

VOLUME FOUR

III. BUSINESS AND SOCIETY (*continued*)

THE PHILOSOPHY OF BUSINESS

They Will Maintain the State of the World   1938
from the Apocrypha

A Philosopher Begrudges a Place to Commerce   1939
Plato

A Probe of the Art of Wealth-Getting   1944
Aristotle

Economic Principles in Ancient China—as Confucius Saith   1948
Chen Huan-chang

A Follower of Confucius Anticipates the Law of Supply and
Demand   1953
Ssū-ma Chien

Jost Amman's *Allegory of Trade*—or, The World of Business
in the Sixteenth Century   1954
Donald T. Clark

Breaking the Bonds of Tradition   1973
Robert L. Heilbroner

Prophetic Title: The Wealth of Nations   1981
Adam Smith

The Views of an Engineer Ahead of His Time   1988
Oliver Evans

Commerce and Free Government Re-enforce Each Other   1989
Philip Hone

An Angry Genius on Capital   1993
Karl Marx

A Sociologist Criticizes Business   2003
Thorstein B. Veblen

The Beginnings of My Political Activity Were in Economics   2011
Adolf Hitler

Constructive Conflict, or How to Deal With Differences in
Business Administration   2013
Mary Parker Follett

[v]

Lady Chatterley Gets a Lecture   2027
    D. H. Lawrence

What Kind of an Animal Is This Here Capitalism?   2033
    David M. Potter

Business Needs Foresight in a Changing World   2045
    Alfred North Whitehead

The Economy of Abundance   2055
    Stuart Chase

An Inveterate Dissenter Supports Capitalism   2065
    H. L. Mencken

The Nature of Executive Responsibility, and the Essence of
   Leadership   2068
    Chester Barnard

Business Leadership and a Creative Society   2074
    Abram T. Collier

American Business and the Soviet Economic Approach   2091
    Henry Cabot Lodge and Nikita Khrushchev

American Capitalism: Trial Balance   2099
    Max Lerner

RELIGION AND BUSINESS

A Hymn for Success in Trade and Banking   2111
    from the Vedas

Go to the Ant, Thou Sluggard . . .   2113
    from the Bible

Religion Enters Every Sphere of Life   2114
    from the Talmud and *The Code of Maimonides*

Those Who Expend Their Wealth in God's Way   2117
    from the Koran

A Churchman Discourses on Profit and Interest   2119
    St. Thomas Aquinas

The Concept of the Just Price   2125
    Raymond de Roover

Every Vocation Is a Post Assigned by the Lord   2138
    John Calvin

He Cannot Be a Good Draper Which Is Not First a Good Man   2139
    William Scott and Sylvia L. Thrupp

Instructions to the Jesuit Brothers Who Manage Haciendas   2160
    Donald B. Campbell

A Seventeenth-Century Merchant Who Still Believed in Profit   2162
    John Winthrop and Robert Keayne

Dress and Undress Thy Soul, According to a 1782 Book on the
   Pleasant Art of Money-Catching   2170
    N. H., Merchant

Trade Knows No Parties, No Politic, No Religious Interests   2171
    Daniel Defoe

Business Virtues Are Religious Virtues in *Poor Richard's Almanac*   2172
    Benjamin Franklin

The Russians Have Something to Say on Business Virtue, Too   2183
    Catherine II and Kosma Petrovich Prutkov

The Rabbit and the Goat   2184
    from *Life*

A Prominent Man in His Church—Asleep or Awake   2185
    Carlsbad

A Vatican View of the Condition of the Working Class   2186
    Pope Leo XIII

The Significance of the Jewish Religion in Economic Life   2197
    Werner Sombart

Religion Is Going to the Dogs—for Businessmen, at Least   2199
    Thorstein B. Veblen

Religious Foundations of Economic Progress   2200
    Kenneth E. Boulding

Power and Morality in a Business Society   2213
    Sylvia Kopald Selekman and Benjamin M. Selekman

The Unfree Economic Position of Modern Man   2220
    Albert Schweitzer

The Business System Is Not Inconsistent With a Good World   2224
    Edward Duff, S.J., and the World Council of Churches

"Skyhooks"—With Special Implications for Monday Through Friday   2225
    O. A. Ohmann

An Administrator's Prayer   2255
    Robert L. Katz

BUSINESS AND THE STATE

At First Commerce Was Not Looked Upon as a Private Matter   2258
    Charles LeTourneau

The Seven Fat Kine and the Seven Lean Kine   2263
    from the Bible

The Emperor Augustus Suppresses Invention   2266
    Arnold J. Toynbee

Usury in Ancient Rome   2273
    Tacitus

The Emperor Hadrian Intervenes in Business   2275
    Marguerite Yourcenar

A Royal Lawmaker Sets a Business Code   2276
   Emperor Justinian I
The State and the Hundred Artisans   2279
   from the *Official System of Chou*
The Scottish Government Promotes Industrial Activity   2280
   R. W. Cochran-Patrick
Government Shouldn't Meddle with Business   2285
   Benjamin Franklin
Prospectus for a Government Finance Corporation   2286
   Alexander Hamilton
The Bitter Debate on Free Trade   2293
   Horace Greeley and S. G. Arnold
The Candlemakers Demand Protection From the Sun's Com-
petition   2296
   Frédéric Bastiat
Locking Horns—or Is It Gears?—with the British Govern-
ment   2301
   Charles Babbage
A British Historian on American Industry   2312
   Lord Macaulay
A Businessman Pleads for Social Legislation in 1867   2315
   Abram S. Hewitt
An 1870 Debate on the Role of Businessmen in Government 2327
   Hamilton A. Hill, and from *The Nation*
An Early Muckraker Interprets American Business Behavior
in the 1890s   2346
   Henry Demarest Lloyd
How a Wall Street Financier Became a Park Bench Statesman 2357
   Bernard Baruch
Men Against Silver, and Silver Against the Country   2365
   John F. Kennedy
Twilight of the Giants, and Dawn of Individuals   2369
   Franklin D. Roosevelt
Defender of the Faith: Orphan Annie   2376
   James A. Kehl
Across the World the Consumer Is King—or Queen   2385
   Donald K. David

THE BUSINESSMAN'S OWN VIEWS

Noble Blood and Business   2390
   Wyndham Beawes
George Washington, the Businessman   2392
   Curtis P. Nettels

This Affluent Society—1784   2397
  Benjamin Franklin
Don't Be Afraid to Stoop—and Pick Up a Pin   2401
  from *Hunt's Merchants' Magazine*
The Trust: Feudalism or Civilization?   2402
  from the *U. S. Investor*, and Charles R. Flint
A Steel Man Prophesies the Future of the World   2413
  Andrew Carnegie
Combinations: Their Uses and Abuses   2424
  S. C. T. Dodd
A Famous Oilman's Concept of the American Businessman 2437
  John D. Rockefeller
The Romance of Commerce   2440
  Harry Gordon Selfridge
While He Is Piling Dung   2443
  Edward C. Bursk
A Creed for Free Enterprise   2445
  Clarence B. Randall
Choosing a Chief Executive   2448
  Cameron Hawley
What Corporation Presidents Think About at Night   2462
  John L. McCaffrey
Du Pont's President—the Uncommon Man   2469
  Crawford H. Greenewalt
Debate at Wickersham Mills   2473
  Abram T. Collier

FUN AND SATIRE

Poverty Pleads That She Is the Mother of Industry   2495
  Aristophanes
Business Is a Little Dull in Hell   2502
  Lucian
An Economical Project   2503
  Benjamin Franklin
Complaint of a Merchant's Wife   2507
  from *Hunt's Merchants' Magazine*
The Romance of the Markets   2508
  from *Punch*
The Hodja's Donkey Goes to Market   2512
  Alice Geer Kelsey
The Shrewd Tin Peddler Who Wouldn't Be Outsmarted   2515
  Hugh Peters
Laughing at Businessmen in the 1880s   2517
  Brown and Metcalfe

[x] THE WORLD OF BUSINESS

The Businessman in American Folklore   2521
    Kenneth Wiggins Porter
John Henry   2537
    Anonymous
A Horse-Trading Country Banker   2541
    Edward Noyes Westcott
The Romance of the Busy Broker   2551
    O. Henry
Babbitt   2555
    Sinclair Lewis
Tom Lachford, Promoter   2561
    Stephen Leacock
Marco Millions   2569
    Eugene O'Neill
I'm a Natural-Born Salesman   2573
    William Hazlett Upson
The Little Prince from Asteroid B-612 Interviews the
  Businessman   2587
    Antoine de Saint-Exupéry
Business in Ireland—or Is It Leprechauns?   2590
    Lord Dunsany
One Minute Please!   2596
    Robert Benchley
As Others Have Seen Us   2599
    George S. Gibb

EPILOGUE

The Managers   2621
    W. H. Auden

Sources of Illustrations   2625
Index   2627

PART THREE

BUSINESS
AND SOCIETY

(Continued)

The Philosophy
of Business

"All men seek one goal: success or happiness. The only way to achieve true success is to express yourself completely in service to society. First, have a definite, clear, practical ideal—a goal, an objective. Second, have the necessary means to achieve your ends—wisdom, money, materials, and methods. Third, adjust your means to that end."

—Aristotle (384–322 B.C.)

As we continue the examination of business as an institution rather than simply as a complex of functions or a series of actions, we come inevitably to the philosophic question of what makes it what it is, what gives it its particular entity, or life. Here the term *philosophy* is used loosely (or, rather, comprehensively) to cover all thoughtful attempts to understand what makes the world tick—including business, as one of the important institutions of the world.

We start with the Bible, followed by some ancient philosophers looking at the economic aspects of human activity and trying to fit these into their metaphysical system or their ideal world (Plato, Aristotle, Confucius).

Then, almost 2000 years later—after the Middle Ages, during which philosophical development was mostly centered in the church—we find philosophy again concerned with matters economic. Only, this time the economic approach seems primary, and philosophy is made to fit human activity, rather than vice versa. Capitalism becomes the focus, or the target (Adam Smith and Karl Marx, for example).

Thenceforward, the philosophical view of business takes two divergent forms. One is preoccupation with the effect of the business spirit *on society* (Veblen, Adolf Hitler, D. H. Lawrence—a weirdly matched trio, to say the least). The other is concern with the dynamics of life *within the business unit* (Follett, Whitehead, Drucker, etc.).

Throughout, the various trends overlap and even conflict. But note

[1937]

that as we move up to today, the philosophy of business does tend to move closer and closer to the scene of operations—represented by such men as Oliver Evans, who ran a flour mill; Frederick Taylor, who worked with steel; Chester Barnard, telephone company executive; Abram Collier, vice president of a life insurance company. And even the professors we cite are likely to be from the faculties of graduate schools of *business.* Which brings us, with some backsliding here and there, smack into the present.

THEY WILL MAINTAIN THE STATE
OF THE WORLD

FROM THE APOCRYPHA

[Ecclesiasticus, 38:24–34, the Apocrypha.]

Here, from an Apocryphal book of the Bible, in the third century B.C., comes this remarkable statement—remarkable because it foreshadowed the fact that for several thousand years philosophy (even philosophy *about* business) was to be the product of nonbusinessmen; and also because it sensed, indeed felt, that the work of the world is important to society, even if its practitioners do not sit in high places.

THE WISDOM of a learned man cometh by opportunity of leisure: and he that hath little business shall become wise.

How can he get wisdom that holdeth the plough, and that glorieth in the goad, that driveth oxen, and is occupied in their labours, and whose talk is of bullocks?

He giveth his mind to make furrows; and is diligent to give the kine fodder.

So every carpenter and workmaster, that laboureth night and day: and they that cut and grave seals, and are diligent to make great variety, and give themselves to counterfeit imagery, and watch to finish a work:

The smith also sitting by the anvil, and considering the iron work, the vapor of the fire wasteth his flesh, and he fighteth with the heart of the furnace: the noise of the hammer and the anvil is ever in his ears, and his eyes look still upon the pattern of the thing that he maketh; he setteth his mind to finish his work, and watcheth to polish it perfectly:

So doth the potter sitting at his work, and turning the wheel about with his feet, who is always carefully set at his work, and maketh all his work by number;

He fashioneth the clay with his arms, and boweth down his strength before his feet; he applieth himself to lead it over; and he is diligent to make clean the furnace:

All these trust to their hands: and every one is wise in his work.

Without these cannot a city be inhabited: and they shall not dwell where they will, nor go up and down:

They shall not be sought for in public counsel, nor sit high in the congregation: they shall not sit on the judges' seat, nor understand the sentence of judgment: they cannot declare justice and judgment; and they shall not be found where parables are spoken.

But they will maintain the state of the world, and their prayer is in the work of their craft.

A PHILOSOPHER BEGRUDGES A PLACE TO COMMERCE

PLATO

[Plato, *The Republic,* trans. by B. Jowett, Clarendon Press, Oxford, 1881, book II, pp. 47–53.]

In the fifth century B.C., Plato, the Greek philosopher, wrote a book setting forth his concept of the ideal state—*The Republic.* In accordance with the classical tastes of his day, he looked down on commerce and industry as a debasing occupation. But he saw that it was necessary, and by a magnificent feat of imagination he reconstructed the beginnings of economic organization and anticipated our modern understanding of the advantages of specialization.

By an interesting twist, too, he shows the process of economic growth leading inevitably to war. This excerpt, in which Socrates is describing a discussion in which he took part, is not to be taken as history but as a look into a great philosopher's mind. For an even blunter view of certain aspects of selling held by Plato, see Marketing Dilemma section in Volume I.

A STATE, I said, arises, as I conceive, out of the needs of mankind; no one is self-sufficing, but all of us have many wants. Can any other origin of a state be imagined?

There can be no other.

Then, as we have many wants, and many persons are needed to

supply them, one takes a helper for one purpose and another for another; and when these partners and helpers are gathered together in one habitation the body of inhabitants is termed a state.

True, he said.

And they exchange with one another, and one gives, and another receives, under the idea that the exchange will be for their good.

Very true.

Then, I said, let us begin and create in idea a state; and yet the true creator is necessity, who is the mother of our invention.

Of course, he replied.

Now the first and greatest of necessities is food, which is the condition of life and existence.

Certainly.

The second is a dwelling, and the third clothing and the like.

True.

And now let us see how our city will be able to supply this great demand: We may suppose that one man is a husbandman, another a builder, some one else a weaver—shall we add to them a shoemaker, or perhaps some other purveyor to our bodily wants?

Quite right.

The barest notion of a state must include four or five men.

Clearly.

And how will they proceed? Will each bring the result of his labors into a common stock?—the individual husbandman, for example, producing for four and laboring four times as long and as much as he need in the provision of food with which he supplies others as well as himself; or will he have nothing to do with others and not be at the trouble of producing for them, but provide for himself alone a fourth of the food in a fourth of the time, and in the remaining three-fourths of his time be employed in making a house or a coat or a pair of shoes, having no partnership with others, but supplying himself all his own wants?

Adeimantus thought that he should aim at producing food only and not at producing everything.

Probably, I replied, that would be the better way; and when I hear you say this, I am myself reminded that we are not all alike; there are diversities of natures among us which are adapted to different occupations.

Very true.

And will you have a work better done when the workman has many occupations, or when he has only one?

When he has only one.

Further, there can be no doubt that a work is spoiled when not done at the right time?

No doubt.

For business is not disposed to wait until the doer of the business is at leisure; but the doer must follow up what he is doing, and make the business his first object.

He must.

And if so, we must infer that all things are produced more plentifully and· easily and of a better quality when one man does one thing which is natural to him, and does it at the right time, and leaves other things.

Undoubtedly.

Then more than our citizens will be required; for the husbandman will not make his own plough or mattock, or other implements of agriculture, if they are to be good for anything. Neither will the builder make his tools—and he too needs many; and in like manner the weaver and shoemaker.

True.

Then carpenters, and smiths, and many other artisans, will be sharers in our little state, which is already beginning to grow?

True.

Yet even if we add neatherds, shepherds, and other herdsmen, in order that our husbandmen may have oxen to plough with, and builders as well as husbandmen may have draught cattle, and curriers and weavers fleeces and hides, still our state will not be very large.

That is true; yet neither will it be a very small state which contains all these.

Then, again, there is the situation of the city—to find a place where nothing need be imported is well-nigh impossible.

Impossible.

Then there must be another class of citizens who will bring the required supply from another city?

There must.

But if the trader goes empty-handed, having nothing which they require who would supply his need, he will come back empty-handed.

That is certain.

And therefore what they produce at home must be not only enough for themselves, but such both in quantity and quality as to accommodate those from whom their wants are supplied.

Very true.

Then more husbandmen and more artisans will be required?

They will.

Not to mention the importers and exporters, who are called merchants?

Yes.

Then we shall want merchants?

We shall.

And if merchandise is to be carried over the sea, skillful sailors will also be needed, and in considerable numbers?

Yes, in considerable numbers.

Then, again within the city, how will they exchange their productions? To secure such an exchange was, as you will remember, one of our principal objects when we formed them into a society and constituted a state.

Clearly they will buy and sell.

Then they will need a market place, and a money token for purposes of exchange.

Certainly.

Suppose now that a husbandman, or an artisan, brings some production to market, and he comes at a time when there is no one to exchange with him; is he to leave his calling and sit idle in the market place?

Not at all; he will find people there who, seeing the want, undertake the office of salesmen. In well-ordered states they are commonly those who are the weakest in bodily strength, and therefore of little use for any other purpose; their duty is to be in the market, and to give money in exchange for goods to those who desire to sell and to take money from those who desire to buy.

This want, then, creates a class of retail traders in our state. Is not *retailer* the term which is applied to those who sit in the market place engaged in buying and selling, while those who wander from one city to another are called merchants?

Yes, he said.

And there is another class of servants, who are intellectually hardly on the level of companionship; still they have plenty of bodily strength for labor, which accordingly they sell, and are called, if I do not mistake, hirelings, hire being the name which is given to the price of their labor.

True.

Then hirelings will help to make up our population?

Yes.

And now, Adeimantus, is our state matured and perfected?

I think so.

Where, then is justice, and where is injustice, and in what part of the state did they spring up?

Probably in the dealings of these citizens with one another. I can not imagine that they are more likely to be found anywhere else.

I dare say that you are right in your suggestion, I said; we had better think the matter out, and not shrink from the inquiry.

Let us then consider, first of all, what will be their way of life, now that we have thus established them. Will they not produce corn, and wine, and clothes, and shoes, and build houses for themselves?

And when they are housed, they will work, in summer, commonly, stripped and barefoot, but in winter substantially clothed and shod. They will feed on barley meal and flour of wheat, baking and kneading them, making noble cakes and loaves; these they will serve up on a mat of reeds or on clean leaves, themselves reclining the while upon beds strewn with yew or myrtle. And they and their children will feast, drinking of the wine which they have made, wearing garlands on their heads, and hymning the praises of the gods, in happy converse with one another. And they will take care that their families do not exceed their means; having an eye to poverty or war.

But, said Glaucon, interposing, you have not given them a relish to their meal.

True, I replied, I had forgotten; of course they must have a relish—salt, and olives, and cheese, and they will boil roots and herbs such as country people prepare; for a dessert we shall give them figs, and peas, and beans; and they will roast myrtle-berries and acorns at the fire, drinking in moderation. And with such a diet they may be expected to live in peace and health to a good old age, and bequeath a similar life to their children after them.

Yes, Socrates, he said, and if you were providing for a city of pigs, how else would you feed the beasts?

But what would you have, Glaucon? I replied.

Why, he said, you should give them the ordinary conveniences of life. People who are to be comfortable are accustomed to lie on sofas, and dine off tables, and they should have saucers and sweets in the modern style.

Yes, I said, now I understand: the question which you would have me consider is, not only how a state, but how a luxurious state is created; and possibly there is no harm in this, for in such a state we shall be more likely to see how justice and injustice originate. In my opinion the true and healthy constitution of the state is the one which I have described. But if you wish also to see a state at fever-heat, I have no objection. For I suspect that many will not be satisfied with the simpler way of life. They will be for adding sofas, and tables, and other furniture; also dainties, and perfumes, and incense, and courtesans, and cakes, all these not of one sort only, but in every variety; we must go beyond the necessaries of which I was at first speaking, such as houses, and clothes, and shoes: the arts of the painter and the embroiderer will have to be set in motion, and gold and ivory and all sorts of material must be procured.

True, he said.

Then we must enlarge our borders; for the original healthy state is no longer sufficient. Now will the city have to fill and swell with a multitude of callings which are not required by any natural want; such as the whole tribe of hunters and actors, of whom one large class have to do with forms and colors; another will be the votaries of music—poets and their attendant train of rhapsodists, players, dancers, contractors; also makers of divers kinds of articles, including women's dresses. And we shall want more servants. Will not tutors be also in request, and nurses wet and dry, tirewomen and barbers, as well as confectioners and cooks; and swineherds, too, who were not needed and therefore had no place in the former edition of our state, but are needed now? They must not be forgotten: and there will be animals of many other kinds, if people eat them.

Certainly.

And living in this way we shall have much greater need of physicians than before?

Much greater.

And the country which was enough to support the original inhabitants will be too small now, and not enough?

Quite true.

Then a slice of our neighbors' land will be wanted by us for pasture and tillage, and they will want a slice of ours, if, like ourselves, they exceed the limit of necessity, and give themselves up to the unlimited accumulation of wealth?

That, Socrates, will be inevitable.

And so we shall go to war, Glaucon. Shall we not?

Most certainly, he replied.

A PROBE OF THE ART OF
WEALTH-GETTING

ARISTOTLE

[Aristotle, *The Politics of Aristotle*, trans. by B. Jowett, Clarendon Press, Oxford, 1885, vol. I, pp. 14–22.]

Our term *economics* comes from a Greek word meaning *household affairs,* as used by Aristotle (384–322 B.C.) in the following selection from his *Politics.*

The etymology of the word reflects a significant and somewhat curious train of thought. Aristotle sees a connection between household management and management of a state; thus, for him, economics is a subspecies of politics! He says, for example, "There is a natural art of acquisition which is practiced by managers of households and by statesmen." And it is this art, particularly in the form of wealth-getting, that connotes the economics of managing. (See the selection from Aristotle in Volume I.)

Also interesting is the fact that although Aristotle realized that wealth-getting covered a much broader field than household management, he still considered the narrower concept the true or natural one. Retail trade is frowned on, and usury is especially condemned—thus starting off two debates that have gone on for centuries.

Aristotle followed Plato by only a few years: he probably even studied under Plato. His approach to philosophy was quite different, however. He started with the realities of this workaday world, while Plato worked down from an ideal superworld. Yet they both agree that trade is ignoble—perhaps because they and their fellow Athenians didn't have to soil their hands with it.

--------♦--------

THE AMOUNT OF PROPERTY which is needed for a good life is not unlimited, although Solon in one of his poems says that

No bound to riches has been fixed for man.

But there is a boundary fixed, just as there is in the other arts; for the instruments of any art are never unlimited, either in number or size, and riches may be defined as a number of instruments to be used in a household or in a state. And so we see that there is a natural art of acquisition which is practiced by managers of households and by statesmen, and what is the reason of this.

There is another variety of the art of acquisition which is commonly and rightly called an art of wealth-getting, and has in fact suggested the notion that riches and property have no limit. Being nearly connected with the preceding, it is often identified with it. But though they are not very different, neither are they the same. The kind already described is given by nature, the other is gained by experience and art.

Let us begin our discussion of the question with the following considerations:

Of everything which we possess there are two uses: both belong to the thing as such, but not in the same manner, for one is the proper, and the other the improper or secondary use of it. For example, a shoe is used for wear, and is used for exchange; both are uses of the shoe. He who gives a shoe in exchange for money or food to him who wants one, does indeed use the shoe as a shoe, but this is not its proper or primary purpose, for a shoe is not made to be an object of barter. The same may be said of all possessions, for the art of exchange extends to all of them, and it arises at first from what is natural, from the circumstance that some have too little, others too much. Hence we may infer that retail trade is not a natural part of the art of getting wealth; had it been so, men would have ceased to exchange when they had enough.

In the first community, indeed, which is the family, this art is obviously of no use, but it begins to be useful when the society increases. For the members of the family originally had all things in common; later, when the family divided into parts, the parts shared in many things, and different parts in different things, which they had to give in exchange for what they wanted, a kind of barter which is still practiced among barbarous nations who exchange with one another the necessaries of life and nothing more; giving and receiving wine, for example, in exchange for corn, and the like. This sort of barter is not part of the wealth-getting art and is not contrary to nature, but is needed for the satisfaction of men's natural wants.

The other or more complex form of exchange grew, as might have been inferred, out of the simpler. When the inhabitants of one country became more dependent on those of another, and they imported what they needed, and exported what they had too much of, money necessarily came into use. For the various necessaries of life are not easily carried about, and hence men agreed to employ in their dealings with each other something which was intrinsically useful and easily applicable to the purposes of life, for example, iron, silver, and the like. Of this the value was at first measured simply by size and weight, but in process of time they put a stamp upon it, to save the trouble of weighing and to mark the value.

When the use of coin had once been discovered, out of the barter of necessary articles arose the other art of wealth-getting, namely, retail trade; which was at first probably a simple matter, but became more complicated as soon as men learned by experience whence and by what exchanges the greatest profit might be made. Originating in the use of coin, the art of getting wealth is generally thought to be chiefly concerned with it, and to be the art which produces riches and wealth; having to consider how they may be accumulated.

Indeed, riches are assumed by many to be only a quantity of coin, because the arts of getting wealth and retail trade are concerned with coin. Others maintain that coined money is a mere sham, a thing not natural, but conventional only, because, if the users substitute another commodity for it, it is worthless, and because it is not useful as a means to any of the necessities of life, and, indeed, he who is rich in coin may often be in want of necessary food. But how can that be wealth of which a man may have a great abundance and yet perish with hunger, like Midas in the fable, whose insatiable prayer turned everything that was set before him into gold?

Hence men seek after a better notion of riches and of the art of getting wealth than the mere acquisition of coin, and they are right. For natural riches and the natural art of wealth-getting are a different thing; in their true form they are part of the management of a household; whereas retail trade is the art of producing wealth, not in every way, but by exchange. And it is thought to be concerned with coin; for coin is the unit of exchange and the measure or limit of it. And there is no bound to the riches which spring from this art of wealth-getting. . . .

There are two sorts of wealth-getting, as I have said; one is a part of household management, the other is retail trade: the former necessary and honorable, while that which consists in exchange is justly censured; for it is unnatural, and a mode by which men gain from one another. The most hated sort, and with the greatest reason, is usury, which makes a gain out of money itself, and not from the natural object of it. For money was intended to be used in exchange, but not to increase at interest. And this term *interest,* which means the birth of money from money, is applied to the breeding of money because the offspring resembles the parent. Wherefore of all modes of getting wealth this is the most unnatural.

Enough has been said about the theory of wealth-getting; we will now proceed to the practical part. The discussion of such matters is not unworthy of philosophy, but to be engaged in them practically is illiberal and irksome. The useful parts of wealth-getting are, first, the knowledge of livestock—which are most profitable, and where, and how—as, for example, what sort of horses or sheep or oxen or any other animals are most likely to give a return. A man ought to know which of these pay better than others, and which pay best in particular places, for some do better in one place and some in another. Secondly, husbandry, which may be either tillage or planting, and the keeping of bees and of fish, or fowl, or of any animals which may be useful to man. These are the divisions of the true or proper art of wealth-getting and come first.

Of the other, which consists in exchange, the first and most important division is commerce (of which there are three kinds— the provision of a ship, the conveyance of goods, exposure for sale— these again differing as they are safer or more profitable), the second is usury, the third, service for hire—of this, one kind is employed in the mechanical arts, the other in unskilled and bodily labor. There is still a third sort of wealth-getting intermediate between this and the first or natural mode which is partly natural; but is also concerned with exchange, viz., the industries that make their profit from the earth, and from things growing from the earth which, although they bear no fruit, are nevertheless profitable; for example, the cutting of timber and all mining. . . .

Those occupations are most truly arts in which there is the least element of chance; they are the meanest in which the body is most deteriorated, the most servile in which there is the greatest use of the body, and the most illiberal in which there is the least need of excellence. . . .

It would be well . . . to collect the scattered stories of the ways in which individuals have succeeded in massing a fortune; for all this is useful to persons who value the art of getting wealth. There is the anecdote of Thales the Milesian and his financial device, which involves a principle of universal application, but is attributed to him on account of his reputation for wisdom. He was reproached for his poverty, which was supposed to show that philosophy was of no use. According to the story, he knew by his skill in the stars while it was yet winter that there would be a great harvest of olives in the coming year; so, having a little money, he gave deposits for the use of all the olive presses in Chios and Miletus, which he hired at a low price because no one bid against him. When the harvest time came, and many were wanted all at once and of a sudden, he let them out at any rate which he pleased, and made a quantity of money. Thus he showed the world that philosophers can easily be rich if they like, but that their ambition is of another sort. He is supposed to have given a striking proof of his wisdom, but, as I was saying, his device for getting wealth is of universal application, and is nothing but the creation of a monopoly. . . .

There was a man of Sicily, who, having money deposited with him, bought up all the iron from the iron mines; afterwards, when the merchants from their various markets came to buy, he was the only seller, and without much increasing the price he gained 200 per cent. Which when Dionysius heard, he told him that he might take away his money, but that he must not remain at Syracuse, for he thought that the man had discovered a way of making money which was injurious to his own interests. He made the same discovery as Thales; they both contrived to create a monopoly for themselves. And statesmen as well ought to know these things; for a state is often as much in want of money and of such devices for obtaining it as a household, or even more so; hence some public men devote themselves entirely to finance.

ECONOMIC PRINCIPLES IN ANCIENT CHINA—AS CONFUCIUS SAITH

CHEN   HUAN-CHANG

[Chen Huan-chang, *The Economic Principles of Confucius and His School*, Columbia University Press, New York, 1911, copyright 1911 by the Faculty of Political Science of Columbia University, vol. II, pp. 483–488.]

Chinese philosophers in the fourth, fifth, and sixth centuries B.C. came closer to anticipating some of our modern ideas of free enterprise than almost anybody else, anywhere else, in between. And this despite the fact that business was government-operated—or, to put it another way, each government was a business unit in competition with other government-business units.

In this selection, a modern Chinese scholar discusses the philosophy of Confucius and others, particularly his follower Mencius. He shows how they developed the theory of the productivity of labor; i.e., that labor should be paid in terms of its productivity. Notice how they differ from the classical philosopher of ancient Greece and Rome in considering the artisan and merchant as more productive than the farmer, and as being one step up the scale to the government officer and the teacher, who are the most productive of all. On the latter point, they really improve on Adam Smith, with his more mechanical interpretation of the division of labor; and dignify the labor that goes into mental products, in a way to put Karl Marx to shame.

(For a breath of refreshing philosophy from *modern* China, see Hu Shih in Volume II and Lin Yutang in Volume III.)

———◆———

THE AMOUNT OF WAGES of the laborer should be according to the product which he contributes. Confucius (*ca.* 551–479 B.C.) says: "By daily examinations and monthly trials, and by making their rations in accordance with their labors: this is the way to encourage all the classes of artisans." This is the principle of justice governing the law of wages. Of course, labor should not be underpaid; yet neither should it be overpaid. If it were overpaid, or to state it clearly, if poor labor were as well paid as good labor, there would be no encouragement for all classes of artisans. The good laborer would be disappointed, the survival would be of the unfit, and the standard of workmanship would be lowered. But if we want to pay wages according to product, daily examinations and monthly trials are necessary; otherwise we cannot know the amount of productivity of labor. This theory is the fundamental law of wages.

What Confucius refers to is the factory system under which the government is the employer. If the government wants to make the state rich, it must give the laborers just wages; this is the principle of inducing all the classes of artisans to come in. If it is not so, the artisans will neither immigrate nor stay, and the wealth of the state will not be sufficient. Kuan Tzŭ [pre-Confucius] also recognizes the importance of encouraging artisans to come in, but his policy for carrying it out is to raise wages to a rate three times as great as that of other states. This policy cannot be a general principle, but simply a temporary measure for an emergent demand for labor. From the statements of Confucius and Kuan Tzŭ, we know that, in the Chou dynasty, there was a free movement of labor, and there was international competition for the labor market; hence, the amount of wages was the determining factor in the movement of labor. The productivity theory is applied not only to manual labor, but also to mental labor. Confucius says:

> In the service of a ruler, when great words are spoken to and accepted by him, great advantages to the state may be expected from them; and when words of small importance are presented to him, only small advantages are to be looked for. Therefore, a superior man will not for words of small importance receive a great salary, nor for words of great importance a small salary.*

Even in regard to the value of words, they would be neither overpaid nor underpaid. This is the principle of justice, and it is the rule of accepting wages.

According to Confucius, however, a superior man may accept underpay, but not overpay. He says:

> The superior man will decline a position of high honor, but not one that is mean; and riches, but not poverty. In this way, disorder will more and more disappear. Hence, the superior man, rather than have his emoluments superior to his worth, will have his worth superior to his emoluments.†

This principle is based on moral and social reasons, but not on economic law. According to economic law, men should never be overpaid, nor underpaid.

According to the principles of the Confucians, division of labor is a very important thing for society, and all labor is productive. Not only is the farmer productive, but also the artisan and the merchant. Again, not only are these three classes of people productive, but also the political officer and the moral teacher. Referring to these two classes of men, there are many arguments saying that they are unproductive. For this reason, let us study their productivity.

First, let us see how the political officer is productive. When Chen Hsiang, formerly a Confucian, but converted by Hsü Hsing, visited Mencius (372–289 B.C.), he quoted the words of Hsü Hsing to the effect that the ruler should cultivate the land equally and along with his people. Mencius said: "I suppose that Hsü Tzŭ sows grain and eats the produce. Is it not so?" "It is so," was the answer. "I suppose also he weaves cloth, and wears his own manufacture. Is it not so?" "No. Hsü Tzŭ wears clothes of hair-cloth." "Does he wear a cap?" "He wears a cap." "What kind of cap?" "A plain cap." "Is it woven by himself?" "No. He gets it in exchange for grain." "Why does Hsü not weave it himself?" "That would injure his

---

* *Li Ki*, bk. xxix, p. 345.
† *Li Ki*, bk. xxvii, p. 286.

husbandry." "Does Hsü cook his food in boilers and earthenware pans, and does he plough with an iron share?" "Yes." "Does he make those articles himself?" "No. He gets them in exchange for grain."

Mencius then said:

The getting those various articles in exchange for grain is not oppressive to the potter and the founder, and the potter and the founder in their turn, in exchanging their various articles for grain, are not oppressive to the husbandman. How should such a thing be supposed? And moreover, why does not Hsü Tzŭ establish the pottery and foundery, supplying himself with the articles which he uses solely from his own establishment? Why does he go confusedly dealing and exchanging with all the artisans? Why does he not spare himself so much trouble?

Chen Hsiang replied: "The business of the artisans can by no means be carried on along with the business of husbandry."

Mencius resumed:

Then, is it the government of the empire which alone can be carried on along with the practice of husbandry? Great men have their proper business, and little men have their proper business. Moreover, even in the case of any single person, he may require various articles which are produced by all classes of artisans; if he must first make them for his own use, this way of doing would lead the whole world into poverty.*

The doctrine of Hsü Hsing is extremely democratic. He teaches that everyone should support his mouth by his own hand, and that all rulers should be farmers. But it is impossible. Mencius' doctrine is based on the principle of division of labor. The governing class supported by others does not oppress the people, because the men of this class cannot cultivate the land at the same time they work in the government, and because their mental work cannot be done by the governed. It is merely an exchange of services, and the governing class and the governed class depend upon each other. The ruler exchanges his governmental work for food from the farmer just as the potter and the founder exchange their articles for the grain of the farmer. From this point of view, we can justify not only the political relation between the ruler and the subject, but also the economic relation between manager and common laborer. Indeed, distribution according to productivity is universal justice.

Second, let us see how the moral teacher is productive. Followed

---

* *Classics*, vol. ii, pp. 247–249.

by "several tens" of carriages and attended by several hundred men, this is the way Mencius traveled from one prince to another, and lived on their hospitality. P'êng Kêng, his pupil, thinking this excessive, says: "For a scholar, doing no business, to receive his support, is improper." Mencius answers:

> If you do not have interchange of service and exchange of productivity, so that one from his overplus may supply the deficiency of another, then the husbandmen will have a superfluity of grain, and the women will have a superfluity of cloth. If you have such an interchange, carpenter, mason, wheelmaker, and carriage-wright may all get their food from you. Here now is a man who is filial at home, and fraternal abroad; who keeps the principles of the ancient kings, awaiting the rise of future learners; and yet you will refuse to support him. How is it that you give honor to the carpenter, mason, wheelmaker, and carriage-wright, and slight him who practices benevolence and righteousness?

Then P'êng Kêng says that those laborers should be fed by society because their purpose is for their living, but that the superior man should not be fed by society because his purpose is not for his living. Mencius replies: "What have you to do with their purpose? Anyone who is of service to you deserves to be supported, and should be supported." Then he asks P'êng Kêng whether he would pay a man for his purpose or for his service. To this P'êng cannot help but answer that he would pay him for his purpose.

Mencius asks him: "There is a man here who breaks your tiles and disfigures your painted walls with his knife; his purpose may be thereby to seek for his living, but will you indeed remunerate him?" "No," says P'êng. Then Mencius concludes: "That being the case, it is not the purpose which you remunerate, but the work done." From Mencius' point of view, the formula of distributive justice is: to each according to his productivity, not his wants.

A FOLLOWER OF CONFUCIUS
ANTICIPATES THE LAW OF SUPPLY
AND DEMAND

SSŬ-MA CHIEN

[Ssŭ Chien, chap. CXXIX, Historical Record (104–97 B.C.); quoted in Chen Huan-chang, *The Economic Principles of Confucius and His School,* Columbia University Press, New York, 1911, vol. I, pp. 176–177.]

Coming along not very long after Plato and Aristotle, a Chinese philosopher of the school of Confucius takes life as it comes and makes the best of it—instead of trying to change human nature and the needs of people.

Two traits are notable (beyond the Oriental calm). One is the acceptance of business as a worth-while activity in its own right—not for either its political or its religious implications; this is unusual in early philosophy. The other is the anticipation of the so-called law of supply and demand, which did not appear in the Western world for another 2000 years.

———◆———

BEFORE THE TIME of Shên Nung [2838 B.C.], I do not know; but since the dynasties of Yü and Hsia, told of by the canons of *Poetry* and *History,* the ear and eye want to exhaust the fineness of sound and beauty; the mouth wants to exhaust the taste of meat; the body wants to be easy and pleasant; and the mind wants to be proud of the glory of power and ability. These economic wants have produced a general habit and have fixed the nature of the people for a very long time. Even though we should persuade them from door after door with a fine speech, we cannot change their habits. Therefore, the best policy is to follow the economic activities of man; the second is to lead them on profitably; the third is to teach them; the fourth is to regulate them; and the worst is to fight with them.

Society depends upon the farmer for the supply of food; upon the miner for the development of the mine; upon the artisan for the manufacturing of goods; and upon the merchant for the exchange of them. Has this natural process anything to do with either political action, or religious teaching, or special order and meeting? It is simply that everyone respectively employs his own ability, and exhausts his own energy, in order to get what he wants. Therefore, when the commodity is cheap, it calls forth demand, and raises its price; and when it is dear, it calls forth supply, and lowers its price. Everyone respectively encourages his own occupation, and enjoys his own work. Such a natural thing is like the water drifting to the low place through day and night without any cessation. There is no one to call for it especially, but it comes itself; there is no one to demand it especially, but the people offer it themselves. Is it not the result of the natural law and the proof of the natural course?

JOST AMMAN'S *ALLEGORY OF TRADE* —OR, THE WORLD OF BUSINESS IN THE SIXTEENTH CENTURY

DONALD T. CLARK

This arrangement of prints, with accompanying explanations, is by Donald T. Clark, member of the faculty and librarian in charge of the Baker Library, Harvard Graduate School of Business Administration. The edition of Amman's work used here by Mr. Clark is in the Baker Library, world's largest unitary collection of business literature.

The next seventeen illustrations are photographs of, first, the whole, and following, various aspects of a very large, extremely rare, highly detailed and beautifully executed print, an allegorical representation of commerce based on the business scene of Northern Europe in the sixteenth century.

Conceived by Johann Neudörfer, engraved by Jost Amman, and printed in Augsberg first in 1585 (our edition is dated 1622), this 30- × 46-inch print is a fantastic storehouse of early business lore, maxims, practices and information.

While the print is clearly intended as an allegory, its artist, Jost Amman, appears to have fashioned the scenes after real life. Everything about it is exceedingly expressive and lifelike. Jost Amman was a Swiss artist. He was born in Zurich in 1539 but moved to Nuremberg in 1560, where he worked and lived until his death in 1591. He was highly skilled as a wood engraver. Employed chiefly as a designer for booksellers, he also worked as an illuminator, miniaturist, and designer of coats of arms. His designs are noted for their richness of detail and their minute and accurate delineation of costumes and ornaments. That he was prolific is attested to by the remark of one of his pupils that "the drawings he made during a period of four years would have filled a hay wagon." That he was a skilled and spirited engraver upon wood is surely proven by the results shown here—particularly the enlargements and details of the print.

Johann Neudörfer, a man of many talents—brilliant mathematician, calligrapher, writing master, teacher of bookkeeping—conceived the idea of creating this *Allegory of Commerce*. Even though the print was not issued until after Neudörfer's death, the *Allegory* was his inspiration—both word and picture. Neudörfer, who also lived (1497–1563) and worked in Nuremberg, was a member of a famous family of calligraphers and writing masters. He designed several new alphabets of German "Fractur-Skript" or Gothic text, and in 1538 he published *Eine gute Ordnung und kurzer Unterricht*, a writing-model book which contained many examples of beautiful handwriting and explanations for learners. Neudörfer's influence on Amman's execution may readily be seen when one compares some of the examples of Neudörfer's work with the text at the top of Amman's print. In still another fashion, his influence upon the print may be detected, for it was Neudörfer's pupil, Caspar Brinner, who supplied the verses on both sides and at the bottom of the engraving and the aphorisms, precepts and descriptive phrases which, usually enclosed in cartouches, are appropriately placed in numerous locations throughout the print.

The print (Figure 275) consists of six individual woodcuts printed on separate sheets which were later joined to form what, from a distance, appears to be a single plate. (Figure 280 clearly shows the corners of four of the woodcuts.)

The size of the composite plate (nearly four feet in height), the number (six) of individual leaves, the absence of protective panes of glass—all contributed to making this an extremely rare work of art. Very few copies are extant today. The blocks, however, are still preserved in the Prince Wallerstein Library in Maihingen, Germany.

The *partial* title of the plate is *Aigentliche abbildung dess gantzen gewerbs der Kauffmanschafft sambtetslicher der Namhafft und Fürnembsten Handelstett Signatur und Wappen darinnen zum theils fürnemblich die Märckt unnd Messen begriffen sein, . . . Erstlich, durch den Nambhafft und weitberumpten alten Herrn Johann Neudörfer seligen, weibandt gewessen Burger und Rechenmaister zu Nurmberg, In grund unnd Ins Fundament gelegt: Jetzund aber durch Casparn Brinner. Burger und Rechenmaister zu Augsburg, . . . mit grosser müe Ins werck . . . verfertigt.*

Here, then, is a veritable potpourri: the symbols of business, pictures of mercantile activity, mixed with aphorisms and precepts and versified history of bookkeeping, a listing of principal commodities of the day, a panorama of the then leading trade center of the world and symbolic representations of those qualities which make for success in business. Truly there is hardly a section of this large plate where one cannot find some detail of business life or activity of interest.

Let us turn now to a closer look at the plate and its details. The most dominant feature is a tall column rising from the basin of a magnificent

FIG. 275.

Fig. 276.

Fig. 277.

fountain symbolizing the source of wealth. All other features of the engraving seem to be grouped about this symbol of riches or source of wealth. On the basin are lettered the names of the principal branches of business and the main commodities of the day: wool, hides, silk, metals, spices, grains, etc.

Above the column—even above Fortune—we find the bold figure of Mercury (Figure 277) surrounded by the signs of the zodiac. Early in Roman mythology, Mercury was the god of merchandise (*merx*) and of merchants. He was the protector of traders. Later, it must be said, he also became known as the god and protector of thieves. Amman portrays him with his usual accoutrements: winged sandals, winged helmet, and, in one hand, a caduceus. In the other hand he clutches a huge scale, or balance (Figure 276).

On either side of Mercury are displayed the coats of arms of the leading commercial centers of sixteenth-century Europe. The seals are arranged in twelve rows according to the months when fairs, the most important trading occasions of the time, took place.

Here is a roll call of market towns. Under the column for July, for example, we readily recognize Augsburg, Florence, Krems, Munich, Rotenberg, Bologna, Frankfurt on the Oder and London—all represented by their seals. Some seals are duplicated, indicating that a major fair was held at other times during the year.

We now turn to the scales (Figure 279) held by Mercury. Each of the arms, which are in perfect balance, supports a scale pan holding an account book. The pans are linked to the basic account book, the journal, by the bonds of debit and credit.

Enclosed by the scales is Fortuna, the goddess of chance and the controller of destinies.

Down through the centuries, the allegorical figure of Fortune has taken many forms (see Figure 1, Vol. I), shown sometimes with a double rudder, or wings, or holding a cornucopia or a ship; sometimes with bound eyes; frequently standing on a ball or wheel. Jost Amman presents us with a balding Fortune! (Figure 280) She seems to have hair on her brow and on one side of her head. The rest is bare. Is this another symbol of the inconstancy of this goddess of pure chance? She is holding wings in one hand and in the other a turtle. The fleeting fugitive nature of chance or fortune is further symbolized by the traditional ball upon which she stands.

"You see fickle luck," writes Brinner in the adjacent cartouche, "which often turns herself around, standing on a flying ball. . . . Chance generally governs a wise merchant's trading, so take a chance on good luck; maybe it will take compassion on you."

Behind the central column and across the entire plate is spread a panoramic view of the city of Antwerp and its harbor, a scene of bustling activity: ships furrowing the River Scheldt—big ships, little ships,

FIG. 278.

ships being loaded, ships being sunk—cranes lifting cargoes, windmills turning, men working.

It is not surprising that Amman and Neudörfer chose Antwerp as part of this allegorical representation of commerce, for Antwerp in the sixteenth century was the "Queen of European commerce." At the time of the execution of this engraving, Antwerp "was the most opulent city of the world" (Thuanus), and was at its highest point of prosperity. Adam Anderson in his *Historical and Chronological Deduction of the Origins of Commerce* (1764) quotes Monsieur Huet, Bishop of Avranches, as saying that Antwerp was "the most celebrated magazine of Commerce in all Europe, if not in the whole world, it having been at this time (1550) a common thing to see 2,500 ships in the Scheld laden with all sorts of merchandize." Others mention the vast number of foreign merchants resident in Antwerp: Spaniards, Danes and Hanses, Italians, English, Portuguese and Germans. Over 2,000 carts entered the city each week,

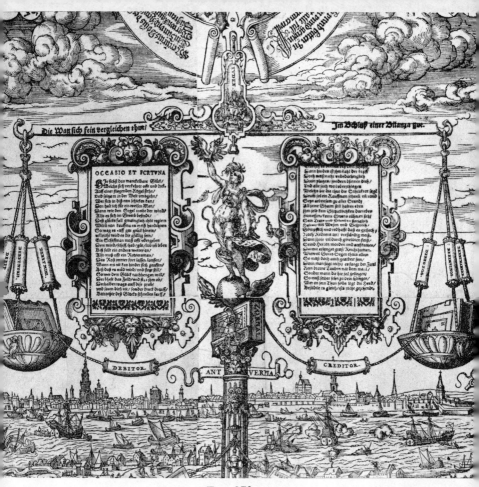

FIG. 279.

while 500 ships sometimes arrived in one day. Venice, while still active as a trade center, had fallen from its first place in European trading. Guicciardini, the Florentine merchant, in explaining the importance of Antwerp, stated that there was as much business done in Antwerp in a fortnight as in Venice in a year.

In the area just below the panorama of Antwerp are depicted conditions and circumstances which affect the balance sheet. On the left (Figure 281): war, plagues, death, risks of travel on land and sea; and on the right (Figure 282): scarcity, begging for food, boredom, exchange troubles, bad justice, highway robbings; on the left under the double safeguards of government protection—treaties and armed escorts—the convoys safely reach their destinations; on the right, they meet up with all sorts of dangers.

Predominant in the lower portion of the allegory are vignettes of business activities which, according to scholars, represent the workings

Fig. 280.

Fig. 281.

Hergegen was zůr rechten steht/
Die Creditores all angeht/

Wann Gott im Berckwerck geben thut/
Groß Glück vnd Segen zu dem Gut/
So sey die Herrschafft nicht so rauch/
So bleibt völlig der Berckman auch/

zNa Glait nimbt man die Kaufleut an/
Durch ein Fürstliche AmptsPerson/
Wer nun solch Glait verachtet gantz/
Derselb bestehl darob sein schantz/

Wann das Getraid wird thewr er sehe/
Dis holtz vnd andre Notturfft mehr/
So mun den Wechsel beschweren thut/
ist die Bezahlung wit fast gut.

So grosse Newerung sich meyt/
daß offt die Recht werden verkehrt/
So man bricht der Freyheiten gantz/
vnd böse arbeit geht im schwang/
Wo man durchauß nit Gleichheit helt/
So man den Habenden nachstellt/
Darauff grosser vnlust einfolle.

FIG. 282.

Fig. 283.

FIG. 284.

Fig. 285.

of one of those powerful commercial houses of the sixteenth century
of which that of Fugger stands as the most celebrated example. In the
center of the court and between the two porticos of four rooms, sits,
ornately robed in fur, the head of the house, a merchant prince (Figure
283, right center). He is shown handing a letter to an armed messenger;
the latter is quoted as saying:

> I travel into the country with letters
> The contents of which I do not know
> But often I make my master jovial with them
> And also cross and weak.

in Journal schreib ich alle tag/
Was sich im Gwerb begeben mag/

FIG. 286.

Immediately above the merchant prince, the *Secretorum Liber Inventarium* is housed, symbolically, in the place of honor.

To the right and left of the head of the house are views of four rooms:

The Weighing House (Figure 285)—"Here all the wares will be selected at random and carefully weighed so that no one will be cheated or unjustly treated"; *The Conference Room* (Figure 286)— "Here will be discussed all the secret and important affairs relating to mines and to groups of merchants and traders so that plans will go well"; *The Counting House* (Figure 287)—"In the counting house here shown, the cashier will perform his official duties publicly so that whatever is taken in or given out will be done properly";

FIG. 287

The Treasure Room (Figure 288)—"Here all the treasures and jewels will be thoroughly described and inventoried so that he who performs these tasks may make a proper report."

In the open court (Figures 283, 284, 289, 290 and 291), many commercial activities are being performed: a bookkeeper makes his record in a journal (Figure 291, left) while another makes entries in a ledger (Figure 291, right); one cashier sorts coins (Figure 290); another (notice his sword—a sixteenth-century status symbol?) tallies the cash, while all around there is a coming and going of merchandise, with workers packing, marking with merchants' marks (two of these identifying marks are clearly shown in this illustration), unpacking, sorting and checking.

mancher hat grosse sorg vnd mühe,
Bey seinem Gut/Oberveit er mit/1
Sein Thun hat bracht zur Richtigkeit,
in deß Buchhaltens gschicklichkeit

FIG. 288.

Fortune presides over the activity of the open court (Figure 291, bottom). She is warning all that she is as fleeting as the smoke that rises from the urn which she carries.

Throughout the court, the artist has placed other figures which symbolize the qualities and knowledge that make for success in business: *Obligatio,* or sense of duty (Figure 283, left corner); *Integritas,* or honesty (Figure 291); *Taciturnitas*, or discretion and reserve in speaking (Figure 291); *Linguarum Peritia,* or knowledge of languages (Figure 291); and *Libertas,* or freedom of trade (Figure 284, lower right).

This, then, is Amman's Allegory of Trade, or the World of Business in Sixteenth-Century Europe—one of the most comprehensive early portrayals of the business scene.

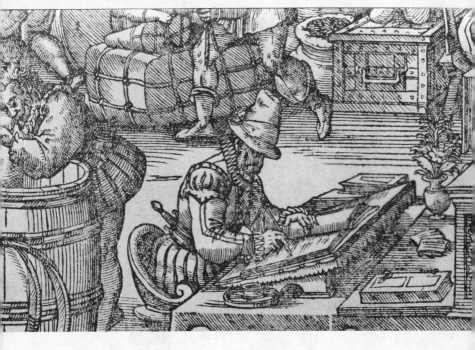

Fig. 289.

Fig. 290.

FIG. 291.

BREAKING THE BONDS
OF TRADITION

ROBERT L. HEILBRONER

[Robert L. Heilbroner, "The Economic Revolution," in *The Worldly Philosophers,* Simon and Schuster, New York, 1953, copyright © 1953, 1961, by the author.]

For almost 2000 years since the time of the earlier selections there was little real development in the philosophical interpretation of business —unless the idea of the guilds and regulation of all aspects of commercial life could be considered an intellectual advancement. Apparently businessmen had learned to live under an umbrella that protected them, and kept others out. Then, around 1700 came the liberalizing of commerce, and the birth pangs of a new capitalism. These were times of smashing change—not violent action, but many small changes adding up over a period of several hundred years to violent effect. Dawn finally came up like thunder—the dawn of modern civilization.

◆

MARKETS HAVE EXISTED as far back as history goes. The Tablets of Tell-el-Amarna tell of lively trade between the pharaohs and the Levantine kings in 1400 B.C.: gold and war chariots were swapped for slaves and horses. But while the idea of exchange must be very nearly as old as man, as with the idea of gain, we must not make the mistake of assuming that all the world has the bargaining propensities of a twentieth-century American schoolboy. Purely by way of curious illustration, it is reported that among the New Zealand Maoris you cannot ask how much food a bonito-hook is worth, for such a trade is never made and the question would be regarded as ridiculous. By way of turnabout, however, in some African communities it is perfectly legitimate to inquire how many oxen a woman is worth—an exchange which we look upon as the Maoris do swapping food and fishhooks (although the delicate practice of dowries may somewhat narrow the gap between us and the savages).

But markets, whether they be exchanges between primitive tribes where objects are casually dropped on the ground or the exciting traveling fairs of the Middle Ages, are not the same as the market system. For the market system is not just a means of exchanging goods; it is a mechanism for sustaining and maintaining an entire society.

And that mechanism was far from clear to the minds of the

medieval world. The concept of widespread gain was blasphemous enough. . . . The broader notion that a general struggle for gain might actually bind together a community would have been held as little short of madness. . . .

Land, labor, and capital as "agents" of production, as impersonal, dehumanized economic entities, are as much modern inventions as the calculus. Indeed, they are not much older.

Take, for example, land. As late as the fourteenth or fifteenth century there was no land, at least in the modern sense of freely salable, rent-producing property. There were lands, of course— estates, manors, and principalities—but these were not just real estate to be bought and sold as the occasion warranted. Such lands formed the core of social life, provided the basis for prestige and status, and constituted the foundation for the military, judicial, and administrative organization of society. Although land was salable under certain conditions (with many strings attached), it was not generally *for sale*. A medieval nobleman in good standing would no more have thought of selling his land than a respectable honorary society or exclusive club today would think of selling memberships. Every society takes some objects of value and places them outside the orbit of transactions; for the Middle Ages, land was one of these.

And the same was true for labor. When we talk of the labor market today, we mean the endless bargaining process in which individuals sell their services to the highest bidder. There simply was no such process in the precapitalist world. There was a vast hodgepodge of serfs, apprentices, and journeymen who labored, but most of this labor never entered a market to be bought and sold. In the country, the peasant lived tied to the lord's estate; he baked at the lord's oven and ground at the lord's mill, tilled the lord's fields and served his lord in war, but he was rarely if ever paid for any of his services; these were his *duties* as a serf, not the "labor" of a freely contracting agent. In the towns the apprentice entered the service of a master; the length of his apprenticeship, the number of his colleagues, his rate of pay, his hours of work, the very methods he used were all regulated by a guild. There was little or no bargaining between servant and master except for sporadic strikes when conditions became intolerable. This was no more of a labor market than is provided by interns in a hospital.

Or take capital. Certainly capital existed in the precapitalist world, in the sense of private wealth. But although the funds existed, there was no impetus to put them to new and aggressive use. Instead of risk and change, the motto was "Safety first." Not the shortest and most efficient, but the longest and most labor-consuming process was the preferred technique of production. Advertising was forbidden and the idea that one master guildsman might produce a better product than his colleagues was regarded as treasonable. In sixteenth-century England, when mass production in the weaving trade first reared its ugly head, the guilds protested to the king. The wonder workshop —two hundred looms and a service staff including butchers and bakers to take care of the working force—was thereupon outlawed by His Majesty; such efficiency and concentration of wealth would set a bad precedent. . . .

[Then] this great self-reproducing, self-sufficient world erupted into the bustling, scurrying, free-for-all of the eighteenth century. *Erupted* is perhaps too dramatic a word, for the change would take place over centuries rather than in a single violent spasm. But the change, long drawn out though it was, was not a peaceful evolution; it was an agonized convulsion of society, a revolution.

Just to commercialize the land—to convert the hierarchy of social relationships into so many vacant lots and advantageous sites—required nothing less than the uprooting of an entrenched way of life. To make "workers" out of the sheltered serfs and apprentices—no matter how exploitative the cloak of paternalism may have been— required the creation of a frightened, disoriented thing called the proletariat. To make capitalists out of guild masters meant that the laws of the jungle had to be taught to the timid denizens of the barnyard.

Hardly a peaceful prospect, any of this. Nobody *wanted* this commercialization of life. How bitterly it was resisted can only be appreciated if we take [a] journey back to watch the economic revolution taking place.

We are back in France. The year, 1666.

The capitalists of the day face a disturbing challenge which the widening market mechanism has inevitably brought in its wake: change.

The question has come up whether a guild master of the weaving industry should be allowed to try an innovation in his product. The verdict: "If a cloth weaver intends to process a piece according to his own invention, he must not set it on the loom, but should obtain permission from the judges of the town to employ the number and length of threads that he desires, after the question has been considered by four of the oldest merchants and four of the oldest weavers of the guild." One can imagine how many suggestions for change were tolerated.

Shortly after the matter of cloth weaving has been disposed of, the button-makers' guild raises a cry of outrage; the tailors are beginning to make buttons out of cloth, an unheard-of thing. The government, indignant that an innovation should threaten a settled industry, imposes a fine on the cloth button-makers and even on those who wear cloth buttons. But the wardens of the button guild are not yet satisfied. They demand the right to search people's homes and wardrobes and even to arrest them on the streets if they are seen wearing these subversive goods.

And this dread of change and innovation is not just the comic resistance of a few frightened merchants. Capital is fighting in terror against change, and no holds are barred. In England, a revolutionary patent for a stocking frame is not only denied in 1623, but the Privy Council orders the dangerous contraption abolished. In France the importation of printed calicoes is threatening to undermine the clothing industry. It is met with measures which cost the lives of sixteen thousand people! In Valence alone on one occasion 77 persons are sentenced to be hanged, 58 broken on the wheel, 631 sent to the galleys, and one lone and lucky individual set free for the crime of dealing in forbidden calico wares.

But capital is not the only agent of production which is frantically seeking to avoid the dangers of the market way of life. What is happening to labor is still more desperate.

Let us turn back to England.

It is the end of the sixteenth century, the great era of English expansion and adventure. Queen Elizabeth has made a triumphal tour of her kingdom. But she returns with a strange plaint. "Paupers are everywhere!" she cries. This is a strange observation, for only a hundred years before, the English countryside consisted in large part of peasant proprietors tilling their own lands, the yeoman, the pride of England, the largest body of independent, free, and prosperous citizens in the world. Now, "Paupers are everywhere!" What has happened in the interim?

What has happened has been an enormous movement of expropriation. Wool has become a new, profitable commodity, and wool demands grazing pastures for the wool producer. The pastures are made by enclosing the common land; the patchwork crazy quilt of small scattered holdings (unfenced and recognizable only by a tree here and a rock there dividing one man's land from another) and the common lands on which all might graze their cattle or gather peat are suddenly declared to be all the property of the lord of the manor and no longer available to the whole parish. Where before there was a kind of communality of ownership, now there is private property. Where there were yeomen, now there are sheep. One John Hales in 1549 wrote: ". . . where XL persons had their lyvings, now one man and his shepherd hath all. . . . Yes, those shepe is the cause of all theise meschieves, for they have driven husbandrie out of the countries, by the which was encreased before all kynde of victuall, and now altogether shepe, shepe."

It is almost impossible to imagine the scope and impact of the process of enclosure. In a single century, the greater part of the yeomanry was converted into a demoralized mob of paupers who would haunt Britain for two hundred years. Riots broke out: in a single uprising in the middle of the sixteenth century 3,500 rioters were killed and their leader, Robert Kett, hanged. In another instance a certain Duchess of Sutherland dispossessed 15,000 tenants from 794,000 acres of land, replaced them with 131,000 sheep, and by way of compensation rented her evicted families an average of two acres of submarginal land apiece. And this happened in 1820, at the tail end of the enclosure movement, nearly fifty years after the American Revolution!

But it was not merely the wholesale land-grabbing which warrants attention. The tragedy is what happened to the yeoman. Driven off the land, he was at a total loss. He could not become a wage-earner in the modern sense, for there were no factories ready to receive him, and nothing like large-scale industry available to absorb him. Deprived of his independent farm, the yeoman became a robber, beggar, vagabond, pauper, a miserable agricultural laborer, or a tenant. Terrified at the flood of pauperism throughout the country, the English Parliament tried to deal with the problem by localizing it. It tied paupers to their parishes for a pittance of relief and dealt with wanderers by whipping, branding, and mutilation. A social reformer of the time of Adam Smith seriously proposed to deal with the migrant pauper by confining him to institutions for which he candidly suggested the name Houses of Terror. But what was worst of all was that the very measures which the country took to protect itself from the pauper—tying him to his local parish where he could be kept alive on poor relief—prevented the only possible solution to the problem. It was not that the English ruling classes were utterly heartless and cruel. Rather, they failed to understand the concept of a fluid, mobile labor force which would seek to work wherever work was to be found according to the dictates of the market. At every step, the commercialization of labor, like the commercialization of capital, was feared, fought, and misconceived.

The market system with its essential components of land, labor, and capital was born in agony—an agony that began in the thirteenth century and did not run its course until well into the nineteenth. Never was a revolution less well understood, less welcomed, less planned. But the great market-making forces would not be denied. Insidiously they ripped apart the mold of custom, insolently they tore away the usages of tradition. For all the clamor of the button-makers, cloth buttons won the day. For all the action of the Privy Council, the stocking frame became so valuable that in another seventy years the same Privy Council would forbid its exportation. For all the breakings on the wheel, the trade in calicoes increased apace.

Over last-ditch opposition from the Old Guard, economic land was created out of ancestral estates, and over the wails of protest from employees and masters alike, economic labor was ground out of unemployed apprentices and dispossessed farm laborers.

The great chariot of society, which for so long had run by gravity down the gentle slope of tradition, now found itself powered by an internal combustion machine. Transactions, transactions, transactions and gain, gain, gain provided a new and startlingly powerful motive force.

What forces could have been sufficiently powerful to smash a comfortable and established world and institute in its place this new unwanted society?

There was no single massive cause. The new way of life grew inside the old, like a butterfly inside a chrysalis, and when the stir of life was strong enough it burst the old structure asunder. It was not great events, single adventures, individual laws, or powerful personalities which brought about the economic revolution. It was a process of internal growth.

First there was the gradual emergence of national political units in Europe. Under the blows of peasant wars and kingly conquest, the isolated existence of early feudalism gave way to centralized monarchies. And with monarchies came the growth of the national spirit; in turn this meant royal patronage for favored industries, such as the great French tapestry works, and the development of armadas and armies with all their necessary satellite industries. The infinity of rules and regulations which plagued Andreas Ryff * and his fellow sixteenth-century traveling merchants gave way to common laws, common measurements, common currency.

An aspect of the political change which was revolutionizing Europe was the encouragement of foreign adventure and exploration. In the thirteenth century the brothers Polo went as unprotected merchants on their fabulous journey into the land of the great Khan; in the fifteenth century Columbus sailed for what he hoped would be the same destination under the royal auspices of Isabella. The change from private to national exploration was part and parcel of the change from private to national life. And in turn the great national adventures of the English and Spanish and Portuguese sailor-capitalists brought a flood of treasure and treasure-consciousness back to Europe. "Gold," Christopher Columbus has said, "is a wonderful thing! Whoever possesses it is master of everything he desires. With gold one can even get souls into heaven." The sentiments of Christopher Columbus were the sentiments of an age and hastened the advent of a society oriented toward gain and chance and activated by the chase after money. Be it noted, in passing, that the treasures of the East were

---

* See pages 256–257 in Vol. I.

truly fabulous. With the share received as a stockholder in Sir Francis Drake's voyage of the *Golden Hynd,* Queen Elizabeth paid off all England's foreign debts, balanced its budget, and invested abroad a sum large enough, at compound interest, to account for Britain's entire overseas wealth in 1930!

A second great current of change was to be found in the slow decay of the religious spirit under the impact of the skeptical, inquiring, humanist views of the Italian Renaissance. The world of today elbowed aside the world of tomorrow, and as life on earth became more important, so did the notion of material standards and ordinary comforts. Behind the change in religious tolerance was the rise of Protestantism, which hastened a new attitude toward work and wealth. The Church of Rome had always regarded the merchant with a dubious eye and had not hesitated to call usury a sin. But now that this merchant was every day climbing in society, now that he was no longer a mere useful appendage but an integral part of a new kind of world, some re-evaluation of his function became necessary. The Protestant leaders paved the way for an amalgamation of spiritual and temporal life. Far from eulogizing the life of poverty and spiritual contemplation, as separate from worldly life, it became the part of positive piety to make the most of one's God-given talents in daily business. Acquisitiveness became a recognized virtue—not immediately for one's private enjoyment, but for the greater glory of God. From here it was only a step to the identification of riches with spiritual excellence, and of rich men with saintly ones.

In the twelfth century a local folk tale tells of a usurer about to be married who was crushed by a falling statue as he was entering the church. On examination, the statue was also of a usurer, thus revealing God's displeasure with dealers in money. Even in the mid-1600s, as we may remember, poor Robert Keayne collided head on with the Puritan religious authorities because of his business practices.* In such an atmosphere of hostility it was not easy for the market system to expand. Hence the gradual acceptance by the spiritual leaders of the innocuousness, indeed the benefits, of the market way was essential for the full growth of the system.

Still another deep current lies in the slow social changes which eventually made the market system possible. We are accustomed to thinking of the Middle Ages as a time of stagnation and lack of progress. Yet in five hundred years the medievalists fathered one thousand towns (an immense achievement), connected them with rudimentary but usable roads, and maintained their population with food brought from the countryside. All this developed the familiarity with money and markets and the buying and selling way of life.

Progress was not only a matter of this slow urbanization. There

* See page 2162 in this volume.

was technical progress, too, of a vastly important sort. The commercial revolution could not begin until some form of rational money-accounting had developed; although the Venetians of the twelfth century were already using sophisticated accounting devices, the merchants in Europe were little better than schoolboys in their accounting ignorance. It took time for the recognition of the need for bookkeeping to spread; not until the seventeenth century was double entry a standard practice. And not until money was rationally accounted for could large-scale business operations run successfully.

Perhaps most important of all in the pervasiveness of its effect was a rise in scientific curiosity. Although the world would wait until the age of Adam Smith for its cataclysmic burst of technology, the industrial revolution could not have taken place had not the ground been prepared by a succession of basic subindustrial discoveries. The precapitalist era saw the birth of the printing press, the paper mill, the windmill, the mechanical clock, the map, and a host of other inventions. The idea of invention itself took hold; experimentation and innovation were looked on for the first time with a friendly eye.

No single one of these currents, acting by itself, could have turned society upside down. Indeed, many of them may have been as much the effects as the causes of a great convulsion in human organization. History turns no sharp corners, and the whole vast upheaval sprawled out over time. Evidences of the market way of life sprang up side by side with older traditional ways, and remnants of the former day persisted long after the market had for all practical purposes taken over as the guiding principle of economic organization. Thus guilds and feudal privileges were not finally abolished in France until 1790, and the Statute of Artificers which regulated guild practices in England was not repealed until 1813.

But by the year 1700, twenty-three years before Adam Smith was born, the world which had tried Robert Keayne, prohibited merchants from carrying unsightly bundles, worried over "just" prices, and fought for the privilege of carrying on in its fathers' footsteps was on the wane. In its place society has begun to heed a new set of "self-evident" dicta. Some of them are:

"Every man is naturally covetous of lucre."

"No laws are prevalent against gaine."

"Gaine is the Centre of the Circle of Commerce."

A new idea has come into being: "economic man"—a pale wraith of a creature who follows his adding-machine brain wherever it leads him. The textbooks will soon come to talk of Robinson Crusoes on desert isles who will organize their affairs as if they were so many corner grocers.

In the world of affairs a new fever of wealth and speculation has gripped Europe. In France in 1718 a Scottish adventurer named

John Law organized a wild blue-sky venture known as the Mississippi Company, selling shares in an enterprise which would mine the mountains of gold in America. Men and women fought in the streets for the privilege of winning shares, murders were committed, fortunes made overnight. One hotel waiter netted thirty million *livres*. When the company was about to topple, the government rounded up a thousand beggars and marched them through the streets of Paris with picks and shovels as a band of miners off for the Land of Eldorado. Of course the structure collapsed. But what a change from the timid capitalists of a hundred years ago to the get-rich-quick mobs jostling in the Rue de Quincampoix; what a money-hungry public this must be to swallow such a bare-faced fraud!

No mistake about it, the travail was over and the market system had been born. The problem of survival was henceforth to be solved neither by custom nor by command, but by the free action of profit-seeking men bound together only by the market itself. The system was to be called capitalism. And the idea of gain which underlay it was so firmly rooted that men would soon vigorously affirm that it was an eternal and omnipresent attitude.

PROPHETIC TITLE: THE WEALTH OF NATIONS

ADAM SMITH

[Adam Smith, *An Inquiry Into the Nature and Causes of the Wealth of Nations*, W. Strahan, and T. Cadell, in the Strand, London, and W. Creech, Edinburgh, 1776; vol. I, book I, pp. 5, 6–7, 9–12, 16–19; vol. II, book IV, pp. 35–36 (abridged).]

Adam Smith, who published *The Wealth of Nations* in 1776, is known as the great prophet of free competition. His doctrine of laissez faire has been taken to mean that businessmen should be *left alone to do* what is in their own self-interest, and the result will be that, as if guided by an invisible or divine hand, they will automatically and inevitably do what is best for the consuming public and/or the national economy. Actually, Smith himself pointed out that there were many limitations to such a doctrine, but he wrote so originally and so cogently that, like other intellectual pioneers, he has come to stand for more than he meant.

The fact remains that he, observing what some businessmen were already doing, took the lead in expounding the idea of division of labor, and in recognizing that the overall effect of individual decisions by individual businessmen tended, under the spur of competition, to work toward impersonal and unintended ends, which could actually be in the public interest. We must remember that for a good many years up to the beginning of the industrial revolution, which Adam Smith was observing, the actions of businessmen had been prescribed and circumscribed by all sorts of regulations, and he is therefore not only protesting against the past but being idealistic about the future—or what the future looked like to him at that time.

———◆———

THE GREATEST IMPROVEMENT in the productive powers of labor, and the greater part of the skill, dexterity, and judgment with which it is anywhere directed, or applied, seem to have been the effects of the division of labor.

The effects of the division of labor, in the general business of society, will be more easily understood, by considering in what manner it operates in some particular manufactures. . . .

To take an example . . . from a very trifling manufacture, but one in which the division of labor has been very often taken notice of, the trade of the pin-maker; a workman not educated to this business (which the division of labor has rendered a distinct trade), nor acquainted with the use of the machinery employed in it (to the invention of which the same division of labor has probably given occasion), could scarce, perhaps, with his utmost industry, make one pin in a day, and certainly could not make twenty. But in the way in which this business is now carried on, not only the whole work is a peculiar trade, but it is divided into a number of branches, of which the greater part are likewise peculiar trades. One man draws out the wire, another straights it, a third cuts it, a fourth points it, a fifth grinds it at the top for receiving the head; to make the head requires two or three distinct operations; to put it on is a peculiar business, to whiten the pins is another; it is even a trade by itself to put them into the paper; and the important business of making a pin is, in this manner, divided into about 18 distinct operations, which, in some manufactories, are all performed by distinct hands, though in others the same man will sometimes perform two or three of them. I have seen a small manufactory of this kind where ten men only were employed, and where some of them consequently performed two or three distinct operations. But though they were very poor, and therefore but indifferently accommodated with the necessary machinery, they could, when they exerted themselves, make among them about 12 pounds of pins in a day. There are in a pound upwards of 4000 pins of a middling size. Those ten persons, therefore, could make among them upwards of 48,000 pins in a day. Each person, therefore, making a tenth part of 48,000 pins, might be considered as making 4800 pins in a day. But if they had all wrought separately and independently, and without any of them having been educated to this peculiar business, they certainly could not each of them have made 20, perhaps not one pin in a day; that is, certainly, not the two hundred and fortieth, perhaps not the four thousand eight hundredth part of what they are at present capable of performing, in consequence of a proper division and combination of their different operations.

In every other art and manufacture, the effects of the division of labor are similar to what they are in this very trifling one; though, in many of them, the labor can neither be so much subdivided, nor reduced to so great a simplicity of operation. The division of labor, however, so far as it can be introduced, occasions, in every art, a proportionable increase of the productive powers of labor. . . .

This great increase of the quantity of work, which, in consequence of the division of labor, the same number of people are capable of performing, is owing to three different circumstances; first, to the increase of dexterity in every particular workman; secondly, to the saving of the time which is commonly lost in passing from one species of work to another; and lastly, to the invention of a great number of machines which facilitate and abridge labor, and enable one man to do the work of many.

First, the improvement of the dexterity of the workman necessarily increases the quantity of the work he can perform; and the division of labor, by reducing every man's business to some one simple operation, and by making this operation the sole employment of his life, necessarily increases very much the dexterity of the workman. A common smith, who, though accustomed to handle the hammer, has never been used to make nails, if upon some particular occasion he is obliged to attempt it, will scarce, I am assured, be able to make about 200 or 300 nails in a day, and those too very bad ones. A smith who has been accustomed to make nails, but whose sole or principal business has not been that of a nailer, can seldom with his utmost diligence make more than 800 or a thousand nails in a day. I have seen several boys under 20 years of age who had never exercised any other trade but that of making nails, and who, when they exerted themselves, could make, each of them, upwards of 2300 nails in a day. The making of a nail, however, is by no means one of the simplest operations. The same person blows the bellows, stirs or mends the fire as there is occasion, heats the iron, and forges every part of the nail; in forging the head too he is obliged to change his tools. The different operations into which the making of a pin, or of a metal button, is subdivided, are all of them much more simple, and the dexterity of the person, of whose life it has been the sole business to perform them, is usually much greater. The rapidity with which some of the operations of those manufactures are performed, exceeds what the human hand could, by those who had never seen them, be supposed capable of acquiring.

Secondly, the advantage which is gained by saving the time commonly lost in passing from one sort of work to another, is much greater than we should at first view be apt to imagine it. It is impossible to pass very quickly from one kind of work to another, that is carried on in a different place, and with quite different tools. A country weaver who cultivates a small farm must lose a good deal of time in passing from his loom to the field, and from the field to his loom. When the two trades can be carried on in the same workhouse, the loss of time is no doubt much less. It is even in this case, however, very considerable. A man commonly saunters a little in turning his hand from one sort of employment to another. When he first begins the new work he is seldom very keen and hearty; his mind, as they say, does not go to it, and for some time he rather trifles than applies to good purpose. The habit of sauntering and of indolent careless application, which is naturally, or rather necessarily, acquired by every country workman who is obliged to change his work and his tools every half hour, and to apply his hand in twenty different ways almost every day of his life, renders him almost always slothful and lazy, and incapable of any vigorous application even on the most pressing occasions. Independent, therefore, of his deficiency in point of dexterity, this cause alone must always reduce considerably the quantity of work which he is capable of performing.

Thirdly, and lastly, everybody must be sensible how much labor is facilitated and abridged by the application of proper machinery. It is unnecessary to give any example. I shall only observe, therefore, that the invention of all those machines by which labor is so much facilitated and abridged seems to have been originally owing to the division of labor. Men are much more likely to discover easier and readier methods of attaining any object when the whole attention of their minds is directed towards that single object than when it is dissipated among a great variety of things. But in consequence of the division of labor, the whole of every man's attention comes naturally to be directed towards some one very simple object. It is naturally to be expected, therefore, that some one or other of those who are employed in each particular branch of labor should soon find out easier and readier methods of performing their own particular work, wherever the nature of it admits of such improvement. A great part of the machines made use of in those manufactures in which labor is most subdivided were originally the inventions of common workmen, who, being each of them employed in some very simple operation, naturally turned their thought towards finding out easier and readier methods of performing it. Whoever has been much accustomed to visit such manufactures must frequently have been shown very pretty machines, which were the inventions of such workmen in order to facilitate and quicken their own particular part of the work. In the first fire [steam] engines, a boy was constantly employed to open and shut alternately the communication between the boiler and the cylinder, according as the piston either ascended or descended. One of those boys, who loved to play with his companions, observed that, by tying a string from the handle of the valve which opened this communication to another part of the machine, the valve would open and shut without his assistance, and leave him at liberty to divert himself with his play-fellows. One of the greatest improvements that has been made upon this machine, since it was first invented, was in this manner the discovery of a boy who wanted to save his own labor. . . .

This division of labor, from which so many advantages are derived, is not originally the effect of any human wisdom, which foresees and intends that general opulence to which it gives occasion. It is the necessary, though very slow and gradual, consequence of a certain propensity in human nature which has in view no such extensive utility; the propensity to truck, barter, and exchange one thing for another.

Whether this propensity be one of those original principles in human nature, of which no further account can be given, or whether, as seems more probable, it be the necessary consequence of the faculties of reason and speech, it belongs not to our present subject to enquire. It is common to all men and to be found in no other race of animals, which seem to know neither this nor any other species of contracts. Two greyhounds, in running down the same hare, have sometimes the appearance of acting in some sort of concert. Each turns her towards his companion, or endeavors to intercept her when his companion turns her towards himself. This, however, is not the effect of any contract, but of the accidental concurrence of their passions in the same object at that particular time. Nobody ever saw a dog make a fair and deliberate exchange of one bone for another with another dog. Nobody ever saw one animal by its gestures and natural cries signify to another, this is mine, that yours; I am willing to give this for that. When an animal wants to obtain something either of a man or of another animal, it has no other means of persuasion but to gain the favor of those whose service it requires. A puppy fawns upon its dam, and a spaniel endeavors by a thousand attractions to engage the attention of its master who is at dinner, when it wants to be fed by him.

Man sometimes uses the same arts with his brethren, and when he has no other means of engaging them to act according to his inclinations, endeavors by every servile and fawning attention to obtain their good will. He has not time, however, to do this upon every occasion. In civilized society he stands at all times in need of the cooperation and assistance of great multitudes, while his whole life is scarce sufficient to gain the friendship of a few persons. In almost every other race of animals each individual, when it is grown up to maturity, is entirely independent, and in its natural state has occasion for the assistance of no other living creature. But man has almost constant occasion for the help of his brethren, and it is in vain for him to expect it from their benevolence only. He will be more likely to prevail if he can interest their self-love in his favor, and shew them that it is for their own advantage to do for him what he requires of them. Whoever offers to another a bargain of any kind proposes to do this. Give me that which I want, and you shall have this which you want, is the meaning of every such offer; and it is in this manner that we obtain from one another the far greater part of those good offices which we stand in need of. It is not from the benevolence of the butcher, the brewer, or the baker, that we expect our dinner, but from their regard to their own interest. We address ourselves, not to their humanity but to their self-love, and never talk to them of our own necessities but of their advantages. Nobody but a beggar chooses to depend chiefly upon the benevolence of his fellow citizens. Even a beggar does not depend upon it entirely. The charity of well-disposed people, indeed, supplies him with the whole fund of his subsistence. But though this principle ultimately provides him with all the necessaries of life which he has occasion for, it neither does nor can provide him with them as he has occasion for them. The greater part of his occasional wants are supplied in the same manner as those of other people, by treaty, by barter, and by purchase. With the money which one man gives him he purchases food. The old clothes which another bestows upon him he exchanges for other old clothes which suit him better, or for lodging, or for food, or for money, with which he can buy either food, clothes, or lodging, as he has occasion.

As it is by treaty, by barter, and by purchase that we obtain from one another the greater part of those mutual good offices which we stand in need of, so it is this same trucking disposition which originally gives occasion to the division of labor. In a tribe of hunters or shepherds a particular person makes bows and arrows, for example, with more readiness and dexterity than any other. He frequently exchanges them for cattle or for venison with his companions; and he finds at last that he can in this manner get more cattle and venison than if he himself went to the field to catch them. From a regard to his own interest, therefore, the making of bows and arrows grows to be his chief business, and he becomes a sort of armorer. Another excels in making the frames and covers of their little huts or movable houses. He is accustomed to be of use in this way to his neighbors, who reward him in the same manner with cattle and with venison, till at last he finds it his interest to dedicate himself entirely to this employment, and to become a sort of house-carpenter. In the same manner a third becomes a smith or a brazier; a fourth a tanner or dresser of hides or skins, the principal part of the clothing of savages. And thus the certainty of being able to exchange all that surplus part of the produce of his own labor, which is over and above his own consumption, for such parts of the produce of other men's labor as he may have occasion for, encourages every man to apply himself to a particular occupation, and to cultivate and bring to perfection whatever talent or genius he may possess for that particular species of business. . . .

As every individual, therefore, endeavors as much as he can both to employ his capital in the support of domestic industry, and so to direct that industry that its produce may be of the greatest value, every individual necessarily labors to render the annual revenue of the society as great as he can. He generally, indeed, neither intends to promote the public interest, nor knows how much he is promoting it. . . . He intends only his own security; and by directing that industry in such a manner as its produce may be of the greatest value, he intends only his own gain, and he is in this, as in many other cases, led by an invisible hand to promote an end which was no part of his intention. Nor is it always the worse for the society that it was no part of it. By pursuing his own interest he frequently promotes that of the society more effectually than when he really intends to promote it. I have never known much good done by those who affected to trade for the public good. It is an affectation, indeed, not very common among merchants, and very few words need be employed in dissuading them from it.

What is the species of domestic industry which his capital can employ, and of which the produce is likely to be of the greatest value, every individual, it is evident, can, in his local situation, judge much better than any statesman or law-giver can do for him. The statesman, who should attempt to direct private people in what manner they ought to employ their capitals, would not only load himself with a most unnecessary attention, but assume an authority which could safely be trusted, not only to no single person, but to no council or senate whatever, and which would nowhere be so dangerous as in the hands of a man who had folly and presumption enough to fancy himself fit to exercise it.

THE VIEWS OF AN ENGINEER
AHEAD OF HIS TIME

OLIVER EVANS

[Quoted in Greville Bathe and Dorothy Bathe, *Oliver Evans*, Historical Society of Pennsylvania, Philadelphia, 1935, p. iv.]

Oliver Evans was an engineer with a real flair for mechanization.* Needless to say, he was well ahead of his times, and failed to get the recognition he deserved during his lifetime, 1755 to 1819. That circumstance may have some bearing on this little piece of philosophy, written in his own hand on the last blank page of his book, *The Abortion of the Young Steam Engineer's Guide*, which he willed to his son, Cadwallader Evans.

WHEN WE SEE A MAN, one of the first ideas that strikes our minds is, that he can know but little more than ourselves.

When we read of a man in some distant country who has made some useful discovery either in art or science, we give more credit to what we hear than we would if we had seen him.

But when we read of a man who lived centuries ago and who laid down theories and rules as fundamental in the sciences, we can place implicit faith in them if we do not plainly see an absurdity in them, for we do not know but that he was more than human.

Therefore he that studies and writes on the improvements of the arts and sciences labors to benefit generations yet unborn, for it is not probable that his contemporaries will pay any attention to him, especially those of his relations, friends and intimates; therefore improvements progress so slowly.

* For an account of his almost fully automated flour mill, see Siegfried Giedion, Volume II.

COMMERCE AND FREE GOVERNMENT
RE-ENFORCE EACH OTHER

PHILIP HONE

[Philip Hone, "Commerce and the Commercial Character," *The Merchants' Magazine* (Freeman Hunt, ed.), New York, Jan. 1844, vol. X, no. 1, pp. 68–71 (abridged).]

Here is the text of "an address delivered before the Mercantile Library Association in Boston, October 3, 1843, by Philip Hone, Honorary Member of the Association, and, up to the present moment, a warm friend and patron." This is the way it is introduced in *Hunt's Merchants' Magazine* of January 4, 1844. Mr. Hone (1780–1851) was in the auction business in New York until the age of 41 when, having made his fortune, he retired to pursue his interests in politics, letters, and the drama. He was a businessman with a typical educated belief in the honor of his calling which characterized that period.

In this address Hone dips into history to prove his point about democracy being the encourager of business. It is notable that he stops quite short of being uncritical or sentimental about the commercialism of the Hanseatic League in the Middle Ages, thus demonstrating, indeed, the high ethical standards which he and his fellow businessmen of the pre-Civil War period were applying, or seeking to apply, to their own conduct.

Hone neatly separates Adam Smith and Karl Marx, just as the golden heyday of Hone's type of mercantilism separated two darker periods of economic history.

THE ONLY VIEW which I intend to take at this time, of commerce, a subject so multifarious in its aspects, and so prolific in its details, is its connection with the free institutions of government, the only soil in which it is raised and nurtured to perfection, and the reciprocity of interests which should bind them to each other. Commerce has never thriven under the retroaction of an arbitrary government, and even the bright gleam of commercial sunshine which flashed for a moment at the close of the fifteenth century over Spain and Portugal, when under the auspices of the, former, Columbus, the daring navigator, made in the great waters a path to the star which he descried in the west, and the discovery of a new passage to India, by the Cape of Good Hope, placed the trident of commerce within the grasp of the latter, these important events in the commercial history of the world serve only to confirm the theory which I have advanced. In vain the seed was planted and sprung up, the icy hand of despotism checked its growth, and the fierce rays of superstition scorched its branches; the genial dews of popular rights were not permitted to visit its roots, and it was denied the healthful culture of equal laws; and thus were the beneficent objects of divine goodness frustrated by the selfish inventions of man.

The principle which it is my desire to establish has an axiom, namely, that commerce can flourish only under the influence of popular laws, is beautifully illustrated by Dr. Watson, in his history of Philip II, where, in speaking of the causes of the commercial prosperity of the Netherlands in the sixteenth century, that accomplished historian discourses thus eloquently:

"The greatest advantages which nature affords for improvement in the arts of life may be rendered useless to the people who possess them, by an injudicious or tyrannical and oppressive exercise of the civil power; and universal experience proves how vain it is to expect that men will apply themselves with vigor to commercial pursuits when their persons are insecure, or when the fruits of their industry may be seized by the rapacious hand of a despotic prince. But happily for the inhabitants of the low countries, the sovereigns of the several provinces (unable, perhaps, from the small extent of their dominions, to execute any plan of tyranny against the people) were at a very early period induced to give their consent and sanction to the above-mentioned system of fundamental laws; by which, although their prerogative was abridged, yet their power and resources were greatly augmented, through that prosperity which their moderate government had enabled their subjects to attain." . . .

The celebrated Hanseatic league, the powerful combination of the Middle Ages, owes its origin and successful continuance for so long a period to the liberal forms of government and the lenient exercise of civil power enjoyed by the several members of the confederacy. Originally entered into by the free cities of Lübeck and Hamburg, with the object of resisting the pirates who infested the Baltic, and to protect their vessels from the barbarous nations, who had very indistinct notions of "free trade and sailors' rights," "they soon derived such advantages from this union," as Gibbon informs us, "that other towns acceded to their confederacy, and, in a short time, eighty of the most considerable cities, scattered through those vast countries, which stretch from the bottom of the Baltic to Cologne on the Rhine, joined in the famous Hanseatic league, which became so formidable that its alliance was courted, and its enmity dreaded by the greatest monarchs."

I am not prepared to say that this mighty combination of aristocratical merchants was the best school in the world for the cultivation of liberty and equality, especially as understood at the present day, and there is abundant evidence that they were not by any means particular in the choice of customers; they bought and sold, alike with Christian, Jew and infidel; they lent their money with equal freedom to arbitrary Austrian emperor and the enlightened Netherlanders, to assist him to rivet more firmly, and then to break asunder, the chains of despotism; and extended pecuniary assistance alike to the holy pontiff and the stubborn reformer. The best security and the largest interest, there is reason to fear, preponderated over the desire to improve the civil condition of mankind or extend the blessings of a reformed religion. But all this, if it be so, does not weaken the position I have assumed; the benefits of this great commercial league, while they were felt by the several confederated cities in the increase of wealth, the consciousness of power, and the diffusion of knowledge, spread far and wide over the civilized world, and the light then kindled on the altar of commerce, illuminated the dark places of superstition, though her priests may have been too much engaged in the pursuit of wealth, to assist in its dissemination. These were substantial benefits and, in my opinion, the causes which produced them could not have existed under an arbitrary form of government. The operations of trade must naturally tend to the diffusion of liberal opinions, albeit men will select their customers where they please, but the pure air of liberty is necessary to the existence of commerce as the favoring breeze which wafts the vessel to the "haven where she would be," and steady laws, administered upon settled principles, indispensable as the compass by which she is steered.

If other examples are necessary to prove that "where liberty dwells there is the country" of commerce, they may be found in the well regulated commercial systems of Holland, the brilliant achievements and extensive influence of the Venetian republic, and a new and better perception of the beauties of elegant literature and refined taste, which the nations imbibed from the Medician merchants of Florence. And in this category we may not omit to mention our good old mother across the waters, who (less free in name and form of government than some countries which have been enumerated, enjoys as large a share of the blessings of rational liberty) owes much of her national prosperity to the wisdom and stability of her laws for the protection of commerce and the security of the persons and property of those engaged in its pursuits. . . .

Commerce . . . prospers best under fixed rules of government, and the only changes it countenances are such as conform to the spirit of improvement in its administration and keep pace with the increasing knowledge of the age, following rather than leading in all such changes. A commercial circle in any country unfettered by bigotry or despotism must necessarily be composed of the most intelligent, enterprising and quick-sighted portions of the community; none other can hold a distinguished station in such a circle. . . .

Now, in all truly liberal and free countries such watchful guardians are allowed to hold an elevated position in the scale of estimate and to enjoy an important share of individual and collective influence; but not so in countries less free, or under governments of a different character, they cannot afford to permit this influence, they could not exist beneath the light of practical intelligence such as this; hence, under all despotic forms of government, the object is to weaken the effect of commercial influence and keep it as far as practicable in the background so that its warning voice shall not be heard from the watchtowers of the nation to disturb the action of its rulers.

A government so constituted will naturally discourage an institution which in its very nature is opposed to the existence of arbitrary power and the perpetuation of error; and the most effectual means of attaining this object is to lower its members in the eyes of the other classes of the community by denying them privileges common to all others; no blame can attach to an arbitrary government for this, it is only part of a principle which unhappily exists in all parts of the world, a struggle for power of the few over the many, which can only be corrected by the extension of liberal opinions and the diffusion of intelligence among the people.

If the autocrat of all the Russias manages, with the aid of the privileged orders who surround his throne, to push back the Russian merchant, even to the denying him a participation in the festivities of the court, which is extended to all other classes, and thereby keeps him in a comparatively degraded position, little distinguished from that of the itinerant peddler, so much the better for the autocrat and his arbitrary edicts.

The same invidious distinction was maintained even by Napoleon, the child of the revolution, nursed by democracy and raised by popular favor; the faubourg St. Antoine could be easily managed at all times, but the stubborn spirit of the Bourse required to be kept in check by the hand of despotism. Political as well as religious truth has ever been most effectually assailed in the persons of its disciples, and the influence of the free principles of commerce can only be counteracted by the proscription of its followers.

AN ANGRY GENIUS ON CAPITAL

~~✺①✺~~

KARL MARX

[Karl Marx, *Capital* (1867), trans. by Eden and Cedar Paul; George Allen &
Unwin, Ltd., London, 1928, vol. I, pp. 3–17 (abridged).]

A specter is haunting Europe—the specter of Communism. All
the powers of old Europe have entered into a holy alliance to
exorcise this specter. . . . Let the ruling class tremble at a
Communist revolution. The proletarians have nothing to lose but
their chains. They have a world to win. Workingmen of all countries unite!

These fiery words from one of the world's great revolutionary documents,
Manifest der Kommunisten, and the words that follow from *Das Kapital*
were, as everyone knows, written by "that angry genius," * Karl Marx
(1818–1883). But we must not forget that Marx was primarily a
philosopher—and such an important one in his effect on history that
we must try to understand him.

Marx was born in Trier, Germany, the second son of a liberal, well-
to-do lawyer, who was to raise his son on the ideas of Locke, Diderot,
and Voltaire. Marx was headed toward a career in law, too, but at the
universities of Bonn and Berlin he was drawn into philosophy and the
great debate over Hegel that was then occupying the minds of the day.
When an academic career became impossible because of Marx's radical
leanings (he was then a member of the "Young Hegelians"), Marx
became editor of a liberal newspaper, the *Rheinische Zeitung.* But
within five months the paper had grown too radical for the Prussian
government, and it was suppressed.

In 1843, Marx married Jenny von Westphalen, daughter of a baron,
and they moved to Paris, where Marx met Friedrich Engels, who was
to become his lifelong friend and collaborator.

Next, in Brussels, Marx and Engels joined a secret communistic
society of German workers, which became known as the "League of
the Communists" (the forerunner of the International Workingmen's
Association, organized in London in 1864). For this League, Marx
and Engels drew up a declaration of principles, and the result was the
Manifest der Kommunisten, or *Communist Manifesto,* in 1848.

That year was a year of revolutions; it seemed to the two young
men and, indeed, to many others, that their prophecy was materializing.

---

* Robert L. Heilbroner, *The Worldly Philosophers,* Simon and Schuster, New York,
1953, p. 130.

In an effort to fan the revolutionary flames, Marx and Engels traveled to Cologne to start another newspaper, but, true to form, they were soon expelled by the Prussian government. After a short sojourn in Paris, Marx went to London, where he was to remain until his death.

In London, Marx faced a desperate financial situation. His family occupied two rooms in the Soho section of the city. Of his six children born, three died in childhood. Although Marx made some money by writing letters on European politics for the New York *Tribune,* he was sometimes forced to stay at home because his coat and shoes were at pawn, and occasionally his work never reached the publisher because he did not have the money for the postage.

It was at this time, amidst great poverty, that Marx published *Das Kapital* (1867), his *magnum opus.*

Here we present the cornerstone of Marx's philosophy, as expressed in the first chapter of *Das Kapital:* that the true value of commodities is determined by the amount of labor that goes into their production. Implicit is the assumption that labor itself is qualitatively uniform; it follows that wage rates should be uniform across jobs or industries of differing difficulty or different demands of skill, although of course in practice the Soviets have abandoned this idea—had to abandon it, in fact, to get the proper incentives for their workers.

It is a little amusing, wryly, that the effect of the Marxian emphasis on the end product of labor is to downgrade labor to a level mediocrity. Adam Smith does almost the same thing for capital and, by implication, management: even self-interest is automatic.

◆

1. THE TWO FACTORS OF A COMMODITY: USE-VALUE AND VALUE (SUBSTANCE OF VALUE, MAGNITUDE OF VALUE)

The wealth of societies in which the capitalist method of production prevails takes the form of "an immense accumulation of commodities," wherein individual commodities are the elementary units. Our investigation must therefore begin with an analysis of the commodity.

A *commodity* is primarily an external object, a thing whose qualities enable it, in one way or another, to satisfy human wants. The nature of these wants, whether for instance they arise in the stomach or in the imagination, does not affect the matter. Nor are we here concerned with the question, how the thing satisfies human want, whether directly or as a means of subsistence (that is to say, as an object of enjoyment) or indirectly as a means of production.

Every useful object, such as iron, paper, etc., must be regarded from a twofold outlook, that of quality and that of quantity. Every such object is an assemblage of numerous properties, and may therefore be useful in various ways. To discover these various ways, and thus to find out the manifold uses of things, is a work of time. Time is likewise needed for the discovery of social standards of measurement for the quantity of useful objects. The variability of the quantitative standards by which commodities are measured is partly dependent upon the varying nature of the objects to be measured and partly upon convention.

The utility of a thing makes it a use-value. But this utility is not a thing apart. Being determined by the properties of the commodity, it does not exist without them. The commodity itself, such as iron, wheat, a diamond, etc., is therefore a use-value or good. Its character in this respect is independent of the amount of human labor required for the appropriation of its useful qualities. In the consideration of use-values, their quantitative determination is always taken for granted, as when we deal with watches by the dozen, linen by the yard, iron by the ton, and so on. The use-value of commodities form the topic of a special study, the science of commodities. Use-value is only realized in use or consumption. Use-values comprise the material content of wealth, whatever its social form may be. In the form of society we are about to examine, they constitute likewise the material depositories of exchange-values.

Exchange-value shows itself primarily as the quantitative ratio, the proportion, in which use-values of one kind are exchanged for use-values of another kind, a ratio continually varying with changes in time and place. Exchange-value thus seems to be something fortuitous and purely relative, and an exchange-value immanent in commodities (intrinsic value) would consequently appear to be a contradiction in terms. Let us look into the matter more closely.

A certain commodity, such as a quarter of wheat, can be exchanged for x blacking, y silk, z gold, etc. In a word, it can be exchanged for other commodities in varying proportions. The wheat, therefore, has numerous exchange-values instead of only one. Since, however, x blacking, y silk, z gold, etc., each represents the exchange-value of one quarter of wheat, it follows that x blacking, y silk, z gold, etc., must be mutually interchangeable, must have equal exchange-values. From this we infer: first, that the valid exchange-values of a commodity are equal one to another; and, secondly, that exchange-value must be the mode of expression, the "phenomenal form," of something contained in the commodity but distinguishable from it.

Now let us take two commodities, such as wheat and iron. Whatever the ratio of exchange may be, it can always be represented by an equation in which a given quantity of wheat is equated with some quantity or other of iron. For instance, our equation may read: one quarter of wheat = x cwt. of iron. What does this equation mean? It tells us that in two different things, namely in one quarter of wheat and in x cwt. of iron, there exists in equal quantities something common to both. They are, therefore, equal to a third something, which differs in essence from them both. Each of them, in so far as it is exchange-value, must be reducible to the third.

A simple geometrical illustration will make this clear. When we wish to ascertain the areas of rectilinear figures, and to compare these one with another, we subdivide them into triangles. The area of a triangle is itself determined by reduction to something very different from the visible shape of the triangle, namely to a rectangle whose area is the altitude of the triangle multiplied by half the base. In like manner, the exchange-values of commodities must be reduced to expressions of something quantitative which is common to them all.

This common "something" cannot be a geometrical, physical, chemical, or other natural property of commodities. The material properties of these only concern us here in so far as they confer utility, so as to render the commodities use-values. On the other hand, the obvious characteristic of the exchange ratio between commodities is precisely this, that it is an abstraction from their use-values. From that outlook, one use-value is just as good as another, if there be enough of it. Barbon said this long ago: "One sort of wares is as good as another, if the values be equal. There is no difference or distinction in things of equal value. . . . A hundred pounds' worth of lead or iron, is of as great value as one hundred pounds' worth of silver and gold." Regarded as use-values, commodities are, above all, of different quality; regarded as exchange-values, they can merely differ in quantity, for from this point of view they have no use-value at all.

When the use-values of commodities are left out of the reckoning, there remains but one property common to them all, that of being products of labor. But even the product of labor has already undergone a change in our hands. If, by our process of abstraction, we ignore its use-value, we ignore also the material constituents and forms which render it a use-value. It is no longer, to us, a table, or a house, or yarn, or any other useful thing. All the qualities whereby it affects our senses are annulled. It has ceased to be the product of the work of a joiner, a builder, a spinner, the outcome of some specific kind of productive labor. When the useful character of the labor products vanishes, the useful character of the labor embodied in them vanishes as well. The result is that the various concrete forms of that labor disappear too; they can no longer be distinguished one from another; they are one and all reduced to an identical kind of human labor, abstract human labor.

Let us now consider the residuum of the labor products. Nothing is left of them but the before-mentioned unsubstantial entity, a mere jelly of undifferentiated human labor, this meaning the expenditure of human labor power irrespective of the method of expenditure. All that now matters in the labor products is that human labor power has been expended in producing them, that human labor power is stored up in them. As crystals of this social substance common to them all, they are values—commodity values.

In the ratio of exchange between commodities, their exchange-value seemed to us something that was completely independent of their use-values. Ignoring the use-value of the labor products, we arrive at their value in the sense above defined. The common element disclosed in the exchange ratio or exchange-value of the commodities is, in fact, their value. The course of our investigation will show that exchange-value is the necessary phenomenal form of value, the only form in which value can be expressed. For the nonce, however, we have to consider value in itself, and independently of this mode of expression.

A use-value or a good [a useful article] has value solely because abstract human labor has been embodied or materialized in it. How are we to measure this value? In terms of the quantity of "value-creating" substance it contains—the quantity of labor. This is itself measured by its duration; and labor time, in turn, is measured by hours, days, etc.

Now, if the value of a commodity be determined by the amount of labor expended during its production, it might seem at the first glance as if the value would be greater in proportion as the worker who made it was lazier or more unskilled, seeing that idleness or lack of skill would increase the time needed for production. But the labor which creates the substance of value is homogeneous human labor, the expenditure of a uniform labor power. The total labor power of society, as embodied in the gross value of all commodities, though comprising numberless individual units of labor power, counts as an undifferentiated mass of human labor power. Each of these individual units of labor power is the same human labor power as all the other units—in so far as it has the characteristics of social average labor power, and functions as such; in so far, that is to say, as in the production of a commodity it uses only the average labor time or the socially necessary labor time. Socially necessary labor time is the labor time requisite for producing a use-value under the extant social and average conditions of production, and with the average degree of skill and intensity of labor. After steam-power looms had got to work in England, only half (or thereabouts) of the previous amount of labor was needed to transform a given quantity of yarn into cloth. The individual hand-loom weaver took just as long to effect this transformation as before the introduction of steam-power into the textile industry, but the product of his one hour's labor under the old conditions represented the product of only half an hour's average social labor under the new, and was therefore worth only half as much as before.

What determines the magnitude of value of a use-value is, therefore, the amount of socially necessary labor it contains, or the social labor time requisite for its production. Speaking generally, in this connection, each individual commodity must be regarded as an average sample of its class. Commodities which contain equal quantities of labor, or can be produced in equal periods of labor time, have therefore the same magnitude of value. The ratio between the respective values of two commodities is identical with the ratio between the periods of necessary labor time occupied in their producton. "As values, commodities are nothing but particular masses of congealed labor time."

The magnitude of value of a commodity would thus remain constant, if the labor time needed for its production were constant. But this latter changes with every change in the productivity of labor. The productivity of labor is determined by various circumstances, among which may be mentioned: the workers' average skill; the development of scientific theory, and the degree to which this theory is applicable in practice; the social organization of production; the supply and the efficiency of the means of production; physical conditions. For example, a specified amount of labor will, in a favorable season, be represented by eight bushels of wheat, and in an unfavorable season by four. The same quantity of labor produces a larger quantity of ore in a rich mine than in a poor one. Diamonds are such scarce products in the earth's crust that, on the average, a very large amount of labor time is needed for their discovery; hence a diamond represents much labor condensed into a small space. Jacob doubts whether gold has ever been paid for at its full value, and this doubt is still more applicable to diamonds. According to Eschwege, by 1823 the total output of the Brazilian diamond mines during the previous eighty years had failed to realize a price equal to that of one and a half year's average produce of the sugar and coffee plantations of the same country, although the diamonds represented far more labor, and therefore more value. If richer diamond mines were discovered, a specified amount of labor would be represented by more diamonds, and the value of diamonds would diminish. Should it become possible, with a small expenditure of labor, to make diamonds out of charcoal, they might be worth less than bricks. Speaking generally, the greater the productivity of labor—the shorter is the period of labor time needed for the production of an article, the smaller the amount of crystallized labor it contains, and the less its value. Conversely, the smaller the productivity of labor—the longer is the period of labor time needed for the production of an article, and the greater its value. Thus the magnitude of value of a commodity varies directly as the amount, and inversely as the productivity, of the labor embodied in it.

A thing can be a use-value though it has no value. That is the case when its utility to mankind is not the outcome of labor. Instances are: air, virgin soil, prairie, primeval forest, etc. . . . A thing can be useful and the product of human labor without being a commodity. One who satisfies his wants with the product of his own labor makes a use-value but does not make a commodity. To produce commodities he must produce, not use-values merely, but use-values for others—social use-values. [Nor does it suffice to say that he produces "for others" without further qualification. The medieval peasant produced cense-corn for the seigneur and tithe-corn for the priest; but the fact that they were produced for others did not make commodities of cense-corn and tithe-corn. To become a commodity, a product must pass by way of *exchange* into the hands of the other person for whom it is a use-value.—FRIEDRICH ENGELS] Finally, nothing can have value unless it has utility. If it is useless, the labor embodied in it has been useless; such labor cannot be counted as labor, and therefore cannot produce value.

2. TWOFOLD CHARACTER OF THE LABOR EMBODIED IN COMMODITIES

We saw at the outset that a commodity is compounded of two things, use-value and exchange-value. Subsequently it became clear that labor, too, in so far as it finds expression in value, acquires characteristics differing from those of labor as the producer of use-values. I was the first to point out and discuss this twofold character of the labor embodied in commodities. Since it is upon this that the understanding of political economy turns, we must look into the matter more closely.

Let us take two commodities, such as a coat and ten yards of linen. The former we will suppose to be worth twice as much as the latter, so that, if ten yards of linen = W, the coat = 2 W.

The coat is a use-value; it satisfies a special want. To produce it, a particular kind of productive activity is requisite. The nature of this activity is determined by its purpose, mode of operation, substance, means, and result. The labor whose utility is thus represented in the use-value of its product, or the labor which thus manifests itself by making its product a use-value, is termed, for short, "useful labor." From this outlook, labor is always regarded with an eye to its effect as producer of utility.

Just as the coat and the linen are qualitatively different use-values, so are the forms of labor that respectively produce them (tailoring and weaving) qualitatively different. Were not the two things qualitatively different use-values, and therefore the products of qualitatively different forms of useful labor, they could not confront one another as commodities. Coats are not exchanged for coats; a use-value is not exchanged for another use-value of the same kind.

In the totality of different kinds of use-values or commodities, there is embodied a totality of equally diversified forms of useful labor. The kinds of useful labor can be divided into genera, species, subspecies, and varieties—for there is a social division of labor. This division of labor is essential to the production of commodities; although it is not true, conversely, that there is no social division of labor in the absence of commodity production. In the primitive communities of India there is social division of labor, but the products of this community production do not become commodities. To take an example that lies nearer to our hand, in every factory there is a systematic division of labor, but this division of labor is not brought into being by an exchange of individual products among the workers in the factory. The only products which confront one another as commodities are those produced by reciprocally independent enterprises.

We have learned, then, that in the use-value of every commodity there is embodied definite, purposive, productive activity, or, in other words, useful labor. Use-values cannot confront one another as commodities, unless they contain qualitatively different forms of useful labor. In a society whose products, in general, take the form of commodities, i.e., in a society of commodity producers, this qualitative differentiation of useful forms of labor carried on by reciprocally independent enterprises develops into a complicated system, a social division of labor.

The coat, as a coat, fulfills its purpose equally well whether it is worn by the tailor who makes it or by one of that tailor's customers. In either case it functions as a use-value. Nor is the relation between the coat and the labor which produces it affected by the fact that tailoring may have become a special trade, an independent branch of the social division of labor. Urged to action by the need for clothing, man made garments for thousands of years before anyone became a tailor. But the existence of the coat, of the linen, of every constituent of material wealth other than those freely provided by nature, must be brought about by a special, purposive, productive activity, one which adapts particular gifts of nature to particular human wants. As creator of use-values, as useful labor, labor is a necessary condition of human existence, and one that is independent of the forms of human society; it is, through all the ages, a necessity imposed by nature itself, for without it there can be no interchange of materials between man and nature—in a word, no life.

The use-values coat, linen, commodities in general, are compounded of two elements, matter and labor. When we abstract the total amount of the various kinds of useful labor embodied in the coat, the linen, or any other commodity, there always remains a material substratum which has been supplied by nature without the help of man. In the process of production, man can only work as nature works—by changing the forms of matter. Nay, more, in this work of changing the forms of matter he is continually aided by the forces of nature. We see, then, that labor is not the only source of the use-values it produces, is not the only source of material wealth. As William Petty phrases it, while labor is the father of material wealth, the earth is its mother.

Let us now pass from the commodity regarded as an object possessing *utility,* to consider the *value* of the commodity.

In our example we assumed the coat to be worth twice as much as the linen. This, however, is merely a quantitative difference, which does not here concern us. Let us bear in mind, however, that, if a coat be worth twice as much as ten yards of linen, then twenty yards of linen will have the same magnitude of value as one coat. As values, coat and linen are of the same substance, are the objective expressions of one and the same kind of labor. Tailoring and weaving are, however, qualitatively different kinds of labor. Nevertheless, there are phases of social life in which a man will sometimes do tailoring work and sometimes weaving. In that case, the two different kinds of labor are but modifications of the labor of the same individual, instead of being peculiar and permanent functions of different individuals; just as the coat which a tailor makes one day and the trousers which he makes the next are but variations of the same individual labor. It is, moreover, obvious that in our capitalist society, in accordance with variations in the demand for labor, a given portion of human labor will be supplied, now in the form of tailoring, and now in the form of weaving. No doubt this change in the form of labor is likely to be attended by friction, but it is inevitable none the less. The essence of productive activity, if we disregard its particular form and consequently ignore the utility of the labor, is this—that it is an expenditure of human labor power. Tailoring and weaving, though qualitatively different productive activities, are both of them productive expenditure of the human brain, muscle, nerve, hand, etc., and in this sense are both of them human labor. They are merely two different ways of expending human labor power. Of course, this human labor power must be more or less developed before it can be expended in varying forms. But the value of any commodity represents human labor unqualified, represents generalized human labors. Just as in bourgeois society a commander-in-chief or a banker plays a great part, whereas a mere "man" plays a small one, so here with human labor. It is the expenditure of simple labor power such as, on the average, the ordinary man, without any special development of faculty, is equipped with in his bodily organism. Simple average labor doubtless varies in character as between one country and another, and as between one cultural epoch and another; but in any given community it is a constant. Skilled labor counts only as intensified, or rather multiplied, simple labor, so that a smaller quantity of skilled labor is equal to a larger quantity of simple labor. Experience shows that skilled labor can always be reduced in this way to the terms of simple labor. No matter that a commodity be the product of the most highly skilled labor, its value can be equated with that of the product of simple labor, so that it represents merely a definite amount of simple labor. The varying ratios in accordance with which different kinds of labor are reduced to simple labor as their standard are determined by a social process which goes on behind the backs of the producers and to them, therefore, seems to be established by custom. In what follows we shall, for simplicity's sake, regard every kind of labor power as simple labor power, thus saving ourselves the trouble of making the reduction.

When we consider coat and linen as values, we ignore differences in their use-values. In like manner, when we consider the labor embodied in these values, we ignore the differences in the kind of utility as between the two forms of useful labor, tailoring and weaving. Just as the use-values coat and linen are combinations of purposive activities with cloth and yarn respectively, whereas the values coat and linen are merely homogeneous aggregates of undifferentiated labor; so do the aggregates of labor incorporated in these values count, not in virtue of their productive relationship to the cloth or the yarn, but simply in virtue of being expenditures of human labor power. Tailoring and weaving are formative elements in the production of the use-values coat and linen for the very reason that the two kinds of useful labor differ in quality; but they are substantial constituents of the coat-value and the linen-value only in so far as their specific qualities as tailoring and weaving are disregarded, and only in so far as both have the same quality of being human labor.

Coat and linen, however, are not merely values in a general sense; they are values of a definite magnitude. According to our primary assumption, the coat is worth twice as much as the ten yards of linen. Whence does this difference in the magnitudes of their values arise? It is due to the fact that the piece of ten yards of linen embodies only half as much labor as the coat; this meaning that, for the production of the coat, labor power was expended for a time twice as long as that needed for the production of the linen.

Whereas, then, in respect of the use-value of a commodity, the labor embodied in it counts qualitatively only; in respect of the magnitude of its value, the labor counts only in a quantitative sense, after it has been reduced to human labor pure and simple. In the former case, we are concerned with the how and the why of the labor. In the latter case, we are concerned with the duration of the labor, must answer the question "How long?" Since the magnitude of the value of a commodity represents only the amount of labor which the commodity embodies, it follows that suitable proportions of various commodities will have values of equal magnitude.

If the productive power (let us say, of all the different kinds of useful labor needed to produce a coat) remains unchanged, the total magnitude of the values of a number of coats will increase as their number increases. If one coat represents the labor of x days, two coats will represent the labor of 2 x days, and so on. Next let us suppose that the amount of labor needed for the production of a coat is doubled or halved. If it be doubled, one coat will now be worth twice as much as two coats were worth before; if it be halved, two coats will now be worth only as much as one coat was worth before. Yet in either case a coat does the same service as before, and the useful labor embodied in it is just as good as of old. What has changed is the amount of labor expended in the production of a coat.

An increase in the quantity of use-value is an increase in material wealth. Two coats are more than one. Two coats serve to cover two men; one coat can cover one man only. Nevertheless, an increase in the amount of material wealth may take place while the magnitude of the value of this wealth falls. Such a contradictory movement is the outcome of the twofold character of labor. Productive power is, of course, in all cases the productive power of useful concrete labor; in actual fact it determines only the efficacy of purposive productive labor in a given space of time. Thus useful labor becomes a more abundant or a less abundant source of products, according as its productive power rises or falls. On the other hand, no change in productive power can, by itself, affect the labor that is embodied in value. Since the productive power appertains to the concrete useful form of labor, it cannot have any bearing on labor when labor is considered in the abstract, apart from its concretely useful form. In equal spaces of time, the same labor always generates equal magnitudes of value, however much the productive power may vary. But in equal spaces of time, the same amount of labor generates varying amounts of use-value; more when productive power rises, less when it falls. The same change in productive power which increases the yield of labor, and therefore increases the amount of use-values it generates, diminishes the magnitude of the value of this increased total mass if it lessens the sum-total of the labor time necessary for its production. The converse is equally true.

On the one hand, all human labor is, physiologically speaking, the expenditure of human labor power; and thus, as homogeneous or abstract human labor, it creates the value of commodities. On the other hand, all labor is the expenditure of human labor power in a special, purposive form; and thus, as concrete useful labor, it creates use-values.

3. THE FORM OF VALUE, OR EXCHANGE-VALUE

Commodities come into the world as use-values, such as iron, linen,

wheat, etc. This is their straightforward natural form. They are, however, commodities only in virtue of their twofold character, simultaneously as useful objects and as depositories of value. Consequently,
they can only manifest themselves as commodities, or can only have
the form of commodities, in so far as they have a twofold form: a
bodily form, and a value form.

The reality of the value of commodities thus resembles Mistress
Quickly, of whom Falstaff said: "A man knows not where to
have her." This reality of the value of commodities contrasts with the
gross material reality of these same commodities (the reality which is
perceived by our bodily senses) in that not an atom of matter enters
into the reality of value. We may twist and turn a commodity this way
and that—as a thing of value it still remains unappreciable by our
bodily sense. Let us recall, however, that commodities only possess
the reality of value in so far as they are expressions of one and the
same social unit, namely human labor. Since the reality of their value
is thus purely social, it is obvious that this reality can manifest itself
only in the social relation between one commodity and another. We
set out, in fact, from the exchange-value or ratio of exchange of commodities in order to get at the value that lies hidden in them. Now we
must return to this phenomenal form of value.

Everyone knows so much, at least, that commodities have a value
form common to them all, the money form; and they know that the
money form contrasts markedly with the manifold bodily forms of
their use-values. But here we are confronted by a task which bourgeois
economics has never even tried to undertake. We have to discover the
origin of the money form; to trace the development of the expression
of value contained in the value ratio of commodities; to follow this up
from its simplest and most inconspicuous configuration to the glar-
ingly obvious money form. Then the enigma of money will cease to
be an enigma.

A SOCIOLOGIST CRITICIZES
BUSINESS

THORSTEIN B. VEBLEN

[All by Thorstein Veblen: *The Theory of Business Enterprise,* Charles Scribner's Sons, New York, 1904, pp. 1–3, 35–37, 66–67. *The Theory of the Leisure Class,* The Macmillan Company, New York, 1912, pp. 22–30, 167–72; reprinted by permission of the Viking Press, Inc. *The Engineers and the Price System,* B. W. Huebsch, Inc., New York, 1921, pp. 131–37; reprinted by permission of the Viking Press, Inc.]

Here philosophy begins to tackle head-on the question of how business values affect society.

Thorstein Veblen was a critic of business, or perhaps, more accurately, of materialistic domination by the financial leaders of big business—what he called, using capital letters, the "Vested Interests." But he was objective, if not aloof; and caustic because he wrote as sharply as he saw. He was a sociologist; perhaps the period in which he lived and looked around did not compare very favorably with the other periods that his scholarly view of the whole range of time and geography provided.

His important writings date from 1899 to 1923. He observed the gilded age first-hand—and there were plenty of instances where gild and guilt were indeed synonymous. Here we present an amalgam from several of his best-known works.

Veblen, like Marx, looked forward to a change in the dominant hold which big business had on society. But he shows two very significant differences from Marx: (1) he saw the indispensability of complex, capitalistic organization, and (2) for betterment (particularly for release from the deadening effect of dollar values) he looked, not to the working masses, but to industrial technicians. But he was wrong in fearing that they would not have the guts and gumption to "rise."

THE MATERIAL FRAMEWORK of modern civilization is the industrial system, and the directing force which animates this framework is business enterprise. To a greater extent than any other known phase of culture, modern Christendom takes its complexion from its economic organization. This modern economic organization is the "capitalistic system" or "modern industrial system," so called. Its characteristic features, and at the same time the forces by virtue of which it dominates modern culture, are the machine process and investment for a profit.

The scope and method of modern industry are given by the machine. This may not seem to hold true for all industries, perhaps not for the greater part of industry as rated by the bulk of the output or by the aggregate volume of labor expended. But it holds true to such an extent and in such a pervasive manner that a modern industrial community cannot go on except by the help of the accepted mechanical appliances and processes. The machine industries—those portions of the industrial system in which the machine process is paramount— are in a dominant position; they set the pace for the rest of the industrial system. In this sense the present is the age of the machine process. This dominance of the machine process in industry marks off the present industrial situation from all else of its kind.

In a like sense the present is the age of business enterprise. Not that all industrial activity is carried on by the rule of investment for profits, but an effective majority of the industrial forces are organized on that basis. There are many items of great volume and consequence that do not fall within the immediate scope of these business principles. The housewife's work, e.g., as well as some appreciable portion of the work on farms and in some handicrafts, can scarcely be classed as business enterprise. But those elements in the industrial world that take the initiative and exert a far-reaching coercive guidance in matters of industry go to their work with a view to profits on investment, and are guided by the principles and exigencies of business. The businessman, especially the businessman of wide and authoritative discretion, has become a controlling force in industry, because, through the mechanism of investments and markets, he controls the plants and processes, and these set the pace and determine the direction of movement for the rest. His control in those portions of the field that are not immediately under his hand is, no doubt, somewhat loose and uncertain; but in the long run his discretion is in great measure decisive even for these outlying portions of the field, for he is the only large self-directing economic factor. His control of the motions of other men is not strict, for they are not under coercion from him except through the coercion exercised by the exigencies of the situation in which their lives are cast; but as near as it may be said of any human power in modern times, the large businessman controls the exigencies of life under which the community lives. Hence. upon him and his fortune centers the abiding interest of civilized mankind. . . .

In current discussion of business, indeed ever since the relation of businessmen to the industrial system has seriously engaged the attention of economists, the point to which attention has chiefly been directed is the businessman's work as an organizer of comprehensive industrial processes. During the later decades of the nineteenth century, particularly, has much interest centered, as there has been much provocation for its doing, on the formation of large industrial consolidations; and the evident good effects of this work in the way of heightened serviceability and economies of production are pointed to as the chief and characteristic end of this work of reorganization. . . . But there are other features of the case, less obtrusive and less attractive to the theoreticians, which need more detailed attention than they have commonly received. . . .

. . . The motives of the businessman are pecuniary motives, inducements in the way of pecuniary gain to him or to the business enterprise with which he is identified. The end of his endeavors is, not simply to effect an industrially advantageous consolidation, but to effect it under such circumstances of ownership as will give him control of large business forces or bring him the largest possible gain. The ulterior end sought is an increase of ownership, not industrial serviceability. His aim is to contrive a consolidation in which he will be at an advantage, and to effect it on the terms most favorable to his own interest.

. . . The spiritual ground of business enterprise . . . is given by the institution of ownership. "Business principles" are corollaries under the main proposition of ownership; they are principles of property—pecuniary principles. These principles are of older date than the machine industry, although their full development belongs within the machine era. As the machine process conditions the growth and scope of industry, and as its discipline inculcates habits of thought suitable to the industrial technology, so the exigencies of ownership condition the growth and aims of business, and the discipline of ownership and its management inculcates views and principles (habits of thought) suitable to the work of business traffic.

The discipline of the machine process enforces a standardization of conduct and of knowledge in terms of quantitative precision, and inculcates a habit of apprehending and explaining facts in terms of material cause and effect. It involves a valuation of facts, things, relations, and even personal capacity, in terms of force. Its metaphysics is materialism and its point of view is that of causal sequence. Such a habit of mind conduces to industrial efficiency, and the wide prevalence of such a habit is indispensable to a high degree of industrial efficiency under modern conditions. This habit of mind prevails most widely and with least faltering in those communities that have achieved great things in the machine industry, being both a cause and an effect of the machine process.

In the sequence of cultural evolution the emergence of a leisure class coincides with the beginning of ownership. This is necessarily the case, for these two institutions result from the same set of economic forces. In the inchoate phase of their development they are but different aspects of the same general facts of social structure. . . .

. . . The motive that lies at the root of ownership is emulation; and the same motive of emulation continues active in the further development of the institution to which it has given rise and in the development of all those features of the social structure which this institution of ownership touches. The possession of wealth confers honor; it is an invidious distinction. . . .

Those members of the community who fall short of this, somewhat indefinite, normal degree of prowess or of property suffer in the esteem of their fellow men; and consequently they suffer also in their own esteem, since the usual basis of self-respect is the respect accorded by one's neighbors.

. . . It is especially the rule of the conspicuous waste of goods that finds expression in dress, although the other, related principles of pecuniary repute are also exemplified in the same contrivances. Other methods of putting one's pecuniary standing in evidence serve their end effectually, and other methods are in vogue always and everywhere; but expenditure on dress has this advantage over most other methods, that our apparel is always in evidence and affords an indication of our pecuniary standing to all observers at the first glance. . . .

The dress of women goes even farther than that of men in the way of demonstrating the wearer's abstinence from productive employment. It needs no argument to enforce the generalization that the more elegant styles of feminine bonnets go even farther toward making work impossible than does the man's high hat. The woman's shoe adds the so-called French heel to the evidence of enforced leisure afforded by its polish; because this high heel obviously makes any, even the simplest and most necessary, manual work extremely difficult. The like is true even in a higher degree of the skirt and the rest of the drapery which characterizes woman's dress. The substantial reason for our tenacious attachment to the skirt is just this: it is expensive and it hampers the wearer at every turn and incapacitates her for all useful exertion. The like is true of the feminine custom of wearing the hair excessively long.

But the woman's apparel not only goes beyond that of the modern man in the degree in which it argues exemption from labor; it also adds a peculiar and highly characteristic feature which differs in kind from anything habitually practiced by the men. This feature is the class of contrivances of which the corset is the typical example. The corset is, in economic theory, substantially a mutilation, undergone for the purpose of lowering the subject's vitality and rendering her permanently and obviously unfit for work. It is true, the corset impairs the personal attractions of the wearer, but the loss suffered on that score is offset by the gain in reputability which comes of her visibly increased expensiveness and infirmity. It may broadly be set down that the womanliness of woman's apparel resolves itself, in point of substantial fact, into the more effective hindrance to useful exertion offered by the garments peculiar to women. . . .

So far, then, we have, as the great and dominant norm of dress, the broad principle of conspicuous waste. Subsidiary to this principle, and as a corollary under it, we get as a second norm the principle of conspicuous leisure. In dress construction this norm works out in the shape of divers contrivances going to show that the wearer does not and, as far as it may conveniently be shown, can not engage in productive labor.

Now, as to the country's industrial system . . . it is a comprehensive and balanced scheme of technological administration. Industry of this modern sort—mechanical, specialized, standardized, running to quantity production, drawn on a large scale—is highly productive; provided always that the necessary conditions of its working are met in some passable fashion. These necessary conditions of productive industry are of a well-defined technical character, and they are growing more and more exacting with every further advance in the industrial arts. This mechanical industry draws always more and more largely and urgently on the natural sources of mechanical power, and it necessarily makes use of an ever increasingly wide and varied range of materials, drawn from all latitudes and all geographical regions, in spite of obstructive national frontiers and patriotic animosities; for the mechanical technology is impersonal and dispassionate, and its end is very simply to serve human needs, without fear or favor or respect of persons, prerogatives, or politics. It makes up an industrial system of an unexampled character—a mechanically balanced and interlocking system of work to be done, the prime requisite of whose working is a painstaking and intelligent coordination of the processes at work, and an equally painstaking allocation of mechanical power and materials. The foundation and driving force of it all is a massive body of technological knowledge, of a highly impersonal and altogether unbusinesslike nature, running in close contact with the material sciences, on which it draws freely at every turn—exactingly specialized, endlessly detailed, reaching out into all domains of empirical fact. . . .

Such is the system of productive work which has grown out of the industrial revolution, and on the full and free run of which the material welfare of all the civilized peoples now depends from day to day. Any defect or hindrance in its technical administration, any intrusion of nontechnical considerations, any failure or obstruction at any point, unavoidably results in a disproportionate set-back to the balanced whole and brings a disproportionate burden of privation on all these peoples whose productive industry has come within the sweep of the system.

It follows that those gifted, trained, and experienced technicians who now are in possession of the requisite technological information and experience are the first and instantly indispensable factor in the everyday work of carrying on the country's productive industry. They now constitute the general staff of the industrial system, in fact; whatever law and custom may formally say in protest. The "captains of industry" may still vaingloriously claim that distinction, and law and custom still countenance their claim; but the captains have no technological value, in fact.

Therefore any question of a revolutionary overturn, in America . . . resolves itself in practical fact into a question of what the guild of technicians will do. In effect it is a question whether the discretion and responsibility in the management of the country's industry shall pass from the financiers, who speak for the Vested Interests, to the technicians, who speak for the industrial system as a going concern. There is no third party qualified to make a colorable bid, or able to make good its pretensions if it should make a bid. . . .

They [the technicians] have hitherto been quite unreflectingly content to work piecemeal, without much of an understanding among themselves, unreservedly doing job-work for the Vested Interests. . . .

. . . The material welfare of all the advanced industrial peoples rests in the hands of these technicians, if they will only see it that way, take counsel together, constitute themselves the self-directing general staff of the country's industry, and dispense with the interference of the lieutenants of the absentee owners. Already they are strategically in a position to take the lead and impose their own terms of leadership, so soon as they, or a decisive number of them, shall reach a common understanding to that effect and agree on a plan of action.

But there is assuredly no present promise of the technicians' turning their insight and common sense to such a use. . . . The technicians are a "safe and sane" lot, on the whole; and they are pretty well commercialized, particularly the older generation, who speak with authority and conviction, and to whom the younger generation of engineers defer, on the whole, with such a degree of filial piety as should go far to reassure all good citizens. And herein lies the present security of the Vested Interests. . . .

THE BEGINNINGS OF MY POLITICAL
ACTIVITY WERE IN ECONOMICS

ADOLF HITLER

[Adolf Hitler, *Mein Kampf*, translated by Ralph Manheim, Houghton Mifflin Company, The Riverside Press, Boston, Mass, copyright 1943, pp. 210, 213-15.]

Economic forces have undoubtedly been responsible for international tensions and open wars. But sometimes the financiers have been used unfairly as pretexts for incendiary action. The following selection is interesting because it provides a lovely (really unlovely) picture of such a distorted use by one of the great distorters of history, Adolf Hitler. Here, in *Mein Kampf* (1925), the Nazi leader describes what he learned from a lecture by Gottfried Feder, a German engineer turned amateur economist. The supernationalism of Hitler's reaction is of course typical; this is how he began his political activity, he says here, and this is how he ended it, except that the latter occasion had more realistic battle sounds in the background.

IN MY EYES, Feder's merit consisted in having established with ruthless brutality the speculative and economic character of stock exchange and loan capital, and in having exposed its eternal and age-old presupposition which is interest. . . .

As I listened to Gottfried Feder's first lecture about the "breaking of interest slavery," I knew at once that this was a theoretical truth which would inevitably be of immense importance for the future of the German people. The sharp separation of stock exchange capital from the national economy offered the possibility of opposing the internationalization of the German economy without at the same time menacing the foundations of an independent national self-maintenance by a struggle against all capital. The development of Germany was much too clear in my eyes for me not to know that the hardest battle would have to be fought, not against hostile nations, but against international capital. In Feder's lecture I sensed a powerful slogan for this coming struggle.

And here again later developments proved how correct our sentiment of those days was. Today the know-it-alls among our bourgeois politicians no longer laugh at us; today even they, in so far as they are not conscious liars, see that international stock exchange capital was not only the greatest agitator for the War, but that especially, now that the fight is over, it spares no effort to turn the peace into a hell.

The fight against international finance and loan capital became the most important point in the program of the German nation's struggle for its economic independence and freedom.

As regards the objections of so-called practical men, they can be answered as follows: All fears regarding the terrible economic consequences of the "breaking of interest slavery" are superfluous; for, in the first place, the previous economic prescriptions have turned out very badly for the German people, and your positions on the problems of national self-maintenance remind us strongly of the reports of similar experts in former times, for example, those of the Bavarian medical board on the question of introducing the railroad. It is well known that none of the fears of this exalted corporation were later realized: the travelers in the trains of the new "steam horse" did not get dizzy, the onlookers did not get sick, and the board fences to hide the new invention from sight were given up—only the board fences around the brains of all so-called experts were preserved for posterity.

In the second place, the following should be noted: every idea, even the best, becomes a danger if it parades as a purpose in itself, being in reality only a means to one. For me and all true National Socialists there is but one doctrine: People and fatherland.

What we must fight for is to safeguard the existence and reproduction of our race and our people, the sustenance of our children and the purity of our blood, the freedom and independence of the fatherland, so that our people may mature for the fulfillment of the mission allotted it by the creator of the universe.

Every thought and every idea, every doctrine and all knowledge, must serve this purpose. And everything must be examined from this point of view and used or rejected according to its utility. Then no theory will stiffen into a dead doctrine, since it is life alone that all things must serve.

Thus it was the conclusions of Gottfried Feder that caused me to delve into the fundamentals of this field with which I had previously not been very familiar.

I began to study again, and now for the first time really achieved an understanding of the content of the Jew Karl Marx's life effort. Only now did his *Kapital* become really intelligible to me, and also the struggle of the Social Democracy against the national economy, which aims only to prepare the ground for the domination of truly international finance and stock exchange capital.

CONSTRUCTIVE CONFLICT, OR HOW TO DEAL WITH DIFFERENCES IN BUSINESS ADMINISTRATION

〜◊〜

MARY PARKER FOLLETT

[Mary Parker Follett, "The Psychological Foundations: Constructive Conflict," in Henry C. Metcalf (ed.), *Scientific Foundations of Business Administration*, The Williams and Wilkins Company, Baltimore, 1926, pp. 114–131.]

With this selection we open a new door in the history of thought to follow philosophy inside the business enterprise.

Is it surprising that the first penetrating studies of the deeper human forces involved in business administration should have been made by a woman, Mary Parker Follett? Or did the first steps *have* to be taken by a person with more intuition than most mere men possess? Of course, she also had the advantage of being a trained psychologist, and having a brilliant mind.

The following selection is the text of a paper which she gave before a Bureau of Personnel Administration conference group in January 1925; it is one of four under the general title of "The Psychological Foundations of Business Administration"—which, incidentally, was not her own title, but the assigned subject on which she was invited to lecture. As she herself said, the subject was far too comprehensive to be covered in four papers, so she chose certain subjects which to her seemed "to go to the heart of personnel relations in industry." And this one, like other Mary Parker Follett pieces, is a classic.

———◆———

I WISH TO CONSIDER in this paper the most fruitful way of dealing with conflict [in business administration]. At the outset I should like to ask you to agree for the moment to think of conflict as neither good nor bad; to consider it without ethical prejudgment; to think of it not as warfare, but as the appearance of difference, difference of opinions, of interests. For that is what conflict means—difference. We shall not consider merely the differences between employer and employee, but those between managers, between the directors at the board meetings, or wherever difference appears.

As conflict—difference—is here in the world, as we cannot avoid it, we should, I think, use it. Instead of condemning it, we should set it to work for us. Why not? What does the mechanical engineer do with friction? Of course his chief job is to eliminate friction, but it is true that he also capitalizes friction. The transmission of power by belts depends on friction between the belt and the pulley. The friction between the driving wheel of the locomotive and the track is necessary to haul the train. All polishing is done by friction. The music of the violin we get by friction. We left the savage state when we discovered fire by friction. We talk of the friction of mind on mind as a good thing. So in business, too, we have to know when to try to eliminate friction and when to try to capitalize it, when to see what work we can make it do. That is what I wish to consider here, whether we can set conflict to work and make it *do* something for us.

METHODS OF DEALING WITH CONFLICT

There are three main ways of dealing with conflict: domination, compromise and integration. Domination, obviously, is a victory of one side over the other. This is the easiest way of dealing with conflict, the easiest for the moment but not usually successful in the long run, as we can see from what has happened since the war [World War I].

The second way of dealing with conflict, that of compromise, we understand well, for it is the way we settle most of our controversies; each side gives up a little in order to have peace, or, to speak more accurately, in order that the activity which has been interrupted by the conflict may go on. Compromise is the basis of trade union tactics. In collective bargaining, the trade unionist asks for more than he expects to get, allows for what is going to be lopped off in the conference. Thus we often do not know what he really thinks he should have, and this ignorance is a great barrier to dealing with conflict fruitfully. At the time of a certain wage controversy in Massachusetts, the lowest-paid girls in the industry were getting about $8.00 or $9.00 a week. The demand made by two of the representatives of the girls was for $22.40 (for a minimum wage, note), obviously too great an increase for anyone seriously to think of getting at one time. Thus the employers were as far as ever from knowing what the girls really thought they ought to have.

But I certainly ought not to imply that compromise is peculiarly a trade union method. It is the accepted, the approved, way of ending controversy. Yet no one really wants to compromise, because that means a giving up of something. Is there then any other method of ending conflict? There is a way beginning now to be recognized at least, and even occasionally followed: when two desires are *integrated,* that means that a solution has been found in which both desires have found a place, that neither side has had to sacrifice anything. Let us take some very simple illustration. In the Harvard Library one day, in one of the smaller rooms, someone wanted the window open, I wanted it shut. We opened the window in the next room, where no one was sitting. This was not a compromise because there was no curtailing of desire; we both got what we really wanted. For I did not want a closed room, I simply did not want the north wind to blow directly on me; likewise the other occupant did not want that particular window open, he merely wanted more air in the room.

I have already given this illustration in print. I repeat it here because this instance, from its lack of any complications, shows my point at once, I think. Let us take another illustration. A Dairymen's Co-operative League almost went to pieces last year on the question of precedence in unloading cans at a creamery platform. The men who came down the hill (the creamery was on a down grade) thought they should have precedence; the men who came up the hill thought they should unload first. The thinking of both sides in the controversy was thus confined within the walls of these two possibilities, and this prevented their even trying to find a way of settling the dispute which would avoid these alternatives. The solution was obviously to change the position of the platform so that both up-hillers and down-hillers could unload at the same time. But this solution was not found until they had asked the advice of a more or less professional integrator. When, however, it was pointed out to them, they were quite ready to accept it. Integration involves invention, and the clever thing is to recognize this, and not to let one's thinking stay within the boundaries of two alternatives which are mutually exclusive.

Take another case. There is sometimes a question whether the meetings of works committees should be held in the plant or outside: the argument for meeting inside is the obvious advantage of being near one's work; the argument against, the fear of company influence. I know one factory that made what I consider an integration by having the meetings of the works committee held in the separate club building of the employees situated within the factory grounds. Here the men felt much freer than in any other part of the plant.

A friend gave me this example. He was called on jury service in a murder trial. The district attorney asked him whether he had any objection to capital punishment. He replied, "Yes, definitely so." The "conflict" was then on, for the judge thought this opinion incapacitated him for service in a murder trial. My friend summed up the incident to me in these words: "After the judge had subjected me to a kind of cross-examination, I was put into the jury box, but neither the judge nor myself was left as victor; the experience had changed us both. We found the solution instead of vindicating the prejudgment of either of us; the solution being that it is possible to render a verdict in accordance with evidence so that you need not evade your duties as a citizen whatever your opinion of capital punishment." . . .

Some people tell me that they like what I have written on integration, but say that I am talking of what ought to be instead of what is. But indeed I am not; I am talking neither of what is, to any great extent, nor of what ought to be merely, but of what perhaps may be.

This we can discover only by experiment. That is all I am urging, that we try experiments in methods of resolving differences; differences on the board of directors, with fellow managers or heads of departments, with employees, or in other relations. If we do this, we may take a different attitude toward conflict.

The keyword of psychology today is *desire*. If we wish to speak of conflict in the language of contemporary psychology, we might call it a moment in the interacting of desires. Thus we take from it any connotation of good or bad. Thus we shall not be afraid of conflict, but shall recognize that there is a destructive way of dealing with such moments and a constructive way. Conflict as the moment of the appearing and focusing of difference may be a sign of health, a prophecy of progress. If the Dairymen's League had not fought over the question of precedence, the improved method of unloading would not have been thought of. The conflict in this case was constructive. And this was because, instead of compromising, they sought a way of integrating. Compromise does not create, it deals with what already exists; integration creates something new, in this case a different way of unloading. And because this not only settled the controversy but was actually better technique, saved time for both the farmers and the creamery, I call this: setting friction to work, making it *do* something.

Thus we see that while conflict as continued unintegrated difference is pathological, difference itself is not pathological. The fights in the Democratic convention were a hopeful sign for the Democratic party. What I think we should do in business organization is to try to find the machinery best suited for the normal appearing and uniting of diversity so that the difference does not stay too long crystallized, so that the pathological stage shall not be reached.

One advantage of integration over compromise I have not yet mentioned. If we get only compromise, the conflict will come up again and again in some other form, for in compromise we give up part of our desire, and because we shall not be content to rest there, sometime we shall try to get the whole of our desire. Watch industrial controversy, watch international controversy, and see how often this occurs. Only integration really stabilizes. But by stabilization I do not mean anything stationary. Nothing ever stays put. I mean only that that particular conflict is settled and the next occurs on a higher level.

Psychology has given us the phrase "progressive integratings"; we need also the phrase "progressive differings." We can often measure our progress by watching the nature of our conflicts. Social progress is in this respect like individual progress; we become spiritually more and more developed as our conflicts rise to higher levels. If a man should tell you that his chief daily conflict within himself is, "Shall I steal or not steal?" you would know what to think of his stage of development. As someone has said, "A man is known by the dilemmas he keeps." In the same way, one test of your business organization is not how many conflicts you have, for conflicts are the essence of life, but *what* are your conflicts? And how do you deal with them? It is to be hoped that we shall not always have strikes, but it is equally to be hoped that we shall always have conflict, the kind which leads to invention, to the emergence of new values.

Having suggested integration as perhaps the way by which we can deal most fruitfully with conflict, with difference, we should now consider the method by which integration can be obtained. But before we do that I want to say definitely that I do not think integration is possible in all cases. When two men want to marry the same woman, there can be no integration; when two sons both want the old family home, there can usually be no integration. And there are many such cases, some of little, some of great seriousness. I do not say that there is no tragedy in life. All that I say is that if we were alive to its advantages, we could often integrate instead of compromising. I have a friend who annoys me in this way. She makes a statement. I say, "I don't agree with that because . . ." and I intend to give my reasons, but before I have a chance she says, "Well, let's not fight about it." But I had no intention of fighting.

BASES OF INTEGRATION

If, then, we do not think that differing necessarily means fighting, even when two desires both claim right of way, if we think that integration is more profitable than conquering or compromising, the first step toward this consummation is *to bring the differences into the open.* We cannot hope to integrate our differences unless we know what they are. I will give some illustrations of the opposite method—evading or suppressing the issue.

I know a factory where, after the war, the employees asked for a 5 per cent increase in wages, but it was not clear to either side whether this meant a 5 per cent raise over present wages or over prewar wages. Moreover, it was seen that neither side wished to know! The employees naturally preferred to think the former, the managers the latter. It was some time before both sides were willing to face the exact issue; each, unconsciously, hoped to win by keeping the whole problem hazy.

One of the longest discussions I ever heard on a minimum wage board was in regard to the question of fares to and from work: first, whether this item should be included at all with board, lodging, etc., in a cost-of-living budget, that is, whether transportation to and from the plant should be a cost on production. When finally it was decided to leave the item in and allow 60 cents a week for it, instead of the $1.20 which the 10-cent Boston carfare would necessitate if this item were to be allowed for in full, it seemed to me a clear case of evasion or suppression. That is, the employers were not willing to face at that moment the question whether wages should include transportation. I sat on that board as a representative of the public, and I suggested more than once during the discussion that we should find out whether most of the girls in that particular industry did live near the plant or at a distance too great for walking. Also I suggested that we should find out whether, if they lived near the plant, the cost of board and lodging in that neighborhood was so high that it would more than offset car fares. But the employers in this instance were not ready to face the issue, and therefore the clearly evasive decision of 60 cents was made.

Another interesting case of suppression occurred in a committee of which I was a member. The question was a disagreement concerning the pay of two stenographers who were working for us. Those who urged the higher amount persisted in speaking of the stenographers' day as an eight-hour day because the hours are from nine to five, although with the hour out for lunch that obviously makes a seven-hour day.

Wherever you have the fight-set, you are in danger of obscurities, conscious or unconscious. As long as trade unionism is a defensive movement, as long as employers' associations are defensive movements, we shall have obscurities. As long as internationalism is what it is, evasion will go on. Of course not to *appear* to evade is part of good diplomacy, for you don't want the other side to think you are trying to "get by" on anything. But we shall continue to evade or suppress as long as our real aim is not agreement, but domination. Lord Shaw, chairman of the Coal Commission, put it as one of the essentials in arbitration that both sides should genuinely desire agreement. Here we get a very direct lesson from psychology.

The psychiatrist tells his patient that he cannot help him unless he is honest in wanting his conflict to end. The "uncovering" which every book on psychology has rubbed into us for some years now as a process of the utmost importance for solving the conflicts which the individual has within himself is equally important for the relations between individuals, or between groups, classes, races, nations. In business, the employer, in dealing either with his associates or his employees, has to get underneath all the camouflage, has to find the real demand as against the demand put forward, distinguish declared motive from real motive, alleged cause from real cause, and to remember that sometimes the underlying motive is deliberately concealed and that sometimes it exists unconsciously.

The first rule, then, for obtaining integration is to put your cards on the table, face the real issue, uncover the conflict, bring the whole thing into the open.

One of the most important reasons for bringing the desires of each side to a place where they can be clearly examined and valued is that evaluation often leads to *revaluation*. We progress by a revaluation of desire, but usually we do not stop to examine a desire until another is disputing right of way with it. Watch the evolution of your desires from childhood, through youth, etc. The baby has many infantile desires which are not compatible with his wish for approbation; therefore he revalues his desires. We see this all through our life. We want to do so-and-so, but we do not estimate how much this really means to us until it comes into conflict with another desire. Revaluation is the flower of comparison.

This conception of the revaluation of desire it is necessary to keep in the foreground of our thinking in dealing with conflict, for neither side ever "gives in" really, it is hopeless to expect it, but there often comes a moment when there is a simultaneous revaluation of interests on both sides and unity precipitates itself. This, I think, happened in Europe at the London Conference last summer, or rather it happened before that and led to the Conference. Integration is often more a spontaneous flowing together of desire than one might think from what I have said; the revaluing of interests on both sides may lead the interests to fit into each other, so that all find some place in the final solution.

The bearing of all this on business administration is, I hope, obvious. A business should be so organized (this is one of the tests for us to apply to our organization) that full opportunity is given in any conflict, in any coming together of different desires, for the whole field of desire to be viewed. Our employees should be able to see, as we should be able ourselves to see, the whole field of desire. The *field of desire* is an important psychological and sociological conception; many conflicts could, I believe, be prevented from ending disastrously by getting the desires of each side into one field of vision where they could be viewed together and compared. We all believe to a certain extent in Freud's "sublimation," but I believe still more that various desires get orientated toward one another and take on different values in the process of orientation.

It will be understood, of course, that all this applies to ourselves as well as to the other side; we have to uncover our subarticulate egoisms, and then, when we see them in relation to other facts and desires, we may estimate them differently. We often think it is a question of eliminating motives when it is only a question of subordinating them. We often, for instance, treat personal motives as more ignoble than we need. There is nothing necessarily discreditable in the politician's "standing by" his friends. The only ethical question is how much that motive is weighing against others. The unethical thing is to persuade yourself that it is not weighing at all.

I have time barely to mention a very important point: the connection between the *realignment of groups* and a revaluation of interests. I have found this important in watching the realignments of political parties. We must in any conflict between groups watch every realignment to see how far it changes the confronting desires, for this means how far it changes the conflict.

I began this section by saying that the first step in integration is to bring the differences into the open. If the first step is to put clearly before ourselves what there is to integrate, there is something very important for us to note—namely, that the highest lights in a situation are not always those which are most indicative of the real issues involved. Many situations are decidedly complex, involve numerous and varied activities, overlapping activities. There is too great a tendency (perhaps encouraged by popular journalism) to deal with the dramatic moments, forgetting that these are not always the most significant moments. We should not follow literary analogies here. You may have a good curtain with, to quote Kipling, the lovers loving and the parents signing checks. Yet, after all, this may not be the controlling moment in the lives of these people. To *find the significant rather than the dramatic features* of industrial controversy, of a disagreement in regard to policy on board of directors or between managers, is essential to integrative business policies.

Such search is part of what seems to me the second step in integration. If the first step is to uncover the real conflict, the next is to take the demands of both sides and break them up into their constituent parts. Contemporary psychology shows how fatal it is to try to deal with conglomerates. I know a boy who wanted a college education. His father died and he had to go to work at once to support his mother. Had he then to give up his desire? No, for on analysis he found that what he wanted was not a college education, but an education, and there were still ways of his getting that. You remember the southern girl who said, "Why, I always thought 'damned Yankee' was one word until I came north."

This method of *breaking up wholes* is the way you deal with business problems; it is the method which precedes business decisions. Take the case of inaugurating a system of approval shipment. A. W. Shaw, in his *Approach to Business Problems,* shows the subproblems involved here:

1. What will be the effect on collections and on the cost of shipment?

2. What is to be the credit policy?

3. Will the stock in transit or in the hands of customers reduce the number of turnovers per year?

4. Will the risk of damage to returned goods be great enough to jeopardize the regular profit?

5. Will the increase in sales more than offset any added cost in the administrative department?

6. Also psychological factors, as customers' curiosity and caution.

I have given this illustration at length because it seems to me that this is the method which should be applied to controversy. I wish indeed that every controversy might be considered a problem.

You will notice that to break up a problem into its various parts involves the *examination of symbols,* involves, that is, the careful scrutiny of the language used to see what it really means. A friend of mine wanted to go to Europe, but also she did not want to spend the money it would cost. Was there any integration? Yes, she found one. In order to understand it, let us use the method I am advocating; let us ask, what did "going to Europe" symbolize to her? In order to do that, we have to break up this whole, "going to Europe." What does "going to Europe" stand for to different people? A sea voyage, seeing beautiful places, meeting new people, a rest or change from daily duties, and a dozen other things. Now, this woman had taught for a few years after leaving college and then had gone away and led a somewhat secluded life for a good many years. "Going to Europe" was to her a symbol, not of snow mountains, or cathedrals, or pictures, but of meeting people—that was what she wanted. When she was asked to teach in a summer school of young men and women where she would meet a rather interesting staff of teachers and a rather interesting group of students, she immediately accepted. This was her integration. This was not a substitution for her wish, it was her *real* wish fulfilled.

I have given other illustrations of symbols in . . . my book, *Creative Experience.* There was an interesting one in the Loeb-Leopold case. I think there should have been taken into consideration in that case what life imprisonment symbolized. As there was no question of freeing the boys, the decision was to be made between death and life imprisonment. Therefore, when the latter sentence was given, that was a symbol, it seemed to me, of victory for the boys, especially since everyone thought that their detention would last only a few years. In many cases, on the other hand, life imprisonment is a symbol of defeat. I do not think that this was taken into account sufficiently in considering the effect of the sentence on the country.

It is, of course, unavoidable to use symbols; all language is symbolic; but we should be always on our guard as to what is symbolized. For instance, the marketing cooperatives say that they want their members to keep their pledges. That statement is a symbol for what they *really* want, which is to get enough of the commodity to control the market. Every day we use many more not-understood symbols, many more whole-words, unanalyzed words, than we ought to. Much of what is written of the "consumer" is inaccurate because *consumer* is used as a whole-word, whereas it is quite obvious that the consumer of large wealth has different desires and motives from the consumer of small means.

We have been considering the breaking up of the whole-demand. On the other hand, one often has to do just the opposite; find the whole-demand, the real demand, which is being obscured by miscellaneous minor claims or by ineffective presentation. The man with a genius for leadership is the one who can make articulate the whole-demand, unless it is a matter of tactics deliberately to conceal it. I shall not stop to give instances of this, as I wish to have time for some consideration of a point which seems to me very important for business, both in dealings with employees and with competing firms, and that is the anticipation of demands, of difference, of conflict.

Mr. Earl Howard, labor manager for Hart, Schaffner and Marx, said to me once, "It isn't enough merely to study the actual reactions of your employees; you must anticipate their reactions, beat them to it." That—to beat them to it—is exactly what each firm does try to do with its competing firms, but I do not think many managers study and anticipate the reactions of their employees as carefully as they do those of competing firms. It would be just as useful.

You could probably give me many illustrations of the *anticipation of response*. We could find innumerable examples in our households. A man liked motoring, his wife walking; he anticipated what her response might be to a suggestion that they motor on Sunday afternoon by tiring her out playing tennis in the morning.

The middlemen are deliberately anticipating response on the part of the farmers. In their struggle with the marketing cooperatives, they are basing their calculations of the future on the assumption that the particularistic tendency of the farmer is such that he cannot be held in line permanently, that he has been carried off his feet by victory and promises; moreover, that the use of legal power in enforcing contracts will in the end defeat the movement, that the farmer will surely rebel against this sort of coercion.

The anticipation of conflict, it should be noted, does not mean necessarily the avoidance of conflict, but playing the game differently. That is, you integrate the different interests without making all the moves. A friend of mine says that my theory of integration is like a game of chess. I think it is something like that. The tyro has to find his solution by making his actual moves, by the crude method of changing the places of his chessmen. A good chess player does not need to do this, he sees the possibilities without playing them out. The businessman in dealing with competitive firms is like the good chess player. As the real conflict between two good chess players is a conflict of possibilities that would be realized if they played them out, so in business you do not have to make all the moves to make your integrations; you deal with antecedents, premonitory symptoms, etc. You do not avoid doing certain things, you have done them without doing them.

But assuming that in our business we do watch response and anticipate response, that still is not going far enough. It is not enough to ask to what our employee or our business confrère or business competitor is responding, nor even to what he is likely to respond. We have to prepare the way for response, we have to try to build up in him a certain attitude. Of course every good salesman does this, but its necessity is not so fully recognized in other departments, and we shall therefore consider this question further in a later paper.

Yet even *preparation for response* is only a small part of the matter; we shall have to go deeper than that. There is *circular* as well as *linear* response, and the exposition of that is, I think, the most interesting contribution of contemporary psychology to the social sciences. A good example of circular response is a game of tennis. A serves. The way B returns the ball depends partly on the way it was served to him. A's next play will depend on his own original serve plus the return of B, and so on and so on. We see this in discussion. We see this in most activity between one and another. Mischievous or idle boys say, "Let's start something"; we must remember that whenever we act we have always "started something," behavior precipitates behavior in others. Every employer should remember this. One of the managers in a factory expressed it to me thus: "I am in command of a situation until I behave; when I act I have lost control of the situation." This does not mean that we should not act! It is, however, something to which it is very important that we give full consideration.

Circular response seems a simple matter, quite obvious, something we must all accept. Yet every day we try to evade it, every day we act and hope to avoid the inescapable response. As someone has said in another connection, "We feed Cerberus raw meat and hope that when we lie between his paws, he will turn out to be a vegetarian."

The conception of circular behavior throws much light on conflict, for I now realize that I can never fight you, I am always fighting you plus me. I have put it this way: that response is always to a relation. I respond, not only to you, but to the relation between you and me. Employees do not respond only to their employers, but to the relation between themselves and their employer. Trade unionism is responding, not only to capitalism, but to the relation between itself and capitalism. The Dawes plan, the London Conference, were obviously moments in circular behavior. Circular behavior as the basis of integration gives us the key to constructive conflict.

OBSTACLES TO INTEGRATION

Finally, let us consider the chief *obstacles to integration*. It requires a high order of intelligence, keen perception and discrimination, [and] more than all, a brilliant inventiveness; it is easier for the trade union to fight than to suggest a better way of running the factory. You remember that the Socialist party in Italy had a majority before Mussolini came in. But they would not take responsibility; they preferred to stay fighting, to attack what others were doing rather than to do themselves. They do not, I think, compare favorably with the English Labour party.

Another obstacle to integration is that our way of life has habituated many of us to enjoy domination. Integration seems to many a tamer affair; it leaves no "thrills" of conquest. I knew a dispute within a trade union where, by the skillful action of the chairman, a true integration was discovered and accepted, but instead of the satisfaction one might have expected from such a happy result, the evening seemed to end rather dully, flatly; there was no climax, there was no side left swelling its chest, no one had conquered, no one had "won out." It is even true that to some people defeat, as well as conquest, is more interesting than integration. That is, the person with decided fight habits feels more at home, happier, in the fight movement. Moreover, it leaves the door open for further fighting, with the possibility of conquest the next time.

Another obstacle to integration is that the matter in dispute is often theorized over instead of being taken up as a proposed activity. I think this important in business administration. Intellectual agreement does not alone bring full integration. I know one factory which deliberately provides for this by the many activities of its many subcommittees, some of which seem rather trivial unless one sees just how these activities are a contribution to that functional unity which we shall consider in a later paper.

I have been interested to watch how often disagreement disappears when theorizing ends and the question is of some definite activity to be undertaken. At a trade union conference, someone brought up the question of waste: how could the workmen help to eliminate waste? But it was found that most of the union men did not think it the job of the workmen to eliminate waste; that belonged to the management. Moreover, they did not think it to their interest to eliminate waste; wages were fixed by the union, by collective bargaining; everything saved went to swell profits; no more went into their pockets. It was seen, however, that there was another side, and the argument went on, but without coming to any agreement. Finally, however, by some maneuvering on the part of the chairman, it was acknowledged that there were certain forms of waste which the unions could be got to take cognizance of. A machinist, a plumber, and a carpenter undertook to take up with their unions the question of how far they could agree to take some responsibility for these particular types of waste. I hope the fact then emerged, when it was considered as a practical issue, that for some forms of waste the management is responsible, for some forms the employees, and for some forms the union.

A serious obstacle to integration which every businessman should consider is the language used. We have noted the necessity of making preparation in the other man, and in ourselves too, for the attitude most favorable to reconciliation. A trade unionist said to me, "Our representatives didn't manage it right. If instead of a 15 per cent increase they had asked for an adjustment of wages, the management would have been more willing to listen to us; it would have put them in a different frame of mind." I don't quite see why we are not more careful about our language in business, for in most delicate situations we quite consciously choose that which will not arouse antagonism. You say to your wife at breakfast, "Let's reconsider that decision we came to last night." You do not say, "I wish to give you my criticism of the decision you made last night."

I cannot refrain from mentioning a personal experience. I went into the Edison Electric Light Company and said to a young woman at a counter, "Where shall I go to speak about my bill?" "Room D for complaints," she replied. "But I don't wish to make a complaint," I said. "I thought there was a mistake in your bill." "I think there is," I said, "but I don't wish to complain about it; it was a very natural mistake." The girl looked nonplused, and as she was obviously speechless a man came out from behind a desk and said: "You would prefer to ask for an adjustment, wouldn't you?" and we had a chat about it.

I think that the "grievance committees" which exist in most factories are a mistake. I do not like the "trouble specialists" of the Ford plant. I wish it were not so often stated that shop or department committees were formed to "settle disputes." If you will get lists of these so-called "disputes," you will find that often they have not so much of the fight element in them as this word implies. But much of the language expressing the relation between capital and labor is that of a fight: "traditional enemies," the "weapon of the union," etc.

I have left untouched one of the chief obstacles to integration— namely, the undue influence of leaders—the manipulation of the unscrupulous on the one hand and the suggestibility of the crowd on the other. Moreover, even when the power of suggestion is not used deliberately, it exists in all meetings between people; the whole emotional field of human intercourse has to be taken fully into account in dealing with methods of reconciliation. I am deliberately omitting the consideration of this, not because I do not feel its importance as keenly as anyone, but because in these few papers we cannot cover everything.

Finally, perhaps the greatest of all obstacles to integration is our lack of training for it. In our college debates we try always to beat the other side. In the circular announcing the courses to be given at the Bryn Mawr Summer School for Workers, I find: "English Composition and Public Speaking; to develop the art of oral and written expression." I think that in addition to this there should be classes in discussion which should aim to teach the "art" of cooperative thinking, and I was disappointed that there was no such course in the program of a school for workers. Managers need it just as much. I have found, in the case of the wage boards which I have been on, that many employers (I ought in fairness to say not the majority) came to these joint conferences of employers and employees with little notion of conferring, but to push through, to force through, plans *previously* arrived at, based on *preconceived* ideas of what employees are like. It seems as if the methods of genuine conference have yet to be learned. Even if there were not the barriers of an unenlightened self-interest, of prejudice, rigidity, dogmatism, routine, there would still be required training and practice for us to master the technique of integration. A friend of mine said to me, "Open-mindedness is the whole thing, isn't it?" No, it isn't; it needs just as great a respect for your own view as for that of others, and a firm upholding of it until you are convinced. Mushy people are no more good at this than stubborn people.

As an indirect summing up of this discussion, I should like to emphasize our responsibility for integration. We saw in our consideration of circular response that my behavior helps create the situation to which I am responding. That implies (what we have daily to take into account) that my behavior is helping to *develop* the situation to which I am responding. The standard of living goes up not only while, but partly because, it is being studied. This conception of the developing situation is of the utmost importance for business administration. It makes it impossible to construct a map of the future, yet all our maxims of foresight hold good; every business should reconcile these two statements. We should work always with the evolving situation, and note what part our own activities have in that evolving situation.

This is the most important word, not only for business relations, but for all human relations: not to adapt ourselves to a situation—we are all more necessary to the world than that; neither to mold a situation to *our* liking—we are all, or rather each, of too little importance to the world for that; but to take account of that reciprocal adjustment, that interactive behavior between the situation and ourselves which means a change in both the situation and ourselves. One test of business administration should be: is the organization such that both employers and employees, or co-managers, co-directors, are stimulated to a reciprocal activity which will give more than mere adjustment, more than an equilibrium? Our outlook is narrowed, our activity is restricted, our chances of business success largely diminished when our thinking is constrained within the limits of what has been called an either-or situation. We should never allow ourselves to be bullied by an "either-or." There is often the possibility of something better than either of two given alternatives. Every one of us interested in any form of constructive work is looking for the plus values of our activity. In a later paper, on *Business as an Integrative Unity,* we shall consider how we can find in business administration those plus values which alone mean progress, progress for the individual and for whatever business or service we have undertaken for ourselves and for our community.

LADY CHATTERLEY GETS A LECTURE

D. H. LAWRENCE

[D. H. Lawrence, *Lady Chatterley's Lover,* Grove Press Inc., New York, 1957, pp. 234–241.]

Here is a biting picture of one kind of industrialist—the kind that, if ever real in the past, was real mostly to writers of fiction and, fortunately, is just about nonexistent today. But whether in 1928 when D. H. Lawrence wrote the novel from which this is taken (*Lady Chatterley's Lover,* famous for its strong wording in other respects) or decades later, there is behind this caricature of an industrial aristocrat the expression of a point of view about business, in fact a very prevalent misunderstanding of industrial values. Here, of course, Lawrence takes the warped soul of crippled Lord Clifford, and contrasts it with an English pastoral landscape in spring with its lovely blossoms, and lovely Constance (his inconstant wife, who blooms for the grounds-keeper—but that's another part of the story).

ON SUNDAY Clifford wanted to go into the wood. It was a lovely morning, the pear blossom and plum had suddenly appeared in the world in a wonder of white here and there.

It was cruel for Clifford, while the world bloomed, to have to be helped from chair to bath-chair. But he had forgotten, and even seemed to have a certain conceit of himself in his lameness. Connie still suffered, having to lift his inert legs into place. . . .

She waited for him at the top of the drive, at the edge of the screen of beeches. His chair came puffing along with a sort of valetudinarian slow importance. As he joined his wife he said:

"Sir Clifford on his foaming steed!"

"Snorting, at least!" she laughed.

He stopped and looked around at the façade of the long, low old brown house [named Wragby].

"Wragby doesn't wink an eyelid!" he said. "But then why should it? I ride upon the achievements of the mind of man, and that beats a horse."

"I suppose it does. And the souls in Plato riding up to heaven in a two-horse chariot would go in a Ford now," she said.

"Or a Rolls-Royce: Plato was an aristocrat!"

"Quite! No more black horse to thrash and maltreat. Plato never thought we'd go one better than his black steed and his white steed, and have no steeds at all, only an engine!"

"Only an engine and gas!" said Clifford.

"I hope I can have some repairs done to the old place next year. I think I shall have about a thousand to spare for that: but work costs so much!" he added.

"Oh, good!" said Connie. "If only there aren't more strikes!"

"What would be the use of their striking again! Merely ruin the industry, what's left of it: and surely the owls are beginning to see it!"

"Perhaps they don't mind ruining the industry," said Connie.

"Ah, don't talk like a woman! The industry fills their bellies, even if it can't keep their pockets quite so flush," he said. . . .

"But didn't you say the other day that you were a conservative-anarchist?" she asked innocently.

"And did you understand what I meant?" he retorted. "All I meant is, people can be what they like and feel what they like and do what they like, strictly privately, so long as they keep the *form* of life intact, and the apparatus."

Connie walked on in silence a few paces. Then she said, obstinately:

"It sounds like saying an egg may go as addled as it likes, so long as it keeps its shell on whole. But addled eggs do break of themselves."

"I don't think people are eggs," he said. "Not even angels' eggs, my dear little evangelist."

He was in rather high feather this bright morning. The larks were trilling away over the park, the distant pit in the hollow was fuming silent steam. It was almost like old days, before the war. Connie didn't really want to argue. But then she did not really want to go to the wood with Clifford either. So she walked beside his chair in a certain obstinacy of spirit.

"No," he said. "There will be no more strikes, if the thing is properly managed."

"Why not?"

"Because strikes will be made as good as impossible."

"But will the men let you?" she asked.

"We shan't ask them. We shall do it while they aren't looking: for their own good, to save the industry."

"For your own good, too," she said.

"Naturally! For the good of everybody. But for their good even more than mine. I can live without the pits. They can't. They'll starve if there are no pits. I've got other provision."

They looked up the shallow valley at the mine, and beyond it, at the black-lidded houses of Tevershall crawling like some serpent up the hill. From the old brown church the bells were ringing: Sunday, Sunday, Sunday!

"But will the men let you dictate terms?" she said.

"My dear, they will have to: if one does it gently."

"But mightn't there be a mutual understanding?"

"Absolutely: when they realize that the industry comes before the individual."

"But must you own the industry?" she said.

"I don't. But to the extent I do own it, yes, most decidedly. The ownership of property has now become a religious question: as it has been since Jesus and St. Francis. The point is *not:* take all thou hast and give to the poor, but use all thou hast to encourage the industry and give work to the poor. It's the only way to feed all the mouths and clothe all the bodies. Giving away all we have to the poor spells starvation for the poor just as much as for us. And universal starvation is no high aim. Even general poverty is no lovely thing. Poverty is ugly."

"But the disparity?"

"That is fate. Why is the star Jupiter bigger than the star Neptune? You can't start altering the make-up of things!"

"But when this envy and jealousy and discontent has once started," she began.

"Do your best to stop it. Somebody's *got* to be boss of the show."

"But who is the boss of the show?" she asked.

"The men who own and run the industries."

There was a long silence.

"It seems to me they're a bad boss," she said.

"Then you suggest what they should do."

"They don't take their boss-ship seriously enough," she said.

"They take it far more seriously than you take your ladyship," he said.

"That's thrust upon me. I don't really want it," she blurted out. He stopped the chair and looked at her.

"Who's shirking their responsibility now!" he said. "Who is trying to get away *now* from the responsibility of their own boss-ship, as you call it?"

"But I don't want any boss-ship," she protested.

"Ah! But that is funk. You've got it: fated to it. And you should live up to it. Who has given the colliers all they have that's worth having; all their political liberty, and their education, such as it is; their sanitation, their health conditions, their books, their music, everything? Who has given it them? Have colliers given it to colliers? No! All the Wragbys and Shipleys in England have given their part, and must go on giving. There's your responsibility."

Connie listened, and flushed very red.

"I'd like to give something," she said. "But I'm not allowed. Everything is to be sold and paid for now; and all the things you mention now, Wragby and Shipley *sell* them to the people, at a good profit. Everything is sold. You don't give one heartbeat of real sympathy. And besides, who has taken away from the people their natural life and manhood, and given them this industrial horror? Who has done that?"

"And what must I do?" he asked, green. "Ask them to come and pillage me?"

"Why is Tevershall so ugly, so hideous? Why are their lives so hopeless?"

"They built their own Tevershall. That's part of their display of freedom. They built themselves their pretty Tevershall, and they live their own pretty lives. I can't live their lives for them. Every beetle must live its own life."

"But you make them work for you. They live the life of your coal mine."

"Not at all. Every beetle finds its own food. Not one man is forced to work for me."

"Their lives are industrialized and hopeless, and so are ours," she cried.

"I don't think they are. That's just a romantic figure of speech, a relic of the swooning and die-away romanticism. You don't look at all a hopeless figure standing there, Connie, my dear."

Which was true. For her dark blue eyes were flashing, color was hot in her cheeks, she looked full of a rebellious passion far from the dejection of hopelessness. She noticed, in the tussocky places of the grass, cottony young cowslips standing up still bleared in their down. And she wondered with rage, why it was she felt Clifford was so *wrong,* yet she couldn't say it to him, she could not say exactly *where* he was wrong.

"No wonder the men hate you," she said.

"They don't!" he replied. "And don't fall into errors: in your sense of the word, they are *not* men. They are animals you don't understand and never could. Don't thrust your illusions on other people. The masses were always the same, and will always be the same. Nero's slaves were extremely little different from our colliers or the Ford motorcar workmen. I mean Nero's mine slaves and his field slaves. It is the masses: they are the unchangeable. An individual may emerge from the masses. But the emergence doesn't alter the mass. The masses are unalterable. It is one of the most momentous facts of social science. *Panem et circenses!* Only today education is one of the bad substitutes for a circus. What is wrong today is that we've made a profound hash of the circuses part of the program, and poisoned our masses with a little education."

When Clifford became really aroused in his feelings about the common people, Connie was frightened. There was something devastatingly true in what he said. But it was a truth that killed.

Seeing her pale and silent, Clifford started the chair again, and no more was said till he halted again at the wood gate, which she opened.

"And what we need to take up now," he said, "is whips, not swords. The masses have been ruled since time began, and, till time ends, ruled they will have to be. It is sheer hypocrisy and farce to say they can rule themselves."

"But can you rule them?" she asked.

"I? Oh, yes! Neither my mind nor my will is crippled, and I don't rule with my legs. I can do my share of ruling: absolutely, my share; and give me a son, and he will be able to rule his portion after me."

"But he wouldn't be your own son, of your own ruling class; or, perhaps not," she stammered.

"I don't care who his father may be, so long as he is a healthy man not below normal intelligence. Give me the child of any healthy, normally intelligent man, and I will make a perfectly competent Chatterley of him. It is not who begets us that matters, but where fate places us. Place any child among the ruling classes, and he will grow up, to his own extent, a ruler. Put kings' and dukes' children among the masses, and they'll be little plebians, mass products. It is the overwhelming pressure of environment."

"Then the common people aren't a race, and the aristocrats aren't blood," she said.

"No, my child! All that is romantic illusion. Aristocracy is a function, a part of fate. And the masses are a functioning of another part of fate. The individual hardly matters. It is a question of which function you are brought up to and adapted to. It is not the individuals that make an aristocracy: it is the functioning of the aristocratic whole. And it is the functioning of the whole mass that makes the common man what he is."

"Then there is no common humanity between us all!"

"Just as you like. We all need to fill our bellies. But when it comes to expressive or executive functioning, I believe there is a gulf and an absolute one, between the ruling and the serving classes. The two functions are opposed. And the function determines the individual."

Connie looked at him with dazed eyes.

"Won't you come on?" she said.

And he started his chair. He had said his say. Now he lapsed into his peculiar and rather vacant apathy, that Connie found so trying. In the wood, anyhow, she was determined not to argue.

In front of them ran the open cleft of the riding, between the hazel walls and the gray trees. The chair puffed slowly on, slowly surging into the forget-me-nots that rose up in the drive like milk froth, beyond the hazel shadows. Clifford steered the middle course, where feet passing had kept a channel through the flowers. But Connie, walking behind, had watched the wheels jolt over the woodruff and the bugle, and squash the little yellow cups of the creeping Jennie. Now they made a wake through the forget-me-nots.

All the flowers were there, the first bluebells in blue pools, like standing water.

"You are quite right about its being beautiful," said Clifford. "It is so amazing. What is *quite* so lovely as an English spring!"

Connie thought it sounded as if even the spring bloomed by Act of Parliament. An English spring! Why not an Irish one? or Jewish? The chair moved slowly ahead, past tufts of sturdy bluebells that stood up like wheat and over gray burdock leaves. Then they came to the open place where the trees had been felled, the light flooded in rather stark. And the bluebells made sheets of bright blue color, here and there, sheering off into lilac and purple. And between, the bracken was lifting its brown curled heads, like legions of young snakes with a new secret to whisper to Eve.

Clifford kept the chair going till he came to the brow of the hill; Connie followed slowly behind. The oak buds were opening soft and brown. Everything came tenderly out of the old hardness. Even the snaggy craggy oak trees put out the softest leaves, spreading thin, brown little wings like young bat wings in the light. Why had men never any newness in them, any freshness to come forth with? Stale men!

Clifford stopped the chair at the top of the rise and looked down.

The bluebells washed blue like flood-water over the broad riding, and lit up the down-hill with a warm blueness.

"It's a very fine color in itself," said Clifford, "but useless for making a painting."

WHAT KIND OF AN ANIMAL IS THIS HERE CAPITALISM?

DAVID M. POTTER

[David M. Potter, "The American Economic System," in Lyman Bryson (ed.), *An Outline of Man's Knowledge of the Modern World*, Doubleday & Co., Inc., Garden City, N.Y., copyright © 1960, pp. 444-445, 449-459 (abridged).]

The facetious title that we have given to this selection is only a clue to the joking in the first paragraph, through which David M. Potter leads us into his very earnest analysis of "The American Economic System" in a 1960 collection, *An Outline of Man's Knowledge of the Modern World*. Potter does a beautiful job of capsulizing 200 years—from the historic influence of Hamilton and Jefferson to the more recent impact of Theodore Roosevelt and Franklin D. Roosevelt, and from the stringent ideas of Karl Marx and David Ricardo to the abundant standard of living we individually enjoy today—to show how America has used capitalism to serve its social aims. (All the people just mentioned are represented in selections in earlier parts of *The World of Business*.)

David Potter, who so frankly and calmly finds much good in capitalism, not because it *is* capitalism but because of what it *does*, is one of the country's most respected educators and historians. He has been Coe Professor of American History at Yale since 1950. During the academic year 1947–48, he was Harmsworth Professor of American History at Oxford. He was reporter for a symposium of the American Round Table on current aspects of the American economy, published under the title *Discussions of People's Capitalism* (1957). He is the author of several significant books, two of the more recent of which are *People of Plenty* and *Economic Abundance and the American Character*. It is interesting to observe how different Potter's economy of abundance in 1960 is from Stuart Chase's 30 years ago.*

IN ENGLAND a railway passenger who carries a pet bird or animal on the train is required to pay a small fee, scaled according to the freight classification into which the pet may fall. An English lady who was

* See page 2055 in this volume.

carrying a turtle inquired whether she would owe a fee, but the agent told her, "No mum, cats is dogs, and squirrels is parrots, but this here turkle is a hinsect, and you don't have to pay for hinsects."

The story illustrates how misleading it can be to force specific and unique things, whether they be turtles or economic systems, into broad categories which lump them together with other things that they do not really resemble. If we were shipping the American economic system to outer space, we would perhaps inform the ticket agent that this here system is a capitalism. This statement might be true without necessarily helping us to understand what the system is really like, and it might hide the fact that our system is rather different from any other capitalism on earth. A term conceals as much as it reveals when it fails to distinguish the economy of present-day America, with its high standard of living, its emphasis on consumption and its huge middle class, from the primitive capitalism of a century ago, with its exploited proletariat and its extremes of wealth and poverty. If we are to place our economic turtle in a class with other economic creatures, therefore, we must at the same time be alert to the great differences which separate it from the others. . . .

THE GOALS OF ABUNDANCE AND WIDESPREAD BENEFITS

In many respects the values that have been ranked high by Americans are the same ones that have been exalted by capitalist theory. Both have placed a great emphasis upon productivity and upon hard work as a means toward productivity. Both have stressed the idea that a man has a right to keep what his personal efforts have produced—his crops, his profits, his earnings. Both have emphasized the importance of leaving him unrestrained, so as not to hamper his initiative. Because of these similarities we sometimes mistake our system for a standard-model capitalism, somewhat modified perhaps to fit the times. But in fact, there are many respects in which capitalist values and American values do not correspond at all closely. For instance, capitalism values saving because saving provides funds for investment, and it values efficiency. Since it values capital formation, it sanctions private property, which will encourage people to save, and it sanctions private enterprise, which, being productive, is more likely to result in saving than nonproductive activities managed by government. Since it values efficiency, it sanctions competition, which will reward efficient enterprises and liquidate inefficient enterprises. Of course, American society sanctions these things also, or seems to, but it sanctions them for quite dissimilar reasons. Private property, with us, has been justified, not because it promoted capital formation, but because we believe in a man's right to keep the rewards of his own skill and labor. But if a man's property rose to be valued in the millions, his claim to the fruits of his own toil no longer seemed to cover the case very exactly, and we imposed a progressive income tax, regardless of its effect upon capital formation. In America private enterprise has been justified less for its superior productivity, though that was valued also, than for the maximum opportunity which it gave to all go-getting citizens to be undisturbed in the process of helping themselves to the potential riches which the economy offers. But if it resulted in some parties', such as railroads, banks, or trusts, getting enough power to interfere with other parties' helping *them*selves, then enterprise had to be regulated in order to keep the opportunity as widespread as possible. In the same way, competition was justified not as a means of maintaining efficiency but as a just basis for the distribution of economic rewards. If "competition" meant that A toiled harder than B and reaped a proportionately bigger crop, the American people approved. If it meant that A and B, both working hard, received sweatshop wages because they were competing to hold their jobs, the American people were prepared to condemn competition as immoral and to arrest its action.

In short, capitalism in the United States has been only an economic means to the attainment of certain basic social goals, and these broader goals have done more than our economic beliefs to control our economic practices. If we try to search out what the essential goals have been, we can define at least two which have had a fundamental bearing on the American economy. One of these is the goal of maximum opportunity for the individual arising from the strong American belief in the dignity and worth of man. The other is the goal of a high and steadily improving standard of living, arising from the fact that American society began its major growth at a moment in history when, for the first time since the beginning of the world, the productive system was capable of yielding a steadily increasing surplus above the bare necessities. This surplus made possible increasingly plentiful and increasingly widespread benefits for the people, that is, a rising standard of living in an economy of abundance. Throughout our history, American economic policy has been controlled by these two goals.

The belief in the worth of the individual has, of course, been a cornerstone. Our independence began with the affirmations that all men are created equal, that all men have rights, that these rights cannot be subverted, and that the body of citizens shall control the government. Our history has been a prolonged record of the fulfillment of this valuation by the establishment of universal education, by the growth of manhood suffrage, by the emancipation of the slaves, by the extension of women's rights, and by all manner of reforms. It is also a record of frustration and self-condemnation when we failed to square our practice with our ideal, as in the case of the Indian or the Negro. People who did not believe in equality could have adjusted to inequality far more easily than we have ever been able to do. The fact is that we had a basic commitment to democracy, which meant that our entire system was geared to democratic methods and goals. That, in turn, implied certain important economic corollaries.

The first of these corollaries is that the men who held economic power, through the working of the free enterprise system, did not necessarily hold political power through the working of the democratic system. This stubborn fact itself ran absolutely counter to the economic theory of Marxian socialists. Their doctrine insisted that in the class struggle between capital and labor, capital would always control the government, and would use the police and the judges and the legislators as its tools against the workers and the common people. Of course, property interests in America, like other interests, have consistently tried to influence the government, and have sometimes succeeded—just as in a democracy the interests of agriculture or of organized labor or of debtor groups have also tried and sometimes succeeded. The traditional unpopularity of "Wall Street" is proof that the American people have been afraid that property interests might gain control, and from this fear it is but a step to the belief, chronically asserted by socialists and even by reformers, that big business does, in fact, dominate. This belief is all the more plausible because there have been periods, notably between 1865 and 1900, when property interests were in the saddle. These were the years when Standard Oil had "done everything to the Pennsylvania legislature except to refine it"; when Cornelius Vanderbilt said, or was reputed to have said, "the public be damned"; when the Supreme Court threw out a New York law which limited work in the baking industry to sixty hours per week on the ground that it interfered with the freedom of the worker to sell his labor; and when Federal troops broke a railroad strike in Illinois. Doctrinaire leftists still rattle the bones of these episodes, but modern businessmen certainly know that they are gone with the wind.

The fact is that property interests never had matters their own way for very long. After the government under the Constitution was established, the owner groups rallied behind Alexander Hamilton, who openly advocated government by and for "the rich, the wellborn, and the able." But in 1800, Thomas Jefferson, with a following of small farmers, turned Hamilton's Federalists out of office, and they never came back. In 1828 the Bank of the United States was so dear to property interests that smart politicians thought no man in public life would dare to attack it. But Andrew Jackson assailed it as a "monster," won re-election on this issue, and drove Nicholas Biddle to the wall. At midcentury, property interests would gladly have let the slavery issue rest, but northern voters made an antislavery man President, and in 1863 the Emancipation Proclamation announced one of the largest confiscations of property in modern history, though Abraham Lincoln, it should be noted, would have preferred to free the slaves in almost any other way.

After the Civil War property came nearer to domination than it has ever come before or since. By the 1890s desperate farmers, caught in the deflationary grip of the gold standard and victimized by monopolies in industry and railroad transportation, saw a rising class struggle which seemed as acute as the one that Karl Marx had predicted. In response the Populists unconsciously translated Marx's doctrine into the American idiom when they said that we were breeding two great classes, tramps and millionaires. When William J. Bryan failed in his bid for election to the Presidency in the bitter Cross of Gold campaign of 1896, it looked as though there really was a class struggle in America and that property was winning it.

But within five years Theodore Roosevelt was President of the United States. T.R. denounced "malefactors of great wealth," dramatically assailed the trusts, and invoked the use of a "big stick" to make big business behave. The Progressive Era, as it was called, extended on beyond Roosevelt himself, and before it was over, the Federal Reserve Act had successfully challenged the control over the country's monetary system by the nation's major financiers. The railroads had been regulated, and some of the trusts had been dissolved.

For twelve years after World War I there was another interlude during which property interests enjoyed a relatively favored position, but this ended abruptly in 1933 when the New Deal launched a program to bring the interests of agriculture and of organized labor into balance with the interests of business and industry. In vain property interests resisted an unprecedented amount of regulation and of redistribution of wealth through taxation. After twenty years in office, the heirs of the New Deal were at last defeated, but under the Eisenhower administration the basic New Deal policies of support for agriculture, of collective bargaining for labor, of regulation for business, of social security, and of redistribution of wealth through taxation, have been maintained as religiously as if they were part of the Constitution itself.

The fact that the masters of capital have never been in really full control means that they have never been able to set the goals of the American economy. Instead, and this is a second major economic corollary of the democratic commitment, the goals of the economy have been set by the democratic philosophy rather than by the theory of capitalism.

Historically, what have the American people expected of their economy? They have not cared very much for maximum efficiency, which is what the theorists of free competition are constantly talking about. In fact, they have tolerated immense waste in the use of natural resources. They have not sought the elimination of inefficient or marginal producers, which again is one of the presumed merits of free competition, but have often gone to the aid of marginal producers, especially in agriculture. If we look not to theory but to experience, we may find that the only economic policy that the American people have always insisted upon and consistently applied is that the system should operate in such a way as to give the bulk of the population access to the sources of wealth. These sources have changed during our historical experience, but the policy of giving access to them has not.

At the birth of American democracy, the chief source of wealth was still in the form of an immense area of land suitable for cultivation. Europe's class society had been built upon the scarcity of land, which made the common people dependent upon the landlords, but in America there was a vast public domain in the hands of government. The policy adopted was not to conserve this asset nor to use it primarily as a source of public revenue but to sell it so cheaply that almost anyone could own land. Beginning in 1863 with the Homestead Act, we actually gave land away in plots of 160 acres to anyone who would occupy and improve it.

As the country developed, new ways of sharing in America's richness began to appear, and when they did, our economic policies were changed accordingly. A time came when ownership of land was no longer enough and when farmers needed to get their crops to market in order to enjoy the benefits of the economy. At that point government did not hesitate to build at public expense a network of turnpikes and canals. In fact, historical studies of several states have shown that state governments in the mid-nineteenth century did not practice nearly as much laissez faire as we sometimes imagine.

Later still, economic opportunity in America took the form of projects that were too large for one man or one group of partners to finance—projects such as manufacturing textiles, constructing railroads, smelting ores, or refining oil. When this happened government responded by adopting laws that enabled men to pool their capital in corporations, which enjoyed certain new privileges such as that of limited liability. Ultimately, the courts recognized these corporations as "persons" and extended to them all the safeguards which the Constitution gave to the property and rights of real persons, that is, human beings. Clearly, we were prepared to sanction collectivized activity when it became necessary as a means of getting access to wealth.

We adjusted our position whenever it became necessary. By the twentieth century millions of Americans found access to their modest share of America's wealth not through land, nor through markets, nor through enterprises of their own, but through jobs—mostly industrial jobs. In the 1930s an economic crisis caused unemployment on so large a scale that this segment of the population lost its means of sharing in the economy. When this happened, government again did, in a new way, what it has consistently done. It took steps through the NRA, through unemployment insurance, through the establishment of collective bargaining, through public works and government spending, and through wage and hour laws to safeguard the position of the wage worker and thus to keep open the channels by which people gained access to the benefits in the economy.

Viewed in this way, the great economic transformation of the 1930s was not, as is so often supposed, a revolutionary departure from our traditional principles, because in fact we had never been committed to government nonintervention. Instead, we had only been committed to the democratic goal of opening the economic possibilities of the nation to the American people. If laissez faire would do it, well and good. But if not, other means could, would, and should be used.

It appears that the democratic goal has played a more vital part than economic theories in shaping American economic policy. At the same time, the second goal, that of abundance, has also been vital, for we have had from the beginning a vision of America as a land of plenty.

The birth of the American republic came at almost precisely the turning point in history when deprivation ceased to be the natural and inevitable condition of mankind. From the dawn of recorded time, man's means of getting food, clothing, and shelter had been so limited that population invariably ran ahead of the supply of necessities. So long as this condition prevailed, poverty seemed a natural fact of life and not a defect in the economy. Equal division would have been no cure, for the supply of goods was so low that equality would only have impoverished the tiny minority of fortunate people without improving the condition of the unfortunate. It is interesting to note that even the early economists who advocated capitalism did not expect it to change this condition. One of the foremost of them, David Ricardo, expressed their general opinion when he said that "there is no way of keeping profits up but by keeping wages down," and he formulated a so-called iron law of wages which clearly condemned the workers to live at the level of bare subsistence. Today we usually overlook the fact that Marx and the capitalist economists held in common the belief that industrialization would degrade the worker. Actually, Marx was not at all original in predicting a vast chasm between the rich and the poor. His ideas were distinctive mostly because he viewed with indignation a prospect which others viewed with indifference, and he predicted that the process would end in revolution.

The American economy today is as far from Ricardo as it is from Marx, and for the same reason. It has been based, from the beginning, upon a rejection of their idea that the exploitation of labor was inevitable. America began with an abundance of physical resources, with more land than men could use. During our history, technological progress has steadily increased our supply of energy, in the form of steam engines, turbines, electric power plants, internal combustion engines, and now jet engines and atomic piles. At the same time, mechanization and, more recently, automation have steadily increased the number of farm and factory tasks that can be performed by inanimate labor. In a century and a half, man has broken all the old barriers which limited his productivity and has revolutionized the proportion of goods to population. When he did this, he could for the first time regard cold and raggedness and hunger not as part of man's sad lot on earth, but as the result of wholly unnecessary social failure. When Franklin Roosevelt proclaimed that one-third of our nation was ill-housed, ill-fed, and ill-clothed, the statement was not, as it would once have been, a mere observation—it was a reproach. Indeed, when he included freedom from want as one of the four freedoms, it seemed far more attainable than the other three. This was because the world is passing from an economy of scarcity to an economy of abundance, and America has stood in the forefront of the change.

When Americans saw that for the first time the possibility of having more than enough to go around was a reality and not a dream, they set themselves another goal which fitted well with the goal of democracy. This was the goal of creating a rich economy with a wide distribution of material benefits. It was an attainable goal but it was an immense job, a new kind of job. It required driving energy, fearless imagination, daring readiness to take chances, and willingness to try things that were new. It needed pioneers, innovators, risk takers, relentlessly hard workers—and also, to some extent, opportunists, gamblers, exploiters, and result-getters. It needed to get everyone into action with a minimum concern for rules, for playing it safe, and for waiting for bureaucratic green lights. For such a purpose, capitalism, with its emphasis upon productivity, competition, and rewards for risk taking, was ideal. Hence the ways of capitalism were adopted wholeheartedly. If the system sometimes worked brutally, and some people got hurt, that was to be expected. But essentially, the goal was a social goal of abundance, and productivity was valued not, for instance, as Hitler valued it, because it strengthened the state, but because it enriched the people. Henry Ford illustrated the way in which American capitalism lent itself to the abundance drive, for his goal was not only to make an automobile which he could sell for a profit, but also one so priced that anyone could hope to own it, after which he would pay wages that would put his own industrial workers in the automobile-buying class. The potentialities of the mass market have now been so thoroughly fulfilled that big business could not survive if it received for itself a disproportionate share of the national income, for it depends in a very sensitive way upon the high purchasing power of wage-earners to keep it going. Both Ricardo and Marx should have witnessed this.

The American commitment to abundance has shown itself in many ways. It shows in our faith that the economy can support a large proportion of the population, namely, those younger than twenty or those older than 65, in nonproductive activities. It shows in our completely realistic expectation that we shall have, at the same time, more leisure and more goods. It showed, less attractively, during World War II, when the consumption of civilian goods rose steadily from $122,000,000,000 worth to $145,000,000,000 worth (measured in constant prices) between 1940 and 1945. The so-called war economy was, in fact, not an economy *converted* to war, but one *expanded* to war. It shows in our respect for spending and in our contempt for stinginess or even frugality. It shows in our steadily expanding conception of what constitutes the necessities of life. Once limited to food, clothing, and shelter, these are now stretching to include the one-family house, indoor plumbing, electricity, hot water, central heating, refrigeration, a television set, an automobile, a telephone, a balanced diet, medical and dental care, a high school education for the children, and an annual vacation. It is said of food that we are killed by too much more often than by too little, and the same thing might be said of horsepower.

THE ECONOMY'S FULFILLMENT OF ITS GOALS

How well has the American economy attained its democratic goal and its goal of abundance? By almost any measure it has succeeded in both goals to an almost incredible degree.

This success has resulted from the high productivity of the American economy. Historically, American productivity has always been high, but by 1948 it had reached a point where the United States, with little more than 6 per cent of the world's population and 7 per cent of the world's area, produced about 41 per cent of the world's output of goods and services, and very close to one-half of the world's industrial output. This statistic, impressive in itself, appears even more impressive in the light of the fact that we have very nearly doubled our productivity since 1930, while holding the proportion of our population in the labor force almost stable and reducing the work week by more than five hours. This amazing productivity has been achieved, of course, by using more and more machinery and power to make each man-hour of work yield more. A century ago, men supplied 15 per cent of all energy used in production, animals supplied 79 per cent, and machines supplied only 6 per cent. By 1960 machines supplied 96 per cent with only 3 per cent furnished by men and 1 per cent by animals. American enterprise has an investment of more than $10,000 in plant for every worker, which means that the employee is less a laborer than a supervisor of the labor performed by machines. With such facilities we have steadily raised output per man-hour of work from 33 cents in 1850 (measured by 1950 prices) to three times this amount in 1930 and to $2.03 by 1952. Our national income in 1952 was $264 billion, which was an average of more than $1,700 per person, or $5,500 per household, before taxes.

Such an economy has been ideally suited to the fulfillment of both the democratic goal of widespread diffusion of benefits and the abundance goal of a high standard of living. As to the diffusion of benefits, it has always been conspicuously true that the bulk of the American population shared in the good things of the economy. Throughout our history, travelers from other countries have remarked how well-dressed American workers were and what attractive homes they lived in. For a long time there were no statistics to back these observations, but for the last generation we have reasonably accurate measurements. These show, for instance, that as late as 1936 only 30 per cent of American families had incomes above $3,000 as measured in 1950 dollars, but by 1953, 63 per cent of all families stood above this figure. In 1936 approximately 20 per cent of all families had incomes of less than $1,000 at 1950 prices (the figure was 43.5 per cent in 1935 prices). By 1953 only 10 per cent stood at this low level.

These changes were accomplished less by increasing the proportionate shares of the groups in question than by raising the totals for everyone. In fact, America has traditionally solved its problems by increasing total wealth rather than by redistributing existing wealth. Despite widespread claims that the New Deal was expropriating the well-to-do and was forcing a revolutionary redistribution of wealth upon the country, the proportions of wealth going to various brackets have remained surprisingly steady through the depression and the New Deal, through the war boom, the war, and the postwar period. The upper 50 per cent of the population got 78 per cent of the money income of the nation in 1929 and it was still getting 77 per cent in 1955, *after taxes*. Redistribution has been gradual, not drastic. Yet it is clear that redistribution is taking place on a significant scale. For instance, in 1913, 16 per cent of the national income was paid in the form of rents, dividends, and interest; while 27 per cent took the form of entrepreneurial income and 57 per cent consisted of wages and salaries. By 1948, rents, interest, and dividends were scarcely 8.5 per cent; entrepreneurial incomes were 19.5 per cent and wages and salaries were 72 per cent. What this has done to the most opulent class is suggested by the fact that in 1917 the top 1 per cent of income recipients received more than half of their income (54 per cent) from dividends, interest, and rents, and less than half from salaries or earnings. By 1948 the proportion from property had shrunk to 14 per cent and that from personal earnings had risen to 86 per cent.

Under the impact of these changes, the proportion of the national income going to the top 1 per cent of recipients has shrunk from 15 per cent in 1929 (the same as 1913) to 12 per cent by 1940 and to 8.3 per cent by 1948 (6.2 per cent after taxes). This is to say that by 1948 the most fortunate twentieth received $3 for every $1 that it would receive on a system of absolutely equal shares, and even here there was still room for the inheritance tax to do its work. As inequality has gone in history, this was not a steep gradient. There is still a class of really poor people whose plight is in some ways worse than ever before, for though they have certain welfare benefits, they are no longer numerous enough to have much political influence. But with due allowance for them, the distribution of income in the United States in large measure reflects the ideal of the dignity of all men and the goal of equality. In fact, the top 1 per cent in the Soviet Union probably enjoys a greater proportion of the nation's personal income than the top 1 per cent in the United States, and in so far as this is true, we face the anomalous fact that the Russians probably have fully as potent an incentive system as we do, at least in certain critically important fields of activity.

As for abundance, the variety of ways in which statisticians have tried to measure the American standard of living is almost unlimited. Some suggestion of the level of living is conveyed by the fact that, in 1951, 66.5 per cent of all American families owned an automobile. In 1950, 63.8 per cent of all the occupied dwelling units in the United States were detached, one-unit buildings, and 60 per cent of them averaged enough space to provide a ratio of four rooms for every three dwellers. Of these dwelling units, 50 per cent boasted central heating, 69 per cent had private baths, 73 per cent had modern cook stoves, 80 per cent had mechanical refrigerators, 83 per cent had running water, 94 per cent had electricity, and 95 per cent had radios. By 1957, 80 per cent had television sets. Two decades earlier, all these advantages, except perhaps radios, had been confined to a minority of the population.

In a comparison with other countries the advantage enjoyed by the United States is proverbially invidious. In 1949 the per capita income in the United States had a value of $1,453. At that time the figure in no other country stood above $900, and only in New Zealand, Canada, and Switzerland was it above $800. In the United Kingdom it was $723 and in the Soviet Union $308. These totals partly reflected postwar conditions, but the highest figure in any country in Latin America was $346, in Argentina, and the lowest was $40, in Haiti and Ecuador. The advantage of the American worker can be expressed even more concretely by saying that in 1950 it took an American who wished to buy a dozen eggs and a pound each of flour, bread, butter, cheese, potatoes, lard, and sugar, ninety-eight minutes of work to earn the value of these purchases. In Australia, Canada, Great Britain, Norway, Sweden, and Israel, something less than 200 minutes of working time would suffice, but more than 500 minutes were required in Austria, Chile, France, Italy, and the Netherlands, and 852 minutes in the Soviet Union. Another way of measuring the discrepancy is to note that in 1949 the American diet contained an average of 3,186 calories per day, while the English diet stood at 2,700 calories, and the diets of Algeria, the Philippines, Japan, India, and (in the Western Hemisphere) El Salvador, fell below 1,800.

Statistical proofs of the high level of material comfort at which Americans live could be spun out indefinitely. But the fact is already almost too well known, both to Americans who boast of it without necessarily understanding the reasons for it and to Europeans who denounce American materialism. Perhaps the most convincing proof of the extent to which the American standard has soared above the physical necessities is not statistical at all, but lies in the fact that Americans no longer buy most of their purchases in response to actual physical need. Need has been transcended as an economic stimulus, and goods are bought for comfort, convenience, recreation, style, or prestige. This is why automobile manufacturers must devise new models in order to make previous models seem obsolete even when most of their mileage is still in them. It is also why advertising plays an essential role in the economy, stimulating consumption by creating new psychological needs in order to keep the economy running, after physical needs have been met.

These items measure the effectiveness of the economy of abundance in terms of release from want. In terms of release from toil, the results are equally striking. In the century from 1850 to 1950, the average number of hours of work per week for the American laborer has been reduced from seventy-two to forty. The worker has been restored to his family; the Friday-afternoon-to-Monday-morning week end has come into very wide use, the annual vacation is a national institution, and leisure is no longer the badge of the privileged class, distinguishing the gentleman from the laborer who toiled from sun to sun. Leisure and increased income are the two benefits which our economy yields, but we often congratulate ourselves that the distribution of income is more equitable than it used to be without taking note of the fact that we have attained an absolutely equalitarian distribution of leisure.

By the middle of the twentieth century the American economy had poured forth more wealth and had rained it upon more of the people than any previous economy in history. It had achieved these results while using the basic methods of capitalism, and apparently because it used them. For although the continent of North America gave us a rich physical endowment, many societies with rich endowments have failed to prosper. Capitalism sped the development of American resources and the growth of American productivity through the sensitive flexibility of the free market, which channeled labor and enterprise and investment into the activities that would be most rewarding, through the propelling force of a strong incentive system that caused millions of men to throw themselves with a will into the drive for production, and through the stimulus to saving, which made investment funds available for industrial growth. These results could not have been attained without modern technology, of course, but the development of technology was itself stimulated by the imperatives of production and the drives of the incentive system, and was thus, in a sense, one of the outgrowths of the capitalistic dynamic.

Yet capitalism though it may be, the American economy of abundance and of wide diffusion of wealth is such a far cry from the capitalism of labor-exploitation and extremes of poverty and opulence that more than one writer has suggested that the term "capitalism," by itself, hardly fits. Professor Sumner Slichter of Harvard called our economy a laboristic economy. Adlai Stevenson called it a democratic capitalism. Recent efforts have been made to win currency for the term "people's capitalism," reclaiming from the Communists a word which they have almost taken away from us—though it is the third word in our Constitution—to characterize a capitalism which has outstripped all socialist programs in the attainment of welfare goals once regarded as distinctively socialist. Whether any of these terms takes a permanent hold is less important than whether the ideas behind them become generally understood. They all suggest that the American economy is a unique system, which uses the capitalistic devices of private property, financial incentives, and the free market but combines these with heavy infusions of governmental regulation and of control of the distribution of wealth through taxation—all as devices to achieve the goals of material abundance democratically shared.

BUSINESS NEEDS FORESIGHT
IN A CHANGING WORLD

ALFRED NORTH WHITEHEAD

[Alfred North Whitehead, "On Foresight," an address delivered at the Harvard Business School, 1930; introduction to Wallace Brett Donham, *Business Adrift*, McGraw-Hill Book Co., Inc., 1931, pp. xi–xxix.]

The great modern philosopher, Alfred North Whitehead (1861–1947) made this address "On Foresight" at the Harvard Business School in

1930, and it was reproduced as the introduction to a book, *Business Adrift,* written by his close friend, Dean Wallace B. Donham of the Harvard Business School. Whitehead disclaims any firsthand knowledge of how to conduct business, but reserves the right to consider what kind of mentality the businessman needs "in the present condition of the world"—and earns that right by an unusually simple but deep analysis.

His discussion of the role of routine in business, as in all society, is delightful, until all of a sudden you realize you are being whip-lashed by your own complaisance. "Well-conditioned responses to completely familiar stimuli" did characterize economic life in the time of Adam Smith,* and "for innumerable centuries in the past." But this century is one of change, and of change at an increasing tempo. Now foresight must supplement routine, and foresight requires understanding. Plato didn't have the foresight to see a civilization like ours, but he did see that philosophers must be kings—and what if plain citizens, including businessmen, are now the kings?

◆

AT THE OUTSET, I must disclaim the foolish notion that it is possible for anyone devoid of personal experience of business to provide useful suggestions for its detailed conduct. There is no substitute for firsthand practice. I am using the word *business* in the largest sense of that term, in which it includes a variety of activities. But any useful theory about them, capable of immediate application to specific instances, must depend on a direct knowledge of the relevant reactions of men and women composing that society, or group of nations, within which the business in question is to flourish.

There remains, however, the question of the general type of mentality which in the present condition of the world will promote the general success of a business community. Such a type is, of course, very complex. But I pick out one unquestioned element in it, namely foresight, and will discuss the conditions for its development and its successful exercise.

Now, some people are born with astounding knacks of the mind. For example, there are calculating boys who can perform intricate operations of mental arithmetic in a flash; there are also other sorts of peculiar faculties of divination; in particular, there are men with a knack of shrewdness in judging circumstances within the narrow range of their immediate observation. But after all, bankers prefer that their clerks should learn arithmetic, and trained geologists are preferred to men with divining rods. In the same way, there are general conditions of training which promote the development of a wider type of foresight.

It is a great mistake to divide people into sharp classes, namely,

* See page 1981 in this volume.

people with such-and-such a knack and people without it. These trenchant divisions are simply foolish. Most humans are born with certain aptitudes. But these aptitudes can easily remain latent unless they are elicited into activity by fortunate circumstances. If anyone has no aptitude of a certain type, no training can elicit it. But, granted the aptitude, we can discuss the ways of training it.

Foresight depends upon understanding. In practical affairs it is a habit. But the habit of foreseeing is elicited by the habit of understanding. Now, to a large extent, understanding can be acquired by a conscious effort and it can be taught. Thus the training of foresight is by the medium of understanding.

The general topic to be understood is the entire internal functioning of human society, including its technologies, the biological and physical laws on which these technologies depend, and including the sociological reactions of humans depending on fundamental psychological principles. In fact, the general topic is sociology in the broadest sense of the term, including its auxiliary sciences. Such a wide range of understanding is, of course, beyond the grasp of any single human. But no part of it is entirely foreign to the provision of foresight in business. Such a complete understanding is a cooperative enterprise; and a business community maintains its success for long periods so far as its average foresight is dominated by some approach to such general understanding.

We shall comprehend better the varieties of individual understanding which go to complete this general equipment of an ideal business community, if we commence by considering the contrast between understanding and routine.

Routine is the god of every social system; it is the seventh heaven of business, the essential component in the success of every factory, the ideal of every statesman. The social machine should run like clockwork. Every crime should be followed by an arrest, every arrest by a judicial trial, every trial by a conviction, every conviction by a punishment, every punishment by a reformed character. Or, you can conceive an analogous routine concerning the making of a motor car, starting with the iron in the ore, and the coal in the mine, and ending with the car driving out of the factory and with the president of the corporation signing the dividend warrants, and renewing his contracts with the mining corporations. In such a routine everyone from the humblest miner to the august president is exactly trained for his special job. Every action of miner or president is the product of conditioned reflexes, according to current physiological phraseology. When the routine is perfect, understanding can be eliminated, except such minor flashes of intelligence as are required to deal with familiar accidents, such as a flooded mine, a prolonged drought, or an epidemic of influenza.

A system will be the product of intelligence. But when the adequate routine is established, intelligence vanishes and the system is maintained by a coordination of conditioned reflexes. What is then required from the humans is receptivity of special training. No one, from president to miner, need understand the system as a whole. There will be no foresight, but there will be complete success in the maintenance of the routine.

Now, it is the beginning of wisdom to understand that social life is founded upon routine. Unless society is permeated, through and through, with routine, civilization vanishes. So many sociological doctrines, the products of acute intellects, are wrecked by obliviousness to this fundamental sociological truth. Society requires stability, foresight itself presupposes stability, and stability is the product of routine.

But there are limits to routine, and it is for the discernment of these limits, and for the provision of the consequent action, that foresight is required.

The two extremes of complete understanding and of complete routine are never realized in human society. But of the two, routine is more fundamental than understanding, that is to say, routine modified by minor flashes of short-range intelligence. Indeed, the notion of complete understanding controlling action is an ideal in the clouds, grotesquely at variance with practical life. But we have under our eyes countless examples of societies entirely dominated by routine. The elaborate social organizations of insects appear to be thoroughgoing examples of routine. Such organizations achieve far-reaching, complex purposes: they involve a differentiation of classes, from cows to serfs, from serfs to workers, from workers to warriors, from warriors to janitors, and from janitors to queens. Such organizations have regard to needs in a distant future, especially if the comparatively short space of life of the individual insects is taken into account as the unit of measurement.

These insect societies have been astoundingly successful, so far as concerns survival power. They seem to have a past extending over tens of thousands of years, perhaps of millions of years. It is the greatest of mistakes to believe that it has required the high-grade intelligence of mankind to construct an elaborate social organization. A particular instance of this error is the prevalent assumption that any social routine whose purposes are not obvious to our analysis is thereby to be condemned as foolish. We can observe insects performing elaborate routine actions whose purposes they cannot possibly understand, which yet are essential either for their own individual survival or for race survival.

But these insect societies have one great characteristic in common. They are not progressive. It is exactly this characteristic that discriminates communities of mankind from communities of insects. Further, this great fact of progressiveness, be it from worse to better, or from better to worse, has become of greater and greater importance in Western civilization as we come to modern times. The rate of change has increased even in my lifetime. It is possible that in future ages mankind may relapse into the stage of stable societies. But such a relapse is extremely unlikely within any span of time which we need take into account.

The recent shortening of the time span between notable changes in social customs is very obvious, if we examine history. Originally it depended upon some slow development of physical causes. For example, a gradual change of physical configuration such as the elevation of mountains: the time span for such a change is of the order of a million years. Again, a gradual change of climate; the time span for such a change is of the order of 5000 years. Again a gradual over-population of the region occupied by some community with its consequent swarming into new territories: having regard to the huge death rate of prescientific ages, the time span for such a change was of the order of 500 years. Again, the sporadic inventions of new technologies, such as the chipping of flints, the invention of fire, the taming of animals, the invention of metallurgy; in the prescientific ages, the average time-span for such changes was, at least, of the order of 500 years. If we compare the technologies of civilizations west of Mesopotamia at the epochs A.D. 100, the culmination of the Roman Empire, and A.D. 1400, the close of the Middle Ages, we find practically no advance in technology. There was some gain in metallurgy, some elaboration of clockwork, the recent invention of gunpowder with its influence all in the future, some advance in the art of navigation, also with its influence in the future. If we compare A.D. 1400 with A.D. 1700, there is a great advance; gunpowder, and printing, and navigation, and the technique of commerce, had produced their effect. But even then, the analogy between life in the eighteenth century and life in the great period of ancient Rome was singularly close, so that the peculiar relevance of Latin literature was felt vividly.

In the 50 years between 1780 and 1830, a number of inventions came with a rush into effective operation. The age of steam power and of machinery was introduced. But for two generations, from 1830 to 1890, there was a singular uniformity in the principles of technology which were regulating the structure of society and the usages of business.

The conclusion to be drawn from this survey is a momentous one. Our sociological theories, our political philosophy, our practical maxims of business, our political economy, and our doctrines of education, are derived from an unbroken tradition of great thinkers and of practical examples, from the age of Plato in the fifth century before

Christ to the end of the last century. The whole of this tradition is warped by the vicious assumption that each generation will live substantially amid the conditions governing the lives of its fathers and will transmit those conditions to mold with equal force the lives of its children.

We are living in the first period of human history for which this assumption is false.

Of course in the past, there were great catastrophes; for example, plagues, floods, barbarian invasions. But, if such catastrophes were warded off, there was a stable, well-known condition of civilized life. This assumption subtly pervades the premises of political economy, and has permitted it to confine attention to a simplified edition of human nature. It is at the basis of our conception of the reliable businessman, who has mastered a technique and never looks beyond his contracted horizon. It colors our political philosophy and our educational theory, with their overwhelming emphasis on past experience.

The note of recurrence dominates the wisdom of the past, and still persists in many forms even where explicitly the fallacy of its modern application is admitted. The point is that in the past the time span of important change was considerably longer than that of a single human life. Thus mankind was trained to adapt itself to fixed conditions. But today this time span is considerably shorter than that of human life, and accordingly our training must prepare individuals to face a novelty of conditions. But there can be no preparation for the unknown.

It is at this point that we recur to the title of this article, Foresight. We require such an understanding of the present conditions as may give us some grasp of the novelty which is about to produce a measureable influence on the immediate future. Yet the doctrine that routine is dominant in any society that is not collapsing must never be lost sight of. Thus the grounds, in human nature and in the successful satisfaction of purpose—these grounds for the current routine must be understood; and at the same time the sorts of novelty just entering into social effectiveness have got to be weighed against the old routine. In this way the type of modification and the type of persistence exhibited in the immediate future may be foreseen.

It is now time to give some illustrations of assertions already made. Consider our main conclusion that our traditional doctrines of sociology, of political philosophy, of the practical conduct of large business, and of political economy, are largely warped and vitiated by the implicit assumption of a stable unchanging social system.

With this assumption it is comparatively safe to base reasoning upon a simplified edition of human nature. For well-known stimuli working under well-known conditions produce well-known reactions. It is safe then to assume that human nature, for the purpose in hand, is adequately described in terms of some of the major reactions to some of the major stimuli. For example, we can all remember our old friend, the economic man.

The beauty of the economic man was that we knew exactly what he was after. Whatever his wants were, he knew them and his neighbors knew them. His wants were those developed in a well-defined social system. His father and grandfather had the same wants, and satisfied them in the same way. So whenever there was a shortage, everyone—including the economic man himself—knew what was short, and knew the way to satisfy the consumer. In fact the consumer knew what he wanted to consume. This was the demand. The producer knew how to produce the required articles, hence the supply. The men who got the goods onto the spot first, at the cheapest price, made their fortunes; the other producers were eliminated. This was healthy competition.

This is beautifully simple and with proper elaboration is obviously true. It expresses the dominant truth exactly so far as there are stable well-tried conditions. But when we are concerned with a social system which in important ways is changing, this simplified conception of human relations requires severe qualification.

It is, of course, common knowledge that the whole trend of political economy during the last thirty or forty years has been away from these artificial simplifications. Such sharp-cut notions as "the economic man," "supply and demand," "competition," are now in process of dilution by a close study of the actual reactions of various populations to the stimuli which are relevant to modern commerce. This exactly illustrates the main thesis of my paper.

The older political economy reigned supreme for about a hundred years from the time of Adam Smith, because in its main assumptions it did apply to the general circumstances of life as led, then and for innumerable centuries in the past. These circumstances were then already passing away. But it still remained a dominant truth that in commercial relations men were dominated by well-conditioned reactions to completely familiar stimuli.

In the present age the element of novelty which life affords is too prominent to be omitted from our calculations. A deeper knowledge of the varieties of human nature is required to determine the reaction, in its character and its strength, to those elements of novelty which each decade of years introduces into social life. The possibility of this deeper knowledge constitutes the foresight of which I am speaking.

Another example which concerns sociological habits, and hence business relations and the shifting values of property, is to be seen in the history of cities.

Throughout the whole span of civilization up to the present moment, the growth of condensed aggregates of humans, which we call cities, has been an inseparable accompaniment of the growth of civilization. There are many obvious reasons, the defense of accumulated wealth behind city walls, the concentration of materials requisite for manufacture, the concentration of power in the form of human muscles and, later, in the form of available heat energy, the ease of mutual intercourse required for business relations, the pleasure arising from a concentration of esthetic and cultural opportunities, the advantages of a concentration of governmental and other directing agencies, administrative, legal, and military.

But there are disadvantages in cities. As yet no civilization has been self-supporting. Each civilization is born, it culminates, and it decays. There is a widespread testimony that this ominous fact is due to inherent biological defects in the crowded life of cities. Now, slowly and at first faintly, an opposite tendency is showing itself. Better roads and better vehicles at first induced the wealthier classes to live on the outskirts of the cities. The urgent need for defense had also vanished. This tendency is now spreading rapidly downwards. But a new set of conditions is just showing itself. Up to the present time, throughout the eighteenth and nineteenth centuries, this new tendency placed the homes in the immediate suburbs, but concentrated manufacturing activity, business relations, government, and pleasure, in the centers of the cities. Apart from the care of children, the periods of sheer rest, the active lives were spent in the cities. In some ways, the concentration of such activities was even more emphasized, and the homes were pushed outwards even at the cost of the discomfort of commuting. But if we examine the trend of technology during the past generation, the reasons for this concentration are largely disappearing. Still more, the reasons for the choice of sites for cities are also altering. Mechanical power can be transmitted for hundreds of miles, men can communicate instantaneously by telephone, the chiefs of great organizations can be transported by airplanes, the cinemas can produce plays in every village, and music, speeches, and sermons can be broadcast. Almost every reason for the growth of cities, concurrently with the growth of civilization, has been profoundly modified.

What then is to be the future of cities, three hundred years hence, a hundred years hence, or even thirty years hence? I do not know. But I venture a guess—that those who are reasonably fortunate in this foresight will make their fortunes, and that others will be ruined by mistakes in calculation.

My second point, that the reasons for the choice of sites for cities have also been modified, is illustrated by recent changes in my own country, England. The first effect of the new industrial age of the eighteenth and nineteenth centuries was to concentrate population round the coal fields. Thus the central portion of England on its northern edge has become one huge city, disguised under different names for its various regional parts. But the novel conditions are shifting population and manufactures to the south of England, near to the great southern ports which look toward the Mediterranean, the South Atlantic Ocean, and the Panama Canal. They are the best ports, with the easiest navigation, and with uncrowded land around them. At present the transmission of electric power is one of the major preoccupations of the government of England.

The effect of new technologies on the sites of cities, and on sorts of cities, is one of the fundamental problems which must enter into all sociological theories, including the forecasting of business relations.

Do not exaggerate the importance of these particular examples. They are just two selected from a whole situation which can be analyzed into innumerable examples with the same moral. I mean nothing so silly as that all of you should meditate on the future of cities. The topic may be quite irrelevant to the future activities of most of us.

But we are faced with a fluid, shifting situation in the immediate future. Rigid maxims, a rule-of-thumb routine, and cast-iron particular doctrines will be the ruin of many people. The business of the future must be controlled by a somewhat different type of men [from] that of previous centuries. The type is already changing, and has already changed so far as the leaders are concerned. The business schools of universities are concerned with spreading this type throughout the nations by aiming at the production of the requisite type of mentality.

I will conclude by a sketch of the business mind of the future. In the first place, it is fundamental that there be a power of conforming to routine, of supervising routine, of constructing routine, and of understanding routine both as to its internal structure and as to its external purposes. Such a power is the bedrock of all practical efficiency.

But for the production of the requisite foresight, something more is wanted. This extra endowment can only be described as a philosophic power of understanding the complex flux of the varieties of human societies: for instance, the habit of noting varieties of character, of demands on life, of serious purposes, of frivolous amusements. Such instinctive grasp of the relevant features of social currents is of supreme importance. For example, the time span of various types of social behavior is of the essence of their effect on policy. A widespread type of religious interest, with its consequent behaviors, has a dominant life of about a hundred years, while a fashion of dress survives any time between three months and three years. Methods of agriculture change slowly. But the scientific world seems to be on the verge of far-reaching biological discoveries. Thus the assumption of slow changes in agriculture must be scanned vigilantly.

This example of time spans can be generalized. The quantitative aspect of social changes is of the essence of business relations. Thus the habit of transforming observation of qualitative changes into quantitative estimates should be a characteristic of business mentality.

I have said enough to show that the modern business mentality requires many elements of discipline, scientific and sociological. But the great fact remains that details of relevant knowledge cannot be foreseen. Thus even for mere success, and apart from any question of intrinsic quality of life, an unspecialized aptitude for eliciting generalizations from particulars and for seeing the divergent illustration of generalities in diverse circumstances is required.

Such a reflective power is essentially a philosophic habit; it is the survey of society from the standpoint of generality. This habit of general thought, undaunted by novelty, is the gift of philosophy.

But the motive of success is not enough. It produces a short-sighted world which destroys the sources of its own prosperity. The cycles of trade depression which afflict the world warn us that business relations are infected through and through with the disease of short-sighted motives. The robber barons did not conduce to the prosperity of Europe in the Middle Ages, though some of them died prosperously in their beds. Their example is a warning to our civilization.

Also we must not fall into the fallacy of thinking of the business world in abstraction from the rest of the community. The business world is one main part of the very community which is the subject matter of our study. The behavior of the community is largely dominated by the business mind. A great society is a society in which its men of business think greatly of their functions. Low thoughts mean low behavior, and after a brief orgy of exploitation, low behavior means a descending standard of life. The general greatness of the community, qualitatively as well as quantitatively, is the first condition for steady prosperity, buoyant, self-sustained, and commanding credit.

The Greek philosopher who laid the foundation of all our finer thoughts ended his most marvelous dialogue with the reflection that the ideal state could never arrive till philosophers are kings. Today, in an age of democracy, the kings are the plain citizens pursuing their various avocations. There can be no successful democratic society till general education conveys a philosophic outlook.

Philosophy is not a mere collection of noble sentiments. A deluge of such sentiments does more harm than good. Philosophy is at once general and concrete, critical and appreciative of direct intuition. It is not—or, at least, should not be—a ferocious debate between irritable professors. It is a survey of possibilities and their comparison with actualities. In philosophy, the fact, the theory, the alternatives, and the ideal are weighed together. Its gifts are insight and foresight, and a sense of the worth of life—in short, that sense of importance which nerves all civilized effort. Mankind can flourish in the lower stages of life with merely barbaric flashes of thought. But when civilization culminates, the absence of a coordinating philosophy of life, spread throughout the community, spells decadence, boredom, and the slackening of effort.

We can now define how the philosophical schools of universities should play their part in the molding of modern life. Every epoch has its character determined by the way its populations react to the material events which they encounter. This reaction is determined by their basic beliefs—by their hopes, their fears, their judgments of what is worth while.

They may rise to the greatness of an opportunity, seizing its drama, perfecting its art, exploiting its adventure, mastering intellectually and physically the network of relations that constitutes the very being of the epoch. On the other hand, they may collapse before the perplexities confronting them. How they act depends partly on their courage, partly on their intellectual grasp.

Philosophy is an attempt to purify those fundamental beliefs which finally determine the emphasis of attention that lies at the base of character.

Mankind is now in one of its rare moods of shifting its outlook. The mere compulsion of tradition has lost its force. It is the business of philosophers, students, and practical men to re-create and re-enact a vision of the world, conservative and radical, including those elements of reverence and order without which, society lapses into riot, a vision penetrated through and through with unflinching rationality. Such a vision is the knowledge which Plato identified with virtue.

Epochs for which, within the limits of their development, this vision has been widespread, are the epochs unfading in the memory of mankind. There is now no choice before us: either we must succeed in providing a rational coordination of impulses and thoughts, or for centuries civilization will sink into a mere welter of minor excitements. We must produce a great age, or see the collapse of the upward striving of our race.

THE ECONOMY OF ABUNDANCE

STUART CHASE

[Stuart Chase, "The Economy of Abundance," in *The Economy of Abundance*, The Macmillan Company, New York, 1934, as adapted in Whit Burnett (ed.), *This Is My Best*, The Dial Press, New York, 1942, pp. 1071–1082 (abridged).]

Stuart Chase, in 1934, made the intellectuals' case for the New Deal—or, if not for the New Deal, for the challenge of optimism in the face of despair, and for the need to rethink our economic traditions. We needed his, and others', correctives. Deep in depression, we had forgotten our destiny, and the reasons for it.

Chase may have confused institutions (such as business or capitalism) with the way they were being operated; or vice versa. For example, he says, "In Russia the march is luminous"—a poor prophecy. But thank God for intellectual courage like his. Otherwise he was highly prophetic. He did foresee the higher truth which we can make true by believing in it and working at it: that ours *is* an economy of abundance.

It might be added that the waste of our system is not so much in unnecessary practices; these may be inevitable, or may be worth the price in liberty or dynamism. Rather, the loss is in taking the wrong direction. We can straighten this as we go along.

A little too popular to be a philosophers' philosopher, Stuart Chase has exerted a considerable liberal influence on modern thinking through such works as *Men and Machines* (1929), *A New Deal* (1932), and *The Economy of Abundance* (from which the following selection, with the same title, is taken). The "Economy of Abundance" is probably his best-known blow for the cause of new, nontraditional thinking.

◆

SUPPOSE that the 13,000,000 people living in the United States in 1830 had awakened on the morning of January 1, 1831, with 40 times the physical energy they had gone to bed with the night before. An active picture meets the mind's eye, a very active picture. A lumberman can fell 40 times as many trees in a week, a housewife sweeps 40 times as many square feet of floor; 40 barns can be built in the time hitherto required for one—and 40 chests, and 40 chairs. Porters can transport 40 times their accustomed load in a day; weavers can ply their shuttles 40 times as fast—if the shuttles can brook the strain; and children can raise 40 times their normal rumpus.

Assuming no increase in the invention of labor-saving devices—and where would be the point with such an exuberance of labor available —what might we logically expect in the way of economic changes? From an economy of scarcity, with barely enough to go around, the young republic would almost immediately enter an economy of abundance. The food supply could be increased, not fortyfold, due to the lack of tools and cleared land, but perhaps fivefold, in a remarkably short time; whereas to double it would probably provide a plethora for all. Every family could have a fine house, filled with fine handmade colonial furniture; every man could have a fine coat, one for every day in the week; and every woman a chest of linen as big as a box stall. . . . Fine horses and fine carriages, books, flat silver, tapestries, gardens, great public buildings, medical attention, education.

The new energy would get through to everybody. It would flower at once into goods for the ultimate consumer. Workshops must be enlarged, tools multiplied, new houses, roads, capitols, libraries, theaters, hospitals built. In a fairly simple economy such as that of 1830, the standard of living for the whole community could not fail to mount enormously within a relatively short time. Indeed, a very high standard in terms of the forthright and durable articles of the day could be achieved with only a fraction of the energy delivered. Rather than fortyfold, perhaps fivefold, or even less, would be enough to achieve the standard, so rapid and direct was the conversion into consumers' goods at that time. Hours of labor could be cut to two or three a day, and still the citizens would have to take to climbing mountains or organizing expeditions to the unknown West, or playing the most strenuous variety of games, or writing long epic poems, or painting miles of murals like Diego Rivera, or even dispensing with work animals, to spend their surplus vitality.

Today, in the United States, we have precisely this equivalent of energy per capita. It is not in our muscles, but in our delivered power resources. Observe that it is not a potential total of installed horsepower, but actual coal, oil and natural gas burned, and water turbines turned. If we counted *capacity* to deliver work, the ratio would be greater than fortyfold. The average working hours for all central power stations in 1933 were only 2800 a year, or about 32 per cent of capacity. The energy we are considering' is given, and has been used, every foot-pound of it. Yet the average standard of living, while including more commodities and services than that of 1830, is still below the margin of health and decency; millions are acutely undernourished, miserably housed, deplorably clothed, while economic insecurity clutches at almost every heart.

Energy, the capacity to do work, is here, a living, demonstrable reality, but it has not got through to the wayfaring man as expressed in his standard of living; the essential work has not been done. Even in 1929, with an average wage of only $1300, it obviously had not been done. The furnaces roar, the turbines whirl, the compression chambers stiffen to the shock of the explosion, but life is a more uncertain business than it was a century ago, and that happiness which Mr. Jefferson bade us pursue is as remote as when he wrote the Declaration of Independence.

The capacity to produce goods, furthermore, is not measured by raw energy alone. Also important is the skill of the mechanism which takes the energy and shapes the product. To use a homely illustration: I can mow about an acre of pasture in a ten-hour day. My neighbor, a farmer all his life, can mow two acres in an equal time, with a smaller expenditure of energy. His muscles are trained to the scythe, where mine are not. Similarly, in the field of mechanical operations, engineers have devised increasingly skillful methods of utilizing a given quantity of energy. For the 20 years from 1909 to 1929, for example, engineers have computed an increase of 66 per cent in kilowatt hours secured from every ton of coal used for the generation of electric power, and a 47 per cent increase in railroad haulage per ton of fuel burned.

But multiplying energy, however efficient its application, cannot proportionately multiply standards of living in industrial societies. Such societies are subject to extreme specialization, and great quantities of energy are required to link the specialized processes together, especially in the form of transportation. The United States has been justly called an "experiment in transportation." Whereas in 1830 the forges of Connecticut obtained iron ore almost in their back yards and delivered horseshoes and hinges to the man across the street, the steel mills of the 1930s haul iron ore by boat and rail from northern Minnesota, coke from Pennsylvania, manganese from Russia, and sell rails, girders, sheet steel and tin plate from Florida to Oregon. It takes energy to mine these raw materials— including the coal, which is potential energy itself—to fabricate them in scores of interlocking processes, and to haul both the partly finished, and the completed article, all about the map.

So in the best-ordered of societies devoted to technology, output for the consumer could not increase so rapidly as total energy. A philosopher would, however, expect to see living standards increase directly with energy delivered, but at a somewhat slower rate. Swinging his dispassionate eye upon the United States of America, he finds a fortyfold increase in energy per capita and a standard of living which, in terms of material well-being, is still deplorably low.

How great is the unavoidable loss due to specialization and to absorption in the process of transforming raw energy into useful heat and work? Even if we assume that this fraction is as large as 75 per cent, which would seem generous, a fortyfold increase in energy would result in a tenfold increase in living standards. But the actual increase in material well-being of 1930 over 1830 is probably not more than twofold. Ninety-five per cent of our energy is doing us no good.

Something is wrong here; something very wrong indeed. The "experiment in transportation" could never account for such a difference. Where has the balance of delivered energy gone? This is no academic question. Somebody has robbed us of that which is more vital than gold.

It is not difficult to analyze where the vanished energy has gone, leaving aside the technical factor of conversion loss. Some of it has gone into uneconomic building—unoccupied skyscrapers, surplus widget factories, and the like. Some has gone into wasteful cross-hauling of raw materials and finished products back and forth across the country. Some has gone into maintaining great cities, where it has been calculated that more than 30 per cent of all delivered energy has to be used for services that offset congestion. Much energy has gone into anticonservation practices—like developing and irrigating submarginal farmland, cutting forests beyond prudent needs—and then into necessary conservation measures to cure the resulting erosion, forest fires, and other devastation. A great deal has been lost through competitive establishments that duplicate each others' facilities on a large scale, and a great deal through style changes, which may render worthless the output of weeks or months of operation.

Too much energy has gone into a monumental obsolescence rate— building and tearing down plants, houses, machines—some of it owing to shoddy construction and some to sales pressure; and far too much into overproduced goods which are destroyed or allowed to spoil. A great deal of our energy has gone into producing goods for export, for which no equivalent imports were exchanged. It is a favorite pastime of generous Uncle Sam, making goods for foreigners, but taking no goods from foreigners. The spirit, of course, is charming, but gifts on this scale require large blocs of energy. Finally, one of the greatest consumers of the new mechanical energy is probably the pleasure motorist, and the energy burned up in his engines is obviously not all waste. Some of it comes under the head of death and destruction, some under escape from intolerable cities, intolerable homes and intolerable monotony, some under the head of putting one's neighbor's eye out, and some under the head of genuine pleasure and use. What the various proportions may be, no sensible statistician would dare to compute.

All these outlets give us a reasonably complete story of where energy has been dissipated, and why so little gets through to the ultimate consumer. It is perfectly obvious that his wants and desires have never been central in the picture. The plant has been built with other ends in view; a crazy patchwork, magnificent in bulk, superb in some of its detail, but not designed for securing the most for the least.

Riding through North Carolina one day, I saw a bright blue motor car, resplendent with chromium fittings, in the yard of a dilapidated shack constructed of rough logs and plastered with red mud. The car and the hut belonged to the same sharecropper. It struck me as a not unreasonable summary of the net gain in living standards since 1830. Measured in tonnage and variety, the wayfaring man has undoubtedly improved his position, but in fundamental well-being, I hold to the conviction that doubling the standard is a fair estimate.

These immense new powers have run to immense new wastes. Our very junk piles would have ransomed a king in the Middle Ages, with their stores of metal and findings. The state of New York undoubtedly contains more fabricated "wealth" than did all Europe in A.D. 1400. But, for all its due capitalization, it is not wealth in terms of human use and enjoyment. It is largely misplaced energy crystallized in stone and steel. The United States was a poor country in 1830 and is a poor country today in terms of the human calculus.

The economy of abundance is self-defined. It means an economic condition where an abundance of material goods can be produced for the entire population of a given community, a condition never obtaining anywhere until within the last few years.

Behind this obvious definition, however, lurk a series of more subtle connotations. The smooth optimism of the phrase is seriously disturbed when, for instance, we set technological abundance into a background of prevailing financial habits. These habits were laid down in an economy of scarcity, and clash bitterly with the facts of plenty. Abundance is not alone a promise to mankind, it is a savage threat to the real or supposed interests of special and powerful groups of men everywhere.

What has been the major economic plague of the past ten years? The plague has been too much wheat to be profitably sold, and not enough bread; too much cotton and not enough clothes; too many bricks and not enough houses; too much drudgery and not enough jobs; too much goods and not enough purchasing power. The paradox of plenty is what has chiefly plagued us. Surplus, surplus everywhere, and often too little to eat. In these circumstances, corporate groups have moved heaven and earth to hold prices up by keeping production down, by sabotaging abundance. The methods they have used are all too familiar—monopolies, mergers, holding companies, price-fixing agreements, international cartels, trade associations punishing "chiselers," suppression of new inventions, even trade union restrictions on output. The facts of technological plenty will not fit into the financial machinery of an age of scarcity.

The economy of abundance is not a mystical force, not a genie from a bottle, despite the fact that its pressures catch us unaware. It is:

A group of buildings, mines, farms, vibrant with machines, and connected by lines of energy and transportation; founded upon

A series of scientific laws, proliferating into specific processes and inventions, and

A set of human habits.

The latter may be further divided into the habits of the scientists and technicians who control and develop the physical processes, and the habits of laymen, connoting everybody else living within the high-energy orbit.

Assuming that the abundance pattern will prevail, what are the terms upon which it will function? Obviously in the melee of transition it can function only by fits and starts. From the foregoing analysis, it is possible concretely to specify the terms. An abundance economy demands:

1. Capacity operation of its plant, or something near capacity, on the balanced-load principle.
2. An unhampered flow of goods to consumers, involving the right to a minimum standard of living, regardless of work performed— *if no work is available.* Distribution must replace exchange. This imperative is practical, not idealistic, arising from the necessity of keeping the plant in operation. It is also likely to become a mass political demand.
3. The elimination of waste, restriction and private monopoly, as methods of maintaining prices.
4. The conservation of natural resources to the degree which, consistent with existing technical knowledge, will maintain adequate supplies of raw materials for the calculable future. Neglect of this imperative may cripple the whole productive mechanism through the failure of one resource—say copper, or oil.
5. The employment of a decreasing number of man-hours in industrial production.
6. The encouragement of research, new invention, and a fairly high obsolescence rate for plant and processes. No more suppressed inventions; no corporate patent monopolies.
7. The capital goods sector to grow only as technological improvement, mass purchasing power, or mass demand requires it. No reliance on this sector, as heretofore, as an automatic distributor of purchasing power.
8. A one-to-one relationship between the growth of physical production and the growth of the interest burden on total debt.
9. A sharp distinction between use property and industrial fixed assets. The latter should be socially controlled in that the units are no longer independent enterprises, but interlock one with another.
10. Economic decentralization; the end of Megalopolis, because it is too wasteful a unit to support. The liquidation of the distinction between city man and country man.
11. The industrialization of most agricultural staples, on a quantity production basis, and a declining number of man-hours in farming.
12. Shorter working hours for all.
13. A wide extension of social services and public works to absorb those inevitably to be displaced from industry, agriculture, and the parasitic trades.
14. The continuation of industrial specialization—though decentralization may be expected to modify the trend somewhat.

15. No narrow economic nationalism. The plant still demands essential raw materials on a reasonable exchange basis from various parts of the world, but this demand is lessening with the development of synthetics.

16. Revised and simplified political forms. The revision of outworn political boundaries—for instance, many county subdivisions.

17. Centralization of government; the overhead planning and control of economic activity. In North America, such planning to satisfy technology should be continental rather than national. In Europe, technology will not tolerate national boundaries indefinitely. A working control over industry is indicated, if the plant is to be efficiently operated. Technical performance cannot be subject to popular vote, but the administrative group and broad policy should be more responsive than at present to the people's wishes.

18. Finally, and exceedingly important, abundance demands no compromise. It will not operate at half speed. It will not allow retreat to an earlier level and stabilization there. Pharaoh did not tell the Nile what to do; the Nile told Pharaoh what to do. The industrial discipline must be accepted—all of it—or it must be renounced. The only retreat is back one hundred years to the economy of scarcity.

Such, substantially, are the terms upon which the economy of abundance will function; such the mold to which new social habits, new institutions, must conform. This is the way, and I think the only way, that a high-energy culture will function in the long run. Some of the imperatives may be subject to modification in detail; other imperatives may arise; but the basic mold is set. This is the direction in which Mr. Roosevelt is now being forced. Underneath political smoke screens, and the alarms of stagecoach champions, those of us who have eyes to see can detect the glacier advancing into Sweden, England, Italy, South America, Canada, Australasia. In Russia the march is luminous.

Do these terms violate human nature; are they inconsistent with normal behavior? Already many have been incorporated into our daily lives. What they do violate is a set of institutions largely developed in the eighteenth century, which in turn displaced an earlier cultural complex based on feudalism, which in turn displaced its predecessor, and so on back to Mesopotamia. Men talk as though the gold standard had been laid down by God, side by side with the law of gravitation. The universal gold standard is not so old as Mr. Roosevelt.

It is not to be gainsaid that these terms carry implications of substantial moral shock to many persons, especially to large owners of property hitherto vendible. The terms are now being bitterly fought, and will continue to be for years to come. Habit complexes do not change overnight. If it requires at least a decade to modify the psychology of stolid Russian peasants, it may require twice as long to modify the psychology of Wall Street.

Technological imperative is impersonal, amoral and nonethical. Like the Nile, it sets the boundaries within which a given culture must operate. The terms imposed by the machine age were onerous to the point of often violating human nature; the terms of the power age are more generous. Fortunate and perhaps fortuitous is the fact that the modern imperative is straight in the direction of an economic system based on serviceability. Machines do not care whom they serve, but they refuse to operate without a high volume of output; they care nothing about human leisure, but the laws of their spinning are inconsistent with the clumsy interference of the human hand. They will not tolerate the wastes and barriers of what Veblen used to call "vendibility."

There the imperatives are, for us to take or to leave. Can we adjust to them? No one can now know whether adjustment is possible; he can only be sure of the negative: that if adjustment is not made, high-energy cultures will presently stand liquidated. He can further be reasonably sure that the liquidation will not be orderly and planned, but cataclysmic. Western man, failing adjustment, will be hurled back, bloodily and painfully, to a low-energy, unspecialized economy.

The timid, with the bold, will do better to push on. If we must die, let it be in the front line. The chances of dying, furthermore, are to my mind appreciably less than of capturing the line. What kind of society would fit these imperatives; would it be bleak and rigorous beyond bearing? I think it would be less bleak than that which we lived through in the later stages of capitalism. If we have been able to adjust to the years 1914 to 1918, and 1930 to 1934 (and I might add, 1940 to 1942), a philosopher might say that we can adjust to anything.

The broad outlines of the future society stand clear in the list of imperatives. Political and economic boundaries will have to widen, not imperialistically but to accord with technological unities. Thus, the United States and Canada will fall into one regional frame; similarly most of Europe. Economically supreme over these frames should sit an industrial general staff to direct the smooth technical operation of all the major sources of raw material and supply. Political democracy will have little to say about the technical detail of economic matters; democracy in consumption will make enormous strides as standards of living are leveled upward; industrial individualism—anarchy is a better term—in the sense of each business-man for himself, each corporation for itself, must be disallowed. The principles of insurance, savings, investment, will be greatly modified in favor of a collective guarantee of adequate living standards. The margin between the relatively rich and the relatively poor will shrink enormously; conspicuous consumption and its emulation will tend to pass. The margin in the United States in 1929 between the richest family ($12,000,000 income), and the poorest family ($300 income), was 40,000 to one. I doubt if in the projected society the margin can much exceed ten to one.

Use property will be extended and protected, but there will probably be an increase in the rental of such property from great service companies.

Income-producing property which one does not use may eventually pass out of individual possession. Title will vest in the community. It will include the bulk of land, mineral deposits, forest stands, public utilities, and most of the producing and distributing plant. Banking, credit and the issue of money will be a strict government function. The interest rate will approximate zero.

Work will be carefully allocated. Perhaps young people will be drafted to perform certain tasks for a year or more. [Because] work is a fundamental instinct, while jobs under integrated power age conditions will be at a minimum, we may see a surprising reversal of the public attitude toward labor. Rather than being envious of the idle, citizens may become envious of those who secure an opportunity to work. Allotments might be at a premium. A great deal of thought and experiment will have to be devoted to obtaining compensation for the instinct of workmanship in the expanded leisure of that society. One would look for a revival of handicrafts on a large scale, not for sale but for amusement, gifts, and exchange.

While industrial and agricultural labor will steadily decline, we may expect a great increase in service occupations, especially doctors, dentists, nurses, hospital attendants, teachers, research workers, technicians, librarians, artists, authors, public administrators, and so on.

A society such as this would not violate the eighteen imperatives. Within it, invention and technology could continue to expand, and mass production would function to a mass demand. I fail to see, furthermore, how it would violate human nature. It holds no terrors for me, in contemplation. It would be irksome for a time, in that it was different, but a retreat to stagecoach days would be even more irksome. I conclude, accordingly, that adjustment to such a society is not beyond human possibility. The administrative task is admittedly very great. Jobs hardly smaller were done in the first World War, however, and are being done today.

The eighteen imperatives must govern the platform of any political advance. Communists, technocrats, Republicans, Democrats, liberals, constitutionalists, what you will, who campaign for ends *that are not in line* with these imperatives are wasting their time and effort. Any political program now before any people anywhere can be quickly judged by this acid test. Hitler is obviously working *against* the imperatives when he proscribes machines, hails back-to-the-land movements, and breaks up industrial combines. . . . Indeed, his whole attitude up to 1934 has been more medieval than modern. Such policies are doomed in advance; they cannot prevail. Russia is working against the imperatives when she tries to teach Marxian physics and Marxian chemistry. President Roosevelt is working against them when he plows under cotton, puts a premium on the destruction of wheat, and tries to bolster up the debt edifice with loans from the Reconstruction Finance Corporation. These are pure scarcity techniques. Mussolini is working against the imperatives when he seeks to make Italy completely self-sufficient.

We can know by this test what is a through road and what is a blind alley. We could come close to formulating a party platform direct from the imperatives. Granted that a statesman made it his own, or that a group of new leaders espoused it, would citizens understand and would they follow? How strong would be the opposition?

These considerations are profound. Politics, too, has a kind of technology. I shall have to leave it to politicians and sociologists, with a solemn warning: They must apply their technique as means to an end in which technological imperatives are dominant. If they create imperatives of their own, beautiful as may be the method for leading the masses, the end of that leading will be down a steep place into the sea.

AN INVETERATE DISSENTER SUPPORTS CAPITALISM

H. L. MENCKEN

[H. L. Mencken, "Capitalism," in the Baltimore *Evening Sun,* Jan. 14, 1935.]

H. L. Mencken was hardly a conservative in the 1920s, unless *conservative* means not accepting the present just because it is new and different; to those who fancied themselves the conservatives of their times, his brittle querulousness seemed somehow unpatriotic, if not outright radical.

But when in the 1930s the fashion was to suggest that maybe traditional capitalism was becoming extinct, his protests sounded truly conservative—not obstructionism, but considered refusal to give up proved values until they were proved inferior. Or maybe he was just being his own self: enjoying being in the minority with as much intellectual flair as possible.

In any event, here is a truly perceptive and affirmative evaluation of capitalism by one who can hardly be called an unthinking sycophant of cant, dogma, or ideology. Marx please take note.

———◆———

ALL THE QUACKS and cony-catchers now crowding the public trough at Washington seem to be agreed upon one thing, and one thing only. It is the doctrine that the capitalistic system is on its last legs, and will presently give place to something nobler and more "scientific." There is, of course, no truth in this doctrine whatsoever. It collides at every point with the known facts. There is not the slightest reason for believing that capitalism is in collapse, or that anything proposed by the current wizards would be any better. The most that may be said is that the capitalistic system is undergoing changes, some of them painful. But those changes will probably strengthen it quite as often as they weaken it.

We owe to it almost everything that passes under the general name of civilization today. The extraordinary progress of the world since the Middle Ages has not been due to the mere expenditure of human energy, nor even to the flights of human genius, for men had worked hard since the remotest times, and some of them had been of surpassing intellect. No, it has been due to the accumulation of capital. That accumulation permitted labor to be organized economically and on a large scale, and thus greatly enhanced its productiveness. It provided the machinery that gradually diminished human drudgery, and liberated the spirit of the worker, who had formerly been almost indistinguishable from a mule. Most of all, it made possible a longer and better preparation for work, so that every art and handicraft greatly widened its scope and range, and multitudes of new and highly complicated crafts came in.

We owe to capital the fact that the medical profession, for example, is now really useful to mankind, whereas formerly it was useful only to the charlatans who practiced it. It took accumulated money to provide the long training that medicine began to demand as it slowly lifted itself from the level of a sorry trade to that of a dignified art and science—money to keep the student while he studied and his teachers while they instructed him, and more money to pay for the expensive housing and materials that they needed. In the main, all that money came from private capitalists. But whether it came from private capitalists or from the common treasury, it was always capital, which is to say, it was always part of an accumulated surplus. It never could have been provided out of the hand-to-mouth income of a noncapitalistic society.

When the Bolsheviki, a gang of frauds almost comparable to our own Brain Trust, took over the control of affairs in Russia, they had to throw overboard at once one of the cardinal articles of their ostensible creed. That article was to the effect that all the sorrows of the world were due to the fact that the workingman, under capitalism, had lost ownership in his tools. All the classical authorities on socialism, from Marx and Engels downward, had stressed this loss heavily, and the Utopia they visioned was always one in which the workingman should get his tools back, and become an independent producer, working for himself alone, and giving none of the value he created to a wicked capitalist. But the moment the Bolsheviki came into power they had to shelve all this, and since then nothing has been heard about it save from their American gulls. A shrewd set of shysters, eager only to run Russia as their private preserve, they saw instantly that their main job was to accumulate capital, for without it half of their victims would starve. The old capital of the country had been destroyed by war. An easy way to get more would have been to borrow it, but no one would lend, so the Bolsheviki had to accumulate fresh capital of their own.

This they managed to do by sweating the Russian workers in a manner never before seen on earth, at all events in modern times. The workers, at the start, resisted, especially the farmers, and in consequence Russia had a couple of famines, and the hat had to be passed in the capitalistic countries to feed the starving. But by slaughtering the rebellious farmers and organizing the jobless into a huge army, the Bolsheviki presently managed to bring the workers of Russia to heel, and since then those poor fish have been worked like prisoners in a chain gang, and have got pretty much the same wages. All the produce of their labor, over and above subsistence far more suitable to rats than to men, has gone into the coffers of the Bolsheviki. Thereby the Bolsheviki have accumulated a store of new capital, and now they use it not only to build ever larger and larger factories, each manned by hordes of workers who own nothing but their hands, but also to provide luxurious quarters for themselves, including an embassy at Washington so gaudy that it is the envy of every banker in the town.

Thus one of the fundamental principles of Marxism has been reduced to absurdity in the house of its professed disciples. They may be scoundrels, and no doubt they are, but they also have considerable cunning, and are thus well aware that nothing properly describable as modern civilization can be carried on without capital. And by capital

I mean precisely what they mean when they denounce it for foreign consumption—that is, I mean a surplus accumulated, not in the pockets of workers, but in the pockets of persons who provide them with the means to work, and not under control of those who produce it, but under the control of those who have managed to collar it. The shabby politicians, puerile pedagogues and briefless lawyers who have raged and roared at Washington since 1933 would go the same way if they had the chance. Some of them, perhaps, are actually stupid enough to believe that the world could get along without capitalism, but others surely must be shrewd enough to note what has happened in Russia. But whether they are only plain idiots or clever rogues, they all talk grandly about capitalism's decay, and even those who allege that they are trying to save it keep on mouthing the nonsense that it is on its deathbed. You will find the same hollow blah in all the organs of the More Abundant Life, and every day it issues from some dotty pedagogue yearning for a government job.

There is no sense in it whatever. The modern world could no more get along without accumulated capital than it could get along without police or paved streets. The greatest change imaginable is simply the change that has occurred in Russia—a transfer of capital from private owners to professional politicians. If you think this would do the individual any good, then all you need do to be un-deceived is to ask any American letter-carrier. He works for a master capitalist named Uncle Sam—and he will be glad to tell you how hard he has to sweat for every nickel he gets.

THE NATURE OF EXECUTIVE
RESPONSIBILITY, AND THE ESSENCE
OF LEADERSHIP

CHESTER BARNARD

[Chester Barnard, "The Nature of Executive Responsibility," in *The Functions of the Executive,* Harvard University Press, Cambridge, 1938, pp. 272-276, 279, 281-284 (abridged). Reprinted by permission of the publishers.]

Chester Barnard, a successful executive himself, president of the New Jersey Bell Telephone Company from 1927 to 1948, was one of the first men to analyze what being an executive means. Plenty of others before him may have discussed the role of the businessman in society, the play of economic forces, the relation of employers and employees, and so on, but Barnard actually tackled the executive process itself.

Barnard packs so much concentrated thought into his telegraphic sentences that he is hard to read; you have to stop and expand his words back into ideas, as you go along—if you do. But many have found the results rewarding. This selection is from his book, *The Functions of the Executive*. It comes toward the end, where he summarizes the implications from the earlier chapters, and then moves on to "the creative function," which he calls the "essence of leadership."

———◆———

EXECUTIVE POSITIONS (*a*) imply a complex morality, and (*b*) require a high capacity of responsibility, (*c*) under conditions of activity, necessitating (*d*) commensurate general and specific technical abilities as a *moral* factor. . . . In addition there is required (*e*) the faculty of creating morals for others. . . .

(*a*) Every executive possesses, independently of the position he occupies, personal moral codes. When the individual is placed in an executive position there are immediately incumbent upon him, officially at least, several additional codes that are codes of his organization. Codes of the organization are themselves accruals largely of intangible forces, influences, habitual practice, which must be accepted as a whole. These codes are quite different among organizations, being affected by their status—supreme, as in the case of governments or churches—or subsidiary, subordinate, dependent; and by their purposes—educational, industrial, commercial, political, party, fraternal, governmental, religious, etc.; and by their technologies.

It will be sufficient for present purposes of illustration to take a hypothetical industrial organization, and to suppose the case of an executive head of an important department. The *organization* codes to which he should conform are: (1) the government code as applying to his company, that is, the laws, charter provisions, etc.; (2) obedience to the general purpose and general methods, including the established systems of objective authority; (3) the general purpose of his department; (4) the general moral (ethical) standards of his subordinates; (5) the technical situation as a whole; (6) the code of the informal executive organization, that is, that official conduct shall be that of a gentleman as *its members* understand it, and that personal conduct shall be so likewise; (7) the code that is suggested in the phrase "the good of the organization as a whole"; (8) the code of the informal organization of the department; (9) the technical requirements of the department as a whole. There will often be others, but these will serve for example.

It will be quite evident from this brief discussion without consideration of specific organizations that the executive, by virtue of his position, adopts a more complex morality than he would otherwise

have. This complexity is not peculiar, however, to executives. Both
executives and professional men differ as a class from nonexecutive
or nonprofessional persons as a class in that the conditions of their
positions impose upon them numerous additional codes. These are
chiefly nonpersonal in their significance; most official or professional
activities can be carried out with no involvement of strictly private
codes. Therefore, the complexity of the individual's moral situation
is not perhaps increased in proportion to the additions arising from
organization and professional functions. But inevitably, at times, some
action or requirement does involve the whole gamut. Then we say
that a man cannot divorce his official or professional conduct from
his private morals. When such issues occur, the alternatives presented
are either to violate one's personal morality or to fail in an official
or professional obligation. Resignation or withdrawal is often a
solution which circumstances "legitimately" permit. Then the result
is maintenance of personal integrity. When, however, resignation or
withdrawal is itself highly immoral, as is sometimes the case, there is
potential tragedy. The penalty for lack of ability to avoid or find
substitute action in such cases is severe. . . .

(b) The capacity of responsibility is that of being firmly governed
by moral codes—against inconsistent immediate impulses, desires,
or interests, and in the direction of desires or interests that are consonant with such codes. Our common word for one aspect of this
capacity is "dependability," by which we mean that, knowing a man's
codes—that is, being aware of his "character"—we can reasonably
foresee what he is likely to do or not to do, usually under a variety of
circumstances.

Almost uniformly, in all types of organizations, persons of executive capacity are assigned initially to executive positions of low
rank. The fact of sense of responsibility is there demonstrated. The
conditions of these lower-rank positions are those of relatively
limited moral complexity and possibly somewhat lower states of
activity. The chief difference between the lower and the higher ranks
is not in the capacity of responsibility but in the condition of moral
complexity. In other words, the higher positions impose more responsibilities, as is often correctly said, but do not require greater
sense of responsibility in important degree.

(c) Generally the conditions of executive work are those of great
activity. This is not obvious, because the word "activity" too much
suggests physical action. But it is clear that the higher the position
the more exposed the incumbent to action imposed from numerous
directions, calling for the activity of decision. The increase of this
activity is in practice not proportional to the level of position because
it is deliberately controlled. . . .

(d) The capacity of responsibility is in executive ranks rather a

constant, and the tendency of activity to increase with scope of
position is often controllable. The increase in complexity of moral
conditions, however, is not controllable by the person affected, so
that despite control of activities the burden increases from conflicts of
morals as the scope of the executive position broadens. For example,
since a preliminary proposal usually raises a conflict of codes, and
since proposals for concrete decision in nonroutine matters increase
with position, an executive position is exposed to more and more
moral conflicts the higher it is, and the process of decision becomes
morally and often technically more and more complex.

Where there is high sense of responsibility, these conflicts can only
be resolved by one of two methods: either to analyze further the
pertinent environment with a view to a more accurate determination
of the strategic factor of the situation, which may lead to the discovery of that "correct" action which violates no codes; or to adopt
a new detailed purpose consistent with general objectives, that is,
the more general purposes. Both methods are tests of general ability,
the first of ability in discrimination, analysis; the second of imagination, invention, innovation. Either process in an important aspect is
an expression of that phase of responsibility which is known as
"determination."

The moral complications of the executive functions, then, can
only be endured by those possessing a commensurate ability. While,
on one hand, the requisite ability without an adequate complex of
moralities or without a high sense of responsibility leads to the hopeless confusion of inconsistent expediencies so often described as
"incompetence," on the other hand, the requisite morality and sense
of responsibility without commensurate abilities leads to fatal indecision or emotional and impulsive decisions, with personal break-
down and ultimate destruction of the sense of responsibility. The
important distinctions of rank lie in the fact that the higher the
grade the more complex the *moralities* involved, and the more necessary higher abilities to discharge the responsibilities, that is, to resolve
the moral conflicts implicit in the positions. . . .

(*e*) The distinguishing mark of the executive responsibility is
that it requires not merely conformance to a complex code of morals
but also the creation of moral codes for others. The most generally
recognized aspect of this function is called securing, creating, inspiring
of "morale" in an organization. This is the process of inculcating
points of view, fundamental attitudes, loyalties, to the organization
or cooperative system, and to the system of objective authority,
that will result in subordinating individual interest and the minor
dictates of personal codes to the good of the cooperative whole. This
includes (also important) the establishment of the morality of
standards of workmanship.

The function of moral creativeness, though not ordinarily described in this way, is of long history. Some aspects of it, such as those related to the organization enthusiasm, are well appreciated; and what has already been said in this study concerning the economy of incentives, and especially concerning the necessity of the method of persuasion in the recruiting of organization forces, makes it unnecessary to elaborate the matter at greater length here. There is enough experience of the subject to make it clear that failure with respect to moral creativeness arises from inadequate attention, lack of persistence in the face of the inertia of human reluctance, and lack of sincerity of purpose. . . .

The creative aspect of executive responsibility is the highest exemplification of responsibility. As to the great proportion of organization decisions required of the executive, the conflict of morals is within organization codes, and personal codes are not directly involved. The "organization personality" alone is concerned. The conflict may be treated with relative objectivity, as a "problem." In fact, probably most executive decisions appear in the guise of technical decisions, and their moral aspects are not consciously appreciated. An executive may make many important decisions without reference to any sense of personal interest or of morality. But where creative morality is concerned, the sense of personal responsibility— of sincerity and honesty, in other words—is acutely emphasized. Probably few persons are able to do such work objectively. Indeed, few can do it long except on the basis of personal conviction—not conviction that they are obligated as officials to do it, but conviction that what they do for the good of organization they *personally* believe to be right.

The creative function as a whole is the essence of leadership. It is the highest test of executive responsibility because it requires for successful accomplishment that element of "conviction" that means identification of personal codes and organization codes in the view of the leader. This is the coalescence that carries "conviction" to the personnel of organization, to that informal organization underlying all formal organization that senses nothing more quickly than insincerity. Without it, all organization is dying, because it is the indispensable element in creating that desire for adherence—for which no incentive is a substitute—on the part of those whose efforts willingly contributed constitute organization.

The most general strategic factor in human cooperation is executive capacity. In the nature of the physical world and of the social world as well, opportunity and ideals outrun the immediate motives and interest and the practical abilities that are required of leaders. The accumulation of capital, the invention of processes, the innovations of human relationships that effective and efficient cooperation need as a preliminary necessity, call for special abilities in the technologies of materials, physical forces, economic systems, and organization arts. Though indispensable, these abilities will not be put forth, will not even be developed, without that sense of responsibility which makes the sacrifices involved a matter of course, and which elicits the initial faith in cooperation. These abilities and capacities are sufficent to bring into life many organizations of low quality and of inferior or antisocial purposes, and to maintain their vitality for a time. The short interest, the immediate purpose, the impulses of the moment, may be as well served by new combinations as by old, and the appeal to individual self-existence is often gratified best by change if only immediate and material needs are at stake. Organizations endure, however, in proportion to the breadth of the morality by which they are governed. This is only to say that foresight, long purposes, high ideals are the basis for the persistence of cooperation.

Thus the endurance of organization depends upon the quality of leadership; and that quality derives from the breadth of the morality upon which it rests. High responsibility there must be even in the lowest, the most immoral, organizations; but if the morality to which the responsibility relates is low, the organizations are short-lived. A low morality will not sustain leadership long, its influence quickly vanishes, it cannot produce its own succession.

Leadership, of course, often is wrong, and often fails. Perhaps frequently the leader believes his personal morality and that of his organization are identical when they are not. Perhaps he is ignorant of the codes in the organization that are necessary by reason of the environment, which he fails to see objectively. Perhaps he mistakes a purely personal motive for an organization purpose. In these cases, the facts destroy his responsibility, his leadership fails, he no longer can create, he is trapped between the incompatibility of purpose and environment, insincerity rots his influence. But until that happens—as perhaps it inevitably does in time to all leaders, since established organizations often seem to outgrow their leaders— until that happens, the creation of organization morality is the spirit that overcomes the centrifugal forces of individual interests or motives. Without leadership in this supreme sense the inherent difficulties often cannot be overcome even for short periods. Leadership does not annul the laws of nature, nor is it a substitute for the elements essential to cooperative effort; but it is the indispensable social essence that gives common meaning to common purpose, that creates the incentive that makes other incentives effective, that infuses the subjective aspect of countless decisions with consistency in a changing environment, that inspires the personal conviction that produces the vital cohesiveness without which cooperation is impossible.

Executive responsibility, then, is that capacity of leaders by which, reflecting attitudes, ideals, hopes, derived largely from without themselves, they are compelled to bind the wills of men to the accomplishment of purposes beyond their immediate ends, beyond their times. Even when these purposes are lowly and the time is short, the transitory efforts of men become a part of that organization of living forces that transcends man unaided by man; but when these purposes are high and the wills of many men of many generations are bound together they live boundlessly.

For the morality that underlies enduring cooperation is multidimensional. It comes from and may expand to all the world, it is rooted deeply in the past, it faces toward the endless future. As it expands, it must become more complex, its conflicts must be more numerous and deeper, its call for abilities must be higher, its failures of ideal attainment must be perhaps more tragic; but the quality of leadership, the persistence of its influence, the durability of its related organizations, the power of the coordination it incites, all express the height of moral aspirations, the breadth of moral foundations.

So among those who cooperate the things that are seen are moved by the things unseen. Out of the void comes the spirit that shapes the ends of men.

BUSINESS LEADERSHIP
AND A CREATIVE SOCIETY

ABRAM T. COLLIER

[Abram T. Collier, "Business Leadership and a Creative Society," *Harvard Business Review*, Jan.–Feb. 1953, vol. 31, no. 1, pp. 29–38.]

Picking up where Chester Barnard left off, another business executive discusses the creative aspects of leadership—Abram T. Collier. Because Mr. Collier is a present-day example of a once more growing trend—i.e., for businessmen to be as intellectually and morally alert as the mercantile aristocracy of the first half of the nineteenth century—we herewith provide more than the usual background.

Mr. Collier was originally a lawyer. His practice involved him with labor-relations problems, and during World War II he served both in this country and in Europe as an administrative officer for the radiation laboratory which was operated by the Office of Scientific Research and Development. The interest that these experiences stimulated led him, after the war, into the management side of business. Several years before he wrote this article he became personnel officer for the home office of

John Hancock Mutual Life Insurance Company, and Second Vice-President.

While attending the Advanced Management Program at the Harvard Business School in 1951, Mr. Collier found the opportunity to discuss business problems with many executives from other industries. Subsequently he was invited to speak before a meeting of the Life Insurance Advertisers Association in Montreal, and for that occasion he gathered together many of the ideas that he had been thinking and talking about. His article is developed from the notes he made for that speech.

As a commentary on this article, it is interesting to observe that the aims and ideals which Mr. Collier sees emerging to guide business administrators are the result not only of business thinking but of religious, scientific, philosophical, and other kinds of insights as well. The ideology itself which he sets forth, in other words, attests to one of the first points in his discussion: the creative value of different viewpoints. In this sense he merges Mary Parker Follett * and Chester Barnard.*

And—just to set the record straight—Mr. Collier is now back on the legal side of business, as General Counsel and Vice-President of the John Hancock company. For more of Collier, see page 2473 in this volume.

———◆———

HIGH ON THE LIST of tasks facing the business administrator are those relating to the basic attitudes, interests, and objectives of his employees. Meeting antagonism and misunderstanding, as he often does, his immediate reaction is to cry out: "How can I get across to my employees some understanding of the objectives I seek?" Well, that question may be important, but perhaps it should not have such priority. It might be better to ask first: "What, in truth, do I seek? What objectives do I have that my employees can also share?"

Some administrators, of course, have not bothered their heads with such intricate problems, feeling that "only results count" or "actions speak louder than words." But advertising and public relations men have demonstrated how inadequate this view is; words and the things they connote are as much a part of our experience as the things that we perceive immediately and directly. And top-rank administrators such as Chester I. Barnard know also that one of the first and greatest functions of leadership is that the leader express for his group the ideals toward which they all, consciously or unconsciously, strive.

Winston Churchill's powerful "blood, sweat, and tears" speech in 1940 has now become a classic model in the political field of the way in which a leader can express the purpose of the people and rally them to common effort. Businessmen, especially those of us con-

———
* See pages 2013 and 2068 in this volume.

cerned with personnel, productivity, and morale, have come to recognize the need for much the same kind of leadership, convinced that only in this way will employees ever have the satisfaction of really feeling they are identified with the enterprise for which they work.

But in seeking to exert such leadership we have already learned that there are some difficult problems of communication in the way. Take the many attempts that have been made in recent years, following the example of such companies as Du Pont, General Electric, and Republic Steel, to give supervisors and workers in business some understanding of the economic and political society in which we live. The general experience is that the terms "capitalism," "competition," "American way of life," "land of opportunity," and "free private enterprise," through excessive repetition, abuse, or otherwise, have lost much of their capacity to convey the meaning intended.

Moreover, where new symbols have been introduced for the old, they too have missed the mark. The editors of *Fortune,* for example, have characterized our society as the "permanent revolution," but we do not think of ourselves as revolutionaries—at least not of the black-bearded and bomb-carrying kind. Other attempts to call our society "open" or "free" have raised the perplexing questions: Open for what? Free for what?

It seems to me that we businessmen ought to aim at articulating an ideology that, in addition to being an accurate expression of management goals, is a little closer to the personal and even religious aspirations of the people than anything we have espoused in the past. Is it not possible that we have been thinking too much in terms of systems, of economics, of products, of laws? Perhaps these approaches should not have failed as they did; perhaps they can be improved. But in any event it seems to me that the fact of their failure (or, at best, their lack of any great success) should be accepted, and that the most profitable line of inquiry is to turn to a different sort of approach altogether.

THE CREATIVE IDEAL

Accordingly, I put forward this simple proposition: that our society is a creative society; that its prime objective, as well as its great genius, is its creativeness; and that, as creative accomplishment is the actual day-to-day goal of modern business, it is also the keystone of our business philosophy.

I am thinking of creativeness in its widest and deepest sense. Thus, business does not exist merely to produce more goods and services, or better goods and services for more people, though that is no small part of its task. Business also, particularly in these days, affords the principal or the only means whereby individual men may gain the satisfaction of accomplishing something more than merely sustaining their own lives. Pleasure, power, and fame appear to be but by-products of the efforts we make to be useful members of society and to leave it with something more than it had when we arrived. Perhaps we leave only the grain of sand that Robert Frost said he wished to leave on the beach of history; but at least, if we do that, we can feel that we have fulfilled our role in living.

What I am suggesting is that the great goals of happiness, freedom, security—even goodness and truth—are values which should be viewed as subordinate to, and resulting from, a new and positive creative ideal. Our people in business and elsewhere seem to be driven by an urge to build; by a longing to explore and reach out; by a desire to realize, through men and for men, such things and experiences as humanity has never known before. In this light, our vaunted freedoms of thought and action, our sought-for freedoms from worry and want, and even our ethical standards of behavior (products as they are of other places and times) are not ends in themselves; rather they emerge as important values just because they support and make possible a creative society of men.

This is the modern heresy: that it is not enough to be good, to lead a blameless life; we must also be creative.

In one sense this ideal is modern in expression only. Wise men in almost every age have been trying to tell us that the greatest individual satisfaction there is comes from a job well done. Samuel Johnson, for example, observed: "Life affords no higher pleasure than that of surmounting difficulties, passing from one step of success to another, forming new wishes and seeing them gratified." And Emerson said: "The *sum* of wisdom is that the time is never lost that is devoted to work."

In another sense, however, this ideal of ours shows some new, significantly new, aspects. Specifically in American business it is now beginning to be recognized that *everyone* has the capacity for the satisfaction that comes from creative accomplishment. As science unleashes vast new sources of power, it appears possible for the first time in history for men of all types and classes to avoid the toil and suffering of hard labor and to experience the joys of work—a satisfaction which in times past was limited to the few.

Contrast this with the older view. We used to classify as creative only those accomplishments that certain individuals could achieve. The writer, the artist, the composer, the scientist—in other words, the rare people who had the genius to find and express new ideas or new truths—were considered the creative members of our society; the classic examples have been the Newtons, the Beethovens, the Kants, the Michelangelos, the Shakespeares. The magnitude of their work often crushed us by making us feel our own inadequacy.

Today, however, we are beginning to recognize that creative work may be accomplished collectively as well as individually. The great and small organizations that have built and operated our industrial plants, farms, transportation and communication networks, financial systems, and distributive organizations, all are examples of the creative genius which comes from the collective effort of administrators and workers, as well as specialists of all degrees.

The first task of business leaders, therefore, is to create an environment in which there can flourish not only individual genius but, more important, the collective capacities of other people in the organization. Some difficult and searching questions must be answered if this task is to be accomplished. What are the basic positive forces operating in a creative business society? What generates their power? What keeps them in balance? What conditions their survival? What controls their direction?

To this end, I should like to submit that the creative ideal depends on the following concepts:

(1) That the forces in business (and many other types of organization) are nurtured by the existence of *differences between individuals and groups.*

(2) That these forces are kept in control and balance by the process of *individuals understanding each other.*

(3) That a creative society depends for its survival upon the belief that *rights must be matched by obligations.*

(4) That the directing force in a creative society is the *faith* of its members in *individual growth.*

THE POWER OF DIFFERENCE

In considering the importance of individual differences, it should first be noted that the goal of many societies—including the goal of Communist society today and of almost every Utopia that has ever been conceived, from Plato to Aldous Huxley—has been to compel men to conform. The theory is that if everyone is induced to accept the same ideas of what is good and proper, conflicts between men and groups of men will disappear and humanity will live happily ever after.

By contrast, one of the cornerstones on which the creative society is built is the incontrovertible fact that men are different, that they cherish these differences, that the joy and fascination of life depends on the existence of differences, and that there are great social values in differences.

Every great ideal has its own theory of the nature of man. The wholly competitive or acquisitive society, which is gone (if it ever in fact existed), assumed that man was motivated only by his own pleasure, that he was egoistic and greedy, and that his wants were insatiable. By assuming that the average man, the economic man, was moved by animal impulses, it was possible to work out satisfactory theoretical explanations of how men acted in the market place.

On the other hand, socialists have assumed, following the notions of Rousseau (and possibly the story of Genesis), that man was essentially good, self-sacrificing, considerate, and loving, but was corrupted by social institutions. On this basis they thought that if institutions were changed or destroyed and if nonconforming individuals and classes were eliminated, then all social problems would cease and the state could and would wither away.

But in a creative society neither of these views is adequate. We observe that men are both egoistic and self-sacrificing—and many things more. While men are, taken as a whole, driven by an urge to create and grow, their characteristics vary with their times, experiences, culture, inheritance, and with all the other circumstances in which they find themselves. To illustrate with a simple example:

> In the company with which I am associated we are using, as an aid in selection and placement, a test of personality or temperament in which the results are described not in imprecise words but in graphic form. Taking several major behavior characteristics, it plots with a fair degree of accuracy where a given individual falls on each of several temperament spectra. For instance, there is a spectrum of gregariousness in which the extreme extrovert falls at one end and the extreme introvert at the other; in between are those having various needs for sociability or a capacity to live within themselves.
>
> Thousands upon thousands of tests of this type have been made, and it is fair to say that in no two cases have the results—the combinations of characteristics on the several spectra—been exactly the same. Similarity of types may be observed, but every man and every woman is found to be unique. Furthermore, research into personality shows that men change their personalities, usually extremely slowly but sometimes dramatically. It also shows that behavior is not wholly a matter for the individual alone but depends in large part on the situation in which he finds himself. That is, the set of values according to which he makes his decisions may vary with his external circumstances.

The driving force of difference—in individuals and in groups—seems well illustrated by the history of the United States and Canada (in contrast to some other countries). While no doubt we have strong forces in many companies, labor unions, churches, and schools which are trying to enforce a high degree of conformity to some particular viewpoint, practice, or belief, nevertheless those forces have been observably less dominant than the forces of individual integrity. In our business world, if a man has felt that he could do a job better than someone else, he has been free to try; indeed, the fact that he saw things differently has given him both the opportunity and the courage to try.

Moreover, there is good reason to believe that the differences between groups of people in the United States and Canada with respect to cultural, racial, and religious backgrounds have been a factor in the dynamic development of these countries. What does it mean that never before in history have so many diverse religious groups been able to live together with so little disharmony? Has our society progressed *in spite of* differences or *because of* them? Possibly the very existence of differences among various people and groups has given people the courage to disagree with prevailing opinions. Every discovery, every invention, every new industry, every new idea has come about because some person or some group of people has had the courage as well as the insight to disagree with the majority or do what the majority has not thought of doing before. This is perhaps part of what David McCord Wright had in mind when he pointed out:

> Our dilemma . . . is that if we make men "free," they will become creative and from their creations will spring the probability of growth and the certainty of trouble.[1]

Differences do, of course, lead to trouble—to misunderstanding and conflict. Yet conflict is essential to constructive work. More than a generation ago Mary Parker Follett, a woman who has since become recognized for her many profound insights into the nature of business organizations, wrote:

> What people often mean by getting rid of conflict is getting rid of diversity, and it is of the utmost importance that these should not be considered the same. We may wish to abolish conflict, but we cannot get rid of diversity. We must face life as it is and understand that diversity is its most essential feature. . . . Fear of difference is dread of life itself. It is possible to conceive conflict as not necessarily a wasteful outbreak of incompatibilities but a *normal* process by which socially valuable differences register themselves for the enrichment of all concerned.[2]

Creativeness in an organization depends to a large extent on people who are not too ready to agree. In our own experience, most of us abhor the attitude of "Well, if you're going to argue about it, let's do it your way." We have found that we must have diversity of

[1] David McCord Wright, *The Impact of the Union*, Harcourt, Brace and Company, Inc., New York, 1951, p. 274.
[2] Mary Parker Follett, *Creative Experiences*, Longmans, Green & Co., New York, 1924, pp. 300, 301.

opinion, firmly as well as fairly expressed, if our business is to make the wise decisions that will enable it to develop and grow.

If we accept difference, it necessarily follows that we are not sure we are right ourselves; we accept the notion that our conclusions about people and society must be treated only as working hypotheses and that there are realities beyond those of our immediate perceptions. It is sometimes forgotten how highly we esteem this concept in the physical sciences. The entire atomic world of neutrons and electrons has never been perceived directly; despite Hiroshima and Nagasaki, it is still a theory or a working hypothesis. The same hypothetical character pertains to all of our knowledge about genes— the transmission of traits from organisms to their offspring.

But if it is necessary to trust to more than our immediate perceptions in the physical sciences, it would seem even more important to do so in social, ethical, and political matters that deal with human beings. The observation of Yale's F. C. S. Northrop, that the ability to live in a world of both immediate perceptions and unperceived hypotheses is the essence of the genius of the West, would apply no less to our industrial and political society than to our scientific progress.

This means that we must subject our old concepts of right and wrong, of good and bad, to a radical change; things are no longer so black and white. Judge Learned Hand, philosopher as well as judge, has described the spirit of liberty as "the spirit that is not too sure that it is right." Tolerance for difference, for the viewpoint that we do not agree with, implies that we are not so sure of our own. We accept our principles of action as working hypotheses, realizing that something may happen to lead us to revise these opinions. While it often sounds as though some of our friends would never change their opinions (particularly on matters of ethics or politics), our great genius lies in the fact that we may talk loudly but, when the chips are down, we seem to act on the basis that all general rules of what is right and wrong must be tempered by common sense.

It can be reasonably contended that the great upheavals of modern history—its wars and its revolutions—are not so much the result of differences between people as of the feeling of a nation or a class that its capacity for creative expression is in some way threatened or thwarted. This was one cause of the Russian revolt of 1917, although the revolutionaries themselves later made the great and historic blunder of seeking to abolish conflict by abolishing difference rather than by accepting difference and in that way removing the barriers to creative work.

Nations such as ours, that have insisted on the freedom of their people to be different, have had to fight and may well fight again to preserve their right to disagree with one another. Yet, if the principle of difference is one of the cornerstones of creativeness, our society has little to fear *in the long run* from the [Communistic or Fascistic dictators] who deny the privilege of difference to their own people.

PROCESS OF UNDERSTANDING

If diversity is the first condition of the creative society, then understanding is the second. The Bible's exhortation, "with all thy getting, get understanding," is particularly appropriate for modern industry. If for their dynamic creative power our businesses depend on continuing differences in viewpoint, for balance and braking power they must equally depend on understanding, on the felt necessity for securing agreement and cooperation.

In the sense that I am using the term, understanding refers both to self-understanding and understanding of others. Self-awareness as a desirable personal attribute is certainly not newer than the Socratic injunction, "Know thyself"; but what is new in our time is the fact that thoughtful social scientists and hardheaded businessmen are coming to see that self-awareness or self-understanding is directly related to an individual's capacity to do creative work with other people. Businessmen are beginning to think not only of the logics of business but also of what Pareto described as the nonlogics or the sentiments of people. They are beginning to see that their own behavior is a factor which influences the behavior of others, and that they are personally involved in more roles than one in every situation in which they play a part.

Let me illustrate from my own personal experience:

For a short time, some years ago, I engaged in the general practice of law. Later I became employed as a lawyer by an insurance company. As a lawyer my clients' problems were not mine; and no matter how hard I tried to solve them, I stood outside of the situation and was not involved in it. But when later I took an administrative position, I found that this detachment was no longer possible, even if I wanted it. I was personally involved in every important decision, and my behavior was affecting others. The shock of being forced to examine my own behavior was by no means small. What I needed to do, however, was no less than what all successful administrators are doing daily in every business.

In addition to self-awareness there is the need for understanding others. What we are learning today is not just that it is a "good thing to see the other fellow's point of view," but also what it is that often makes it difficult to do so. We are learning that we cannot really understand another if we agree with him, nor can we understand him if we disagree! When we feel either love or hate, we lose our power to see the world as others see it. We blur our own perceptions, and we cut off the normal flow of words which help us see into another's mind.

This conclusion has tremendous significance. If understanding the needs and desires of others is an essential for collective creative effort, it means that we can no longer be quick to evaluate people or their opinions as either good or bad. During the understanding process at least, we must throw our ethical judgment out the window.

Carl R. Rogers and F. J. Roethlisberger made this same point when in essence they said that the great barrier to communication is our tendency to evaluate, to approve or disapprove the statements that other people make.[3] For example:

> If you say to me, "I prefer Englishmen to the French," there is almost an overwhelming urge for me to say either "So do I" or "No, I think they are stuffy." We may then talk for hours without a meeting of the minds. If, on the other hand, I want to find out whether we really agree or disagree about this matter, if I want to listen intelligently and to understand what you mean, thus opening the gateway to communication, then I must restrain my natural inclination to presume what you mean and instead make an effort to draw you out. I might ask something like, "Do you mean Englishmen are more to be admired?" You may reply, "Yes, they are really facing up to their economic problems better than the French." And if I continue in that way, rephrasing your comments in question form to test out what you are *trying* to tell me, there is a much better chance that we can have a fruitful discussion.

This brief explanation of a gateway to understanding, of receiving communications, of listening, may sound extremely obvious and somewhat simple. We spend most of our time learning to express ourselves, which is difficult enough but still easier than listening. Indeed, it is fair to say that listening is one of the most difficult things in the world to do. When someone charges into your office and criticizes some action that you have taken, it is not easy to find out what is really on his mind when your first impulse is to tell him to "go to hell." Or take the case where somebody asks you for your advice because he cannot make up his mind about a personal problem; most of us are inclined to comply with such a request without knowing what the real problem is, or without realizing that the decision will be sound only if it is made by the troubled person himself.

It takes real insight to be able to express in words what someone else is trying to tell us. It also takes great effort and even courage. If we put ourselves in someone else's position, if we try to express

---

[3] Carl R. Rogers and F. J. Roethlisberger, "Barriers and Gateways to Communication," *Harvard Business Review*, July–August 1952, p. 46; see Volume III.

adequately his point of view, we may find that our own views become changed in the process. Professor Rogers says, "The risk of being changed is one of the most frightening prospects many of us can face." [4]

There are, of course, many other ways of securing understanding; some of them have been outlined by Stuart Chase in his recent popularization of social science, *Roads to Agreement*.[5] One is particularly worth mentioning:

> This way is modeled on the long-established custom of the Quaker business meeting. Quakers as a class are great individualists, but in handling the business affairs of their churches they act only with unanimity. They have no formal voting, no sense of a majority imposing its will on a reluctant minority. If a problem cannot be settled by unanimous agreement, they invoke periods of silence or put over the question until some future meeting. Some solution is usually forthcoming.
>
> This rule of unanimity, it seems, is now being practiced by boards of directors and executive committees in businesses throughout the land. What a far cry this is from deciding what is the greatest good for the greatest number by a mechanical counting of hands! Where difference is accepted, it is possible also to accept the notion that a minority may be right.

The concept of integration as opposed to compromise is also achieving a wider recognition. Integration may be called the means of solving a conflict of opinion in such a way that both sides prevail. The idea behind it is that the basic interests underlying many disputes are not inconsistent. For example:

> If two people in an office want to use the same desk, it may appear at first that a major conflict is in the making, which can be solved only if one or the other wins the decision. On investigation, however, it may appear that one of the persons wants the desk in order to have better light, whereas the other wants it in order to be near some friend. If these facts come out, it will be apparent that neither wants the desk as such and that it may well be possible to satisfy the basic interests of both.

In order to achieve integrations, says Miss Follett, we should "never, if possible, allow an either/or situation to be created. . . . There are almost always more than two alternatives in a situation and our job is to analyze the situation carefully enough for as many as possible to appear. A yes-or-no question is in itself a prejudgment." [6]

[4] *Ibid.*, p. 48.
[5] Harper & Brothers, 1951, p. 45 ff.
[6] *Dynamic Administration—The Collected Papers of Mary Parker Follett*, Harper & Brothers, New York, 1940, pp. 219, 220.

May there not be some relationship between these methods of reaching understanding and the spirit which is not too sure that it is right? Is there not some connection between these techniques of agreement and our capacity for collective creativeness? Can it not be said that in a creative society we must have both conflict and agreement?

RIGHTS AND OBLIGATIONS

A third standard of a creative society, and an essential ingredient in our workaday world, has been foreshadowed by our discussion of difference and of understanding. It is the belief that human relationships are two-way matters and that rights are matched by obligations.

Karl Marx predicted that in Western society it was inevitable that the rich would become richer and the poor would become poorer. This increasing division between the classes would, as he saw it, accelerate class warfare and the revolution. If our society had indeed been basically competitive and acquisitive, instead of creative and cooperative, Marx may well have been proved right. But the fact is that today, through our collective creativeness, the poor have become richer. Our society has been able to create wealth at a vastly greater rate than it has increased its population.

By and large, we have been able to maintain the viewpoint that our economic and political problem is not so much to redistribute the wealth that exists as to create more wealth for all. As the eminent economist, Kenneth Boulding, has written, "Economic life is not a 'zero-sum' poker game in which a fixed volume of wealth is circulated among the players, but a 'positive-sum' enterprise in which the accumulation of each person represents something he brings to the 'pot' rather than something he takes out." [7] In other words, we are engaged in a creative task of producing more and better things. We recognize that we share as we contribute, that no society can long give something for nothing (to the poor *or* the rich), and that we cannot do great work unless *everyone* shares both in the work and in its results.

This concept has been called by many names. Mutuality is one; give-and-take is another. Professor Charles I. Gragg of the Harvard Business School calls it the "double plus." As he sees it, business transactions and other relationships can be described in one of three ways:

(1) There is first the kind of a transaction in which the plus is all on my side, leaving a big minus for you. If I take all the profit, however, through my power or my cleverness, then I have really

---

[7] Kenneth Boulding, "Religious Foundations of Economic Progress," *Harvard Business Review,* May–June 1952, p. 36; see page 2206 in this volume.

lost the bargain, because you will come to distrust me and will refuse to do business with me for long.

(2) The reverse situation is equally disastrous. If I, through an excess of altruism or with misguided notions of humanity, permit you to take the entire profit, with nothing for myself, I put you in the unhappy role of being a recipient of my charity; moreover, I leave myself unable to do further business with anyone.

(3) But there is still another and more satisfactory form. Only if you profit moderately and I profit moderately, only if there is a plus for you and a plus for me—a double plus—can we continue to deal with one another steadily and with confidence.

In our business lives we are beginning to see that by consciously fashioning our relationships with our employees, with our suppliers, with our customers—and, indeed, even with our competitors—we are not making suspicious and careful deals so much as common-sense arrangements that are carried on in this spirit of mutual give-and-take. That does not mean anything petty like back-scratching; every service and every kindness is not to be immediately returned, nor is every service to be performed in the hope of return. The correct attitude, rather, is a healthy respect for the well-being and personal integrity of the other fellow.

What does all this imply? Only in an atmosphere of profit (in the broad sense) to all parties can we meet the creative objectives that our society sets. If, in times past, we erred on the side of taking too much for ourselves, it is equally essential that we do not err in the future on the side of trying to do too much for others. A too-literal application of the Sermon on the Mount—the turn of the cheek—does small damage to us but great damage to him who strikes the blow.

Why is it, otherwise, that the problem of providing for the aged worker has once more raised its head, when we thought a few years ago that we had safely tucked it away with compulsory retirement and pensioning at age 65? From the point of view of sympathy for the aged and of convenience in administering our business enterprises, the practice is as desirable today as it was 15 years ago. We have discovered, however, that many individual men who retire are hurt because they lose their sense of being creative, of being useful members of society. Moreover, when we contemplate that 11 per cent of our population will be over 65 in another 20 years, we begin to realize that the real economic cost of compulsory retirement is not the money that goes into pensions but the lost productivity of these older people.

It seems that people, individually and in groups, must continue to be creative; if they are not, the individual or society, or both, will suffer. If we do not intend to keep people over 65 in business, some other way must be found to permit them to continue active membership in the world's work.

The same kind of thinking underlies our concern for other noncontributors to society. Society has been doing an increasingly successful job of minimizing sickness of almost all kinds, not so much out of solicitude for the feelings of persons who are ill as out of its own self-interest in having the benefit of their contribution. Programs undertaken with this motive quickly earn common respect, for the galling part of illness to the sufferer is the necessity of having to depend on others, of not being able to contribute his share.

We are concerned for similar reasons about the criminal and the indolent. It is true that we have not as yet learned enough to be confident of our ability to rehabilitate these people. But we have at least learned that it is no answer to judge them or to punish them; our first task is to understand them. We consider them "cured" only when they join the majority of their fellows, contributing commensurately to what they receive.

Why do businessmen fight against the welfare state? Are businessmen actually heartless and callous? Don't they recognize that the sick and the poor need the aid of the rest who are well and able? Of course they do. But their experience says to them that doctors do not give pills to everyone because a few are sick; that when a man is given something for which he has not worked, he feels degraded; that a man who is well and able wants to earn what he receives.

Businessmen, who have learned from experience that paternalism has failed, hope that government will learn from their mistakes. Businessmen have good reason for believing that government will not really serve the poor and sick until it stops regarding them as "little people" and undertakes instead the harder job of giving them an honest chance to do useful and creative work.

FAITH IN MEN'S GROWTH

The fourth and last condition of maintaining and strengthening a creative society, the force that provides direction and control, is a clear faith in the growth and development of men. The machine age poses a great challenge to our willingness to demonstrate this faith. All of the new wealth we can produce with modern technology is of little avail if in the process men are reduced to the levels of the machines they tend. But fortunately we are not confronted with a Hobson's choice between wealth and men. We have found that the more we are able to train and develop men as individuals, leaving repetitive work to machines, the greater satisfactions they obtain and the more productive (in a material sense) they become.

Take a business with a large content of routine clerical work, e.g., life insurance. In this business we stand on the threshold of a new era in adapting electronics to office workers' problems. When any business reaches this point, to be sure, management is bound to face the problem of securing the cooperation of people who may prefer things as they are. It may even have to face a problem of technological unemployment. But however real and thorny these difficulties are, they are insignificant compared to the human values that are gained. Instead of a business in which, say, 75 per cent of the employees are engaged in routine tasks, the modern machine makes it possible for 75 per cent to be engaged in tasks requiring skill and judgment. The machine eliminates human toil; but, much more important, it also provides opportunities for men to do only those tasks men alone can do.

The development of the machine economy has numerous important implications for management. For one thing, it is fast bringing about a new concept of business organization. No longer can the boss know all the details and the intricacies of the operation he supervises. He is being forced more and more to rely on his subordinates, to consult with them, to be guided by their joint conclusions —in short, to permit them to share and to grow in breadth of vision.

This in turn means, of course, a gradual abandonment of authoritarian principles. Administrators have begun to conceive of their role not as manipulators of labor but as coordinators of functions. Re-examining themselves and their jobs, they have discovered that they have no special claim to superior wisdom, no vested authority over the work and lives of others. They have found, rather, that they have a function to perform: to plan ahead, to coordinate the others, to secure their interest and cooperation.

Society will not, as a result, tend to become classless in any Marxian sense. Far from it. We may reasonably anticipate, however, that members of future "elites" will come to occupy positions of status and power less because of wealth, position, or birth and more because of the kind of contributions they make or because of the kind of functions they fulfill. Key positions will tend more and more to be occupied by those who are best able to conceive new ideas and the application of old ones, who are best able to communicate ideas and events, and who are best able to pull together people and things to achieve creative ends. Today's inheritance tax and management's increased interest in personnel development are fast speeding this process along.

In an important sense the role of the administrator seems destined to become more and more that of the instructor—the kind of teacher who understands his pupils, accepts their differences, commands their respect, and inspires them to creative work of every kind. In such a role, administrators will have less of a problem of discipline to the degree that they are able to develop an environment for creative experience and to lead their students (their workers) to savor the satisfying taste of personal accomplishment. In so doing they will have gone far to eliminate the distinction between "schooling" and "education" which Mark Twain quite properly made when he quipped, "I have never let my schooling interfere with my education."

In their new role as teachers, administrators are learning that attitudes and viewpoints which affect behavior can frequently be communicated effectively only if they are reduced to concrete terms. In their efforts at training and development, particularly, they are recognizing the need to start from real case situations. Witness the growing attention to discussions of actual business problems rather than the oft-repeated clichés on general principles of management.

Abstract ideas, however, are not to be discarded simply because they so often fail to influence behavior. Indeed, as the mark of civilized men they are necessary tools of communication which are quite adequate *if* both writer and reader start from the same premises. They are easily accepted, in other words, if they seem meaningful in relation to one's own experience. Aneurin Bevan's autobiography affords an example of this:

> Bevan's life as a young Welsh miner was filled with frustrations. Then he read Karl Marx. This experience "had all the impact of divine revelation. Everything fell in place. The dark places were lighted up and the difficult ways made easy." [8] Marx is most abstract, but nevertheless his words have had a great effect on people whose experience has led them to feel like chained and exploited men.

The moral of this fact has not been lost on businessmen and statesmen, who know that the only real and lasting bulwark against Marxism is in the experience of the large body of our workers and our citizens. If that experience is basically creative and satisfying— and it is management's task to see that it is so—the stultifying conformities of the socialist state will always be bitter to their taste.

But businessmen and statesmen, while often seeing what is the best *defense* against Marxism, have not been so quick to see what needs to be done in a *positive* way. Like Marxians, we too must have an appropriate body of abstract ideas—ideas that can constitute a simple article of faith but are also capable of profound extension, ideas that are consistent with experience but are also adaptable to new insights and new truths.

---

[8] *In Place of Fear,* Simon and Schuster, New York, 1952, p. 19.

Perhaps this discussion will stimulate others to work out such ideas—each in his own way, as a part of our individual differences, but all toward the same goal, in the spirit of mutuality. What I have written can be no more than a preface.

The problems of production, distribution, and finance are usually foreign to a worker's experience and interests. It is therefore just as silly for top management to hope that workers will be anxious to understand the problems of business as it would be to fear that they are interested in gaining control of the business. What workers do appear to want is a chance to increase their usefulness and creativeness, a chance to develop their full potential as individuals within the scope of their environment and experience. It has become part of management's function to see not only that they have had that chance but that the philosophy behind it is made articulate.

But the creative society is based on more than the relationship between management and workers, indispensable though that is in our industrial age. It depends on close relationships between all fields of human endeavor. Business is not "just business." The Chinese wall between business and the home, the community, the school, and the church has long since been stormed. Business is all people, places, and things; it is physics, economics, politics, sociology, psychology, philosophy, ethics, and aesthetics.

In the same broad sense, business is also religion. One of the recurring themes in most religions is that God is viewed as the Creator and that creativeness is one of His essential attributes. Another recurring theme is that man's spirit, his conscious "self," his unique ability to transcend his material and animal limitations, is the essence of God in man. To suggest that creativeness may be a basic attribute of men in society is thus merely to relate these two ageless insights.

Moreover, it seems that a religious sense of wonder, humility, and faith helps us to see the vision of a boundless future built by the inherent capacities of men from all walks of life and of all races, creeds, natures, and backgrounds. It is a vision of cooperation, togetherness, and sharing the great adventure. It is a vision of independence and courage the explores the far reaches of the universe and probes deep into the essence of what we call man. It is, in short, a vision of a changing, growing, and infinitely exciting world which depends for its existence on the spirit that is not too sure it is right, on a deep-seated desire to open our minds and our hearts to the lives of others, on the practical sense of give-and-take, on our faith in the growth and development of ourselves and our fellow men.

AMERICAN BUSINESS AND THE SOVIET ECONOMIC APPROACH

~⟨◊⟩~

HENRY CABOT LODGE AND NIKITA KHRUSHCHEV

["Dinner Given by the Economic Club of New York for N. S. Khrushchev," in *Let Us Live in Peace and Friendship*, Foreign Languages Publishing House, Moscow, 1959, pp. 114–128 (abridged).]

In this interchange between Lodge and Khrushchev, which occurred during Khrushchev's "friendly" visit to the United States, one can see the sharp difference between the Soviet economic approach and ours. We present his speech to you in the form in which it was published by the Russian government (applause and all) because even with the Soviet editing the reasoning seems to us unsound, if not actually false—perhaps all the more clearly so because the editing is so patently devised. But it is history, unmistakably history, and just as unmistakably a live influence in the world.

◆

IN THE EVENING OF SEPTEMBER 17, the members of the Economic Club of New York gave a dinner for N. S. Khrushchev, Chairman of the Council of Ministers of the U.S.S.R.

The Economic Club of New York is an organization of influential U.S. businessmen. The ballroom of the Waldorf-Astoria Hotel was filled by nearly two thousand people—directors of big banks, commercial and industrial firms and prominent financiers and economists. Prolonged applause greeted the appearance in the hall of N. S. Khrushchev and his party.

The president of the club, Herbert Woodman (president of Inter-Chemical Corporation) noted in his introductory speech that everybody was now aware of the historic importance of the exchange of visits between N. S. Khrushchev and Dwight D. Eisenhower. The Soviet people, the club president declared, may be justly proud of their economic achievements. At the same time Woodman went out of his way to extol the capitalist system, claiming, for example, that monopolies were being combated in the U.S.A.

The Representative of the U.S.A. at the United Nations Organization Henry Cabot Lodge spoke next.

SPEECH BY HENRY CABOT LODGE

The Economic Club effectively symbolizes the leadership of our economic system—a leadership which genuinely respects the material achievements of the Soviet Union.

This club is a good place in which to point out that the "robber baron"—the predatory villain—which is the phrase used by some to describe capitalism a century ago—a monopolistic system in which a few controlled and exploited the efforts of many—is something to which we are opposed. In fact on July 2, 1890, we declared war on monopoly capitalism when the Sherman Anti-Trust Act became law. That law is still being actively enforced. If "robber baron" is the definition of the word *capitalist,* then we are not capitalists at all.

There are, for example, 14,000,000 Americans who own shares in American industry. In our country, two-thirds of the gross national product goes into consumption: food, entertainment, refrigerators, automobiles, etc. Three out of four families own their own automobile. More Americans are engaged in providing services to the American consumer than in producing goods—although our production of goods is the highest in the world. Three-fifths of all homes in America which are not on farms are owned by the families who occupy them, and three out of four of our farms are operated by people who own them.

One out of every ten families makes $10,000 a year or more—which is triple the proportion of ten years ago. Family income, adjusted for change in the value of the dollar, has gone up 50 per cent in ten years. A coal miner gets between $25 and $28 a day.

Economic humanism rather than monopoly capitalism perhaps best describes such a system.

I have been told that in the Soviet Union a man can own his own home, make a will, and use a bank. And that there is no limit on what his income could become. Such things have been generally considered to be attributes of capitalism.

In our country, all corporations above the smallest must pay 52 per cent of this profit to the Federal government, in addition to many other taxes. And we have a steeply graduated income tax which at the upper levels rises above 80 per cent and is almost entirely confiscatory. Eleven per cent of the American taxpayers—those earning over $8,000 a year—pay 51 per cent of the personal income taxes. Such things are generally considered to be attributes of socialism.

So *capitalism* and *socialism* are confusing words which can mean many different things in different places.

Here in this room are men who symbolize American business—which is one of America's principal activities. It is a way of doing things which retains the confidence of the American people. It is what makes us thrive. Only two years ago it was the recuperative power of American business which played an indispensable and vital part in leading us away from the then threatening recession.

American business prospers at the same time that the Federal government, in ways large and small, pervades our lives—that one adult in every five gets regular checks from the government and that countless others receive occasional payments, that Federal warehouses give out food to more than 5,000,000 persons—and that 2,000,000 persons live in government-subsidized housing.

We live in a welfare state which seeks to put a floor below which no one sinks, but builds no ceiling to prevent man from rising. Our own experience with wartime economic planning and controls centered in Washington convinces us that the plans of tens of thousands of independent producers lead to greater production, a more dynamic economy and a richer life for all than can ever be achieved by a few plans by public officials.

American business recognizes the deep desire of people for peace and they recognize that there is no profit, but only disaster, in war.

Therefore it would be a mistake to think that our business leaders are America's "ruling class" or that you are in the presence of men who want other than a peaceful world.

There is only one ruling class in this country and that is the American voter.

The men in this audience have great capacities and great responsibilities. They are creators and innovators. They are Americans all, who are in harmony with all the great national aspirations of the country.

In conclusion, Mr. Chairman, let me say that I was struck—as I am sure your audience was—by your statement at lunch to the effect that you could see no difference between the abuses of early capitalism that Marx described and our modern system of economic humanism.

The difference is as great as the difference between black and white, and we believe this will become crystal clear to you as you see things for yourself on your tour around the country. This country exists for the benefit of the everyday rank and file of citizens. And whenever they have wanted to change it in the past, they have done so through the ballot box.

They can do so again whenever they want to. We have this system today because the rank and file approves it, and because it has given them the highest standard of living in the world.

SPEECH BY N. S. KHRUSHCHEV

Mr. Chairman,

Gentlemen,

Before proceeding with the address, which I prepared prior to coming to your club, I should like to say a few words on some of the points brought up here by the chairman, Mr. Woodman, and by Mr. Lodge.

Mr. Woodman said that never in the history of your club has there been such a large number of people as today, wishing to attend a meeting with a guest. Before our meeting began I jokingly told Mr. Woodman that in some parts of my country, where the people have never seen, say, a camel, large crowds assemble if a camel appears. Everybody wants to take a look at it, and some even wish to pull its tail. [*Laughter, applause*]

Forgive me my joke, but I should like to draw something of a parallel. The flower of the capitalist world of New York, and not only of New York, is gathered here. And suddenly a Communist appears in such select company, a company you are accustomed to. Understandably, the wish arises to take a look at him, and to pull him by the tail if he proves to have one. [*General hilarity, burst of applause*]

I don't know if Mr. Marshall MacDuffie is present here. I saw him today at the luncheon given by the mayor of New York. During the first years after the war, when I was Chairman of the Council of Ministers in the Ukraine, Mr. MacDuffie came to the Soviet Union as representative of UNRRA, the American war relief organization. I was on very good terms with him and with the late La Guardia, the former mayor of New York and head of UNRRA. Marshall MacDuffie came to us again when I was already working in Moscow. In one of our conversations he told me then that it would be very useful if I were to visit America. I asked him why. MacDuffie replied that some Americans thought I had horns. If they were to see I had no horns, that would be a great achievement. [*Laughter, applause*]

I did not make that up. Ask MacDuffie, he will confirm our conversation. I think that now all of you here can see for yourselves that I really have no horns. [*Laughter, applause*] Having convinced yourselves of this, the victory will be half won if you also convince others. People will realize that Communists are human beings like everybody else. The only difference between us is the difference in our views on the political structure and social system of states. And we must get agreement on the point that each people must choose for itself what system to maintain.

As far as I know, you do not let your competitors look into your account books. Don't look into our accounts, then, for we have our own, communist system of bookkeeping. [*Animation*] Let's better live in peace. There are cases with you too, aren't there—though they may be rare—when competing corporations come to an agreement not to attack each other. Why then, to use your language, should not we, representatives of the communist corporation, and you, representatives of the capitalist corporation, agree on peaceful co-existence? Let each abide by his own views. [*Prolonged applause*]

I know that you like capitalism, and I don't want to dissuade you. I think it would be beneath my dignity if I were to take advantage of the hospitality of the biggest capitalists and begin moralizing to you on the superiority of communism. That would be a senseless thing to do before this audience. Let history be the judge! [*Prolonged applause*]

Why then did Mr. Lodge so zealously defend capitalism here? He did it zealously, and that is only natural. If he did not defend capital-ism so fervently, he would not hold such an important post in your country. [*Laughter, applause*] The only question I have is what made Mr. Lodge plead the benefits of capitalism with such ardor today. Is it possible that he wished to talk me into adopting the capitalist faith? [*Laughter*] Or perhaps Mr. Lodge is afraid that if a Bolshevik addresses capitalists he will convert them and they will espouse the communist faith? I want to reassure you: I have no such inten-tions—I know who I am dealing with. [*Laughter, prolonged applause*]

If Mr. Harriman will allow me, I will tell you about our exchange of jokes in a conversation we had in Moscow. I said in jest that Mr. Harriman was "jobless" after having been ousted by Rockefeller from the post of governor of your state [*animation*], and that now he was at a loose end. Whereupon Comrade Mikoyan observed that he could be found a job in the Soviet Union [*laughter, applause*], and I said, "If you like, I offer you the position of economic adviser to the Chairman of the Council of Ministers of the U.S.S.R., with a good salary and a good country house." [*Laughter, applause*] You, of course, realize that this was said in jest.

That is my reply to Mr. Lodge. . . .

I know that businessmen are wont to talk without diplomatic niceties, with utter frankness. That is why I take the liberty of telling you in all frankness what may not perhaps be to the liking of some of you, but would yet be good for you.

Some people—blinded, to put it mildly, by their dislike of socialism and communism—dream in their sleep, as the saying goes, of the ruin of the countries that have taken that path of development. In his dreams a person usually sees his cherished desires, and all too often awakening brings him disappointment: he opens his eyes and finds the same faces and the same environment that surrounded him when he plunged into his vain dream.

Some people frequently dream that socialist Russia is the same as it was before the revolution. But let's compare the rates at which the Soviet Union has been developing since we overthrew the old, rotten system, and the rates of development in the United States during the same period. Compared with the 1913 level, output in the Soviet Union has increased 36-fold, and only fourfold in your country. Why does our economy and culture develop more rapidly than yours? I am not imposing my ideology upon you, though I do not conceal my allegiance to the Communist Party and my political views—they are known to you. But the figures show convincingly that the source of our rapidly growing strength is the socialist revolution, which enables our country to take a road of development along which the locomotive of Soviet economy is racing at an ever-increasing speed. Old Russia could never have even dreamed of such a pace.

Possibly you disagree with me. But can you explain, then, what miracles brought those results about? What miracles, I ask you?

In old Russia 76 of every 100 people over nine years of age were illiterate. Nearly 80 per cent of the children and teenagers had no opportunity of going to school. Whereas today all our children go to school and there are practically no illiterate people in the country. We now have 40 times more specialists with a higher or special secondary education than there were in prerevolutionary Russia, and our higher schools train almost three times as many engineers as American universities and colleges. Last year, for example, we trained 94,000 engineers, while you trained 35,000.

We have now worked out and begun a titanic seven-year plan of economic development. I shall name just one figure to give you an idea of its scale: our capital investments alone will amount to approximately $750,000 million in these seven years. Fulfillment of this plan will bring us close to the level of economic development in the United States.

Where do we get the funds for all this? Where do we get the accumulations? All this can only be explained by the advantages of the socialist system, for, as we know, miracles don't happen.

Some people may, as before, doubt the feasibility of our plans. But that is ostrich policy; when an ostrich sees that its rival is overtaking it, it is said to hide its head in the sand. Our development will not cease if you close your eyes to reality.

Already now I can disappoint the people who are playing ostrich. Do you happen to know how we are fulfilling the first year of the seven-year plan?

Our plan for 1959 envisaged a 7.7 per cent rise in industrial output. Actually, we have increased output by 12 per cent in the first eight months of this year. There is reason to believe that we will produce more than $10,000 million worth over and above this year's plan. This means that, far from planning any impossible rates of economic development, we have, on the contrary, provided favorable conditions for industry, so as not to overtax the economy, and to receive additional accumulations through overfulfillment of the plan and to make the work of our enterprises more rhythmical. Consequently, we shall be able to overtake the U.S.A. in economic development first in volume and then per head of population, more rapidly than projected in our plans.

Before my departure, Comrade Kosygin, Chairman of the State Planning Committee, reported to me on the plan prepared by the committee for 1960, which has been worked out in the main. True, it is still a tentative plan, but it has already been coordinated with all the Union republics, and is therefore close to the form in which it will be approved. It will probably be approved soon after my return from America, at the close of October or early in November. The figures of this plan are not without interest. For example, in 1960 we shall be able to produce two million metric tons more rolled stock than initially projected for the second year of the seven-year plan. With regard to oil, we are planning to increase output by more than 14 million metric tons in 1960 alone. This, too, is not bad for our economy.

Excellent prospects are opening up for our gas industry. For the time being America ranks first in the world for output and known reserves of gas, but in recent years we have been making increasing use of natural gas. Our geologists have discovered such huge gas deposits as will suffice for decades to come. This enables us to expand the extraction and consumption of gas still more and to overtake you in this respect as well.

These, gentlemen, are only a few words about our potentials. We have everything we need. Our people are solidly behind their government, full of enthusiasm. They strive to do their duty to the best of their ability and thereby strengthen their socialist system still further.

Possibly some people thought I would come to the United States to solicit for the development of Soviet-American trade, without which, it is alleged, the seven-year plan cannot be fulfilled. I want to say in all frankness that I have not come here to beg. We have always, ever since the inception of the Soviet state, urged the development of international trade. And we are by no means raising this question today because lack of such trade prejudices the fulfillment of the seven-year plan. Whoever thinks so is making a big mistake.

We attach considerable importance to the development of international trade, acting upon the same rule as many people in your country, too, if we are to believe the motto reproduced on a postage stamp recently issued in the United States: "World peace through world trade."

We agree with this approach. True, when I said something of the kind some time ago, indicating that trade is important as a means of relaxing international tension, I was criticized by some people in America. Your newspapers wrote at that time that Khrushchev spoke of trade only because for him trade is no more than politics. But if we are really to speak about who has turned trade into a political instrument, it is an American institution you all know that invented a special list of embargoes, which you, businessmen, are compelled to observe when trading with the Soviet Union. Let's not argue, however. History will establish who associated trade with politics, and in what way.

I want to emphasize that the Soviet government has always advocated, and continues to advocate, equitable, mutually beneficial international trade without any discrimination whatsoever—the trade spoken of by Benjamin Franklin, whose words, "Commerce among nations should be fair and equitable," are engraved above the front entrance of the U. S. Department of Commerce.

The establishment of all sorts of embargo lists in trade is something we oppose and will always oppose as an unreasonable practice. If you do not wish to trade in so-called strategic, or any other goods, you don't have to. That is your affair. But do not introduce discrimination against any one country or group of countries. This practice disrupts normal international trade and leads to political complications. Indeed, history tells us that governments resort to such restrictions only when they contemplate a military campaign against the country subjected to discrimination. Let us then clear the path to normal trade relations between all countries, irrespective of their social systems.

We are trading on a basis of equality with many countries. Suffice it to say that last year the volume of Soviet foreign trade exceeded the 1938 level sevenfold and amounted to 34,589 million rubles.

Our trade relations with Britain are shaping out quite well. Trade is expanding with businessmen in West Germany. It should be noted that the Government of West Germany also has a correct understanding of the interests of its country in this matter, and cooperates in the development of trade contacts rather than obstructs them. We welcome this. Good economic relations are shaping between us and Italy. Relations with France are not bad. Why then must America stand apart? However, that is up to you. The question of trade is a question of profit. If you find it unprofitable to buy from us, or to sell us some goods, do as you think best.

But bear one thing in mind. It sometimes happens that too choosy a girl lets time slip, stays unmarried too long, and is left empty-handed.

[*Laughter*] Such maidenly indecision is doubly out of place in business, where the rule, "First come, first served," perpetuated in an English proverb, operates more than anywhere else. We too have a good saying to that effect: "He who comes late gets a picked bone." [*Animation*] . . .

From time immemorial lively trade has been considered a good omen in relations between countries. In the now obtaining situation international trade acquires still greater importance as a kind of barometer of the relations between countries. Then may the pointer of this barometer move at least toward "variable," and once it passes that line we are sure that—given the effort of both sides—it will soon point to fair weather.

You are all well informed of the fact that we are offering you economic competition. Some describe this as our challenge to the United States. But speaking of challenges, one might say perhaps— and it would even be more precise—that it was the United States that first challenged the whole world. The U.S.A. developed its economy to a higher level than any other country. For a long time nobody ventured to dispute your supremacy. But the time has now come when a country has appeared which accepts your challenge, which takes into account the level of development in the United States and in its turn challenges you. You may rest assured that the Soviet Union will hold its own in this economic competition; it will overtake you and leave you behind.

But what harm is there in that? No matter who wins in this competition—you or we—both the Soviet Union and the United States will gain by it, because our people will have peace and live still better than today.

AMERICAN CAPITALISM:
TRIAL BALANCE

MAX LERNER

[Max Lerner, "American Capitalism: Trial Balance," in *America as a Civilization,* Simon and Schuster, New York, copyright © 1957 by the author, pp. 267–274. Reprinted by permission of the publishers.]

Here Max Lerner, noted author and lecturer, with a record of penetrating, inquiring and objective judgment, casts a trial balance for American capitalism in his book, *America as a Civilization* (1957). This analysis should appeal to all citizens, businessmen and others, who honestly want to look at both the credit and the debit sides—the positive accomplishments of our predominant form of business organization, and the costs that we pay for allowing it to be as strong as it is.

Lerner gets away from broad abstractions like "the American system" or "the free-enterprise economy," and from epithets like "serfdom" or "totalitarianism" applied to noncapitalist systems, and tackles the basic arguments underlying those catchwords. His point would have been even stronger if he had seen that growth and dynamism are not to be found in only a few places like large corporations. Thus, for example, we now see that the number of small businesses has more than kept pace with the growth of the population—literally hundreds of thousands of service stations having been created by the automobile alone while it was destroying livery stables and harness manufacturers.

———◆———

GIVEN THIS CULTURE OF SCIENCE and the machine, how about the system of American capitalism which organizes it? The appraisal of American capitalism as a going concern must be made largely in terms of a balance sheet. Whoever embraces its achievements should not flinch from acknowledging its costs; whoever condemns the costs should be candid enough to recognize the achievement.

The record of achievement is clear enough: a continuously rising curve of man-hour productivity; a high rate of capital formation; steadily rising profits which have made a corpse of the Marxist predictions about profits under capitalism; employment levels which in the mid-1950s were at their top peacetime pitch; a wilderness of available commodities and a strong "propensity to consume," reflecting the spread of high and increasing living standards even among middle- and low-income levels; a steadily increasing growth in real wages; a continuing secular increase in the national product; a production record which has provided the military production for two World Wars and the current "readiness economy" for defense, while increasing the products available for civilian consumption; a capacity to take in its stride an ever-heavier tax structure without destroying freedom of economic movement and decision within the economy; a continuing sense of economic dynamism, and finally an economy with the capacity for changing its forms under pressure so that it could in the mid-1950s lay claim to being a "people's capitalism" even while being to a high degree a corporate and monopoly capitalism.

The debit side is also clear: a haste for profits which has used up too rapidly the land and resources of the continent and built unplanned cities; an economy which made heavy productive gains (especially in World War II) through the expansion of war industries and seems still to be buttressed by a government budget for arms which runs to 15 or 20 per cent of the gross national product; one which has lived like a fever-chart patient by constantly taking its pulse and has not been able to control firmly the periodic swings of prosperity and depression; one in which the big-enterprise corporations create private empires challenging the state itself; one in which the chances for a competitive start in the race for the big money are less open to small businessmen and depend more upon upward movement in a corporate bureaucracy; an economy in which, despite its production levels, much remains to be done in distributing the final product more fairly.

The observer is tempted to say (with Hamlet): "Look at this picture, and here at this one."

The defense of American capitalism runs largely in broad abstractions like "the American system" or "the free-enterprise economy," or in epithets like "serfdom" or "totalitarian" applied to noncapitalist systems. Underlying these catchwords are some basic arguments. One is the *argument from incentive:* that men's brains and energy work best when they have no hampering restrictions, and when they see an immediacy of relation between effort and reward. The second is the *argument from a free market:* that an economy runs best as the result of millions of individual decisions made through the operations of a free production, wage, and price system; that when it goes off kilter, it can generally set itself right again by individual adjustments within a frame of government spurs and checks; and that even government regulation is best accomplished by the indirect methods of inducements and pressures on the free market, rather than the direct method of planning and control. The third is the *argument from managerial efficiency:* that the corporate managerial group is recruited from the men with the best skills, who deal with the problems of industrial production more flexibly than a governmental bureaucracy could.

The arguments, though vulnerable, are basically valid. True, the free market no longer exists in anything like its historic form, and big enterprise and the giant corporation, with prices largely reached by administrative decision, have in part taken its place. Yet the economy has developed its own distinctive forms of freedom, and the decisions reached in it are still freer than in a cartelized or largely government-directed economy. The system of profit and property incentives has been transformed in the giant corporation; yet new incentives have emerged that keep the corporate managers alert and drive the productive system on. The argument from corporate efficiency has much in its favor, provided we do not forget that a corporate bureaucracy has a strong inner impulse toward conformism of spirit and, like government bureaucracies, runs the danger of stagnation.

Some corollaries of these doctrines that emerge in the capitalist apologia are more open to question: the argument that the big corporations and their managers administer their power *as a trust* for the people as a whole; and the argument that there is a *harmony of interests* which ties labor and the farmers to business prosperity and therefore business decisions. While most Americans are too realistic to accept the view that big property is being held in trust for them, they do not resent the power of the possessing groups because they hope themselves someday to be secure enough to "take it easy." As for the harmony of interests, they may have some skepticism about it, yet they have never been caught by the European idea that class cleavages must deepen until the whole system breaks.

The real problems of capitalism, however, are not the doctrinal struggles but the operational strains—the periodic breakdowns, the sense of insecurity, the shadow of monopoly, the dependence upon war expenditures, the question of distributive justice. The American economy, because of its power and prosperity, has become the last, best hope of free economies in the world. But by the same token the issues of its capacity for survival, its social costs, and its impact on the human spirit have called in question the nature and survival value of the system of capitalism itself.

What are the elements of American capitalism as a going concern, distinguishing it from other going systems? It is customary to say that capitalism is organized as a "private-enterprise system," for private (individual or corporate) profit, with the resulting rewards protected by the state as private property. This is valid enough, except for the fact that far-reaching changes have taken place in the structure and functioning of American capitalism. The profit incentive, for example, does not operate in corporate management as it used to operate in individual enterprise, since ownership and management have split apart: it still holds, however, if it is rephrased as the drive within the manager to make the best possible profit record for the corporation. The idea of private property has also suffered a change, since industrial ownership is now widely scattered in the form of stock ownership, some of the stocks being owned by trust funds, investment trusts, other corporations, life insurance companies, and even trade unions.* The earlier picture of capitalism as a competitive system has also had to be changed. To some extent competition has been inhibited by price agreements and "oligopoly"— the control of an industry by a handful of big corporations competing only partly in price and mainly in packaging, advertising, and brand names, as in meat packing, automobiles, or cigarettes. Yet the impressive fact about the American economy is the extent to which

* Which in turn are owned by or made up of many individuals.

it has effectively resisted the monopoly tendencies. The concept of bigness is not the same as the concept of monopoly, and something that can fairly be called competition is still a power regulator of the economy.

The core of capitalism then is still present. It is in essence concerned with decision-making within a profit-competitive framework. Under communism the decisions are made by a small group of political functionaries assigned to strategic industrial posts. Under democratic socialism they are made by technicians operating largely within government corporations, responsible ultimately to the people. Under American capitalism the decisions on production, pricing, advertising, and sales policies are private decisions—that is to say, they are made by individual businessmen or heads of small corporations, whether they be producers, middlemen, or retailers, and in the case of big corporations they are made by the managers to whom the power of decision is delegated by the stockholders; the decisions on wages and labor policy are generally made through collective bargaining by the managers and trade union leaders. Obviously there are restrictions placed on these decisions by price and wage legislation, sometimes by priorities and the allocation of scarce materials in a defense economy. But within these limits the decisions are linked with ownership and management, and they are made always with a view to profit and in competition with other enterprises. At the other end of the capitalist process there are millions of decisions made by the consumer: production and investment policies are guided not by governmental decisions or by what might be considered socially necessary production but in the light of consumers' decisions about how they will spend their money and for what.

Thus at one end American capitalism is guided by decisions made by businessmen, managers, and trade union leaders, at the other end by consumer decisions. This decision-making operates within a frame in which there are strong surviving elements of private property, private and corporate profits, and competition.

In assessing American capitalism as a going concern, one important test is the test of *productivity*. Here American capitalism shows the most impressive facet of its record. Socialists might argue that, given the resources of America and the accidents of its history, some other system of organization, ownership, and power could have attained the same productivity with a better distribution of the products. This is one of those iffy questions that will never be resolved. On the other hand it is hard to sustain the claim that the creative force in the American record of increased productivity is the capitalist entrepreneur and manager, and he alone. Science, technology, the legal and governmental framework, and the skill of the worker all belong in the larger pattern along with the supplier of risk capital and the business organizer. Yet the American record of an increase of productivity running between 2 per cent and 3 per cent a year must be counted one of the overall achievements of capitalism. Nor has this production record been only a matter of technology and resources. The drive toward productivity has also been due to the elements within the social structure which have invested the whole productive process with the *élan* of freedom. This is as true today as it was a century ago, as John Sawyer has shown, basing himself on the accounts of European travelers in America in the 1840s and 1850s.

All this brings us to the question of *incentive,* which is more troublesome. Those who contend that profit alone has furnished the effective incentive for industrial production must plead guilty to a lower view of human motive than applies even in an imperfect world. The fact is that the managerial function in the big corporation has been performed through incentives quite different from those of ownership profits or dividends, and more closely related to competitive performance and pride in a job well done. Through a complex mingling of profit, salary, bonus, and craftsmanship incentives, capitalism as a going concern has enlisted considerable talents in the processes of production and selling; and it has plowed back into increased production a steady portion (recently around 7 per cent) of the national product, keeping the process of capital formation an active and growing one.

It is on the test of *stability* that American capitalism is most vulnerable. American economic thought is crisscrossed by conflicts of opinion about the underlying causes of the periodic swings and breakdowns of the system, resulting in cycles of prosperity and recession, boom and depression. There are still die-hard critics of the system who believe that boom and bust are inherent in the system and will never yield to anything short of full-scale socialism. There are also True Believers of another stripe who feel, as their forerunners felt in the boom days of the 1920s, that Americans have somehow found the golden key to perpetual prosperity.

Aside from these two groups there is fairly general agreement, however, that, while the swings in the "business cycle" may not yet have been mastered, American business, labor, and government leaders have learned to detect the danger signals and put in motion some preventive measures, and have learned also—once the cycle is on its way—how to cut the length and severity of the downward swing and cushion its impact. In the mid-1950s there was an upsurge of conviction that the cycle had to a large extent been mastered and need never again operate drastically. The bitter experience after

1929 taught the nation's leaders how to use "countercyclical" measures in the form of tax and fiscal policies, rediscounting rates, Federal expenditures for defense and public works, state and Federal programs for building roads, schoolhouses, and hospitals. The President's Council of Economic Advisers, working with a committee of Congress, is now accepted under Republican as well as Democratic administrations. Its reports, carefully studied in business, labor, and government circles, are in effect an embryonic form of corrective and preventive planning. The government's massive role in a war-geared "readiness economy" has also given it a leverage in guiding, checking, and stimulating business activity and as such it is a form of indirect planning.

America has thus characteristically used an indirect approach to the control of the swings of business activity, aiming at stability without embracing a direct program of planning and without transferring the crucial decisions from the corporate managers and the consumers to government managers. The specter of depression is, of course, always present. At the close of World War II there were widespread prophecies of economic castastrophe, yet the real danger proved to be not mass unemployment but inflation, not a paralysis of production but a boom induced by high demand and sustained by the armament race. This mood has lasted into the mid-1950s. Obviously there is a serious problem in the steady inflationary movement of American prices, year after year, largely due to the pressure of rising consumer demand, with its tragic effect in wiping out much of the substance and meaning of savings. Yet, while Americans are still far from solving the basic problem of boom and bust, they have at least a heightened awareness of what is involved and are willing to take decisive action. There are few economists who would accept the European notion, seemingly as widespread among scholars as among the people, that American capitalism will once again in the calculable future be as helpless as it was in the years following 1929.

On the test of *security and insecurity* American capitalism has made steady if reluctant progress. So far from interfering with prosperity, it is now accepted that effective, well-administered insurance programs make the economy more stable as well as adding to personal security. Every person must confront the tragic elements in life, but the pathetic elements can be whittled down by common action. To the degree that America has become a welfare state it is not because of effeminacy or the importation of "foreign" ideas, but of practical grappling with a deeply felt need to make the individual fate more secure.

Judged by another test—that of *income spread and distribution*—the going economy has in the past evoked strong self-criticism from American writers, if not from the economists. Especially in the decade before World War I, and in the 1920s and 1930s, they unsparingly subjected the economy to the test of equity. The extremes of wealth and poverty, the discrepancies between the Babylonian living at the top of the pyramid and the scrimping and degradation at its base, became staples of the American self-portrait. There was a time when the prospects of the future for many Americans seemed precarious. Any European or Asian who thinks that Americans need to be prodded about this should read the almost unparalleled record in which sensitive Americans have made their own indictment of their own vaunted system. But the note of self-criticism has recently grown fainter because of the overwhelming evidence of American living standards. These have improved all through the class system as productivity has increased and the trade unions have been able to claim a share of it for their members. The problem of poverty in America is now circumscribed within the lower fourth of the population.

One could argue, of course, that the depressed groups in back-ward areas in other countries are far worse off than this lower fourth in America. This would be sound if American living standards were judged by productivity in other areas of the world, but they must be judged by American productivity. In every economy, as Sumner put it, "there are dinners without appetites at one end of the table, and appetites without dinners at the other." The American economy as a production miracle has evoked life claims in America not roused in the underdeveloped economies; what would be a full meal elsewhere is a skimpy one at the table of the American business system.

The final test of a going economy is the *creativeness* it evokes and makes possible. Few systems in history have attracted so much talent and put it to use, and in no other economy have men's business abilities been so continuously tapped. The problem is not whether the economy gives scope to creativeness, but what kind of creativeness it gives scope to. The question asked is always whether a new idea or a new insight is "practical"—that is, whether it can be translated into dollars-and-cents terms. The creativeness that is not vendible is likely to be ignored and to wither. Yet within this pecuniary framework there has been broader scope for the creation of use values and life values than the critics of the money calculus have been ready to admit.

This then would be a rough trial balance of American capitalism as a going concern: that it has done brilliantly in productivity and national product; that it has done less well with the swings of the business cycle and with boom and bust, but that substantial steps have been taken to meet this; that its greatest weakness on this score lies in the dependence of the recent prosperity on the war-geared economy; that its growth in the areas of concentrated economic power has been at the expense of small business; that in its income distribution it is a good deal better than its opponents would admit but not nearly as good as its apologists claim, good enough to retain the faith of those who are fulfilled by it but not good enough to exact the loyalty of those who feel left out; that it allows for creativeness but within a limited sense of that word; that as a whole it is an economy which has wrested from the world its envy along with a grudging respect, but not its imitation.

Religion and Business

"Seest thou a man diligent in his business?
He shall stand before kings; he shall not
stand before mean men."

—Proverbs 22:29

———◆———

As in the case of philosophy, the first relations between business and religion were initiated not by business but by the other party. The early church, which played a more central part in society and in human life than today, laid down rules, among other things, for the conduct of trade, to protect those who were involved in or affected by it. (It also, of course, proscribed usury, as set forth in the section on Usury in Volume II.)

But it has been a long time since the Greek historian Polybius, in the second century B.C., could say: "At Carthage, nothing which results in profit is regarded as disgraceful." Not that particular situations do not arise where executive behavior is unwise or unprincipled, but the point is that today there is general censure—both outside and within business. And increasingly we see businessmen looking at themselves, and self-consciously attacking the problems of how to be a businessman and make decisions which are right by moral and religious standards.

To appreciate this change in approach, one must understand a little of why it happened. Therefore, as part of the introduction to this selection, we present herewith a short analysis by one of the editors of *The World of Business,* which appeared originally as an editorial in the Boston *Sunday Globe* of December 21, 1958.

Do business and religion mix—or is religion something for Sundays only? This question is worrying businessmen across the country, in big companies and small companies, and in all kinds of industries.

It may seem strange that such a basic question should not have been answered long ago. But it was not even raised until recently—at least not in such a strong and pervasive way.

Now magazines for businessmen carry articles on the subject; and reprints of these articles are in great demand. For example, the *Harvard Business Review* published one on " 'Skyhooks'—With Special Implications for Monday Through Friday," of which 50,000 reprints have been

2108

bought by businessmen. The article was written by a businessman too—
O. A. Ohmann, Assistant to the President of Standard Oil of Ohio. [See
p. 2225.]

Other evidences of businessmen's interest in the question of whether
religion should be applied to business are in speeches, conferences, and
seminar meetings where businessmen and church people sit down and
talk out their common problems.

There are two reasons for the great surge of businessmen's concern
about their religious problems. One is that business has changed over
the last quarter century. The other is that the churches have changed too.

Businessmen today are more likely to be professional career men
who work in business firms which they do not own (beyond maybe a
few shares of stock); they are managers rather than owners. Obviously
they cannot hold their jobs unless they help the company to be a financial
success, but their drive for immediate profits is bound to be a little
less intense than if all the earnings came to them. In short, they are
in a better position to temper their money-making viewpoint with consideration for the long-run health of the business, which includes the
well-being of employees, the good will of customers, the confidence of
suppliers, and so on.

So businessmen have become more concerned with their human relations and their social responsibilities. Whether they deserve the credit
for the improvement or not hardly matters. Certainly union pressures
have pushed in this direction; certainly economic conditions have been
such that it has been easier for business to afford the luxury of a
conscience. But the point is that businessmen have responded to the
challenge of the times, and that this has created a new kind of climate
within the industrial organization, which now can never be reversed.

Actually, a substantial part of this change must have come from inside
businessmen themselves. Increasingly they have attended schools where
they have had courses in business subjects; and in many such courses the
long-run effects of business actions are brought into the picture. But
even more important may be the change in religious attitudes which
has accompanied the change in business.

Whereas formerly many of the churches emphasized the "minor
virtues" of thrift and hard work—particularly the churches descended
from the old Puritan faith—today they are turning more and more to
the importance of the dignity of man as a creation of God.

The older attitude insisted on obedience to the Ten Commandments
and on support of the church with money and Sunday attendance, but
it left a man free to be the most practical businessman he could be the
rest of the week—in fact, encouraged him to make as much money
as he could. The modern attitude, however, requires him also to look at
people for their own sake. Are all the people that work for his company
fulfilling their God-given potentials? . . . and is he? . . . they as

productive workers finding satisfaction in their jobs, he as a manager responsible for seeing they have that opportunity.

When one looks at this change closely, it shows up as a shift in emphasis. Businessmen in the past had to consider social values; businessmen of today still have to go after profits. Consequently for many businessmen there is often a conflict. Situations do arise where the financial success of the company requires that a certain action be taken— like firing a long-service employee or moving a plant from a community. Such action entails some hardship to people. Should dollars or human needs be the final determinant?

Sometimes, because of the complexity of modern large-scale organizations, the decision must be made between two needs, both of which are human or social. The rest of the personnel may be happier because the man dismissed had a bad influence on morale; in the end more people may be benefited than are hurt by the plant's moving because now the company will be able to survive and grow.

Religious creeds are not clear on such points. One has only to listen to a Protestant minister, a Catholic priest, or a Jewish rabbi to realize that they agree on the fundamental point: the businessman must, at the very least, conduct his business with due regard to the rights of people. But they either disagree or are vague when it comes to telling the businessman how he should decide when two important values are in opposition.

In this sense business and religion do not mix. There are no religious rules by which a man can run his business. Further, in the long run, the businessman makes his biggest contribution to society by being an efficient businessman—an employer of people, a purchaser of materials, a supplier of products to serve the public. If he becomes so preoccupied with the details of his social responsibilities that he neglects the end purpose of being a businessman, then he is not fulfilling his own God-given potential.

So perhaps it is just as well that religion does not tell businessmen exactly what to do. Modern business is too complex; a set of rules would be a strait jacket, and society would suffer. Also, the values in question are too intangible, too fine, for anyone to try to weigh on a scale, measure with calipers, or add up on a computer. It may be tough on businessmen, but the only solution is for every businessman to be his own Solomon— and it is a thousand times tougher today than it used to be.

Conflicts between different sets of values are inevitable in a business today; they always were, but now they are more so. The important point, however, is that such issues are actually coming up for decision. In other words, businessmen are sensitive to what is involved in these problem areas, and are increasingly taking the enlightened view of what is best for all parts of the business for the long pull. That is the big, significant change.

So religion does play a vital role in business. In one sense, it creates problems for the businessman; that is, it makes him conscious of conflicts of values to be decided, which of course are there even if he does not see them. At the same time, however, it can help him to solve them, not by providing a set of rules that can be applied without thinking, but by instilling in him the very desire to think his problems out and solve each one of them as wisely as possible.

Thus, if he is a religious man, he will try harder to make wise decisions whenever he has to balance the interests of managers and employees, of employees and stockholders, of stockholders and customers, because he will be more understanding and perceptive of other people. And, again, if he is a religious man, he actually will make wiser decisions, simply because as an individual he will have more strength of character. He will have higher personal standards; and, to achieve those standards, he will have fuller confidence in himself—not just as a single human being but as one responsible for many other human beings.

A HYMN FOR SUCCESS IN TRADE AND BANKING

FROM THE VEDAS

["A Merchant's Prayer," in *Hymns of the Atharva-Veda,* adapted from the trans. of Maurice Bloomfield, The Clarendon Press, Oxford, 1897, pp. 148–149. This is vol. XLII from Max Müller (ed.), *The Sacred Books of the East,* trans. by various Oriental scholars.]

From 1000 B.C., or earlier, comes this hymn to some of the ancient Vedic Gods of India—to Indra, Agni, Prajapati, and so on—praying for good fortune in trade.

The fifth verse is interpreted by some to refer to moneylending rather than trade. The key phrase is "seeking riches with riches." If this is taken to mean lending money at interest, then the sense of the verse is: "O God, I engage myself in moneylending from my sum in order to earn money. . . ."

In any event, it is perfectly clear from the subsequent history of India that both commerce and banking were considered respectable until the period of the Mohammedan dominance around the twelfth century A.D. (the Koran considers usury a grave crime; see page 2118 in this volume).

Bills of exchange circulated widely, and many kinds of loans were made at interest. Interestingly enough, the amount of interest charged was a matter of religious law; it is dealt with in the Code of Manu, written down about A.D. 100 but reflecting Hindu thought of the epic period 500 or 600 years earlier. (Manu was the Indian Noah.) Rates varied for the different castes or classes. Thus, at one point, the rates for unsecured loans were 2 per cent for Brahmans (the nobility), 3 per cent for Kshatizas, 4 per cent for Vaishyas, and 5 per cent for Shudras (at the bottom of the social ladder). There were also maximum limits, set by religious law, apparently in inverse proportion to the social utility of the commodity in question.

For the most part, the traders and bankers themselves, that is, the businessmen, were Vaishyas, but some Kshatizas and even Brahmans (whose mission in life was the observation of religious ceremonies) were attracted to business. An old story tells of a prince who resigned his share in the kingdom in favor of his sister to become a trader and a banker.

So why shouldn't the gods be asked to help?

———◆———

1. INDRA, the merchant, do I summon: may he come to us, may he be our van; driving away the demon of grudge, the waylayers, and wild beasts, may he, the possessor, bestow wealth upon me!

2. May the many paths, the roads of the gods, which come together between heaven and earth, gladden me with milk and ghee [soft butter], so that I may gather in wealth from my purchases!

3. Desirous do I, O Agni, with firewood and ghee offer oblations to thee, for success and strength; according to ability praising thee with my prayer, do I sing this divine song, that I may gain a hundredfold!

4. Pardon, O Agni, this sin of ours incurred upon the far road which we have traveled! May our purchases and our sales be successful for us; may what I get in barter render me a gainer! May ye two [Indra and Agni] in accord take pleasure in this oblation! May our transactions and the accruing gain be auspicious to us!

5. With what riches I practice bargaining, seeking riches with riches, ye gods—let that become more for me, not less. Drive away, O Agni, in return for the oblation, the gods who shut off gain!

6. With what riches I practice bargaining, seeking riches with riches, ye gods—may Indra, Prajapati, Savitar, Soma, Agni, place luster into it for me!

7. We praise with reverence thee, O priest [Agni] Vaisvânara. Do thou over our children, selves, cattle, and life's breath watch!

8. Daily, never failing, shall we bring oblations to thee, O Gâtavedas, as if fodder to a horse standing in the stable. In growth of wealth and nutriment rejoicing, may we, O Agni, thy neighbors, not take harm!

GO TO THE ANT, THOU SLUGGARD . . .

FROM THE BIBLE

[The Bible, Proverbs 6:6–11.]

There have been two broad currents of opinion in the history of business and religion. One is that business practices, business values, are anti-religious or at least have to be tempered to be acceptably moral. The other is that religion teaches the virtues which make for success in business or, conversely, that the businessman cannot succeed unless he is a good man to begin with. The following verses from the Bible obviously belong to the latter category. They are from the Proverbs, usually ascribed to Solomon, around the tenth century B.C.

Go to the ant, thou sluggard;
Consider her ways, and be wise;
Which having no chief,
Overseer, or ruler,
Provideth her bread in the summer,
And gathereth her food in the harvest.
How long wilt thou sleep, O sluggard?
When wilt thou arise out of thy sleep?
Yet a little sleep, a little slumber,
A little folding of the hands to sleep—
So shall thy poverty come as a runner,
And thy want as an armed man.

RELIGION ENTERS EVERY
SPHERE OF LIFE

FROM THE TALMUD AND
The Code of Maimonides

[*The Code of Maimonides, Book Thirteen, The Book of Civil Laws,* trans. from the Hebrew by Jacob J. Rabinowitz; Yale University Press, New Haven, 1949, pp. 109–110, 111.]

[Madison C. Peters (ed.), *Wit and Wisdom of the Talmud,* The Baker & Taylor Co., New York, 1900, pp. 30, 42, 43, 47, 82–84, 87, 89–90.]

[*The Babylonian Talmud,* Seder Neziken; trans. by Rabbi Dr. I. Epstein; The Soncino Press, London, 1935, Yebamoth—pp. 420–421.]

The Talmud, in which the abstract word of the Old Testament is translated into rules for daily living, is one of the oldest codes of conduct still in use today. Evolving from over 700 years of experience, the Talmud was finally reduced to writing during the second, fourth, and sixth centuries. It is a mélange of laws, stories with morals, and wise sayings; snatches from each of these categories are presented in the following selection.

The first part on the selling price of goods is similar to St. Thomas Aquinas' concern with just price versus market price.* This article is from *The Code of Maimonides,* a commentary on the section of the Talmud which contains a systematic collection of religious-legal decisions developing the laws of the Old Testament. An important document in its own right, the *Code* was written by Maimonides, a Jewish philosopher and scholar of the twelfth and thirteenth centuries (1135–1204).

Also included are a story with a moral and various proverbs directly from the Talmud.†

---◆---

I. CREDITOR AND DEBTOR

No agreement may be made with respect to produce until the market price has been published; but once the market price has been published, such an agreement may be made, for even if the seller does not have the produce, another man has it. How is this to be understood? If the market price has become fixed at four *sĕ'ah* to the *sela',* one may make an agreement with a vendor for the purchase of 100 *sĕ'ah,*

---

* See page 2119 in this volume.
† For additional material from the Talmud and *The Code of Maimonides,* refer to index listing in this volume.

giving him 25 *sela'*, and if the vendor delivers 100 *sĕ'ah* of wheat after the lapse of some time, when wheat sells at a *sela'* per *sĕ'ah*, there is no usury at all in the transaction, even though the vendor had no wheat at the time when he made the agreement.

This applies only if the vendor, at the time when the agreement is made, has none of the kind which he agrees to sell, but if he has some of that kind, although it has not been completely processed, it is permissible to make an agreement with respect thereto, even if the market price has not yet been published.

How is this to be understood? If a man is the first among the reapers, he may make an agreement with respect to the wheat even though it is still in the sack. One may also make an agreement with respect to wine as soon as he cuts the grapes and places them in the pressing vat, or with respect to oil as soon as he places the olives in the vat, or with respect to lime as soon as the limestone is sunk in the kiln.

One may likewise make an agreement with respect to pottery as soon as the potter makes the clay balls. This applies only to pottery made of white clay, but in the case of pottery made of black clay one may make an agreement with respect thereto, even though none of it has yet been made, because black clay is readily available and if the seller does not have it another man has it.

One may likewise make an agreement with respect to manure at any season of the year, even though he has none, because manure is always available. . . .

No agreement may be made on the basis of the market price in small towns, because the market price there is not a stable one, but only on the basis of the market price in the principal town of the region. . . .

II. FROM THE TALMUD

A certain man who was once hired to work for a stipulated daily wage, and who worked for three years without having drawn his earnings, at length desired to go home and demanded his accumulations from his employer. "I have no money just now," said the employer. "Give me then some of your produce," demanded the employee. "I regret very much," said the master, "that I cannot comply with thy request." He asked him for cattle, for wine or vineyard, but the master declared he was unable to give him anything. With a heavy sigh the poor laborer took his tools and without a murmur departed. Scarcely had he gone when the employer ordered three asses laden with eatables, drinkables and wearing apparel, and personally rode to the residence of the laborer, who at once prepared a meal for his master, and they ate and drank together. After a while the employer drew forth a bag of money and handing it to the astonished employee, told him that the provisions-laden asses were his also. Thereupon the following dialogue ensued:

Employer: "What was in thy mind when I told thee I had no money?"

Employee: "I thought thou hadst unfortunately lost it."

Employer: "And when I told thee I had no cattle?"

Employee: "That others claimed it for a debt incurred prior to mine."

Employer: "What couldst thou have thought when I told thee I had no field?"

Employee: "That it might have been mortgaged."

Employer: "And when I told thee I had no fruit?"

Employee: "That it might not have been tithed yet."

Employer: "But what didst thou think when I told thee I had no vineyard nor wine?"

Employee: "It came to my mind that, perchance, thou hadst sanctified both wine and vineyard as gifts to the Temple."

Employer: "Ah, thou art a godly man. Faithfully hast thou complied with the ethical doctrine 'Judge everybody favorably.' Thou hast judged me favorably and God judge thee favorably."

PROVERBS

Attend no auctions if thou hast no money.

Keep partners with him whom the hour favors.

If thy business does not prosper in one town try another.

He who looks daily after his field finds a corn.

Credit and mutual trust should be the foundation of commercial intercourse.

Who is rich? He who is satisfied with his lot.

Go to sleep without supper, but rise without debt.

Beautiful is the intellectual occupation, if combined with some practical work.

Lend to the poor in the time of their need.

Never take the clothes of wife or children in payment of a debt.

If you have taken of a man his plough or his pillow for debt, return his plough in the morning and his pillow at night.

III. FROM THE BABYLONIAN TALMUD

Rab once entered among the growing ears of corn. Seeing that they were swaying he called out to them, "Swing as you will, engaging in business brings more profit than you can do."

THOSE WHO EXPEND THEIR WEALTH IN GOD'S WAY

FROM THE KORAN

[Mohammed, The Koran, Oxford University Press, London, 1954, pp. 37-41.]

These excerpts from the Mohammedan Qur'ân (or, as it is more famil-
iarly written in English, Koran) again show the closeness of early religious
teaching and the practices of daily life. The Koran was "revealed" to
Mohammed over the years from about A.D. 611 to 632; the first authorized
text was issued in 660.

Notice the classic condemnation of usury. We have a whole section
devoted to this subject from the philosophical viewpoint in Volume II.

THE LIKENESS of those who expend their wealth in God's way is as
the likeness of a grain that grows to seven ears, in every ear a
hundred grains, for God will double unto whom He pleases; for God
both embraces and knows. . . .

But the likeness of those who expend their wealth craving the
good will of God, and as an insurance for their souls, is as the likeness
of a garden on a hill. A heavy shower falls on it, and it brings forth
its eatables twofold; and if no heavy shower falls on it, the dew does;
and God on what ye do doth look. . . .

O ye who believe! expend in alms of the good things that ye have
earned, and of what we have brought forth for you out of the earth,
and do not take the vile thereof to spend in alms, what you would
not take yourselves save by connivance at it,* but know that God is
rich and to be praised.

Thou † art not bound to guide them; but God guides whom He
will; and whatever good ye expend, it is for yourselves, and do not
expend save craving for God's face.

And what ye expend of good, it shall be repaid you, and ye
shall not be wronged—unto the poor who are straitened in God's
way, and cannot knock about ‡ in the earth. The ignorant think them

---

* I.e., by a mutual understanding between seller and buyer.

† I.e., Mohammed.

‡ I must remind the reader that the language of the Qur'ân is really rude and
rugged, and that although the expressions employed in it are now considered as
refined and elegant, it is only because all literary Arabic has been modeled on the
style of the Qur'ân. The word which I have ventured to translate by this somewhat
inelegant phrase (*dharban*) means literally, "to beat or knock about," and as
colloquial English affords an exact equivalent I have not hesitated to use it.—Trans-
lator.

to be rich because of their modesty; you will know them by their mark, they do not beg from men importunately; but what ye spend of good God knows.

Those who expend their wealth by night and day, secretly and openly, they shall have their hire with their Lord. No fear shall come on them, nor shall they grieve.

Those who devour usury shall not rise again, save as he riseth whom Satan hath paralyzed with a touch; and that is because they say "selling is only like usury," but God has made selling lawful and usury unlawful; and he to whom the admonition from his Lord has come, if he desists, what has gone before is his *; his matter is in God's hands. But whosoever returns [to usury], these are the fellows of the Fire, and they shall dwell therein for aye. God shall blot out usury, but shall make almsgiving profitable, for God loves not any sinful misbeliever.

Verily, those who believe, and act righteously, and are steadfast in prayer, and give alms, theirs is their hire with their Lord; there is no fear on them, nor shall they grieve.

O ye who believe! fear God, and remit the balance of usury, if ye be believers; and if ye will not do it, then hearken to the proclamation of war from God and His Apostle; but if ye repent, your capital is yours. Ye shall not wrong, nor shall ye be wronged.

And if it be one in difficulties, then wait for easy circumstances; but that ye remit it as alms is better for you, if ye did but know.

Fear the day wherein ye shall return to God; then shall each soul be paid what it has earned, and they shall not be wronged.

O ye who believe! if ye engage to one another in a debt for a stated time, then write it down, and let a scribe write it down between you faithfully; nor let a scribe refuse to write as God taught him, but let him write, and let him who owes dictate; but let him fear God his Lord, and not diminish therefrom aught; but if he who owes be a fool, or weak, or cannot dictate himself, then let his agent dictate faithfully, and let them call two witnesses out from amongst their men; or if there be not two men, then a man and two women, from those whom he chooses for witnesses, so that if one of the two should err, the second of the two may remind the other; and let not the witnesses refuse when they are summoned; and let them not tire of writing it, be it small or great, with its time of payment. That is more just in the sight of God, and more upright for testimony, and brings you nearer to not doubting. Unless, indeed, it be a ready-money transaction between you, which ye arrange between yourselves, then it is no crime against you that ye do not write it down; but bring witnesses to what ye sell one to another, and let not either scribe or witness come to harm, for if ye do it will be

---

* I.e., his former conduct shall be pardoned.

abomination in you; but fear God, for God teaches you, and God knows all things. But if ye be upon a journey, and ye cannot find a scribe, then let a pledge be taken. But if one of you trust another, then let him who is trusted surrender his trust, and let him fear God his Lord, and conceal not testimony, for he who conceals it, verily, sinful is his heart; God knows what ye do.

God's is what is in heaven and in the earth, and if ye show what is in your souls, or hide it, God will call you to account; and He forgives whom He will, and punishes whom He will, for God is mighty over all.

The Apostle believes in what is sent down to him from his Lord, and the believers all believe on God, and His angels, and His Books, and His apostles—we make no difference between any of His apostles—they say, "We hear and obey, Thy pardon, O Lord! for to Thee our journey tends. God will not require of the soul save its capacity. It shall have what it has earned, and it shall owe what has been earned from it. Lord, catch us not up, if we forget or make mistake; Lord, load us not with a burden, as Thou hast loaded those who were before us. Lord, make us not to carry what we have not strength for, but forgive us, and pardon us, and have mercy on us. Thou art our Sovereign, then help us against the people who do not believe!"

A CHURCHMAN DISCOURSES ON PROFIT AND INTEREST

~~⚭~~

ST. THOMAS AQUINAS

[St. Thomas Aquinas, "Of Cheating Which is Committed in Buying and Selling," "Of the Sin of Usury," in *Summa Theologica*, trans. by the Fathers of the English Dominican Province; Benziger Brothers, Inc., New York, 1947, vol. II, 2nd part, pp. 1513–1519 (abridged).]

Here the great Catholic philosopher St. Thomas Aquinas (1225–1274) discusses the questions of selling at a profit and lending money upon interest. Thus Christianity shows the same concern about these business practices that earlier philosophers did (see, for example, Plato and Aristotle *). It is also noteworthy that lending at interest has been frowned on or prohibited by the Jewish and Mohammedan religions.

After discussing questions of fraud, such as whether it is lawful to sell a thing for more than it is worth or whether the seller is bound to reveal a fault in the thing sold (these are omitted here), St. Thomas

_____
* See pages 1939 and 1944 in this volume.

Aquinas tackles the question of profit itself—is it lawful to sell a thing at a higher price than was paid for it?—and then moves on to usury.

———◆———

WE MUST NOW CONSIDER those sins which relate to voluntary commutations. First, we shall consider cheating, which is committed in buying and selling: secondly, we shall consider usury, which occurs in loans. In connection with the other voluntary commutations no special kind of sin is to be found distinct from rapine and theft. . . .

WHETHER, IN TRADING, IT IS LAWFUL TO SELL A THING AT A HIGHER PRICE THAN WHAT WAS PAID FOR IT . . .

Objection 1. It would seem that it is not lawful, in trading, to sell a thing for a higher price than we paid for it. For Chrysostom says on Matthew 21:12: *He that buys a thing in order that he may sell it, entire and unchanged, at a profit, is the trader who is cast out of God's temple.* Cassiodorus speaks in the same sense in his commentary on Psalms 70:15, *Because I have not known learning or trading,* [or] according to another version: *What is trade,* says he, *but buying at a cheap price with the purpose of retailing at a higher price?* and he adds: *Such were the tradesmen whom Our Lord cast out of the temple.* Now, no man is cast out of the temple except for a sin. Therefore suchlike trading is sinful.

Obj. 2. Further, it is contrary to justice to sell goods at a higher price than their worth, or to buy them for less than their value, as shown above. . . . Now, if you sell a thing for a higher price than you paid for it, you must either have bought it for less than its value, or sell it for more than its value. Therefore this cannot be done without sin.

Obj. 3. Further, Jerome says (*Ep. ad Nepot* lii): *Shun, as you would the plague, a cleric who from being poor has become wealthy, or who, from being a nobody has become a celebrity.* Now, trading would not seem to be forbidden to clerics except on account of its sinfulness. Therefore it is a sin in trading, to buy at a low price and to sell at a higher price.

On the contrary, Augustine commenting on Psalms 70:15, *Because I have not known learning,* says: *The greedy tradesman blasphemes over his losses; he lies and perjures himself over the price of his wares. But these are vices of the man, not of the craft, which can be exercised without these vices.* Therefore trading is not in itself unlawful.

I answer that, A tradesman is one whose business consists in the exchange of things. According to the Philosopher [Aristotle] (*Politics* i. 3), exchange of things is twofold; one, natural as it were, and necessary, whereby one commodity is exchanged for another, or money taken in exchange for a commodity, in order to satisfy the needs of life. Suchlike trading, properly speaking, does not belong to tradesmen, but rather to housekeepers or civil servants who have to provide the household or the state with the necessaries of life. The other kind of exchange is either that of money for money, or of any commodity for money, not on account of the necessities of life, but for profit, and this kind of exchange, properly speaking, regards tradesmen, according to the Philosopher (*Politics* i. 3). The former kind of exchange is commendable because it supplies a natural need: but the latter is justly deserving of blame, because, considered in itself, it satisfies the greed for gain, which knows no limit and tends to infinity. Hence trading, considered in itself, has a certain debasement attaching thereto, in so far as, by its very nature, it does not imply a virtuous or necessary end. Nevertheless gain which is the end of trading, though not implying, by its nature, anything virtuous or necessary, does not, in itself, connote anything sinful or contrary to virtue: wherefore nothing prevents gain from being directed to some necessary or even virtuous end, and thus trading becomes lawful. Thus, for instance, a man may intend the moderate gain which he seeks to acquire by trading for the upkeep of his household, or for the assistance of the needy: or again, a man may take to trade for some public advantage, for instance, lest his country lack the necessaries of life, and seek gain, not as an end, but as payment for his labor.

Reply Obj. 1. The saying of Chrysostom refers to the trading which seeks gain as a last end. This is especially the case where a man sells something at a higher price without its undergoing any change. For if he sells at a higher price something that has changed for the better, he would seem to receive the reward of his labor. Nevertheless the gain itself may be lawfully intended, not as a last end, but for the sake of some other end which is necessary or virtuous, as stated above.

Reply Obj. 2. Not everyone that sells at a higher price than he bought is a tradesman, but only he who buys that he may sell at a profit. If, on the contrary, he buys not for sale but for possession, and afterwards, for some reason wishes to sell, it is not a trade transaction even if he sell at a profit. For he may lawfully do this, either because he has bettered the thing, or because the value of the thing has changed with the change of place or time, or on account of the danger he incurs in transferring the thing from one place to another, or again in having it carried by another. In this sense neither buying nor selling is unjust.

Reply Obj. 3. Clerics should abstain not only from things that are evil in themselves, but even from those that have an appearance of evil. This happens in trading, both because it is directed to worldly gain, which clerics should despise, and because trading is open to so many vices, since a *merchant is hardly free from sins of the lips* * (Ecclesiasticus [Apocrypha] 26:28). There is also another reason, because trading engages the mind too much with worldly cares, and consequently withdraws it from spiritual cares; wherefore the Apostle says (2 Timothy 2:4): *No man being a soldier to God entangleth himself with secular businesses.* Nevertheless it is lawful for clerics to engage in the first mentioned kind of exchange, which is directed to supply the necessaries of life, either by buying or by selling.

OF THE SIN OF USURY

We must now consider the sin of usury, which is committed in loans: and under this head there are four points of inquiry: (1) Whether it is a sin to take money as a price for money lent, which is to receive usury. (2) Whether it is lawful to lend money for any other kind of consideration, by way of payment for the loan. (3) Whether a man is bound to restore just gains derived from money taken in usury. (4) Whether it is lawful to borrow money under a condition of usury.

FIRST ARTICLE

Whether It Is a Sin to Take Usury for Money Lent . . .

Objection 1. It would seem that it is not a sin to take usury for money lent. For no man sins through following the example of Christ. But Our Lord said to Himself (Luke 19:23): *At My coming I might have exacted it,* i.e., the money lent, *with usury.* Therefore it is not a sin to take usury for lending money.

Obj. 2. Further, according to Psalms 18:8, *The law of the Lord is unspotted,* because, to wit, it forbids sin. Now, usury of a kind is allowed in the Divine law, according to Deuteronomy 23:19, 20. *Thou shalt not generate [lend money upon interest] to thy brother, . . . nor corn, nor any other thing, but to the stranger:* nay more, it is even promised as a reward for the observance of the Law, according to Deuteronomy 28:12: *Thou shalt generate to many nations, and shalt not borrow of any one.* Therefore it is not a sin to take usury.

Obj. 3. Further, in human affairs justice is determined by civil laws. Now, civil law allows usury to be taken. Therefore it seems to be lawful.

Obj. 4. Further, the counsels are not binding under sin. But among other counsels we find (Luke 6:35): *Lend, hoping for nothing thereby.* Therefore it is not a sin to take usury.

Obj. 5. Further, it does not seem to be in itself sinful to accept

---

* A merchant is hardly free from negligence, and a huckster shall not be justified from the sins of the lips.

a price for doing what one is not bound to do. But one who has money is not bound in every case to lend it to his neighbor. Therefore it is lawful for him sometimes to accept a price for lending it.

Obj. 6. Further, silver made into coins does not differ specifically from silver made into a vessel. But it is lawful to accept a price for the loan of a silver vessel. Therefore it is also lawful to accept a price for the loan of a silver coin. Therefore usury is not in itself a sin.

Obj. 7. Further, anyone may lawfully accept a thing which its owner freely gives him. Now, he who accepts the loan, freely gives the usury. Therefore he who lends may lawfully take the usury.

On the contrary, It is written (Exodus 22:25): *If thou lend money to any of thy people that is poor, that dwelleth with thee, thou shalt not be hard upon them as an extortioner, nor oppress them with usuries.*

I answer that, To take usury for money lent is unjust in itself, because this is to sell what does not exist, and this evidently leads to inequality which is contrary to justice.

In order to make this evident, we must observe that there are certain things the use of which consists in their consumption: thus we consume wine when we use it for drink, and we consume wheat when we use it for food. Wherefore in suchlike things the use of the thing must not be reckoned apart from the thing itself, and whoever is granted the use of the thing is granted the thing itself; and for this reason, to lend things of this kind is to transfer the ownership. Accordingly if a man wanted to sell wine separately from the use of the wine, he would be selling the same thing twice, or he would be selling what does not exist, wherefore he would evidently commit a sin of injustice. In like manner he commits an injustice who lends wine or wheat, and asks for double payment, viz., one, the return of the thing in equal measure, the other, the price of the use, which is called usury.

On the other hand, there are things the use of which does not consist in their consumption: thus to use a house is to dwell in it, not to destroy it. Wherefore in such things both may be granted: for instance, one man may hand over to another the ownership of his house while reserving to himself the use of it for a time, or vice versa, he may grant the use of the house, while retaining the ownership. For this reason a man may lawfully make a charge for the use of his house, and, besides this, revendicate the house from the person to whom he has granted its use, as happens in renting and letting a house.

Now, money, according to the Philosopher (*Ethics* v. 5; *Politics* i. 3) was invented chiefly for the purpose of exchange; and consequently the proper and principal use of money is its consumption or alienation whereby it is sunk in exchange. Hence it is by its very nature unlawful to take payment for the use of money lent, which payment is known as usury: and just as a man is bound to restore other ill-gotten goods, so is he bound to restore the money which he has taken in usury.

Reply Obj. 1. In this passage usury must be taken figuratively for the increase of spiritual goods which God exacts from us, for He wishes us ever to advance in the goods which we receive from Him: and this is for our own profit, not for His.

Reply Obj. 2. The Jews were forbidden to take usury from their brethren, i.e., from other Jews. By this we are given to understand that to take usury from any man is evil simply, because we ought to treat every man as our neighbor and brother, especially in the state of the Gospel, whereto all are called. Hence it is said without any distinction in Psalms 14:5: *He that hath not put out his money to usury,* and (Ezekiel 18:8): *Who hath not taken usury.* They were permitted, however, to take usury from foreigners, not as though it were lawful, but in order to avoid a greater evil, lest, to wit, through avarice to which they were prone according to Isaiah 56:11, they should take usury from the Jews who were worshipers of God.

Where we find it promised to them as a reward, *Thou shalt generate to many nations,* etc., *generating* is to be taken in a broad sense for lending [upon interest], as in Ecclesiasticus 29:10, where we read: *Many have refused to generate not out of wickedness,* i.e. they would not lend. Accordingly the Jews are promised in reward an abundance of wealth, so that they would be able to lend to others.

Reply Obj. 3. Human laws leave certain things unpunished, on account of the condition of those who are imperfect, and who would be deprived of many advantages, if all sins were strictly forbidden and punishments appointed for them. Wherefore human law has permitted usury, not that it looks upon usury as harmonizing with justice, but lest the advantage of many should be hindered. Hence it is that in civil law it is stated that *those things according to natural reason and civil law which are consumed by being used, do not admit of usufruct, and that the senate did not (nor could it) appoint a usufruct to such things, but established a quasi-usufruct,* namely by permitting usury. Moreover the Philosopher, led by natural reason, says (*Politics* i. 3) that *to make money by usury is exceedingly unnatural.*

Reply Obj. 4. A man is not always bound to lend, and for this reason it is placed among the counsels. Yet it is a matter of precept not to seek profit by lending: although it may be called a matter of counsel in comparison with the maxims of the Pharisees, who deemed some kinds of usury to be lawful, just as love of one's enemies is a matter of counsel. Or again, He speaks here not of the hope of usurious gain, but of the hope which is put in man. For we ought not to lend or do any good deed through hope in man, but only through hope in God.

Reply Obj. 5. He that is not bound to lend, may accept repayment for what he has done, but he must not exact more. Now he is repaid according to equality of justice if he is repaid as much as he lent. Wherefore if he exacts more for the usufruct of a thing which has no other use but the consumption of its substance, he exacts a price of something nonexistent: and so his exaction is unjust.

Reply Obj. 6. The principal use of a silver vessel is not its consumption, and so one may lawfully sell its use while retaining one's ownership of it. On the other hand the principal use of silver money is sinking it in exchange, so that it is not lawful to sell its use and at the same time expect the restitution of the amount lent. It must be observed, however, that the secondary use of silver vessels may be an exchange, and such use may not be lawfully sold. In like manner there may be some secondary use of silver money; for instance, a man might lend coins for show, or to be used as security.

Reply Obj. 7. He who gives usury does not give it voluntarily simply, but under a certain necessity, in so far as he needs to borrow money which the owner is unwilling to lend without usury. . .

[The other three articles on usury are omitted here.]

THE CONCEPT OF THE JUST PRICE

RAYMOND DE ROOVER

[Raymond de Roover, "The Concept of the Just Price: Theory and Economic Policy." in the *Journal of Economic History*, December 1958, pp. 418–434 (abridged). Reprinted by permission of Economic History Association, New York University.]

Did the scholastic thinkers of the Middle Ages really distinguish between just price and market price? In this article a modern scholar answers with a definite "No!" In his estimation at least, the leading scholastics equated just price with market price, thus supporting the doctrine of competition in most situations. Under this interpretation, religious thought of the late Middle Ages proves to be much more modern than we had hitherto realized. The Puritans in New England in Keayne's case * were deviating from—or misunderstanding—the influential thinkers of the preceding centuries.

Perhaps it should be explained that the "scholastics" were learned men, like our Doctors of Philosophy, who studied and wrote on law and theology. In the Middle Ages law and theology were inextricably bound together—indeed, were almost one and the same thing.

---

* See page 2162 in this volume.

◆

IN THE VIEW of many economists the just price is a nebulous concept invented by pious monks who knew nothing of business or economics and were blissfully unaware of market mechanisms. It is true that certain writers, Catholics and non-Catholics alike, have done their best to accredit this fairy tale and to propagate the notion that the just price, instead of being set by the allegedly blind and unconscionable forces of the market, was determined by criteria of fairness without regard to the elements of supply and demand or at least with the purpose of eliminating the evils of unrestrained competition.

According to a widespread belief—found in nearly all books dealing with the subject—the just price was linked to the medieval concept of a social hierarchy and corresponded to a reasonable charge which would enable the producer to live and to support his family on a scale suitable to his station in life. This doctrine is generally thought to have found its practical application in the guild system. For this purpose the guilds are presented as welfare agencies which prevented unfair competition, protected consumers against deceit and exploitation, created equal opportunities for their members, and secured for them a modest but decent living in keeping with traditional standards. . . .

The purpose of this paper is to demonstrate that the generally accepted definition of the just price is wrong and rests on misinterpretation of the scholastic position on the matter. According to the majority of the doctors, the just price did not correspond to cost of production as determined by the producer's social status, but was simply the current market price, with this important reservation: in cases of collusion or emergency, the public authorities retained the right to interfere and to impose a fair price. In order to straighten out the existing confusion, it will also be shown how this doctrine was translated into policy, particularly in connection with the guilds.

For the inception of the scholastic doctrine of the just price, one of the fundamental texts is the canon *Placuit,* which is really a capitulary issued in 884 by Karloman, King of France, but incorporated by Raymond of Pennaforte (1180–1278) in the canon law. This canon states that parish priests should admonish their flocks not to charge wayfarers more than the price obtainable in the local market (*quam in mercato vendere possint*). Otherwise, the wayfarers can complain to the priest, who is then required to set a price with "humanity." This text, it seems to me, clearly equates just price with market price and does not lend itself to a different interpretation.

In the works of Albertus Magnus (1193–1280) and especially

in those of Thomas Aquinas (1226–1274), the passages relating to price are so scattered and seemingly so conflicting that they have given rise to varying interpretations. By selecting only those passages favorable to their thesis, certain writers even reached the conclusion that Albertus Magnus and Thomas Aquinas had a labor theory of value and adumbrated Karl Marx (1818–1883). To prove their point these writers used chiefly the comments of the two theologians on Aristotle's *Nicomachean Ethics,* where it is stated that commutative or contractual justice requires strict equivalence between what is received and what is given and that any exchange violating this rule is unfair. This is then construed in a Marxian sense as meaning that price, to be just, should always correspond to cost, which in the Middle Ages was chiefly labor cost. The trouble is that such an explanation contradicts statements made elsewhere by Albertus Magnus and Thomas Aquinas. Moreover, the texts in question are open to another interpretation which would do away with any inconsistency. In their comments on Aristotle both Albertus and Aquinas insist that arts and crafts would be doomed to destruction if the producer did not recover his outlays in the sale of his product. In other words, the market price could not fall permanently below cost. If so, there is no contradiction, since the market price would then tend to coincide with cost or to oscillate around this point like the swing of a pendulum. Besides, Thomas Aquinas himself recognizes that the just price cannot be determined with precision, but can vary within a certain range, so that minor deviations do not involve any injustice. This second interpretation, of course, is not in accord with Marxian dialectics; but it agrees with classical and neoclassical economic analysis. It is also consonant with the later development of scholastic thought.

Whatever the meaning of these obscure passages, Albertus Magnus and Thomas Aquinas are more explicit, if less analytical, in other works where they give their own opinions and do not try to elucidate Aristotle's. The first, in his comments on the *Sentences* of Peter Lombard, defines the just price as follows: What goods are worth according to the estimation of the market (*secundum aestimationem fori*) at the time of the sale. Thomas Aquinas nowhere puts the matter so clearly, but he tells the story of a merchant who brings wheat to a country where there is dearth and knows that others are following with more. May this merchant, Aquinas asks, sell his wheat at the prevailing price (*pretium quod invenit*) or should he announce the arrival of fresh supplies and thus cause the price to fall? The answer is that he may sell his wheat at the current price without infringing the rules of justice, although, Aquinas adds almost as an afterthought, he would act more virtuously by notifying the buyers. In my opinion this passage destroys with a single blow the thesis of those who try to make Aquinas into a Marxist, and proves beyond doubt that he considered the market price as just.

This interpretation, moreover, agrees with that of Cardinal Cajetan (1468–1534), the authoritative commentator on the *Summa*. In connection with question 77 *secunda secundae,* which deals with the sales contract, he concludes that according to Aquinas the just price is "the one, which at a given time, can be gotten from the buyers, assuming common knowledge and in the absence of all fraud and coercion." He then goes on to describe the market mechanism and to show how prices rise or fall in response to changes in demand or supply.

Those who say Thomas Aquinas favored cost of production rather than market valuation as the criterion of justice claim that the later scholastic doctors, yielding to the pressure of rising capitalism, modified his doctrine in this respect. Since Aquinas upheld market valuation instead of cost, however, there was no change, but a continuous tradition involving, it is true, elaboration and refinement as economic development raised new problems and as discussion revealed flaws in previous analysis.

Some of the most valuable contributions were made by Bernardino of Siena (1380–1444), perhaps the ablest economist of the Middle Ages. Although usually a follower of John Duns Scotus, he espouses the Thomist position on price. According to San Bernardino, price is a social phenomenon and is set not by the arbitrary decision of individuals, but *communiter,* that is, by the community. How? There are two possibilities: The price of a commodity can be fixed either by the public authorities for the common good, or by the estimation currently arrived at in the market (*secundum aestimationem fori occurrentis*). The first is the legal price; the second is called later the natural price. Citing Henricus Hostiensis (died 1271), San Bernardino stresses the fact that the market price has to be accepted by the producer and is fair whether he gains or loses, whether it is above or below cost. This point was further elaborated by the Dominican friar, Tommaso Buoninsegni (died 1609). In his treatise on licit traffics he points out that the just price does not have gradations, because buyers, if they are well informed, as they usually are in a wholesale market, will not pay more than the current price. In other words, for the same commodity there can be only one price in the same market.

By the sixteenth century the majority of the scholastic doctors agreed that the just price was either fixed by law or determined by common estimation (*communis aestimatio*). There has been some discussion about the meaning of this phrase, but it appears to be identical with *aestimatio fori,* or market valuation, since the two expressions were used interchangeably by the scholastics. Moreover, it is not clear how a community acting collectively could arrive at a price except by the chaffering of the market, certainly not by taking a vote, for example.

The dissenters were only a few followers of John Duns Scotus (1265–1308), such as John Mayor (1469–1550), another Scot, and Johannes Consobrinus, or João Sobrinho (died 1486), a Portuguese who taught for some time in England. Like their leader, they maintained that the just price corresponded to cost including normal profit and compensation for risk. . . .

The theory of Duns Scotus was denounced most vehemently as fallacious by the School of Salamanca, founded by the great jurist, Francisco de Vitoria (*ca.* 1480–1546). More than ever emphasis was put on the fairness of the current market price. Without exception, Vitoria and his disciples insist that attention be paid only to supply and demand, without regard for labor costs, expenses, or incurred risks; inefficient producers or unfortunate speculators should simply bear the consequences of their incompetence, bad luck, or wrong forecasting.

Although the whole discussion on the just price assumed the existence of competitive conditions, it is strange that the word "competition" never occurs in scholastic treatises until the end of the sixteenth century, when it is used by Luis de Molina (1535–1601). Discussing price formation in an open market, he states that "competition (*concurrentium*) among buyers—brisker at one time than at another—and their greater avidity will cause prices to go up, whereas paucity of purchasers will bring them down." The Spanish school accepted as a matter of course the quantity theory of money and the proposition that prices "generally" will rise or fall in response to expansion or contraction of the monetary circulation.

Whenever the free market failed to function properly, the public authorities, according to the scholastic doctrine, had not only the right but the duty to step in by means of price regulation. When there was a legal price, it superseded the market price and was binding, unless the regulations were manifestly out of date or openly disobeyed, with the authorities making no attempt at enforcement. In other words, the moralists realized perfectly well that it was useless to fix prices by decree if nothing was done to make them effective.

Discussion of this issue does not start until the fourteenth century, and one of the first advocates of price fixing was the Frenchman Jean Gerson (1362–1428), *doctor christianissimus* and at one time chancellor of the University of Paris. He suggested that price fixing be extended to all commodities, on the ground that no one should presume to be wiser than the lawmaker. This suggestion, however, found few supporters, as the impracticality of the whole scheme became apparent. In fact, medieval price regulation usually embraced

A PROCLAMATION CONCER-

NYNGE BOVCHERS.

289 ... Regis Henrici Octaui xxij°

OR AS MOCHE AS THE KINGES maiestie is credibly aduertised and infourmed, th beafes, muttons, and veales, are lykely to be moze scarse and dere nowe ayenst this holy tyme of Ester, th in other seasons of the yere, by reason of the charges of keppynge of suche cattelle with hey and other f uer, in the wynter: by occasion wherof the bouchers and other that shall sell such beaues muttons and ve les by retaple by weighte, can not bye theym of the bzeders bzoggers fermours dzouers owners and feders of suche cattell suche reasonable pzices in grosse, as they may sell the same ayene by weight by retaple at suche pzices as are limitted in the a made fozf ynge of flesshe by weight, onlesse it shulde be to their vtter losse and vndoinge: His highenes therfoze wyllyng that the same bouchers, and other sellyng flesshe by retaple foz the tyme hereafter lymitted in this pzoclamation, shuld be so co uentiently pzouided foz in the pzemissis, as they shulde not haue any cause reasonable to fozbere they: pzouisions foz suche vit to be solde by retaple ayenst this holy tyme of Easter, foz reliefe and succour of his subiectis, in as ample maner as heretofo hath ben accustomed: Is therfoze contented and pleased, that from hensefoth vnto the. xxiiii. day of June next commyng, bo chers and all other, that shall sell flesshe of the kyndes afozesayde by weyghte by retaple, shall and may sell from tyme to tyn vnto the sayde. xxiiii. day of June nexte commynge, euery pounde of beefe good and holsome foz mans bodye, foz an halfepe and one halfe farthynge and no moze: And euery pounde of mutton foz thze farthynges onely and no moze: And euery poun of veale foz an halfepeny and halfe farthynge, and no moze. The sayde acte of pzouision heretofoze had and made foz sellyn flesshe by weight by retaple, oz any thinge therin conteyned, to the contrarie herof not withstondinge.

¶ Pzouyded alwayes, that no bouchers oz other shall kylle any calues to selle by retaplle foz the terme of two yeres ensuin from the first day of Januarye laste, vpon the peynes lymitted in the acte made foz kyllynge of calues, this pzoclamation withstandyng. And his highnes hath ozdeyned, that if any boucher oz other sellyng by retaple, do selle any of the kyndes of talles afozesayde, otherwyse then by weight, oz at any other pzices than is afoze lymptted, oz refuse to selle accozdinge to t pzoclamation: thenne euery boucher, oz other so offendynge shall suffre lose and fozfayte all suche peynes and penalities, a also be ozdered in all thinges as is conteyned and limitted in the acte made foz the pzemisses. This pzoclamation in a wyse not lettynge.

¶ And fu. hermoze the kynges hyghnes straytely chargeth and commaundeth all and euerye the sayde bzeders bzoggers d uers fermours feders and owners of suche cattell, that they and euery of them furnysshe the fayzes & markettes with suche cattall as they haue to selle from tyme to tyme, in as large and ample maner as hath ben accustomed: And to sell they: sayde tell at suche reasonable pzices, as the sayd bouchers oz suche other, as shall retaple the same ayene by weight, may vtter and the same to his louynge subiectes, at suche pzices as are aboue lymptted, as they wyll auoyde his graces hygh dyspleasure, a answere to the same at they: vttermoste perylles.

¶ AND THAT after the sayde. xxiiii. day of June, the sayde bouchers and other sellyng flesshe by retaple, shal from the fozthe sell by weyght by retaple, accozdynge to the pzyces limitted in the sayd act made and pzoupded foz the same, vpon the p nes and penalities conteyned in the sayd acte, without any abstinence oz redzesse to be hadde therof after the sayde. xxiiii. da Wherfoze the kynges hyghnes straytely chargeth and commaundeth all and synguler Maires, Justyces of peace, Shireff aplisses, constables, and other his officers and faythfull subiectes, to whom it shall oz in any maner of wyse may appertay at they and euery of them cause this his pzoclamation to be put in due and effectuall execution accozdynge to the tenour th , as they wyll aunswere to his hyghnes at their vttermoste perys.

GOD SAVE THE KYNGE.

Tho. Berthelet. regius impres
excudebat.
CVM PRIVILEGIO.

FIG. 292. Price Fixing in the Time of King Henry VIII. This extremely rare proclamation, issued by order of King Henry VIII on March 25, 1535, preserved in the Kress Library, fixed the prices of beef, mutton and veal during a period from Easter up to the 28th of June. A translation of the black-letter text follows:

A PROCLAMATION CONCERNING BUTCHERS

25th day of March, the 26th year of the reign of Henry VIII
[i.e., 1535]

For as much as the Kings majesty is credibly advertised and informed, that beefs, muttons, and veals, are likely to be more scarce and dear now against this holy time of Easter, than in other seasons of the year, by reason of the charges of keeping of such cattle with hay and other stover, in the winter: by occasion whereof the butchers and other that shall sell such beefs, muttons and veals by retail by weight, can not buy them of the breeders brokers farmers drovers owners and feeders of such cattle at such reasonable prices in gross, as they may sell the same again by weight by retail at such prices as are limited in the act made for [selling] of flesh by weight, unless it should be to their utter loss and undoing: His Highness therefore willing, that the same butchers, and other selling flesh by retail for the time hereafter limited in this proclamation, should be so conveniently provided for in the premises, as they should not have any cause reasonable to forbear these provisions for such victual to be sold by retail against this holy time of Easter, for relief and succor of his subjects, in as ample manner as heretofore hath been accustomed: Is therefore contented and pleased, that from henceforth unto the 24th day of June next coming, butchers and all other, that shall sell flesh of the kinds aforesaid by weight by retail, shall and may sell from time to time, unto the said 24th day of June next coming, every pound of beef good and wholesome for mans body, for an halfpenny and one half farthing and no more: And every pound of mutton for three farthings only and no more: And every pound of veal for an halfpenny and half farthing, and no more. The said act of provision heretofore had and made for selling flesh by weight by retail, or any thing therein contained, to the contrary hereof not withstanding.

Provided always, that no butchers or other shall kill any calves to sell by retail for the term of two years ensuing, from the first day of January last, upon the pains limited in the act made for killing of calves, this proclamation not withstanding. And his highness hath ordained, that if any butcher or other selling by retail, do sell any of the kinds of victuals aforesaid, otherwise than by weight, or at any other prices than is afore limited, or refuse to sell according to this proclamation: then every butcher, or other so offending shall suffer loss and forfeit all such pains and penalties, and also be ordered in all things as is contained and limited in the act made for the premises. This proclamation in any wise not letting.

And furthermore the kings highness straightly chargeth and commandeth all and every the said breeders brokers drovers farmers feeders and owners of such cattle, that they and every of them furnish the fairs and markets with such fat cattle as they have to sell from time to time, in as large and ample manner as hath been accustomed: And to sell only a few basic necessities, such as wheat, bread, meat, wine, and beer. Legal prices were usually ceiling prices. But they could be minima, below which a buyer could not go, if the rate was set in favor of the seller.

One weakness of the scholastic doctors was that they were interested only in laying down principles and tended to overlook practical difficulties, which, they claimed, did not concern the theologians but were the province of the "politicians." An extreme position was taken by Martin Azpilcueta (1493–1587), better known as Navarrus, who opposed all price regulation because it was unnecessary in times of plenty and ineffective or harmful in times of dearth. Several others, among them Molina, looked upon price regulation with the same disfavor.

Since scholastic doctrine favored competition, it is logical that all forms of price discrimination were condemned. Already in the thirteenth century both Thomas Aquinas and John Duns Scotus formulated the rule that a seller was not allowed to sell dearer because his wares were greatly wanted by a prospective buyer. An even better statement is found in San Bernardino of Siena who, citing the canon *Placuit* mentioned above, underscores the point that price should be the same to all and that no one is allowed to charge strangers more

---

their said cattle at such reasonable prices, as the said butchers or such other, as shall retail the same again by weight, may utter and sell the same to his loving subjects, at such prices as are above limited, as they will avoid his graces high displeasure, and answer to the same at their uttermost perils.

AND THAT after the said 24th day of June, the said butchers and other selling flesh by retail, shall from thence forth sell by weight by retail, according to the prices limited in the said act made and provided for the same, upon the pains and penalties contained in the said act, without any abstinence or redress to be had thereof after the said 24th day. Wherefore the kings highness straightly chargeth and commandeth all and singular Mayors, Justices of peace, Sheriffs, bailiffs, constables, and other his officers and faithful subjects, to whom it shall or in any manner of wise may appertain, that they and every of them cause this his proclamation to be put in due and effectual execution according to the tenor thereof, as they will answer to his highness at their uttermost perils.

GOD SAVE THE KING.

Printed by Thos. Berthelet,
royal printer.

With privilege.

than local customers or to take advantage of a buyer's ignorance, rusticity, or special need. Instead of *Placuit,* certain writers quote a text from the *Digest,* which says that the seller may not exploit a buyer's affection or desire for a particular article, whence the expression *pretium affectionis,* which in scholastic literature designates a discriminatory price. In any case there was no disagreement about the unethical character of price discrimination.

The scholastics, theologians as well as jurists, were also unanimous in regarding monopoly as a deleterious practice, inimical to the commonweal. Monopoly was defined broadly so as to include any pacts or rings formed to keep up or to depress prices above or below the competitive level. . . . In the opinion of the scholastics monopoly was an offense against liberty; it assumed a criminal character because it rested usually on collusion or "conspiracy"—this phrase actually occurs again and again in scholastic treatises. Perhaps the best treatment on the subject is found in the writings of the Belgian Jesuit Leonardus Lessius (1554–1623). He admits that not all monopolies are iniquitous and that a prince, if he has good reasons, may grant exclusive privileges. He must then, however, fix a fair price giving due consideration to all attending circumstances (*spectatio circumstanciis omnibus*), such as cost, risk, and market conditions, presumably by striking a compromise between conflicting criteria, as public utility commissions do today. To my mind there is no doubt that the conspiracy idea of the antitrust laws goes back to scholastic precedents and is rooted in the medieval concept of the just price.

The doctrine of the market price of course applied only to staple products, on which competition, to use David Ricardo's phrase, operated without restraint. The scholastics also discussed the case of luxuries, such as thoroughbred dogs, birds of paradise, rare pictures, rich tapestries, and the like, for which there was no regular market. On this subject the doctors were unable to reach an agreement. Some, as for example Francisco de Vitoria, proclaimed that the seller of such superfluities and frivolities could accept what an informed buyer offered to pay, provided of course that there was no fraud, deceit, or coercion. Others, such as Lessius, contended that the price of such articles should be set by experts (*ex judicio intelligentis mercatoris*). The Blessed Angelo Carletti da Chivasso (died 1495) found it difficult to make a rule but thought that the seller should determine the price honestly after considering such pertinent facts as scarcity, trouble, and risk.

For completeness it should perhaps be added that the Reformation wrought little change and that the Protestant divines, Max Weber notwithstanding, continued to expound the scholastic doctrine on the just price without altering it in the least. I do not see, for example, why the Puritan preacher Richard Baxter (1615–1691) should be denounced as an abbeter of capitalism because he mentions that the just price is the market price in the absence of a rate set by law. The doctrine of the just price was brought to the shores of America by the Puritan ministers. As a sample of their doctrines I shall merely mention the five rules for trading proposed by the Reverend John Cotton (1584–1642). They differ from scholastic doctrine only in one respect: the medieval doctors did not approve of price increases on credit sales, because such a practice involved concealed usury.

A few words need to be said about the practical application of the doctrine of the just price. How was it translated into policy? And was this policy consistent with its theoretical postulates? Perhaps the authorities followed a vacillating course and wavered between the enforcement of competition on the one hand and the protection of monopoly on the other hand. In the Middle Ages the implementation of economic policy rested to a large extent, if not exclusively, with the municipal authorities of cities, towns, and boroughs. This is especially true of the Italian city states and the quasi-independent *Reichsstädte* in Germany. In England and France, however, royal government had not entirely renounced its sovereign rights and often took advantage of economic and social conflicts to assert its authority. Nevertheless, even in these two monarchies the towns were the main policy-making agencies. They followed one policy with respect to foodstuffs that they drew from the countryside and another with regard to the manufactured products that were made within the walls. "Thus," in the words of John M. Clark, "there were laws, of town origin, aiming to enforce competition in the things the townsmen bought, while the guild regulations limited and controlled competition in the things they sold." Although this may be an oversimplification, it contains a great deal of truth. One has to remember, however, that realities involve complications too readily overlooked in making general statements.

With regard to victuals the aim of town policy was very simply to secure abundant supplies as cheaply as possible. For this purpose reliance was placed on the enforcement of competition, and the peasants of the surrounding district were encouraged and, if necessary, compelled to bring their products to the market and to sell them directly to the consumer, thereby eliminating all middlemen, hawkers, or brokers. As Hans van Werveke correctly points out, this provisioning policy (*politique de ravitaillement*) was practiced throughout western Europe from Sicily to England. Everywhere measures were taken against engrossers (*accapareurs*), forestallers (*recoupeurs*), and regraters (*regrattiers*) who tried to accumulate stocks, to prevent supplies from reaching the market, or to form corners in order to drive prices up. Medieval records are full of references to engrossers or forestallers who were caught, dragged into court, and fined or punished with exposure on the pillory. This applies not only to England but to the Continent as well. Those who escaped conviction in the secular courts were still punishable *in foro conscientiae;* according to canon law, monopoly profits were *turpe lucrum,* which, like usury, was subject to restitution. In dealing with the Middle Ages it would be a grievous error to ignore the confessional as a means of enforcement.

Unfortunately, crop failures created a recurrent problem, especially in the case of grain, because bread was the staple food and there were no suitable substitutes. Since the demand for cereals was highly inelastic, prices went up to fantastic heights in case of dearth. Under those circumstances it would have been folly to rely on the automatic operation of competition. In order to avoid bread riots and mass starvation the authorities were forced to resort to regulation, and it is here that difficulties began. The scholastic authors were full of illusions about the omniscience, honesty, and efficiency of public authorities.

The history of price regulation remains to be written, but we know it to be a tale of woe. In the absence of a well-organized system of allocation and rationing, price controls were bound to break down, and it is not surprising that previous to 1800 their administration was often haphazard, vexatious, inefficient, and arbitrary. A crude form of rationing, common all over Europe, was to freeze the price of bread but to vary the size of the loaf with the price of breadstuffs. As the latter increased, the penny or twopenny loaf became smaller and smaller. Price fixing usually made matters worse instead of better and inevitably led to the emergence of a black market and widespread concealment of available stocks. A more successful device was to store supplies in public granaries and to sell them to the poor below market price in time of dearth. The creation of such granaries, unfortunately, did not become a regular policy until the eighteenth century, when it was adopted by the Prussian state. Another expedient was to appropriate public funds for purchases abroad and to sell the imported grain at a loss in the local market. The result was usually to relieve the situation, to lower prevailing prices, and to bring stocks out of hiding. In many instances panicky authorities were only goaded into action by the fear of mob violence and then proceeded to seize stocks and to find scapegoats among minor offenders.

The public authorities, for all their inefficiency, probably achieved some measure of success in avoiding worse troubles. I am convinced that the problem was not one that could have been solved by reliance on the free operation of competition. The theologians of the Spanish school were doubtless overoptimistic in assuming that removal of controls was the best solution in times of critical shortage of essential commodities. As the experience of two world wars has shown, the institution of controls is an unavoidable measure when demand greatly exceeds the available supply at reasonable prices.

The scholastic writers, in their weighty treatises, rarely mention the guilds, but when they do, it is not to praise them for their humanitarian livelihood policy but to blame them for their monopolistic practices. Thus, San Antonino (1389–1459) accuses the clothiers, or *lanaiuoli*, of Florence of paying their workers in truck or in debased coins. In England John Wycliffe (*ca.* 1324–1384) curses the free masons and other craftsmen because they "conspire" together to ask more than a rightful wage and to oppress other men. An equally virulent attack is found in the so-called *Reformation of Emperor Sigismond* (1437); the author of this proposal would abolish all guilds because they abuse their control of town governments to exploit the public.

Monopoly was the essence of the guild system. This statement applies chiefly to the craft guilds, which were associations of small independent masters. They often entered into secret compacts to fix prices at the expense of the consumer. There was, however, another kind of guild—much less common—which was mainly found in the textile industry. Instead of being composed of independent masters it was made up of artificers, such as weavers, dyers, fullers, or finishers, who worked for wages and combined to protect themselves against exploitation by their employers and to obtain better pay. They even went so far as to organize strikes. This second type resembled more closely the modern labor union. It is important to distinguish between these two kinds of guilds. No such distinction was made by the scholastics, who were not favorably disposed toward any alliances, whether of masters or of workers. Molina, for example, condemns them both indiscriminately as detrimental to the commonweal.

In order to avoid confusion it may be desirable to deal first with the ordinary craft guild of independent artisans, such as bakers, butchers, shoemakers, and so forth. It is often asserted that such guilds set prices supposedly enabling their members to earn a decent living. It cannot be denied that they did so in many cases, but it must be stressed that such action was an abuse, unless the rates established by the guilds had received official sanction.

According to scholastic doctrine the fixing of prices was entrusted to the public authorities, but I have not found that this function was delegated to private interests, such as guilds. In this matter practice corresponded to theory. In England at least the law forbade the guilds to set prices "for their singular profit and to the common hurt and damage of the people"; victualers especially were not permitted to form "confederacies" for this purpose. The same rule prevailed in Germany as long as the territorial princes retained some control over the towns. Thus, in Cologne, according to a decision of 1258, the archbishop retained the right to police the market because the guilds depressed prices when they bought and raised prices when they sold. Even in Italy municipal statutes usually restrained the guilds from making any secret agreements to keep prices up or down. The best example is perhaps Florence; although it was a stronghold of the guild system, the ordinances of justice of 1293 and later statutes contained provisions outlawing all "conspiracies," monopolies, leagues, or pacts for the purpose of manipulating prices. Delinquents incurred a heavy fine of £1,000 *di piccioli,* although I know of no instance in which this penalty was ever imposed.

This leniency contrasts sharply with the drastic measures taken in Florence to thwart any attempt by the workers in the woolen and silk industries to form brotherhoods. In both these industries the guild was controlled by the master manufacturers or industrial entrepreneurs. The statutes of these industrial guilds most severely proscribed any conjurations, machinations, or conventicles among the artificers and journeymen subject to the guilds' jurisdiction. In 1345 a wool carder, Ciuto Brandini, actually suffered capital punishment, although his only crime was that he had tried to organize a confraternity among his fellow workers. In the indictment he is described as a man of ill fame and foul language and is accused of forming an illegal "congregation," threatening peace and order, and imperiling the life and property of the citizens. Similar conditions existed in other textile centers, not only in Italy, but also beyond the Alps, even in Toulouse, a minor center. In Flanders, around 1300 still the major cloth-producing region in Europe, the patricians and clothiers who ran the town governments passed the most cruel legislation to cow the workers, to ban suspicious assemblies, and to put down strikes. In Ypres the penalty was blinding and perpetual banishment. In 1280 or 1281 ten strikers were thus disfigured. This inhuman punishment did not prevent an outburst which swept the patricians out of power and caused a long period of unrest. In any case, the evidence is clear. The theory of the just price was applied also to wages and was used or misused to brand workers' associations as intolerable conspiracies, even when they were concealed under the form of religious fraternities.

The general conclusion of this study can be briefly stated. The scholastics were more favorable to freedom or competition than is generally assumed. Their hostility toward monopoly was especially marked. Contrary to a widespread belief they certainly did not rely on the price system to maintain the social hierarchy. As a matter of fact, small masters operating under conditions of competition were not likely to accumulate great wealth. Social status in the Middle Ages depended chiefly on inequality in the distribution of property, mainly land, and the levying of dues (feudal payments or tithes) for the benefit of the ruling classes. There was one exception: in Italy the merchants and bankers outrivaled the feudal nobility.

EVERY VOCATION IS A POST ASSIGNED BY THE LORD

JOHN CALVIN

[John Calvin, *Institutes of the Christian Religion* (1536), trans. by John Allen, Presbyterian Board of Publication, Philadelphia, 1813, vol. I, pp. 649-650.]

John Calvin (1509–1564), the militant Swiss divine and reformer who became the leading Protestant influence in France, was the precursor of Puritanism. He believed in austerity of ritual and of living, and preached the complete freedom of the church from state control.

While the following selection from his *Institutes of the Christian Religion* (1536) says little directly about business, it indirectly sets the foundation for much of our modern attitude toward commercial and industrial life. The man who performs efficiently (in business, as anywhere else) is carrying out God's mission for him; that is Calvin's point.

LASTLY, it is to be remarked that the Lord commands every one of us, in all the actions of life, to regard his vocation. For he knows with what great inquietude the human mind is inflamed, with what desultory levity it is hurried hither and thither, and how insatiable is its ambition to grasp different things at once. Therefore, to prevent universal confusion being produced by our folly and temerity, he has appointed to all their particular duties in different spheres of life. And that no one might rashly transgress the limits prescribed, he has styled such spheres of life *vocations,* or *callings.* Every individual's line of life, therefore, is, as it were, a post assigned him by the Lord, that he may not wander about in uncertainty all his days.

And so necessary is this distinction that in his sight all our actions are estimated according to it, and often very differently from the sentence of human reason and philosophy. There is no exploit esteemed more honorable, even among philosophers, than to deliver our country from tyranny; but the voice of the celestial Judge openly condemns the private man who lays violent hands on a tyrant. It is not my design, however, to stay to enumerate examples. It is sufficient if we know that the principle and foundation of right conduct in every case is the vocation of the Lord, and that he who disregards it will never keep the right way in the duties of his station. He may sometimes, perhaps, achieve something apparently laudable; but however it may appear in the eyes of men, it will be rejected at the throne of God; besides which, there will be no consistency between the various parts of his life.

Our life, therefore, will then be best regulated, when it is directed to this mark; since no one will be impelled by his own temerity to attempt more than is compatible with his calling, because he will know that it is unlawful to transgress the bounds assigned him. He that is in obscurity will lead a private life without discontent, so as not to desert the station in which God has placed him. It will also be no small alleviation of his cares, labors, troubles, and other burdens, when a man knows that in all these things he has God for his guide. The magistrate will execute his office with greater pleasure, the father of a family will confine himself to his duty with more satisfaction, and all, in their respective spheres of life, will bear and surmount the inconveniences, cares, disappointments, and anxieties which befall them, when they shall be persuaded that every individual has his burden laid upon him by God. Hence also will arise peculiar consolation, since there will be no employment so mean and sordid (provided we follow our vocation) as not to appear truly respectable, and be deemed highly important in the sight of God.

HE CANNOT BE A GOOD DRAPER
WHICH IS NOT FIRST A GOOD MAN

WILLIAM SCOTT AND SYLVIA L. THRUPP

[William Scott, *An Essay of Drapery* (1635), reprinted in Publication No. 9, Kress Library of Business and Economics, printed at Harvard University Printing Office, Cambridge, copyright 1953, pp. 1–13 (introduction, abridged), 17–22, 30–39 (abridged).]

For the following words of introduction we are indebted to Sylvia L. Thrupp of the University of Chicago. They come from her introduction to Scott's *An Essay of Drapery* (1635), published from the original by the Baker Library, Harvard Graduate School of Business Administration, in 1953.

William Scott's *Essay of Drapery,* published in 1635, is the first substantial piece of writing known in English that exalts business as a career. It is not a technical book. It prescribes the study of accounting and the acquiring of a very thorough knowledge of one's trade, but does not itself expound any material details. Scott is concerned, rather, to exhibit the life of business as a life of moral and religious discipline. . . .

In a dedicatory preface addressed to "The Worshipfull Mr. George Scott esquire . . . Reverenced Uncle," he describes himself as a "Yong Citizen." As a citizen of London he must have been at least out of his teens, and a member of a guild. "That I have manag'd businesse, may authorize me to write of it," he begins, adding that he has not done so for long. The book, it seems, was written in further proof of his worth: "he who at 20 hath not given some token of his sufficiency, will hardly doe it afterward."

From his subsequent eulogy of the "Complete Citizen" as one who has served a seven years' apprenticeship, and from the evident limitation of his experience to business in drapery, one may infer that he had served his term and had been admitted as a member of one of the important cloth-trading guilds, or companies. The political and legal privileges of citizenship, which were essential to the setting up of any wholesale business in London, could be obtained only after admission into a recognized guild. There were three means of obtaining admission. It was possible simply to buy one's way in, by paying a high fee set by the guild. This was to enter by redemption. A citizen's son, if he wished to enter the same guild as his father, could, on coming of age, claim the privilege known as patrimony, and be admitted free, or for a very low fee. Most men, however, whether they were sons of citizens or not, served an apprenticeship in the guild to which they wished to belong. This involved paying their master a cash premium for their support and instruction. In the great cloth-trading guilds, premiums were at a maximum. Young Scott must, therefore, have had relatives or friends of means to help him make his start.

Whether his life exemplified the success on which his mind was so bent, we do not know. . . .

[According to] Scott, the just or reputable businessman is a free spirit, in harmony with God's design, with his own nature, and with his fellows. There is no conflict save with tendencies to run to extremes, such as excessive greed of gain for its own sake, sloth, and carnal abandon. . . . Our citizen's world is a whole, complete.

In religion, at the time of writing, Scott was a Puritan of that cautious variety that did not believe in venturing outside the shelter of the established church. A reference to "the elect" suggests a Calvinist leaning, as also does his respect for Bishop Jewel, who had been prominent in the earlier Elizabethan church for anti-Romanist preaching and for Calvinistic theology. Scott's piety is immoderate. A man should make prayer and meditation a constant habit, "his soule still panting after Heaven, stealing up thither in the midst of business." He should read his Bible and study divinity, but always checking his interpretation by authority: "so as the Priests' lipps may bee still said to preserve knowledge." This is Anglican piety, equally opposed to Catholicism and to the sects: "Superstition and Schisme are both bad; the one erects an absolute Tyranny in the mindes of men, the other gives way to all loosenesse."

Scott's ideas on the ethical standards that should govern a business-man's life are derived from three different sources, from his observation or experience of what was actually considered good business practice in his time, from his reading in Christian ethics, and from his own strong personal sense of what a man's relation to God should imply. Most of what he has to say about market practices could have been derived from observation. For example, when he says that a man who creates fear of grain shortage in order to raise prices will be considered a harsh and unjust dealer, he is merely reporting a fact. On the other hand, in speaking of contracts, he refers directly and explicitly to Christian ethical doctrine as supplying a guiding principle, the principle that both parties should benefit equally. These, his basic ethical points, are obviously not peculiar to his own time. On these, both a medieval merchant and a modern businessman could agree with the Puritan. . . .

Scott seems to view the economy as static. The object of work is not to increase wealth and welfare, but simply to "maintain" the world. This may help to explain many of his negative attitudes, his lack of any genuine spirit of enterprise. In turn, one way of explaining the static character of his view would be to point out that the philosophical idea of material progress as a fact and as a value, a goal to guide one's aim, was not yet current. It is true that as recently as the probable year of Scott's birth, 1613, Sir Walter Raleigh had finished writing his great history of the world around the opposite idea, the notion that the world was in decay and near its end. Such a belief would certainly not encourage thought on capital accumulation. To the extent that ordinary men depended on the ideas that philosophical writers formulated for them, they may have been hampered in conceiving of new possibilities in business, by lack of a clear notion of progress. This would be most nearly true of periods and areas of trade depression. Practical men in the great ages of expansion in the central Middle Ages, men who found new uses for water power, who rolled the town-building movement eastward in Germany, who saw wealth and population everywhere increasing, could hardly have felt that the economy was static.

Young Scott had been depression-scared at an impressionable period of his life. This circumstance may go far to explain why he leaned so heavily on religious and ethical sources in his thinking about business. He was totally lacking in the modern businessman's confidence that business activity will always in the long run contribute to the increase of wealth and welfare. He felt acutely the need of other justification. . . .

IT IS A HAPPIE THING for a man to goe through his affaires without Injustice, which he cannot doe but by bringing his spirit into liberty, *In omnes ejus actus contemplationem suam mittens,* contemplating upon all his actions: so by due consultation, and discreete action, hee may live justly, pleasingly, profitably. . . .[1]

. . . thus it is in Drapery, the foundation whereof is Honesty: Hee cannot bee a good Draper which is not first a good man, *Conscientiam suam aperiens, semperque tanquam in publico vivens, se magis veritus quam alios,* opening his conscience, living as if he were allwaies in publique, rather fearing himselfe then others; by this hee raiseth himselfe above and beyond all feare, contemning the blowes of Fortune: His wisedome without this will bee eroneous, his policie will bee knavery; yet honesty without wisedome is unprofitable. Wisedome is the beautifull and noble composition of him in his words, his actions, and all his motions, *si oculis ipsis cerneretur, mirabiles amores excitaret sui,* could the eyes see wonderfull love; by her he doth emancipate his spirit from unjust subjection, unto things out of his calling not necessary: though no knowledge is unfruitfull; yet the course of a generall knowledge being too long, the knowledges most pertinent to himselfe, are to bee chosen, which hee shall hardly end before his course bee ended; so much there is to be knowne of his trade and about it; of his commodity, as it is cloth, and as it is his cloth, and so lives by it.

For the first, as no humane action is delivered to the World without many circumstances, so no cloth without them; there is no circumstance in it but is a step mounting the understanding to the true value of it, *Cæca regens filo vestigia:* by laying the circumstances together, the body of an action is fully knowne. In cloth is to bee considered wooll, the matter of it, whether it bee course or fine, which are *qualitates tangibiles,* perceived with the exterior sence, the touch, the eye: but seeing is more conversant about colour, which is *qualitas visibilis.* . . .

Next for quantity. Weight is the quantity of the matter, Measure is of the forme; which two controwling each other, the number of both must decide the difference, the number of Weight shewes the substance, which is too often abused by increasing the number of measure, that both bee according to the Statute is desired by those who would buy good cloth good cheape. These circumstances with others considered, the Judgement which can *bona & mala distinguere,* puts a difference between good and ill, compares all with the price, and so makes bargaines, not inverting the end of Trade, which should bee for the good of both parties. But whither doe I goe? *Diogenes* at a Faire full of those things which curiosity calls necessary, pro-

---

[1] Scott here deplores the tendency to trust in Fortune, "The Goddesse of rashnesse and sloth."

claimes his abundance such, as not to need them; So may these be thought *potiùs subtilia quāutilia,* rather curious than necessary: I therefore spend no more time upon them. Thus he considers his commodity, as Cloth. Now as his Cloth in trading; with which that hee may carry himselfe, *Justly, Pleasingly,* and *Profitably,* I descend to particulars: yet some one trade as well as another shal have interest in my discourse.

THE

COMPLEAT

CITIZEN.

I define him to be a man whom seven yeeres service having made a Citizen: now just, pleasing, profitable wayes, have made compleat.

He shall live justly.

Saint *Augustine* makes mention of a certain Jester; who undertook to tell the people what they all most desired; standing up he said with a loud voice, *vili vultis emere, & carè vendere,* you will buy cheap, and sell deare: to doe so, as it was in his time, so is in ours common, but a common vice, unlesse it consist in certaine limits. That Justice may bee kept in prizing commodities, the common estimation of wise Goodmen is to bee followed: upon some the Law hath pitcht a price, which may bee diminisht, not increased; because that price was set in favour of the buyer, of all which with their sorts, it is impossible for Law to determine the value; yet the Civill Law saith, that's the just price of commodity, *Si tanti vendatur, quanti vendi potest,* if it be sold for so much as it can be sold for; that, is, saith, *Amesius, quanti vendi potest communiter,* for how much it can be sold commonly; the affection or profit of this or that particular man not considered: But where taxation or common estimation cannot, there *seclusâ fraude,* without deceit, the judgement of the Owner must set the price. A Contract must be made according to the equality of the thing; and that must bee measured by the price that is given. For as time is the measure of businesse, so is price of Wares. If the price exceed the worth of the thing, or the thing exceed the price, the equality of justice is taken away; that both agree is the just rule of trading, against which deceit is opposite, *decipere est unum ostentare, & aliud præter opinionem inferre,* to deceive is, to make shew of one thing, and bring in another, beside the opinion of the party; by which more is given for Wares so sold, than they are worth: taking lesse for them then they are worth, a man deceives himselfe: to prevent which, my discourse of his living profitably shal endeavour. His rule was peremptory, that said a wise man will not deceive, neither can hee bee deceived; So was his profession of honesty and wisedome, lowd who chose this Motto, *fallere vel falli res odiosa mihi,* to deceive or be deceived, is hatefull to me. . . .

The unjust wayes of deceit which I would have my Citizen to shun, are many: as Flattery, Dissimulation, Lying, &c. of which in their order.

There bee some whom Gaine will transforme into all shapes; let the Customer looke how hee will, they like a Looking-glasse will have something in them like him. . . .[2]

. . . But it is not alwayes so in the way of Trade. Some Customers will grow dull and displeased, if they bee not often whetted by a Flatterer; downe-right honest speeches discontent them. For this cause, as the Apostle said; *Be angry but sin not:* So I say, Flatter, but sin not, if that be possible. Yet it is my opinion, that amiable lookes and faire speeches will goe farre enough, wee need seeke no by-wayes. Flattery is the corruption of truth, a thing as pernicious, as truth excellent. Among other things this is one the Flatterer is known by, *Non imitatur amicitiam, sed præterit,* hee doth not onely imitate friendship, but goes beyond it.

Dissimulation is a thing more tollerable with a Citizen; it is with him as with one who hath married a wife, whom hee must use well, pretending affection to her, though hee cannot love her: and indeed Divines hold it in some cases lawfull, to pretend one thing and intend an other; as in the case of our Saviour, going with the two Disciples to *Emaus,* he made as if hee would goe further, to stirre up their desire of his presence; what ever hee pretended, hee intended to stay with them that night. If a man pretends a long journey by being booted and spurrd, but intends to returne suddainely, to see what those whom hee puts in trust would doe; if he had gone is no sinne: whereas if he had said hee would have gone such a journey, and not performed it, had been a lye: But woe to them which dissemble to an ill end: these have the voyce of *Iacob,* but the hands of *Esau;* they are smooth in their words, rough in their actions. . . .[3] he that dissembles, must have still a fearefull eye upon himselfe, lest hee be discovered; his mystery is poore, for hee is ere long found out, and then not credited; all he speaks is held Apocryphal. O how excellent a thing is freedome! there is no better life then to live according to a mans nature, resolving alwaies, *Lingua calamum in corde tingere,* to dip the penne of the Tongue in the Incke of the heart, speaking but what hee thinkes; to doe otherwise is impiety, yet to utter all hee thinkes is eminent folly.

---

[2] A discourse is added here to the effect that flattery need not be deceitful.
[3] Further condemnation is added here of lying as cowardly and servile.

Lying is a base vice: therefore said an ancient Philosopher, it is the part of slaves to lie; and the Poet wisely,

Dare to bee true, nothing can neede a lye,
A fault that needes it most, growes two thereby.

Lying is pernicious to humane society: for silence is more sociable than untrue speech; it is the worse because so various: if it had but one visage, there were some remedy for it, a man might take the contrary to it for truth: . . .[4]

. . . Lying then is to be banisht: but this rule must bee observed; as wee may not lie, so we need not speake all the truth. . . .[5]

Now I discover some false lights; their end is to make the Wares seeme better than they are, that the seller may receive for them more than they are worth. But doe they which use them think Light can look upon the Wares, and not he that made the light? Or will they thinke to enjoy the perfect light hereafter which adulterate it here? . . .[6]

. . . It is to bee lamented, that men have too darke shops: but more, that they have too darke mindes; let them remember who it was which said, *There is nothing hid which shall not be made manifest.* A shop may bee too darke, and it may bee too light: therefore it is, or should bee so ordered, that least Commodities bee sold too deare, shops shall not be too darke; and lest they be sold too cheap, they shall not bee too light.

It is ordinary to prey upon the Sellers occasion to use money, or the Buyers to use the commodity: but this should move pitty, not cruelty. *Pliny* saith of the Lyon, *parcit semper subjectis,* and shall man bee so unjust as to doe lesse? or if man, far bee it from a Citizen, who conversing with most men, should have most humanity.

As it is likewise unjust, so it is ordinary, to buy wares for time, yet pay not for them at the time agreed upon. The Indians of *Guiana,* when they promise any thing, will deliver a bundle of sticks equall to the number of dayes or moneths that they appoint, and for themselves will have another bundle of the like number: every day or moneth they take away a sticke; when all is taken away, they know the time of their appointment is come. Thus carefull are they in observing their time, but how negligent are we! It was well said by reverend *Jewell* (the Jewell of his time) *O nos miseros qui Christiani dicimur! hoc tempore gentes agimus sub nomine Christi.* 'Tis our misery, that we are called Christians, yet live like Heathen under that name: but here it were well if wee could *gentes agere* doe like these Heathen:

---

[4] An insistence is made here that one should take a loss rather than act unjustly.

[5] Further elaboration is here made of St. Augustine's casuistry on lying. There is also a long condemnation of swearing.

[6] There is an elaboration here of the theme that one should go in fear of punishment by God.

they which are so backward in payment, are like ill Singers (saith one) they should be sent to the compter, a good Singing school for them to learn to keepe better time in. . . .

The last way of deceit, of which I will discourse, is inhaunsing and raysing the prizes of commodities above measure; which the very light of nature condemneth, as *Cicero* honestly.

If a man in time of dearth bring a Ship laden with Corne, and know that there are a great many more Ships comming within few dayes; if hee dissemble this, taking advantage of the present want, to sell his Corne at too high a rate, he is condemned for hard and unjust dealing: so a consideration of what cases doe lessen and increase the price, doth here offer it selfe.

There is as much injustice in selling commodities too cheap, as too deere: the beginning of the evill may seeme small, but the end is great, saith the French phrase.

A commoditie may bee worth more, being sold to one man then to an other; as Cloth, if by the English private trades it bee sold cheap, without respect of persons; Farreners can in other Countries sell it as cheape as the English Merchant, which must spoyle his trade; the decay of the trade into *Russia* came by this meanes.

Commoditie increaseth its price, victualls or household provision being deare; otherwise those many thousands which live by making, dying, dressing, selling them or the like, must fare the worse.

When the buyers seeke the wares, they or a sort of them being scarce, the common estimation is increased, so the price may be raised.

Commodities sold by retayle, must bee sold dearer then when they are sold otherwaies; the labour and care in selling them thus being the greater: not to doe so, is to undervalew the labour and care of the whole profession.

Lastly, commodities may bee sold dearer for time, then ready money: sale is a perpetuall alienation of the property for a price; but that that price should bee alienated for a time, is not the most ancient nor most true way; it should be payed upon the receipt of the wares, which so payed may by industry bee increased, not payd; thence followes a sensible want of what might have beene gained, which the buyer in conscience ought to recompence; and the seller may take, if the other be not poore, or a looser by the wares thus bought: I have heard and read words against this, but not arguments.

The price is to bee lessened, when a man hath foolishly bought his wares; for it may happen that he may sell them cheaper than hee bought them, and yet doe unjustly: or the estimation of his commodities after his buying them is lesned, then the price is to bee lesned with it.

When one sells a great deale together, here the manner of selling, lessening the number of buyers, but increasing his takings, lessens the price; and giving thus occasion of selling them againe; they must bee sold cheaper, lest many thousands, as it may fall out, suffer detriment by them in buying them at too deare a hand.

When wares seek buyers, *Merces oblatæ vilescunt,* profered wares grow cheap yet this is no sufficient reason of lessening the price, unlesse the things thus sold be little profitable to the buyer; or such as hee would not buy, but because of its cheapenesse, or buying it, rather respecting the seller than himselfe.

When a commodity proves faulty, or is any wayes perisht in the substance or circumstance, the price is to bee lessened. I might insist upon some other petty cases lessening and increasing the price, but let this suffice: all contracts must tend *Ad bonum ipsorum contrahentium,* to the good of them which make them. So shall all injustice bee avoyded. That my Citizen may doe so: I desire that he may never forget, that God is *Totus oculus,* all eye; and so must see all his Actions. . . .[7]

. . . So if it be demanded; who is a flatterer, dissembler, lyer, deceitfull person? I answere, he who thinkes not that God takes notice of his doings. . . .[8]

. . . But lest I bee censured for putting my Sickle into the Divines Harvest, I turne this discourse into a Prayer; beseeching God to guide my Citizen so in the way of Justice, that he may follow him who said, *Ego sum veritas,* I am the truth: let him endeavour to bee with him; truth in words, not knowing how to deceive; Truth in thoughts, not knowing how to be deceived: Truth in deeds, conforming his Actions to the Divine will; is the truth; hee followes him which is the way too, *Et illa via quæ ducit ad vitam,* and that way which leades to life, to a good life here, to a better hereafter.

So I come to my second thing.

He shall live Pleasingly

$$to \begin{cases} Himselfe. \\ Others. \end{cases}$$

But how shall he live so to himselfe? Philosophie professes sorrow to be naturall to all conditions, pleasure is but a stranger. All parts of a man are capeable of sorrow, few of delight. The parts capeable of pleasure, can receive but on or two sorts at once, but all parts can receive the greatest number of griefes. Man hath no continuance in pleasure, it quickly vanisheth: so he tastes of happinesse, but drinkes deepe of misery, according to the French Proverb; evill comes by pounds, but goes away by ounces: the best condition of this life hath

---

[7] Reference is made here to St. Basil as having reminded his disciples that God is the beholder of all thoughts and actions.

[8] London is here cautioned that God might ruin her for wickedness.

bin so undervalewed, that even wise men have said: had man bin worthy to have known what life was before hee received it, he would have bin loath to have accepted it. . . .[9]

. . . And I have observed that the condition of a Citizen is full of trouble, more than ordinary. As no man hath pleasure or profit without the price of some evill, so hee payes a greater price for them, then most men doe. God makes men his Balls; and of these Balls, who is more tost up and downe then the Citizen? He never rests: thus his state seemes miserable. But nothing is so which custome hath brought into nature: every milke soppe can swim in hot bathes; but he is the man that can endure violent Tides, and still swim aloft. *In eam intravimus Civitatem, ubi his legibus vivitur.* Wee have entred into the Citie, where wee must live by these Lawes: to desire Freedome from all trouble is vaine, yet that my Citizens trouble may not bee so great, I now endeavour.

A deepe inspection into his trade is necessary, they take least delight in their businesse, which know least of it.

It is necessary that he be accomplisht with sufficient skill in *Arithmetick,* and a right way of keeping Books; by these a great Trade may be drawne into a little compasse, bring forth that with pleasure, which the nature of most could not doe without excessive paine.

Let him not tye himselfe too strictly to any thing beyond nature; the least wrested and most naturall proceedings are most pleasing. 'Tis worth the time to observe, that wisedome doth a good office to those whose desires shee squareth according to their power, as one may, was the favoured saying of *Socrates,* a Sentence of great Weight. If hee study the liberall Arts, he must doe it superficially; so as not to bee swallowed up of them, lest hee bee brought to say with *Ovid,* I can utter nothing but Art. . . .[10]

. . . Policy when it is naturall, workes free and quietly; it is without noise, whereas the other is of an ambitious clamour. I speak not this against Learning; for a Citizen may use her, so she be not imperious, but assistant: yet let me say, that Discretion, which is above Learning, doth sufficiently inable a man to improve in all his affaires, what ever he is or hath, to the best advantage; the other stands in Comtemplation, this is busie in action. 'Tis neither Wit, Wisdome, Learning, Arts, liberall, or illiberall; but that which shewes how to governe them all conveniently, and every other thing with them, like *Iphicrates,* who was neither *Legionary,* Souldier, nor Archer, nor Targeter: but one who could rule and use all these.

Again, let him not have too great a care of the future: Future things shall in their times become present, therefore the care of the present

---

[9] More is presented here on the Stoic view of pleasure.

[10] Scott expresses here his preference for Sparta over Athens, and his admiration for the early Romans' preference for virtue over learning.

sufficeth. It was said at first, *In the sweat of thy browes thou shalt eate thy bread.* Hee did not say (saith *Augustine*) *In solicitudine & cura,* in solicitude and care; wee may bee carefull, but our care must not have a kinde of sicknesse with it, like that of covetous men. A good Bishop could have preacht against this humour a whole houre together, and have said nothing but beware of Covetousnesse; 'tis a wonder to see what anxious thoughts men have, and all for the world, which is bitter, and yet 'tis loved: but how would it be loved, if it did become sweet? What extreme care doe men take to encrease their wealth? Yet 'tis worth knowing, that this care hath not successe; for Divine Providence will not be bound by our provisions; those have beene most quiet and prosperous in the Actions that have beene ready at hand to apprehend the present occasion with alacrity: a man may bee carefull for to morrow with content; if too carefull, hee misseth it: to bee negligent in our affaires is a defect; to dwell longer in them then will serve for due deliberation, and firme resolution, is excesse; both disturbe our peace. As the Emperour would adde City to City, Country to Country, Nation to Nation: so men strive to joyne hundreds to hundreds, thousands to thousands; thinking that when their proposed estate is acquir'd, they can then rest; O fooles, they may doe so before if they please; for every man is rich, or may be so if his minde hinder not: that man is truely wealthy, which wanting a great estate, wants not a minde which doth not desire it.

All things which we suffer are by our opinion made greater, there are more things which affright, than oppresse us: some things trouble us more than they should, some things before they should, and some things trouble us which should not. It is strange to consider that most of our trouble should arise from most small causes, and that accidents should touch us more than the principall. The Robe of *Cæsar* troubled *Rome* more than his twenty two stabs, and the lesser circumstances move us more many times than the Subjects themselves: in all these wee are all so miserable, as we think our selves; how quietly might we then live, if finding our selves disturb'd, we lie not swelling in our passion, but get up to the top of our reason, and fall into some contrary qualification. So the Dolphins at the beginning of a Tempest, which arising from the bottome of the Sea when it is troubled with hot exhalations and vapours, mount up to the top of the water for refrigeration.

'Tis ordinary for a Citizen to trust, and hee commonly loseth much by it. I thinke there is no Citizen can say hee hath had no losses. *Democritus* promised to resuscitate *Artaxerxes* his dead friend, upon condition that the Inscription of his Tombe might be the names of thirty men that had lived to the twentieth yeere of their age without griefe; they sought thirty, but found none. I might promise the like impossibility upon condition, that I might see the names of thirty Citizens which have traded twenty, nay ten yeers, whose Bookes are without some debts, which they never hope to see discharg'd: but what of that? *Quid miraris bonos viros ut confirmentur, concuti?* Why dost thou wonder that good men are smitten, to bee confirmed? . . .[11]

. . . a man must suffer losses, but let him not be so unwise, as with vexation to debarre himselfe of rest, when even his teares cannot recover a losse, or recall time: make things ill done, better, we may; to make them not to bee at all, requires more than humane strength or finite power. Actions once past may admit a correction, not a nullity; why then should losses trouble a man, or make his heart not his owne? 'Twas well said of one; who hath himselfe, hath lost nothing.

But of all losses, I must not passe over the losse of all. *Versa est in cineres Troja, Troy* is turned into ashes. Suppose my Citizen broken; he hath endeavoured to prosper, but divine providence hath not seconded his care, which is a question; hee hath surely neglected some meanes, hee hath bin an ill husband, and spent too much time and money in vaine: let him have my advice before my comfort: I would have him, though hee leave himselfe worth nothing, to pay every man all their owne; or if he compound for a part, let him resolve to pay all, and endevour to be able.

Heer's his comfort; by suffering he shall overcome, *Romani sedendo vincunt,* the Romanes overcome with sitting still; his soule because his intentions are sincere, is quiet, sits still: And by how much the more quiet, by so much the more stronge. Great aspersions lye heavy upon his name, great sorrow lyes heavy upon his soule; now patience being added to give him, and *Sic vinci est vincere,* so to bee overcome is to conquer. His blessings which hee had before, were of the Lord: how then can hee want, who by patience keepes him that gave them? He that hath taken away, can give more: what wicked *Cain* said of his sinnes, they are greater then can be forgiven, no Christian may say of his losses; they are greater than can be given: God can blesse above losses, so hee blessed *Jobs* latter end, more than his beginning. Perhaps he had not seene fortunes both faces before: now providence sends adversity to make his wisedome greater. . . .[12]

. . . My experience, which is not of much more than seaven yeares standing in the City hath furnisht me with examples of those, who have fallen from a meane estate, and risen to a greater; which are examples not of falling, but of rising, in case thou fallest. He was a wise King that would bee pictured swimming, with this motto, *Lucter, non mergor,* I strive, I am not drowned. And the famous Admirall *Chabotco* would bee symboliz'd by a ball, with this inscription, *Concussus surgo,* being smitten I rise higher.

---

[11] A discourse is given here on the theme that affliction does the Christian good.
[12] The story is added here of how Hannibal claimed that as a general he learned most from adversity.

But above all examples take this: our Saviour calling to *Saul,* said, arise, and stand upon thy feete: as if he had said (saith one), *Ideo te dejeci, ut fortior surgeres,* I have therefore thrown thee down, that thou mightest rise more strong. And this was the voyce of that great Apostle, *Cum infirmor, tunc potens sum,* when I am weakened, I then grow mighty: This I speake that hee may doe his soule good, that hee may by his affliction rise in his Religion, as well as in his estate; men are seldome Religious in prosperity: he therefore, and onely he gets by his breaking, that is after it more humble, more pittifull, more mortified, more given to prayer, and the like duties; doing thus, if he be poore without, he is rich within, *Habet intus quo gaudeat,* he hath that within him, whereof he may rejoyce. Our wealth and gold is Christ, come to him and you shall abound with true riches. He now breaks off his former carelesse way, *Et mutatus mutatum invenit,* and findes God that was angry before, to be now kind. Nothing but his sinning could keepe off Gods blessing, now nothing but a continued serious repentance breakes off sinning; which repentance with the whole course of piety, I advise may not fall short, but reach out as farre as the blessing expected: for that fals not upon the beginning of a spirituall grace, but the latter end; he and onely hee that endures to the end, shall receive the Crowne. Nothing can lay claime to the eternall blessings of God, but perseverance, which is the eternity of man. If thou wouldst then from the losse of temporall blessings, get those which are spirituall, if thou wouldst by *Iacobs* ladder clyme from from the blessings of Earth, which are the foote of it, to the blessings of Heaven, which are the top of it; Remember that upon that ladder were Angells ascending and descending, but none standing still; therefore persevere.

To conclude this; if hee would live Pleasingly, let him live Religiously. I would not have his Bible stand in his Hall so much for ornament, as use: Let him study Divinity, yet so as the Priests lipps may bee still said to preserve knowledge. 'Tis the fault of these times, to make that their and others destruction, which should be their solace, by mistaking Schisme, for true Religion: They would not runne from Religion to superstition, yet they runne from it to prophanenes. Superstition and Schisme, are both bad; the one erects an absolute Tyranny in the mindes of men, the other gives way to all loosenesse. He was a wise Statist that said, he had rather have a man an Atheist, then either of them, because he seldome perturbs states, and is ever most wary: but to our purpose, let his Religion teach him to have his soule still panting after Heaven, stealing up thither in the midst of busines, as if he were there evermore conversant, whence hee lookes for a Saviour. Man is made *De terra & ex terra,* in the earth, and of the earth, *non tamen ad terram, nec propter terram, sed ad Cælum & propter Cælum,* (saith one) but not to the earth, or for the earth; but to Heaven, and for Heaven. He whom no business should put out of our mindes, is in Heaven, *Resurrexit non est hic,* he is risen, hee is not here: Looke for him in the Church, you shall heare of him there: looke for him by invocation, and a conscionable diligence in thy Calling, and the holy Ghost will shew him there: and when thou hast thus found him, hee will take thee up to Heaven, to raigne with him there. Saint *Chrysostom* and *Hierome* wonder at the Eunuch mentioned in the eighth Chapter of the *Acts,* He was a Barbarian distract with many businesses hee read: and though hee did not understand, yet he read, and that in the way in the Chariot: *Si talis in ipso itinere qualis in quiete domi fuisse credendus est,* if hee were thus devoted in his journey; how would hee have beene in quiet at home? if hee a Heathen did thus much upon the way; shall not wee Christians doe much more in our Shops? . . . to minde the affaires of the soule, is the way to prevent distraction, not to further it; as Physicians say of sorrow for sin, it hurts not the heart as worldly sorrow doth: so I may say, it is worldly care, not this care that troubles our peace. So much of his living pleasingly to himselfe.

Hee shall live Pleasingly to others.

Which that hee may performe, he must be assisted by behaviour: without this, his other qualities will not help him. It cannot but bee distastfull to any man, comming into a Shop, when he sees a man stand as if hee were drown'd in flegme and puddle; having no other testimony of his being awake, than that his eyes are open. It is expected that the outward carriage should promise what's within a man.

Except liberality, courtesie is more regarded of men than any vertue: it payes a great deale, yet is never the poorer: it satisfies every man, yet lessens not the Stock: it is a good Character of a good nature, and it hath beene observed that few men have risen to great Fortunes, which have not been courteous. These small ceremonious matters win great commendations, because they are continually in use and note; whereas the occasion of a great vertue commeth but seldome. To use these not at all, is to teach others not to use them, and so to diminish respect: they have in them a certaine well-becomming majestie, if they bee used without pride or affectation. To make no difference in the use of them, to a Lord, and a Ploughman kissing their hands, and bowing as low to a Chamber-maide, as to her Lady, is uncomely. It was well said of one, *Corpus animum tegit & detegit,* the body, the outward carriage of it covers and uncovers the mind, which should bee to some more open, to some more hid. Let my Citizen then use Ceremonies, but not with affectation, neither let him use them too often. He cannot comprehend great matters, that breaketh his minde too much to small observations.

But there is an inward thing, which unlesse it bee added to these, makes them all nothing. A Schoolemaster had in his place of exercise, a Glasse, wherein hee caus'd his Schollers to behold themselves. If they were comely, he would tell them what pitty it was that goodly bodies should bee possest with defective mindes: if they were ill-favoured, he would tell them they should make their bodies faire, with dressing their mindes handsomely.

If the behaviour and countenance bee good; the adorning the minde, doubles the excellency: If ill, it will make it good, when a mans minde performeth what his body promiseth not.

His minde must be stuf't with sufficiency to produce pleasing discourse, wherein he must not bee so lavish as to hinder his observation, and become tedious to him he deales with. To speake all he can at once (as if hee were making his Will) is not the way to please: the best way to doe that, is to know how to be silent; and when he speakes, to let his speech not be accompanied with vehemency: his words should flow from his mouth, so that it might bee said of them, they are *non tam verba quàm mella,* not so much words as Honey. And I would have these words tyed to his Commerce, for therein his Customer will commonly take more delight to heare, than hee to speake. All hee speakes of, that must bee true: However the Dresse be, Truth is constantly the same; it still keepes the same Splendor, that if it met with masculine and true elocution fitted to the matter and circumstances, is praise worthy: but note that it alwaies gives more grace and lustre to the speech, than possibly it can borrow from it. Yet because men are most taken with pleasing words, let them be discreetly chosen, and properly applied: For as speech makes a man more excellent than a Beast, so eloquence will make him more excellent than other men; but to this must bee added a grave naturall action, wherein a man may see the visage, hands, and members of the man to speake with his mouth; and thus per-swading his Customer to the liking of his commodity, hee must put on the same liking himselfe; for putting on the same passion hee would stir up in others, he is most like to prevaile: Yet in as much as hee is to deale with men of divers conditions, let him know that to speake according to the nature of him with whom he commerceth, is the best Rhetorick.

I must needs condemne the using of one phrase to all men, and the mistrusting of every mans sences with, doe you heare Sir, and to tell every man he will make a word; as if he would be thought an augmenter of learning is vaine: but if he meanes to speake his mind, at once I wish him so to doe, for that's the old and the best way. He that sold *Abraham* the field for buriall, askt what he would, and had it; but the custome of our times is contrary, *Et quod consuetum præsumitur esse justum,* and what is usuall is presumed to be just: yet

I desire every man to use as few words as possible hee may; so the
way of making bargaines, may in time be brought to the first and best
state.

I shall not taxe the ordinary phrase, what lacke ye; it being great
policy, for a man to entreat for his own necessities, by asking others
what they want; but the too common use of it sounds harsh. I would
not have a mans throate worne like a high way, let him step a little
out of the common Road: but taking heede of the other extreame, he
must not become a wilfull maker of complements, and so a tyran-
nous torment to his customer, who will count him for a man of a
troublesome spirit, if he finds him infected with impertinent ceremonies.

To his superiour, his words must carry much humility in them; to
his equalls familiarity, which because he shall be sure of from them,
must bee mingled with a little state.

To his inferiours familiarity too, but not too much of it, lest hee
breed contempt; yet his words may carry a great deale, for with
inferiours he shall be sure of reverence. To conclude this, that my
Citizen may deale pleasingly with all men; I would have him be a
good Linguist, getting so many Languages, and those so well, that if it
were possible, every man he deales with, should thinke him his
Countrey-man. These observations are necessary to his profit; for he
shall hardly get by that man, whom he cannot please.

So I come to my third part.

He shall live Profitably.

to $\begin{cases} \textit{Himselfe.} \\ \textit{Others.} \end{cases}$

To Himselfe.

It cannot be denied but outward accidents conduce much to a mans
Fortune, as death of others, occasion fitting vertues; but most commonly the folly and fall of one man, is the fortune of an other: no man
prospers so sodainely, as by others errours: therefore *Dæmades* the
Athenian needed not to have condemned a man of the City for selling
necessaries, belonging to burialls, saying, his great profit could not
come unto him without the death of many; for what man almost
profiteth, but by the losse of others? Was not Romes rising by the
ruine of her neighbour Cities? doe not most Traders thrive by the
licentiousnesse of youth? the Husband man by the dearth of Corne:
the Architect by the ruine of houses, the Lawyer by contentions betweene men, the Physitians by others sicknesses? this is not contrary
to the generall policy of nature; for Physitians hold, that the birth and
augmentation of every thing, is the alteration & corruption of another;

God takes from one, and gives to another; but let no man desire it; for the Commandment is, thou shalt not covet: there are then and must be externall causes of a mans rising.

But there is some hidden vertue, which must beare a great stroake in the busines. *Salomon* saith, he that considereth the wind, shall not sow; and he that looketh to the cloudes shall not reape: whereupon sayth one; a wise man will make more opportunities than he finds.

Is the maine thing which raiseth a mans estate without him, or within him? *Quæritur.*

Livy tells us of *Cato senior,* that he was so well accomplisht in minde and body; that in what place soever he had bin borne, he could have made himselfe a fortune. There are than open vertues which bring forth praise; but hidden and secret ones which bring forth fortune.

Certaine deliveryes of a mans selfe, which have no name; like the milkie way in the skie, which is a meeting of many small starres, not seene asunder, but giving light together, for there are a number of scarse discerned vertues, which make men fortunate.

For that which is without a man, instead of providence; let me call it Divine providence: it can make him fortunate, which is not wise; and him that is wise to be miserable: sometimes simple men bring to a happy end great matters, both publique and private; and againe sometimes the best counsells, have the worst issues: the same counsell doth happily succeed to one, unhappily to another; in the same case, with the same man many things went luckely yesterday, unluckely to day: so that wee cannot judge of mens sufficiency by event. One wondering why ill successe should follow upon the mature deliberation of wise men, was answered thus; they were Masters of their deliberation, not of the sucesse of their affaires. *Timotheus* the Athenian, when he had in the account, he gave to the State, often interlaced this speech; and in this fortune had no part: it was noted of him, that he never prospered afterwards. Divine providence must have it's due, there is no rising without it: laying both these together, the question will be resolved thus; a mans industry with Gods blessing upon it, is that which makes him fortunate; both have force in the businesse; it is clerely false, that one doth all, and the other nothing. The advice of wisedome then, is not wholly to settle our selves to one, for they mutually attend each other. . . .

My Citizen must not be ambitious, if he would be honour'd, he must be vertuous as well as rich; why he must endeavour for riches, hath beene shewed. So I now proceed; as I would have him labour, so let not his labour be overlong; there is a difference betweene providing for a mans selfe and family, and doing nothing else: the affaires of the soule, the refreshing of the body must be lookt after, beside the publique good hath some interest in every mans time.

The labours of lesse then the third part of the World, maintaine all the World: how many live idlely? almost all women, which are halfe of the number; or if women be imploy'd, in their stead men be idle; put to those candid men, and great men; then adde the last and worst sort, the great number of beggers, and you shall see that few labour, and of those, few be well imployed. If the labour of lesse then the third part maintaynes the World, lesse then the third part of my Citizens time, one day with another, will be sufficient for him; unlesse his private affaires be extraordinary, or he be imployed in the publique.

But before I speake any thing of his getting by his endeavour; let me say something of his spending. I would have him think it more honourable to stoope to petty savings, then to base gettings; let him imitate the thriftie King of *France,* who thought it no discredit to tye a knot in a broken poynt, and reweare it.

Let him not haunt Taverns too much which is the Epidemicall fault of the Citie; I know it is not company, but want of discretion in the choyce and use of it, which overthrowes a man; but besides needlesse expenses; how can that man be fit for busines, who makes his body a continuall quagmire? The refined wits of the separation, love brotherhood, not fellowship: we may with the Apostle love brotherly fellowship, so making use of both, yet drink as they did in the Primitive times, thinking *Deum esse per noctem memorandum,* that God is to be remembered in the night, as well as in the day.

And what shall I say of superfluous dyet? *In mea patria venter est Deus* (saith one) in my Countrey the belly is the God; and is it not so in ours? What infinite summes of money are sacrificed to it, in procuring the Earth, the Ayre, the Sea, to centre at one Table, making Table-clothes like *Peters* sheets, including creatures, cleane, and uncleane? Our Fathers were they alive now, surely they could not tell the names of our needlesse variety of dishes, without the helpe of a Kitching Dictionary; they would wonder that Art should keepe Schoole in the Kitchen, and that the palats of these times should be so ingenious. . . .

Let him not keepe inferiours so distant, that he cannot afterwards imploy them at his need: It was the wisedome of a French King, to doe any thing to win that man to him, which might benefit or hurt him; let him be liberall in his words, so he bestows favours which cost him nothing; let him be free in his deeds, for a benefit is the Father of a benefit. It was observed of *Sejanus,* that he could not have bin advanced, without an infinite number of men obliged by his favours; yet here let his discretion direct him, for small benefits are easily forgotten; great ordinarily surcharge: some ungratefull ones neglect them, and some would not there should be any, to whom they may account themselves as debtors, wishing nothing more than the death of him that hath done them good.

In conversing with equalls, let him professe himselfe to be lesse than they; let him be courteous and affable to them; for they that are so, will find their enemies to bee greater friends to them, then naturall brothers will be to men highminded.

If he deale with superiours, let him make what use he can of them, but not trust in them; among all mortall things, there is nothing more fading then that power which hath not support from it selfe; it is common for that man to be unfortunat, which depends upon another. Let him indevour by good courses to winne speedily the opinion of all honest men, which much imports to the shortning that way, which guides to an eminent esteeme: so let him strive to be in his rising, assisted by many; other wise, he will find himselfe opprest with age, before hee be rich, or well knowne.

Thus let him be diligent in the Quest of riches, and credit; but not over-violent and long; he knowes not how to enjoy, which knowes not how to make an end of having: therefore let him be content with what he may have, for aboundance is not the end of evils, but the muta-tion. If doing these things, hee misse of wealth & esteeme, let him not misse of vertue; for though every fortune faile him, it is no meane for-tune to be vertuous.

There is *Sancta avaritia,* a holy covetousnesse, let him never be satisfied with doing good to his better part; I would have him thinke, that by every man with whom he shall trade, he may benefit his mind something. If those which trade with most men did so, wee might wonder more at their wisedome, than we doe now at their wealth.

Thus my Compleat Citizen shall live in his calling; that's a mans proper calling, for which God hath fitted him with ability. Secondly, it is his calling, if he came to it by the ordinary way, of the place wherein he lives: in stead of divers sorts of men which I might here taxe, I will instance but one.

Many Petitions have bin put up to the high Court of Parliament, for the suppressing of those brokers, which deale in cloth, and other commodities; the reason of which alleadg'd, I know not, but imagine this.

They wrong the whole Republique, wanting sufficiency of skill, to buy and order the commodity: hee that buyes it of them, payes too deare for it; or if hee buyes it cheape, it is too bad for his use.

Not knowing how to order their trade, they cannot hold out long so, breaking they hurt the seller too; for I have observed that all, (or most) suddainely breake, which meddle in those businesses, in which they have no skill: the reason of these two inconveniences, is their not comming into what they professe, by the way of the City, a seven yeeres Apprentiship, having beene most of them before Taylors, Tapsters, or the like which is the cause of a third evill.

Many of them comming in, and not by the ordinary way, raise the number of Traders to such a multitude, that in the end (without redresse) they will undoe themselves and others, for there will bee more of them, then our people or strangers wee deale withall shall have occasion to imploy.

Thus I have shewed how my Citizen shall live profitably to himselfe in his way: but himselfe is too poore an end for an honest mans actions: let him not be right earth, which onely stands fast upon its one Centre, whereas all things which have affinity with the Heavens, move upon the Centre of another, which they benefit therefore.

Hee shall live Profitably to others.

First, to his Wife. We are taught by the light of nature, that *In Familia, prima cura Vxoris habenda sit,* in a Family, the first and chiefe care should be of the Wife; shee is a great Officer in the little Common-wealth the House; she is I know an impediment to great enterprizes: the best workes of merit have proceeded from the unmarried, which have sought eternity in memory, not in posterity: and in regard of liberty, the unmarried man is most happy. Some have said wittily, and in my opinion devoutly: marriage fills the earth, and virginity Heaven: but others have better said, how should Heaven be full, if the Earth were empty? or how should the earth but bee empty without marriage? which the best Common-wealths have so esteemed, that they have freed him from taxation and Offices, that had many Children, but punisht him for an unprofitable member that lived long single.

It is commendable for a Citizen to marry: but since his negligence may bee his Wifes undoing, let him live so profitably to her, as by his discretion to direct her.

The ancient Heathen useed to place *Mercury* by *Venus,* to shew what need the affections of marriage have of the rule of Reason and wisedome to order them. God cast *Adam* into a heavy sleepe, whilest he made him a Wife of one of his Ribs: upon which one moralizeth very well thus: the affections ought to sleepe about this worke, and reason to wake: as in the choice of a wife, so in the governing of her when shee is chosen.

As he married, or should have done, respecting his posterity, and the Common-wealth: so now he must not let her spend too much, lest his posterity rue it, or he be disabled to doe good to others.

Among many faults of Shee-Citizens, their pride stands as a *Saul,* higher by the head and shoulders than the rest; not that it is greater, or more common than their secret sins, but more seene; and so with lesse danger I may speake against it. Doe any of them beare the minde of *Philons* wife, who being demanded why she alone went so plainely apparelled, made answer, that her Husbands vertues were ornament sufficient for her.

For redresse of their pride, let Husbands shew them good examples by going plainely themselves: so they, if they have any goodnesse in them, will bee ashamed to doe otherwise; if this will not doe, let them be restrain'd.

Let not a woman rule, it is the counsell of the Apostle, *Let wives be subject to their husbands,* he considered that the woman rul'd, nay over-ruled so ill at first, as that it were pitty shee should bee permitted to rule againe. Let the uxorious man, who will let his wife doe any thing, rather than displease her, harken to St. *Hierom;* a wise man must love his wife with judgement, not with blinde affection.

As hee may not dote on his wife, so let him not bee bitter towards her: opprobrious termes and dealings have made women doe that which otherwise they would never have done. *Clytemnestra* being injured by her Husband, fell into adultery, and consequently slew him. . . . Let him beare with her infirmities, remembering that she is the weaker vessell: let him practice lenity, not severity; clemency, not tyranny; otherwise a good womans patience may bee turned to fury: if she doe not performe such businesse as hee puts upon her, with that wisedome he expects, let him beare with her; he was a wise man that expected no more wit from a woman, then to know her Husbands bed from a strangers. If he perceive her angry, let him beare with her infirmitie in that also, and not bee angry, at the same time, for a house divided cannot stand. *Socrates* was the more able to converse quietly with perverse persons abroad, hearing with patience dayly the scolding of his Zantippe at home.

Let him bee willing and endeavour to be able to instruct her; it is not onely necessary that hee walke with his Wife as a man of love, but before her, as a man of understanding: It is monstrous to see the head stand where the feet should be; and a double pitty, when a *Nabal* and *Abigail* are matcht together; but if thou hast a Wife whose wisedome needs none of thy instruction, thank God for her; *houses and riches are the Inheritance of the Fathers, but a prudent Wife is of the Lord.* . . .

In the next place, he shall live profitably to the poore.

Art thou a great man, and wouldst make thy greatnes known? make it known by thy gifts. *Marcus Antonius* said of the Romane greatnes, that it was not so much discern'd by what it tooke, as what it gave: if occasions of doing good be not offered, seeke for them; It was *St. Augustines* advice, *Emamus occasiones,* let us buy occasions of doing good; mercifull workes are, *Pro sacrificiis, imo præ sacrificiis,* accepted of God as sacrifice; yea more than sacrifice. *Anthony* Prince of *Salern* a liberall man, being askt what he would leave himselfe, answered, *Quod dedi,* that which I have given; but avaritious men thinke they lose what they give. When they beg in *Italy,* they use this phrase, *Fate ben per voi,* doe good for your selves, *Fæneratur Domino qui miseretur pauperis,* he that giveth to the poore, lendeth to the Lord. *Qui prohibet to esse fæneratorem, jubet te esse fæneratorem,* so he that forbids thee to be an usurer, doth command thee to be so; To conclude this, let all covetous wretches consider *Dives, desideravit guttam qui non dedit micam,* he that denyed a crumme of bread in his life, was denyed a drop of water in hell: alas what are 10000. Rivers, or that whole Sea of water to that infinit world of fire? yet *Dives,* unhappy *Dives,* who wasted in his life so many tuns of wine, cannot now procure water enough, a pot of water, a drop of water to coole the tip of his scorched tongue. In the last place, let him live profitably to the whole Republique. An Ant is a wise creature for it selfe, but a shrewd thing in an Orchard or Garden; and certainly men that are great lovers of themselves, wast the Publique. My Citizen must then with reason divide betweene selfe-love and society; so walking profitably to himselfe, as hee hinder not the good of the Commonwealth, but further it. . . .

INSTRUCTIONS TO THE
JESUIT BROTHERS
WHO MANAGE HACIENDAS

DONALD B. CAMPBELL

[Donald B. Campbell, "Books for Businessmen," *Mexican American Review,* April 1961, pp. 38–39.]

Here Donald B. Campbell, Executive Director of the Mexican Institute of Business Administration, draws from a fascinating little book, *Instructions to the Jesuit Brothers who Manage Haciendas* (*Instrucciones a los Hermanos Jesuitas Administradores de Haciendas*). The book was written by an unknown hand (or hands) sometime in the 18th century, was seized along with other documents by the vice-regal government soon after the expulsion of the Jesuits from New Spain in 1767, and lay unnoticed in the National Archives of Mexico for nearly two centuries. (The quotations from the original have been translated by Mr. Campbell.)

The book is of interest here, not only because it affords glimpses of how a large estate was managed in colonial times in Mexico, but also because it provides a little picture of the Church itself engaged in business and meeting operating problems—the other side of the coin from the effect of religion on business.

As the Spanish priest Baltasar Gracián said in 1647, in his manual of advice for prospective sages and saints (*Oráculo manual y arte de prudencia*), even in such unworldly roles it is necessary to "be a bit of a businessman." *

. . . Such matters as bookkeeping, stores keeping, maintenance, daily routines, and the like, are treated with great clarity and in exhaustive detail. In fact it would seem that no detail is overlooked, and one gets the impression that few of the shrewd and canny Jesuit administrators ever had the wool pulled over their eyes: "In order that there be no shortage of plowshares, let [the Administrator] have if possible a competent blacksmith on the premises; and if not, let him make arrangements with a blacksmith in some neighboring town; and in order not to be cheated, let him inquire of the neighbors what is usually paid for such work, and what shrinkage takes place when an iron is on the forge, and therefore let him always weigh the iron and steel before handing it over to the blacksmith, and then let him weigh it when the work is delivered."

The book begins with instructions on how the personal life of the administrator is to be ordered, then proceeds to what we might term in modern parlance "the objectives of the enterprise": "If the Brothers Administrators wish God to bestow his blessings upon the fields and crops, they should look with greater care to the cultivation of souls and the moral training of their laborers and servants than to the cultivation of the fields." But neither is it contemplated that the business shall be conducted at a loss: "for God has promised abundant harvests of temporal fruits to those who keep his Holy Law."

Though much good advice is given on tilling, sowing, and harvesting, the subject of personnel and manpower management is likewise given careful attention: "According to the quality of the laborers and the instruction they are given, so will be the results of the work in the fields and the fruits of the soil: therefore let the Administrators find laborers who will be good, faithful, practical, and intelligent workers."

But we find the Brothers' personnel practices very much on the paternalistic side; paternalism is, in fact, extolled in the highest terms; "Let them remember, then, that they are the fathers of their families, and that they have the same close obligations that all fathers of families have toward their domestic servants. . . .

"Let them take care that all the laborers and household servants . . . go to Mass on Sundays and feast days at the accustomed time.

---

* The actual injunction was "*Tener unpunto de negociante.*"

. . . They shall have a list of names of all the Indians of the hacienda
with their wives and children; when Mass is over, they shall go to
the door of the chapel . . . and as they call out the names . . . the
Indians shall come out and respond: *'Ave María Santísima.'* Then
they shall mark on the list those who have been absent, and on the
following Sunday, if these are unable to give a rational excuse, they
shall instruct the assistant to the parish priest to apply six or eight
lashes. The same shall be done with the slaves, if there be any."

Not altogether a pretty picture, we gather. Yet we feel that these
priestly administrators of a bygone day tried always to act justly
as well as severely, and, from what we can gather from other sources,
labor conditions on the Jesuit-run haciendas were probably somewhat
better than on the majority of the neighboring estates under lay
management. . . .

A SEVENTEENTH-CENTURY
MERCHANT WHO STILL BELIEVED
IN PROFIT

JOHN WINTHROP AND ROBERT KEAYNE

["Excerpts From the Will of Keayne, 1653," in N. S. B. Gras and Henrietta M.
Larson, *Casebook in American Business History,* F. S. Crofts & Co., New York,
1939, pp. 55–60. The will is printed (in modernized form) in *A Report of the
Record Commissioners of the City of Boston,* document 150–1886; pp. 27,
30–32, 35 (abridged).]

In 1639, when trade and commerce were just gaining a foothold in the
New World, a Boston merchant, Robert Keayne, was "tried" by his
church for charging too large a profit. In a sense, this intervention in the
form of religion was not new, as the preceding selections have clearly
shown. But here the religious body taking action was the whole group
of his peers, and they were actually considering expelling him from
the church.

There follows first the report of John Winthrop, three-time governor
of Massachusetts over the period 1629 through 1649, which sums up
the arguments pro and con of Keayne's conduct, and reveals the
decision that the church took. Then there is an excerpt from Keayne's
will, wherein he tells how *he* felt about it.

Entirely apart from the question of whether Keayne went too far or
not, we should keep in mind that he was running counter to a long-held
concept of profit in trade as being static and somehow related to the
intrinsic worth of the goods rather than to the strength of the demand.

Mo. 9.) At a general court holden at Boston [1639], great complaint was made of the oppression used in the country in sale of foreign commodities; and Mr. Robert Keayne, who kept a shop in Boston, was notoriously above others observed and complained of; and, being convented, he was charged with many particulars; in some, for taking above sixpence in the shilling profit; in some above eightpence; and, in some small things, above two for one; and being hereof convict (as appears by the records) he was fined £200, which came thus to pass: The deputies considered, apart, of his fine, and set it at £200; the magistrates agreed but to £100. So, the court being divided, at length it was agreed that his fine should be £200, but he should pay but £100, and the other should be respited to the further consideration of the next general court. By this means the magistrates and deputies were brought up to an accord, which otherwise had not been likely, and so much trouble might have grown, and the offender escaped censure. For the cry of the country was so great against oppression, and some of the elders and magistrates had declared such detestation of the corrupt practice of this man (which was the more observable because he was wealthy and sold dearer than most other tradesmen, and for that he was of ill report for the like covetous practice in England, that incensed the deputies very much against him).

And [since] the course was very evil, especial circumstances considered: 1. He being an ancient professor of the gospel: 2. A man of eminent parts: 3. Wealthy, and having but one child: 4. Having come over for conscience' sake, and for the advancement of the gospel here: 5. Having been formerly dealt with and admonished, both by private friends and also by some of the magistrates and elders, and having promised reformation; being a member of a church and commonwealth now in their infancy, and under the curious observation of all churches and civil states in the world. These added much aggravation to his sin in the judgment of all men of understanding.

Yet most of the magistrates (though they discerned of the offense clothed with all these circumstances) would have been more moderate in their censure: 1. Because there was no law in force to limit or direct men in point of profit in their trade. 2. Because it is the common practice, in all countries, for men to make use of advantages for raising the prices of their commodities. 3. Because (though he were chiefly aimed at, yet) he was not alone in his fault. 4. Because all men through the country, in sale of cattle, corn, labor, &c., were guilty of the like excess in prices. 5. Because a certain rule could not be found out for an equal rate between buyer and seller, though much labor had been bestowed in it, and divers laws had been made, which, upon experience, were repealed, as being neither safe nor equal.

Lastly, and especially, because the law of God appoints no other punishment but double restitution; and, in some cases, as where the offender freely confesseth, and brings his offering, only half added to
the principal. After the court had censured him, the church of Boston
called him also in question, where (as before he had done in the
court) he did, with tears, acknowledge and bewail his covetous and
corrupt heart, yet making some excuse for many of the particulars,
which were charged upon him, as partly by pretense of ignorance of
the true price of some wares, and chiefly by being misled by some
false principles, as, 1. That, if a man lost in one commodity, he might
help himself in the price of another. 2. That if, through want of skill
or other occasion, his commodity cost him more than the price of the
market in England, he might then sell it for more than the price of the
market in New England, &c. These things gave occasion to Mr. Cotton,
in his publick exercise the next lecture day, to lay open the error of
such false principles, and to give some rules of direction in the case.

Some false principles were these:

1. That a man might sell as dear as he can, and buy as cheap as he
can.

2. If a man lose by casualty of sea, &c., in some of his commodities,
he may raise the price of the rest.

3. That he may sell as he bought, though he paid too dear, &c.,
and though the commodity be fallen, &c.

4. That, as a man may take the advantage of his own skill or ability, so he may of another's ignorance or necessity.

5. Where one gives time for payment, he is to take like recompense of one as of another.

The rules for trading were these:

1. A man may not sell above the current price, i.e., such a price
as is usual in the time and place, and as another (who knows the worth
of the commodity) would give for it, if he had occasion to use it; as
that is called current money, which every man will take, &c.

2. When a man loseth in his commodity for want of skill, &c., he
must look at it as his own fault or cross, and therefore must not lay
it upon another.

3. Where a man loseth by casualty of sea, or, &c., it is a loss cast
upon himself by Providence, and he may not ease himself of it by
casting it upon another; for so a man should seem to provide against
all providences, &c., that he should never lose; but where there is a
scarcity of the commodity, there men may raise their price; for now
it is a hand of God upon the commodity, and not the person.

4. A man may not ask any more for his commodity than his selling
price, as Ephron to Abraham, the land is worth thus much.

The cause being debated by the church, some were earnest to have
him excommunicated; but the most thought an admonition would

be sufficient. Mr. Cotton opened the causes, which required excommunication, out of that in 1 Corinthians 5:11. The point now in question was whether these actions did declare him to be such a covetous person, &c. Upon which he showed that it is neither the habit of covetousness (which is in every man in some degree), nor simply the act, that declares a man to be such, but when it appears, that a man sins against his conscience, or the very light of nature, and when it appears in a man's whole conversation. But Mr. Keayne did not appear to be such, but rather upon an error in his judgment, being led by false principles; and, beside, he is otherwise liberal, as in his hospitality, and in church communion, &c. So, in the end, the church consented to an admonition.

[But apparently Keayne never changed his belief in the idea of charging as much as people would pay. Here is how he unburdened himself in his will in 1653, fourteen years and many frustrations later.]

But the truth is that [I have received] unkindness and ill requital of my former love, cost, and pains, both in Old England and here, which I have taken to promote the good of the place, being answered by divers [persons] here with unchristian, uncharitable, and unjust reproaches and slanders since I came hither (as if men had the liberty of their tongues to reproach any that were not beneficial to them), together with that deep and sharp censure that was laid upon me in the country and carried on with so much bitterness and indignation of some (contrary both to law or any foregoing precedent, if I mistake not, and I am sure contrary or beyond the quality and desert of the complaints that came against me, which indeed were rather shadows of offense), [more] out of a desire of revenge made great by the aggravations of some to make them heinous and odious than that they were so indeed (and this not in my judgment only, which may be looked at as partial, but in the judgments of hundreds that have expressed themselves, both then and especially since).

And yet by some it was carried on with such violence and pretended zeal as if they had had some of the greatest sins in the world to censure, [and] that had it been in their power or could they have carried it, they would not have corrected or reformed but utterly have ruined myself and all that I had (as if no punishment had been sufficient to expiate my offense) for selling a good bridle for 2s. [than which] now worse are sold without offense for 3s., and [for selling] sixpenny nails for 7d., and eightpenny nails for 10d. per hundredweight, which since and to this day are frequently sold by many for a great deal more, and so in all other things proportionably, as selling gold buttons for 2s. 9d. a dozen that cost above

two in London and yet were never paid for by them that complained.
These were the great matters in which I had offended, when
myself have often seen and heard offenses, complaints, and crimes
of a high nature, against God and men, such as filthy uncleanness,
fornications, drunkenness, fearful oaths, quarreling, mutinies, Sab-
bath breakings, thefts, forgeries, and suchlike, which have passed
with fines or censures so small or easy as have not been worth
the naming or regarding, which I cannot think upon but with sad
thoughts of [the] inequality of such proceedings, which have been
the very cause of tying up my heart and hands from doing such
general and public good acts as in my heart I both desired and
intended. . . .

I did not then, nor dare not now, go about to justify all my actions.
I know God is righteous and does all upon just grounds, though
men may mistake in their grounds and proceedings. Councils have
erred and courts may err, and a faction may be too hard and
outvote the better or more discerning part. I know the errors of
my life; the failings in my trade and otherwise have been many.
Therefore, from God it was most just; though it had been much
more severe I dare not so open my mouth against it, nor never did,
as I remember, but justify Him. Yet I dare not say, nor did I ever
think (so far as I can call to mind), that the censure was just and
righteous from men. Was the price of a bridle, not for taking but
only asking 2s. for it which cost here 20d., such a heinous sin, [such
bridles] which have since been commonly sold and are still for 2s. 6d.
and 3s. or more, though worse in kind?

Was the selling of two or three dozen of great gold buttons for
2s. 10d. per dozen, that cost 2s. 2d. ready money in London and
bought at the best hand, such a heinous sin (as I showed to many
by my invoice, though I could not at that instant find it when the
court desired to see it, and since was confirmed by special testimony
from London, and yet the buttons not paid for when the complaint
was made, nor, I think, not yet)? Neither did the complaint come
from him that bought and owed [for] them, nor with his knowledge
or consent, as he has since affirmed, but merely from the spleen
and envy of another, whom it did nothing concern. Was this so
great an offense? Indeed, that it might be made so, some out of
their ignorance would needs say that they were copper and not
worth 9d. per dozen; but these were weak grounds to pass heavy
censure upon.

Was the selling of sixpenny nails for 8d. per pound and eightpenny nails for 10d. per pound such a crying and oppressive sin?
Though as I remember it was above two years before he that bought
them paid me for them; and [they were] not paid for, if I forget
not, when he made that quarreling exception and unrighteous

complaint in the court against me (he then being of the court himself), as if I had altered and corrupted my book in adding more to the price than I had set down for them at first delivery. Which if I had set down 8d. for that after two years' forbearance, which I would have sold for 7d. if he had paid me presently, I think it had been a more honest act in me than it was in him that promised, or at least pretended, to pay me presently, that he might get them at a lower price than a man could well live upon, and when he had got my goods into his hands to keep me two or three years without my money, and though all that while there was no fault found at the prices but when he could for shame keep the money no longer, yet he will requite it with a censure in the court.

For my own part, as I did ever think it an ungodly act in him, so I do think in my conscience that it had been more just in the court to have censured him than me for this thing though this was the chief crime alleged and most powerfully carried against me and, [though] other things [were] drawn in to make this the more probable and to help to make up a censure, [such] as some farthing skeins of thread, etc.

But the truth of the thing was this: This man sent unto me for two or three thousand of sixpenny nails. I sent to him a bag full of that sort just as they came to me from Mr. Ffoot's of London, never opened nor altered by me. These I entered into my book at 8d. per pound, thinking he would have paid me in a very short time. It fell out that these nails proved somewhat too little for his work. He sent them again and desired me to let him have bigger [nails] for them. I took them and sent him a bag of eightpenny nails of the same quantity at 10d. a pound. Now, because I was loath to alter my book and to make a new charge, I only altered the figures in my book and made the figure of 6 a figure of eight for eightpenny nails, and the figure of 8 that before stood for 8d. a pound, I made 10d. Now, though he knew of the change of these sixpenny nails for 8d., which I had quite forgot through my many other occasions and the length of time that they had stood in the book unpaid, yet this he concealed from me and from the court also. But to make the matter more odious, he challenged me and my book of falsehood, supposing that because he had kept me so long from my money, therefore I had made the price higher by altering the figures than at first I had charged them down and that I required 10d. per pound for sixpenny nails. And so [he] carried it in the court, who was the more easily believed because he was a magistrate and of esteem therein (though it was a most unjust and untrue charge, and only from his own imagination) till I cleared it by good testimony from an honest man in his own town.

. . . [This was the man] whom he sent for the first nails and

did so bring them back and received the bigger nails for them, who
came to me of his own accord and told me he heard there was a
difference between such a man and I which he said he could clear.
And [he] related the matter fully to me, which I was very glad to
hear, which brought all things to my mind and what was the ground
of altering the figures in the book, which before I had forgot, though
I saw it was done with my own hand. And this was the very truth
of the thing.

I presently acquainted our honored governor, Mr. John Winthrop,
and some others, who were very glad that the truth of that reproach
was so unexpectedly discovered and cleared. And many, if not most
of the court, was satisfied with it and saw the thing to be very
plain in my debt book. But the party, himself, would not be satisfied but [that] they were sixpenny nails set down at 10d. per pound,
though [he], himself, saw the figure of 8 as plain as the figure of 10.

Now I leave it to the world to judge, or any impartial man or any
that has understanding in trade, whether this was a just offense, or so
crying a sin that I had such cause to be so penitent for (this being
the chief [charge] and pressed on with so great aggravation by my
opposers), except it should be that my actions innocent in themselves were so misconstrued and I knew not how to help myself.
Especially considering it was no oppressive price, but usual with
others at that time to sell the like so, and since, for almost half as
much more frequently (as I think all know), and yet both given
and taken without exception, or at least without public complaint.

Yes, and the same gentleman, himself, since he has turned
merchant and trader seems to have lost his former tenderness of
conscience that he had when he was a buyer and [seems] not to be
so scrupulous in his own gainstaking. For (if I be not misinformed
and I think I had it from very good information, of some of his
neighbors yet living, that knew well what they said), he agreed with
some of the neighbors in his own town that he would send for or
bring with him £1,000 worth of English goods for the good of the
country, which they should have at easy rates and he would take
wheat, peas, or any sort of corn and cattle for the pay. They provided
their pay according to agreement.

But he failed them in their first expectation, having no goods come
at all. Yet another year he had a less quantity come, and amongst
them nails, and I believe taken up upon credit and not paid for
before they came. Yet, when they were come, corn nor cattle would
not serve for pay, nor trust he would not, but his demands are ready
money. And for the gains he will have 6d. in the shilling profit
(which was oppression and exaction in the highest degree when he
was a buyer).

But that was not all either, for, if they paid in Spanish money, they must pay him the dollars at 4s. 6d. a piece, which here went currently at 5s. And for his nails, they being scarce at that time, his neighbors being in want would have given him any price or pay for them, but he would part with none of them. No necessity would prevail except they would buy all his other goods with them (which no doubt came at prices high enough, which made his parcel lie somewhat long upon his hands and possibly was fain to fall both in his price and pay after so many had refused them) and to retail some of them, for I was shown myself some cloth bought of him at 18 or 20s. per yard that, if some others had sold the like at 15s. per yard, it would have been thought worthy [of] complaint. . . .

It is true that in anything wherein I might justly take shame or sorrow to myself God inclined my heart not to withstand it. For he that hides his sins shall not prosper, but he that confesses and forsakes them shall find mercy. In many [things] we sin all, and who can say his heart is clean? Yet, for the chief of the things that was most urged against me in court and for which the sentence [was] passed against me (as the gold buttons, the bridle, the nails, the falsifying of my books), I did justify and stand to maintain that they were evident mistakes and that I was wronged about [them] (as that they were eightpenny nails at 10d. per pound and not sixpenny, that the buttons were gold and not copper and that they cost 2s. 2d. per dozen in London [and] sold here at 2s. 10d. per dozen and that there was no oppression in that price, that though the figures in my book were altered, yet it was not for any such end as was pretended and urged against me but upon that very cause that before I have related here). I had no cause of penitence or confession of guilt except it was for that I had been so used and reproached about them against all equity. But, if they should have cast me out of the church 20 times for this, I should have chosen it rather than to have confessed myself guilty, for the satisfaction of any, wherein I knew myself (better than anyone else did) to be innocent. . . .

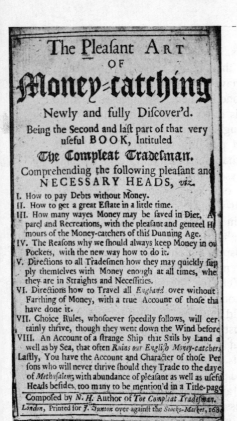

The Pleasant ART
OF
Money-catching
Newly and fully Discover'd.

Being the Second and last part of that very
useful BOOK, Intituled
The Compleat Tradesman.
Comprehending the following pleasant and
NECESSARY HEADS, *viz.*

I. How to pay Debts without Money.
II. How to get a great Estate in a little time.
III. How many wayes Money may be saved in Diet, Ap-
parel and Recreations, with the pleasant and genteel Hu-
mours of the Money-catchers of this Dunning Age.
IV. The Reasons why we should always keep Money in our
Pockets, with the new way how to do it.
V. Directions to all Tradesmen how they may quickly sup-
ply themselves with Money enough at all times, when
they are in Straights and Necessities.
VI. Directions how to Travel all *England* over without a
Farthing of Money, with a true Account of those that
have done it.
VII. Choice Rules, whosoever speedily follows, will cer-
tainly thrive, though they went down the Wind before.
VIII. An Account of a strange Ship that Sails by Land as
well as by Sea, that often *Ruins our English Money-catchers.*
Lastly, You have the Account and Character of those Persons who will never thrive should they Trade to the daye
of *Methusalem*; with abundance of pleasant as well as useful
Heads besides, too many to be mention'd in a Title-page.

Composed by *N. H.* Author of *The Compleat Tradesman.*
London, Printed for *J. Junton* over against the *Stocks-Market,* 168.

FIG. 293.

The Pleasant Art of
MONEY CATCHING
Frontispiece

P.M.   R.M.

R.M.Whilst others Plots against the State are hatching
My Study is, the Art of MONEY CATCHING
P.M.And I, poor I, by sad Experience know,
That want of MONEY brings a deal of Woe,

*London, Printed by John Lever att little Moorgate next Lon-
don wall near Moorfields.*

FIG. 294.

DRESS AND UNDRESS THY SOUL,
ACCORDING TO A 1782 BOOK ON
THE PLEASANT ART OF
MONEY-CATCHING

N. H., MERCHANT

[N. H., Merchant, from "Excellent Rules of Thriving, in Verse," in *Pleasant
Art of Money-Catching,* printed by John Lever, London, 1782, p. 79.]

This little verse, out of a much longer piece, is more than a century
and a half old. It is typical of the closeness which was seen between
business and moral values, at a time when it was possible to make
good profits by hard work, and even better profits by a little sharp
practice.

Sum up at Night what thou hast done by day;
And in the Morning, what thou hast to do;
Dress and undress thy Soul; mark the decay
And growth of it; if with thy Watch, that too
Be down, then wind up both; since we shall be
Most surely judged, make thy Accounts agree.

TRADE KNOWS NO PARTIES, NO POLITIC, NO RELIGIOUS INTERESTS

DANIEL DEFOE

[Daniel Defoe, *The History of the Principal Discoveries and Improvements, In the Several Arts and Sciences* . . . , printed for W. Mears, etc., London, 1727, pp. 143, 171–173 (abridged). Adapted from the original by the editors.]

Daniel Defoe, erstwhile businessman and author of *Robinson Crusoe,* covered "all parts of the known world" in the book from which this selection is taken. He also wrote at a time when trade was opening up the riches of the world to England—a heady experience. In his view of history, commerce spread, and was spread by, religion; indeed, for him, commerce, or trade, is almost a religion itself. For more details about this interesting man, see the introduction to his piece in Volume I.

TRADE KNOWS NO PARTIES, no politic, no religious interests; commerce is a certain communication of nations occasioned by the necessities, and for the good of mankind; the enemies of trade are enemies to all men; pirates and high-sea robbers are wild beasts that should have no law, and whom all men should join to destroy, without inquiring what or who they are: If a bear or a wolf set upon a traveler you do not inquire whether he be Papist or Protestant in delivering him, 'tis enough the one is a man, the other a beast. . . .

Add to this, though it be but an observation by the by, that religion spreading itself through the world soon after these conquests of the Romans, and very much by the help of those conquests; I say religion spreading among the nations introduced (with it) principles of morality, and civilized the people.

For take it with you as you go, religion (I mean the Christian religion) did not at its first beginning to spread itself in the world, indulge, or so much as allow the vices common now to Christians;

and winked at in Christian nations, such as avarice, craft, sly, and cunning circumventing one another, overreaching, and fraudulently cheating in their dealings, and all the little nameless cheats and chicaneries of trade.

The Christian religion infused principles of honesty and plain dealing; it recommended a general rectitude of the mind, a known integrity of principle, a just and upright conduct under the awe of an invisible Being, who inspected the minutest actions, and would call to account for the most secret concealed wickedness; so that in short, where the Christians became traders, or engaged in arts, manufactures, and commerce, there, whoever dealt with them were sure to find upright dealing, punctual performance of every agreement; the hand laid upon the heart was as sacred as an oath, and what the mouth spoke the hands were solemnly bound by; in a word, a general probity and exact honest procedure governed all their dealings; and this we cannot doubt encouraged trade, as to this day we see that foul, unjust, and dishonest usage discourages trade, and drives away the merchants even from cities, and nations, as well as persons.

But this country and the Belgi, that is the Flemings and Dutch, embracing the Christian religion, within sixty or seventy years after their first coming under the Roman dominion, it may be said of them, with truth, that they sooner than other pagan nations felt the civilizing influences of religion; by how much they with a greater willingness and forwardness embraced the religion itself; for 'tis remarked by the writers of our histories, in the story of Joseph of Arimathea, who was the first Apostle of the Britains, that the people most gladly, and with the greatest simplicity, that is honesty and integrity, received the knowledge of Christ.

Thus, and I think with great justice, I observe the settling commerce in this part of the world to be the genuine, natural product of the planting of religion, and Roman liberty here together; and 'tis observable to this very day, that trade flourishes upon the same foundation, and declines as that foundation sinks and decays, (viz.)

I. Liberty, for securing and preserving property, without which commerce cannot be safe.

II. Honesty, for the introducing just dealings between man and man, on which depends credit, which we find by experience is the life of trade.

Now, in these two cases the juncture I speak of was particularly eminent; (1) The just government of the Romans established peace and liberty; and (2) The Christian religion coming in upon the very track or footsteps of the Roman conquests, that religion (to the immortal honor of its very name in the world) inspired its professors with just principles, forming their minds by the rules of all moral virtues, as well as with the awe and fear of a divine Power, a righteous judgment, and a futurity of reward; on both these foundations the world became more habitable than before, and men enjoying the tranquility, which was the consequence of just government, applied themselves to industry and labor; hence arts and learning flourished, and in consequence of the first,

Trade and Navigation.

BUSINESS VIRTUES ARE RELIGIOUS VIRTUES IN *POOR RICHARD'S ALMANAC*

BENJAMIN FRANKLIN

[Benjamin Franklin, "The Way to Wealth," preface to *Poor Richard's Almanac* for 1757, John B. Alden, New York, 1889, pp. 1–12.]

Benjamin Franklin was a great man, no doubt of it. He also was one of the few businessmen to succeed in politics as well as in running an enterprise for profit. The fifteenth son of a not very prosperous candlemaker, Franklin became a successful printer (for some of his business life, see the selection from his *Autobiography* in Volume III). But perhaps there is some clue to his ability to advance in political affairs and government service in that, as a businessman, he made much of his progress through the favor he won in influential quarters; for example, he had a number of good orders for printing currency.

Ben was not a completely moral man by strict standards; he had a notable weakness for women. Also, he was hardly altogether modest about his own merits and accomplishments. But that did not keep him from moralizing about modesty and humility, and of course (here he *was* an authority) thrift and honesty.

One of the publications that came off his presses regularly was an annual almanac. Franklin says in the *Autobiography:*

> Observing that it [the Almanac] was generally read, scarce any neighborhood in the province being without it, I consider'd it as a proper vehicle for conveying instruction among the common people, who bought scarcely any other books: I therefore filled all the little spaces that occurr'd between the remarkable days in the calendar with proverbial sentences, chiefly such as inculcated industry and frugality, as the means of procuring wealth and thereby securing virtue; it being more difficult for a man in want, to act always

honestly, as, to use here one of those proverbs, *it is hard for an empty sack to stand upright.*

This was the so-called Poor Richard's Almanac, since it contained advice from Franklin writing under the nom de plume of Richard Saunders. Again, turning to Franklin's own explanation:

These proverbs, which contained the wisdom of many ages and nations, I assembl'd and form'd into a connected discourse prefix'd to the Almanack of 1757, as the harangue of a wise old man to the people attending an auction. The bringing all these scattered counsels thus into a focus enabled them to make greater impression. The piece, being universally approved, was copied in all the newspapers of the Continent: reprinted in Britain on a broadside, to be stuck up in houses; two translations were made of it in French, and great numbers bought by the clergy and gentry, to distribute gratis among their poor parishioners and tenants. In Pennsylvania, as it discouraged useless expense in foreign superfluities, some thought it had its share of influence in producing that growing plenty of money which was observable for several years after its publication.

It is this preface, known as "The Way to Wealth," that everyone in the nineteenth century regarded as the height of Franklin's literary— and philosophical—accomplishment. For those who want to see Franklin in a lighter vein than either the *Autobiography* or the *Almanac,* turn to his farcical plan to save daylight on page 2503 in this volume.

———◆———

COURTEOUS READER,

I have heard that nothing gives an author so great pleasure, as to find his works respectfully quoted by other learned authors. This pleasure I have seldom enjoyed; for tho' I have been, if I may say it without vanity, an *eminent author* of Almanacks annually now a full quarter of a century, my brother authors in the same way, for what reason I know not, have ever been very sparing in their applauses; and no other author has taken the least notice of me, so that did not my writings produce me some solid *pudding,* the great deficiency of *praise* would have quite discouraged me.

I concluded at length, that the people were the best judges of my merit; for they buy my works; and besides, in my rambles, where I am not personally known, I have frequently heard one or other of my adages repeated, with, *as Poor Richard says,* at the end on't; this gave me some satisfaction, as it showed not only that my instructions were regarded, but discovered likewise some respect for my authority; and I own, that to encourage the practice of remembering

FIG. 295. Franklin's Wisdom Cast as a Rebus.

THE ART OF MAKING MONEY PLENTY
IN EVERY MAN'S POCKET

BY

DOCTOR FRANKLIN

At this time when the general complaint is that money is so scarce it must be an act of kindness to inform the moneyless how they can reinforce their purses. I will acquaint all with the true secret of money catching, the certain way to fill empty purses & how to keep them always full. Two simple rules well observed will do the business. 1st Let honesty and labor be thy constant companions: 2d Spend one penny every day less then thy clear gains: Then shall thy purses soon begin to thrive, thy creditors will never insult thee nor want oppress nor hunger bite, nor naked freeze thee, the whole hemisphere will shine brighter, and pleasure spring up in every corner of thy heart.

Now thereby embrace these rules and be happy.

—B. Franklin

and repeating those wise sentences, I have sometimes *quoted myself* with great gravity.

Judge then how much I must have been gratified by an incident I am going to relate to you. I stopt my horse lately where a great number of people were collected at a vendue of merchant goods. The hour of sale not being come, they were conversing on the badness of the times, and one of the company call'd to a plain clean old man, with white locks, *Pray Father* Abraham *what think you of the times? Won't these heavy taxes quite ruin the country? How shall we be ever able to pay them? What would you advise us to?*—— Father *Abraham* stood up, and reply'd, if you'd have my advice, I'll give it you in short, for *a word to the wise is enough,* and *many words won't fill a bushel,* as *Poor Richard* says. They join'd in desiring him to speak his mind, and gathering round him, he proceeded as follows:

Friends, says he, and neighbors, the taxes are indeed very heavy, and if those laid on by the government were the only ones we had to pay, we might more easily discharge them; but we have many others, and much more grievous to some of us. We are taxed twice as much by our *idleness,* three times as much by our *pride,* and four times as much by our *folly,* and from these taxes the commissioners cannot ease or deliver us by allowing an abatement. However, let us hearken to good advice, and something may be done for us; *God helps them that help themselves,* as *Poor Richard* says, in his Almanack of 1733.

It would be thought a hard government that should tax its people one tenth part of their *time,* to be employed in its service. But *idleness* taxes many of us much more, if we reckon all that is spent in absolute *sloth,* or doing of nothing, with that which is spent in idle employments or amusements, that amount to nothing. *Sloth,* by bringing on diseases, absolutely shortens life. *Sloth, like rust, consumes faster than labor wears, while the used key is always bright,* as *Poor Richard* says. But *dost thou love life, then do not squander time, for that's the stuff life is made of,* as *Poor Richard* says.—— How much more than is necessary do we spend in sleep! forgetting that *the sleeping fox catches no poultry,* and that *there will be sleeping enough in the grave,* as *Poor Richard* says. If time be of all things the most precious, *wasting time* must be, as *Poor Richard* says, *the greatest prodigality,* since, as he elsewhere tells us, *lost time is never found again;* and what we call *time enough, always proves little enough.* Let us then be up and doing, and doing to the purpose; so by diligence shall we do more with less perplexity. *Sloth makes all things difficult, but industry all easy,* as *Poor Richard* says; and *he that riseth late, must trot all day, and shall scarce overtake his business at night.* While *laziness travels so slowly, that poverty soon overtakes him,* as we read in *Poor Richard,* who adds, *drive thy business, let not that drive thee;* and *early to bed, and early to rise, makes a man healthy, wealthy and wise.*

So what signifies *wishing* and *hoping* for better times? We may make these times better if we bestir ourselves. *Industry need not wish* as *Poor Richard* says, and *he that lives upon hope will die fasting. There are no gains, without pains;* then *help hands, for I have no lands,* or if I have, they are smartly taxed. And, as *Poor Richard* likewise observes, *he that hath a trade hath an estate,* and *he that hath a calling hath an office of profit and honor;* but then the *trade* must be worked at, and the *calling* well followed, or neither the *estate* nor the *office* will enable us to pay our taxes.——If we are industrious we shall never starve; for as *Poor Richard* says, *at the working man's house hunger looks in, but dares not enter.* Nor will the bailiff or the constable enter, for *industry pays debts, while despair encreaseth them,* says *Poor Richard.*——What though you have found no treasure, nor has any rich relation left you a legacy, *diligence is the mother of good luck,* as *Poor Richard* says, and *God gives all things to industry.* Then *plough deep, while sluggards sleep, and you shall have corn to sell and to keep,* says *Poor Dick.* Work while it is called today, for you know not how much you may be hindered tomorrow, which makes *Poor Richard* say, *one today is worth two tomorrows;* and farther, *have you somewhat to do to-morrow, do it today.* If you were a servant, would you not be ashamed that a good master should catch you idle? Are you then your own master, *be ashamed to catch yourself idle,* as *Poor Dick* says. When there is so much to be done for yourself, your family, your country, and your gracious king, be up by peep of day; *let not the sun look down and say, inglorious here he lies.* Handle your tools without mittens; remember that *the cat in gloves catches no mice,* as *Poor Richard* says. 'Tis true there is much to be done, and per-haps you are weak handed, but stick to it steadily, and you will see great effects, for *constant dropping wears away stones,* and by *diligence and patience the mouse ate in two the cable;* and *little strokes fell great oaks,* as *Poor Richard* says in his Almanack, the year I cannot just now remember.

Methinks I hear some of you say, *must a man afford himself no leisure?*——I will tell thee, my friend, what *Poor Richard* says, *employ thy time well if thou meanest to gain leisure;* and, *since thou art not sure of a minute, throw not away an hour.* Leisure is time for doing something useful; this leisure the diligent man will obtain, but the lazy man never; so that, as *Poor Richard* says, *a life of leisure and a life of laziness are two things.* Do you imagine that sloth will afford you more comfort than labor? No, for as *Poor Richard* says, *trouble springs from idleness, and grievous toil from needless ease.*

Many without labor would live by their wits only, but they break for want of stock. Whereas industry gives comfort, and plenty, and respect: *fly pleasures, and they'll follow you. The diligent spinner has a large shift;* and *now I have a sheep and a cow, everybody bids me good morrow;* all of which is well said by *Poor Richard.*

But with our industry, we must likewise be *steady, settled* and *careful,* and oversee our own affairs *with our own eyes* and not trust too much to others; for, as *Poor Richard* says,

> I never saw an oft removed tree,
> Nor yet an oft removed family,
> That throve so well as those that settled be.

And again, *three removes is as bad as a fire;* and again, *keep thy shop, and thy shop will keep thee;* and again, *if you would have your business done, go; if not, send.* And again,

> He that by the plow must thrive,
> Himself must either hold or drive.

And again, *the eye of a master will do more work than both his hands;* and again, *want of care does us more damage than want of knowledge;* and again, *not to oversee workmen, is to leave them your purse open.* Trusting too much to others' care is the ruin of many; for, as the *Almanack* says, *in the affairs of this world, men are saved, not by faith, but by the want of it;* but a man's own care is profitable; for saith *Poor Dick, learning is to the studious,* and *riches to the careful,* as well as *power to the bold,* and *Heaven to the virtuous.* And farther, *if you would have a faithful servant, and one that you like, serve yourself.* And again, he adviseth to circumspection and care, even in the smallest matters, because sometimes *a little neglect may breed great mischief;* adding, *for want of a nail, the shoe was lost; for want of a shoe the horse was lost; and for want of a horse the rider was lost,* being overtaken and slain by the enemy, all for want of care about a horseshoe nail.

So much for industry, my friends, and attention to one's own business; but to these we must add *frugality,* if we would make our *industry* more certainly successful. A man may, if he knows not how to save as he gets, *keep his nose all his life to the grindstone,* and die not worth a *groat* at last. *A fat kitchen makes a lean will,* as *Poor Richard* says; and,

> Many estates are spent in the getting,
> Since women for tea forsook spinning and knitting,
> And men for punch forsook hewing and splitting.

If you would be wealthy, says he, in another Almanack, *think of saving as well as of getting: The* Indies *have not made* Spain *rich, be-*

cause her outgoes *are greater than her* incomes. Away then with your expensive follies, and you will not have so much cause to complain of hard times, heavy taxes, and chargeable families; for, as *Poor Dick* says,

> Women and wine, game and deceit,
> Make the wealth small, and the wants great.

And farther, *what maintains one vice would bring up two children.* You may think perhaps, that a *little* tea, or a *little* punch now and then, diet a *little* more costly, clothes a *little* finer, and a *little* entertainment now and then, can be no *great* matter; but remember what *Poor Richard* says, *many* a little *makes a mickle;* and farther, *beware of* little *expenses; a small leak will sink a great ship;* and again, *who dainties love, shall beggars prove;* and moreover, *fools make feasts, and wise men eat them.*

Here you are all got together at this vendue of *fineries* and *knicknacks.* You call them *goods,* but if you do not take care, they will prove *evils* to some of you. You expect they will be sold *cheap,* and perhaps they may for less than they cost; but if you have no occasion for them, they must be *dear* to you. Remember what *Poor Richard* says, *Buy what thou hast no need of, and ere long thou shalt sell thy necessaries.* And again, *at a great pennyworth pause a while;* he means that perhaps the cheapness is *apparent* only and not *real;* or the bargain, by straitning thee in thy business, may do thee more harm than good. For in another place he says, *many have been ruined by buying good pennyworths.* Again, *Poor Richard* says, *'tis foolish to lay out money in a purchase of repentance;* and yet this folly is practiced every day at vendues, for want of minding the Almanack. *Wise men,* as *Poor Dick* says, *learn by others harms, fools scarcely by their own;* but, *felix quem faciunt aliena pericula cautum.** Many a one, for the sake of finery on the back, have gone with a hungry belly, and half starved their families; *silks and sattins, scarlets and velvets,* as *Poor Richard* says, *put out the kitchen fire.* These are not the *necessaries* of life; they can scarcely be called the *conveniences,* and yet only because they look pretty, how many *want* to *have* them. The *artificial* wants of mankind thus become more numerous than the *natural;* and, as *Poor Dick* says, *for one* poor *person, there are an hundred* indigent. By these, and other extravagancies, the genteel are reduced to poverty, and forced to borrow of those whom they formerly despised, but who through *industry* and *frugality* have maintained their standing; in which case it appears plainly, that *a ploughman on his legs is higher than a gentleman on his knees,* as *Poor Richard* says. Perhaps they have had a small estate left them, which they knew not the getting of;

---

* He is lucky who is made cautious by other men's perils.

THE LADDER OF FORTUNE.

Fig. 296. The Ladder of Fortune, or, Poor Richard, illustrated by Currier and Ives. "Behold, my children, follow the steps of industry, temperance, and all the other virtues, and you will find success, the favor of God, long life and other rich rewards," the father counsels his children. In the background are depicted the vices: lottery, gambling, swindling, strikes, betting and the stock exchange.

they think *'tis day, and will never be night;* that a little to be spent out of *so much,* is not worth minding; (*a child and a fool,* as *Poor Richard* says, *imagine twenty shillings and twenty years can never be spent*) but, *always taking out of the meal-tub, and never putting in, soon comes to the bottom;* then, as *Poor Dick* says, *when the well's dry, they know the worth of water.* But this they might have known before, if they had taken his advice; *If you would know the value of money, go and try to borrow some;* for, *he that goes a borrowing goes a sorrowing;* and indeed so does he that lends to such people, when he goes *to get it in again.*———*Poor Dick* farther advises, and says,

> Fond *pride of dress,* is sure a very curse;
> E'er *fancy* you consult, consult your purse.

And again, *pride is as loud a beggar as want, and a great deal more saucy.* When you have bought one fine thing you must buy ten more, that your appearance may be all of a piece; but *Poor Dick* says, *'tis easier to* suppress *the first desire, than to* satisfy *all that follow it.* And 'tis as truly folly for the poor to ape the rich, as for the frog to swell, in order to equal the ox.

> Great estates may venture more,
> But little boats should keep near shore.

'Tis however a folly soon punished; for *pride that dines on vanity sups on contempt,* as *Poor Richard* says. And in another place, *pride breakfasted with plenty, dined with poverty, and supped with infamy.* And after all, of what use is this *pride of appearance,* for which so much is risked, so much is suffered? It cannot promote health, or ease pain; it makes no increase of merit in the person, creates envy, it hastens misfortune.

> What is a butterfly? At best
> He's but a caterpillar drest.
> The gaudy fop's his picture just,

as *Poor Richard* says.

But what madness must it be to *run in debt* for these superfluities! We are offered, by the terms of this vendue, *six months' credit;* and that perhaps has induced some of us to attend it, because we cannot spare the ready money, and hope now to be fine without it. But, ah, think what you do when you run in debt; *you give to another power over your liberty.* If you cannot pay at the time, you will be ashamed to see your creditor; you will be in fear when you speak to him; you will make poor pitiful sneaking excuses, and by degrees come to lose your veracity, and sink into base downright lying; for, as *Poor Richard* says, *the second vice is lying, the first is running in debt.* And again, to the same purpose, *lying rides upon debt's back.* Whereas a freeborn *Englishman* ought not to be ashamed or afraid to see or speak to any man living. But poverty often deprives a man of all spirit and virtue: *'tis hard for an empty bag to stand upright,* as *Poor Richard* truly says. What would you think of that prince, or that government, who should issue an edict forbidding you to dress like a gentleman or a gentlewoman, on pain of imprisonment or servitude? Would you not say, that you are free, have a right to dress as you please, and that such an edict would be a breach of your privileges, and such a government tyrannical? And yet you are about to put yourself under that tyranny when you run in debt for such dress! Your creditor has authority at his pleasure to deprive you of your liberty, by confining you in gaol for life, or to sell you for a servant, if you should not be about to pay him! When you have got your bargain, you may, perhaps, think little of payment; but *creditors, Poor Richard* tells us, *have better memories than debtors;* and in another place says, *creditors are a superstitious sect, great observers of set days and times.* The day comes round before you are aware, and the demand is made before you are prepared to satisfy it. Or if you bear your debt in mind, the term which at first seemed so long, will, as it lessens, appear extremely short. *Time* will seem to have added wings to his heels as well as shoulders. *Those have a short Lent,* saith *Poor Richard, who owe money to be paid at Easter.* Then, since, as he says, *the borrower is a slave to the lender, and the debtor is to the creditor,* disdain the chain, preserve your freedom; and maintain your independency: be *industrious* and *free;* be *frugal* and *free.* At present, perhaps, you may think yourself in thriving circumstances, and that you can bear a little extravagance without injury; but,

> For age and want, save while you may;
> No morning sun lasts a whole day,

as *Poor Richard* says.———Gain may be temporary and uncertain, but ever while you live, Experience is constant and certain; and *'tis easier to build two chimneys than to keep one in fuel,* as *Poor Richard* says. So *rather go to bed supperless than rise in debt.*

> Get what you can, and what you get hold;
> 'Tis the stone that will turn all your lead into gold,

as *Poor Richard* says. And when you have got the philosopher's stone, sure you will no longer complain of the bad times, or the difficulties of paying taxes.

This doctrine, my friends, is *reason* and *wisdom;* but after all, do not depend too much on your own *industry* and *frugality* and *prudence,* though excellent things, for they may all be blasted without the blessing of heaven; and therefore ask that blessing humbly, and be not uncharitable to those that at present seem to want it, but comfort and help them. Remember *Job* suffered, and was afterwards prosperous.

And now to conclude, *experience keeps a dear school, but fools will learn in no other, and scarce in that;* for it is true, *we may give advice, but we cannot give conduct,* as *Poor Richard* says; however, remember this, *they that won't be counseled can't be helped,* as *Poor Richard* says; and farther, that *if you will not hear reason, she'll surely rap your knuckles.*

Thus the old gentleman ended his harangue. The people heard it, and approved the doctrine, and immediately practiced the contrary, just as if it had been a common sermon; for the vendue opened, and they began to buy extravagantly, notwithstanding all his cautions, and their own fear of taxes.——I found the good man had thoroughly studied my Almanacks, and digested all I had dropt on those topics during the course of five-and-twenty years. The frequent mention he made of me must have tired anyone else, but my vanity was wonderfully delighted with it, though I was conscious that not a tenth part of this wisdom was my own which he ascribed to me, but rather the *gleanings* I had made of the sense of all ages and nations. However, I resolved to be the better for the echo of it; and though I had at first determined to buy stuff for a new coat, I went away resolved to wear my old one a little longer. *Reader,* if thou wilt do the same, thy profit will be as great as mine.

I am, as ever,
Thine to serve thee,
RICHARD SAUNDERS

July 7, 1757

THE RUSSIANS HAVE SOMETHING TO SAY ON BUSINESS VIRTUE, TOO

CATHERINE II *and*
KOSMA PETROVICH PRUTKOV

["Choice Russian Proverbs" by Catherine II and Kosma Petrovich Prutkov, in Bernard Guilbert Guerney (ed. and trans.), *The Portable Russian Reader,* The Viking Press, copyright 1947, pp. 636–637, 640, 642. Reprinted by permission of the publishers.]

Here are some Russian equivalents of Poor Richard's sayings—two of them from rich Catherine, Empress of Russia.

Profit and loss are next-door neighbors.

He that ploughs with zeal will always have luck and weal.

—Catherine II (1729–1796)

Undeserved wealth is like unto water cress: it will grow anywhere.

A dog sitting on hay is harmful; a hen sitting on eggs is useful; because of sedentary life men put on flesh—thus every money-changer is fat.

Toil like an ant, if you would be likened to a bee.

Before deciding on a business enterprise, make inquiries: Is a Jew or a German to be found in such a one? If so, go ahead; you will profit.

—Kosma Petrovich Prutkov (1801– or 1803–1863)

THE RABBIT AND THE GOAT

FROM *Life*

["The Rabbit and the Goat," in *Life*, Oct. 8, 1885, vol. VI, no. 145, p. 208.]

Here, from an 1885 issue of the old humor magazine *Life*, is an Aesopian sort of fable about one of the fine points of business morality—that is, fine in the sense of being "cut fine," into little pieces, rather than something good or splendid. Whether or not the moral is impressive, or can be of much help to the conscientious businessman, it does illustrate that the kind of workaday problems of ethics we all face in this century also challenged our ancestors in the last century, as no doubt in all preceding centuries too.

A GOAT ONCE APPROACHED a peanut stand that was kept by a Rabbit, purchased five cents worth of peanuts, laid down a dime, and received a punched nickel in change. In a few days the Goat came back, called for another pint of peanuts, and offered the same nickel in payment; but in the meantime had stopped the hole in it with a peg.

"I can't take that nickel," said the Rabbit.

"This is the very nickel you gave me in change a few days ago," replied the Goat.

"I know it is," continued the Rabbit, "but I made no attempt to deceive you about it. When you took the coin the hole was wide open, and you could see it for yourself. In working that mutilated coin off on you I simply showed my business sagacity; but now you bring it back with the hole stopped up and try to pass it, with a clear intent to deceive. That is fraud. My dear Goat, I'm afraid the grand jury will get after you if you are not more careful about little things of this sort."

Moral: This Fable teaches that the moral quality of a business transaction often depends upon the view you take of it.

A PROMINENT MAN IN HIS CHURCH
—ASLEEP OR AWAKE

CARLSBAD

[Carlsbad, "The Latest Quotation," in *Life,* Nov. 26, 1885, vol. VI, no. 152, p. 301.]

Do business and religion mix? That is a profound problem which many men have pondered seriously, as indicated by all the other articles in this section. But in this light bit, also from *Life* in 1885, the question is resolved quite readily in the affirmative. Even in church our hero dreams of his investments.

NOT MANY SUNDAYS AGO a well-known Wall Street man went to church (as his roadster had gone lame), and with his wife and family occupied a pew on the middle aisle, not many seats from the front. He was somewhat tired and the peaceful air of the sanctuary had such a soothing effect upon his nervous system that as soon as the sermon began he quietly dozed off. He took his little nap in a very unobtrusive manner, and meanwhile dreamed of his heavy operations in Oregon Transportation.*

"My brethren," thundered the preacher, working up to a climax. "Did they not cry as with one voice, St. Paul! St. Paul!——" and the suddenly awakened broker jumped excitedly to his feet, and bid 96 for a thousand shares. For once in his life it could be said of him, "He was a prominent man in his church."

* This was part of a transport system connecting the Columbia River with St. Paul, Minnesota.

A VATICAN VIEW OF
THE CONDITION OF
THE WORKING CLASS

POPE LEO XIII

[Leo XIII, "The Condition of the Working Class," from the Papal Encyclical "Rerum Novarum," May 15, 1891. From Anne Fremantle (ed.), *The Papal Encyclicals in Their Historical Context*, G. P. Putnam's Sons, New York, copyright © 1956 by Anne Freemantle, pp. 166–177. Reprinted by permission of the publisher.]

Here one of the great modern Catholic Popes, Leo XIII (1878–1903), issues one of his famous *Letters* on social problems. He takes the strong position that there are excesses in business practice that need to be corrected; that government (particularly socialistic or communistic government) is *not* the proper remedial agency; and that action depends on private men "whom fortune favors," recognizing their responsibility under religious guidance to use their resources for the common good. Significantly, he includes "gifts of the mind" within the temporal blessings that, as "the steward of God's providence," man should employ for the benefit of others.

These observations on "The Condition of the Working Class" are from the Papal Encyclical, *Rerum Novarum,* or *Of New Things,* May 15, 1891. This marks a very historic occasion: the Catholic Church's recognition of the change taking place under industrialism, and the early enunciation of a liberal, constructive policy to meet it.

THAT THE SPIRIT of revolutionary change, which has long been disturbing the nations of the world, should have passed beyond the sphere of politics and made its influence felt in the cognate sphere of practical economics is not surprising. The elements of the conflict now raging are unmistakable in the vast expansion of industrial pursuits and the marvelous discoveries of science; in the changed relations between masters and workmen; in the enormous fortunes of some few individuals, and the utter poverty of the masses; in the increased self-reliance and closer mutual combination of the working classes; as also, finally, in the prevailing moral degeneracy. The momentous gravity of the state of things now obtaining fills every mind with painful apprehension; wise men are discussing it; practical men are proposing schemes; popular meetings, legislatures, and rulers of nations are all busied with it—and actually there is no question which has taken a deeper hold on the public mind.

Therefore, Venerable Brethren, as on former occasions when it seemed opportune to refute false teaching, We have addressed you in the interest of the Church and of the commonweal, and have issued Letters bearing on "Political Power," "Human Liberty," "The Christian Constitution of the State," and like matters, so have We thought it expedient now to speak on *The Condition of the Working Classes*. It is a subject on which We have already touched more than once, incidentally. But in the present Letter, the responsibility of the Apostolic office urges us to treat the question of set purpose and in detail, in order that no misapprehension may exist as to the principles which truth and justice dictate for its settlement. The discussion is not easy, nor is it void of danger. It is no easy matter to define the relative rights and mutual duties of the rich and of the poor, of capital and of labor. And the danger lies in this, that crafty agitators are intent on making use of these differences of opinion to pervert men's judgments and to stir up the people to revolt.

But all agree, and there can be no question whatever, that some remedy must be found, and found quickly, for the misery and wretchedness pressing so heavily and unjustly at this moment on the vast majority of the working classes.

For the ancient workingmen's guilds were abolished in the last century, and no other organization took their place. Public institutions and the very laws have set aside the ancient religion. Hence by degrees it has come to pass that workingmen have been surrendered, all isolated and helpless, to the hardheartedness of employers and the greed of unchecked competition. The mischief has been increased by rapacious usury, which, although more than once condemned by the Church, is nevertheless, under a different guise, but with the like injustice, still practiced by covetous and grasping men. To this must be added the custom of working by contract, and the concentration of so many branches of trade in the hands of a few individuals; so that a small number of very rich men have been able to lay upon the teeming masses of the laboring poor a yoke little better than that of slavery itself.

To remedy these wrongs the socialists, working on the poor man's envy of the rich, are striving to do away with private property, and contend that individual possessions should become the common property of all, to be administered by the state or by municipal bodies. They hold that by thus transferring property from private individuals to the community, the present mischievous state of things will be set to rights, inasmuch as each citizen will then get his fair share of whatever there is to enjoy. But their contentions are so clearly powerless to end the controversy that were they carried into effect the workingman himself would be among the first to suffer. They are, moreover, emphatically unjust, because they would rob the lawful possessor, bring state action into a sphere not within its competence, and create utter confusion in the community.

It is surely undeniable that, when a man engages in remunerative labor, the impelling reason and motive of his work is to obtain property, and thereafter to hold it as his very own. If one man hires out to another his strength or skill, he does so for the purpose of receiving in return what is necessary for sustenance and education; he therefore expressly intends to acquire a right full and real, not only to the remuneration, but also to the disposal of such remuneration, just as he pleases. Thus, if he lives sparingly, saves money, and, for greater security, invests his savings in land, the land, in such case, is only his wages under another form; and, consequently, a workingman's little estate thus purchased should be as completely at his full disposal as are the wages he received for his labor. But it is precisely in such power of disposal that ownership obtains, whether the property consist of land or chattels. Socialists, therefore, by endeavoring to transfer the possessions of individuals to the community at large, strike at the interests of every wage earner, since they would deprive him of the liberty of disposing of his wages, and thereby of all hope and possibility of increasing his stock and of bettering his condition in life.

What is of far greater moment, however, is the fact that the remedy they propose is manifestly against justice. For every man has by nature the right to possess property as his own. This is one of the chief points of distinction between man and the animal creation, for the brute has no power of self-direction, but is governed by two main instincts, which keep his powers on the alert, impel him to develop them in a fitting matter, and stimulate and determine him to action without any power of choice. One of these instincts is self-preservation, the other the propagation of the species. But both can attain their purpose by means of things which lie within range; beyond their verge the brute creation cannot go, for they are moved to action by their senses only, and in the special direction which these suggest. But with man it is wholly different. He possesses, on the one hand, the full perfection of the animal being, and hence enjoys, at least as much as the rest of the animal kind, the fruition of things material. But animal nature, however perfect, is far from representing the human being in its completeness, and is in truth but humanity's humble handmaid, made to serve and to obey. It is the mind, or reason, which is the predominant element in us who are human creatures; it is this which renders a human being human, and distinguishes him essentially and generically from the brute. And on this very account—that man alone among the animal creation is endowed with reason—it must be within his right to possess things not merely for temporary and momentary use, as other living things do, but to have and to hold them in stable and permanent possession; he must have not only things that perish in the use of them, but those also which, though they have been reduced into use, remain his own for further use.

This becomes still more clearly evident if man's nature be considered a little more deeply. For man, fathoming by his faculty of reason matters without number, and linking the future with the present, becoming, furthermore, by taking enlightened forethought, master of his own acts, guides his ways under the eternal law and the power of God, whose providence governs all things. Wherefore it is in his power to exercise his choice not only as to matters that regard his present welfare, but also about those which he deems may be for his advantage in time yet to come. Hence man not only can possess the fruits of the earth, but also the very soil, inasmuch as from the produce of the earth he has to lay by provision for the future. Man's needs do not die out, but recur; although satisfied today they demand fresh supplies for tomorrow. Nature accordingly owes to man a storehouse that shall never fail, affording the daily supply for his daily wants. And this he finds solely in the inexhaustible fertility of the earth.

Neither do we, at this stage, need to bring into action the interference of the state. Man precedes the state, and possesses, prior to the formation of any state, the right of providing for the sustenance of his body. Now, to affirm that God has given the earth for the use and enjoyment of the whole human race is not to deny that private property is lawful. For God has granted the earth to mankind in general, not in the sense that all without distinction can deal with it as they like, but rather that no part of it has been assigned to anyone in particular, and that the limits of private possession have been left to be fixed by man's own industry, and by the laws of individual races. Moreover, the earth, even though apportioned among private owners, ceases not thereby to minister to the needs of all, inasmuch as there is no one who does not sustain life from what the land produces. Those who do not possess the soil contribute their labor; hence it may truly be said that all human subsistence is derived either from labor on one's own land, or from some toil, some calling which is paid for either in the produce of the land itself, or in that which is exchanged for what the land brings forth.

Here, again, we have further proof that private ownership is in accordance with the law of nature. Truly, that which is required for the preservation of life, and for life's well-being, is produced in great abundance from the soil, but not until man has brought it into cultivation and expended upon it his solicitude and skill. Now, when man thus turns the activity of his mind and the strength of his body toward procuring the fruits of nature, by such act he makes his own that portion of nature's field which he cultivates—that portion on which he leaves, as it were, the impress of his individuality; and it cannot but be just that he should possess that portion as his very own, and have a right to hold it without anyone being justified in violating that right.

So strong and convincing are these arguments that it seems amazing that some should now be setting up anew certain obsolete opinions in opposition to what is here laid down. They assert that it is right for private persons to have the use of the soil and its various fruits, but that it is unjust for anyone to possess outright either the land on which he has built, or the estate which he has brought under cultivation. But those who deny these rights do not perceive that they are defrauding man of what his own labor has produced. For the soil which is tilled and cultivated with toil and skill utterly changes its conditions: it was wild before, now it is fruitful; was barren, but now brings forth in abundance. That which has thus altered and improved the land becomes so truly part of itself as to be in great measure indistinguishable and inseparable from it. Is it just that the fruit of a man's own sweat and labor should be possessed and enjoyed by anyone else? As effects follow their cause, so it is just and right that the results of labor should belong to those who have bestowed their labor.

With reason, then, the common opinion of mankind, little affected by the few dissentients who have contended for the opposite view, has found in the careful study of nature, and in the laws of nature, the foundations of the division of property, and the practice of all ages has consecrated the principle of private ownership, as being pre-eminently in conformity with human nature, and as conducing in the most unmistakable manner to the peace and tranquility of human existence. The same principle is confirmed and enforced by the civil laws—laws which, so long as they are just, derive from the law of nature their binding force. The authority of the divine law adds its sanction, forbidding us in severest terms even to covet that which is another's: *Thou shalt not covet thy neighbor's wife; nor his house, nor his field, nor his man-servant, nor his maid-servant, nor his ox, nor his ass, nor anything which is his.*[1]

The rights here spoken of, belonging to each individual man, are seen in much stronger light when considered in relation to man's social and domestic obligations. In choosing a state of life, it is indisputable that all are at full liberty to follow the counsel of Jesus Christ as to observing virginity, or to bind themselves by the marriage tie. No human law can abolish the natural and original

---

[1] Deuteronomy 5:21.

right of marriage, nor in any way limit the chief and principal purpose of marriage, ordained by God's authority from the beginning. *Increase and multiply.*[2] Hence we have the family; the "society" of a man's house—a society limited indeed in numbers, but no less a true "society," anterior to every kind of state or nation, invested with rights and duties of its own, totally independent of the civil community.

The right of property, therefore, which has been proved to belong naturally to individual persons, must in like wise belong to a man in his capacity of head of a family; nay, such person must possess this right so much the more clearly in proportion as his position multiplies his duties. For it is a most sacred law of nature that a father should provide food and all necessaries for those whom he has begotten; and, similarly, nature dictates that a man's children, who carry on, so to speak, and continue his own personality, should be by him provided with all that is needful to enable them to keep themselves honorably from want and misery amid the uncertainties of this mortal life. Now, in no other way can a father effect this except by the ownership of lucrative property, which he can transmit to his children by inheritance. A family, no less than a state, is, as we have said, a true society, governed by a power within its sphere, that is to say, by the father. Provided, therefore, the limits which are prescribed by the very purposes for which it exists be not transgressed, the family has at least equal rights with the state in the choice and pursuit of the things needful to its preservation and its just liberty.

We say, at least equal rights; for inasmuch as the domestic household is antecedent, as well in idea as in fact, to the gathering of men into a community, the family must necessarily have rights and duties which are prior to those of the community, and founded more immediately in nature. If the citizens of a state—in other words the families—on entering into association and fellowship, were to experience at the hands of the state hindrance instead of help, and were to find their rights attacked instead of being upheld, such association should be held in detestation, rather than be an object of desire.

The contention, then, that the civil government should at its option intrude into and exercise intimate control over the family and the household, is a great and pernicious error. True, if a family finds itself in exceeding distress, utterly deprived of the counsel of friends, and without any prospect of extricating itself, it is right that extreme necessity be met by public aid, since each family is a part of the commonwealth. In like manner, if within the precincts of the household there occur grave disturbance of mutual

---

[2] Genesis 1:28.

rights, public authority should intervene to force each party to yield to the other its proper due; for this is not to deprive citizens of their rights, but justly and properly to safeguard and strengthen them. But the rulers of the state must go no further: here nature bids them stop. Paternal authority can be neither abolished nor absorbed by the state; for it has the same source as human life itself. "The child belongs to the father," and is, as it were, the continuation of the father's personality; and, speaking strictly, the child takes its place in civil society, not of its own right, but in its quality as member of the family in which it is born. And for the very reason that "the child belongs to the father," it is, as St. Thomas of Aquin says, "before it attains the use of free will, under power and charge of its parents." [3] The socialists, therefore, in setting aside the parent and setting up a state supervision, act *against natural justice,* and break into pieces the stability of all family life.

And not only is such interference unjust, but it is quite certain to harass and worry all classes of citizens, and subject them to odious and intolerable bondage. It would throw open the door to envy, to mutual invective, and to discord; the sources of wealth themselves would run dry, for no one would have any interest in exerting his talents or his industry; and that ideal equality about which they entertain pleasant dreams would be in reality the leveling down of all to a like condition of misery and degradation.

Hence it is clear that the main tenet of socialism, community of goods, must be utterly rejected, since it only injures those whom it would seem meant to benefit, is directly contrary to the natural rights of mankind, and would introduce confusion and disorder into the commonweal. The first and most fundamental principle, therefore, if one would undertake to alleviate the condition of the masses, must be the inviolability of private property. This being established, We proceed to show where the remedy sought for must be found.

We approach the subject with confidence, and in the exercise of the rights which manifestly appertain to Us, for no practical solution of this question will be found apart from the intervention of religion and of the Church. It is We who are the chief guardian of religion and the chief dispenser of what pertains to the Church, and We must not by silence neglect the duty incumbent on Us. Doubtless this most serious question demands the attention and the efforts of others besides ourselves—to wit, of the rulers of states, of employers of labor, of the wealthy, aye, of the working classes themselves, for whom We are pleading. But We affirm without hesitation that all the striving of men will be vain if they leave out the Church. It is the Church that insists, on the authority of the Gospel, upon those teachings whereby the conflict can be brought to an end,

---

[3] St. Thomas, *Summa Theologica,* 2a 2ae, Q. x. Art. 12.

or rendered, at least, far less bitter; the Church uses her efforts not only to enlighten the mind but to direct by her precepts the life and conduct of each and all; the Church improves and betters the condition of the workingman by means of numerous useful organizations; does her best to enlist the services of all ranks in discussing and endeavoring to meet, in the most practical way, the claims of the working classes; and acts from the positive view that for these purposes recourse should be had, in due measure and degree, to the intervention of the law and of state authority.

Let it, then, be taken as granted, in the first place, that the condition of things human must be endured, for it is impossible to reduce civil society to one dead level. Socialists may in that intent do their utmost, but all striving against nature is in vain. There naturally exist among mankind manifold differences of the most important kind; people differ in capacity, skill, health, strength; and unequal fortune is a necessary result of unequal condition. Such inequality is far from being disadvantageous either to individuals or to the community. Social and public life can only be maintained by means of various kinds of capacity for business and the playing of many parts; and each man, as a rule, chooses the part which suits his own peculiar domestic condition.

As regards bodily labor, even had man never fallen from *the state of innocence,* he would not have remained wholly unoccupied; but that which would then have been his free choice and his delight became afterwards compulsory, and the painful expiation for his disobedience. *Cursed be the earth in thy work; in thy labor thou shalt eat of it all the days of thy life.*[4] In like manner, the other pains and hardships of life will have no end or cessation on earth; for the consequences of sin are bitter and hard to bear, and they must accompany man so long as life lasts. To suffer and to endure, therefore, is the lot of humanity; let them strive as they may, no strength and no artifice will ever succeed in banishing from human life the ills and troubles which beset it. If any there are who pretend differently—who hold out to a hard-pressed people the boon of freedom from pain and trouble, and undisturbed repose, and constant enjoyment—they delude the people and impose upon them, and their lying promises will only one day bring forth evils worse than the present. Nothing is more useful than to look upon the world as it really is—and at the same time to seek elsewhere, as we have said, for the solace to its troubles.

The great mistake made in regard to the matter now under consideration is to take up with the notion that class is naturally hostile to class, and that the wealthy and the workingmen are intended by nature to live in mutual conflict. So irrational and so false is

---

[4] Genesis 3:17.

this view, that the direct contrary is the truth. Just as the symmetry of
the human frame is the resultant of the disposition of the bodily
members, so in a state is it ordained by nature that these two
classes should dwell in harmony and agreement, and should, as it
were, groove into one another, so as to maintain the balance of the
body politic. Each needs the other: Capital cannot do without
labor, nor labor without capital. Mutual agreement results in pleasant-
ness of life and the beauty of good order; while perpetual conflict
necessarily produces confusion and savage barbarity.

Now, in preventing such strife as this, and in uprooting it, the
efficacy of Christian institutions is marvelous and manifold. First
of all, there is no intermediary more powerful than religion (whereof
the Church is the interpreter and guardian) in drawing the rich,
and the poor breadwinners, together, by reminding each class of
its duties to the other, and especially of the obligations of justice.
Thus religion teaches the laboring man and the artisan to carry
out honestly and fairly all equitable agreements freely entered into;
never to injure the property, nor to outrage the person, of an employer; never to resort to violence in defending their own cause,
nor to engage in riot or disorder; and to have nothing to do with
men of evil principles, who work upon the people with artful
promises, and excite foolish hopes which usually end in useless
regrets, followed by insolvency. Religion teaches the wealthy owner
and the employer that their work-people are not to be accounted
their bondsmen; that in every man they must respect his dignity
and worth as a man and as a Christian; that labor is not a thing
to be ashamed of, if we lend ear to right reason and to Christian
philosophy, but is an honorable calling, enabling a man to sustain
his life in a way upright and creditable; and that it is shameful
and inhuman to treat men like chattels to make money by, or to
look upon them merely as so much muscle or physical power. Again,
therefore, the Church teaches that, as religion and things spiritual
and mental are among the workingman's main concerns, the employer is bound to see that the worker has time for his religious
duties; that he be not exposed to corrupting influences and dangerous occasions; and that he be not led away to neglect his home
and family, or to squander his earnings.

Furthermore, the employer must never tax his work-people beyond
their strength, or employ them in work unsuited to their sex or age.
His great and principal duty is to give everyone a fair wage.
Doubtless, before deciding whether wages are adequate, many things
have to be considered; but wealthy owners and all masters of labor
should be mindful of this—that to exercise pressure upon the
indigent and the destitute for sake of gain, and to gather one's profits
out of the need of another, is condemned by all laws, human and

divine. To defraud anyone of wages that are his due is a crime which cries to the avenging anger of heaven. *Behold, the hire of the laborers . . . which by fraud hath been kept back by you, crieth aloud; and the cry of them hath entered into the ears of the Lord of Sabaoth.*[5]

Lastly, the rich must religiously refrain from cutting down the workmen's earnings, whether by force, by fraud, or by usurious dealing; and with all the greater reason because the laboring man is, as a rule, weak and unprotected, and because his slender means should in proportion to their scantiness be accounted sacred.

Were these precepts carefully obeyed and followed out, would they not be sufficient of themselves to keep under all strife and all its causes?

But the Church, with Jesus Christ as her Master and Guide, aims higher still. She lays down precepts yet more perfect, and tries to bind class to class in friendliness and good feeling. The things of earth cannot be understood or valued aright without taking into consideration the life to come, the life that will know no death. Exclude the idea of futurity, and forthwith the very notion of what is good and right would perish; nay, the whole scheme of the universe would become a dark and unfathomable mystery. The great truth which we learn from nature herself is also the grand Christian dogma on which religion rests as on its foundation— that when we have given up this present life, then shall we really begin to live. God has not created us for the perishable and transitory things of earth, but for things heavenly and everlasting; He has given us this world as a place of exile, and not as our abiding-place. As for riches and the other things which men call good and desirable, whether we have them in abundance, or lack them altogether—so far as eternal happiness is concerned—it matters little; the only important thing is to use them aright. Jesus Christ, when He redeemed us with *plentiful redemption,* took not away the pains and sorrows which in such large proportion are woven together in the web of our moral life. He transformed them into motives of virtue and occasions of merit; and no man can hope for eternal reward unless he follow in the blood-stained footprints of his Saviour. *If we suffer with Him, we shall also reign with Him.*[6] Christ's labors and sufferings, accepted of His own free will, have marvelously sweetened all suffering and all labor. And not only by His example, but by His grace and by the hope held forth of ever-lasting recompense, has He made pain and grief more easy to endure; *for that which is at present momentary and light of our*

---

[5] St. James 5:4.
[6] 2 Tim. 2:12.

tribulation, worketh for us above measure exceedingly an eternal weight of glory.[7]

Therefore those whom fortune favors are warned that freedom from sorrow and abundance of earthly riches are no warrant for the bliss that shall never end, but rather are obstacles;[8] that the rich should tremble at the threatenings of Jesus Christ—threatenings so unwonted in the mouth of Our Lord[9]—and that a most strict account must be given to the Supreme Judge for all we possess. The chief and most excellent rule for the right use of money is one which the heathen philosophers hinted at, but which the Church has traced out clearly, and has not only made known to men's minds, but has impressed upon their lives. It rests on the principle that it is one thing to have a right to the possession of money, and another to have a right to use money as one wills. Private ownership, as we have seen, is the natural right of man; and to exercise that right, especially as members of society, is not only lawful, but absolutely necessary. "It is lawful," says St. Thomas of Aquin, "for a man to hold private property; and it is also necessary for the carrying on of human existence."[10] But if the question be asked, How must one's possessions be used? the Church replies without hesitation in the words of the same holy Doctor: "Man should not consider his outward possessions as his own, but as common to all, so as to share them without hesitation when others are in need. . . ."

Whoever has received from the divine bounty a large share of temporal blessings, whether they be external and corporeal, or gifts of the mind, has received them for the purpose of using them for the perfecting of his own nature, and, at the same time, that he may employ them, as the steward of God's providence, for the benefit of others. "He that hath a talent," says St. Gregory the Great, "let him see that he hide it not; he that hath abundance, let him quicken himself to mercy and generosity; he that hath art and skill, let him do his best to share the use and the utility thereof with his neighbor."[11]

---

[7] 2 Cor. 4:17.
[8] St. Matt. 19:23, 24.
[9] St. Luke 6:24, 25.
[10] 2a 2ae Q. lxvi. Art. 2.
[11] St. Gregory the Great, Hom. ix. in Evangel. n. 7.

THE SIGNIFICANCE OF THE JEWISH
RELIGION IN ECONOMIC LIFE

~∽◇∽~

WERNER SOMBART

[Werner Sombart, "The Significance of the Jewish Religion in Economic Life,"
in *The Jews and Modern Capitalism*, trans., with notes, by M. Epstein; T. Fisher
Unwin, London, 1913 (1st English ed.), pp. 192–212 (abridged).]

This selection is taken from a chapter, with the same title, in Werner
Sombart's *The Jews and Modern Capitalism* (original German edition
1911, English translation 1913). Sombart was a professor of economics
at the University of Berlin, and a man of many words and ideas.*

Sombart is criticized for the enthusiasm with which he developed his
concepts—or, perhaps, allowed his concepts to carry him along. But in
spite of certain apparent inaccuracies his approach is always provocative.
What he thinks is worth thinking about, even if one does not swallow it
whole. Thus he says in an early part of the chapter (not reproduced
here), "Jewish religion has the same leading ideas as capitalism. I see
the same spirit in the one as in the other." That idea sounds as if it
ought to be examined, doesn't it?

———◆———

IF PURITANISM has had an economic influence, how much more so has
Judaism, seeing that among no other civilized people has
religion so impregnated all national life. For the Jews religion was
not an affair of Sundays and Holy Days; it touched everyday life
even in its minutest action, it regulated *all* human activities. At
every step the Jew asked himself, Will this tend to the glory of God
or will it profane His name? Jewish law defines not merely the
relation between man and God, formulates not merely a metaphysical
conception; it lays down rules of conduct for all possible relationships, whether between man and man or between man and nature.
Jewish law, in fact, is as much part of the religious system as are
Jewish ethics. The Law is from God, and moral law and divine
ordinances are inseparable in Judaism. Hence in reality there are
no special ethics of Judaism. Jewish ethics are the underlying
principle of the Jewish religion. . . .

The kinship between Judaism and capitalism is . . . illustrated
by the legally regulated relationship—I had almost said the businesslike connection, except that the term has a disagreeable connotation—between God and Israel. The whole religious system is in

* For another sample of his thinking and writing, see his piece in Volume
III.

reality nothing but a contract between Jehovah and His chosen people, a contract with all its consequences and all its duties. God promises something and gives something, and the righteous must give Him something in return. Indeed, there was no community of interest between God and man which could not be expressed in these terms —that man performs some duty enjoined by the Torah and receives from God a *quid pro quo*. Accordingly, no man should approach God in prayer without bringing with him something of his own or of his ancestors' by way of return for what he is about to ask.

The contract usually sets forth that man is rewarded for duties performed and punished for duties neglected; the rewards and punishments being received partly in this and partly in the next world. Two consequences must of necessity follow: first, a constant weighing up of the loss and gain which any action needs must bring, and secondly, a complicated system of bookeeping, as it were, for each individual person.

The whole of this conception is excellently well illustrated by the words of Rabbi [probably Judah Ha-Nasi] (A.D. 164–200): "Which is the right course for a man to choose? That which he feels to be honorable to himself and which also brings him honor from mankind. Be heedful of a light precept as of a grave one, for you do not know what reward a precept brings. Reckon the loss incurred by the fulfillment of a precept against the reward secured by its observance, and the gain gotten by a transgression against the loss it involves. Reflect on three things and you will not come within the power of sin. Know what is above thee—a seeing eye, and a hearing ear, and all your deeds written in a book." . . .

Another conception is bound up with this of divine bookkeeping and is closely akin to a second fundamental trait of capitalism—the conception of profit. Sin or goodness is regarded as something apart from the sinner. Every sin, according to rabbinic theology, is considered singly and by itself. "Punishment is according to the object and not the subject of the sin." The quantity of the broken commandments alone counts. No consideration whatever is had for the personality of the sinner or his ethical state, just as a sum of money is separated from persons, just as it is capable of being added to another abstract sum of money. The ceaseless striving of the righteous after well-being in this and the next world must needs therefore take the form of a constant endeavor to increase his rewards. Now, as he is never able to tell whether at a particular state of his conscience he is worthy of God's goodness or whether in his "account" the rewards or the punishments are more numerous, it must be his aim to add reward after reward to his account by constantly doing good deeds to the end of his days. The limited conception of all personal values thus finds no admission into the world of his religious ideas and its place is taken by the endlessness of a pure quantitative ideal.

Parallel with this tendency there runs through Jewish moral theology another which regards the getting of money as a means to an end. The conception is frequently found in books of religious edification, the authors of which realizing but seldom that in their warnings against the acquisition of too much wealth they are glorifying this very practice. Usually the treatment of the subject is under the heading "covetousness," forbidden by the tenth commandment. "A true Israelite," remarks one of the most popular of modern "helps to faith," "avoids covetousness. He looks upon all his possessions only as a means of doing what is pleasing in the sight of God. For is not the entire purpose of his life to use all his possessions, all enjoyment as the means to this end? Indeed it is a duty . . . to obtain possessions and to increase one's enjoyments, not as an end in themselves but as a means to do God's will on earth."

RELIGION IS GOING TO THE DOGS —FOR BUSINESSMEN, AT LEAST

THORSTEIN B. VEBLEN

[Thorstein Veblen, *The Theory of Business Enterprise*, Charles Scribner's Sons, New York, 1904, pp. 359–360.]

Here Thorstein Veblen, the famous sociologist of the early 1900s, makes an uncomfortable contrast between religious and business values. This is typical Veblen, and as such shows the bias of the man (to see the worst underneath the best) and the bias of the age in which he lived (where the worst was indeed the worst).*

SO, AGAIN, as regards the religious life. Men trained by the mechanical occupations to materialistic, industrial habits of thought are beset with a growing inability to appreciate, or even to apprehend, the meaning of religious appeals that proceed on the old-fashioned grounds of metaphysical validity. The consolations of a personal relation (of subservience) to a supernatural master do not appeal to men whose habit of life is shaped by a familiarity with the relations of impersonal cause and effect, rather than by relations

---

* For more details about the man and his philosophy, see page 2003 in this volume.

of personal dominance and fealty. It does not come as a matter of course for such men to give the catechism's answer to the question, What is the chief end of man? Nor do they instinctively feel themselves to be sinners by virtue of a congenital, hereditary taint or obliquity. Indeed, they can only with great difficulty be seriously persuaded that they are sinners at all. They are in danger of losing the point of view of sin. The relation of status or fealty involved in the concept of sin is becoming alien to their habit of mind. They are therefore slow to realize that their past life has violated such a relation of fealty, on the one hand, and that it is of vital consequence to re-establish such a relation of status by a work of salvation or redemption. The kindly ministrations of the church and the clergy grate on the sensibilities of men so trained, as being so much ado about nothing. The machine, their master, is no respecter of persons and knows neither morality nor dignity nor prescriptive right, divine or human; its teaching is training them into insensibility of the whole range of concepts on which these ministrations proceed.

RELIGIOUS FOUNDATIONS OF ECONOMIC PROGRESS

KENNETH E. BOULDING

[Kenneth E. Boulding, "Religious Foundations of Economic Progress," *Harvard Business Review,* May–June 1952, vol. XXX, no. 3, pp. 33–40.]

Kenneth E. Boulding is Professor of Economics at the University of Michigan. He was awarded the John Bates Clark Medal of the American Economic Association in 1949, and his numerous books and articles on economic subjects have established his reputation in many quarters. Accordingly, when Mr. Boulding analyzes the deep and far-reaching influence which religion has had on economic institutions—as he does here—he demands and deserves careful attention.

"My interest in this subject goes back a long time," Mr. Boulding told the *Harvard Business Review,* where his analysis was published in May–June 1952. "Of course, it arises mainly out of the fact that I am both a Quaker and an economist—a combination not always too easy to hold together!"

ONE OF THE MOST CHALLENGING—and tantalizing—propositions of what may be called the "larger economics" is that the success of economic institutions depends to a large extent on the nature of the whole culture in which they are embedded, and not on the nature of these institutions in themselves. This proposition is of particular importance in two current fields of economic inquiry: (a) the study of the complex forces which underlie economic development and (b) the study of the stability and survival power of the characteristic institutions of capitalism.

Indeed, it is only a slight exaggeration to say that the wealth of a nation is a by-product of certain elements in its culture, cumulated through the years. Over a broad range of human societies within the extremes of the Eskimo and the desert nomad, if one area is rich and another poor, it is not because of anything inherent in the natural resources or in the genetic make-up of the people, but because of the cumulative effect of certain familial, educational, and religious practices. Thus the forbidding soil and climate of New England provided a comfortable—if not opulent—homeland for the Puritan, while under the Turk, in his unspeakable days, the ancient cradles of civilization became barren and starveling deserts.

Of all the elements of culture which shape economic institutions, religious practices particularly play a key role—a doubly important one because many other elements of the pattern of life, such as sex, child rearing, work habits, agricultural and industrial practices, are themselves profoundly affected by the prevailing religious beliefs. That religion plays such an important role is not, however, sufficiently recognized by most people, and it is my purpose here to throw more light on it. More specifically, I shall attempt to survey certain aspects of our own society in the light of the contribution which religious ideas, practices, and institutions have made to its economic development and to its power of survival.

PROCESS OF ECONOMIC DEVELOPMENT

To appraise the role of religion in economic development, we must understand the process by which economic change takes place. All change may not be for the better, but it is clear that there can be no betterment without some change.

There are, then, three essential features of any process of economic development in a society—innovation, imitation, and displacement; and two further features which, though conceivably not indispensable, are almost certain to be present in any kind of economic improvement process of which we have knowledge— accumulation of capital and limitation of population. Let us look more closely at these five features:

(1) There must be an *innovator*, who first makes the change. He can be divided, as was done by Schumpeter, into an inventor and an

entrepreneur. But the point here is that whether the function is specialized or not, or whether it is performed by a single individual or by a number, the function itself is necessary. If we are to have progress, somebody, somewhere, must do something in a way that has never been done before.

(2) If, however, there is no freedom to *imitate* a change—still more, if the innovator himself is suppressed by the conservative institutions of his society—there can be no testing out of the innovation to see whether it in fact constitutes a "betterment" or not. It would be rash to say that all innovations which are widely imitated are in fact "betterments," for even the mass may be wrong. But we can say that unless there is opportunity for imitation, an innovation *cannot* be tested, and nobody can ever find out whether it is in fact a "good" innovation, that is, a "better" way of doing things.

(3) Imitation cannot take place, in turn, unless there is *displacement* of the old methods. It is the resistance to displacement (that is, to "competition") on the part of those whose interests are bound up with the old ways, and who are not flexible enough in their habits or opportunities to change, which is likely to be one of the main obstacles to change.

(4) Next, practically all economic innovation of which we have knowledge involves the *accumulation of capital,* in the broad sense of the increase in "valuable objects." The objects so accumulated are not only material; the acquisition of skills, traits, and abilities constitutes capital accumulation just as much as does the stockpiling of materials and material equipment.

If capital is to be accumulated, production must exceed consumption—production being gross additions to the total stock of capital, and consumption being subtractions from it. Such accumulation is far from automatic. In poor societies it is difficult because the minimum needs of consumption press daily on the meager and hard-won product; most of the activity of the society is concerned with mere maintenance, and little is left for accumulation. In rich societies the threat may be from more subtle sources—from unwillingness to accumulate (i.e., to invest) leading to unemployment and from levels of production below the society's capacity.

(5) Even if there is an increase in the total capital or income of a society, however, economic progress will not necessarily result. Economic well-being must rise on a per-capita basis. Hence the accumulation of capital will not constitute "improvement" unless capital increases, in some sense, faster than population. And hence a permanent high-level economy is not possible unless there is *limitation of population*—that is, unless population is checked by methods other than starvation and poverty (according to the familiar "dismal theorem" of Malthus that if nothing checks the growth of

population but misery and starvation, then the population will grow until it is miserable and starves).

Even if a society starts on the road of economic improvement, then, there are many elements in its culture which may prevent the improvement in techniques from resulting in an actual improvement in welfare. The newly won powers may be used merely for the support of larger populations at the old level of poverty, or they may also be squandered in the luxury of a foolish ruling class or in the waste of total war. The pyramids of Egypt and the endless wars of Rome are good examples of the waste of resources liberated by technical improvement.

INFLUENCE OF THE PROTESTANT ETHIC

The past three centuries have witnessed a rate of economic development in the "western world" which, measured by any standard we choose, almost certainly exceeds the achievement of any other period of equal length in human history. We are so much accustomed to this rapid progress, both in techniques and in general levels of income, that we are likely to take it for granted. Nevertheless, looking over the whole range of human history and prehistory, we can clearly see that these last 300 years represent an episode in human development which has no parallel, except perhaps in that dim period when settled agriculture was invented and gave rise to the first civilizations.

The unique nature of the achievement makes it all the more important that we should not take it for granted, but should inquire very carefully into its sources in the culture of the western world. The history of civilizations reveals that it is perfectly possible, indeed easy, to dry up the springs of progress in a society, and that virtually all past civilizations have eventually done so. Therefore, unless we are aware of the nature of those elements in our total pattern of life which are responsible for this rapid rate of development, we may run into grave danger of changing that pattern, without knowing it, in a way that destroys those peculiar elements in the culture from which development springs.

Important among the elements in our complex culture having favorable influence on the rate of economic development are certain religious ideas and practices which comprise the so-called "Protestant ethic."

The thesis of Max Weber and his school that the Protestant ethic has influenced the development of capitalism is now well accepted. Though one's estimate of the quantitative importance of this influence will depend to a great extent on the interpretation of history which one favors, the direction of the influence can hardly be in doubt.

What has not, I think, been pointed out with sufficient force is that the Protestant ethic has contributed to the *success* of capitalist institutions, particularly in regard to their fostering a high rate of economic progress. Economic sociologists like Weber, Sombart, and Tawney, who have emphasized the close connection between religious and economic ideas, have been on the whole unfriendly to capitalist institutions and have consequently tended to lay stress on their failures rather than their successes. This is perhaps because the ethical systems of these writers were conceived in fairly static terms—in terms, for instance, of the problem of justice in the distribution of a given total income, rather than in terms of the encouragement of a growing total income.

It has now become clear, however, that the consequence of even a small rate of economic progress, persistently raising average incomes, is so enormous over even a few decades that from the point of view of long-run human welfare the capacity of a system to generate economic development has come to overshadow all other criteria in judging it "good" or "bad." (Curiously enough, this has also become true of Communism; in the interest of inducing a rapid rate of economic development the rulers of Russia have thrown overboard practically every other ideal of their ethical system, and have developed degrees of inequality which even the most uncontrolled period of capitalist development could hardly rival.)

In other words, we see now that in practice the abolition of poverty can come only from development—not from redistribution, not from taking from the rich to give to the poor, but by making everybody richer. And it is on this score that the Protestant ethic, which was born with the Reformation, has been so influential.

Innovation, imitation, and displacement in economic life have their counterparts in religious life. Thus the Reformation marked the beginning of a series of innovations in religion. Men like Luther, Calvin, Menno Simons, George Fox, John Wesley, General Booth, and even in our own day Frank Buchman, represent a disturbance of the previously established equilibrium, with a new form of religious enterprise and new arrangements of human time and spiritual energy. They are widely imitated, and the spread of the new technique forces profound adjustments even in those older institutions which do not go over completely to the new ideas.

It generally seems to be true that these innovations in religion have preceded and in some sense paved the way for innovations in economic life. Indeed, the most important innovation in any society is the *idea* of innovation itself, for this represents the Rubicon between the traditional stationary type of society, in which each generation repeats the pattern of its elders, and the "economic," dynamic society, in which innovation becomes an accepted and profitable role. A strong case can be made out for the claim that the principal historical agency bringing about this critical change is a reformation (or revolution) in religion, that this liberates the society from its previous equilibrium and exposes it to all the terrors and delights of dynamics. Once iconoclasm has succeeded in the most traditional and "sacred" area of life, once "free enterprise" has been successful in religion, the spirit of innovation seizes upon all other areas of life.

What in our western society we call *the* Reformation is of course only one among many. The period of rapid innovation which followed the rise of Mohammedanism is another and spectacular example. Within Christianity itself the monastic reformations—especially of the Benedictines and Cistercians—paved the way for the economic development of medieval Europe. Again—if only to remind us that Protestantism is not the whole story—the Counter-Reformation within the Catholic Church also represents a period of "innovation," though of a less dramatic and less iconoclastic nature.

The fact remains that the Protestant Reformation has certain specific features of its own which have increased its importance for economic development. I am not referring to the sanctification of economic activity through the extension of the concept of "vocation," as emphasized by earlier writers. The concept of vocation is not peculiar to Protestantism, nor is it so important as what I have in mind.

First of all, there is the "unmediated" character of Protestant religion, that is, the emphasis on the individual's own responsibility for his religious life and salvation without the intermediary of priest or prescribed ritualistic "works." It is this unmediated quality of Protestant religion which underlies the sociological significance of the doctrine of justification by faith. Protestantism, that is to say, represents private enterprise in religion, as opposed to the great organized collectivism of the Catholic Church.

It is not surprising that private enterprise in religion carried over into the economic field. The full effect of this is seen in the eighteenth century, where the immense economic innovations which constituted the beginnings of the technical revolution in banking, trade, and industry were to an astonishing extent the work of the British nonconformists, and especially of the Quakers, who had developed the most unmediated of all Protestant varieties of religion.

Another aspect of Protestantism which relates closely to economic development is its perfectionism. Like the earlier monastic reformations, Protestantism reflects a discontent with compromise with the "world" and a serious attempt to return to the pristine revelation of perfection implied in the Christian vision of perfect love. Unlike the monastic reformation, however, the Protestant Reformation—because one of the things against which it was protesting was the corruption of the monastery and nunnery prevalent in the time of Luther—rejected the monastic solution and became an attempt to lead the life of Christian perfection in the workaday world rather than in cloistered separation.

Such an attempt, however, is almost doomed to fail, and the difficulty of practicing the major virtue of charity will lead to an insensible substitution of the "minor virtues" as attainable ends of the religious group. So the perfectionist subsides into the Puritan, and groups of people arise practicing, with some success, the minor virtues of thrift, hard work, sobriety, punctuality, honesty, fulfillment of promises, devotion to family, and so on. The minor virtues, however, lead almost inevitably to accumulation and increased productivity, and eventually therefore to an escape from poverty.

THE LOST ECONOMIC GOSPEL

This all adds up to what I call the "lost economic gospel" of Protestantism. Poverty is the result of "sin," sin being defined in terms of intemperance, loose living, prodigality, laziness, dishonesty, and so on (that is, in terms of violation of the "minor virtues").* On yielding to the power of Christ and the discipline of the congregation the individual is converted, gives up his evil ways, and becomes temperate, frugal, thrifty, hard working, honest, and so on; as a result of which he begins to accumulate skill and other capital and raises his standard of life. Thus he becomes respectable, and incidentally, but only incidentally, he may become rich by hitting on a successful innovation.

In the process of the individual's becoming richer, society also becomes richer. Indeed, the improvement of society is nothing more than the sum of the improvements of individuals. In a dynamic and improving society, therefore, the increase in riches of the individual is not thought of as a redistribution of wealth (one individual gaining at the expense of others) but rather as a creation of wealth (the gains of one individual representing net additions to the total and being taken from no man). Economic life is not a "zero sum" poker game in which a fixed volume of wealth is circulated around among the players, but a "positive sum" enterprise in which the accumulation of each person represents something which he brings to the "pot" rather than something which he takes out.

Another doctrine which Protestantism shares with other forms of Christianity has combined with the "lost gospel" to contribute to the success of capitalist institutions: the doctrine of stewardship, of charity in the narrower sense of the word. Those whose virtue, energy, or plain good fortune have brought them material success are

---

* Kenneth E. Boulding, "Our Lost Economic Gospel," the *Christian Century*, August 16, 1950, pp. 970–972.

expected to regard their riches as in some sense a trust, to be used for the benefit of the less fortunate. Over the long pull, this aspect of Christian culture has proved of great importance in modifying the inequalities of capitalism. As in the middle ages the establishment of monasteries was an important agency in the redistributon of wealth and income, so in the nineteenth and twentieth centuries the establishment of universities and foundations has provided a means whereby private accumulations have found their way into public uses.

The habit of mind engendered by the doctrine of stewardship has also been important in removing obstacles to legislative methods of correcting inequalities, such as progressive income and inheritance taxation. It is quite possible that this factor may have something to do with the different impact of capitalist institutions in the West and, say, in China, where the acquisitive opportunities have been less likely to be modified by the sense of responsibility for the welfare of those outside the circle of kinship.

It can hardly be doubted, then, that the "lost gospel"—the old gospel of individualism, of self-help—is in many respects a sound one. Indeed, the middle-class nature of Protestantism is a testimony to its long-run success. If Protestants are middle-class, it is largely because their Protestantism has made them so—has developed a culture in which hard work, thrift, family limitation, productivity, and frugality have been important values. There is hardly any better over-all recipe for economic development, whether for the individual or for a society.

Nevertheless to a considerable degree the old doctrines are discredited in the churches today, especially, oddly enough, in the more prosperous ones. The old gospel of self-help flourishes among the little rising sects, the pentecostal people, and the store-front churches, it is actually the poor who seem to be least aware of the new "social gospel" and who cling to the old-time individual virtues. In the large Protestant denominations, as represented by the National Council of Churches, it is not perhaps unfair to say that there is more awareness of the weakness of the individualist gospel than of its strength, and that even where the older gospel is preached, it is often the result of the momentum of tradition rather than of any continuing spiritual insight.

There are significant reasons for the decline of the gospel of self-help and the rise of the "social gospel." Part of the cause lies in sheer misunderstanding, stemming from failure to appreciate the ethical significance of economic progress, and a resultant economic ethic based on static assumptions, in which an undue stress is laid on distributing a fixed sum of wealth fairly rather than on increasing the total to be distributed.

More fundamental is a certain inevitable tension between the ethic of the New Testament and the ethic of Samuel Smiles (the old Scottish biographer of industrialists and extoller of thrift and self-reliance). There is an anti-economic strain in the teaching of almost all the prophets and poets. The careful, calculating, economizing way of life is neither prophetic nor poetic. It counts the cost; it asks for reward; it has no fine frenzies; it is humdrum, commonplace, even a little sordid. The stimulus to economic progress, therefore, is not in the ethic of the New Testament itself; rather it is in the "Puritan" substitute-ethic, the product of the impact of the ethic of love on the iron laws of the world.

The substitute-ethic, however, is itself somewhat unstable, because it is always subject to criticism by the pure ethic which generates it. Hybrids are vigorous but can generally only be reproduced from pure stock! Thus when the New Testament makes a fresh impact on a sensitive and vigorous mind—as it is likely to do at least once in a generation—the gospel of "be righteous and grow rich," for all its truth and practicality, looks cheap and pharisaical beside the poetic vision of "sell all thou hast and give to the poor"; and radical forms of Christianity tend to appear. There is something in Toynbee's suggestion that Communism is a Christian heresy!

Perhaps a still more fundamental reason for the failure of capitalism to sustain the ethic which supports its most characteristic institutions is to be found in certain technical failures of these institutions themselves.

The ethic of capitalism is based firmly on the proposition that wealth is produced by saving and that saving is accomplished by producing much and consuming little. That is why the principal recipe for riches includes hard work and thrift and the other Protestant virtues. Under some circumstances, however, wealth is not produced by saving. Hard work works the worker out of a job, parsimony produces unemployement, and the fluctuations of the price system redistribute wealth without regard to any of the soberer virtues. The thrifty and hard-working find their net worth disappearing in deflation and their hard-earned interest and pensions evaporating in inflation, while the speculator and the manipulator reap what others have sown.

In conditions of general price and output instability the poker-game aspects of capitalism come to the fore. Instead of wealth being accumulated by carefully contributing to the physical stock more than one takes from it, it is accumulated by taking advantage of the shifting structure of relative values, by buying cheap and selling dear. Every economist will recognize, of course, that there is a legitimate function of speculation, and that some flexibilty of the price structure is necessary to reflect changing structures

of productivity and tastes. In fact, however, the characteristic institutions of capitalism—especially the organized commodity
and security markets and the real estate market—have lent themselves to fluctuations far beyond what the flexibility of the system
requires, and have therefore been the instrument of redistributions
of wealth which have created a gap between economic virtue (in
the sense of contribution to the progress of real wealth) and reward.

The phenomenon of depression has been particularly destructive
to the capitalist ethic, because the misery which it has entailed
has seemed to be so meaningless: why work and save when the end
result is the foreclosure of a mortgage and selling apples in the
street! The whole technical weakness of an ungoverned market
economy can be summed up in two concepts: (a) speculative instability in price levels due to the dynamics of self-justified expectations and (b) the limited or imperfect market resulting either from
monopolistic imperfections in the market structure or from general
deflation. Speculative instability leads to essentially meaningless
redistributions of wealth. The limited market leads to an undue shift
of emphasis away from production, to wasteful advertising and selling
costs, to restrictions of output, to featherbedding, and to other
familiar devices by which individuals or segments of the economy
seek to protect themselves from the impact of general deflations or
seek to enhance their own particular power position at the expense
of others.

The all-important question is whether these defects are to be
regarded as diseases of the free economy, potentially curable within
the general framework of market institutions, or whether they are
to be regarded as essential genetic characteristics of it, quite incurable
without a radical overthrow of the whole market economy itself.

CHANCES OF SURVIVAL

It is this connection that the contribution of Keynes to the survival of capitalism is so important, for it is the essence of the
Keynesian view that the defects of capitalism are curable diseases
rather than incurable deformities. While the actual cures may be a
matter still in considerable dispute, it is the great virtue of the
Keynesian analysis that it gives us a clearer picture than we have
ever had before of the nature of the disease, and it has consequently
engendered the hope that institutions can be devised within the
general framework of a free market economy which will prevent
deflation and unemployment, on the one hand, and inflation, on the
other.

If such a "governor" can insure the overall stability of the economy
(and it is not the purpose of this article to say how this should be

done), most of the ethical objections to a market economy fall to the ground. Given a reasonable degree of stability of the overall price and output system, the old-fashioned virtues of hard work, thrift, honesty, and so on come into their own.

Perhaps the crucial test of the capitalist system will turn on its ability to solve what is by far the greatest single economic problem facing the world today: the development of the so-called under-developed areas—inhabited by about three-quarters of the world's population—to the point where at least the grim consequences of extreme poverty (malnutrition, early death, constant ill health, superstition, squalor, and misery) are mitigated.

There are, roughly speaking, two kinds of society in the world today. The "high-level" societies have low birth and death rates, an expectation of life at birth rising up toward 60 or 70 years, disease well under control, malnutrition rare, literacy universal, education wide-spread, a high status and much freedom for women, complex economic and political institutions, and so on. The "low-level" societies, on the other hand, have high birth and death rates, an expectation of life around 30 years, disease and malnutrition rampant, literacy and education confined to a small upper class, a low status for women among the mass of the people, burdensome and exploitative financial institutions, often a colonial status, and so on.

The crux of the problem is how to raise the three-quarters of the world that live on a low level to the high level of the other quarter, for it is precisely this wide disparity that makes our world so unstable. American-Russian relations, for instance, would not constitute the apparently insoluble problem which they now pose if the relationship were simply one of America and Russia; in that event they could perfectly well leave each other alone! The relation-ship is complicated almost unbearably by the fact that each power is competing for the support of the vast fringe of underdeveloped countries which divide them on the globe, from Poland to Korea. These countries are dissatisfied with their present state and are hover-ing between the two cultures, wondering which offers them the best chance of shifting from their present low-level to a high-level economy.

In this whole difficult situation it is of vital importance to ap-preciate the relation of economic institutions and economic de-velopment to the *whole* culture pattern, and to realize that the success of any set of economic institutions depends on the total culture setting in which they are placed. The success, even of modern tech-nology, therefore, may depend quite as much upon the missionary as upon the engineer. One of the tasks of human inquiry is to discover exactly what the elements are in any culture which per-petuate poverty—whether in family life, in religious life, in education, in politics, or in economic and financial institutions—and then to effect a *minimum* change in the culture which is necessary to eradicate these germs of poverty.

We do not want, of course, the kind of cultural imperialism that insists on giving the Fiji Islanders Coca-Cola and Christmas trees whether these things are meaningful extensions of their present culture or not. Cultural change and cultural impact, however, there must be. Such impact is immensely dangerous and may result in disaster to both cultures; yet with the collapse of isolation such impact is inevitable. If it is to be ultimately fruitful, it must be understood much better than we understand it now; the marriage of economics and cultural anthropology must be accomplished, even at the point of a shotgun!

It must not be thought, however, that all that is needed for world salvation is a stiff dose of social science, no matter how well documented empirically and no matter how well integrated analytically. The rise of social science presents man with problems of an ethical and spiritual nature of which he is still for the most part not aware. The spectacular "success" of the physical sciences in expanding the power of man, both for good and for evil, is dramatically symbolized in the atom bomb. The worst that a physicist can do for anybody, however, is to cause pain and death. The social scientist, when he knows a little more, may be able to destroy the soul, that inner core of freedom and integrity which constitutes at once the humanity and the divinity of man.

The nightmare of the "manipulative society"—the brave new world of Aldous Huxley or George Orwell—is not too far from reality. We see it foreshadowed in the crudely manipulative society of Soviet Russia, and it is this aspect of Communism which rightly fills us with disgust and fear. In its very conflict with Communism, however, the West may find itself sliding imperceptibly into a manipulative society more horrible, because more efficient, than the Soviet counterpart.

A world of unseen dictatorship is conceivable, still using the forms of democratic government, in which education has been replaced by training, in which government creates artificially the public opinion which keeps it in power, in which "loyalty" investigations corrupt the whole system of communications, in which only "safe" ideas are expressed, in which love of country is corroded by conscription and integrity is swallowed up in expediency, and in which the springs of technical, as well as of moral, progress are eventually dried up. The cleverer we are and the more we know, the more thoroughly we may damn ourselves.

INCREASED SIGNIFICANCE OF RELIGION

When the final history of the human race comes to be written, therefore, the part played by religion and religious experience may be even more significant than I have suggested earlier. I have argued that religion is an important autonomous force in the development of the technical revolution. It may turn out to be even more important in the control of this revolution.

We do not yet realize, I believe, what a portentous watershed in human history we are now treading. Civilization is a product of the increase in human control over environment which resulted from the invention of settled agriculture. All past civilizations, however, have proved to be unstable; the "iron laws" of social dynamics have eventually caught up with them and destroyed them. It is by no means improbable that our own civilization will suffer the same fate.

Yet there is reason for hope. As our knowledge not only of nature but of man and society expands, we may get to the point where man comes not to be ruled by history but to rule it. He may be able to take the iron laws and fashion them into an instrument for his own purposes, to mold the unconscious dynamic which drives him to destroy his civilizations into a conscious dynamic which will empower him to perpetuate them indefinitely.

The possibility of permanent and universal civilization therefore rises before us, though the prospect is not necessarily one to be approached without fear. It might be the kingdom of heaven on earth, but it might also be an indestructible and universal tyranny, securely based on the power of both physical and social science. A world of refugees is bad enough, but a world in which there is no place of refuge would be worse.

An increase in human power, therefore, makes all the more urgent the question of the discipline of the human will. Economic development means an increase in our ability to get what we want. Religion, however, raises the question of whether we want the right things. As long as we are impotent, it does not perhaps matter so much in regard to externals whether we want the right things or the wrong things. We cannot get what we want in any case. But if we can get what we want, the question of whether we want the right things becomes acutely important.

There are those who think that as economic development comes to fruition in a humanistic heaven on earth where war, poverty, and disease are abolished, religion will wither away. In that millennium faith will be swallowed up in knowledge, hope in fulfillment, and love in psychoanalysis and group dynamics! Such a belief seems to be naïve. As power and knowledge increase, the question of the *truth* of religion—of what is the "will of God," and how it is discovered and incorporated into the human will—becomes all-important. The feather of religious experience may then tip the great scales toward either heaven or hell on earth.

POWER AND MORALITY IN A BUSINESS SOCIETY

~~~◊~~~

SYLVIA KOPALD SELEKMAN AND BENJAMIN M. SELEKMAN

[Sylvia Kopald Selekman, Benjamin M. Selekman, "Power: Liberator or Enslaver?" in *Power and Morality in a Business Society*, McGraw-Hill Book Co., New York, copyright © 1956, pp. 3–14 (abridged). Reprinted by permission of author and publisher.]

Professor Benjamin M. Selekman, of the Harvard Business School Faculty, has long been a student of labor relations, as well as a teacher in the same field and an arbitrator in industrial disputes. As can be inferred from this article, he has had an intense feeling of sympathy for all people; he has known laborers from his early years, and he has increasingly come to know managers. So it was with a rare background of experience and of informed spirit that he wrote, in collaboration with his wife, *Power and Morality in a Business Society* (1956), of which this selection is a chapter, "Power: Liberator or Enslaver?" He has reduced the whole confused labor issue to a clear and essential conflict, for which there is no resolution, but which becomes bearable and even constructive through morality on the part of those who hold power.

———◆———

IT IS A LIFETIME of exposure to the impact of power on human relationships which has led us to undertake this exploration into power and morality. For both of us have seen and felt power from childhood on, not only in the usual daily disciplines experienced as one grows up but also in the much harsher forms resorted to in the struggle shaking the social structure of the communities and the times in which we lived.

POWER AND HUMAN EXPLOITATION AT BEGINNING OF CENTURY

One of us grew up, for instance, amidst coal and steel in western Pennsylvania. Here, during the first two decades of this century, I was a witness to the intermittent battles between miners and steelworkers on the one hand and their employers on the other over the right to have any voice in the conditions of work and life. And literally it was *life,* for in those days most of the miners not only worked in the pits of the employing companies but also lived in the company towns and bought all their provisions, clothing, and other necessities in the company stores. Rent and store bills were automatically deducted from earnings on payday.

The strikes of those times were violent—invariably accompanied with damage to property, personal injury, and loss of life. The workers resorted to the use of naked power when picketing; the employers resorted to naked power when importing strikebreakers. These strikebreakers enjoyed the protection of private police such as Baldwin Fels' detectives and specially deputized sheriffs. The state constabulary, nominally neutral in their duty to maintain the peace, usually ended up in any particular strike by protecting property and strikebreakers. During one strike, I saw the brutal dispersal by the state constabulary of men, women, and children assembled on the main street of the town to hear a union organizer. The method was a simple one. The constabulary put spurs to their trained horses at the head of the street and rode through the crowd six abreast swinging their maces until most of their victims fell dazed or unconscious to the cobblestones. Those who escaped the horses' hoofs and the policemen's clubs scattered to the four winds.

During my last year in high school, I was so shocked at such brutal denial of the basic liberty of free assemblage—which I had been studying in my civics course—that I devoted my graduation oration to berating those in power, dragging in "Wall Street," of course, as well as "economic determinism" and "capitalistic imperialism"! The respectable townspeople blamed the school superintendent for permitting such a "subversive" speech to be made. They also snubbed me as I went on my wonted errands to the grocer, the butcher, and the landlord, though I had been an erstwhile hero and a source of pride because I was planning to go to college (something very few from industrial towns did in those days).

Similarly, both of us witnessed the degradation of the sweatshops in the large cities—my late wife as she grew up in New York, and I as from time to time I visited friends who held jobs in the needle trades. Several of our friends became exhausted under the harsh conditions prevailing in those unsanitary, makeshift shops. Some became invalids with chronic illness. A few died prematurely. Most of them were active participants in building unions which were destined, after many strikes and much violence, not only to eliminate so miserable a working environment but also to collaborate with management in pioneering in such progressive measures as housing, banking, workers' education, and arbitration machinery. Having witnessed, as young people, the degradation of workers, both of us rejoiced when as grownups we were given an opportunity to participate in these new forms of self-government, particularly in workers' education and in arbitration.

On my first job, I again witnessed a power struggle. I was assigned to make a field study of the aftermath of the bitter and violent strike which the miners had waged for fifteen months in 1913 and 1914 against the Colorado Fuel and Iron Company in Huerfano and Las Animas counties. In one of the battles between striking miners and militia at Ludlow, eleven children and two women had been smothered to death when the tents in which they lived after eviction from company houses were ignited by flying bullets exchanged between miners and soldiers. In addition, I observed events and interviewed the steelworkers of the same company at the Pueblo works as they participated, almost to a man, in the nationwide steel strike in 1919.

Fortunately, I was to observe in Colorado not only the impact of economic and political power, with all its grim manifestation in naked violence, but also the influence of moral power. For John D. Rockefeller had been shocked and stung into action by the exposure of President Wilson's Industrial Relations Commission of what went on in a company which his family controlled. With the help of Clarence Hicks, recruited from the YMCA movement, and W. L. Mackenzie King, then ex-deputy Minister of Labor and later Prime Minister of Canada, he drafted a plan of employee representation, known in time as the Rockefeller Plan. It aimed to give the miners and the steelworkers a vehicle for voicing their grievances, as well as for participating in determining wages and working conditions. So dedicated was Rockefeller in his moral purpose that he personally visited the working communities in Colorado—not without risk—and himself explained to the miners the intent and purpose of his plan.

POWER AND HUMAN EMANCIPATION BY MIDCENTURY

One could go on at length portraying the human suffering and maladjustments arising out of clashes of power in industry in those early years. But it is better to draw the curtain on that scene and lift it again approximately a quarter of a century later. We see now a complete and dramatic change. The unions representing steelworkers, coal miners, clothing, and garment workers are now fully established and recognized. Their legitimacy, like that of all organized labor, is now explicitly sanctioned by law and upheld by the vigorous administration of a Federal agency. The miners, the steelworkers, the tailors, enjoy not only the highest wages in the world (real wages, not just money wages!) but also holidays and vacations with pay, pensions, sickness and hospital benefits, and, well on the way, assured minimum earnings when laid off. In the communities where they live, they and their unions now occupy an important and, not infrequently, a dominant position. In the affairs of their respective industries, the unions exercise a potent voice, heard with respect and sometimes with misgiving by management. For in the eyes of the latter—by this time a professionally trained corps of men as compared with the hard-boiled superintendent and foreman of a generation ago—the constant pressure for wage increases, greater benefits, and an ever wider "say" in industry may imperil the capacity of business to function efficiently; the whole economy, indeed, may be upset by these pressures. With the threats of inflation or rigidities in costs, business may find it difficult to keep competitive and to plan and develop new enterprises—a necessity for the economic growth and prosperity of the nation.

It is not our purpose here to examine the pros and cons in the positions of unions or corporations, but, rather, to etch with a few broad strokes the contrast between the 1950s and the situation as it prevailed before the 1930s. For economic and political power— reinforced by moral power—has brought about a complete change during our lifetime in the social and economic structure of the nation. The acceleration of scientific power, moreover, during two World Wars has laid the basis not only for great material wealth and strength but also for the nightmare vision of the destruction of the civilization which the same scientific power has helped to preserve and foster.

And, just as both of us were witnesses to the unsocial exploitation of power in the early years of this century, so have we been privileged to witness and to participate as teachers, researchers, consultants, and arbitrators, in the socializing of power in the past quarter century.

But power was seen by one of us in still another phase. My wife grew up under the influence of Daniel De Leon's Socialist Labor Party, a form of socialism more akin to the Russian Marxism of Lenin than to the American socialism of Debs or Thomas. At first, she rejoiced when the czars were displaced by the Bolsheviks. But the joy was destined to prove short-lived. She recoiled with distaste and disillusionment as Lenin, and later Stalin, imposed a massive slavery upon the Russian people, a slavery soon to be copied by Mussolini and Hitler as they merged collectivism and nationalism into fascism and Nazism as a façade for completely subjugating and brutalizing their peoples. What a contrast America offered as it grappled with its problems from day to day to emerge into the humanitarian nation of the 1950s.

Indeed, anyone who has lived through the first half of this century in this country cannot help being impressed with the changed and changing status of women, of minorities, of wage earners. To be sure, the movement for greater freedom has been an uneven one, particularly in the matter of equality for racial and ethnic minorities.

Nevertheless, in contrast with the enslavement of whole peoples by Nazism, fascism, and communism, the period in the United States amounts to one of liberation. There is even a contrast, not so sharp, to be sure, between events in this country and the nations of western Europe, from whom we inherited the great basic liberties of mankind. The contrast is not between freedom and enslavement, but rather between the vitality of the American people and in Europe a sort of dead-center standstill—even perhaps timidity—in carrying out an early promise for the liberation of man.

AMERICAN POWER AND HUMAN FREEDOM ON GLOBAL SCALE

We do not intend to pause and examine the probable causes of these striking differences between this country and Europe. Two World Wars constitute an obvious factor; for in eastern and central Europe the aftermath in misery and destruction enabled ruthless men with fixed ideologies to seize power and, under the guise of collectivism, mislead and subjugate their demoralized and disillusioned fellow nationalists. The same wars exhausted France and Great Britain. For over a year, indeed, Britain stood alone in the breach in a life-and-death struggle against evil tyranny.

We entered both wars, but we entered them late. Our allies were well-nigh exhausted before we fully awoke to the peril of a victory for the forces of tyranny. Our power, in spite of its tardy mobilization, turned the scales. But instead of finding ourselves exhausted, we emerged with our strength augmented to greater heights than it had ever known before. Indeed, both times we came out as the strongest nation of the globe. We withdrew from the world scene after World War I. In retrospect, our withdrawal constituted an abdication of responsibility, but this is not to say that, even had we stayed in, World War II would have been prevented. For Nazism and fascism were new forms of tyranny. It is questionable whether we, any more than the British and French with their much greater experience in statecraft and diplomacy, would have had the wisdom to lead the free world so as to discourage the evil forces within Germany before Hitler could let loose upon the world the most horrible war ever waged.

After World War II, however, we did stay in with the rest of the civilized world, and the results, whatever the initial discouragement, have been most heartening. Without us, Russian communism would no doubt by now be ensconced on the Eurasian continent, from the English Channel to the Pacific, with still more satellites within her domain than she boasts of now. For this time, sensing at last our self-interest, we not only stayed with our friends but also assumed the responsibility of leadership and, together with our allies, forged the North Atlantic community, a power bloc strong enough to counterbalance Russian power. And by means of the Marshall Plan and other forms of assistance, we have helped the European democracies gradually regain their spirit and their strength. While we differ in many things, the Western community is becoming more an alliance of self-respecting and articulate nations. It now looks, indeed, as if Russia, checkmated as she is, may seriously enter into negotiations with the West to work out a possible pattern of coexistence.

Now, what is impressive in all this is that power has constituted the primary factor in bringing about critical changes for good or for evil. Our power proved decisive in winning two World Wars, and, as this is written, may be turning the scales toward a workable peace—or at least a stalemate under which Russia may rely on diplomacy and subversion, rather than physical attack, to gain her ends. So long as a resort to raw power is thus avoided and the tests shifted to the diplomatic front, the hope remains strong that not only may destructive war be prevented but also that we may have a more than equal chance of winning the battle for men's minds.

SHIFTS OF POWER AND INEVITABLE SCAPEGOATS

Within the national scene, too, power constituted the primary factor behind the movement for liberation. It was by mobilizing their political power and making alliances with liberal and reform groups that women gained their right to participate equally with men in government. Labor achieved its new status by unremittingly building its strength on the economic and political front. Progress in this instance was, it is true, retarded until the great depression of the thirties; and, in those prostrate days, many workers became as disillusioned as their European brethren. But it was our good fortune that the leaders of the incipient labor movement had not become discouraged by the rebuffs historically received at the hands of industry. For this was the time when Hitler and Mussolini rose to strength. It was the time when Stalin strengthened his vise on the Russian people. In our country, fortunately, more conservative labor leaders were followed, and in a short period of twenty years, we witnessed the growth of a powerful labor movement. Farmers also rose to new strength in the economic and political arena. Massive social and welfare legislation was enacted.

In the heat of the moment there were also negative outbursts, and attacks of one group upon another filled the air. Business became a convenient scapegoat; having been at the direction of the economic life of the nation for so long a period, it could hardly escape the searching, if unfriendly, criticism which followed. Nor could it escape the legislation enacted to regulate its activities and minimize the abuses, real or fancied, which the people thought had brought about the great depression. Thus again the century was shaken by a shift in power.

NATURE OF POWER

Power shifts such as these have long been the subject of study and observation. What has not been adequately studied, however—and what we must consider if we are to understand the time in which we live—is the nature of power itself: power as liberator and creator; power as enslaver and destroyer. By power we mean all the essential phases of energy which help to free man from backbreaking drudgery and thus make his life actually and potentially more productive and creative. But we must hasten to add that power also includes those phases of energy which threaten man with servitude and, in its latest form, with destruction. To be more specific, by power we mean the power of nature uncovered by science; the power of man as he organizes himself and his fellow men through a multiplicity of economic and political activities and institutions to do better cooperatively (and competitively) what he cannot do by himself; and finally, the power of morality—the body of religious and ethical doctrines which every man socially inherits, and which thus, in the American ethos, shapes men's ideals toward the kind of society envisioned by the Judaic-Christian and the Greco-Roman traditions.

THE CHALLENGE OF DEPLOYING POWER CREATIVELY

We stand, thus, in the middle of the twentieth century with new groups in positions of great power within the nation, and, as a nation among nations, with a vitality that has been paralleled only in a few periods of history. One would think that, with this peak strength, America would be secure, sure of itself, ready to move forward. A malaise, however, seems to be besetting us. We are unsure of ourselves. We are sensitive to criticism. We are misunderstood. We find that people elsewhere are not happy with our leadership. Even our generosity is turned against us. Internally, we are ill at ease and suspicious of one another—so much so that at times we seem in danger of forgetting our fundamental belief in the dignity of man. We enjoy a standard of living unparalleled in the world or in all history; but we do not enjoy life. We are mobile in our cars and see the whole world in television. Yet we are not sure where we want to go or what we want to see. Our very power baffles us, and we do not know how to turn it into creative expression both as a nation and as individual citizens. We recoil from the charge of materialism and the challenge that a system based on private enterprise can never achieve a moral life. And so we answer defensively. We deny. We scold. Sometimes we are tempted to with-draw—and, indeed, threaten with "agonizing reappraisals." We suffer from a gnawing sense of guilt and sin and from a lack of confidence and mutual trust. Most of all, incredible as it may seem, America is afraid. Indeed, at times it seems as if the most powerful people on the face of the earth are suffering from one of the worst cases of jitters known.

Such a situation, if continued, is in danger of eventually sapping our vitality. Unless we try to understand the fundamental nature of our society as interrelated systems of power—scientific, business, political, and moral—we are in danger of failing in our mission, the mission to establish a great civilization on this continent and to lead the way toward peace and security for mankind. . . .

America's power has made her fearful all the more because its dimension is so great. For as a people we hesitate to accept the fact that power is an essential for progress and freedom. We are haunted by the age-old suspicion that power is evil, as indeed it is, unless it is checked, contained, and directed. How may such an objective be attained and how can the objective be worked out in day-to-day living—the objective of diminishing the evil and enhancing the beneficent aspects of power? . . .

The fulfillment of man's aspirations for effective and moral living is, and must be, a never-ending quest. What we wish above all is to get our fellow Americans excited about the great opportunity which has come to them because of the vast power they have in-herited and developed—not to fear it or apologize for it, but, rather, to deploy it in a way to enrich and ennoble us and the rest of the world.

THE UNFREE ECONOMIC POSITION
OF MODERN MAN

ALBERT SCHWEITZER

[Albert Schweitzer, *The Philosophy of Civilization*, The Macmillan Company, New York, copyright © 1949, 1957, pp. 9–12 (abridged). Reprinted by permission of the Macmillan Company and A. & C. Black, Ltd., London.]

Albert Schweitzer is too good a man for any of us to doubt his motives— great musician, great doctor, who has devoted his life to serving the unfortunate people of one of the least civilized parts of the world. His physical retreat from civilization is symbolic of his disappointment in people and events; they fall so far short of his own high standards. His views do deserve our consideration. But we can still challenge his perception of what life is like in this world; for instance, there are many employees of large corporations who have freedom to think just because their work does not dominate all their days and hours, while many shopkeepers are locked in such a struggle to keep alive that they have no opportunity to enjoy the rest of living at all.

EVEN IF THE ABDICATION of thought has been . . . the decisive factor in the collapse of our civilization, there are yet a number of other causes which combine with it to hinder our progress in this regard. They are to be found in the field of spiritual as well as in that of economic activity, and depend, above all, on the interaction between the two, an interaction which is unsatisfactory and continually becoming more so.

The capacity of the modern man for progress in civilization is diminished because the circumstances in which he finds himself placed injure him physically and stunt his personality.

The development of civilization comes about—to put it quite generally—by individual men thinking out ideals which aim at the progress of the whole, and then so fitting them to the realities of life that they assume the shape in which they can influence most effectively the circumstances of the time. A man's ability to be a pioneer of progress, that is, to understand what civilization is and to work for it, depends, therefore, on his being a thinker and on his being free. He must be the former if he is to be capable of comprehending his ideals and putting them into shape. He must be free in order to be in a position to launch his ideals out into the general life. The more completely his activities are taken up in any way by the struggle for existence, the more strongly will the impulse to improve his own condition find expression in the ideals of his thought. Ideals of self-interest then get mixed up with and spoil his ideals of civilization.

Material and spiritual freedom are closely bound up with one another. Civilization presupposes free men, for only by free men can it be thought out and brought to realization.

But among mankind today both freedom and the capacity for thought have been sadly diminished.

If society had so developed that a continually widening circle of the population could enjoy a modest, but well-assured, condition of comfort, civilization would have been much more helped than it has been by all the material conquests which are lauded in its name. These do, indeed, make mankind as a whole less dependent upon nature, but at the same time they diminish the number of free and independent lives. The artisan who was his own master becomes the factory hand through the compulsion of machinery. Because in the complicated business world of today only undertakings with abundant capital behind them can maintain their existence, the place of the small, independent dealer is being taken more and more completely by the employee. Even the classes which still possess a larger or smaller amount of property or maintain a more or less independent activity get drawn more and more completely into the struggle for existence because of the insecurity of present conditions under the economic system of today.

The lack of freedom which results is made worse still because the factory system creates continually growing agglomerations of people who are thereby compulsorily separated from the soil which feeds them, from their own homes and from nature. Hence comes serious psychical injury. There is only too much truth in the paradoxical saying that abnormal life begins with the loss of one's own field and dwelling place.

Civilization is, it is true, furthered to a certain extent by the self-regarding ideals produced by the groups of people who unite and cooperate in defense of their similarly threatened interests, in so far as they seek to obtain an improvement in their material, and thereby also in their spiritual, environment. But these ideals are a danger to the idea of civilization as such, because the form which they assume is either not at all, or very imperfectly, determined by the really universal interests of the community. The consideration of civilization as such is held back by the competition between the various self-regarding ideals which go under its name.

To the want of freedom we have to add the evil of overstrain. For two or three generations numbers of individuals have been living as workers merely, not as human beings. Whatever can be said in a general way about the moral and spiritual significance of labor has no bearing on what they have to do. An excessive amount of labor is the rule today in every circle of society, with the result that the laborer's spiritual element cannot possibly thrive. This overwork hits him indirectly even in his childhood, for his parents, caught in the inexorable toils of work, cannot devote themselves to his upbringing as they should. Thus his development is robbed of something which can never be made good, and later in life, when he himself is the slave of overlong hours, he feels more and more the need of external distractions. To spend the time left to him for leisure in self-cultivation, or in serious intercourse with his fellows or with books, requires a mental collectedness and a self-control which he finds very difficult. Complete idleness, forgetfulness, and diversion from his usual activities are a physical necessity. He does not want to think, and seeks not self-improvement, but entertainment, that kind of entertainment, moreover, which makes least demand upon his spiritual faculties.

The mentality of this mass of individuals, spiritually relaxed and incapable of self-collectedness, reacts upon all those institutions which ought to serve the cause of culture, and therewith of civilization. The theater takes a second place behind the pleasure resort or the picture show, and the instructive book behind the diverting one. An ever increasing proportion of periodicals and newspapers have to accommodate themselves to the necessity of putting their matter before their readers in the shape which lets it be assimilated most easily. A comparison of the average newspapers of today with those of fifty or sixty years ago shows how thoroughly such publications have had to change their methods in this respect.

When once the spirit of superficiality has penetrated into the institutions which ought to sustain the spiritual life, these exercise on their part a reflex influence on the society which they have brought to this condition, and force on all alike this state of mental vacuity.

How completely this want of thinking power has become a second nature in men today is show by the kind of sociability which it produces. When two of them meet for a conversation each is careful to see that their talk does not go beyond generalities or develop into a real exchange of ideas. No one has anything of his own to give out, and everyone is haunted by a sort of terror lest anything original should be demanded from him.

The spirit produced in such a society of never-concentrated minds is rising among us as an ever growing force, and it results in a lowered conception of what man should be. In ourselves, as in others, we look for nothing but vigor in productive work, and resign ourselves to the abandonment of any higher ideal.

When we consider this want of freedom and of mental concentration, we see that the conditions of life for the inhabitants of our big cities are as unfavorable as they could be. Naturally, then, those inhabitants are in most danger on their spiritual side. It is doubtful whether big cities have ever been foci of civilization in the sense that in them there has arisen the ideal of a man well and truly developed as a spiritual personality; today, at any rate, the condition of things is such that true civilization needs to be rescued from the spirit that issues from them and their inhabitants.

THE BUSINESS SYSTEM IS NOT
INCONSISTENT WITH
A GOOD WORLD

EDWARD DUFF, S.J. AND THE
WORLD COUNCIL OF CHURCHES

[Edward Duff, S.J., *The Social Thought of the World Council of Churches,* Association Press, New York, 1956, p. 220.]

The World Council of Churches held its second assembly at Evanston, Illinois, in 1954. While in general taking a strong stand for the intelligent control of the forces, economic as well as scientific, that now affect the world, the Council was noteworthy in feeling that the business system was *not* inconsistent with a *good* world. Thus, in *The Social Thought of the World Council of Churches,* written with the cooperation of the Council, there is this lonely but striking paragraph:

THE PREPARATORY COMMISSION'S MEMORANDUM on the Responsible Society acknowledged that in expressing alarm over the ideology or practice of laissez faire capitalism it would be beating a dead horse. Indeed, the Memorandum pointed to the need for surveillance of trends towards excessive state intervention in the economic process with consequent dangers of centralization and rigidity. Both these cautions were adopted at Evanston. "Capitalism" was accorded a measure of praise: "At its best the business system has provided incentives for the responsible initiative and hard work which produce economic progress, and has embodied the wisdom of decentralized decisions and widely distributed power. These are virtues needed in any system."

"SKYHOOKS"—WITH SPECIAL IMPLICATIONS FOR MONDAY THROUGH FRIDAY

~∧◯∧~

O. A. OHMANN

[O. A. Ohmann, " 'Skyhooks'—With Special Implications for Monday Through Friday," *Harvard Business Review*, May–June 1955, pp. 1–18.]

This provocative discussion is an attempt to think through the constantly changing and expanding role of the business executive rather than to state clearly formulated conclusions. In fact, Mr. Ohmann himself considers it "frankly experimental. It stems," he reports, "from the repeated experience I have had with certain executives who seem to know all about the art and science of management and yet are quite ineffective, and with other executives who seem to violate most of the rules in the book and yet are extremely successful. Experiences of this sort led me to conclude that the explanation lies in the value structure of the individual's philosophy."

For three years prior to 1955 (the date of this *Harvard Business Review* article), management development was Mr. Ohmann's full-time assignment as Assistant to the President, The Standard Oil Company of Ohio. Before entering business he was head of the Department of Psychology at Cleveland College of Western Reserve University.

———◆———

DURING THE LAST SEVERAL YEARS, while my principal job assignment has been management development, I have become increasingly impressed with the importance of intangibles in the art of administration. With the managerial revolution of the last generation and the transition from owner-manager to professional executive, there has appeared a growing literature on the science and art of administration. A shift in emphasis is noticeable in these writings over the past 30 years.

Following the early engineering approach typified by the work of Frederick Taylor and others, there next developed a search for the basic principles of organization, delegation, supervision, and control. More recently, as labor relations became more critical, the emphasis has shifted to ways of improving human relations. The approach to the problems of supervisory relationships was essentially a manipulative one. Textbooks on the techniques of personnel management mushroomed. Still later it became more and more apparent that the crux of the problem was the supervisor himself, and this resulted in a flood of "how to improve yourself" books. Meanwhile the complexities of the industrial community increased, and the discontents and tensions mounted.

It seems increasingly clear, at least to me, that while some administrative practices and personnel techniques may be better than others, their futility arises from the philosophical assumptions or value judgments on which this superstructure of manipulative procedure rests. We observe again and again that a manager with sound values and a stewardship conception of his role as boss can be a pretty effective leader even though his techniques are quite unorthodox. I am convinced that workers have a fine sensitivity to spiritual qualities and want to work for a boss who believes in something and in whom they can believe.

This observation leads me to suspect that we may have defined the basic purposes and objectives of our industrial enterprise too narrowly, too selfishly, too materialistically. Bread alone will not satisfy workers. There are some indications that our people have

SIX DAYS WITH THE DEVIL AND ONE WITH GOD.

FIG. 297. Six Days with the Devil and One with God. Thomas Nast in this 1869 *Harper's Weekly* cartoon shows the Business Man telling Christianity, "I am too Busy to see you Now. Wait till Sunday."

lost faith in the basic values of our economic society, and that we need a spiritual rebirth in industrial leadership.

Certainly no people have ever had so much, and enjoyed so little real satisfaction. Our economy has been abundantly productive, our standard of living is at an all-time peak, and yet we are a tense, frustrated, and insecure people full of hostilities and anxieties. Can it be that our *god of production* has feet of clay? Does industry need a new religion—or at least a better one than it has had?

I am convinced that the central problem is not the division of the spoils as organized labor would have us believe. Raising the price of prostitution does not make it the equivalent of love. Is our industrial discontent not in fact the expression of a hunger for a work life that has meaning in terms of higher and more enduring spiritual values? How can we preserve the wholeness of the personality if we are expected to worship God on Sundays and holidays and mammon on Mondays through Fridays?

I do not imply that this search for real meaning in life is or should be limited to the hours on the job, but I do hold that the central values of our industrial society permeate our entire culture. I am sure we do not require a bill of particulars of the spiritual sickness of our time. The evidences of modern man's search for his soul are all about us. Save for the communist countries there has been a world-wide revival of interest in religion. The National Council of Churches reports that 59 per cent of our total population (or 92 million) now claim church affiliation. The November 22, 1954, issue of *Barron's* devoted the entire front page to a review of a book by Barbara Ward, *Faith and Freedom*.[1]

Perhaps even more significant is the renaissance in the quality of religious thought and experience. Quite evidently our religion of materialism, science, and humanism is not considered adequate. Man is searching for anchors outside himself. He runs wearily to the periphery of the spider web of his own reason and logic, and looks for new "skyhooks"—for an abiding faith around which life's experiences can be integrated and given meaning.

WHY "SKYHOOKS"?

Perhaps we should assume that this need for "skyhooks" is part of man's natural equipment—possibly a function of his intelligence—or if you prefer, God manifesting Himself in His creatures. It seems to me, however, that the recent intensification of this need (or perhaps the clearer recognition of it) stems in part from certain broad social, economic, political, and philosophical trends. I shall not attempt a comprehensive treatment of these, but shall allude to only a few.

[1] Barbara Ward, *Faith and Freedom*, W. W. Norton & Company, Inc., New York, 1954.

I have already indicated that on the economic front we have won the battle of production. We have moved from an economy of scarcity to one of abundance. We have become masters of the physical world and have learned how to convert its natural resources to the satisfaction of our material wants. We are no longer so dependent and so intimately bound to the world of nature. In a way we have lost our feeling of being part of nature and with it our humble reverence for God's creation.

While the industrialization of our economy resulted in ever-increasing production, it also made of individual man a production number—an impersonal, de-skilled, interchangeable production unit, measured in so many cents per hour. For most employees, work no longer promotes the growth of personal character by affording opportunities for personal decision, exercise of judgment, and individual responsibility. A recent issue of *Nation's Business* quotes the modern British philosopher, Alexander Lindsay, on this point as follows:

> Industrialism has introduced a new division into society. It is the division between those who manage and take responsibility and those who are managed and have responsibility taken from them. This is a division more important than the division between the rich and poor.[2]

Certainly the modern industrial worker has improved his material standard of living at the cost of becoming more and more dependent on larger and larger groups. Not only his dignity but also his security has suffered. And so he reaches out for new "skyhooks"—for something to believe in, for something that will give meaning to his job.

A second trend which seems to bear some relation to our urgent need for a faith grows out of our disillusionment with science. As a result of the rapid advance of science, the curtains of ignorance and superstition have been pulled wide on all fronts of human curiosity and knowledge. Many of the bonds of our intellectual enslavement have been broken. Reason and scientific method were called on to witness to the truth, the whole truth, and nothing but the truth. We were freed from the past—its traditions, beliefs, philosophies, its mores, morals, and religion. Science became our religion and reason replaced emotion.

However, even before the atom bomb there was a growing realization that science did not represent the whole truth, that with all its pretensions it could be dead wrong, and, finally and particularly, that without proper moral safeguards the truth did not necessarily

---

[2] John Kord Lagemann, "Job Enlargement Boosts Production," *Nation's Business*, Dec. 1954, p. 36.

make men free. Atomic fission intensified the fear and insecurity of every one of us who contemplated the possibility of the concentration of power in the hands of men without morals. We want science to be in the hands of men who not only recognize their responsibility to man-made ethical standards (which are easily perverted) but have dedicated themselves to the eternal and absolute standards of God. Thus, while the evidence of material science has been welcomed, our own personal experiences will not permit us to believe that life is merely a whirl of atoms without meaning, purpose, beauty, or destiny.

A third factor contributing to our insecurity is the trend toward bigness and the resulting loss of individuality. This is the day of bigger and bigger business—in every aspect of life. The small is being swallowed by the big, and the big by the bigger. This applies to business, to unions, to churches, to education, to research and invention, to newspapers, to our practice of the professions, to government, and to nations. Everything is getting bigger except the individual, and he is getting smaller and more insignificant and more dependent on larger social units. Whether we like it or not this is becoming an administrative society, a planned and controlled society, with ever-increasing concentration of power. This is the day of collectivism and public-opinion polls. It is the day when the individual must be *adjusted to the group*—when he must above all else be sensitive to the feelings and attitudes of others, must get an idea of how others expect him to act, and then react to this.

This is the insecure world which David Riesman has described so well in his book, *The Lonely Crowd*.[3] He pictures man as being no longer "tradition directed" as was primitive man, nor as in Colonial days is he "inner directed" as if by the gyroscope of his own ideals, but today he is "outer directed" as if by radar. He must constantly keep his antenna tuned to the attitudes and reactions of others to him. The shift has been from morals to morale and from self-reliance to dependence on one's peer group. However, the members of one's peer groups are each responding to each other. Obviously these shifting sands of public opinion offer no stable values around which life can be consistently integrated and made meaningful. The high-water mark of adjustment in such a society is that the individual be socially accepted and above all else that he appear to be *sincere*.

This is certainly not a favorable environment for the development of steadfast character. It is essentially a neurotic and schizophrenic environment which breeds insecurity.

This socially dependent society also offers an ideal market for the wares of the "huckster," the propagandist, and the demagogue.

[3] David Riesman, *The Lonely Crowd*, Yale University Press, New Haven, 1950.

Lacking a religious interpretation of the divine nature of man, these merchants in mass reaction have sought the least common denominator in human nature and have beamed the movies and newspapers at the ten-year mental level. One wonders if this approach to people does not make them feel that they have been sold short and that they are capable of much better than is expected of them. Has this demoralizing exposure of the cheapness of our values not intensified our search for something better to believe in?

On top of all these disturbing socioeconomic trends came the war. This certainly was materialism, science, and humanism carried to the logical conclusion. The war made us question our values and our direction. It left us less cocksure that we were right, and more fearful of ourselves as well as of others. It made us fearful of the power which we had gained, and led us to search our soul to determine whether we had the moral strength to assume the leadership role that had been given to us. We have been humbled in our efforts to play god and are about ready to give the job back. Note, however, that this is not a characteristic reaction to war. Typically wars have been followed by a noticeable deterioration of moral standards, traditional values, and social institutions.

Perhaps none of these rationalizations for our return to religion is entirely valid. I suspect that the search for some kind of overarching integrative principle or idea is the expression of a normal human need. Certainly history would indicate that man's need for a god is eternal even though it may be more keenly sensed in times of adversity. A religion gives a point of philosophical orientation around which life's experiences can be organized and digested. Without the equivalent, a personality cannot be whole and healthy. Short-term goals which need to be shifted with the changing tide do not serve the same integrative function as do the "skyhooks" which are fastened to eternal values. I do not personally regard the current religious revival as a cultural hangover, nor as a regression. Being a mystic I prefer instead to view the need for such a faith as the spark of the Creator in us to drive us on to achieve His will and our own divine destiny.

WHY MONDAY THROUGH FRIDAY?

If we may grant for the moment that modern man *is* searching for deeper meanings in life, we may then ask, what has this to do with industry. If he needs "skyhooks," let him get them in church, or work out his own salvation. The business leaders of the past insist that "business is business" and that it had little bearing on the individual's private life and philosophy.

There are several reasons why "skyhooks" must be a primary concern of the business administrator:

(1) For the individual the job is the center of life, and its values must be in harmony with the rest of life if he is to be a whole and healthy personality.

(2) This is an industrial society, and its values tend to become those of the entire culture.

(3) The public is insisting that business leaders are in fact responsible for the general social welfare—that the manager's responsibilities go far beyond those of running the business. They have delegated this responsibility to the business executive whether he wishes to play this role or not.

(4) Even if the administrator insists on a narrow definition of his function as merely the production of goods and services as efficiently as possible, it is nevertheless essential that he take these intangibles into account since they are the real secrets of motivating an organization.

(5) Besides all this the administrator needs a better set of "skyhooks" himself if he is to carry his ever-increasing load of responsibility without cracking up. The fact that so many administrators are taking time to rationalize, defend, and justify the private enterprise system is an outward indication of this need for more significant meanings.

ANYTHING WRONG WITH CAPITALISM?

We may ask, then, what specifically is wrong with our capitalistic system of private enterprise. What is wrong with production or with trying to improve our standard of living? What is wrong with a profit, or with private ownership of capital, or with competition? Is this not the true American way of life? [4]

Nothing is necessarily wrong with these values. There are certainly worse motives than the profit motive. A refugee from communism is reported to have observed: "What a delight to be in the United States where things are produced and sold with such a nice clean motive as making a profit."

I am not an economist, and it is beyond the scope of this article to attempt a revision of our economic theory. I am tempted, however, to make a couple of observations about these traditional economic concepts:

1. That while the values represented by them are not necessarily wrong, they are certainly pretty thin and do not challenge the best in people.

2. That many of the classical economic assumptions are outmoded and are no longer adequate descriptions of the actual operation of our present-day economy.

[4] For a comprehensive treatment of the criticisms of business see J. D. Glover, *The Attack on Big Business*, Division of Research, Harvard Business School, Boston, 1954.

For example, the concept of economic man as being motivated by self-interest not only is outmoded by the best current facts of the social sciences, but also fails to appeal to the true nobility of spirit of which we are capable.

The concept of the free and competitive market is a far cry from the highly controlled and regulated economy in which business must operate today. General Motors does not appear to want to put Chrysler out of business, and apparently the union also decided to take the heat off Chrysler rather than to press its economic advantage to the logical conclusion. The assumption that everyone is out to destroy his competitors does not explain the sharing of technology through trade associations and journals. No, we also have tremendous capacity for cooperation when challenged by larger visions. We are daily denying the Darwinian notion of the "survival of the fittest" which, incidentally, William Graham Sumner, one of the nineteenth-century apologists for our economic system, used for justifying unbridled self-interest and competition.

Certainly the traditional concept of private ownership of capital does not quite correspond to the realities of today's control of large blocks of capital by insurance companies and trusteed funds.

The notion of individual security through the accumulation of savings has largely given way to the collectivist means of group insurance, company annuities, and Social Security.

The concept that all profits belong to the stockholders is no longer enthusiastically supported by either the government or the unions since both are claiming an increasing cut.

And so, while we may argue that the system of private enterprise is self-regulatory and therefore offers maximum individual freedom, the simple, cold fact is that it is in ever-increasing degree a managed or controlled economy—partly at the insistence of the voters, but largely as the result of the inevitable economic pressures and the trend toward bigness.[5]

Regardless of the rightness or wrongness of these changes in our system of enterprise, the changes have been considerable, and I doubt that classical economic theory can be used as an adequate rationale of its virtues. I am therefore not particularly optimistic about the efficacy of the current campaign to have businessmen "save the private enterprise system and the American way of life" by engaging in wholesale economic education, much of which is based on outmoded concepts.

Much as economic theory needs revision, I fear that this is not likely to cure our ills. Nor do I believe that profit-sharing or any other device for increasing the workers' cut (desirable as these

[5] See John Kenneth Galbraith, *American Capitalism*, Houghton Mifflin Company, Boston, 1952.

efforts may be) will give us what we really want. It is rather another type of sharing that is needed, a sharing of more worthy objectives, a sharing of the management function, and a sharing of mutual respect and Christian working relationships.

What is wrong is more a matter of goals and purposes—of our assumptions about what we are trying to do and how we can dignify and improve ourselves in the doing. There is nothing wrong with production, but we should ask ourselves: *"Production for what?"* Do we use people for production or production for people? How can production be justified if it destroys personality and human values both in the process of its manufacture and by its end use? Clarence B. Randall of Inland Steel in his book, *A Creed for Free Enterprise*, says:

> We have come to worship production as an end in itself, which of course it is not. It is precisely there that the honest critic of our way of life makes his attack and finds us vulnerable. Surely there must be for each person some ultimate value, some purpose, some mode of self-expression that makes the experience we call life richer and deeper.[6]

So far, so good, Mr. Randall. But now notice how he visualizes industry making its contribution to this worthy objective:

> To produce more and more with less and less effort is merely treading water unless we *thereby release time and energy for the cultivation of the mind and the spirit* and for the achievement of those ends for which Providence placed us on this earth.[7]

Here is the same old dichotomy—work faster and more efficiently so that you can finish your day of drudgery and cultivate your soul on your own time. In fact he says: "A horse with a very evil disposition can nevertheless pull the farmer's plow." No, I am afraid the job *is* the life. *This* is what must be made meaningful. We cannot assume that the end of production justifies the means. What happens to people in the course of producing may be far more important than the end product. Materialism is not a satisfactory "skyhook." People are capable of better and want to do better. (Incidentally I have the impression that Mr. Randall's practices line up very well with my own point of view even if his words do not.)

Perhaps we should ask what is the really important difference between Russian communism and our system. Both worship production and are determined to produce more efficiently, and do. Both worship science. Both have tremendously improved the standard of living of their people. Both share the wealth. Both

---

[6] Clarence B. Randall, *A Creed for Free Enterprise*, Little, Brown and Company, Boston, 1952, p. 16 (see page 2445 in this volume).
[7] *Ibid.*

develop considerable loyalties for their system. (In a mere 40 years since Lenin started the communist revolution a third of the world's people have come to eccept its allegiance.) True, in Russia capital is controlled by the state while here it is theoretically controlled by individuals, although in actual practice, through absentee owner- ship, it is controlled to a considerable extent by central planning agencies and bureaus, both public and private.

No, the real difference is in the philosophy about people and how they may be used as means to ends. It is a difference in the assumptions made about the origin of rights—whether the individual is endowed with rights by his Creator and yields these only volun- tarily to civil authority designated by him, or whether rights originate in force and in the will of the government. Is God a myth, or is He the final and absolute judge to whom we are ultimately re- sponsible? Are all standards of conduct merely man-made and relative, or absolute and eternal? Is man a meaningless happenstance of protoplasm, or is he a divine creation with a purpose, with potential for improvement, and with a special destiny in the over-all scheme of things?

These are some of the differences—or at least I hope that they still are. And what a difference these intangible, perhaps mythical, "skyhooks" make. They are nevertheless the most real and worth- while and enduring things in the world. The absence of these values permitted the Nazis to "process" people through the gas chambers in order to recover the gold in their teeth.

THE ADMINISTRATOR CONTRIBUTES

This, then, is part of our general cultural heritage and is passed on to us in many ways. However, it really comes to life in people—in their attitudes, aspirations, and behaviors. And in a managerial society this brings us back to the quality of the individual administrator. He interprets or crystallizes the values and objectives for his group. He sets the climate within which these values either *do* or *do not* become working realities. He must define the goals and purposes of his group in larger and more meaningful perspective. He integrates the smaller, selfish goals of individuals into larger, more social and spiritual objectives for the group. He provides the vision without which the people perish. Conflicts are resolved by relating the immediate to the long-range and more enduring values. In fact, we might say this *integrative function* is the core of the administrator's contribution.

The good ones have the mental equipment to understand the business and set sound long-term objectives, but the best ones have in addition the philosophical and character values which help them to relate the over-all goals of the enterprise to eternal values. This is precisely the point at which deep-seated religious convictions can serve an integrative function since they represent the most long-range of all possible goals.[8] Most really great leaders in all fields of human endeavor have been peculiarly sensitive to their historic role in human destiny. Their responsibility and loyalty are to some distant vision which gives calm perspective to the hot issues of the day.

This function of the administrator goes far beyond being a likable personality, or applying correct principles of organization, or being skillful in the so-called techniques of human relations. I am convinced that the difficulties which so many executives have with supervisory relationships cannot be remedied by cultivation of the so-called human relations, skills. These difficulties spring rather from one's conception of his function or role as a boss, his notion about the origin and nature of his authority over others, the assumptions he makes about people and their worth, and his view of what he and his people are trying to accomplish together. To illustrate:

> If, for example, my personal goal is to get ahead in terms of money, position, and power; and if I assume that to achieve this I must best my competitors; that the way to do this is to establish a good production record; that my employees are means to this end; that they are replaceable production units which must be skillfully manipulated; that this can be done by appealing to the lowest form of immediate selfish interest; that the greatest threat to me is that my employees may not fully recognize my authority nor accept my leadership—if these are my values, then I am headed for trouble—all supervisory techniques notwithstanding.

I wish I could be quite so positive in painting the picture of the right values and approaches to management. I suspect there are many, many different right answers. No doubt each company or enterprise will have to define its own long-term purposes and develop its own philosophy in terms of its history, traditions, and its real function in our economy. I am also certain that no one philosophy would be equally useful to all managers. The character of an organization is, to a large extent, set by the top man or the top group, and it is inevitable that this be the reflection of the philosophy of these individuals. No one of us can operate with another's philosophy. I have also observed that in most enterprises the basic faith or spirit of the organization is a rather nebulous or undefined something, which nevertheless has very profound meaning to the employees.

Recognizing then the futility of advocating any one pattern of values, it occurs to me that it might, however, be suggestive or

---

[8] For further elaboration see Gordon W. Allport, *The Individual and His Religion,* The Macmillan Company, New York, 1953.

helpful if I told you something of the philosophy of one extremely successful executive whom I have pumped a good deal on this subject (for he is more inclined to live his values than to talk about them):

As near as I can piece it together, he believes that this world was not an accident but was created by God and that His laws regulate and control the universe and that we are ultimately *responsible to Him*. Man, as God's supreme creation, is in turn endowed with creative ability. Each individual represents a unique combination of talents and potentials. In addition, man is the only animal endowed with freedom of choice and with a high capacity for making value judgments. With these gifts (of heredity and cultural environment) goes an obligation to give the best possible accounting of one's stewardship in terms of maximum self-development and useful service to one's fellows in the hope that one may live a rich life and be a credit to his Creator.

This executive also assumes that each individual possesses certain God-given rights of self-direction which only *the individual* can voluntarily delegate to others in authority over him, and that this is usually done in the interest of achieving some mutual cooperative good. The executive therefore assumes that his *own* authority as boss over others must be exercised with due regard for the attendant obligations to his employees and to the stockholders who have temporarily and voluntarily yielded their rights in the interest of this common undertaking. (Notice that he does not view his authority as originating with or derived from his immediate superior.) This delegated authority must, of course, be used to advance the common good rather than primarily to achieve the selfish ambitions of the leader at the expense of the led.

He further assumes that the voluntary association of employees in industry is for the purpose of increasing the creativity and productivity of all members of the group and thus of bringing about increased benefits to all who may share in the ultimate use of these goods and services. What is equally important, however, is that in the course of this industrial operation each individual should have an opportunity to develop the maximum potential of his skills and that the working relationships should not destroy the individual's ability to achieve his greatest maturity and richness of experience. As supervisor he must set the working conditions and atmosphere which will make it possible for his employees to achieve this dual objective of increasing productivity and maximizing self-development.

These goals can best be achieved by giving employees maximum opportunity to exercise their capacity for decision making and judgment within their assigned area of responsibility. The supervisor is then primarily a coach who must instruct, discipline, and motivate all the members of the group, making it possible for each to exercise his special talent in order to maximize the total team contribution. Profits are regarded as a measure of the group's progress toward these goals, and a loss represents not only an improper but even an immoral use of the talents of the group.

There is nothing "soft" about his operation. He sets high quality standards and welcomes stiff competition as an additional challenge to his group. He therefore expects and gets complete cooperation and dedication on the part of everyone. Incidentally, he views the activity of working together in this manner with others as being one of life's most rewarding experiences. He holds that this way of life is something which we have not yet fully learned, but that its achievement is part of our divine destiny. He is firmly convinced that such conscientious efforts *will* be rewarded with success. He manages with a light touch that releases creativity, yet with complete confidence in the outcome.

This is probably a poor attempt at verbalizing the basic philosophy which this man lives so easily and naturally. I hope, however, that it has revealed something of his conception of his role or function as an executive, and his view of what he and his organization are trying to do together. With this account of his values I am sure that you would have no difficulty completing the description of his administrative practices and operating results. They flow naturally from his underlying faith, without benefit of intensive training in the principles and art of administration.

As you would suspect, people like to work for him—or with him. He attracts good talent (which is one of the real secrets of success). Those with shoddy values, selfish ambitions, or character defects do not survive—the organization is self-pruning. Those who remain develop rapidly because they learn to accept responsibility. He not only advocates but practices decentralization and delegation. His employees will admit that they have made mistakes, but usually add with a grin that they try not to make the same one twice. People respond to his leadership because he has faith in them and expects the best in them rather than the worst. He speaks well of the members of his organization, and they appear to be proud of each other and of their record of performance. He takes a keen interest in developing measurements of performance and in bettering previous records or competitive standards. He feels that no one has a right to "louse up a job"—a point on which he feels the stockholders and the Lord are in complete agreement.

While he does not talk much about "employee communications" nor stress formal programs of this type, his practice is to spend a large proportion of his time in the field with his operating people rather than in his office. He is "people oriented" and does a particularly good job of listening. The union committee members have confidence in his fairness, yet do a workmanlike job of bargaining. In administering salaries he seems to be concerned about helping the individual to improve his contribution so that a pay increase can be justified.

In his general behavior he moves without haste or hysteria. He is typically well organized, relaxed, and confident, even under trying circumstances. There is a high degree of consistency in his behavior and in the quality of his decisions because his basic values do not shift. Since he does not operate by expediency, others can depend on him; and this consistency makes for efficiency in the discharge of delegated responsibility. Those operating problems which do come to him for decision seem to move easily and quickly to a conclusion. His long-term values naturally express themselves in well-defined policies, and it is against this frame of reference that the decisions of the moment easily fall into proper perspective.

In policy-level discussions his contributions have a natural quality of objectivity because "self-concern" does not confuse. Others take him at face value because his motives are not suspect. When differences or conflicts do arise, his approach is not that of compromise; rather he attempts to integrate the partisan views around mutually acceptable longer-range goals. The issues of the moment then seem to dissolve in a discussion of the best means to the achievement of the objective. I have no doubt that he also has some serious problems, but I have tried to give a faithful account of the impression which he creates. There is a *sense of special significance* about his operation which is shared by his associates.

THIS IS THE KEY

It is precisely this "sense of special significance" which is the key to leadership. We all know that there are many different ways of running a successful operation. I am certainly not recommending any particular set of administrative practices—although admittedly some are better than others. Nor am I suggesting that his set of values should be adopted by others, or for that matter could be. What I am saying is that a man's real values have a subtle but inevitable way of being communicated, and they affect the significance of everything he does.

These are the vague intangibles—the "skyhooks"—which are difficult to verbalize but easy to sense and tremendously potent in their influence. They provide a different, invisible, fundamental structure into which the experiences of every day are absorbed and given meaning. They are frequently unverbalized, and in many organizations they defy definition. Yet they are the most real things in the world.

The late Jacob D. Cox, Jr., formerly president of Cleveland Twist Drill Company, told a story that illustrates my point:

> Jimmy Green was a new union committee member who stopped in to see Mr. Cox after contract negotiations had been concluded. Jimmy said that every other place he had worked, he had always gone home grouchy; he never wanted to play with the children or take his wife to the movies. And then he said, "But since I have been working here, all that has changed. Now when I come home, the children run to meet me and we have a grand romp together. It is a wonderful difference and I don't know why, but I thought you would like to know." [9]

As Mr. Cox observed, there must be a lot of Jimmy Greens in the world who want an opportunity to take part freely in a cooperative effort that has a moral purpose.

* * *

I regard the ideas expressed here as unfinished business—as experimental thinking rather than final answers, as something that needs some good, hard-boiled criticism. Any reader who has an inclination to challenge my thinking or to suggest further refinement of it will do me a service, and his fellow readers too, by putting his ideas together for possible publication. The Editors of the *Harvard Business Review* tell me they will welcome such letters.

[A sample of the letters received by the *Harvard Business Review* follows.]

LETTERS OF COMMENT

[In answer to Mr. Ohmann's invitation for readers to give "Skyhooks" some good, hard-boiled criticism, both Mr. Ohmann and the Editors of the *Harvard Business Review* have received hundreds of letters of comment. Some of them have been enthusiastic, some critical, but the response has been overwhelmingly favorable. The letters which follow are selected to illustrate different points of view.]

FROM:
    Weyman C. Huckabee, Secretary-Treasurer
    The Laymen's Movement for a Christian World, Inc.

---

[9] Jacob D. Cox, Jr., *Material Human Progress*, Cleveland Twist Drill Company, Cleveland, 1954, p. 104.

We are happy to announce that the Board of Directors of The Laymen's Movement recently voted to award a citation to the *Harvard Business Review* for a series of . . . articles which you have published,[10] and a special citation to O. A. Ohmann "for his insight concerning the spiritual basis of a free society as set out in his article 'Skyhooks.' "

The purpose of The Laymen's Movement is to help build high moral and spiritual values in the everyday life of the world. When a significant job is done in this field, we like the privilege of expressing our appreciation. . . .

Though there are a few prominent members of The Laymen's Movement, such as Thomas J. Watson, Conrad Hilton, Herman Steinkraus, Lee H. Bristol, Howard Sheperd, Arthur J. Morris, J. C. Penney, Maxey Jarman, Saul Dribben, and Harry A. Bullis, most of our members hold less prominent positions in business or professional life. They are scattered throughout America, and a very small number are in thirteen foreign countries.

FROM:
    R. S. Owen, Senior Partner
    R. S. Owen & Company

Mr. Ohmann opens up an avenue of thinking that makes interesting walking, and I would like to accept this challenge to walk with him for at least one thought.

A few years back I brought together several men (heads of their businesses), each of whom wanted to improve his own production by exchanging know-how and experience. This was to be carried out by their production supervisors in subsequent clinics and monthly exchange of production and cost information.

During our first luncheon together there was the customary patter of exploratory talk; many were meeting for the first time. Someone mentioned an incident in his church, and it developed that every man in the room held a position of responsibility in a church. The companies represented were small companies, all in the same business. I thought at the time that it augured well for the success of a venture which is dependent on a high degree of individual honesty and integrity that these men had accepted responsibilities in their churches and lived their lives accordingly.

As I have come to know this group of men better, I have observed a similar pattern of administrative behavior. This becomes most apparent in matters that concern people—there is always a calm consideration of all the aspects of any given situation. Also, as I

---

[10] This series also included Kenneth E. Boulding, "Religious Foundations of Economic Progress," page 2200 in this volume.

have come to know the personnel within these various companies, I find an unusually high degree of loyalty to the company's interests and the bossman.

Another experience of the past two years that bears on the subject concerns the field of wage incentives. In the particular industry in which we operate, wage incentive systems have had a varied record. It is my business to install such arrangements. In several instances recently I have urged that production standards be established and allowed to run for some time before the impact of the financial incentive is injected. There are several reasons for this, but the primary one is that leadership from the personal interest of supervisors is of such importance to the success of a management plan that, painful though it is, the production improvement should start to come through the leadership medium rather than through the prospect of increase in direct pay. The financial incentive can come later. Leadership that is motivated by personal interest in the other fellow is natural among supervisors who have the stewardship concept.

From these experiences and others, I have a thought to offer along the lines of Mr. Ohmann's article. I submit that a man, particularly in management, is only in his best position to exercise judgment when he himself is feeling his best, things are fine at home, his garden is in good shape, his opportunities for service in the church and community have been accepted, the bird house is in good repair and filled with seed, and his roses are properly pruned and fertilized. In other words, when a man is in tune with all the things that are God's, he is in tune with God, and when he is in tune with God, he is in the best possible position to handle a situation involving people.

FROM:
John Rhodes, Vice President
Interstate Wells

On finishing Mr. Ohmann's article, I was convinced that he was either a minister or a professor. Turning to the biographical sketch, I was surprised to find that he had been an industrial relations manager and is now assistant to the president of an oil company. Possibly he entered business on a high enough level to have escaped a good deal of what I have observed.

I do not know Mr. Ohmann's complete background, but I suspect it diverges vastly from mine. I went to work at fourteen, and in succession was delivery boy, stock clerk, office boy, laborer, truck driver, stenographer, personnel clerk, a series of other positions, and ultimately industrial relations manager. College was a night affair, with the day's work dominating my existence. I came to know the working staff thoroughly from laborer through clerk on through section heads, department managers, plant superintendents, staff people, and line people. And I have reached some vastly different conclusions from Mr. Ohmann's, probably because of that background.

Before going into these, I hasten to agree with certain points. A manager with sound values can be effective though unorthodox. People do need satisfaction for spiritual cravings in the work scene. Man should be more than a beast. There should be a sharing of management function, mutual respect, and Christian working relationships. I cannot too strongly *emphasize* the profoundly spiritual side of my own character which seems to match Mr. Ohmann's. Emphasize, because what follows may seem to deny it. But it is not a question of what I feel. It's what I find.

And what I find is an industrial economy which should be the despair of any deep thinker. Its broad base is populated by all kinds of people, uneducated and educated, but essentially good and kind. But as soon as you rise above the lowest levels, you begin to see why Jesus taught resignation and humility rather than ambition. Ambition turns these ordinary, kindly people into something almost unnatural. For from the first supervisory levels to the top, industry is shot through with monsters who do not know they are evil, who through indifference, neglect, or deliberate intention perpetrate cruelties that are the more horrible because undramatic.

There is no disemboweling of men or stretching them on a rack. That would be preferable, for then the perpetrators would have to face the concrete evidence of what they were doing. But there is a stifling of ambition where it is found, a denial of participation, a lack of natural love and affection, a thwarting of brotherhood, a suppression of creativity, a general attitude which says, "Do just what you're told; take your pay and go home." Any attempt at a warm and full relationship is stiff-armed away by suspicion, greed, and envy.

It is no happenstance that people turn to their churches, their fraternal organizations, and their hobbies for outlets for creative instincts and spiritual communion. The flight to the suburbs, with its concomitant do-it-yourself craftsmanship, is partially the result of personal inability to fulfill oneself in the business field. Managers wistfully wish that they could engender the same fine craftsmanship, the meticulous attention to detail, the fierce concentration, the love, if you will, of the man in his home building a barbecue pit. This they could do, for the man is often putting into his home activities an ardor which has been coldly rejected by industry.

In the plant, he has no sense of belonging, no identification; and all the supervisors, from foreman to superintendent, concert to prevent this sense. They are too busy manifesting their own personalities, protecting their own positions, or destroying that of another to care what happens to the esprit de corps of the worker. Abstractly they intensely desire it, on the one hand, and concretely crush it, on the other.

And even where there are top executives like Mr. Randall, men of goodwill who sincerely want to do the right thing, they are thwarted, first, by not knowing quite how to go about it, and, second, by the impassivity of the great supervisory mass. There may be kindliness above, but right down the line there is indifference, jealousy, and downright cruelty. There are men of tiny stature, who will never take thought to add one cubit.

This is where Mr. Ohmann and I differ. It is my finding that there are so many men consciously or unconsciously evil in the supervisory ranks that nothing can be done about them; and Mr. Ohmann will go to his grave, and I to mine, without any real change in this picture.

Maybe I should not say evil. Say rather that they are psychoneurotic, psychotic, unhappy, frustrated, disturbed. We should feel sorry for them. But the misery they cause by what they do—or do not do—adds up to a staggering total of evil, all of it unnecessary.

And also we should not say, perhaps, that nothing can be done. Psychiatrists could find out why they are overly ambitious, fearful, petty, jealous, and spiteful, and abate their symptoms. But only in theory, since they outnumber the psychiatrists available for their treatment hundreds of times over.

My advice to Mr. Ohmann is to do what good he can in industry, but never expect the millennium of the kindly, competent supervisor and the consequently happy, fulfilled employee. Experience is against it.

FROM:
Wallace C. Speers, Vice President
James McCutcheon & Co.[11]

My only hesitation on complete agreement with Mr. Ohmann's article comes from experience. The spiritual factor or nonphysical love or whatever you want to call it is not soft or sanctimonious, nor is it just sweetness and light. Christ, Himself, said again and again that "the law must be fulfilled." I take that to mean economic law or any part of the natural law.

The danger in approaching the reaching out for the spiritual factor in terms of everyday life comes from the false conception that it *replaces* everything. It doesn't. It *conditions* everything.

[11] Mr. Speers is Chairman of The Laymen's Movement for a Christian World.

The result is that if a cleric approaches this idea without direct personal experience and appreciation of the hard knocks of real life, he is in danger of ending up with something that may be wishy-washy at best or pink at worst.

Even if an experienced businessman approaches it with the idea that the spiritual factor replaces energy, efficiency, skill, imagination, or ability, he will fall flat on his face in terms of economics.

The best hope of success is a hard-boiled businessman who is eminently successful at getting a vision of the place the spiritual factor must play in business and letting it condition his approach to every phase of it without letting it affect any of the economic or natural laws in his operation.

I have almost ruined a department and perhaps more than one man by trying to substitute kindness for discipline and the natural strict requirements of method.

The best example of what I mean is contained in an experience of mine. In doing an act of kindness by taking an elderly lady home late at night, I turned too sharply into her driveway and crumpled my fender on a retaining wall. No matter how wonderful the motivation or how good the deed, God does not withdraw His natural laws.

Skill, ability, experience, imagination, and so forth, still have to be maintained; otherwise the spiritual factor loses its effectiveness entirely. That does not deny its critically important central position in everyday life if we are to find satisfaction or provide a workable pattern. It merely points out the setting in which it must be used.

FROM:
Walter H. Rupp, Technical Adviser
Esso Research and Engineering Company

I would like to try adding a few thoughts and perhaps a suggested refinement to the excellent Ohmann article.

Factually, individuals in the United States are turning toward God increasingly. Some embrace Him; some merely glance His way. There is great comfort for all men in God's Church, and if it is possible for us only to worship on Sundays, that is a start. But what of Monday through Friday (and Saturday too)? Where are these individuals then?

Are not the "Sunday individuals" being "teamized" on Monday through Friday, and sometimes on Saturday too? "Teamized" by being led into paths where the robe of individualism is tattered and the tent of group action rises to shelter the faceless people comprising the "team." In return for this loss of individuality, we have achieved a higher standard of material living (sometimes even a higher standard than we need or want). The "Abundance without Satisfaction" result that Ohmann discussed is our lot five-sevenths or six-sevenths of the time.

And why should this be? Of course I don't know "why." I can only tell how a few individuals seem to feel about it. Industrial living often has failed to supply *life* to its members. Rather it tends to sap the individual's will and asks him to abdicate in favor of a fictitious being—a "corporation." And in return for work and loyalty, he receives material possessions—pensions, group insurance, social security, and discounts on company products.

How can we bring the five-sevenths or six-sevenths of the week closer to the Sunday one-seventh? Can business and love of the individual be made compatible? I think they can. With frank admission of oversimplification, I'm sure that love can be practiced in everyday business life. Now the definition of "business love" is far different from "love" as used on Sunday and in our family circles. The English language has room for many words denoting love of different kinds. Other languages often have five or six words describing love of different degrees and applications.

By "business love" is meant the desire to help other people up the ladder, to rehabilitate workers who have some blind spots in talent or personality, to show concern for feelings ahead of the dollar sign, to think more of some individual's progress than maybe even he himself thinks of it, and finally to look beyond the daily job and find a true meaning in our industrial life as one of God's necessary operations for human welfare. In other words, our daily work is a means of sustaining life to be used for His improvement of all humanity.

This expression is not as clear as crystal. But in my own mind, it is crystal clear that if those of us in business will look at each individual man as what he *might be,* then the spirit of God's hope will be with us seven-sevenths of the time. In my personal view, this is "business love." It can give meaning to business life.

FROM:
Esther I. Persson
Editorial Staff, *Banking*

Some weeks ago I read "Skyhooks" in the May–June issue of the *Harvard Business Review*. The uneasy feeling I have had ever since is like the old jingle:

> I do not like thee, Dr. Fell;
> The reason why I cannot tell.

Partly for my own peace of mind, and partly because of the author's disarming invitation, I have tried to analyze and to set down the reasons for my vague dislike and fear of the ideology implied in the article.

First, the underlying philosophy has an unpleasant familiarity. Where have I met its counterparts? In the theories of communism, fascism, and nazism. Does this sound shocking? Perhaps. But when an attempt is made to equate a philosophy of life with a philosophy of industrial production, the result looks much like Mussolini's corporate state, in which a man works in conformity with the philosophy of his economic master. All forms of thought control and brainwashing—whether actuated by good or evil intent—are repulsive.

This particular brand of thought control is perhaps more repellent than the communist variety, because it masquerades under the guise of goodness, and offers itself as a counteroffensive to communism. But opposing one evil with another, more subtle evil will not cure or improve whatever ails the Western industrial world.

Second, Mr. Ohmann expresses opinions as if they were facts. He has a right to believe, for example, that "no people have ever had so much, and enjoyed so little real satisfaction. . . . we are a tense, frustrated, and insecure people full of hostilities and anxieties." That's one man's opinion, but I don't agree with it. Of course all adults have worries, but that does not make us a nation of neurotics. When in the history of the human race has man not had worries and even frustrations?

The so-called revival of interest in religion may only be a search for social conformity. Whether or not a business or industry executive goes to church does not affect his talent to get along with subordinates and peers, his creative and imaginative understanding of others, or any other admirable quality of character.

We look with amusement on the smug conformity of the Victorians, and we admire men like Darwin and Huxley who let in a breath of fresh air. They, too, were mystics, although not in the Victorian sense. And now again it looks as if the only people who are "mystics" are those who conform to a specific ritual way of life. We are fairly well along to becoming smug Victorians. No one had a deeper feeling of being part of nature than men like Darwin. How can we define "God" and "God's creation"? And if each one of us *could* adequately define these terms, we would find as many definitions as definers—and who would presume to affix the *imprimatur* on the ultimate "correct" definition?

"For the individual the job is the center of life." This, too, is opinion, not fact. For the vast majority of persons who depend on their jobs, the getting, and the keeping, and the bettering of their jobs is important *economically,* but surely their job is not the center of life.

And, finally, I am glad I do not have to work either for or with the "extremely successful executive" whose portrait the author draws in such detail. Of course such an organization is "self-pruning" just as any thought-controlled organization must be. For my own part, I'd rather work for Clarence Randall.

FROM:
    Claude Robinson, President
    Opinion Research Corporation

I should like to send this extremely interesting article to several of my business friends as an indication of some of the mental stirrings that are currently going on in industry.

Here we have long been impressed by the research evidence that says that man does not live by bread alone and the motivational power of what we call the nonfinancial reward, or reward of the spirit. We have not undertaken to link our philosophy to a religious system, for obvious reasons, but we are quite conscious of the values that are being discussed.

A year ago I had the pleasure of spending a week walking up and down the beach with an Episcopal bishop discussing all manner of affairs, including problems of industry. I was quite struck by the fact that we came to many of the same conclusions—he by the theological route and I by the research route.

As a matter of fact, we think we note an increasing interest in the whole area of nonfinancial job values. More companies such as Du Pont, Standard Oil Company of New Jersey, and others, for example, are giving thought to this subject in practical terms.

One specific point: the article appears to argue that the trend toward bigness is incompatible with individuality. When I was doing graduate work in sociology, we used to talk a good deal about this issue; and I am inclined to believe that what the sociologists call "primary group controls" are more tyrannical in small population units than in large population units. In a big city there is possibly a greater diversification of labor and therefore more opportunity for individuals to exercise their individuality. If you desire to ride your bicycle down a street on a moonlit night, you can possibly find other people in a big city who desire to do likewise; but in a smaller community you are only subject to ridicule.

FROM:
    E. L. Quirin, Director of Research
    Babson's Reports, Inc.

Most of the following thoughts are only nuances, but important ones, I believe. Assuredly my views pertain to perhaps only one per cent of the article masterpiece—I shall not dwell at length in "Amens"!

Naturally, we all hope for the best from the notable revival of attendance and sincere participation in religious services. However, I am inclined to wonder whether *so far* this may have meant more a bonanza for the churches as organizations than an awakening to spiritual freedom for the individual. The "disillusionment with science" should not go so far as to cause us to forget the "many bonds of our intellectual enslavement which it has broken" and to drive us back to the peaceful drug of orthodoxy's false authority which still proclaims its right to enslave minds for the promise of rewards. Let us not endanger stifling the seed of honest introspection, such as "Skyhooks," by placing it among the same weeds, or in the same pasture, as the dogmatically intolerant castes which are still the most tempting refuge to the lost soul.

In other words, I do believe in encouraging introspection and the seeking of spiritually healthy truths and codes of behavior, which one associates with "going to church," but I believe today's world requires that one go to church with a questioning mind, and not an obediently blind one which is demanded of some adherents. This may seem trite. Yet we must not overlook the fact that lost souls will grab at any seeming hope. Politically lost Germany followed Hitler. Should our religion-lost people follow the church that promises most in its humble-seeming, self-appointed role (whichever religion it may be among the many in that category)? Should we not question whether our organized religions are in harmony with present-day life? Are they really the spiritual conveyance they claim to be?

Elsewhere Mr. Ohmann mentions that in Russia capital is controlled by the state and that everywhere capital is controlled by bureaus and agencies, public or private. It seems to me that the world has been suffering for several centuries now from the frustration caused by overlooking the fact that a state, a bureau, a corporation, all are individuals. We should all forever be aware that such legal concepts do not alter nature. I do not believe that the United States exists in God's view of world responsibilities, or, in that sense, the corporation I work for. These are inventions of the mind—like clubs, churches, political parties. So regardless of the artifice "legal ownership," such as the state, the corporation, the churches, only individuals must be recognized as the owners through, and under the terms of, the organization which they, the controlling individuals, operate.

FROM:
Kermit Fischer, President
Fischer and Porter Company

This article gave me much encouragement and nourishment. I think the five reasons Mr. Ohmann has given why "skyhooks" must be a primary concern of the business administrator are particularly valuable and give me much gratification because they express so lucidly thoughts which I have at various times tried to convey without too much success to other industrial executives.

While we have emerged from the "beat them over the back" stage of industrial exploitation, we have as yet only graduated into the "optimum carrot determination" stage. Our industrial managers do "feed" the workers instead of "beating" them, but the main effort seems to be directed toward determining the optimum length and diameter of the carrot which shall be dangled in front of the worker and the optimum interval at which he shall be permitted to have a nibble. Granted, the carrot is getting bigger and longer every year. And, furthermore, the worker is taking ever larger bites out of the carrot. However, there seems to be too little recognition among the management class that "business leaders are in fact responsible for the general social welfare" and that it is their obligation to see that their employees have the greatest opportunity for health, happiness, security, and the full realization of their latent capacities.

FROM:
Rev. Charles B. Aziere, O.S.B., Editor
Catholic Business Education Review [12]

We were agreeably surprised by this article: first, because there is so much Catholic philosophy of business in it; secondly, because we found it in the *Harvard Business Review*. We are not going to challenge Mr. Ohmann's thinking, for we agree with most of it, but we are going to suggest some further refinement.

What we would like to refine in Mr. Ohmann's thinking is the "why" of his philosophy, or the lack of a philosophy, since he doesn't seem to be very sure of himself in this portion of his article. We are not going to be quite as positive as Mr. Ohmann that "no one philosophy would be equally useful to all managers," but we hope to show why we *believe* that one is.

We do believe there is one philosophy equally useful to all managers—the philosophy of Jesus Christ. And we believe that all managers *can* operate in accordance with this philosophy, especially

[12] This comment is based on an editorial written by Father Aziere and published in the *Catholic Business Education Review* of June 1955.

if they will accept the interpretation of St. Thomas Aquinas, as correlated to the philosophy of Aristotle. We believe Mr. Ohmann and some of his readers might be very much surprised at the *one* right answer, as applied to our times, which can be found in the social teachings of Popes Leo XIII, Pius XI, and Pius XII. For a starting point in the refinement of his views, we would recommend to Mr. Ohmann and his readers *The Church Speaks to the Modern World* by Etienne Gilson.

Now, the fact that we believe there is one right answer, and Mr. Ohmann believes there are many, many right answers, isn't the basic question. The basic question is this: *On what authority?* If there are many, many right answers, and if each individual is privileged to interpret basic values as he finds them useful to himself or his kind of society, by what right or value basis can he judge Karl Marx, Adam Smith, François Quesnay? Or Descartes, Hegel, or Spencer? Or Lenin, Hitler, or Jefferson? Or Martin Luther, John Wesley, or Leo XIII? Or, for that matter, A Successful Executive? We purposely limit these questions to leaders of Western (Christian?) civilization, because we interpret Mr. Ohmann's views on God as applying to the God of Christianity.

We believe the question of authority is the heart of the matter of the "why" of Mr. Ohmann's philosophy. We recognize, also, that this is contrary to Protestantism's basic precept—namely, that every individual can interpret basic values, that there can be many, many different right answers. But if this were true, we could never quite see why the right would not be granted to Karl Marx or Adolf Hitler as well as to Martin Luther and John Wesley. What makes one less free than another to interpret basic values, if all are equally free? We doubt that enough leaders of the Western civilization of our times are yet ready to accept a Supreme Court in the economic and social spheres, as they have long since accepted one in the political field. They will continue to grope for the right answer because they are not ready to go to the source where the right answer will be found.

Yet we like the trend of thinking exemplified by Mr. Ohmann and many others in recent years. It offers a definite movement of reversal of the trend set in motion by the Protestant reformation. The reformers first denied the *authority* of the Church founded by Jesus Christ. In a later age the rationalists and illuminati denied the *authority* of Christ Himself. It was but a further development for many scientists and social thinkers to deny the *authority* of God as well. The crisis of our age has forced men to take sides on the existence and authority of God. Perhaps this is but a trend of reversal and return to one fold and One Shepherd. At least we may hope that the groping for some kind of unity among those separated from the Catholic Church, the evident attempts at spiritual revival, and the search for a satisfactory theology among Protestant churches will at least lead mankind back to Jesus Christ in our Western society.

FROM:
J. M. Barker, Chairman, Board of Directors
Allstate Insurance Company

I disagree with what Mr. Ohmann says in spots, but that does not mean that I am critical of what he says. For instance, at the bottom of the first page, "Certainly no people have ever had so much and enjoyed so little real satisfaction." That is a pretty broad statement. It is the common coin of present-day comment about Americans in general, but I do not agree with it. I have no real basis for comparison, even though I have been a student of history for many years. Perhaps it is because I do not know how to measure "real satisfaction."

If he is saying that real satisfaction does not stem from material well-being alone, I agree. I consider that the great problem of our civilization is: How do we withstand the ravages of prosperity? I am one of those who think that evolution is a very slow process and that it takes many thousands of years to change man's nature perceptibly. What Mr. Ohmann calls the search for "skyhooks" has characterized man throughout his whole history. We know more about the dissatisfactions of present-day man than we do about the dissatisfactions of the past, because our system of communication is better. Dissatisfaction is one of the penalties of living in an evolutionary world. The stage settings may be different in different ages, but the human elements seem to me to be unchanged. As Karr, the old Frenchman said, "Plus ça change, plus c'est la même chose."

I think Mr. Ohmann is too severe on William Graham Sumner, whom he calls a nineteenth-century apologist for our economic system. Actually Sumner lived from 1840 to 1910, and was the rector of an Episcopal church in Morristown, New Jersey, until 1872, when he went to Yale as a professor of economics. The book Mr. Ohmann probably has in mind is *What Social Classes Owe to Each Other,* published in 1882. In it Sumner made the famous statement that A and B got together and decided what C should do for D. C, the fellow who bore the burden, was the one he called "the forgotten man." Franklin D. Roosevelt twisted Sumner's presentation so that D became the forgotten man, which was good politics and quite in line with the Rooseveltian ideals.

I am inclined to differ, also, in the examination of "the really important difference between Russian communism and our system." Has communism in Russia "tremendously improved the standard of living of their people"? I wish that he had defined what the term "communism" means as practiced in Russia. I do not agree with the statement that "here [capital] is theoretically controlled by individuals, although in actual practice, through absentee ownership, it is controlled to a considerable extent by central planning agencies and bureaus, both public and private." Suppose I have some capital invested in The Standard Oil Company of Ohio. I certainly cannot dictate the company's use of capital, and in that narrow sense I have lost control of the capital. When, however, at a moment's notice I can sell my shares in a public market and get cash for them and use the capital for some other purpose, I maintain that I have a considerable degree of control. I admit freely that I have lost control of the capital which I turn over to the government in tax payments.

I agree with Mr. Ohmann that "the character of an organization is, to a large extent, set by the top man or the top group, and it is inevitable that this be the reflection of the philosophy of these individuals." I should be tempted to make the statement even more emphatic.

The great Egyptologist and philosopher, James H. Breasted, wrote a great book a good many years ago called *The Dawn of Conscience.* In it he showed by translations from the pyramid inscriptions the first faint appearance of what we call conscience in human affairs. In other words, he put his finger on that point in history when historical man in the saddle first accepted some responsibilities for the welfare of the man on the ground. That appears to be the first recorded instance of man accepting any responsibility as his brother's keeper. As time goes on, man has accepted more and more responsibility for his fellow man. Again, an evolutionary process. I have lived a long and active life, and I should say that in it I have seen more progress along that line in this country than has previously taken place over the ages in the world.

Perhaps the most pointed difference of opinion I have is that it does not seem to me that Mr. Ohmann has thought through the implications of the vastly increased world population of a century or two or three hence. In an overpopulated world, all our ideals of the golden rule, the fellowship of man, honesty, decency, and kindliness are bound to go by the board when there are just too many people for the means of subsistence. Let the scientists say that they can take care of the problem by feeding people proteins grown from algae and such stuff. Sooner or later the geometric increase of population is going to catch up with the means of subsistence. I do not mean to be unfair in bringing up this point, but I wish that Mr. Ohmann had looked farther into the future and examined the implications of the continued denial of the principle of the survival of the fittest.

FROM:
J. C. Tugman, Application Engineering
General Electric Company

The article by Mr. Ohmann declares that the enterprise system is so negligent about its impact upon the human spirit that its expanding drive puts the whole economic institution on dangerous tension by weakening the foundations of the social structure and developing a new type of individual whose loyalty to the system largely depends upon what he can get from it. Mr. Ohmann says that our society is really very sick.

How far we have drifted from the outlook of the colonial pioneers who regarded the primary purpose of their industry as a discipline to develop them for divine favor! It is not hard to see how succeeding generations confused the enriching fruits of the discipline with the divine favor. It is not hard either to understand how their present heirs have built up a magnificent but narrowly conceived institution to produce the fruits on a fabulous scale. It is no wonder we have shifted our reverence from the Lord to the system of production. In the only nation so overfed that weight reduction is systematically advocated, we have yet to awaken to the fact that the life we lead stifles us in our most significant need. We habitually cost-account our activities and interests. We have taken over the logic of production as the guide to what is good for us.

The events in our cultural development which have led us to our present situation are related in Reinhold Niebuhr's *The Irony of American History*. Long ago, he relates, we began to identify prosperity with virtue. He points out that "from the later Puritans to the present day, we have variously attributed American prosperity to our superior diligence, our greater skill or (more presently) to our more fervent devotion to the ideals of freedom." Niebuhr quotes De Tocqueville who said of American preachers of 1835 that "it is often difficult to ascertain from their discourses whether the principal object of religion is to obtain eternal felicity or prosperity in this world."

"Skyhooks" discusses some of the more damaging consequences of this concentration upon economic progress. The author agrees with Clarence Randall that we worship production. Monday through Friday we are so absorbed with it there is no room for another religion. We do reserve Sunday to recall the dear departed faith we honor but no longer rely on to help us in our really important activities. At the same time we have become vaguely aware of the malady that afflicts our society. The discontent with plenty and the restless searching for dependable values are symptoms of our distress.

"Skyhooks" is chiefly concerned with the effect of our religion of production upon industrial leadership. Mr. Ohmann notes that it obstructs natural man-to-man feeling in the handling of human relations. Social science is explored for techniques to process the human elements conformably with the logic of production. These efforts are futile, he thinks, although he concedes the social type of individual has been noticeably altered. Following David Riesman, he agrees that we have become an insecure, other-directed people. Management training has become more difficult since management itself is so strongly affected by other-directedness. The intensity of effort that goes into pleasing the superior leaves the individual drained of energy for personal convictions.

Thus "Skyhooks" has renewed some anxieties Dean Wallace B. Donham mentioned in *Education for Responsible Living* (1944). Loss of purpose in our national life in the period between the world wars had bothered him:

> Twenty years ago, in the period of great prosperity around 1923–27, I felt that this nation was one of the least stable nations on the face of the globe. I still feel that way. . . . In times of peace our capacity to work together, to cooperate, and our long term ideals for the nation were nearly lost. . . . We must refuse to accept dollar tests as final. There are more fundamental things to be thinking about.

If we are to halt the mischief Mr. Ohmann and others see, before we exhaust our resources of character and stamina, we must take pains to give management a broader outlook. Management must sense the world of the spirit and seek to serve it in order to produce balance and purpose in its own and the community outlook. In this connection we shall have to be careful about people with quick, comfortable, spiritual remedies. Cults of reassurance seem to be trying to adapt man to the defects of too much unassimilated economic progress. The fellows who want to save us with dated economics (whom Mr. Ohmann regards dubiously) are not the only ones to watch.

We are in need of a completely new revelation which will restore perspective. Economic progress must be maintained, but in a context which will permit managers and workers to develop wholeness of personality. After all, a social order which has to be sustained by the amount of satisfaction its economic system can produce is inherently unstable. Life is not given as ready-made. We need work which can help us develop our character and self-respect as well as our income.

Some of the things Mr. Ohmann recommends for change may

take some time. We shall probably have to live with the trend toward bigness for quite a while—national defense requires it. But there may be some hope that jobs can be redesigned to provide the scope and challenge to help men develop character. Peter Drucker's recent articles in *Harper's* suggest that automation may presently make such a demand for high-grade talent that we may have to keep people past 65 in the work world. Whatever promise this holds, let us hope that we may be spared the anomaly of having to work at our pleasures, an alternative Riesman has observed in our other-directed society.

A better alternative might be the discovery of a mystic like Mr. Ohmann. The distinction and leadership his company has so long exhibited probably lies in its appreciation of a man who can speak with authority in the important field of the spirit. A. A. Berle in *The 20th Century Capitalist Revolution* says:

"There is solid ground for the expectation that 20 years from now the men of the greatest renown in the United States will be the spiritual, philosophical and intellectual leaders for the sufficient reason that they will be more needed than any other type. Society still tends to produce and to honor the kinds of men it needs most."

AN ADMINISTRATOR'S PRAYER

ROBERT L. KATZ

[Robert L. Katz, "An Administrator's Prayer," in *Harvard Business Review,* January–February 1957, vol. 35, no. 1, p. 136.]

Here Robert L. Katz, a member of the Harvard Business School faculty when he wrote this, and now with Opto-Electronic Devices, Inc., catches the spirit of businessmen who bring to their work a high sense of social values, rooted in the teachings of their churches. Since most of the preceding selections have represented Catholic and Protestant points of view, it may not be amiss to point out that the Jewish religion has long been outstanding for its concern with social objectives.

This prayer was first published as a magazine piece in January 1957. Since then it has had a wide distribution in reprint form, for company bulletin boards and office walls, among businessmen of all faiths.

Grant me the self-awareness to know honestly what I am, what I can do, and what I cannot;

Grant me the judgment to channel my energies into those avenues which best utilize my abilities and do not require talents which I do not possess;

Grant me the wisdom to admit error cheerfully and learn from my experiences, that I may grow and develop and avoid repetition of mistakes;

Grant me the humility to learn from others, even though they be younger, less experienced, or of humbler station than I;

Grant me the courage to make decisions whenever they are necessary and to avoid rashness when they are not;

Grant me the sensitivity to judge the reactions of others that I may modify my actions to meet the needs of those affected;

Grant me the consideration to recognize the worth of each individual, and to respect all those with whom I have contact, neither stifling their development nor exalting myself at their expense;

Grant me the perspicacity to acknowledge that I can be no more effective than my subordinates enable me to be, and to deal with them so that they can help me by helping themselves;

Grant me the tolerance to recognize mistakes as a cost of true learning and to stand behind my subordinates, accepting my responsibility for their actions;

Grant me the insight to develop a personal philosophy, that my life may have more meaning and satisfaction and that I may avoid capricious action under the pressures of expediency;

Grant me the patience to live realistically with my circumstances, striving always for the better, but recognizing the perils of too rapid or too drastic change;

Grant me all these things, dear Lord, that I may live a more useful life, through serving my fellow men, and, through them, serve Thee.

Business and the State

"Men in great place are thrice servants: servants
of the sovereign or state, servants of fame, and
servants of business."

—Francis Bacon (1561–1626)

The state, of course, is a collective organization of people to accomplish
some purpose that applies to all of them. In this sense it is business—
public business but business just the same. So it is not surprising that
in the past people have used government to act as a superbusiness for
all citizens, including private businessmen. The businessmen depended
on being protected by the government's umbrella—and sometimes government borrowed the money from businessmen to pay for the umbrella!

This was particularly true before the day when Adam Smith spoke
for giving private businessmen more freedom, on the ground that the
greater initiative and flexibility thus gained would point business activity
even more firmly in the direction of the public good. Then, for a while,
the pendulum swung to the other extreme, and business was almost
completely independent. Now the state does act as a social guardian of
the people's health and welfare, and to this extent there has been a
swing part way back; but with management responsibility as a self-
regulating governor, the state refrains—except in need (war, depression,
monopoly) or on request (e.g., the tariff-free trade controversy)—from
trying to steer the conduct of daily business.

The following selections give some of the highlights in this long
history of government–business relations.

AT FIRST COMMERCE WAS NOT
LOOKED UPON AS A PRIVATE
MATTER

~~◆~~

CHARLES LE TOURNEAU

[Charles LeTourneau, "Commerce, Debts, Money," in *Property: Its Origin and Development*, Charles Scribner's Sons, New York, 1892, pp. 345–352 (abridged).]

A French sociologist of the early 1900s writes perceptively and charmingly about trade as a *tribal* or *state* activity. From the very beginning trade with others outside the home group has been subject to "government regulation," from very primitive taboos through embargoes (which started wars) to the protection of industry by tariffs in modern times. At the beginning of this selection the practices of people of 5,000 or more years ago are recaptured by looking at primitive tribes of the twentieth century.

———————————◆———————————

I. COMMERCE

To civilized populations commercial exchange seems a very simple matter. Nevertheless, during the lengthy childhood of humanity many centuries must have elapsed ere the little ethnic groups even formed any idea of amicable barterings among themselves. All over the world the first intercourse between hordes and tribes must have been of the nature of warlike conflicts, and brutal struggles for existence. Hence evidently sprang the formalities, or rather obstacles, in trading among the savage peoples.

At first commerce was not looked upon as a private matter; it concerned the whole group by whom it was controlled. In Australia, among the Narrinyeri, when two tribes wish to enter into commercial relations, or to maintain them, they proceed as follows: On each side the duties of business agent are entrusted to an individual chosen for the purpose at his birth, and whose umbilical cord has been carefully preserved, wrapped in a tuft of feathers. This object is called the *Kalduke*, and the fathers of the two children dedicated to trade exchange it with each other. These children must never speak to each other, and at an adult age they become commercial agents in the name of their respective tribes.

In uncivilized countries it is so customary to regard strangers, and even neighbors, as hereditary enemies that commercial exchanges are often made by means of a depot for goods in a given spot and at a given time. In Russian Columbia this is the mode of procedure: The stranger began by depositing his goods on the bank, then withdrew; the Indian afterwards came and placed by the side of the first deposit what he thought a fair exchange and then went away. The stranger then came back and carried off the Indian's goods, if they seemed to him of sufficient value; if not, he simply withdrew again, and waited until something else was added. If they did not come to an agreement each took back his goods. There was a like manner of procedure in New Mexico, between the Spanish soldiers of the *Presidios* and the Indians. Along the road leading from Chihuahua to Santa Fe the Indians, when inclined to trade, erected little crosses, on which they hung a leathern pouch with a piece of venison; then, at the foot of each cross, they deposited buffalo hides to be exchanged for victuals. The soldiers took the skins, and in return left at the foot of the cross some salt meat.

These customs, exhibiting so singular a mixture of trust and distrust, are not peculiar to America, and they bear further witness to the fundamental sameness of mankind. Herodotus tells how the Carthaginians traded in a like manner with the Lybians, beyond the columns of Hercules, on the African coast. "The Carthaginians disembark their cargo, return to their ship, and make a great smoke. The inhabitants come and leave gold near the goods. If there is sufficient left the Carthaginians carry it off; if not, they go on board again, and the natives add to the gold. They do not touch the cargo until the gold has been removed." The Nubians of our day have slightly altered the process; both parties draw up in battle array opposite each other; then between the two bands exchanges are made by a few individuals. Among themselves the Redskins act similarly, but as individuals and under the chief's protection. The caçiques and warriors of two tribes begin by exchanging presents, then they trade from wigwam to wigwam, sending in the goods for sale, the goods being returned or else some equivalent. In Chile the chief warns his subjects by sound of trumpet when the merchants arrive. The Indians who are thus summoned, hasten to divide the goods among themselves. Later on, when the merchants wish to depart, there is a fresh summons, and then each purchaser brings an article in exchange.

Everywhere when tribes are under monarchic organization the chief interferes at will in these barterings to authorize or control them, but chiefly to collect dues. Thus the Chilean caçiques just mentioned levied tolls on the rivers; *they had a bar across the stream.* About a few years ago, in a district of New Caledonia, some French missionaries, manufacturers of coconut oil, bought the nuts through the medium of the chief, who made a profit out of them. On the Gaboon, the tribes of the interior, in order to bring their goods to the mouth of the river, are obliged, under pain of fine, and even slavery, to let them pass from tribe to tribe; the price paid returns in like fashion, and on its way each chief levies toll. In Polynesia, however, barter is carried on freely between individuals. But this is not usual. Savages or barbarians have nearly always a horror of free trade. Of this I will give instances.

In Abyssinia, where home trade is rather brisk, since nearly every village has its market, the toll-gatherers watch the passengers night and day in order to exact from them the varying dues for which there is no tariff. Furthermore, only merchants are taxed in Abyssinia; there is open thoroughfare for everyone else. In the petty barbarous monarchies of Central Africa, where Berber and Negro blood are largely mingled, there is a very active trade in slaves, commodities, stuffs, etc. There are even regular markets, sometimes daily. These are sometimes fortified to protect the merchants from sudden attacks. The petty kings, governors, princelings naturally levy dues, sometimes extremely heavy ones, on the wares. At Kano, in the Houssa, the governor simply carries off two-thirds of the dates and other fruits brought to market. This town of Kano has besides, thanks to the nomadic Tuaregs, a trading connection with extremely distant countries, with Murzuk, Ghât, Tripoli, Timbuktu, etc.

We must go among the republican Kabyles to find a free, though protected, trade. The Kabyle markets belong to the tribe. To each market (sûk) there are appointed salesmasters; but the markets are free of all dues, save for the tribal school (mâmera), when there is one. Furthermore, the market-ground is declared neutral, and placed under the ânaia of the proprietors; even in time of war it is possible to go to and from it with impunity. Any offense committed against the sûk is a violation of the public ânaia, and it is punished on the spot with extraordinary severity; for example, the smallest theft entails immediate stoning.

This freedom and respect for trade among the Kabyles is a kind of anomaly. In nearly all barbarous states of antiquity and of the present time, even in the most civilized of them, commerce and the manufactures which supply it have been always subjected to extremely harassing impediments. We know well with what reluctance China and Japan have been opened up to European trade. I have already told how distrustful ancient Egypt was of foreign traders, how they were only allowed to enter the country at certain spots on the frontier or seacoast, the Egyptians being forbidden to join the caravans, and the ass and camel declared unclean. Before Psametck, foreign sailors landing in Egypt were put to death or reduced to slavery. But love of gain is tenacious, and under the

Pharaohs, as elsewhere, merchants in the end organized and carried on an important export trade in cereals, stuffs, glass, pottery.

Now, exportation necessarily evolves importation. But against the latter, and in general against all competition, barbarous states take defensive and offensive precautions, harsh in proportion to their lack of civilization. We have just seen how ancient Egypt began by closing her frontiers. The Carthaginians, keen traders, forbade the Sardinians, under pain of death, to till their own land; they had corn to find a market for, and they went so far as to run down every vessel sailing on the coast of Sardinia, Portugal, or Mauritania. Roman merchants were only allowed into Carthage and certain Sicilian ports. They were shut out from all trade along the coasts of Libya, Sardinia, Portugal, and from all rivers west of the Mediterranean. Treaties to this effect were explicit: "Unless by superior force, the Romans shall not sail beyond the lofty promontory, that is, the first cape situated to the north of Carthage. If they force their way in by dint of arms, they shall not be allowed to sell anything there." [1] "The Romans and their allies shall neither trade nor build towns in Sardinia or Africa." [2] If compelled to harbor in forbidden ports, they could not stay there longer than five days. These severe rules furnish us with a reason for the chronic rage against Carthage which burned in Cato the Elder, Cato the Usurer. The *Delenda Carthago* merely meant, "I have corn to sell; I do as much as possible in maritime usury at exorbitant rates. Destroy these competitors for me!"

Greece, although so intellectual, did not escape the mania for excessive protection, and the folly of gain at all cost. Solon, the wise Solon, launched divine maledictions against those who exported from Athens any agricultural produce besides figs, oil, and honey. Solon's mind with regard to economics was merely that of his time and his country, and this attitude persisted in Greece even up to her most glorious age. In the lifetime of Demosthenes capital punishment was incurred by the exportation of cereals.[3] The import duties in Attica were from 10 to 20 per cent. The Peloponnesian war was prolonged simply because the Athenians absolutely refused to open their ports and the market of Athens to the Megarians.[4]

Rome was no more a free-trader than the other Mediterranean states. In early times she carried on a maritime trade along the coasts of the islands and of Africa, where she encountered the formidable rivalry of the Syrians, Cathaginians, etc. She bought from Carthage and Egypt much more than she sold there, but none the less she imposed an enormous duty on all foreign products,

[1] Polybius, iii.
[2] Livy, vi.
[3] Demosthenes, *Philippic, X.—Oration against Nicostratus*, etc.
[4] Thucydides, *Peloponnesian War*, cxxxix.

from 12½ per cent *ad valorem*.[5] I have already told how the Romans uprooted the vines of Gaul to get rid of competition.

All this agrees but ill with the superb disdain professed for trade by well-born Romans. "We ought," said Cicero, "to despise traders . . . because for the sake of gain they needs must lie. What is there noble about a shop?" But Cicero meant only retail trade. "Wholesale trade," said he, "is not so contemptible." But why? The Roman knights, it is certain, and especially those called *publicani,* farmers-general of Rome, carried on export and import trade on a large scale. Egypt sent into Rome corn, black slaves, ivory, Indian products, etc. Forty thousand luckless beings labored in the Carthaginian mines. Puteoli, in Italy; Marseilles, Lyons, Bordeaux, Nantes, in Gaul, were important markets. In Rome retail trade employed numerous shops, which were mere sheds against the houses, but fetching a high rent. The various kinds of trades and arts exercised either by slaves or by freedmen, clients of their former masters, and working for their benefit, were grouped in certain quarters and in guilds as in every country. The early organization of these industrial guilds, such as lasted in France up to the Revolution, is attributed to Numa Pompilius.

Space will not allow me to mention in detail the great Asiatic nations of China, Japan, and India; but all that has been just told of our classical antiquity is applicable to them: the hatred and mistrust of foreigners, extreme protection, excessive and inquisitorial regulations. For a very long while the Chinese never, so to speak, traded outside their own country. In India, Strabo tells us, to prevent the exportation of a certain grain, the *bosphorum,* it was parched after being threshed.[6] Weights and measures, and the delivery of fruits in due season, were minutely regulated; the same merchant could not vend two different commodities without paying double duty. "The King," says Manu, "every five or fifteen days, with the advice of experts, ought to fix the price of goods; he has the right to control, forbid, or claim for himself the importation or exportation of such and such a commodity." [7] Every six months the king must fix the value of precious metals, etc.[8]

Europe, up to a very recent date, was no wiser. At Lübeck, Hamburg, etc., woolen stuffs manufactured in England were excluded; at Venice Germans could offer their goods only to Venetian merchants, and had no right to take them away again. Such wares were even confiscated if they happened to be the same as those imported over sea by the Venetians. In France, during the Middle Ages and up to a period close to our own, a great many vexatious

[5] Code of Justinian, iv, tit. 65—Code of Theodosius, xv, tit. 12.
[6] Strabo, xv, p. 10.
[7] Code de Manou, viii.
[8] *Ibid.,* viii, p. 403.

and absurd edicts and ordinances relating to commerce were enacted. "Considering," says an edict of Philip the Fair, "that our
enemies would be able to benefit by our victuals, and that it is also
of consequence to them to get rid of their goods, we have ordained
that the first go not out nor the latter enter." An ordinance of
Charles IX forbids the exportation of "wool, flax, hemp, yarn," and
the importation of "cloths, linens, striped stuffs, harness, swords, etc."

I stop, not wishing to vex the shades of Sully and Colbert, nor
especially would I, what is still more serious, seem to criticize our
protectionists of today, who abuse the present system of liberty to
throw us back into the customs and manners of the past. Old
inherited instincts form the basis of the human mind, and the super-
position of innate tendencies is exactly comparable with that of
the earth in geology. The spirit of progress and liberty is only a
thin bed, scarce covering the mighty moral strata bequeathed by our
forefathers.

THE SEVEN FAT KINE AND
THE SEVEN LEAN KINE

FROM THE BIBLE

[Holy Bible (King James version), Genesis, 41:1–16, 25–43, 46–49, 53–57.]

Here, from around 2000 B.C., is an early example of governmental
intervention in economic affairs. It reminds one of New Dealer Henry
Wallace's "ever normal granary" plan in the 1930s—buying and storing
grain when it is plentiful, to be sold when it is scarce. However, this
proposal of Joseph's, as described in Genesis, was more to keep the
supply even than it was to keep the price even, which was Wallace's
aim. In both cases, however, governmental action was planned to take
care of a situation that appeared to be too big or too complex to be
handled adequately by the ordinary mechanism of the market place.

AND IT CAME TO PASS at the end of two full years, that Pharaoh
dreamed: and, behold, he stood by the river.

And, behold, there came up out of the river seven well favored
kine and fatfleshed; and they fed in the meadow.

And, behold, seven other kine came up after them out of the
river, ill favored and leanfleshed; and stood by the other kine upon
the brink of the river.

And the ill favored and leanfleshed kine did eat up the seven well favored and fat kine. So Pharaoh awoke.

And he slept and dreamed the second time: and, behold, seven ears of corn came up upon one stalk, rank and good.

And, behold, seven thin ears and blasted with the east wind sprung up after them.

And the seven thin ears devoured the seven rank and full ears. And Pharaoh awoke, and, behold, it was a dream.

And it came to pass in the morning that his spirit was troubled; and he sent and called for all the magicians of Egypt, and all the wise men thereof; and Pharaoh told them his dream; but there was none that could interpret them unto Pharaoh.

Then spake the chief butler unto Pharaoh, saying, I do remember my faults this day:

Pharaoh was wroth with his servants, and put me in ward in the captain of the guard's house, both me and the chief baker:

And we dreamed a dream in one night, I and he; we dreamed each man according to the interpretation of his dream.

And there was there with us a young man, an Hebrew, servant to captain of the guard; and we told him, and he interpreted to us our dreams; to each man according to his dream he did interpret.

And it came to pass, as he interpreted to us, so it was; me he restored unto mine office, and him he hanged.

Then Pharaoh sent and called Joseph, and they brought him hastily out of the dungeon: and he shaved himself, and changed his raiment, and came in unto Pharaoh.

And Pharaoh said unto Joseph, I have dreamed a dream, and there is none that can interpret it: and I have heard say of thee, that thou canst understand a dream to interpret it.

And Joseph answered Pharaoh, saying, It is not in me: God shall give Pharaoh an answer of peace. . . . [And Pharaoh related his dream to Joseph.]

And Joseph said unto Pharaoh, The dream of Pharaoh is one: God hath shewed Pharaoh what he is about to do.

The seven good kine are seven years; and the seven good ears are seven years: the dream is one.

And the seven thin and ill favored kine that came up after them are seven years; and the seven empty ears blasted with the east wind shall be seven years of famine.

This is the thing which I have spoken unto Pharaoh: What God is about to do he sheweth unto Pharaoh.

Behold, there come seven years of great plenty throughout all the land of Egypt:

And there shall arise after them seven years of famine; and all the plenty shall be forgotten in the land of Egypt; and the famine shall consume the land;

And the plenty shall not be known in the land by reason of that famine following; for it shall be very grievous.

And for that the dream was doubled unto Pharaoh twice; it is because the thing is established by God, and God will shortly bring it to pass.

Now therefore let Pharaoh look out a man discreet and wise, and set him over the land of Egypt.

Let Pharaoh do this, and let him appoint officers over the land, and take up the fifth part of the land of Egypt in the seven plenteous years.

And let them gather all the food of those good years that come, and lay up corn under the hand of Pharaoh, and let them keep food in the cities.

And that food shall be for store to the land against the seven years of famine, which shall be in the land of Egypt; that the land perish not through the famine.

And the thing was good in the eyes of Pharaoh, and in the eyes of all his servants.

And Pharaoh said unto his servants, Can we find such a one as this is, a man in whom the Spirit of God is?

And Pharaoh said unto Joseph, Forasmuch as God hath shewed thee all this, there is none so discreet and wise as thou art:

Thou shalt be over my house, and according unto thy word shall all my people be ruled: only in the throne will I be greater than thou.

And Pharaoh said unto Joseph, See, I have set thee over all the land of Egypt.

And Pharaoh took off his ring from his hand, and put it upon Joseph's hand, and arrayed him in vestures of fine linen, and put a gold chain about his neck;

And he made him to ride in the second chariot which he had; and they cried before him, Bow the knee: and he made him ruler over all the land of Egypt. . . .

And Joseph went out from the presence of Pharaoh, and went throughout all the land of Egypt.

And in the seven plenteous years the earth brought forth by handfuls.

And he gathered up all the food of the seven years, which were in the land of Egypt, and laid up the food in the cities: the food of the field, which was round about every city, laid he up in the same.

And Joseph gathered corn as the sand of the sea, very much, until he left numbering; for it was without number. . . .

And the seven years of plenteousness, that was in the land of Egypt, were ended.

And the seven years of dearth began to come, according as Joseph had said: and the dearth was in all lands; but in all the land of Egypt there was bread.

And when all the land of Egypt was famished, the people cried to Pharaoh for bread: and Pharaoh said unto all the Egyptians, Go unto Joseph; what he saith to you, do.

And the famine was over all the face of the earth: And Joseph opened all the warehouses, and sold unto the Egyptians; and the famine waxed sore in the land of Egypt.

And all countries came into Egypt to Joseph for to buy corn; because that the famine was so sore in all lands.

THE EMPEROR AUGUSTUS SUPPRESSES INVENTION

ARNOLD J. TOYNBEE

[Arnold J. Toynbee, "Thinking Ahead—Will Businessmen Be Civil Servants?" in the *Harvard Business Review*, Sept.–Oct. 1958, vol. 36, no. 5 (abridged).]

There always has been misunderstanding of the effect of innovations which "threaten" to make existing products or procedures obsolete. From the point of view of those who may be put out of business by a new invention, *threaten* may be right. But from the larger point of view, or in the longer run, the proper verb is *promise*. This is what raises our standard of living. Furthermore, the alert businessman shifts from buggy whips to automobile accessories, and employment rises. There are bound to be areas and industries where the adjustment is not smooth; progress is not smooth, ever. Change always exacts some sacrifice. But without change there is no progress.

In the following selection a truly great man, the Emperor Augustus of ancient Rome's golden age (which coincides with Christ's birth), makes a classic mistake—classic in the sense that it reflects the classical period's prevailing failure to understand the dynamism of change; classic also in the sense that a certain segment of people in *all* places and *all* times have continued to make the same mistake. No wonder Rome, and all past civilizations, have had in them the seed of their own destruction: the inability to keep on growing *after* they have attained prosperity and become self-satisfied.

Observe, also, that the Roman government was largely responsible for what business there was at this time. Says the author: "The Roman businessman's opportunities came from the subject peoples' economic distress and from the Roman government's administrative inefficiency."

This piece is by Arnold J. Toynbee, who has been honored many times for his historical research and writing, and is the author of the ten-volume classic, *A Study of History* (Oxford University Press, 1935–54), *The World and the West* (Oxford University Press, 1953), and many other books. He is a professor emeritus at the University of London and was formerly Director of Studies at the Royal Institute of International Affairs in London. He gave this account of Roman business to a group of 70,000 American businessmen (readers of the *Harvard Business Review*) to warn them against being too complacent, too afraid of change, too dependent on government.

◆——————

THE STORY of Roman business is part of our historical background. The English word *business* is a literal translation of the Latin word *negotium. Negotium* means "the opposite of leisure," and the Latin word for *businessman* is *negotiator*—which means, of course, not a negotiator in our English sense of the word, but a man who denies himself leisure in order to get business done.

The Marxian critics of our modern Western businessmen have had some hard things to say about them. To many of us in the West, some of these things seem to be untrue, or at least to be overstated. But the worst that the severest critic has ever said about our modern businessmen would hardly be bad enough for their Roman predecessors. When modern business is accused of being exploitative, it can afford to plead guilty because it is in a position to point out that, in seeking its own economic advantage, it has enabled the human race to achieve an unheard-of increase in its productivity.

But Roman business was really mostly predatory and parasitical. Large-scale industrial production—e.g., the manufacture of crockery or of clothing—played a minor part in it. A bigger affair was the introduction of cattle ranching and plantation farming into areas in Sicily and southern Italy that had been devastated in the second and worst of the three wars between Rome and Carthage. The Roman businessman made profits by stocking these areas with manpower in the shape of slave shepherds and slave plantation hands. But their energy and efficiency in running the slave trade can hardly be placed on the credit side of their account. And the bulk of their business, and the most lucrative items in it, consisted of contracts with the Roman government and loans on outrageously extortionate terms to the conquered and subject communities that could find no other source of ready money for paying the war indemnities and the taxes which the victorious Roman government was exacting from them.

The Roman businessmen's opportunities came from the subject peoples' economic distress and from the Roman government's administrative inefficiency. When the Roman government carried the

Roman commonwealth into its second war with Carthage in 218 B.C., its administrative organization was that of a small peasant state. In other words, it was almost nonexistent. Within little more than 50 years, Rome had made herself both militarily and politically supreme round all the shores of the Mediterranean, but her administrative machinery still remained rudimentary. Faced with the problem of managing a vast empire, the government helped itself out by farming out every possible branch of public activity to private business enterprise. It farmed out the collection of custom duties, the collection of the grain tithe in the provinces, the collection of fees payable for maintaining livestock on the public pasture, the operation of mines confiscated from the governments of conquered states, and the provisioning of Roman armies, which were at this time campaigning overseas at long distances from home.

The rise of the Roman businessmen was as sudden as the spread of Roman rule, and was indeed a consequence of it. They made themselves conspicuous at an early stage of the second Romano-Punic War in an incident that was characteristically discreditable. After a few years of conducting this tremendous and, at the outset, disastrous war, the Roman government went bankrupt. With an empty treasury, how was it to keep up the all-important flow of food, clothing, and munitions to the Roman armies fighting far away from Italy, in Spain? The contractors who had been supplying these armies offered to continue without asking for further payment till after the war was over; but this offer to supply on credit was accompanied by two conditions: the contractors must be given personal exemption from military service, and their shipments must be insured by the government against risks on the voyage. The government had no choice but to accept these terms; and the contractors then augmented their deferred profits by lading a certain number of rotten ships with rubbishy cargoes, valuing them for insurance purposes as if they were good cargoes and sound ships, and arranging for these vessels to be wrecked on route.

This would have been shocking behavior, even if the fraudulent contractors' country had not been fighting for her life. When the knowledge of what they were doing leaked out, there was public indignation. The government, however, was afraid to prosecute, for fear that this might stop the flow of such supplies as *were* being duly delivered—and the government had no other source of supply to which it could resort. When a magistrate did finally institute legal proceedings in the national assembly, the guilty contractors organized a gang and broke up the meeting. This was too much, and several of them only evaded being brought to book by taking asylum in allied states where they were secure against being extradited.

But most of the profits from this discreditable business were eventually collected from the government by the contractors, and this was one of the sources of the capital with which the new Roman business community operated during the next two centuries. This was an ominous beginning; those next 200 years were an age of agony for the countries round the Mediterranean. The Roman businessmen exploited them mercilessly, and the Roman government never intervened more than halfheartedly and ineffectively to protect its subjects from its agents. How could the government afford to do justice, when it was dependent for the receipt of its revenues on the businessmen's unprincipled activities?

Halfway through the last century B.C., civilized society at the western end of the ancient world seemed to be on the brink of dissolution. Society was then snatched out of the jaws of destruction by two great statesmen, Caesar and Augustus. They conceived and executed a number of constructive reforms, and this gave the Greco-Roman civilization a reprieve that lasted for two centuries. One of the key reforms was the transformation of wolves into shepherd dogs: they converted the children of the predatory businessmen into dutiful civil servants.

Like many strokes of genius, this one was based on a simple idea—obvious in retrospect, but not so easy to think of, and not at all easy to carry out. Rome had conquered the Mediterranean world, had overthrown or hamstrung all the previous states, but had failed to set up any adequate substitute for them. The consequence had been two centuries of chaos and misery. What the world needed was an efficient, honest, benevolent world government; what it had been getting was efficient, dishonest, and heartless exploitation by the Roman businessmen whom the Roman conquests had called into existence by giving them their opportunity. The point on which Augustus seized was that the efficiency was there, and his problem was to redirect it and harness it to constructive, instead of its present destructive, activities.

To judge by the record of the Roman republican government during those previous two centuries, it might have looked as if the Romans were incapable of organizing public administration on the grand scale. But the lie was given to any such verdict by the record of the Roman businessmen during the same period. This record was morally disgraceful, but it was impressive if the criterion was to be that of material achievement. That is, under the stimulus of the opportunity for making lucrative profits, the businessmen had improvised large-scale organizations that worked. It was beside the point that they had been working havoc. Their effectiveness in accomplishing the purposes for which they had been set up demonstrated that there was a fund of first-rate organizing ability in the Roman people. And the fact that the Roman government's own official organization had remained so rudimentary was evidence merely of the callousness, the unimaginativeness, and the conservatism of the Roman governing class. They could have found the men to staff a world government if they had chosen to. They had not cared to try, but Augustus intended to achieve this. He had to achieve it, or see civilization collapse and himself meet the same fate as his adoptive father, Caesar.

The business community was the tool lying ready for Augustus to use; and he made the Roman businessmen serve his enlightened purpose by doing two things to them simultaneously. While he diminished their opportunities for making business profits, at the same time he offered them a new career as salaried civil servants. By establishing a world-wide peace, which lasted, with some short lapses, for another 200 years, he struck at the slave trade's source of supply and so reduced the trade itself, and the profits from it, to less monstrous dimensions. By taking over the collection of the public revenues from the companies that had been farming them, he forced the children of the tax farmers to become employees of the state. He could do without the farming system because he could draw on the business experience of the tax-farming class to do the same work as efficiently, but more honestly and humanely, as government officials.

This administrative reform was an immense success. It was perhaps the chief reason why in the Mediterranean world for the next 200 years life was less insecure and less unhappy than it had been during the 200 years immediately preceding Augustus' generation.

But what happened? All things—and especially good things—have to be paid for. And, in the Mediterranean world under the Augustan peace, the price of orderliness and justice was uncreativeness and dullness.

Under the Augustan regime, creativeness was deliberately discouraged and, in extreme cases, was victimized, because the activities of creative personalities are a disturbing factor in society. That is the price of creativeness; but Augustus and his successors were intent on "freezing" society, as a precaution against the resurgence of disorder and violence. Hence they looked askance at all manifestations of independent-mindedness and private initiative. They frowned on aristocracies; they frowned on private associations, even those as remote from politics as burial societies; and they frowned, for the same reason, on inventors.

There is a thrice-told tale of the horrid fate of an inventor of unbreakable glass. The foolish fellow proudly reported his invention to the authorities and then suggested to them that he deserved a reward; the junior officials concerned were sufficiently impressed to send the case up to the Emperor.

"Sir," said the Emperor's secretary to his master one morning, "I have been directed to inform you that a man has made the astonishing invention of unbreakable glass, and to ask what action it pleases you to take."

"Oh, have the man put to death," said the Emperor, without raising his eyes from the pile of papers on his desk.

The secretary supposed that he has misheard. "I do not think, Sir," he went on, "that I can have managed to make quite clear what I have been instructed to tell you."

"You did make it perfectly clear, so have him put to death."

"But, Sir," the kindhearted secretary persisted, "the poor man has made a most remarkable and most useful invention, and we were wondering whether you wouldn't think him worthy of a reward."

At this point the overworked Emperor lost his temper. "How dare you plague me," he snapped out, "by forcing me to explain the obvious when it is your duty simply to carry out my orders. Don't you see that if this man's invention is put on the market, it will throw the makers of ordinary glass out of employment; unemployment will lead to unrest; and unrest to revolution, then civil war? My predecessors' and my own immense labors for bringing happiness to the human race will run the risk of being undone. You will understand that we can't have that, so, I tell you for the third time, see that the man is put to death and, still more important, see that the blueprint of his invention is incinerated."

Round about this time, a man called Heron in Alexandria—the greatest industrial and commercial city in the Mediterranean world of the day—discovered the principle of the steam turbine engine. In an age in which the whole Mediterranean basin was united under a single government, the application of steam power to locomotion would have done wonders for long-distance trade and still greater wonders for the defense of the Roman Empire's dangerously extended frontiers. But Heron's invention never came to be treated as anything more than a curiosity and a plaything.

The inventive genius was there, as no doubt it is present everywhere at all times; but in the Roman Empire the seed fell on stony ground. The will was lacking to turn inventions to practical account for improving the material conditions of life.

The imperial government's success in making life static had the unintended effect of making it dull. The historian Tacitus, writing in the second century of the Augustan peace, raises, in an imaginary conversation, the question why the public speakers of his own day made such a poor performance by comparison with those of the age before the establishment of the Augustan world order. The explanation that he offers rings true, and it is illuminating. We have the good fortune, he says, to find ourselves, in our day, living in such a well-administered and such a respectable world that there is really nothing to make speeches about.

Cicero, living in that terrible pre-Augustan age, was less lucky as a man—he met a violent death—but he was luckier as a public speaker as long as he escaped assassination. Sensational cases in court and shattering public events were everyday occurrences in his time, so his genius as an advocate and as a political speaker had full scope. He never had to search for a theme. During the Augustan peace, public speakers did have to search for themes, and they usually had no better resource than to hunt up academic ones drawn from well-worn commonplaces of ancient history and classical literature.

Dullness and uncreativeness—these seemed a small price to pay for good government and social justice in the eyes of generations that had not forgotten their grandparents' tales of a dreadful previous age of anarchy and oppression. Yet the price turned out to be greater than was realized by the generations which paid it without complaint.

When society stifles human creativeness, it is depriving man of the use of his fundamental asset; for unless man sets his creative powers to work on his environment, he cannot unlock the cupboard in which all his other potential assets are stored. And, if there is no zest in life, there will be no impulse to make the most of those creative achievements that will break their way out, here and there, in spite of all the well-meaning impediments which a paternal government may have devised.

One reason why the Augustan peace eventually broke down was that it failed to arouse enthusiasm in the hearts of its beneficiaries. And besides this psychological reason there was an economic one. The elaborate and expensive Greco-Roman civilization placed too heavy a burden on the agricultural economy on which it was imposed. This economy might have been made much more productive in the Greco-Roman world, as it has been made in our modern world, by a practical application of technological inventions. But under the Roman Empire the climate of opinion was as adverse to this as it has been favorable to it in the modern world. So eventually the static agricultural economy broke down under the burden of civilization, and the house of cards collapsed.

I have suggested that society cannot afford to stifle human creativeness. Fortunately it is also true that it cannot succeed in stifling it in the long run. Whatever you may do to suppress it, it will break out sooner or later, and the history of the Augustan peace illustrates this truth, too. While most of the men and women living under the Augustan peace were content just to "get by," there were awkward and irrepressible minorities that insisted on devoting themselves to ideals, up to the point of giving their lives for them if necessary. For instance, there were the Roman soldiers, holding the frontiers of the world state, and there were the Christian martyrs. Of these two sets of earnest, exalted, unmanageable people, the martyrs were the more surprising, because they came out of an unheroic social setting in the sordid overgrown cities of the interior. Life was not dull for either martyrs or soldiers; so these two minorities made history and, in making it, undid Augustus' shrewd and painstaking work.

I have ventured to take you back with me into this episode of past history because of the bearing that I believe it to have on our own situation and prospects. Our situation today is not unlike that of the Greco-Roman world just before it was salvaged by Augustus.

Here and now, there is a crying need, as there was then and there, for peace, harmony, teamwork, organization, administration, and efficiency on a world-wide scale. We are in the same danger of seeing civilization destroy itself by revolution and war.

Indeed, in our case, the degree of both the danger and the urgency is considerably higher. Our modern society has surpassed the Greco-Roman society in scale and complexity. It has become literally world-wide. It includes all sections of the human race, from the richest to the poorest. And it is now armed with atomic weapons. For us today, world order, peace, and social justice are literally necessities of life. We know that we shall destroy ourselves if we do not achieve these goals, so there can be no question of boggling over the price. We have to pay it, whatever it may be; and I think it is going to be the same price that the Greco-Roman world paid in and after the generation of Augustus. Knowing, as we do, how that story ended, can we use our hindsight to save ourselves from stumbling into the pitfalls in the road that we, in our turn, have perforce to take?

USURY IN ANCIENT ROME

TACITUS

[*The Annals of Tacitus,* trans. by George Gilbert Ramsay; John Murray, London, 1904, pp. 378–381.]

Here is an account by Tacitus, the great Roman historian of the first century A.D., which is a beautiful example of what happens when the government tries to institute measures that are contrary to the needs

and wants of society. In this case the attempt was to stop the lending of
money at interest, and at the same time to get those who had money for
lending to invest it instead in farm land, thus improving the state of
Roman agriculture, which apparently was being neglected by the wealthy
citizens.

[IN THE TIME OF TIBERIUS] a host of prosecutors rose up against
persons who were enriching themselves by usury in violation of
the law passed by the Dictator Caesar. That law had laid down
certain limits as to the lending of money and the holding of landed
estate inside Italy; but as private interest always gets the better of
the public good, it had long fallen into abeyance. The lending
out of money upon usury had long been a trouble in the city, a
constant cause of strife and discord; and attempts had been made
to check it even in ancient times, when manners were less corrupt
than they are now. First, the Twelve Tables limited the rate of
interest which might be charged to 10 per cent; for up to that
time wealthy persons had exacted what rate they chose. Next, a
tribunitian law reduced the rate to 5 per cent. At last, the lending
out of money on interest was forbidden altogether; and many
measures were passed to meet the fraudulent evasions which, continually repressed, were being continually devised, with an ingenuity
truly marvelous. On the present occasion, the Praetor Gracchus,
who was president of the court in which such cases were tried,
embarrassed by the number of persons brought into court, referred
the matter to the Senate; and the senators, scarce one of whom was
free from blame in the matter, threw themselves on the mercy of
the Emperor. He was pleased to allow a period of eighteen months,
during which everyone should bring his money affairs into conformity with the requirements of the law.

This step brought about a scarcity of money; not only because
all lenders were calling in their loans at once, but also because the
coined metal which had come in from the many recent condemnations
and confiscations was all locked up in the Imperial Treasury, or in
the Fiscus of the Emperor. To meet this scarcity, the Senate had
ordained that lenders should invest two-thirds of their capital in
landed property in Italy. The creditors, however, asked for payment
in full; and the debtors, when called upon, could not honorably be
in default. So at first they all ran to the moneylenders, entreating
their forbearance; next, the Praetor's court rang with notices of
suits; and the plan devised to bring relief, the buying and selling
of land, turned out to have exactly the opposite effect, since the
capitalists hoarded up their money with a view to purchasing landed
properties. The quantity of land for sale brought about a fall of

prices; and the greater a man's indebtedness, the greater his difficulty in selling. Thus many were ruined, the loss of property carrying with it loss of position and reputation also. At last Tiberius came to the rescue by distributing through the banks a sum of one hundred million sesterces, and allowing landowners to borrow for three years without interest, provided that they could offer security to the Treasury for double the amount. Thus credit was restored, and by degrees private lenders came into the market. The purchase of lands, however, was not carried out on the conditions laid down by the Senate. These were enforced with much strictness at the beginning, as is usual in such cases, but with very little in the end.

THE EMPEROR HADRIAN
INTERVENES IN BUSINESS

MARGUERITE YOURCENAR

[Marguerite Yourcenar, *Hadrian's Memoirs*, Farrar, Straus and Young, New York, copyright 1954 by Marguerite Yourcenar, pp. 120–121. Reprinted by permission of Farrar, Straus and Cudahy, Inc., and Martin Secker and Warburg, Ltd., London.]

Regulation of business by government is no recent development. The old empires were too dependent on trade not to want to see it developed in the national interest. Some of the ancient agricultural states too actually exploited their own mineral resources; Athens, for example, worked the Laurentium silver mines as a government operation (with slave labor), and the resulting revenue enabled her to finance a successful navy and a leisured civilization—leisured, that is, in the sense of working a little at business, and working hard at play (play including the serious pursuit of culture).

In the selection that follows we have an imaginative reconstruction of the Emperor Hadrian's measures to see that business served the interests of the Roman Empire in the second century A.D. As novelist Marguerite Yourcenar interprets history, Hadrian speaks in the first person. (The details may not all be documented, but the tone is authentic.)

OUR MERCHANTS are sometimes our best geographers, our best astronomers, and our most learned naturalists. Our bankers number among our ablest judges of men. I made use of these special capacities, but fought with all my strength against their possibilities for encroachment. Subsidies given to shipbuilders had multiplied tenfold our trade with foreign nations; thus I succeeded in reinforcing our costly imperial fleet with but slight expense. So far as importations from the Orient and Africa are concerned, Italy might as well be an island, dependent upon grain dealers for its subsistence, since it no longer supplies itself; the only means of coping with the dangers of this situation is to treat these indispensable men of business as functionaries to be watched over closely.

In recent years our older provinces have attained to a state of prosperity which can still perhaps be increased, but it is important that that prosperity should serve for all, and not alone for the bank of Herod Atticus, or for the small speculator who buys up all the oil of a Greek village. No law is too strict which makes for the reduction of the countless intermediaries who swarm our cities, an obscene, fat and paunchy race, whispering in every tavern, leaning on every counter, ready to undermine any policy which is not to their immediate advantage.

In time of shortage a judicious distribution from the state granaries helps to check the scandalous inflation of prices, but I was counting most of all on the organization of the producers themselves, the vineyard owners in Gaul and the fishermen in the Black Sea (whose miserable pittance is devoured by importers of caviar and salt fish who batten on the produce of those dangerous labors). One of my best days was the one on which I persuaded a group of seamen from the Archipelago to join in a single corporation in order to deal directly with retailers in the towns. I have never felt myself more usefully employed as ruler.

A ROYAL LAWMAKER SETS A BUSINESS CODE

~~~◊~~~

EMPEROR JUSTINIAN I

["The Code of Justinian," compiled by Justinian; from *The Civil Law,* translated and edited by Samuel P. Scott. The Central Trust Company, Cincinnati. 1932, vol. XV, pp. 175-177, 180 (abridged). Reprinted by permission of Jefferson Medical College, Philadelphia, John F. Rankin, trustee, and the beneficiaries of the Trust.]

The Roman Emperor, Justinian I, surnamed The Great, has gone down in history as a legislator and codifier of the law. Thus, in A.D. 528–534, he assembled the *Corpus Juris Civilis,* the body of civilian law. Many edicts of previous emperors concerning business matters were included; altogether they add up almost to a code of fair practices. Clearly, government took a strong hand in those days! This selection is from the part "Concerning Manufacturers" and "Concerning the Pork Butchers."

————

CONCERNING MANUFACTURERS

1. *The Emperors Valentinian, Theodosius, and Arcadius to Tatianus, Praetorian Prefect*

We order that all manufacturers shall deliver the articles made by them, and not pay money in their stead, and that the iron furnished shall be of good quality, and readily melted, in order that there may be less opportunity for fraud, and the public welfare be the better provided for. . . .

2. *The Emperors to Rufinus, Master of the Offices*

We order that the chief of the manufacturers shall, after the lapse of two years of continuous service, be not only discharged, but also treated with honor; and be included among the protectors of the guild of manufacturers, as well as sent every two years for the purpose of congratulating the Emperor. . . .

3. *The Emperors Arcadius and Honorius to Osius, Master of the Offices*

Indelible marks, that is to say, well-known brands, should be placed upon the arms of apprentices to manufacturers, so that in this way they may easily be recognized, if they should attempt to conceal themselves, and that those who are marked in this way, as well as their children, can unquestionably be identified by their guild whenever they surreptitiously, for the purpose of avoiding labor, have succeeded in obtaining admission to membership in any other guild. . . .

4. *The Emperors Honorius and Theodosius to Anthemius, Praetorian Prefect*

When anyone desires to be enrolled in the Organization of Manufacturers in the city in which he was born, or in which he has fixed his domicile, after they have been assembled, and before any documents are drawn up, he must prove that neither his grandfather nor his father was a decurion, and that he owes nothing to the Order of the Decurionate, and is under no liability to any citizen, and, after the proper formalities have been complied with before the Governor of the province, or (if he should be absent) before the defender of the city, the candidate shall be admitted into the association which he has selected.

If, in violation of the provisions of this law, anyone should secretly obtain admission to the guild of manufacturers, he is hereby notified that he shall be returned to the order to which he belongs, and compelled to discharge his duties to his country, and that no privilege of time, or previous service will entitle him to exemption. . . .

5. *The Emperors Theodosius and Valentinian*

It has been provided by law that artisans must confine themselves to their own trades, and, together with their children, remain in the one to which they belong, until their labors are ended by death.

Finally, any offense committed by one renders the entire number responsible, which rule has been established to cause them to be more careful in the selection of their members, and exercise supervision over their acts, since the loss sustained by one is felt by all. Therefore, all of them constitute, as it were, but a single body, and are compelled to answer for the delinquency of one, when circumstances demand it. . . .

6. *The Emperors Leo and Anthemius to Eufirmius, Master of the Offices*

We order that those artisans engaged in manufactures for the Emperor, as well as their wives and children, who are also said to be artisans, shall not be required to answer in court, unless before the tribunal of Your Highness, to whose jurisdiction they belong and under whose power they are. Nor shall they, after their term of service has expired, under any circumstances, be liable to civil or curial obligations, or be illegally molested by the illustrious Governors of provinces or their subordinates. . . .

7. *The Emperor Anastasius to the Master of the Offices*

No member of the guild of manufacturers shall hereafter lease property, or engage in the management or cultivation of land belonging to another; and any owner who ventures to violate this law by knowingly entrusting his personal effects or land to the administration of artisans shall lose it; and the latter, after having undergone severe punishment and the confiscation of their property, shall be sentenced to perpetual exile.

Every time that it may be necessary to require the transport of arms, Your Highness shall notify the eminent Prefecture, and state the quantity of arms, and the place from which they are to be transferred, in order that the Prefect may immediately order the illustrious Governor of the province to provide ships or vehicles out of those belonging to the public, for the conveyance of said arms, in accordance with the notice served upon him by Your Highness. If, after notice has thus been given by Your Highness to the Prefecture as aforesaid, delay or negligence on the part of the authorities should occur, and the transport of the arms should, for this reason, be prevented, We order that the accountant at that time in office in the Prefecture shall, with the other officials responsible for the delay, be sentenced to a fine of fifty pounds of gold, and that the said amount of gold shall be paid into the Treasury as soon as it is collected. In addition to this, We subject the illustrious Governor of the province, as well as his subordinates, to a fine of thirty pounds of gold, when, through their connivance, the transport of arms was delayed. . . .

CONCERNING THE PORK BUTCHERS . . .

1. *The Emperors Valentinian, Theodosius, and Arcadius to Albinus, Prefect of the City*

As dealers in hogs in the Eternal City are engaged in an occupation advantageous to the Roman people, they shall forever be exempt from the performance of ignoble services.

THE STATE AND THE HUNDRED ARTISANS

FROM THE *Official System of Chou*

[*Official System of Chou*, chap. XXXIX; quoted in Chen Huan-chang, *The Economic Principles of Confucius and His School*, Columbia University, New York, copyright 1911, p. 406.]

The Chinese, in the fifth century B.C., had a highly polished civilization, in terms of both art and society. Their elaborately simple wares were matched by an equally simple and just as carefully arranged system of human activity. And all of it—including the various kinds of production (which the Chinese lumped together in a stylized word picture, the "hundred artisans")—was organized into one unit: the state. We are reminded of the same thing, except that it is more primitive, among the early Greeks, where the economic unit was the king's household (see Homer in the Perspective section, Volume I).

This selection is from the "Official System of Chou"—Chou being a follower of Confucius. This was an *official* system, you see.

A STATE HAS SIX FUNCTIONS, and the "hundred artisans" take up one of them. Some are sitting down and discussing the principles. Some are rising and executing them. Some are judging the curve, the plane and all the conditions of the materials, for the utilization of the five elements and the preparation of the articles. Some are transporting the valuable and strange goods of the four corners and storing them up. Some are using their energy for the increase of wealth from the land. Some are making the silk and flax ready for the finishing of clothes.

Those who are sitting down and discussing the principles are called emperor and princes. Those who are rising and executing them are called students and great officials. Those who are judging the curve, the plane and all the conditions of the materials, for the utilization of the five elements and the preparation of the articles, are called the hundred artisans. Those who are transporting the valuable and strange goods of the four corners and storing them up are called merchants. Those who are using their energy for the increase of wealth from the land are called farmers. Those who are making the silk and flax ready for the finishing of clothes are called working women.

THE SCOTTISH GOVERNMENT PROMOTES INDUSTRIAL ACTIVITY

R. W. COCHRAN-PATRICK

[R. W. Cochran-Patrick, *Mediaeval Scotland*, James Maclehose and Sons, Glasgow, 1892, pp. 30–42 (abridged).]

One of the most revealing tributes to the importance of business as a part of our society is the way governments often stepped in to promote different kinds of industrial activity. Businessmen today are likely to complain about "government intervention," and no doubt with good cause in many situations, but the plain fact is that they have often enjoyed government's helping hand too. Here is a description from the early history of Scotland, starting with "William the Lion" (A.D. 1027–1087), showing how the government helped to bring in Flemish workmen to assist Scotch manufacturers, and also some of the problems thus created. An interesting sidelight is the large role that the "burghs" or towns played in economic regulation.

The pardonable pride in things Celtic which is displayed in the following excerpt is not surprising considering the name of the book's author (R. W. Cochran-Patrick) and its place of publication (Glasgow).

To THOSE WHO BELIEVE that the national greatness of this country depends in no small measure on the prosperity of its manufacturing and commercial industries, it will not be without interest to trace the origin and growth of these amongst ourselves. And the most prominent point in the history of early Scottish manufactures is the persistent national desire to promote and develop them. Often the means adopted seem to our ideas to be erroneous, and very often they fail. But the object aimed at was never lost sight of. From the days when William the Lion founded his royal burghs with practically exclusive monopolies of manufactures and commerce in order to encourage trade, to the times when James VI crowded the statute books with Acts of Parliament for the same purpose, the one idea was to stimulate by every means commercial enterprise. . . .

During the prehistoric ages our knowledge of the arts and industries of the early tribes is extremely limited. It would be rash to assume that absolute barbarism prevailed in every part of the country and at all periods. Every now and then some relic of the forgotten past turns up which shows a technical skill and artistic knowledge which can hardly be reconciled with the commonly received notions of the state of the primitive inhabitants of this country. Celtic traditions point to the very high antiquity, and to a very remarkable development, of native industries. Fifteen centuries before the Christian era, Tigherumas Mac Ollaig was the first, according to these venerable legends, to put colors into cloth and ornamental borders to garments. The catalogue of the possessions of Ailill and Medbh given in the ancient tale of the Táin Bo Chuailgue enumerates raiment of crimson, blue, black, green, yellow, speckled, gray, and striped, and other colors not easily identified. The costumes of the chiefs described in the same story also display a wonderful variety of manufactured stuffs. Conchobar Mac Nessa wore a crimson five-folding fuan or tunic with a shirt of cloth of gold. Another warrior, Munremur Mac Gercin, was attired in a dark long-wooled cloak and a shirt of striped silk. Amargin Mac Ecelsalach shone conspicuous among the clans in a blue five-bordered shirt, with carved clasps of white bronze (*findruine*) and buttons of gold, and "a cloak mottled with the splendor of all the most beautiful colors." . . .

It is remarkable that the Scots of Dalriada do not seem to have brought with them from their Ulster homes arts and cultures which undoubtedly flourished there, though probably at a later period than that assigned by their traditions. And it is still more curious that the same race remained inert and unmoved by the various influences which in other parts of Scotland began to stimulate commercial enterprise. On the other hand, the Saxon settlers, if they did not leave a high civilization behind them, possessed a capability for

future development, which soon began to tell on national progress.
Of the state of the native Caledonian tribes we can say very little.
But whenever these various races began to be blended in one
nationality, and settled down under a recognized government, the
latent energies immediately, though gradually, came into activity,
and ultimately have risen into the first rank. . . .

Even when history begins, a long period elapses before any notice
is taken of manufactures of any kind. During the century and a half
of peace and prosperity which closed with the death of Alexander
III, there is some ground for believing that textile manufactures
existed to a certain extent in this country. In the *Leges Burgorum,*
or laws of the burghs of Scotland, we find the twenty-second law
prohibiting any one but a burgess from making cloth or dyeing it.
Part of this ancient code dates back to the reign of David I. In
the original Cartulary of Glasgow, a volume of venerable antiquity,
written in a hand of the thirteenth century, is a little capitular,
giving the privileges of the burghs at that period. The second of
these provides that no one without the burgh shall presume to make
cloth, on pain of the king's amercement unforgiven—an enactment
probably of the reign of William the Lion. In the charter granted
by the same king to the city of Perth all manufacture of cloth in the
sheriffdom is prohibited except by those who were burgesses of that
royal and favored town. Similar provisions exist in the charters
granted during the same reign to Aberdeen and the burgh and shire
of Inverness. And it is to this period and to the policy of William
the Lion that we must date the exclusive privileges of the burghs
which can be traced down to a very much later time.

In 1398 cloth exported to foreign parts was to pay 2s. of custom
in the pound. Woolen cloth was to be measured by the rig [1] and not
by the selvidge [2] in 1469.

The weavers of Edinburgh received a seal of cause [3] in 1475. In
1491 six weavers were tried by the magistrates of Dunfermline.
Woolen cloth manufactured in Scotland was exported to Amsterdam
in 1495. The "Walkers" [4] of Edinburgh were incorporated in 1500.
The Convention of Royal Burghs sitting at Edinburgh in 1529
ordered that "no manner of walcar nor wobster [5] mak ony claith of

[1] *rig:* that part of the web which is folded down or doubled.
[2] *selvidge:* the rest of the web as distinguished from the rig.
[3] *seal of cause:* A writ under the seal of the municipality conferring certain
privileges on the particular craft. Thus the Cordiners of Glasgow had a seal
of cause from the Lord Provost, Bailies, Council, and Community of the Burgh and
City of Glasgow in 1558 in their favor which was confirmed under the seal of
James, Archbishop of Glasgow.
In other cases the seal of cause was confirmed by Parliament.
[4] *Walker:* To "walk" or "wauk" cloth is to thicken it. Garnett in his tour in
Scotland gives an ingenious derivation of the term. He considers the operation as
so called because the women sit round a board and work the cloth with their feet
as if walking. Wauk mills were in existence in Ayrshire and Renfrewshire till a very
recent period.
[5] *wobster:* a weaver. The word also occurs in the form of *webster* and *wabster.*

thar awin to sell agane." In 1473 the importation of cloth from
England was prohibited, the reason assigned being that the Scotch
only got cloth, which they could make at home, for their salmon
and other fish, instead of gold and silver as formerly; and ten
years later a duty of four ounces of standard silver was imposed on
every "serplath" [6] of cloth brought into the country by the merchants.
In 1540 the Parliament of Scotland enacted that in every burgh
there should be a qualified man chosen to seal all cloth in token
of its good quality; and if any cloth of inferior sort was found, half
of the goods of the offender were to be forfeited to the king, and
the other half to the burgh. It would be interesting to know if
any of these old seals, probably of lead, are still in existence. In
the Parliament of 1567 it was provided that the old Acts anent
"wobsters," "walkers," and makers of white cloth were to be put in
force, with this addition, that care was to be taken that the cloth was
not "flokkit," or, in other words, with the nap raised or improperly
thickened. In order to promote woolen manufactures and to give
employment to poor persons it was forbidden in 1581 to export
wool out of the country.

Shortly after this period James VI made a strong effort to improve
native industries, and among other expedients three skilled workmen from the Low Countries named John Gardin, Philip Fermant,
and John Banko were brought to Scotland for the purpose of establishing a textile manufactory. They were engaged to remain in the
country for five years, and were to be accompanied by thirty attendants, including a skilled "litster" or dyer. They were to manufacture as good cloth as was made in Flanders, Holland, or England,
and of the same patterns and quality; and they were further bound
to teach Scottish-born apprentices all the secrets of their trade.
Nicolas Vduart, burgess of Edinburgh, was appointed overseer of
the factory, and was ordered to see that the strangers had everything
provided for them, including a wright to set up their looms. Each
piece of cloth of satisfactory quality was to be stamped, and to
have a seal of lead attached to it. They were to manufacture "serges," [7]
"growgrams," [8] "Bombesies," [9] "stemmingis," [10] "beyis," [11] fustians,
bed covers, and other fabrics; they were to have a proper place in
Edinburgh, and other principal towns, for selling their goods on
market days; all necessary materials for their machinery were to be
supplied free; they were to be exempt from all taxation and public
burdens, and were to have, if they required, a church and minister of

---

[6] *serplath:* A measure of wool equal, according to Skene, to eighty stones.
[7] *serges:* a sort of light cloth.
[8] *growgrams:* otherwise grogranes or grograms: a kind of coarse silk taffety [taffeta].
[9] *Bombesies:* a thin hard stuff.
[10] *stemmingis:* a cloth originally made of goat's hair, afterwards of wool or silk.
It is called also taminy.
[11] *beyis,* or bayis: the cloth now called baize.

their own. In spite of this care for their spiritual welfare the strangers were evidently not beyond the supervision of the clergy of the "gude toon" of Edinburgh. For in 1588 it is recorded in the records of the burgh that "be ressoun of the difference in materis of relligion betuix the kirk and the twa Flemyng wobsters," they were to end their work between the date of the entry (May 8) and September 1 next to come, and in the meantime to confer with the ministers "anes at the leist ilk owlk in the ile of the kirk"; and if they did not make their peace with the kirk they were to depart the realm on the date named. The town of Edinburgh paid them £68 6s. 8d. for their traveling expenses, which was afterwards repaid the burgh by the Laird of Dairsie and Mr. Arch Wilkin, and finally given to the Trinity Kirk for making repairs on it. . . .

At an extraordinary sederunt of the Privy Council on the twenty-fourth of July [1601] the Bailies of Edinburgh appeared to answer to a charge made against them by the strangers lately brought into the country from Flanders for improving the cloth manufacture that they were neither "intertaneit nor putt to the werk," and "that they were sinderit,[12] quhilk wald be a grit hinder to the perfectioun of the said werk," and the Bailies were ordered to keep them together in Edinburgh, notwithstanding any ordinance set down by the Commissioners of burghs anent separating the strangers and planting them severally in other towns. And until they were set to work Edinburgh was to provide them with meat and drink and to be proportionately relieved by the other burghs. Another Act of the Estates in February 1601 is referred to in the minute of February 14 of the Convention of Burghs, but it is not to be found in the Record Edition. Apparently it provided that twenty more craftsmen, "makeris of claith and lauboureris of woll" should be brought from abroad, and the burghs accordingly agreed to uplift 12,000 merks toward the expense. . . .

A difference of opinion still existed between the king and the burghs as to the best method of utilizing the services of the strangers. The king accordingly addressed a letter to the convention urging the Commissioners further to consider the matter, but it does not appear what the result was.

From a minute of the Convention of Burghs on the second of February, 1605, it would appear that an Act of Parliament had been passed on the seventh of June giving an offer to the burghs to work the cloth factories, though no mention is made of it in the Record Edition of the Acts. The burghs declined the offer on the double ground that they had no more interest in cloth manufacture than any other part of the realm, and that they had sustained great losses by the former attempts to set it up; but they agreed to

---

[12] *sinderit:* parted or separated.

give their "fortefecatioun and concurrence" to anyone who would undertake the work.

The next notice to be found of these foreigners is in 1609, when they were established in the Canongate of Edinburgh, and were being still molested by the magistrates; but, on appeal to the Privy Council, they were exempted from their interference. During the remainder of the reign of James VI, who consistently and perseveringly took every opportunity of promoting and improving native manufactures, considerable progress seems to have been made in the woolen industries. In 1613 Scottish cloth, plaiding, and kerseys [13] were exported to the Low Countries, showing that home wants were not only fully supplied, but a surplus left for foreign trade.

GOVERNMENT SHOULDN'T MEDDLE WITH BUSINESS

BENJAMIN FRANKLIN

[Benjamin Franklin, *Extracts from the Works of Dr. Franklin, on Population, Commerce, &c.* (1751), from John Ramsay McCullough (ed.), *A Select Collection of Scarce and Valuable Economical Tracts,* printed by Lord Overstone, London, 1859, pp. 224–225.]

Ben Franklin, speaking out early in the life of the young republic, before the battle lines in the tariff question had really been drawn, nonetheless shows that he would have been a vigorous protagonist for free trade in the bitter controversy which developed soon after his death. In spirit, here, this businessman-turned-statesman is closer to Jefferson than to Hamilton.*

OUR PRINCIPLES, we apprehend, may hold good for all nations, and ought to be attended to by the legislative power of every nation. We will not discuss every particular point: nor is it to our purpose to examine the pretended principles or utility whereon monopolies are generally established. That the wisdom of government should weigh and nicely consider any proposed regulation on those principles we humbly judge to be self-evident; whereby may be seen whether it coincides with the general good. Solomon adviseth *not to counsel with a merchant for gain.* This, we presume, relates to the merchant's own particular profit; which, we repeat, must ever be the spring of his actions. Government ought, notwithstanding, to endeavor to

---

[13]*kerseys:* or kairsays: a sort of cloth.

* For more of Ben Franklin, refer to index listing in this volume.

procure particular informations from everyone; not only from those actually employed, or those who have been concerned in particular branches of trade, but even from persons who may have considered of it theoretically and speculatively.

Perhaps, in general, it would be better if government meddled no farther with trade than to protect it, and let it take its course. Most of the statutes, or acts, edicts, arrets, and placarts of parliaments, princes, and states, for regulating, directing, or restraining of trade, have, we think, been either political blunders, or jobs obtained by artful men for private advantage, under pretense of public good. When Colbert assembled some wise old merchants of France, and desired their advice and opinion, how he could best serve and promote commerce, their answer, after consultation, was, in three words only, "Laissez nous faire": Let us alone. It is said, by a very solid writer of the same nation, that he is well advanced in the science of politics who knows the full force of that maxim, "Pas trop gouverner": Not to govern too much. Which, perhaps, would be of more use when applied to trade than in any other public concern. It were therefore to be wished that commerce was as free between all the nations of the world as it is between the several counties of England *; so would all, by mutual communication, obtain more enjoyments. Those counties do not ruin one another by trade; neither would the nations. No nation was ever ruined by trade; even seemingly the most disadvantageous.

Wherever desirable superfluities are imported, industry is excited; and therefore plenty is produced. Were only necessaries permitted to be purchased, men would work no more than was necessary for that purpose.

PROSPECTUS FOR A GOVERNMENT FINANCE CORPORATION

ALEXANDER HAMILTON

[Arthur Harrison Cole (ed.), *Industrial and Commercial Correspondence of Alexander Hamilton*, publ. under auspices of The Business Historical Society, Inc.; A. W. Shaw Company, Chicago, 1928, pp. 192–199.]

Here is an early prospectus for a state corporation that is significant on many counts. One, it is written by none other than Alexander Hamilton, first Secretary of the Treasury (who believed very strongly in encouraging the development of manufacturing in the United States; see the piece by

---

* Trade was not free between the American colonies, nor indeed between the early states; in fact, there are still some barriers in the form of state taxes.

him in Volume II). Two, it envisages use of a lottery to raise funds, a prevalent governmental device in those days. Three, it contains a very interesting list of provisions covering the scheme of organization. And, finally, it is a very clear example of government fostering industry—a construction finance corporation, one step ahead of the Reconstruction Finance Corporation we had to devise in the dark 1930s.

———◆———

THE DEARNESS OF LABOR and the want of capital are the two great objections to the success of manufactures in the United States.

The first objection ceases to be formidable when it is recollected how prodigiously the proportion of manual labor in a variety of manufactures [has] been decreased by the late improvements in the construction and application of machines—and when it is also considered to what an extent women and children in the populous parts of the country may be rendered auxiliary to undertakings of this nature. It is also to be taken into calculation that emigrants may be engaged on reasonable terms in countries where labor is cheap, and brought over to the United States.

The last objection disappears in the eye of those who are aware how much may be done by a proper application of the public debt— here is the resource which has been hitherto wanted. And while a direction of it to this object may be made a mean of public prosperity and an instrument of profit to adventurers in the enterprise, it at the same time affords a prospect of an enhancement of the value of the debt, by giving it a new and additional employment and utility.

It is evident that various fabrics [manufacturing enterprises] under every supposed disadvantage are in a very promising train. And that the success has not been still more considerable may be traced to very obvious causes.

Scarcely any has been undertaken upon a scale sufficiently extensive or with a due degree of system. To ensure success it is desirable to be able to enter into competition with foreign fabrics in three particulars—quality, price, term of credit. To the first, workmen of equal skill [are] an essential ingredient. The means employed have not generally been adequate to the purpose of procuring them from abroad, and those who have been procurable at home have for the most part been of an inferior class. To cheapness of price, a capital equal to the purpose of making all necessary advances and procuring materials on the best terms is an indispensable requisite—and to the giving of credit a capital capable of affording a surplus beyond what is required for carrying on the business is not less indispensable. But most undertakings hitherto have been bottomed on very slender resources.

To remedy this defect an association of the capitals of a number of individuals is an obvious expedient—and the species of capital which consists of the public stock is susceptible of dispositions which will render it adequate to the end. There is good reason to expect that as far as shall be found necessary money on reasonable terms may be procured abroad upon an hypothecation of the stock. It is presumable that public banks would not refuse their aid in the same way to a solid institution of so great public utility. The pecuniary aid even of government, though not to be counted upon, ought not wholly to be despaired of. And when the stock shall have attained its due value so that no loss will attend the sale, all such aids may be dispensed with. The stock may then be turned into specie without disadvantage whenever specie is called for.

But it is easy to see that upon a good capital in stock an effective credit may be raised in various ways which will answer every purpose of specie; independent of the direct expedient of borrowing.

To effect the desired association an incorporation of the adventurers must be contemplated as a mean necessary to their security. This can doubtless be obtained. There is scarcely a state which could be insensible to the advantage of being the scene of such an undertaking. But there are reasons which strongly recommend the State of New Jersey for the purpose. It is thickly populated—provisions are there abundant and cheap. The state having scarcely any external commerce and no waste lands to be peopled can feel the impulse of no *supposed* interest hostile to the advancement of manufacturers. Its situation seems to insure a constant friendly disposition.

The great and preliminary desideratum, then, is to form a sufficient capital. This, it is conceived, ought not to be less than $500,000. Toward forming this capital, subscriptions ought immediately to be set on foot, upon this condition, that no subscriber shall be bound to pay until an act of incorporation shall have been obtained—for which application may be made as soon as the sums subscribed shall amount to $100,000.

As soon as it is evident that a proper capital can be formed means ought to be taken to procure from Europe skilful workmen, and such machines and implements as cannot be had here in sufficient perfection. To this the existing crisis of the affairs of certain parts of Europe appears to be particularly favorable. It will not be necessary that all the requisite workmen should be brought from thence—one in the nature of a foreman for each branch may in some branches suffice. In others it may be requisite to go further and have one for each subdivision. But numbers of workmen of secondary merit may be found in the United States; and others may be quickly formed.

It is conceived that there would be a moral certainty of success in manufactories of the following articles: *

1st Paper and pasteboard
2nd Paper hangings
3rd Sailcloth and other coarse linen cloths, such as sheetings, shirtings, diaper, oznaburgs &c.
4th The printing of cottons and linens; and as incident to this but on a smaller scale the manufacturing of the article to be printed.
5th Women's shoes of all kinds
6th Thread, cotton and worsted stockings
7th Pottery and earthenware
8th Chip hats
9th Ribbands and tapes
10th Carpets
11th Blankets
12th Brass and iron wire
13th Thread and fringes

It will be unnecessary to enter into the details of the execution further than to observe that the employment of the labor-saving mills and machines is particularly contemplated.

In addition to the foregoing a brewery for the supply of the manufacturers, as a primary object, may be thought of.

When application shall be made for an act of incorporation it ought to include a request that provision may be made for incorporating the inhabitants of the district within a certain defined limit which shall be chosen by the company as the principal seat of their factories and a further request that the company may have permission to institute a lottery or lotteries in each year for the term of five years for a sum or sums not exceeding in one year $100,000. The State of Jersey if duly sensible of its interest in the measure will not refuse encouragement of this nature.

An incorporation of this sort will be of great importance to the police of the establishment. It may also be found eligible to vest a part of the funds of the company in the purchase of ground on which to erect necessary buildings &c. A part of this ground divided into town lots may be afterwards a source of profit to the company.

The lottery will answer two purposes. It will give a temporary command of money and the profit arising from it will go toward indemnifying for first unproductive efforts.

* A few months later this scheme had shrunk to "the making and printing of cotton cloth."

The following scheme for the organization of the company will probably be an eligible one:

1st   The capital of the company as before remarked to consist of $500,000 to be divided into 5000 shares, each share being $100.

2nd   Any person, copartnership or body politic may subscribe for as many shares as he, she or they may think fit. The sums subscribed to be payable one half in the funded 6 per cent stock, or in 3 per cent stock at two dollars for one, and the other half in deferred stock.* The payments to be in four equal parts. The first at the time of incorporation, the second in six months after, the third in six months after the second and the fourth in six months after the third. Those who prefer paying in specie to be permitted to do so, computing the funded 6 per centum at par and the deferred according to its present value at the time of payment, discounting the interest thereupon during the suspension of the payment at the rate of 6 per centum per annum.

3rd   The affairs of the company to be under the management of thirteen directors to be chosen annually on the first Monday of October in each year by plurality of suffrages of the stockholders. The directors by plurality of voices to choose from among themselves a governor and deputy governor.

4th   The number of votes to which each stockholder shall be entitled shall be in proportion to the number of shares he shall hold; that is to say, one vote for each share. But neither the United States nor any state which may become a subscriber shall be entitled to more than 100 votes. The United States or any state nevertheless which may subscribe for not less than 100 shares may appoint a commissioner who shall have a right at all times to inspect the proceedings of the company and the state of its affairs, but without any authority to control. Every subscriber may vote by attorney duly constituted.

5th   There shall be a stated meeting of the directors on every first Monday of January, April, July and October at the place which is the principal seat of the manufactory. But the governor for the time being or any three directors may, by writing under his or their hands directed to the other directors and left at their respective places of abode at least fourteen days prior to the day for meeting, or by advertisement in one public gazette printed in the state where the corporation shall be established and in another public gazette

---

* The "stock" here mentioned is unquestionably the funded debt of the United States for which provision had been made in the funding act of 1790—a scheme elaborated by Hamilton himself. According to this act, the debt was evidenced by bonds of three sorts: 6 per cent bonds and 3 per cent bonds which bore interest at once, and 6 per cent bonds upon which interest was "deferred" until after 1800. (Holders of existing government obligations received such bonds in specified proportions.)

printed in the City of Philadelphia, and in another public gazette printed in the City of New York, for the space of thirty days prior to the time of meeting, convene a special meeting of the directors for the purpose of transacting business of the company.

6th No director shall receive any emolument unless the same shall have been allowed by the stockholders at a general meeting. But the directors may appoint such officers and with such compensations as they shall think fit.

7th Not less than seven directors, if the governor or deputy governor be not one, shall constitute a board for the transaction of business. But if the governor or deputy governor be one, five shall suffice. In case it should at any time happen that there are two separate meetings of five or more directors each, but both less than a majority of the whole, one having the governor and the other the deputy governor, that at which the governor shall be present shall be the legal one.

8th The directors to have power to make all bylaws, rules and regulations requisite for conducting the affairs of the company.

9th At every annual meeting of the stockholders for the purpose of choosing directors, the directors shall lay before them a general state of the affairs of the company, exhibiting the amount of its stock debts and credits, the different kinds of manufactures carried on, the number of persons employed in each and their respective compensations together with an account of profit and loss.

10th The persons not exceeding five in number who at any general meeting shall have next after the directors chosen the highest number of votes for directors shall by force thereof be a committee of inspection and shall have a right of access to all the books of the company and of examination into all its affairs and shall at each succeeding meeting report all such authentic facts as shall come to their knowledge to the stockholders for their information. The stockholders may also, if they think fit, at any general meeting appoint by plurality of suffrages any five of their number for the purpose of making such enquiries and investigations as they may think necessary.

11th The stockholders at a general meeting may annul or alter any of the regulations established by the directors and make such others as they may think necessary.

12th Any board of directors or either of the committees above mentioned may at any time call a general meeting of the stockholders, giving thirty days' previous notice thereof in three gazettes, one published in the state in which the factory shall be established, another in the City of Philadelphia and another in the City of New York.

13th Every cashier or treasurer of the corporation shall before he enters on the duties of his office give bond with one or more sureties to the satisfaction of the directors for the faithful execution of his duty in a sum not less than $20,000.

14th So much of the capital stock of the company as may consist of public debts shall be placed on the books of the Treasury of the United States in the name of the corporation, and every stockholder shall be entitled to a license under the seal of the corporation to inspect the account of the said stock at his pleasure as far as may comport with the rules of the Treasury. This however shall not prevent the investment of the said debt in stock of the Bank of the United States, reserving to each stockholder the like right of inspection in relation to the stock of the company to be invested.

15th There shall be a yearly dividend of the profits of the company for the first five years, and after that period a half-yearly dividend.

16th The stock of the corporation shall be assignable and transferrable according to such rules as shall be instituted in that behalf by its laws and ordinances.

17th The corporation shall be at liberty to make and vend all such articles as shall not be prohibited by law; provided that it shall only trade in such articles as itself shall manufacture in whole or in part or in such as shall be received in payment or exchange therefor.

18th It shall be understood that a majority of the stockholders may at any time dissolve the corporation; but this shall be only done at a general meeting which shall have been specially summoned for the purpose with public notice of the intent. And upon such dissolution the directors for the time being shall be *ipso facto* trustees for settling all the affairs of the corporation, disposing of its effects, paying its debts, and dividing the surplus among the stockholders in proportion to their respective interests in the stock.

19th The stock and other property of the corporation to be exempt from Taxes.

The management of the affairs of this company will require that an agent shall be appointed to superintend all the different works and the disposition of the articles manufactured in conformity to the general regulations of the directors. This agent ought to have such a compensation as will command the services of a man every way competent and trustworthy. Such a man may doubtless be found; it is not necessary that he should be a technical man in any of the branches of manufacture, but a man of information, thoroughly a man of business, of probity and diligence and energy.

THE BITTER DEBATE ON
FREE TRADE

~~◦⁀◦~~

HORACE GREELEY AND S. G. ARNOLD

[Horace Greeley & S. G. Arnold, "Free Trade," *The Merchants' Magazine and Commercial Review*, Freeman Hunt, ed. and publ., New York, March 1841, vol. IV, no. 3, pp. 232–238 (abridged).]

One of the big areas where government has had an influence on industrial activity—indeed, where business has often *asked* government for help—is the use of tariffs and quotas to protect home industry against foreign imports.

The debate on free trade versus protectionism has been a long one. As a matter of fact, it is only in the last few years that the bitterness of the past debate has subsided. Now most of us accept, in principle, the desirability of a high degree of freedom in international trade; of course in our present high state of development, we have less need to nurture new struggling industries in competition with established industries in other countries.

In any event, the following selection is now primarily of historical interest. But it is important to realize how vigorous the polemics used to be; how live the issue was to government and business people. Here Horace Greeley, the famous newspaper publisher and statesman of the 1800s, who advised "Go west, young man," presents the case for protection; by analogy to the effect of *state* subsidies (for example, to encourage the growing of wheat in Maine), he attempts to show that *internationally* the same thing happens, and tariffs on foreign products serve as a "bounty" to domestic producers. And S. G. Arnold, a well-known historian of that day (whose father and grandfather were prominent Rhode Island merchants), refutes him on the same grounds.

Few people remember that Greeley was both the Democratic and the Liberal Republican candidate for the Presidency against General Grant. This particular debate, which occurred in the pages of Freeman Hunt's *Merchants' Magazine and Commercial Review*, is from the early part of Greeley's career, the 1840s.

———◆———

IS IT . . . COMMERCIALLY EXPEDIENT that the great producing interests of the country be fostered and stimulated to their highest possible activity and force, or that they be left entirely to take care of themselves, and in each department to encounter the depressing and disastrous rivalry of whatever portion of the globe may be able to undersell our productions in its particular staple? . . .

Let me now adduce some illustrative examples; we all know that certain bounties are paid by our government to our citizens engaged in the cod and mackerel fisheries; will my opponent contend that no more fish are caught than there would be if no bounties were given? Again: until very recently, Maine was a timber-cutting and commercial state, her breadstuffs being in great part purchased from abroad. In 1836 (I believe), her legislature enacted that a bounty should be paid thereafter to the producers of wheat within her territory. Under the operation of that act, in the course of two or three years, the annual production of wheat in Maine has been quadrupled. Now, my opponent will not deny that this act is clearly a protective one, and directly in the teeth of the "free trade" principles which Maine has ever professed to cherish. . . .

My opponent, then, has no chance of escape from the natural conclusion, but through the presumption that the skill and labor employed in the production of wheat has been diverted from some other equally profitable employment; that therefore Maine has gained nothing by her protective policy. But is this presumption justified by fact? Will any man seriously contend that if Maine had not raised the two millions of bushels extra of wheat, during the last three years, she would necessarily have produced something in its stead of equal or greater value? *I trust not.* . . .

ANSWER BY S. G. ARNOLD

We could have wished that Mr. Greeley had drawn from his inexhaustible store of facts something a little more satisfactory than is contained in those three words ["I trust not"], as without them we must still come to the conclusion that Maine has, in fact, been the *loser* by her "protective policy." The reason why wheat was not raised before the bestowment of this bounty, was because the wheat culture was less profitable than some other modes of industry. The bounty had the effect to raise it to the general average, and consequently to invite the culture. Had the bounty been paid by the king of France, it is possible that Maine might not have been the loser. It was, however, taxed in some way on her own citizens, and was therefore merely taken from the pockets of one class to be put into those of another; and if, after all, wheat cannot be raised in Maine cheaper than it can be procured by exchange, she has, clearly, been the *loser* by her "protective policy."

To illustrate this position. A farmer in Maine can raise on a certain piece of land $25 worth of potatoes, and only $20 worth of wheat. It is consequently to his interest to raise potatoes. But if the wheat bounty was sufficient to raise the value of his crop from

$20 to $25, it would then be indifferent to him whether he raised wheat or potatoes, inasmuch as his profits would be the same in either case. But although he is, *individually,* just as well off by turning his attention to the culture of *wheat,* yet it is evident that his ground has produced less *value.* His wheat is, after all, worth only $20. He is a loser to the amount of $5 on his crop, but the state has kindly come forward to make up his loss. The wheat growers of Maine, then, are not, as a class, losers by their change of occupation; but the state, that is, the taxpayers, are losers to the full amount of the bounty.

. Now, what is true of protection in Maine is true of protection anywhere else. The article protected can be procured by exchange cheaper than it can be produced, and the protective duty is laid to make it so dear as to give the advantage to the home producer. It was not produced before because some other mode of industry was more profitable. The duty raises it to the general average, and consequently the producer suffers no loss, although really engaged in a losing business, the community having agreed to sustain him, that is, to pay his losses. . . .

In a country like ours, where everything is progressive, an article which may not be profitably produced now may be profitably produced at some future time, when capital shall have become more abundant, and labor less productive. To attempt to anticipate that time by means of the forcing system of protection can never prove advantageous to a country, as it must inevitably be attended with public loss, and by injuring the accumulating capital of the nation have a direct tendency to put off that time to a more distant day.

Besides, it must not be forgotten that our situation, located, as we are, some thousands of miles from the most producing nations, is itself a natural protection, and that this protection is still further increased by the duties which are required for the support of government. These give us an advantage without the special interposition of the state, which is quite sufficient to stimulate our enterprising citizens to the pursuit of wealth in every mode of industry which offers the least prospect of success.

In short, we are fully satisfied that the only sure guide to wealth and prosperity is FREEDOM, *entire and unrestricted* FREEDOM. It is, we think, a great mistake for governments to compel men into this or that mode of production. We believe it to be no part of their duty; and it seldom fails of leading, in the end, to disaster and ruin. Under a system of free trade, men are guided by the instinct of their own interests, and the cotton planter, the wheat grower, the manufacturer, the blacksmith, hatter, shoemaker, tanner, &c., all fix themselves in such situations as they believe will be most profitable to themselves; and unless they greatly mistake their own interests, their choice will be best calculated to produce the greatest amount of products to the country.

The best protection, then, is the protection of all men in their persons and property—the protection of society by means of general education—and the protection of our flag wherever it shall be unfurled to the four winds of heaven. It is such protection which gives nerve to enterprise, spirit to industry, and wing to commerce; and which is destined to carry forward our country in that mighty and glorious progress which she has commenced with such Herculean and lofty strides.

THE CANDLEMAKERS DEMAND
PROTECTION FROM THE
SUN'S COMPETITION

FRÉDÉRIC BASTIAT

[Frédéric Bastiat, "Petition," in *Economic Sophisms*, trans. by Patrick James Stirling, Oliver and Boyd, Edinburgh, 1873, pp. 49–53.]

Here, from France, in the year 1845, is a little fun at the expense of all the businessmen who were clamoring for the government to protect them from foreign competition. It is a truism to comment that over the years businessmen have always *silently* liked government intervention when it has been in their favor, and have denounced it *loudly* when it has been for somebody else's benefit.

The story of the authorship is just about as interesting as the piece itself. From Palgrave * we learn this about the French economist who wrote it—Frédéric Bastiat (1801–1850)—a man who deserves to be better known to Americans, and whose career brings out some of the issues involved in business-government relations:

But for a few casual circumstances which drew out his literary powers, Bastiat would have died comparatively unknown, his first book only appearing in 1845, five years before his death. He had lived up to that date in retirement, working hard, but producing little. The son of a merchant in the Spanish trade, he was left an orphan when nine years old. As a man, he tried his hand, without great success, first in business, in the establishment of his uncle, then in farming at Mugron, near Bayonne, on the estate which he inherited at the death of his grandfather, 1825. Appointed after the

* Henry Higgs (ed.), *Palgrave's Dictionary of Political Economy*, Macmillan and Co., Ltd., London; 1925, pp. 123–124.

revolution of 1830 *juge de paix* of his canto, he seemed destined to
die in the little town where he had been born, limiting his ambition
to the direction of a small scientific society. . . . His first pamphlets
were little memoirs on local matters, the interest of which, notwithstanding the high qualities of style and form they possessed,
was necessarily limited to a narrow circle.

To England belongs the honor of having lighted up in Bastiat the
sacred fire of thought. An English journal to which he subscribed
almost by accident, the *Globe,* informed him of the foundation and
progress of the Anti-Corn Law League, the existence of which was
barely known in France. . . . A few weeks later, and the *Journal
des Économistes* received from the farthest end of the district of the
Landes a manuscript signed with an unknown name, "De l'influence
des tarifs français et anglais sur l'avenir des deux peuples." The
article appeared October 1844, and excited a good deal of attention. The author was asked for more; and the file of *Sophismes
Économiques* commenced, to the joy of the opponents, and the
confusion of the defenders, of privilege. Nothing is more brilliant,
nothing more *French,* in the best sense of the word, than these
amusing pamphlets, in which the most delicate irony and the most
pitiless logic are combined, as in the famous "Pétition des fabricants
de chandelles, bougies, lampes, chandeliers, reverbères, mouchettes,
éteignoirs, et des producteurs de suif, huile resine, alcool, et
généralement de tout ce qui concerne l'éclairage" [which is the selection presented here]. This petition of the candlemakers is a humorous
complaint against the sun for spoiling their trade, a petition based
on protectionist lines. . . .

Bastiat soon became the most active and dreaded antagonist of the
protectionist policy. The war tariffs of the first empire had been
continued after the restoration by the monarchy of July (Louis
Philippe). The first Association pour la liberté des échanges was
formed at Bordeaux, February 1846; another was established at
Paris the same year with Bastiat as general secretary, and *Le Libre
Échange* as its journal. This free-trade campaign was roughly interrupted by the revolution of 1848; and the French economists,
and Bastiat among them, found themselves compelled to direct
their efforts and their forces against the spread of socialism. Bastiat
harassed those who followed the socialists, with epigrams and
refutations, and thus assisted in enlightening the country as to the
perils with which the revolutionary utopia threatened it. . . .

After having victoriously refuted the errors of protection and
socialism, he thought it was time for him to formulate what he
considered the true economic doctrine, and commenced the publication of his *Harmonies.* In this brilliant work, unhappily never
finished, Bastiat shows the contrast between the internal weakness

of the artificial organizations which are founded on constraint, and the prosperity spontaneously arising in an economic condition in which the equilibrium of individual and collective forces results from their free and reciprocal balance. (For an amusing counterpoint to this piece, see Benjamin Franklin's proposal to the people of Paris that they should not waste the free sunlight of early morning by sleeping so late, page 2503 in this volume.)

———◆———

Petition of the Manufacturers of Candles, Wax Lights, Lamps, Candlesticks, Street Lamps, Snuffers, Extinguishers, and of the Producers of Oil, Tallow, Rosin, Alcohol, and, Generally, of Everything Connected with Lighting.

TO MESSIEURS THE MEMBERS OF THE CHAMBER OF DEPUTIES

GENTLEMEN,

You are on the right road. You reject abstract theories, and have little consideration for cheapness and plenty. Your chief care is the interest of the producer. You desire to emancipate him from external competition, and reserve the *national market* for *national industry.*

We are about to offer you an admirable opportunity of applying your—what shall we call it? your theory? No; nothing is more deceptive than theory; your doctrine? your system? your principle? but you dislike doctrines, you abhor systems, and as for principles, you deny that there are any in social economy: we shall say, then, your practice, your practice without theory and without principle.

We are suffering from the intolerable competition of a foreign rival, placed, it would seem, in a condition so far superior to ours for the production of light, that he absolutely *inundates* our *national market* with it at a price fabulously reduced. The moment he shows himself, our trade leaves us—all consumers apply to him; and a branch of native industry, having countless ramifications, is all at once rendered completely stagnant. This rival, who is no other than the sun, wages war to the knife against us, and we suspect that he has been raised up by *perfidious Albion* (good policy as times go); inasmuch as he displays toward that haughty island a circumspection with which he dispenses in our case.

What we pray for is that it may please you to pass a law ordering the shutting up of all windows, skylights, dormer windows, outside and inside shutters, curtains, blinds, bull's-eyes; in a word, of all openings, holes, chinks, clefts, and fissures, by or through which the light of the sun has been in use to enter houses, to the prejudice of the meritorious manufactures with which we flatter ourselves we have accommodated our country—a country which, in gratitude, ought not to abandon us now to a strife so unequal.

We trust, gentlemen, that you will not regard this our request as a satire, or refuse it without at least previously hearing the reasons which we have to urge in its support.

And, first, if you shut up as much as possible all access to natural light, and create a demand for artificial light, which of our French manufactures will not be encouraged by it?

If more tallow is consumed, then there must be more oxen and sheep; and, consequently, we shall behold the multiplication of artificial meadows, meat, wool, hides, and, above all, manure, which is the basis and foundation of all agricultural wealth.

If more oil is consumed, then we shall have an extended cultivation of the poppy, of the olive, and of grape. These rich and exhausting plants will come at the right time to enable us to avail ourselves of the increased fertility which the rearing of additional cattle will impart to our lands.

Our heaths will be covered with resinous trees. Numerous swarms of bees will, on the mountains, gather perfumed treasures, now wasting their fragrance on the desert air, like the flowers from which they emanate. No branch of agriculture but will then exhibit a cheering development.

The same remark applies to navigation. Thousands of vessels will proceed to the whale fishery, and in a short time we shall possess a navy capable of maintaining the honor of France, and gratifying the patriotic aspirations of your petitioners, the undersigned candle-makers and others.

But what shall we say of the manufacture of *articles de Paris?* Henceforth you will behold gildings, bronzes, crystals, in candlesticks, in lamps, in lusters, in candelabra, shining forth, in spacious warerooms, compared with which those of the present day can be regarded but as mere shops.

No poor *resinier* from his heights on the seacoast, no coal miner from the depth of his sable gallery, but will rejoice in higher wages and increased prosperity.

Only have the goodness to reflect, gentlemen, and you will be convinced that there is, perhaps, no Frenchman, from the wealthy coalmaster to the humblest vender of lucifer matches, whose lot will not be ameliorated by the success of this our petition.

We foresee your objections, gentlemen, but we know that you can oppose to us none but such as you have picked up from the effete works of the partisans of free trade. We defy you to utter a single word against us which will not instantly rebound against yourselves and your entire policy.

You will tell us that, if we gain by the protection which we seek, the country will lose by it, because the consumer must bear the loss.

We answer:

You have ceased to have any right to invoke the interest of the consumer; for, whenever his interest is found opposed to that of the producer, you sacrifice the former. You have done so for the purpose of *encouraging labor* and *increasing employment.* For the same reason you should do so again.

You have yourselves obviated this objection. When you are told that the consumer is interested in the free importation of iron, coal, corn, textile fabrics—yes, you reply, but the producer is interested in their exclusion. Well, be it so; if consumers are interested in the free admission of natural light, the producers of artificial light are equally interested in its prohibition.

But, again, you may say that the producer and consumer are identical. If the manufacturer gain by protection, he will make the agriculturist also a gain; and if agriculture prosper, it will open a vent to manufactures. Very well; if you confer upon us the monopoly of furnishing light during the day, first of all, we shall purchase quantities of tallow, coals, oils, resinous substances, wax, alcohol— besides silver, iron, bronze, crystal—to carry on our manufactures; and then we, and those who furnish us with such commodities, having become rich will consume a great deal, and impart prosperity to all the other branches of our national industry.

If you urge that the light of the sun is a gratuitous gift of nature, and that to reject such gifts is to reject wealth itself under pretense of encouraging the means of acquiring it, we would caution you against giving a death blow to your own policy. Remember that hitherto you have always repelled foreign products, *because* they approximate more nearly than home products to the character of gratuitous gifts. To comply with the exactions of other monopolists, you have only *half a motive;* and to repulse us simply because we stand on a stronger vantage-ground than others would be to adopt the equation, $+ \times + = -$; in other words, it would be to heap *absurdity* upon *absurdity.*

Nature and human labor cooperate in various proportions (depending on countries and climates) in the production of commodities. The part which nature executes is always gratuitous; it is the part executed by human labor which constitutes value, and is paid for.

If a Lisbon orange sells for half the price of a Paris orange, it is because natural, and consequently gratuitous, heat does for the one, what artificial, and therefore expensive, heat must do for the other.

When an orange comes to us from Portugal, we may conclude that it is furnished in part gratuitously, in part for an onerous consideration; in other words, it comes to us at *half price* as compared with those of Paris.

Now, it is precisely the *gratuitous half* (pardon the word) which we contend should be excluded. You say, How can natural labor sustain competition with foreign labor, when the former has all the work to do, and the latter only does one-half, the sun supplying the remainder? But if this *half,* being *gratuitous,* determines you to exclude competition, how should the *whole,* being *gratuitous,* induce you to admit competition? If you were consistent, you would, while excluding as hurtful to native industry what is half gratuitous, exclude *a fortiori* and with double zeal, that which is altogether gratuitous.

Once more, when products such as coal, iron, corn, or textile fabrics are sent us from abroad, and we can acquire them with less labor than if we made them ourselves, the difference is a free gift conferred upon us. The gift is more or less considerable in proportion as the difference is more or less great. It amounts to a quarter, a half, or three-quarters of the value of the product, when the foreigner asks us for only three-fourths, a half, or a quarter of the price we should otherwise pay. It is as perfect and complete as it can be, when the donor (like the sun in furnishing us with light) asks us for nothing. The question, and we ask it formally, is this, Do you desire for our country the benefit of gratuitous consumption, or the pretended advantages of onerous production? Make your choice, but be logical; for as long as you exclude, as you do, coal, iron, corn, foreign fabrics, *in proportion* as their price approximates to *zero,* what inconsistency would it be to admit the light of the sun, the price of which is already at *zero* during the entire day!

LOCKING HORNS—OR IS IT GEARS? —WITH THE BRITISH GOVERNMENT

CHARLES BABBAGE

[Charles Babbage, "Difference Engine No. 2," in *Passage from the Life of a Philosopher,* Longman, Green, Longman, Roberts, & Green, London, 1864, pp. 97–111.]

Charles Babbage was not a crackpot; quite the contrary. He was a respected mathematician and member of the Royal Society in England, and made many contributions to advanced mathematical techniques (calculus, logarithms, etc.).

Babbage's attention seems to have been very early drawn to the number and importance of the errors introduced into astronomical and other calculations through inaccuracies in the computation of tables.

He contributed to the Royal Society some notices on the relations between notation and mechanism; and in 1822, in a letter to Sir Humphry Davy on the application of machinery to the calculation and printing of mathematical tables, he discussed the principles of a calculating machine, to the construction of which he devoted many years of his life. Government was induced to grant its aid, and he traveled in Europe, examining different systems of machinery. The great calculating machine was never completed; the constructor apparently desired to adopt a new principle when the first specimen was nearly complete, to make it not a difference but an analytical machine, and the government declined to accept the further risk.

What we have in this selection is a description by Babbage (in his autobiographical *Passages from the Life of a Philosopher*) of his attempts to get his Difference Engine No. 2 constructed by the government. This would be the full-fledged analytical machine that had frustrated the building of the first model. He didn't run into the same opposition as the inventor of safety glass in the time of Caesar Augustus,* but the result was about the same.

Babbage apparently was something of a "character," however sound as a scientist and (or) philosopher. One can imagine how well he got on with the Chancellor of the Exchequer, whom he describes as witheringly as you can find it done anywhere, any time.

———◆———

Difference Engine No. 2—The Earl of Rosse, President of the Royal Society, proposed to the government a plan by which the Difference Engine No. 2 might have been executed. It was addressed to the Earl of Derby, and rejected by his Chancellor of the Exchequer.

It was not until 1848, when I had mastered the subject of the Analytical Engine, that I resolved on making a complete set of drawings of the Difference Engine No. 2. In this I proposed to take advantage of all the improvements and simplifications which years of unwearied study had produced for the Analytical Engine.

In 1852, the Earl of Rosse, who, from its commencement, had looked forward with the greatest interest to the application of mechanism to purposes of calculation, and who was well acquainted with the drawings and notations of the Difference Engine No. 2, inquired of me whether I was willing to give them to the government, provided they would have the engine constructed. My feeling was, after the sad experience of the past, that I ought not to think of sacrificing any further portion of my life upon the subject. If, however, they chose to have the Difference Engine made, I was ready

———

* See page 2270 in this volume.

to give them the whole of the drawings, and also the notations by by which it was demonstrated that such a machine could be constructed, and that when made it would necessarily do the work prescribed for it.

My much valued friend, the late Sir Benjamin Hawes, had also been consulted, and it was agreed that the draft of a letter to Lord Derby, who was then prime minister, should be prepared, in which I should make this offer. Lord Rosse proposed to place my letter in Lord Derby's hands, with his own statement of a plan by which the whole question might be determined.

Lord Rosse's suggestion was that the government should apply to the president of the Institution of Civil Engineers to ascertain,

1st. Whether it was possible from the drawings and notations, to make an estimate of the cost of constructing the machine.

2nd. In case this question was answered in the affirmative—then, could a mechanical engineer be found who would undertake to construct it, and at what expense?

The Institution of Civil Engineers was undoubtedly the highest authority upon the first question. That being decided in the affirmative, no other body had equal power to find out those mechanical engineers who might be willing to undertake the contract.

Supposing both these questions, or even the latter only, answered in the negative, the proposition, of course, fell to the ground. But if they were both answered in the affirmative, then there would have arisen a further question for the consideration of the government: namely, whether the object to be obtained was worthy of the expenditure.

The final result of this eminently *practical* plan was communicated to the Royal Society by their president, in his address at their anniversary on November 30, 1854. The following is an extract:

> The progress of the work was suspended: there was a change of government. Science was weighed against gold by a new standard, and it was resolved to proceed no further. No enterprise could have had its beginning under more auspicious circumstances: the government had taken the initiative—they had called for advice, and the adviser was the highest scientific authority in this country—your Council; guided by such men as Davy, Wollaston, and Herschel. By your Council the undertaking was inaugurated, by your Council it was watched over in its progress. That the first great effort to employ the powers of calculating mechanism, in aid of the human intellect, should have been suffered in this great country to expire fruitless, because there was no tangible evidence of immediate profit, as a British subject I deeply regret, and as a Fellow my regret is accompanied with feelings of bitter disappointment. Where a question

has once been disposed of, succeeding governments rarely reopen it; still I thought I should not be doing my duty if I did not take some opportunity of bringing the facts once more before government. Circumstances had changed, mechanical engineering had made much progress; the tools required and trained workmen were to be found in the workshops of the leading mechanists, the founder's art was so advanced that casting had been substituted for cutting, in making the change wheels, even of screw-cutting engines, and therefore it was very probable that persons would be found willing to undertake to complete the Difference Engine for a specific sum.

That finished, the question would then have arisen, how far it was advisable to endeavor, by the same means, to turn to account the great labor which had been expended under the guidance of inventive powers the most original, controlled by mathematics of a very high order; and which had been wholly devoted for so many years to the great task of carrying the powers of calculating machinery to its utmost limits. Before I took any step I wrote to several very eminent men of science, inquiring whether, in their opinion, any great scientific object would be gained if Mr. Babbage's views, as explained in Ménabrèa's little essay, were completely realized. The answers I received were strongly in the affirmative. As it was necessary the subject should be laid before government in a form as practical as possible, I wrote to one of our most eminent mechanical engineers to inquire whether I should be safe in stating to government that the expense of the calculating engine had been more than repaid in the improvements in mechanism directly referable to it; he replied, unquestionably. Fortified by these opinions, I submitted this proposition to government: that they should call upon the president of the Society of Civil Engineers to report whether it would be practicable to make a contract for the completion of Mr. Babbage's Difference Engine, and if so, for what sum. This was in 1852, during the short administration of Lord Derby, and it led to no result. The time was unfortunate; a great political contest was impending, and before there was a lull in politics, so that the voice of science could be heard, Lord Derby's government was at an end.

The following letter was then drawn up, and placed in Lord Derby's hands by Lord Rosse:

June 8, 1852

My Lord,

I take the liberty of drawing Your Lordship's attention to the subject of the construction of a Difference Engine, for calculating and printing astronomical and nautical tables, which was brought under the notice of the government so far back as the year 1823, and upon which the government of that day desired the opinion of the Royal Society.

I annex a copy of the correspondence which took place at that time, and which Your Lordship will observe was laid before Parliament.

The committee of the Royal Society, to which the subject was referred, reported generally that the invention was one "fully adequate to the attainment of the objects proposed by the inventor," and that they considered Mr. Babbage as "highly deserving of public encouragement in the prosecution of his arduous undertaking."— *Report of Royal Society,* May 1, 1823. *Parliamentary Paper* 370, May 22, 1823.

And in a subsequent and more detailed Report, which I annex also, they state:

> The committee have no intention of entering into any consideration of the abstract mathematical principle on which the practicability of such a machine as Mr. Babbage's relies, nor of its public utility when completed. They consider the former as not only sufficiently clear in itself, but as already admitted and acted on by the Council in their former proceedings. The latter they regard as obvious to everyone who considers the immense advantage of accurate numerical tables in all matters of calculation, especially in those which relate to astronomy and navigation, and the great variety and extent of those which it is the object and within the compass of Mr. Babbage's engine to calculate and print with perfect accuracy.—*Report of Committee of the Royal Society,* Feb. 12, 1829.

Upon the first of these reports, the government determined to construct the machine, under my personal superintendance and direction. The engine was accordingly commenced and partially completed. Tables of figures were calculated, limited in extent only by the number of wheels put together.

Delays, from various causes, arose in the progress of the work, and great expenses were incurred. The machine was altogether new in design and construction, and required the utmost mechanical skill which could be obtained for its execution. "It involved," to quote again from the Report of the Committee of the Royal Society, "the necessity of constructing, and in many instances inventing, tools and machinery of great expense and complexity (and in many instances of ingenious contrivances likely to prove useful for other purposes hereafter), for forming with the requisite precision parts of the apparatus dissimilar to any used in ordinary mechanical works;

that of making many previous trials to ascertain the validity of proposed movements; and that of altering, improving, and simplifying those already contrived and reduced to drawings. Your committee are so far from being surprised at the time it has occupied to bring it to its present state that they feel more disposed to wonder it has been possible to accomplish so much." The true explanation both of the slow progress and of the cost of the work is clearly stated in this passage; and I may remark in passing, that the tools which were invented for the construction of the machine were afterwards found of utility, and that this anticipation of the committee has been realized, as some of our most eminent mechanical engineers will readily testify.

Similar circumstances will, I apprehend, always attend and prolong the period of bringing to perfection inventions which have no parallel in the previous history of mechanical construction. The necessary science and skill specially acquired in executing such works must also, as experience is gained, suggest deviations from, and improvements in, the original plan of those works; and the adoption or rejection of such changes, especially under circumstances similar to those in which I was placed, often involves questions of the greatest difficulty and anxiety.

From whatever cause, however, the delays and expenses arose, the result was that the government was discouraged, and declined to proceed further with the work.

Mr. Goulburn's letter, intimating this decision to me, in 1842, will be found in the accompanying printed statement. And that the impediments to the completion of the engine, described by the Royal Society, were those which influenced the government in the determination they came to, I infer from the reason assigned by Mr. Goulburn for its discontinuance, viz., "the expense which would be necessary in order to render it either satisfactory to yourself or generally useful." I readily admit that the work could not have been rendered satisfactory to myself unless I was free to introduce every improvement which experience and thought could suggest. But that even with this additional source of expense its general usefulness would have been impaired, I cannot assent to, for I believe, in the words of the report I have already quoted, the "immense advantage of accurate numerical tables in all matters of calculation, especially in those which relate to astronomy and navigation, cannot, within any reasonable limits, be overestimated." As to the expense actually incurred upon the first Difference Engine, that of the government was about £17,000. On my own part, and out of my own private resources, I have sacrificed upon this and other works of science upwards of £20,000.

From the date of Mr. Goulburn's letter, nothing has been done toward the further completion of the Difference Engine by the government or myself. So much of it as was completed was deposited in the Museum of King's College, where it now remains.

Three consequences have, however, resulted from my subsequent labors, to which I attach great importance.

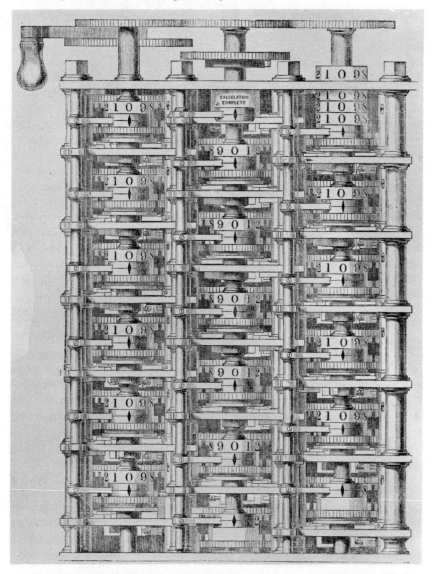

FIG. 298. Babbage's Calculating Engine. A woodcut of a small part of Charles Babbage's Difference Engine No. 1. Started in 1823, this portion was put together in 1833; construction was abandoned in 1842.

First, I have been led to conceive the most important elements of another engine upon a new principle (the details of which are reduced accurately to paper), the power of which over the most complicated analytical operations appears nearly unlimited; but no portion of which is yet commenced. I have called this engine, in contradistinction to the other, the Analytical Engine.

Secondly, I have invented and brought to maturity a system of signs for the explanation of machinery, which I have called mechanical notation, by means of which the drawings, the times of action, and the trains for the transmission of force are expressed in a language at once simple and concise. Without the aid of this language I could not have invented the Analytical Engine; nor do I believe that any machinery of equal complexity can ever be contrived without the assistance of that or of some other equivalent language. The Difference Engine No. 2, to which I shall presently refer, is entirely described by its aid.

Thirdly, in laboring to perfect this Analytical Machine of greater power and wider range of computation, I have discovered the means of simplifying and expediting the mechanical process of the first or Difference Engine.

After what has passed, I cannot expect the government to undertake the construction of the Analytical Engine, and I do not offer it for that purpose. It is not so matured as to enable any other person, without long previous training and application, even to attempt its execution; and on my own part, to superintend its construction would demand an amount of labor, anxiety, and time which could not, after the treatment I have received, be expected from me. I therefore make no such offer.

But that I may fulfill to the utmost of my power the original expectation that I should be able to complete, for the government, an engine capable of calculating astronomical and nautical tables with perfect accuracy, such as that which is described in the *Reports of the Royal Society,* I am willing to place at the disposal of government (if they will undertake to execute a new Difference Engine) all those improvements which I have invented and have applied to the Analytical Engine. These comprise a complete series of drawings and explanatory notations, finished in 1849, of the Difference Engine No. 2—an instrument of greater power as well as of greater simplicity than that formerly commenced, and now in the possession of the government.

I have sacrificed time, health, and fortune, in the desire to complete these Calculating Engines. I have also declined several offers of great personal advantage to myself. But, notwithstanding the sacrifice of these advantages for the purpose of maturing an engine of almost intellectual power, and after expending from my own private fortune a larger sum than the government of England has spent on that machine, the execution of which it only commenced, I have received neither an acknowledgment of my labors, nor even the offer of those honors or rewards which are allowed to fall within the reach of men who devote themselves to purely scientific investigations. I might, perhaps, advance some claims to consideration, founded on my works and contributions in aid of various departments of industrial and physical science, but it is for others to estimate those services.

I now, however, simply ask Your Lordship to do me the honor to consider this statement and the offer I make. I prefer no claim to the distinctions or the advantages which it is in the power of the crown or the government to bestow. I desire only to discharge whatever *imagined* obligation may be supposed to rest upon me, in connection with the original undertaking of the Difference Engine; though I cannot but feel that whilst the public has already derived advantage from my labors, I have myself experienced only loss and neglect.

If the work upon which I have bestowed so much time and thought were a mere triumph over mechanical difficulties, or simply curious, or if the execution of such engines were of doubtful practicability or utility, some justification might be found for the course which has been taken; but I venture to assert that no mathematician who has a reputation to lose will ever *publicly* express an opinion that such a machine would be useless if made, and that no man distinguished as a civil engineer will venture to declare the construction of such machinery impracticable. The names appended to the Report of the Committee of the Royal Society fully justify my expressing this opinion, which I apprehend will not be disputed.

And at a period when the progress of physical science is obstructed by that exhausting intellectual and manual labor, indispensable for its advancement, which it is the object of the Analytical Engine to relieve, I think the application of machinery in aid of the most complicated and abstruse calculations can no longer be deemed unworthy of the attention of the country. In fact, there is no reason why mental as well as bodily labor should not be economized by the aid of machinery.

With these views I have addressed Your Lordship, as the head of the government; and whatever may be my sense of the injustice that has hitherto been done me, I feel, in laying this representation before Your Lordship, and in making the offer I now make, that I have discharged to the utmost limit every implied obligation I originally contracted with the country.

I have the honor to be,
&c., &c., &c.,
CHARLES BABBAGE

Dorset Street, Manchester Square

As this question was one of finance and of calculation, the sagacious premier adroitly turned it over to his Chancellor of the Exchequer— that official being, from his office, *supposed* to be well versed in both subjects.

The opinion pronounced by the novelist and financier was that "Mr. Babbage's projects appear to be so indefinitely expensive, the ultimate success so problematical, and the expenditure certainly so large and so utterly incapable of being calculated, that the government would not be justified in taking upon itself any further liability."—*Extract from the Reply of Earl Derby to the application of the Earl of Rosse, K. P., President of the Royal Society.*

The answer of Lord Derby to Lord Rosse was in substance:

That he had consulted the Chancellor of the Exchequer, who pronounced Mr. Babbage's project as

1. "Indefinitely expensive."
2. "The ultimate success problematical."
3. "The expenditure utterly incapable of being calculated."

1. With regard to the "indefinite expense." Lord Rosse had proposed to refer this question to the president of the Institution of Civil Engineers, who would have given his opinion after a careful examination of the drawings and notations. These had not been seen by the Chancellor of the Exchequer; and, if seen by him, would not have been comprehended.

The objection that its success was "problematical" may refer either to its mechanical construction or to its mathematical principles.

Who, possessing one grain of common sense, could look upon the unrivaled workmanship of the then existing portion of the Difference Engine No. 1, and doubt whether a simplified form of the same engine could be executed?

As to any doubt of its mathematical principles, this was excusable in the Chancellor of the Exchequer, who was himself too practically acquainted with the fallibility of his own figures, over which the severe duties of his office had stultified his brilliant imagination. Far other figures are dear to him—those of speech, in which it cannot be denied he is indeed pre-eminent.

Any junior clerk in his office might, however, have told him that the power of computing tables by differences merely required a knowledge of simple addition.

As to the impossibility of ascertaining the expenditure, this merges into the first objection; but a poetical brain must be pardoned when it repeats or amplifies. I will recall to the ex-Chancellor of the Exchequer what Lord Rosse really proposed, namely, that the government should take the opinion of the president of the Institution of Civil Engineers upon the question, whether a contract could be made for constructing the Difference Engine, and if so, for what sum.

But the very plan proposed by Lord Rosse and refused by Lord Derby, for the construction of the *English* Difference Engine, was adopted some few years after by another administration for the *Swedish* Difference Engine. Messrs. Donkin, the eminent engineers, *made an estimate,* and a *contract was* in consequence executed to construct for government a facsimile of the *Swedish* Difference Engine, which is now in use in the department of the Registrar-General, at Somerset House. There were far greater mechanical difficulties in the production of that machine than in the one the drawings of which I had offered to the government.

From my own experience of the cost of executing such works, I have no doubt, although it was highly creditable to the skill of the able firm who constructed it, but that it must have been commercially unprofitable. Under such circumstances, surely it was harsh on the part of the government to refuse Messrs. Donkin permission to exhibit it as a specimen of English workmanship at the Exhibition of 1862.

But the machine upon which everybody could calculate had little chance of fair play from the man on whom nobody could calculate.

If the Chancellor of the Exchequer had read my letter to Lord Derby, he would have found the opinion of the Committee of the Royal Society expressed in these words:

> They consider the former [the abstract mathematical principle] as not only sufficiently clear in itself, but as already admitted and acted on by the Council in their former proceedings.
>
> The latter [its public utility] they consider as obvious to everyone who considers the immense advantage of accurate numerical tables in all matters of calculation, especially in those which relate to astronomy and navigation.—*Report of the Royal Society,* Feb. 12, 1829.

Thus it appears:

1st. That the Chancellor of the Exchequer presumed to set up his *own idea* of the utility of the Difference Engine in direct opposition to that of the Royal Society.

2nd. That he *refused* to take the opinion of the highest mechanical authority in the country on its probable cost, and even *to be informed* whether a contract for its construction at a definite sum might not be attainable: he then boldly pronounced the expense to be "utterly incapable of being calculated."

This much-abused Difference Engine is, however, like its prouder relative the Analytical, a being of sensibility, of impulse, and of power.

It can not only calculate the millions the ex-Chancellor of the Exchequer squandered, but it can deal with the smallest quantities;

nay, it feels even for zeros. It is as conscious as Lord Derby himself is of the presence of a *negative quantity,* and it is not beyond the ken of either of them to foresee the existence of *impossible ones.*

Yet should any unexpected course of events ever raise the ex-Chancellor of the Exchequer to his former dignity, I am sure he will be its *friend* as soon as he is convinced that it can be made *useful* to him.

It may possibly enable him to un-muddle even his own financial accounts, and to——

But as I have no wish to crucify him, I will leave his name in obscurity.

The Herostratus of science, if he escape oblivion, will be linked with the destroyer of the Ephesian Temple.

A BRITISH HISTORIAN ON AMERICAN INDUSTRY

LORD MACAULAY

[Lord Macaulay, "Lord Macaulay on American Institutions," *Harper's New Monthly Magazine,* Feb. 1877, vol. LIV, no. CCCXXI, pp. 460–461. The letter was written May 23, 1857.]

In the mid-nineteenth century (1857), Lord Macaulay, English statesman and most widely read historian of his time, did about as complete a job of underestimating the power of industry to raise the standard of living in a democracy as anyone can possibly imagine. He wrote this letter to Henry S. Randall, an American, who was the author of a biography of Thomas Jefferson.

HOLLY LODGE, KENSINGTON,
LONDON, MAY 23, 1857

DEAR SIR,

The four volumes of the *Colonial History of New York* reached me safely. I assure you that I shall value them highly. They contain much to interest an English as well as an American reader. Pray accept my thanks, and convey them to the Regents of the University.

You are surprised to learn that I have not a high opinion of Mr. Jefferson, and I am surprised at your surprise. I am certain that I never wrote a line, and that I never, in Parliament, in conversation, or even on the hustings—a place where it is the fashion to court the populace—uttered a word indicating an opinion that the supreme authority in a state ought to be intrusted to the majority of citizens told by the head; in other words, to the poorest and most ignorant part of society. I have long been convinced that institutions purely democratic must, sooner or later, destroy liberty or civilization, or both.

In Europe, where the population is dense, the effect of such institutions would be almost instantaneous. What happened lately in France is an example. In 1848 a pure democracy was established there. During a short time there was reason to expect a general spoilation, a national bankruptcy, a new partition of the soil, a maximum of prices, a ruinous load of taxation laid on the rich for the purpose of supporting the poor in idleness. Such a system would, in twenty years, have made France as poor and barbarous as the France of the Carlovingians. Happily the danger was averted; and now there is a despotism, a silent tribune, an enslaved press. Liberty is gone, but civilization has been saved. I have not the smallest doubt that, if we had a purely democratic government here, the effect would be the same. Either the poor would plunder the rich, and civilization would perish, or order and prosperity would be saved by a strong military government, and liberty would perish.

You may think that your country enjoys an exemption from these evils. I will frankly own to you that I am of a very different opinion. Your fate I believe to be certain, though it is deferred by a physical cause. As long as you have a boundless extent of fertile and unoccupied land, your laboring population will be far more at ease than the laboring population of the Old World, and, while that is the case, the Jefferson politics may continue to exist without causing any fatal calamity. But the time will come when New England will be as thickly peopled as old England. Wages will be as low, and will fluctuate as much with you as with us. You will have your Manchesters and Birminghams, and in those Manchesters and Birminghams hundreds of thousands of artisans will assuredly be sometimes out of work. Then your institutions will be fairly brought to the test.

Distress everywhere makes the laborer mutinous and discontented, and inclines him to listen with eagerness to agitators who tell him that it is a monstrous iniquity that one man should have a million while another cannot get a full meal. In bad years there is plenty of grumbling here, and sometimes a little rioting. But it matters little. For here the sufferers are not the rulers. The supreme power is in the hands of a class, numerous indeed, but select; of an educated class; of a class which is, and knows itself to be, deeply interested in the security of property and the maintenance of order. Accordingly, the malcontents are firmly yet gently restrained. The bad time is got over without robbing the wealthy to relieve the indigent. The springs of national prosperity soon begin to flow again: work is plentiful, wages rise, and all is tranquillity and cheerfulness. I have seen England pass three or four times through such critical seasons as I have described.

Through such seasons the United States will have to pass in the course of the next century, if not of this. How will you pass through them? I heartily wish you a good deliverance. But my reason and my wishes are at war, and I cannot help foreboding the worst. It is quite plain that your government will never be able to restrain a distressed and discontented majority. For with you the majority is the government, and has the rich, who are always a minority, absolutely at its mercy.

The day will come when in the State of New York a multitude of people, none of whom has had more than half a breakfast, or expects to have more than half a dinner, will choose a legislature. Is it possible to doubt what sort of a legislature will be chosen? On one side is a statesman preaching patience, respect for vested rights, strict observance of public faith. On the other is a demagogue ranting about the tyranny of capitalists and usurers, and asking why anybody should be permitted to drink champagne and to ride in a carriage while thousands of honest folks are in want of necessaries. Which of the two candidates is likely to be preferred by a workingman who hears his children cry for more bread? I seriously apprehend that you will, in some such season of adversity as I have described, do things which will prevent prosperity from returning; that you will act like people who should in a year of scarcity devour all the seed corn, and thus make the next year not of scarcity, but of absolute famine.

There will be, I fear, spoliation. The spoliation will increase the distress. The distress will produce fresh spoliation. There is nothing to stop you. Your Constitution is all sail and no anchor. As I said before, when a society has entered on this downward progress, either civilization or liberty must perish. Either some Caesar or Napoleon will seize the reins of government with a strong hand, or your republic will be as fearfully plundered and laid waste by barbarians in the twentieth century as the Roman empire was in the fifth, with this difference, that the Huns and Vandals who ravaged the Roman empire came from without, and that your Huns and Vandals will have been engendered within your own country by your own institutions.

Thinking thus, of course, I cannot reckon Jefferson among the benefactors of mankind. I readily admit that his intentions were good and his abilities considerable. Odious stories have been circulated about his private life; but I do not know on what evidence those stories rest, and I think it probable that they are false or monstrously exaggerated. I have no doubt that I shall derive both pleasure and information from your account of him.

I have the honor to be, dear Sir, your faithful servant,

T. B. MACAULAY

H. S. Randall, Esq., etc., etc., etc.

A BUSINESSMAN PLEADS FOR
SOCIAL LEGISLATION IN 1867

∿◯∿

ABRAM S. HEWITT

[Abram S. Hewitt, "The Production of Iron and Steel in Its Economic and Social Relations," in Allan Nevins (ed.), *Selected Writings of Abram S. Hewitt*, Columbia University Press, New York, 1937, pp. 19–20, 69–85 (abridged).]

Abram S. Hewitt (1822 to 1903), while not so well known as some of those men we consider great in our history, was nonetheless their equal in stature in many ways. He was all his life a practicing businessman, one of the two partners who operated the successful iron works of Cooper and Hewitt; yet he took a deep interest in the broadest range of problems, civic and cultural.

His contribution to history reflects his business career, in fact, for he understood and interpreted the role of industry and of wealth in society more practically than any of his nonbusiness contemporaries—and in a more enlightened way (considering how far ahead of his times he was) than almost any businessman before or since.

The following selection is taken from his report as United States Commissioner to the Paris Exposition, in 1867; with a preface by Allan Nevins, the historian. It shows both Hewitt's intellectual perspicuity and his moral sensitivity.*

◆

PREFACE BY ALLAN NEVINS (abridged)

Hewitt in 1867 was easily the foremost American ironmaster. During most of the preceding twenty years the Cooper, Hewitt works at Trenton had been the largest and best equipped in the country, and they had always been the most progressive. Hewitt was the first American ironmaster to experiment (unsuccessfully, his ores not being adapted to it) with the Bessemer process; he was the first to roll wrought-iron structural beams of large size; his works were known for the high quality of the rails they produced with ore taken from a deposit at Andover, N.J., and for their excellent wire and rods. It was therefore fitting that he should be sent by the American government as a commissioner to Paris to report on the progress of the European industry. He had done great service to the Union cause in the Civil War, particularly in the production of the first good American gun-

---

* For more of Hewitt, refer to index listing in this volume.

metal. His keen mind was certain to pick out what was significant in European exhibits and mills. Though he knew that Europeans had outstripped the United States, he was staggered when he saw the tremendous strides that had been taken abroad. At every point—in size of product, in quality, in new inventions, in the production of cast iron, wrought iron, and steel alike—the British, French, and German mills were far superior to anything in the United States. The new rolling mills, he wrote Edward Cooper, "beat us to death"; and he might have said as much for other departments. He did his best to carry home some of the new European processes. He hired an expert Swedish metallurgist, one of the first technicians of the kind employed in America. He obtained the American rights to the Siemens-Martin or open-hearth process, which has since outstripped the Bessemer process in America as in the rest of the world. And he laid before the American public . . . an admirably clear and thorough exposition of the recent advances made in Europe. [This part of the report is not included in the selection here.] It will be noted that Hewitt was interested not merely in technical progress but in the relations of capital and labor, in living conditions, and in the contributions of large-scale industry to general human welfare. . . .

REPORT AS UNITED STATES COMMISSIONER TO THE PARIS EXPOSITION, 1867

With such vast possessions of raw material, we are naturally brought to the consideration of the elements which enter into the cost of producing iron in the United States as compared with the other iron-producing countries of the world. And first the distinction must be drawn between the cost determined by the quantity of labor expended in the production of a ton of iron and the cost of money as determined by the price paid for the labor. The former is the absolute and natural cost, and it is the only just standard of comparison between nations if national wealth is defined as the amount of capital in existence plus the amount of labor available for production. The other is the artificial or accidental cost, of which, indeed, we may take advantage in our buying or selling, but which forms no just standard of comparison in estimating the relative cost of production in different countries. There is a difference, familiar to all in the United States, between the cost of articles measured by gold or by currency, which makes it, for the time, easy to understand the difference in cost measured by money or by day's labor.

England, having the largest and most accessible stores of coal and iron ore, can produce a ton of iron with less labor than any other European nation; and hence it will be most profitable to institute the comparison of cost measured by labor, first, with Great Britain. In the Cleveland [England] region, which is most favorably situated for the cheap production of iron, the cost of producing a ton of pig iron is about 40 shillings, which at the average rate of wages paid around the blast furnace, is equivalent to 11 days' labor—that is to say, the labor of 11 men for one day. It is possible that in one or two works this may be reduced to 10 days, but in others it rises to 12 or 13. In the United States the cheapest region for the manufacture of pig iron as yet extensively developed is on the Lehigh River, in the State of Pennsylvania, where, taking coal and ore at their actual cost of mining, pig iron is produced at an average cost of $24 per ton, which represents, at the present rate of wages, the labor of about 13 days. But when the iron business is established along the great valley which extends from Virginia to Alabama, the labor of bringing the coal and ore together will be considerably less than on the Lehigh River, and it is safe to say that there iron can be made in any required quantity, [and] when the avenues of communication are sufficiently opened, with as little labor, to say the least, as it can be produced in the Cleveland region. In France, Belgium, and Prussia, each now requiring a larger expenditure of human labor to produce a ton of iron than is required in England, there are no such possibilities of reduction, because every year their ore is becoming more expensive, and the cost of mining coal will increase more rapidly than in England in consequence of the size and character of the veins. Hence follows the deduction that if France, Belgium, and Germany are to compete with England in the open markets of the world, the competition can only be maintained by the payment to labor of a lower rate of wages; or, to state it in another form, the greater the natural advantages possessed by a country for the production of iron, the larger will be the rate of wages paid to the workman; and this is found to be verified by existing facts. . . .

The difference between the cost of French iron and Belgium and English, aside from cost of transportation, which is very light, is compensated by the import duty, which, on iron from England and Belgium amounts to 60 francs per ton. Independently of this tariff, which admits of a considerable importation of iron into France, it would not be possible for the iron business to be continued on any considerable scale, for the reason, as will be seen, that the wages are already at the lowest possible point consistent with the maintenance of human life in a condition fit for labor; the average earnings of all the workmen, skilled and unskilled, employed in an iron work being at the rate of 3.45 francs per day, or about 66¢ per day in gold; the great mass, however, of common labor receiving less than 50¢ per day in gold. In order to estimate the purchasing power of this sum, it is necessary to give the prices of the principal articles required for the support of life, and for this purpose I have selected the department in which Le Creusot is situated as the proper locality for comparison, with the rate of wages there paid:

Wheat bread ...0.25 francs per lb., equal to 5¢ in gold
Rye bread .....0.20 francs per lb., equal to 4¢ in gold
Beef ....0.65 francs per lb., equal to 13¢ in gold
Mutton ....0.75 francs per lb., equal to 15¢ in gold
Veal ....0.75 francs per lb., equal to 15¢ in gold
Pork ....0.75 francs per lb., equal to 15¢ in gold
Chickens ....1.00 to 2.50 francs, equal to 20¢ to 50¢ in gold
Geese ....3.00 francs, equal to 60¢ in gold
Ducks ....1.50 to 2.00 francs, equal to 30¢ to 40¢ in gold
Butter ....1.00 francs per lb., equal to 20¢ in gold
Dozen eggs .....0.50 to 1.00 francs, equal to 10¢ to 20¢ in gold
Potatoes ....0.50 francs per decaliter, equal to 40¢ per bu.
Ordinary wine ..0.40 francs per liter, equal to 5¢ per pint
Beer ....0.25 francs per liter, equal to 3¢ per pint

House rent is cheap, a small, ordinary, but comfortable house, with a garden, renting for $16 per year in gold. Clothes are also cheap, costing not more than half the price of similar articles in the United States; but fuel is rather dearer on the average. It does not require any very extensive observation in order to verify the obvious conclusion deducible from the above figures, that the general condition of the working classes in France, from a material point of view at least, is simply deplorable. It requires the utmost economy on the part of the laboring man and the united labor of his wife and his children to keep his family in existence; and it is the accepted rule and practice for such a family to have meat but once a week. Any change in this condition of affairs, involving a change in the remuneration paid to the common laborer, would put it out of the power of the ironmasters of France to carry on their business in competition with Belgium and England, in the absence of a higher tariff on imports. The existence of the iron business in France, therefore, as a national branch of industry, may be said to rest upon the elementary condition of giving meat once a week only to the great mass of laborers who are engaged in iron production. In Belgium substantially the same state of affairs prevails. In the despatch of Lord Howard de Walden, the British minister at Brussels, to Lord Stanley, dated February 11, 1867, on the subject of Belgian industry, he says: "The characteristics of the Belgian workmen are steadiness and perseverance, combined with great intelligence in working after models; their habits are not so expensive as those of English artificers; their diet is more humble, they consume less meat, and their bread is seldom purely wheaten or white in quality; rye, and the cheaper quality of wheat called *épeautre,* enter in great proportion into the composition of the loaf; beer and spirits are both lower in price than in England; they seldom use tea, and the chicory root constitutes a very economical and wholesome substitute for coffee. . . . The system of schools for infants from two to seven years, and from seven to twelve years, is very general, and affords great facilities—the children being cared for—to both their parents to occupy themselves in daily service, and by combined industry to ameliorate the condition of their family. In all these respects, therefore, the necessaries of life being the base of wages, the Belgian enjoys advantages over the British workman."

From our American point of view, these "advantages over the British workman" in dispensing with meat and tea and in substituting chicory for coffee and in appropriating the labor of both parents for a mere existence are not so apparent. But we are naturally brought by it to consider the condition of the British laborer.

It has been seen that the natural advantages of Great Britain in the possession of its vast stores of coal afford a fund for the payment of better wages to the laborer in England than on the Continent, and the British workman has not been slow to assert his rights to all he can get, and his physical condition is undoubtedly superior to that of his French and Belgian neighbors. If he is not better lodged, he is at least better fed, and in the iron works it is probable that the workmen generally get meat once a day. But, as a general rule, the labor of the women and children is required in order to eke out the subsistence of the family. In Wales women are extensively employed in the works, doing the labor for which a man would be required in America and earning from ten pence to one shilling, three pence per day, or rather less than half the wages that would be paid to a man for the same labor, which they perform equally well. In Staffordshire and in the north of England and in Scotland women and children are still extensively employed above ground about the mines and around the coal heaps at the mouth of the pits, the substantial result of which is that the labor of the whole family is procured for the sum which would be paid to its male head if he alone labored for the support of the family, of course at a far lower cost in the resulting production of iron than would otherwise be possible. Restraining laws have been enacted in England of late years in regard to women and children, limiting the number of hours during which they may be employed and also providing that they shall not be employed during the night, except in certain specified cases. But if the women and children were altogether withdrawn from those occupations, as they are in the United States, it would not be possible to produce iron except at a considerable advance on its present cost.

Passing from the material to the intellectual condition of the workmen in France and England, the provision for the education of the children is upon a very limited scale indeed, and although there are creditable exceptions in particular localities, mainly due to the enlightened conscience of the proprietors, the great mass of the working classes out of the large cities are deplorably illiterate. In the department of Saône-et-Loire, where the works of Le Creusot are situated and where the most commendable efforts are being made by Messrs. Schneider & Co. to educate the rising generation, it appears that 36.19 per cent of those who were joined in marriage in 1866 could not write their names, and of the conscripts drawn for the army from the same department in the same year, 24.51 per cent were unable to read. And the same statistics show that, taken as a whole, in nearly two-thirds of France the number of those who cannot write their names on marriage is between the limits of 30 and 75 per cent of the total number. This deplorable state of affairs has, of late, led to the establishment of schools for the instruction of adults, mostly voluntary, upon which there were in attendance during the present year 829,555 adults, of whom 747,002 were men and 82,553 were women. Of 110,503 who could neither read nor write on entering the course in October, 1866, 87,211 had learned to read by the first of April, 1867; 12,632 instructors have given their services gratuitously, and the whole movement and the statistics above given prove both the depth of ignorance into which the working classes have been plunged and their earnest desire to emerge from it. . . .

The moral condition of men is so dependent upon their physical and mental status that it is probably unnecessary for me to enlarge upon the obvious conclusions that might be inferred from the facts above recorded; but the conviction in my own mind was so profound, after a very careful survey of the whole field, that I deemed it my duty to accept an invitation to testify before the Trades Union Commission in England, in the hope that a full discussion of the physical and moral elements involved in the organization of industry would result in the ultimate elevation of the working classes of Europe to such a standard, at least, as would render the conditions of competition between our own country and Europe more just and equitable. It is quite evident that in the effort to produce cheap commodities and to undersell each other in the markets of the world, the rightful claims of humanity have been disregarded to such an extent that the reorganization of labor, in its relation to capital, is felt by all thoughtful men to be an imperative necessity.

It cannot be that the aim of society is only to produce riches. There must be moral limits within which the production of wealth is to be carried on, and these limits have been and are being so obviously transgressed that a spirit of discontent pervades the entire industrial world; and in the very countries where this competition has been pressed to its utmost limits capital has ceased to become remunerative, although humanity itself has been sacrificed to its demands. . . .

The truth is that the whole system is false, and now, when pressed by the energy, enterprise, and competition of the age to its legitimate results, humanity is in rebellion, and there is a general cry from all classes, laborers, employers, philanthropists, philosophers, and statesmen alike, for relief. The necessity for this relief becomes painfully apparent when the poor-law returns made in England are carefully examined, from which it is evident that there is an army of paupers pressing upon the occupations of the common laborer and striving to push him over the almost insensible line which divides these two classes from each other. It is not possible that the laborer should receive more than bare subsistence wages, and there can be no relief for his patient suffering so long as there are thousands who, unable to earn any wages at all, stand ready to fill up every gap in the ranks of industry; and to the honest laborer himself, standing on the edge of this line over which he is liable at any moment to be forced into the ranks of pauperism, the anxiety and miserable state of uncertainty for himself and his family must be fatal to all rational happiness and is well calculated to drive him into vicious indulgences and temporary excesses whenever a transient opportunity is afforded as a momentary relief from a condition of hopeless misery.

From the returns made to the British Parliament as to pauperism in the month of September, A.D. 1867, it appears that out of a population of 19,886,104, dwelling in the area for which the returns are made, 872,620 persons were on the list of paupers supported by public charity, of which number 129,689 were in the workhouses and 738,726 were relieved in their own houses. This latter portion constitutes the army which substantially regulates the rate of wages for labor, as they are ready, to a greater or less extent, to take any vacant place which may offer itself. And this state of the case exists not in midwinter, but just after the close of the harvest, and the returns show that the evil is an advancing one, as there is an increase of 27,521, or 3.3 per cent, in 1867 over the corresponding week in 1866. . . .

By another parliamentary return it appears that the average number of scholars attendant upon the schools under government inspection in the year 1866 was 871,309 in England and Wales, showing this suggestive fact, that the paupers receiving public relief and the children receiving instruction in schools aided by the public funds were about equal in number. This statement alone, if other evidence were lacking, would serve to prove that the working classes of Great Britain have not yet achieved the position in point of education and social comfort to which humanity is entitled. Nor can it be alleged that this is due to any deficiency in the resources provided by nature for the reward of industry. The coal and iron-ore mines of England afford the most magnificent fund to be found on the face of the globe for the abundant remuneration of the capital and labor engaged in their development, and every class in the community, except the operatives themselves, have enjoyed a bountiful return for their interest in this national endowment. The landowner has been largely paid, not only by the royalties derived from the minerals, but in the enormous increase in the value of the soil by the rapid growth of population engaged directly and indirectly in the manufactures based on their consumption. The capital invested in manufactures in Great Britain has, in the main, reaped a most abundant reward, and the general result has been an accumulation of capital in the hands of the higher and middle classes unequaled in the history of mankind.

That the working classes have not been equally well rewarded is due simply to the improvident and even reckless manner in which these great natural resources have been employed, giving rise to a competition unlimited by any other consideration than the immediate profit to be derived by the capital invested in the business. Of course, the less the rate of wages, the longer the number of hours of work to be got from the laborer, the greater the number of women and children that could be employed, the lower will be the cost of the product, and the more decided the ability to undersell all foreign competitors in the markets of the world. Hence, in the absence of restraining laws and an enlightened conscience on the part of the operators and manufacturers, and in the presence of a large population in a restricted area, governed in the interests of special classes, it was inevitable that the superior natural resources of Great Britain should be used, as they have been, rather to crush out foreign competition than to elevate the working classes; and this very attempt to undersell foreign nations in their own markets necessarily involved the lowest possible rate of wages, in those countries, consistent with mere existence; reacting, in turn, upon the English labor market and compelling lower rates of wages than would otherwise have been required, if the aim of the nation had been directed to the payment of the largest possible compensation to its own working classes rather than to the control of the markets of the world even at the expense of humanity itself.

The possession of these wonderful deposits of coal and iron as a fund for the payment of adequate wages to labor in Great Britain is equivalent to our virgin soil in the United States, enabling both nations to pay the highest possible rate of wages consistent with the conservation of capital; but this advantage in Great Britain has been deliberately and recklessly thrown away by a competition between the English manufacturers themselves, resulting in overproduction and compelling a steady pressure upon the wages of labor in order to keep up the production and secure larger consumption by lower prices for the commodities. It is a mistake to suppose that this reduction in price has been caused by the competition of foreign nations with Great Britain, for we have seen that France cannot produce enough iron for its own consumption and that Belgium turns out only one-tenth as much iron as Great Britain, and is therefore governed as to price solely by the rate at which Great Britain is willing and able to furnish the remaining nine-tenths. If it were possible for Belgium to alter the ratio of production, she might in the long run make the price for the total product; but it is simply ridiculous to apprehend, in view of the natural resources of the two countries, that any such change can ever be effected.

The most interesting industrial and social question of the age is, therefore, the policy which will be pursued by Great Britain in the administration of its mines of coal and iron. And the royal commission, now making an official inquiry into the exhaustion of the coal fields, will stop far short of the real scope of the question if it fails to investigate whether by wise and suitable regulations the annual production of coal cannot be so regulated as to secure a far better remuneration to the labor engaged in its production than it has heretofore received. I am perfectly aware that such regulations must necessarily be restrictive in their character, and, at the first glance, will appear to be at war with the commercial policy of free trade advocated in Great Britain. Very little reflection, however, is required to show that by far the greater portion of the legislation of all enlightened nations is necessarily of a protective and restrictive character; and at this day no enlightened statesman would advocate the deliberate sacrifice of local advantages for the sake of any mere abstract theory, which might be ever so well founded in reason, but fails to be applicable in the presence of exceptionable facts and resources. The protection of life, liberty, property, and social order, the title to lands and personal property, rest entirely upon protective laws; and all provisions for the protection of capital and health and the establishment of police are so many restraints upon the natural freedom of the individual; and surely legislation looking to the wisest possible use of national resources and the prevention of the waste or misapplication of the raw material upon which the structure of the national industry and prosperity and the welfare of the working classes rest is not merely a natural but a necessary step in the progress of industry and the development of civilization.

In no country in the world are so many proofs of the wisdom of this course to be found as in the history of British legislation in reference to the working classes during the last thirty-five years. The repeal of the corn laws was a measure of eminent protection to the working classes, relieving them of the taxes imposed upon food for the benefit of the landowner, and of the landowner alone; because the condition of the agricultural laborer could not be made worse, but could only be improved by any change. The series of laws regulating the employment of women and children in factories and mines are not merely highly restrictive, but by common consent have produced the happiest results on the moral and physical condition of the working classes. The laws recognizing the legal existence of friendly societies; for the encouragement of building associations; [for] the conversion of the post offices into savings banks for the working classes; for the granting of annuities and life assurance guaranteed by the government to the working classes, on the payment of small periodical install- ments; for the encouragement of cooperative stores and associations; for "partnerships of industry" in which the workman is allowed to have an interest in the profits of the business without becoming liable as a partner for the debts; the statutes authorizing the establishment of free reading rooms, libraries, and museums by a vote of the rate- payers in any borough, town, or city, constitute a course of wise legis- lation unmistakably protective, restrictive, and enabling; persistently advocated and successfully established by the most sagacious, liberal, and philanthropic statesmen of the present age and resulting in so marked an improvement in the condition of the working classes, ac- companied with so decided an advance in the rate of wages that it is scarcely possible longer to deny that the first step toward securing to the working classes an adequate reward for their labor is such legis- lation as protects them from the evils which seem to be inseparable from the spirit of unrestrained competition between nations and be- tween men, which experience has shown to result in the utter disre- gard of the moral and physical condition and social welfare of the working classes, unless regulated by positive legal enactment.

This wise course of legislation may be said to be but fairly initiated in England, but the intelligent observer cannot fail to be convinced that it will be persisted in until all special privileges which interfere with the normal distribution of the proceeds of labor and capital will be removed. The effect will undoubtedly be a rise in wages, [which is] already apparent; and this result is unquestionably a matter of deep concern to the manufacturers and capitalists of Great Britain, who fear that it will deprive them of their ability to control the mar- kets of the world, as they now do, with the products of their mills.

There is in reality no just ground for this apprehension. The distribution between capital and labor may, and must, undoubtedly, be changed, but the aggregate income will not on the average of years be reduced, because the control of the fuel of the world, that is to say, of the condensed power which has been stored up by divine Providence for its use, is in the hands of the Anglo-Saxon race in Europe and America, who alone have reduced prices by a competition with other nations, impossible but for the possession of the mineral fuel in such vast quantities and for the violation of the natural laws which should govern the employment and the compensation of labor. The transition to a more equitable basis of production will simply enable other countries, who, as we have seen, cannot do more than supply themselves with coal and iron, to raise their laboring classes out of a condition still more deplorable than exists in England, without by any possibility enabling them to keep up any effective competition in the markets of the world, for the supply of the iron required for the future progress, development and civilization of mankind. A rise in wages in England, therefore, will not only be a blessing to the workmen of that favored country, relieving it of pauperism, so far as it may be possible to extinguish poverty at all, but will be a harbinger of light to the unpaid, unfed, and unhappy operatives throughout all lands in which human industry is now weighed down by the effects of British competition, based upon superior natural resources. And to me it is a suggestive and for humanity an encouraging fact, that the agitation and restlessness which characterize the working classes of our age are mostly apparent in Great Britain and the United States, who are not only so far in advance of all other countries in the possession of natural industrial resources, but who from the habit of free discussion and prompt obedience to the popular voice (the result of constitutional government long in force) will be most ready to accept the conclusions deduced by the stern logic of experience and facts, and [to] modify their legislation so as to conform to the just demands of humanity whenever the proper course is discovered and made plain to the common sense of the people.

When by reason of such legislation the wages of labor in Great Britain have reached their normal condition there will no longer be any occasion for us to consider the question of protective or prohibitory tariffs; but in the meantime, to the people of the United States, who in consequence of the possession of a virgin soil have in comparison with their European neighbors suffered but little from violations of the fundamental principles of social science, two courses are open. We can either take advantage of the unnaturally cheap rate at which our wants can and will be supplied from abroad, while the present system lasts, and by throwing open our ports to foreign iron, purchase foreign labor at a far lower rate than we are willing to sell our own, and thus abandon a business which so long as our present rates of wages are maintained cannot be conducted in the United States even without profit, or we can impose such a duty on foreign iron as will make up for the difference in the amount of wages paid for making a ton of iron in Europe or in this country, less the expense of transportation.

The decision of this question is mainly of interest to the working classes themselves and to the great body of the farmers, because if the iron business is abandoned for the present in the United States, the labor now employed in it must in the main take to the soil, and a larger yield of agricultural products [will] be insured. The surplus so produced must seek its market in the open marts of the world, and the mouths that would have been fed on this side of the Atlantic will simply be fed elsewhere, although not so abundantly and so generously. But it must be remembered that whatever may be the price of bread in Europe at the works where the iron will be made will be the price which the same operatives could afford to pay if the iron works had been placed where the grain is grown, and the cost of transportation thence is just so much deducted from the price which the farmer would have received if the grain had been consumed at home.

The question is one, also, which more concerns the West than the East, because the loss caused by transportation from the West is greater; and the final decision of this great question should therefore be well considered, especially with reference to the point whether the saving produced by the purchase of cheap iron and other articles will compensate for the loss entailed by the transportation of the grain.

It forms no part of the purpose of this report to deduce any conclusion on this subject, but only to state the facts in such form as will enable intelligent legislation to be enacted, keeping in view the interests of all classes and above all the considerations of independence essential to the dignity of the American republic and the welfare of mankind. But in the discussion of this question, and in the legislation which may be proposed to meet the best interests of the nation in regard to a supply of iron and steel, the broad distinction which exists between the nature of the question in Europe and the United States must never be lost sight of. On the Continent, protective duties on iron are imposed in order to counterbalance the superior natural resources and advantages of Great Britain for the production of iron, and not to secure higher wages to the laborer; whereas, in the United States, protective duties, if imposed at all, are not necessary because our natural advantages for making iron are inferior in any particular to those of Great Britain, but simply because the wages of labor are fixed upon a more just and liberal scale to the workmen in the first instance, and by the law of equivalents to the whole industrial force engaged in the great work of production, of whatever form and nature.

If the facts and suggestions contained in this report, the result of half a year of careful study of the exposition and the knowledge which it enabled me to acquire in reference to the social condition of the working classes in Europe, shall in any way aid Congress in arriving at a judicious solution of these grave questions, involving so many and such varied interests, and if, as I hope, the terrible evils of pauperism shall be even for a time, and possibly forever, averted from our own country by legislation based upon sound, social, and economical principles, I shall cease to regret the strange and cruel misrepresentations to which I have been subjected among the working classes, in whose behalf mainly the duty confided to me was undertaken.

Whatever policy may be finally adopted with reference to American industry, it is a source of profound satisfaction, and should be a subject of general congratulation, that a careful survey of the natural resources of those nations who stand in the van of European progress and civilization justifies the declaration that the great problem of democratic institutions is being solved in a land having in addition to a fruitful soil the largest and best supplies of the fundamental elements upon which industry, progress, and civilization are based; and that there is good reason to hope that here it may be shown how wealth may be created without the degradation of any class which labors for its production, the only advantage (if advantage it may be termed) possessed by Europe over the United States for the cheap production of iron and steel being in the lower and inadequate rate of wages which there prevails, and not in any superior natural resources in ore, fuel, or geographical position.

AN 1870 DEBATE ON THE ROLE OF BUSINESSMEN IN GOVERNMENT

HAMILTON A. HILL AND FROM *The Nation*

[Hamilton Andrews Hill, "The Relations of the Businessmen of the United States to the National Legislation," in the *Journal of Social Science: Containing the Transactions of the American Association,* no. III, 1871; published for the American Social Science Association by Hurd and Houghton, New York, and The Riverside Press, Cambridge, Mass., 1871, pp. 148–168 (abridged). Read at the general meeting in Philadelphia, Oct. 26, 1870.]

["Businessmen as Legislators," in *The Nation,* Nov. 3, 1870, no. 279, pp. 290–292.]

On October 26, 1870, a paper was read before a meeting of the American Social Science Association, on the subject of "The Relations of the Businessmen of the United States to the National Legislation." Its author was Hamilton A. Hill (1827–1895) of Boston—a businessman with a law degree whose varied career included politics when he became a member of the Massachusetts House of Representatives. As a business-man, Hill was first a shipping merchant in Boston, and later the first secretary of the National Board of Trade.

Then, in the November 3, 1870, issue of *The Nation,* Mr. Hill's position was attacked in an editorial on "Businessmen as Legislators."

Mr. Hill shows how important economic issues have become in national government, yet our legislators are disproportionately lawyers. Urging businessmen to participate more actively, he says: "The present time is favorable for commencing such a movement. The issues between the two political parties are less sharply defined than they have been for years, and there seems to be a growing disposition on the part of moderate men on both sides to work together."

But the editorial writer of *The Nation* is skeptical, even cynical. According to him, "nothing in the training or experience of men of business is likely to develop in them, to any special degree, either the moral or mental qualifications necessary to make good legislators."

The debate is noteworthy for its thoughtfulness, and also for its relevance today, more than 90 years later. We are still arguing about the role of businessmen in government, although they clearly play a larger part than they used to; thus, in Congress alone, the ratio of lawyers to businessmen, deplored by Hill in his paper, has dropped from about 5 to 1 in 1870 to 2 to 1 in 1960 (and the two groups together now account for some 90 per cent of the total, compared with 80 per cent in 1870).

————◆————

PAPER BY MR. HILL

WHILE THE SPIRIT OF CLASS, like the spirit of sectionalism, in certain of its manifestations, ought always to be discouraged and condemned, there can be no question that every class in a nation, like every section of a country, has peculiar interests of its own, which, unless it shall concern itself about them, will probably fail to receive proper consideration, and that it has also duties to perform to the state, growing out of its own conditions and relations, which cannot be misunderstood or neglected by it without public loss.

For the purposes of the present discussion, the people of the United States may be divided into four classes, the professional, the agricultural, the mechanical, and the commercial. We have no nonindustrial class among us; we are all workers, either of necessity or by choice, and almost every man may be appropriately assigned to one or another of the groups mentioned.

In the professional class we should include all those who study, practice, or teach in the departments of divinity, medicine, or law, or in the arts and sciences, also all other literary men and educators, and all who belong to the army or navy; in the agricultural class, those who devote themselves to the cultivation of the soil; in the mechanical class, all artisans and artificers; and in the commercial class, all who are engaged in the manufacture, transportation, or distribution of commodities, or in the regulation and control of money and credit, which lie at the foundation of all mercantile exchange. It is to the last of these that we propose to invite attention in this paper, and an inquiry will be raised as to the relations which the commercial class sustains to the community as a whole, the extent of the dependence under which it rests, on national legislation, and the degree to which it ought to participate, first in its own interest, but secondly and especially in the interest of the nation, in framing this legislation. . . .

The commercial class . . . embraces all manufacturers, miners, importers, wholesale and retail dealers, ship-owners, managers of transportation lines by land or by water, railroad proprietors and officials, capitalists, bankers and brokers, and all employed by them. Its importance numerically should not be overlooked. The present population of the United States is about 40,000,000 souls; it is estimated that of this number 33 per cent, or upwards of 13,000,-000, are in receipt of an income, and 11,000,000 add directly by their labor to the wealth of the country. These 11,000,000 may be subdivided with approximate accuracy as follows; agriculturists, 6,500,000; mechanics, 1,000,000; laborers, 1,500,000; and the commercial class, as already defined, 2,000,000, or 18 per cent of the whole.

But this statement falls far short of illustrating the relative importance of the class under consideration, as we shall see if we glance at the nature and scope of its operations. It keeps afloat 4,000,000 tons of shipping under the American flag, employed on the inland waters of the country, along the coasts, and upon the ocean. It has built 50,000 miles of railway, over which 48,000,000 tons of merchandise pass annually, not including coal. It has constructed 125,000 miles of telegraph lines at a cost of $9,000,000. It controls the export and import of merchandise valued for the last year at $900,000,000. It produces from the spindles, looms, forges, and benches of our numberless manufacturing establishments the value of from $500,000,000 to $600,000,000 a year. It directs the operations of 1600 banks, scattered all over the country, the paid-up capital of which is $400,000,000, and the resources of which amount to $1,500,000,000.

But this is not all. The industry of the mechanic and laboring classes relies largely, if not mainly, on our merchants, manufacturers, and capitalists; while the entire product of our national agriculture, valued at more than $3,000,000,000, enters the domain of commerce almost immediately after its ingathering, and is altogether dependent on the commercial class for the money which enables it to be brought to the home market or shipped abroad, no less than for the vessels or railways by which it is conveyed, or for the elevators or warehouses in which it is stored. In a word, the total product of the industry of the people of the United States, estimated for last year at $6,825,000,000, does no more than measure the scope and extent of the influence exerted by businessmen in one way or another, directly or remotely, sooner or later, on the material prosperity and development of the nation.

"The merchants of a country," says Lord Bacon, "are *vena porta,* and if they flourish not, a kingdom may have good limbs, but will have empty veins, and nourish little." Is not this emphatically true among ourselves in the United States?

We need hardly stop to explain how closely dependent these commercial and other related interests are upon the national legislation for their welfare and security. It is true that no legislation, however hostile, could annihilate the vast annual product of our industry. Our businessmen have often prospered in the past in spite of acts of Congress, and they will probably do the same in frequent instances in the future. Legislation has not made this nation what it is, commercially or otherwise; and legislation will never unmake it. At the same time, it may do, and, as we know, has at various periods done much to quicken or to retard commercial progress; to encourage or to embarrass the efforts of businessmen; to give confidence to, or to frighten capital. Sometimes it is negative, sometimes positive in its character, but in all cases it will be potential in its effect for good or for evil.

If under given circumstances, no legislation is what is required, as when the merchants of France, in reply to a question from Louis XIV as to what he could do for them, said, "Let us alone," then any interference whatever will only work mischief. On the other hand, if the fostering care of the government is needed permanently or temporarily by a particular branch of industry, then to fail to legislate in its behalf will prove mischievous, and to fail to legislate intelligently and judiciously may be hardly less hurtful. If also, in the progress of affairs, it becomes necessary to change a long-established policy in relation to some one or more branches of commercial enterprise, then to adhere tenaciously to legislation once justifiable but now obsolete is sure to be injurious, and in particular instances may prove fatal.

Who can estimate the extent to which our domestic exchanges are influenced by the action of Congress from time to time, on the subject of the currency? The exchangeable value of the billions of our annual products may be determined in one direction or the other by the adoption of a particular policy of expansion or of contraction. The consequences of a serious error in finance at Washington will in the process of time be felt in every bank, every warehouse, and every village store, and in every farmhouse in the United States; and this being so, how many of our population will escape from them? Upon our tariff legislation, whether in its provisions it be stable or fluctuating, simple or complex, moderate or prohibitory, depend, for both the method and the extent of their increase, our multiform manufactures in leather, iron, cotton, wool, wood, and other materials. Our established position as a competing maritime power upon the oceans of the globe, the traffic on which is regulated by unchanging and universal principles and not by municipal rules, must always be decided in the long run by the degree of harmony which we succeed in securing between what we call our navigation laws and those principles. Questions are arising in reference to internal improvements, the relation of the general government to them, their amenability to national control, and their right to claim the aid of the national treasury, and upon the manner in which these questions are answered, the permanent efficiency of the transportation service of the country hinges.

There can be no doubt that from this time forward it will be incumbent upon Congress to devote its time and thought chiefly to the material interests of the nation. Fortunately we are so completely isolated from the other great powers by our geographical position that we need not involve ourselves in their misunderstandings, jealousies, and quarrels. Still more fortunately, our own internal dissensions upon subjects purely political and governmental have so far abated that we may hope soon to see substantial and practical accord upon them among all intelligent and patriotic citizens. What remains for us then, but to set ourselves diligently to the solution of the problems bearing upon the development of the national resources? This is now the duty of the people, and it is especially the duty to which Congress is called, in order that the national wealth may be increased in every direction, and to the utmost possible extent.

Nor is this an unworthy or sordid end, if properly understood. What is a rich nation? Assuredly not of necessity a nation in which there are numerous instances of large personal accumulation or acquisition. A nation may contain many very wealthy men, and yet be poor; it may contain very few, and yet be rich. To entitle it to be called rich, it must possess large aggregated wealth, and the more equally this is diffused among all classes of its population, the greater its prosperity. We want to raise the general standard among ourselves, of comfort, of intelligence, and of morality, to the highest practicable point; and, to secure for the millions of our fellow citizens, native or adopted, now dwelling on this continent, and for the millions more who will inevitably come hither, whether we desire it or not (perhaps in greater crowds than ever before), opportunity for labor according to individual fitness or preference, adequate remuneration, and the possibilities of home. Who shall say that this purpose is not worthy of the choice and devotion of every American citizen, whether he be in private or in public life? Grander than any epitaph carved on the tomb of military conqueror or hero is the inscription on a monument raised to commemorate the public services of one of England's greatest and purest statesmen: He gave the people bread.

We have endeavored to show the extent and value of the material interests represented by what we have termed the commercial class of our country, the importance of these interests to the entire population and to the national prosperity, and the manner in which they may be affected, favorably or adversely, by legislation. We have said also that it has become the duty of Congress to direct its thought and attention chiefly to their protection and promotion. It is proper now to inquire concerning the adaptation of Congress, as at present constituted, for sustaining the responsibilities and for performing the services which all this implies.

At the time of the adoption of the Federal Constitution, it seems to have been anticipated that the representative body would be composed of "land-holders, merchants, and men of the learned professions," and the opinion was expressed that "there was no danger that the interests and feelings of the different classes of citizens would not be understood and attended to by these three descriptions of men." But it could hardly have been foreseen that a branch of one of these classes, a single one of the learned professions, would attain so large a preponderance in numbers and influence over all others, as we find that it has done. We refer of course to the profession of the law. In the Senate of the United States at the present time, out of seventy-two members, 44, or 61 per cent, are members of the bar, while nine only, or 12½ per cent, are connected with trade, transportation, or finance. The proportion is precisely the same in the House of Representatives, in which, out of 238 members, 146 are lawyers, and 31 are members of the commercial class in its broadest definition.

It would be a liberal estimate to state the number of lawyers in the country in 1870 at 40,000; the number according to the census, in 1860, was 33,193. Assuming it to be 40,000 now, the profession of the law contains one tenth of 1 per cent of the population, while its representation in the National Legislature equals, as we have seen, 61 per cent. At the same time the commercial class, comprising within itself 18 per cent of all those who add directly to the wealth of the country by their industry, and 5 per cent of the entire population, has a representation in Congress of only 13 per cent. . . .

We have no disposition to call in question the peculiar fitness of able and experienced practitioners at the bar, in view of the special training received by them during preparation for and in the practice of their profession, for participation in the duties of legislative bodies; nor will we raise an issue as to the relative rank among their legal brethren, of members of Congress who are lawyers, although we have sometimes heard from that source sharp criticisms in reference to both their professional and their general standing. Carefully avoiding all personal allusions and reflections in the course of what we have to say, we will admit that these men, as a whole, fairly represent the average respectability and learning of their class. But we cannot concede that legal studies and attainments are the sole or chief qualification for legislative service, or that any sound argument can be deduced from their possession to prove that it is desirable that lawyers should be so largely in the majority in Congress as for many years past they have been and as they now are.

However well qualified lawyers may be by training and experience to deal with general principles, they must often lack that practical knowledge of affairs which is essential to the right and opportune application of principles and to the working out of details in commercial legislation. They are obliged, therefore, to rely upon others for much of the information which they require, and if they have to go for this beyond the limits of their own body, they obtain their knowledge under many disadvantages. Hence, in part, the reason why Congress has been so slow, as the commercial class feel that it has been, to deal with some of the problems growing out of the War of the Rebellion. Few of its members, comparatively, possessing any practical knowledge of business, the majority have been compelled, in various ways, to solicit expressions of opinion promiscuously from individuals or corporations in their constituencies, and these expressions have been so various and so contradictory, given from so many different viewpoints, and prompted by such conflicting motives, that Congress, having no convictions of its own, well-defined and matured, intelligently formed and confidently held, has been unable to unite upon a commercial or financial policy calculated to meet the approval of the country, or to relieve the embarrassments under which various interests are now suffering. . . .

It is to a Congress thus comprising professional men not versed in the practical details of business, and politicians too often indifferent to these subjects, that the merchants of the country are obliged to have recourse for legislation in reference to our material interests. As has been intimated, the late Civil War disturbed in various ways the course of our domestic and our foreign commerce. Political reconstruction having been secured, our businessmen now desire a careful review and readjustment of all the legislation of the last ten years relating to general business and finance, in order that the conditions of trade may be restored as fully and as rapidly as practicable to the status quo ante bellum.

They desire also a thorough examination of our navigation laws, and other commercial statutes enacted in years long past, for the purpose of ascertaining whether in any essential particulars modifications are needed to make them conformable to changes which have taken place in our own circumstances, or in those of other nations. More than this, they ask that a commercial policy be devised and adopted which shall be broad, flexible, liberal, and comprehensive, free from all suspicion of sectionalism, recognized in its essential principles by both political parties, and worthy of transmission from one administration to another.

But how shall Congress be brought to understand and to sympathize with the commercial class in these desires? Our merchants cannot explain all their views by correspondence; and if they visit Washington for the purpose, they find themselves in corridors crowded with office seekers, with men having personal and selfish schemes to promote, and with professed lobbyists, or they chafe in anterooms, as did Dr. Johnson when waiting to see Lord Chesterfield. If they obtain admission to the committee rooms, they find the members preoccupied and pressed for time, and they have to explain themselves briefly and hurriedly; their motives are liable to misconception; and they are often treated with indifference, sometimes with positive rudeness. Is it strange, then, that they decline to place themselves in a position at once so thankless and so unpleasant?

For this state of things what remedy shall we propose? How shall Congress as a body be brought rightly to understand the financial and commercial wants of the nation, and wisely and adequately to legislate in view of these wants? Answering this question generally, we should say that we must be more rigid and exacting in the selection of candidates, putting forward only men of recognized character, ability, and experience, and choosing only those who are both competent and willing to be the leaders of public opinion, and who will have sufficient confidence in themselves and sufficient independence to initiate measures of reform, instead of waiting until the nation, after a long and patient endurance of evils, can be aroused to unite in demanding their removal.

Our subject, however, requires us to be more explicit than this, and it suggests the nature of the specific fitness which must be insisted on certainly in a fair proportion of those who are to constitute the Houses of Congress. It teaches us that we must send a larger number of thoroughly trained, first-class businessmen to Congress, and especially to the lower branch, than we have of late been in the habit of doing. If it be true, as has been stated, that from henceforth the paramount duty of Congress will largely be to pass upon questions relating to finance, the tariff, ocean commerce, railway transportation, and kindred topics, the most natural course to pursue to insure proper action thereupon would seem to be to elect to seats in Congress, bankers, manufacturers, merchants, and railroad officials. Far better to introduce the practical knowledge and experience of such men into the body itself than to attempt to infuse into it any information by means of written communications or hearings before committees.

If the condition of a bank, or a factory, or a railway become embarrassed, it is customary in the commercial world to select some man especially skilled in the banking, manufacturing, or railway business, as the case may be, to retrieve if possible the position of the failing institution, or, if there must be disaster, to make this as light as possible. Under such circumstances no one would think of selecting a man to stand at the head of a corporation who could bring no practical knowledge to the performance of his duties, and whose only claim to such a position was based on a legal education or good standing in a political party. And yet we are in a measure intrusting the welfare of sixteen hundred banks to men to whom we would not confide the management of any one of them. We are placing the well-being of our whole manufacturing system in the hands of men whom we would not put in charge of a single mill. We are sending men to frame our navigation policy whose advice we would not accept in reference to the model of a ship, or the merits of a sea captain or mate. We are charging men with the transportation interests of a continent who would be utterly incompetent to manage one of our shortest railway lines.

Of course we shall not be understood as urging that every legislator should possess in himself the requisite qualifications for each one of the positions to which we have referred; that would be absurd. Nor can anything we have said be construed as intimating that every legislator should be competent to fill some one or other of them. We do not desire to see the Halls of Congress occupied exclusively by the commercial class; we would simply recur to the original idea of the framers of the Constitution, which was, as we have said, that the representative body should consist in the right proportions of members of the learned professions, businessmen, and landholders or agriculturists. We expect that in Congress, as well as in other legislative assemblies, there will always be a large number of lawyers, and we shall be content to have it so if only the best men at the bar are chosen; but we claim that side by side with them should sit merchants and other members of the commercial class, and in about equal numbers. There ought to be not less than 100 of these men in the House of Representatives today. All the large cities of the Union should, in part at least, be represented by them. They should be selected, not because they are party politicians, and are therefore available, their occupation as businessmen being the accident or incident; but distinctly for the reason that they are businessmen and not partisans at all. The influence for good of such a body of men in rightly molding and shaping our commercial legislation, it would be impossible to estimate. . . .

How can we secure the election to Congress of a proper number of commercial men of the right kind? We have said that in our opinion there ought to be 100 of them in the House of Representatives today, sitting for the great commercial constituencies. How can they be placed there? This is a matter in reference to which the businessmen of these constituencies must bestir themselves; they may not be really more deeply interested in the character of the legislation enacted at Washington on subjects relating to the material welfare of the country than are men in other walks of life, but they are so apparently, and the majority of their fellow citizens believe them to be so in fact.

With them therefore rests the responsibility of taking the first steps in the direction of reform. That they have the power to carry the point there can be little doubt, if they will use proper means. Numerically, as we have seen, they are not weak. We have estimated the commercial class in the United States, employers and employed inclusive, to be 18 per cent of the total of real producers; it is of course the strongest proportionately in the communities in which it is proposed that its influence for reform shall be exerted. But it possesses another element of strength; it holds the purse strings which it is necessary to untie at the commencement of every political canvass. Nearly all the money raised in the cities for party purposes is contributed by businessmen and capitalists, and it would be quite legitimate for them not only to insist, when making their subscriptions, upon a due recognition of their class in the nominations to be presented to the people, but also, if their just claims and reasonable expectations fail to be met, to quietly allow those who thus overrule their preferences, with their supporters, to pay all the election bills. Their moral power, however, would be their greatest source of strength; they would be heartily sustained by the best men in the learned professions, and by thoughtful citizens of every class. A movement to obtain proper representation in Congress for the monetary, manufacturing, importing, and transportation interests would be seen to be so just in itself, and so desirable for the country at large, that it would receive prompt and hearty approval and cooperation on every hand.

The local Boards of Trade and Chambers of Commerce are educating businessmen for legislative service, and they are beginning to create a public sentiment which will sustain them in this service when they shall enter upon it. They cannot be safely used in their character of commercial organizations, for making nominations or carrying elections, but they will be found to be of much use indirectly. The individual members know each other, understand each other, and estimate each other, generally, at about the right value. Their acquaintanceship, and their habit heretofore of consulting and working together, have prepared the way for further concert of action; so that outside of their organizations, but closely related to them, they are in a situation to form in every large business community a nucleus for a movement in favor of representative reform which, with proper effort, will rapidly grow and finally prevail.

The present time is favorable for commencing such a movement. The issues between the two political parties are less sharply defined than they have been for many years, and there seems to be a growing disposition on the part of moderate men on both sides to work together. If, therefore, the members of the Boards of Trade and Chambers of Commerce will informally meet each other for consultation, manifesting a conciliatory and unselfish spirit, and subordinating all personal and party preferences to the public good, if they will agree among themselves in reference to the man or men who are best fitted to act upon commercial questions in Congress, and if they will firmly insist upon the nomination of such, and of such only, it will not be long before their expressed wishes will be regarded, and they will have the satisfaction of seeing themselves, their class, and the enterprise and industry of the country fairly represented and properly cared for. They will not accomplish their purpose all at once; it will be less difficult to succeed in some constituencies than in others; but every additional commercial man sent to Washington will make it the more easy to elect others.

This brings us to the second inquiry: How can we obtain the consent of the men whom we wish to nominate and elect? We admit that this is a more serious difficulty than that which we have just been treating; for with the acceptance of a nomination by an unexceptionable candidate in any commercial constituency in which the businessmen are earnest and united, the battle will be more than half won. But the trouble is, the men upon whom we should all be likely to agree would generally be those who would most hesitate to enter Congress.

In the first place, with many of them, going there would involve some pecuniary sacrifice; they would have to leave their business affairs altogether for months at a time, and they would have to divide their attention between their public and private duties, even when at home. Still, we think that, under certain circumstances, enough of such men could be induced to forego personal advantage, at the solicitation of their brother merchants, supported by their fellow citizens generally, to represent the more important constituencies. There is such a thing as disinterestedness in the world, and there is a proper ambition in the heart of many a high-toned man which will prompt him to serve his country when called to do so by the unsought suffrages of his associates; and when there seems to be a probability that his efforts will be appreciated, and in a measure successful, one or both of these considerations might be expected to influence favorably those whom we should ask to represent the commercial class in the national councils. We know that our most experienced and successful businessmen are constantly induced to accept new responsibilities from which they would gladly excuse themselves, were it not for what they conceive to be their duty to their friends or to the public. It is hard to have to believe that convictions of what the necessities of the country require, confirmed by a knowledge of what is desirable for local interests also, will not induce men to make a temporary sacrifice for the sake of the results which they may hope thereby to achieve.

But there is a lower ground on which an argument might be based, and it ought to be mentioned, although let us hope that it would not be necessary to make use of it in urging upon businessmen their duty to take part in legislative affairs. They have a very direct personal and pecuniary concern in the character of the legislation of the country; the value of their property, the nature of their operations, the extent of their profits, all depend upon the laws which are passed relating to internal taxation, the tariff, and the currency. They may suppose that by their own prudence they can protect themselves personally, no matter how widely the course of legislation may be at variance with the general welfare; but in this they will find themselves mistaken sooner or later, for they cannot permanently escape from the effect of embarrassments and disabilities, involving both the class of which they are members and the country of which they are citizens.

There are other reasons, however, why many of our best merchants would at the present time refuse to allow their names to be used as candidates for Congress. They would not feel at their ease in an assembly composed mainly of professional men, or of politicians. To obtain their consent, it would be necessary to assure them that they would not stand alone, that they would not be in a hopeless minority, and that the subjects especially represented by them would not be treated as of secondary importance. Above all, they would have to be relieved from the annoyances connected with the distribution of patronage, and from the drudgery of party work. Even professed politicians begin to find this a burden too heavy to be borne; and merchants of the character indispensable to such a representation as we now plead for will never willingly assume it. If some comprehensive measure of civil service reform shall be enacted, the most serious impediment will be removed to our obtaining the consent of just such men as the country now needs, to serve not as party leaders but as legislators and practical statesmen.

A third inquiry awaits our reply: How can we guard against the use of their position in Congress by businessmen to promote their personal gain? This question might as well be proposed whenever a man is to be chosen to take the presidency of a bank, or to be placed at the head of a railway or manufacturing corporation. There is always danger in connection with every important appointment; and how is it avoided? By electing to these offices men of probity, standing, and long-tried character, who value their good name and their high standing on 'Change as worth more than bags of gold. There are hundreds of such men in the United States, administering large trusts honestly and well; and having proved faithful in that which is less, they would not probably be false in that which is greater.

Moreover, it is usually considered a pledge and guarantee of good administration when the head of a corporation is pecuniarily interested in its success; and everything else being equal, the soundest and safest legislation on commercial and financial questions might be expected from those who themselves have the most at stake in the prosperity of the country. It is true that a man sometimes enriches himself at the expense of a company in which he is a large stockholder, and a legislator may make a corrupt use of his place for the benefit of himself or of his associates; but cases like these must be left to be dealt with as they arise. We do not know that a respectable merchant would be more likely to yield to this kind of temptation than a lawyer or a politician; but whenever a commercial member of Congress shall be found to devote himself to his own interests, or too exclusively to the interests of the district where he lives, or the branch of business to which he belongs, forgetting that while sent to Congress to represent his own constituency, he is sent there to legislate for the whole people, the public sentiment of the country will not tolerate him for any length of time, and a moral pressure will be brought to bear which will compel the electors of his locality to choose a purer and a better man.

Believing . . . that the shortest way to reform and to all good government is to make the representation as true as possible, we have endeavored in the foregoing pages to show that an essential change is called for in the composition of our national legislature, and to suggest how this change may be brought to pass. Our object has been not so much to secure justice for a class, the claims of which have been too long neglected, although such a purpose would call for no apology; nor exclusively to advance the material wealth of the nation by appropriate legislation, although the desirableness of this it would be difficult to overestimate. But such a body of businessmen as we desire to see upon the floor of Congress would do more than shape financial and commercial legislation; they would prove themselves competent to deal with the various social and political questions which would come before them, and especially they would give powerful support to every wise measure of reform. They would closely scrutinize the expenses of the government; and they would be unsparing in their treatment of all abuses. They would be as unwilling to accept perquisites as to wield patronage; they would therefore speedily abolish the franking privilege, and they would seek to redeem the civil service from the contaminating contact of party politics.

Under their influence, also, it might be anticipated that a change for the better would be introduced into the method of conducting Congressional business. They would legislate not altogether on theory, but in view of the pressing necessities of the time; they would frame fewer laws perhaps, but this might be no calamity, seeing that often it is the duty of the legislator not so much to make laws as to bring to light those which inhere in the nature of things. Fewer long speeches would be made than at present, and fewer still would be printed; but more work would be done, and in a shorter time. In a word, these men would insist upon an honest, economical, intelligent, and faithful administration of the government in all its branches; and they would infuse into all somewhat of the vitality and efficiency which characterize their own warehouses and counting rooms.

We have confined our remarks to legislation, and have refrained from saying anything in reference to the influence which our businessmen should exert in the direct administration of the government. This latter logically comes after the former, for laws must be first made and then executed; but this is a distinct subject and should be separately treated. It may be said, however, that when the commercial class shall exercise its proper influence in Congress, it will soon begin to participate in the management of governmental affairs. It was after Richard Cobden had won his spurs in many a hotly contested debate in the House of Commons that he was offered a baronetcy and a seat in the Privy Council. At the time referred to, we shall have a Department of Commerce presided over by a cabinet minister who will be a merchant; and it will be the rule to select the Secretary of the Treasury and perhaps other heads of departments from among prominent members of the commercial class.

In the United States we are favored with a good government; but we cannot safely rest contented with the excellence of the fundamental law on which it is based. We should be satisfied with nothing less than a good government, well conducted. There is no occasion for our adopting the fallacy of Pope's couplet,

> For forms of Government let fools contest;
> Whate'er is best administered is best.

Having a form which is theoretically sound, we should seek for the best administration possible under it, for the wisest application of the principles to which we are attached, and for the equitable and universal enforcement of statutes which shall doubly command themselves to every citizen, because they are in harmony with his own enlightened convictions, as well as with the spirit of the Federal Constitution. To this end, the intelligence, the industry, and the property of the country should have fair and full representation in both branches—the legislative and the executive—of the national government.

EDITORIAL IN *THE NATION*

A paper by Mr. Hamilton A. Hill, of Boston, was read . . . before the Social Science Association at Philadelphia, on "The Relations of Businessmen to National Legislation," which is, especially at this moment, deserving of more attention than it is likely to receive as merely a part of the discussions of a society commanding unfortunately but a limited share of public attention. The essential part of this paper commences with a statement which is not new to our readers, but which seems to be entirely lost sight of by the great majority of even the more thinking portion of our voters: "From this time forward," says Mr. Hill, "it will be incumbent upon Congress to devote its time and thought chiefly to material questions. What is the adaptation of Congress, as now constituted, for meeting such a responsibility? Sixty-one per cent of the members of both Houses of Congress are members of the bar, while only 12½ per cent are connected with trade, transportation, or finance."

Few persons are aware to what an extent Mr. Hill's description of the future duties of Congress is correct. The seemingly vague term, "material questions," disguises to many minds his true meaning. He should perhaps have said, questions affecting the material welfare, the business prosperity, the income and expenditure, the profits and earnings, the bread and butter, as it were, of every citizen. It is unfortunately true that, in a large measure, all these things are dependent upon the action of Congress in relation to measures which affect them all. The great War of the Rebellion rendered necessary,

or was at least thought to have rendered necessary, a series of
Congressional enactments the result of which has been far different
from what was anticipated; which have led to the most remarkable
change in the distribution of wealth ever before accomplished without
violence; which have entirely arrested the production of wealth in some
directions, and in others have led to an unprofitable production;
which nothing but the intelligence of our people and the ampli-
tude of our resources have made possible without individual exhaustion and national prostration. It is these enactments that the people
are determined to have changed. It is this change that now lies
before Congress as its most imperative duty.

There can be no doubt of the correctness of Mr. Hill's statement
of the issues to come before the Congress now elected; for the
platforms of both leading parties, whether issued by Congressional
committees or state committees, or more local organizations, give,
almost without exception, most prominence to questions affecting
the material welfare of the people. From a very imperfect list of
the platforms issued during the pending canvass, we find that no
less than eighteen make important planks of the tariff question,
eleven take strong ground on the subject of the public lands, eight
make an important issue of the national-bank privileges, five complain of legislation injuriously affecting our shipbuilding and navigation interests, almost every one has reference to the internal revenue,
while only three make it a distinct issue. Only two demand a civil-
service reform. While these platforms of themselves, or separately,
are not entitled to overmuch consideration; while many of them
display a profound ignorance of the true nature of the questions
with which they attempt to deal; while some of them are contradictory in their various parts and inconsistent with themselves; and
while our collection of them is quite imperfect—and a full list might
materially change the result—yet the figures given show conclusively
enough what questions the politicians at least thought were upper-
most in the public mind, on what issues they could best hope to
gain popular support. The politicians agree with Mr. Hill, and they
are right. The questions now before the country *are* material ones.

Mr. Hill's conclusion is that, the questions now before the country
being material ones, the best men to solve them are those who are
most in the habit of dealing with material questions—the businessmen of the community. He proceeds to show, upon somewhat
questionable data, that the businessmen of the community amount
to 18 per cent of the whole, and that the entire wealth of the country
is either produced by them or else is constantly passing through
their hands—while they are represented in the councils of the nation
by only 12½ per cent of the whole, against 61 per cent of lawyers
and 26 per cent of all other professions. But here occurs a complete

hiatus in the argument; for he does not attempt to prove that evil results from this imperfect representation, or that a more perfect representation is possible, or that merchants would necessarily make better legislators than lawyers. The speaker assumes that a more perfect representation of commercial interests by commercial men is highly desirable, and then goes on to show how that may be obtained. But it is precisely this assumption that we feel inclined to contest.

Judging by analogy, we should certainly not be disposed to look to businessmen for good legislation on business questions, since in a Congress consisting of 61 per cent of lawyers, almost any work is better done than the regulation of legal proceedings or the administration of justice. The various Reconstruction Acts, and, above all, the Georgia Bill, were striking illustrations of the confusion which is allowed to make its way into legislation even under legal auspices; the spirit displayed by Congress in its actual and proposed legislation concerning the Supreme Court of the United States is a still better illustration; the Bankrupt Act, exclusively the work of Congressional lawyers, needs endless tinkering, and furnishes probably more business to our courts of law than any other statute; and, not to go further, the very enactments in which Congress expresses its own will on miscellaneous subjects are frequently so imperfectly constructed as to accomplish results the very reverse of what was intended.

But if analogy leads us to doubt the superior fitness of men of any one occupation to legislate upon the interests of their class or of any other class, what is there in the training and experience of businessmen to make them an exception to this rule? Nothing whatever. From the earliest ages, when a merchant or a trader was an object of contempt to soldiers, priests, and princes, the mercantile community has been looked upon as the convenient victim of rapacious or necessitous rulers. Even to this day the commerce of all civilized countries is called upon to contribute the largest portion of the expenses of the state, and half the evils suffered by our people during the last ten years of war and war consequences are systematically attributed not by the ignorant only, but by those who ought to know better, to the trading portion of the people—from the hucksters that disturb the rest of the *Times* and the *Tribune,* through the foreign importers who absorb the profits of the interior dealers, to the bankers and brokers of Wall Street, who revel in their ill-gotten gains at the expense of every member of the rural districts, and in open violation of every rule of public and private morality. Since merchants have been merchants, they have been victims of law. Law has hampered them, regulated them, interfered with them, injured their business, and taxed them beyond all patience; and hence the one prominent sentiment regarding law in all business communities is that it is almost certain to be inexpedient and to discriminate against them unjustly, but that it is useless to struggle against an overwhelming majority, and that all they can do is to adapt their business, as far as possible, to the laws as they find them, or else transfer their skill, knowledge, activity, enterprise, and capital to other fields of operation less injuriously affected by mischievous enactments. No one at all acquainted with men of business can fail to hear our assertion emphatically confirmed, or can have any difficulty in learning detailed cases of the immense injury inflicted upon business by legislation during the last few years alone.

It may be said that this is only another argument in favor of electing more businessmen to Congress, and apparently the argument is good. But we are considering the question of their fitness for legislation acquired by the training and experience of business, and we say that the habitual struggle with bad laws, the almost unavoidable contempt for all laws, and, worse than all, the daily necessity of seeking to adapt one's self to the consequences of injudicious legislation (and adaptation often means evasion) is the worst possible school for a lawmaker.

There is another reason fully as weighty, and just as little thought of. Trade of all kinds is an endless succession of bargains, a ceaseless repetition of petty struggles between two individuals, each striving to get as much as possible, and to give as little. Whatever the nature of commercial, financial, or even of manufacturing business, it ultimately resolves itself into giving as little as possible and getting the largest possible return. Let us not be understood as joining the silly outcry against bargaining or dickering. There is nothing dishonest or dishonorable in it; there is no deception connected with it; it is perfectly fair and aboveboard. But it is just the nature of trade that success in it depends upon always getting much and giving little. Of no other occupation is this true in the same degree. The lawyer—the more time, skill, study, and labor he gives to his clients' cases, the more likely he is to win; the more certainly his practice will increase. The mechanic, the artist—the better work they give, the better their pay. The farmer looks for larger crops from fields bountifully manured and industriously tilled. The physician, the clergyman, need no bargain to obtain their reward; their talent, their conscientious labor, bring prompt recognition and pecuniary advantage. The merchant alone at every stage of his career is compelled to keep up the daily struggle to give little and to get much. In no other occupation is it necessary to keep the ultimate gain so constantly before the eyes, and look so steadily at the profit in dollars and cents.

This habit, this necessity, while it creates men of clear, practical insight, of incessant industry, of rapid decision, men of much knowledge of men and of much knowledge of things, at the same time diminishes the ability to look on any subject except for its prospective profit; it disables men, incessantly occupied in the study of their own interests, from examining, much less understanding, the interests of others; it incapacitates them for deep thought on all questions the direct, practical results of which are not readily visible; it produces the habit of considering the entire community as engaged in incessant trade, where each one is supposed to be capable of driving his own bargain, and thereby fosters the belief that no consideration is due to the helpless, feeble, or ignorant.

The very first quality of a legislator should be unselfishness; not only the minor principle which prevents a man from prostituting his position to individual gain, but the broader virtue which enables him to understand the wishes, to study the interests, to assume in thought the position of those for whom he is to legislate. Unselfish, fair-minded, earnest—these are what might be called his moral qualifications. His mental qualifications should be of an equally high order. Nothing is more erroneous than the belief that so-called practical men would make good laws. Lawmaking is essentially a matter of theory; and although theory without a knowledge of facts is a nonexistent delusion, or, at best, the dream of a brain imperfectly developed, yet the knowledge of facts alone is useless, nay, injurious, without the theory that classifies them, that knows their relative importance and their connection with one another as cause and effect. It is only too evident that nothing in the training or experience of men of business is likely to develop in them, to any special degree, either the moral or mental qualifications necessary to make good legislators. They may not make worse lawmakers than lawyers are generally found to be; but it is idle to anticipate that a larger infusion of the business element into Congress would necessarily lead to better legislation on the material questions now before the country.

AN EARLY MUCKRAKER INTERPRETS
AMERICAN BUSINESS BEHAVIOR
IN THE 1890s

<del>~~~~</del>

HENRY DEMAREST LLOYD

[Henry Demarest Lloyd, "The Old Self-Interest," in *Wealth Against Commonwealth,* Harper & Brothers, New York, 1894, pp. 494–515 (abridged).]

"We are very poor. The striking feature of our economic condition is
our poverty, not our wealth. We make ourselves 'rich' by appropriating
the property of others by methods which lessen the total property of all."
In these words Lloyd epitomized in the late nineteenth century what
he thought was happening in the United States. Accumulators of wealth—
"syndicates," "captains of industry"—pulled the strings of the whole
economy through red tape, bureaucracy, and conspiracy. Ordinary citizens, thought this "angry young man," had become mere puppets. The
concepts of duty and self-interest had been prostituted. The "great
money-makers" had "sprung in one generation into seats of power kings
do not know," and in so doing had become public enemies. Combinations
in coal, whisky, bread, meat, and oil (especially oil) provided examples
horrifying to Lloyd.

More important, this journalist-turned-reformer succeeded in conveying his anger and horror to millions of people, not only in the United
States but everywhere that the English language was read. *Wealth
Against Commonwealth* proved to be an opening gun in a veritable
literary barrage on large-scale enterprise in the United States. Lloyd
was really the first of the muckrakers, those writers who so effectively
induced the public to insist on control of big business in the years prior
to World War I. For that reason alone, even if not for the literary
quality of the work, can any literate citizen be denied the opportunity
to share the thoughts and feelings of a man who pushed us along
the road to the present democratic, but regulated, welfare state?

———◆———

THE CORN OF THE COMING HARVEST is growing so fast that, like
the farmer standing at night in his fields, we can hear it snap and
crackle. We have been fighting fire on the well-worn lines of old-
fashioned politics and political economy, regulating corporations,
and leaving competition to regulate itself. But the flames of a new
economic evolution run around us, and we turn to find that compe-

tition has killed competition, that corporations are grown greater than the state and have bred individuals greater than themselves, and that the naked issue of our time is with property becoming master instead of servant, property in many necessaries of life becoming monopoly of the necessaries of life. We are still, in part, as Emerson says, in the quadruped state. Our industry is a fight of every man for himself. The prize we give the fittest is monopoly of the necessaries of life, and we leave these winners of the powers of life and death to wield them over us by the same "self-interest" with which they took them from us. In all this we see at work a "principle" which will go into the records as one of the historic mistakes of humanity. Institutions stand or fall by their philosophy, and the main doctrine of industry since Adam Smith has been the fallacy that the self-interest of the individual was a sufficient guide to the welfare of the individual and society. Heralded as a final truth of "science" this proves to have been nothing higher than a temporary formula for a passing problem. It was a reflection in words of the policy of the day. . . .

The true law of business is that all must pursue the interest of all. In the law, the highest product of civilization, this has long been a commonplace. The safety of the people is the supreme law. We are in travail to bring industry up to this. Our century of the caprice of the individual as the lawgiver of the common toil, to employ or disemploy, to start or stop, to open or close, to compete or combine, has been the disorder of the school while the master slept. The happiness, self-interest, or individuality of the whole is not more sacred than that of each, but it is greater. They are equal in quality, but in quantity they are greater. In the ultimate which the mathematician, the poet, the reformer projects the two will coincide.

Our world, operated by individual motive, is the country of the Chinese fable, in which the inhabitants went on one leg. Yes, but an "enlightened self-interest"? The perfect self-interest of the perfect individual is an admirable conception, but it is still individual, and the world is social. The music of the spheres is not to be played on one string. Nature does nothing individually. All forces are paired like the sexes, and every particle of matter in the universe has to obey every other particle. When the individual has progressed to a perfect self-interest, there will be over against it, acting and reacting with it, a correspondingly perfect self-interest of the community. . . . Our century, given to this laissez faire—"leave the individual alone; he will do what is best for himself, and what is best for him is best for all"—has done one good: it has put society at the mercy of its own ideals, and has produced an actual anarchy in industry which is horrifying us into a change of doctrines. . . .

The true laissez faire is, let the individual do what the individual can do best, and let the community do what the community can do best. The laissez faire of social interest, if true, cannot conflict with the individual self-interest, if true, but it must outrank it always. What we have called "free competition" has not been free, only freer than what went before. The free is still to come. The pressure we feel is notice to prepare for it. Civilization—the process of making men citizens in their relations to each other, by exacting of each that he give to all that which he receives from all—has reached only those forms of common effort which, because most general and most vital, first demanded its harmonizing touch. Men joining in the labors of the family, the mutual sacrifices of the club or the church in the union of forces for self-defense and for the gains of cooperation on the largest scale in labors of universal concern, like letter-carrying, have come to be so far civilized. . . .

Where the self-interest of the individual is allowed to be the rule both of social and personal action, the level of all is forced down to that of the lowest. Business excuses itself for the things it does—cuts in wages, exactions in hours, tricks of competition—on the plea that the merciful are compelled to follow the cruel. "It is pleaded as an excuse by those [common carriers] who desire to obey the [Interstate Commerce] law that self-preservation drives them to violate it because other carriers persist in doing so," says Senator Cullom. When the self-interest of society is made the standard, the lowest must rise to the average. The one pulls down, the other up. That men's hearts are bad and that bad men will do bad things has a truth in it. But whatever the general average of morals, the anarchy which gives such individuals their head and leaves them to set the pace for all will produce infinitely worse results than a policy which applies mutual checks and inspirations. Bad kings make bad reigns, but monarchy is bad because it is arbitrary power, and that, whether it be political or industrial, makes even good men bad.

A partial truth universally applied as this of self-interest has been is a universal error. Everything goes to defeat. Highways are used to prevent travel and traffic. Ownership of the means of production is sought in order to "shut down" production, and the means of plenty make famine. All follow self-interest to find that though they have created marvelous wealth it is not theirs. We pledge "our lives, our fortunes, and our sacred honor" to establish the rule of the majority, and end by finding that the minority—a minority in morals, money, and men—are our masters whichever way we turn. We agonize over "economy," but sell all our grain and pork and oil and cotton at exchanges where we pay brokerage on a hundred or a thousand barrels or bushels or bales of wind to get one real one sold. These intolerabilities—sweatshops where model merchants buy and sell the cast-off scarlet-fever skins of the poor, factory and mine where childhood is forbidden to become manhood and manhood is forbidden to die a natural death, mausoleums in which we bury the dead rich, slums in which we bury the living poor, coal pools with their manufacture of artificial winter—all these are the rule of private self-interest arrived at its destination.

A really human life is impossible in our cities, but they cannot be reconstructed under the old self-interest. Chicago was rebuilt wrong after the fire. Able men pointed out the avenues to a wider and better municipal life, but they could not be opened through the private interpositions that blocked the way. The slaughter of railway men coupling cars was shown, in a debate in the United States Senate, to be twice as great as it would be if the men were in active service in war. But under the scramble for private gain our society on its railway side cannot develop the energy to introduce the improved appliances ready to hand which would save these lives, all young and vigorous. The cost of the change would be repaid in 100 per cent dividends every year by the money value alone to us of the men now killed and wounded. . . .

We are very poor. The striking feature of our economic condition is our poverty, not our wealth. We make ourselves "rich" by appropriating the property of others by methods which lessen the total property of all. Spain took such riches from America and grew poor. Modern wealth more and more resembles the winnings of speculators in bread during famine—worse, for to make the money it makes the famine. What we call cheapness shows itself to be unnatural fortunes for a very few, monstrous luxury for them and proportionate deprivation for the people, judges debauched, trustees dishonored, Congress and state legislatures insulted and defied, when not seduced, multitudes of honest men ruined and driven to despair, the common carrier made a mere instrument for the creation of a new baronage, an example set to hundreds of would-be commercial Caesars to repeat this rapine in other industries and call it "business," a process set in operation all over the United States for the progressive extinction of the independence of laboring men, and all business men except the very rich, and their reduction to a state of vassalage to lords or squires in each department of trade and industry. All these—tears, ruin, dishonor, and treason—are the unmarked additions to the "price marked on the goods." . . .

The new wealth now administers estates of fabulous extent from metropolitan bureaus, and all the profits flow to men who know nothing of the real business out of which they are made. Red tape, complication, the hired man, conspiracy have taken the place of the watchful eye of the owner, the old-fashioned hand at the plough

that must "hold or drive." We now have Captains of Industry, with
a few aids, rearranging from office chairs this or that industry,
by mere contrivances of wit compelling the fruits of the labor of
tens of thousands of their fellows, who never saw them, never
heard of them, to be every day deposited unwilling and unwitting
to their own credit at the bank; setting, as by necromancy, hundreds

FIG. 299. The Bosses of the Senate.

Roger Butterfield in his *The American Past* says of this cartoon: "Keppler's
'Bosses of the Senate' is an accurate allegory. By 1889 the upper chamber
of Congress was known as a millionaires' club. The presiding officer was
a Wall Street banker, and the principal Senators represented oil, lumber,
railroads, insurance, silver, gold, utility and manufacturing interests. "

of properties, large and small, in a score of communities, to flying
through invisible ways into their hands; sitting calm through all
the hubbub raised in courts, legislatures, and public places, and by
dictating letters and whispering words remaining the master magicians
of the scene; defying, though private citizens, all the forces and
authorities of a whole people; by the mere mastery of compelling
brain, without putting hand to anything, opening or closing the
earth's treasures of oil or coal or gas or copper or what not; pulling
down or putting up great buildings, factories, towns themselves;
moving men and their money this way and that; inserting their will
as part of the law of life of the people—American, European, and

Asiatic—and, against the protest of a whole civilization, making themselves, their methods and principles, its emblematic figures.

Syndicates, by one stroke, get the power of selling dear on one side, and producing cheap on the other. Thus they keep themselves happy, prices high, and the people hungry. What model merchant could ask more? The dream of the king who wished that all his people had but one neck that he might decapitate them at one blow is realized today in this industrial garrote. The syndicate has but to turn its screw, and every neck begins to break. Prices paid to such intercepters are not an exchange of service; they are ransom paid by the people for their lives. The ability of the citizen to pay may fluctuate; what he must pay remains fixed, or advances like the rent of the Irish tenant to the absentee landlord until the community interfered. Those who have this power to draw the money from the people—from every railroad station, every streetcar, every fireplace, every salt cellar, every bread pan, washboard, and coal scuttle—to their own safes have the further incentive to make this money worth the most possible. By contracting the issue of currency and contracting it again by hoarding it in their banks, safe-deposit vaults, and the government treasury, they can depress the prices of all that belongs to the people. Their own prices are fixed. These are "regular prices," established by price lists. Given, as a ruling motive, the principles of business—to get the most and give the least; given the legal and economic, physical and mechanical control, possible under our present social arrangements, to the few over the many, and the certain end of all this, if unarrested, unreversed, can be nothing less than a return to chattel slavery. There may be some finer name, but the fact will not be finer. Between our present tolerance and our completed subjection the distance is not so far as that from the equality and simplicity of our Pilgrim Fathers to ourselves.

Everything withers—even charity. Aristocratic benevolence spends a shrunken stream in comparison with democratic benevolence. In an address to the public, soliciting subscriptions, the Committee of the United Hospitals Association of New York said, in December, 1893: "The committee have found that, through the obliteration of old methods of individual competition by the establishment of large corporations and trusts in modern times, the income of such charitable institutions as are supported by the individual gifts of the benevolent has been seriously affected." . . .

In the worst governments and societies that have existed one good can be seen—so good that the horrors of them fall back into secondary places as extrinsic, accidental. That good is the ability of men to lead the life together. The more perfect monopoly makes itself the more does it bring into strong lights the greatest fact of our industry, of far more permanent value than the greed which has for the moment made itself the cynosure of all eyes. It makes this fair world more fair to consider the loyalties, intelligences, docilities of the multitudes who are guarding, developing, operating with the faithfulness of brothers and the keen interest of owners properties and industries in which brotherhood is not known and their title is not more than a tenancy at will. One of the largest stones in the arch of "consolidation," perhaps the keystone, is that men have become so intelligent, so responsive and responsible, so cooperative that they can be intrusted in great masses with the care of vast properties owned entirely by others and with the operation of complicated processes, although but a slender cost of subsistence is awarded them out of fabulous profits. The spectacle of the million and more employees of the railroads of this country despatching trains, maintaining tracks, collecting fares and freights, and turning over hundreds of millions of net profits to the owners, not one in a thousand of whom would know how to do the simplest of these things for himself, is possible only where civilization has reached a high average of morals and culture. More and more the mills and mines and stores, and even the farms and forests, are being administered by others than the owners. The virtue of the people is taking the place Poor Richard thought only the eye of the owner could fill. If mankind, driven by their fears and the greed of others, can do so well, what will be their productivity and cheer when the "interest of all" sings them to their work?

This new morality and new spring of wealth have been seized first by the appropriating ones among us. But, as has been in government, their intervention of greed is but a passing phase. Mankind belongs to itself, not to kings or monopolists, and will supersede the one as surely as the other with the institutions of democracy. Yes, Callicles, said Socrates, the greatest are usually the bad, for they have the power. If power could continue paternal and benign, mankind would not be rising through one emancipation after another into a progressive communion of equalities. The individual and society will always be wrestling with each other in a composition of forces. But to just the extent to which civilization prevails, society will be held as inviolable as the individual; not subordinate—indeed inaudible—as now in the counting room and corporation office. We have overworked the self-interest of the individual. The line of conflict between individual and social is a progressive one of the discovery of point after point in which the two are identical. Society thus passes from conflict to harmony, and on to another conflict. Civilization is the unceasing accretion of these social solutions. We fight out to an equilibrium, as in the abolition of human slavery; then upon this new level thus built up we enter upon the struggle for a new equilibrium, as now in the labor movement. The man for himself destroys himself and all men; only society can foster him and them.

The greatest happiness of the greatest number is only the doctrine of self-interest writ large and made more dangerous by multitude. It is the self-interest of the majority, and this has written some of the unloveliest chapters of history. There have never been slaves more miserable than those of Sparta, where the state was the owner. American democracy prepares to repeat these distresses of the selfishness of the many, and gives notice to its railway employees of a new divine right—"the convenience of the public"—to which they must forego every right of manhood. No better definition of slave could be found than one who must work at the convenience of another. This is the position into which recent legal decisions and acts of the Federal executive force railway men. These speak in the name of interstate commerce, but their logic can be as easily applied by state judges to state commerce, and all workingmen are manifestly as necessary, each in his function, to the convenience of the public as the men of the rail. The greatest happiness of all must be the formula. When Lamennais said, "I love my family more than myself, my village more than my family, my country more than my village, and mankind more than my country," he showed himself not only a good lover, but the only good arithmetician.

Children yet, we run everything we do—love or war, work or leisure, religion or liberty—to excess. Every possibility of body and mind must be played upon till it is torn to pieces, as toys by children. Priests, voluptuaries, tyrants, knights, ascetics—in the long procession of fanatics a newcomer takes his place; he is called "the model merchant"—the cruelest fanatic in history. He is the product of ages given to progressive devotion to "trading." He is the high priest of the latest idolatry, the self-worship of self-interest. Whirling dervish of the market, self, friends, and family, body and soul, loves, hopes, and faith, all are sacrificed to seeing how many "turns" he can make before he drops dead. Trade began, Sir Henry Sumner Maine tells us, not within the family or community, but without. Its first appearances are on the neutral borderland between hostile tribes. There, in times of peace, they meet to trade, and think it no sin that "the buyer must beware," since the buyer is an enemy. Trade has spread thence, carrying with itself into family and state the poison of enmity. From the fatherhood of the old patriarchal life, where father and brother sold each other nothing, the world has chaffered along to the anarchy of a "free" trade which sells everything. One thing after another has passed out from under the regime of brotherhood and passed in under that of bargainhood.

The ground we move on, the bodies we work with, and the necessaries we live by are all being "exchanged," by "rules fetched with cupidity from heartless schools," into the ownership of the Jacobs of mankind. By these rules the cunning are the good, and the weak and the tender the bad, and the good are to have all the goods and the weak are to have nothing. These rules give one the power to supply or deny work to thousands, and to use the starvation terms of the men he disemploys as the measure of the cost of subsistence of all workmen. This must be near the end. The very churches have become mercantilized, and are markets in which "prophets" are paid fancy prices—"always called of God," as Milton said, "but always to a greater benefice"—and worshipers buy and sell knee-room.

Conceptions of duty take on a correspondingly unnatural complexion. The main exhortations the world gives beginners are how to "get on"—the getting on so ardently inculcated being to get, like the old man of the sea, on somebody's back. "If war fails you in the country where you are, you must go where there is war," said one of the successful men of the fourteenth century to a young knight who asked him for the laws of life. "I shall be perfectly satisfied with you," I heard one of the great business geniuses of America say to his son, "if you will only always go to bed at night worth more than when you got up in the morning." The system grows, as all systems do, more complicated, and gets further away from its first purposes of barter of real things and services. It goes more under the hands of men of apt selfishness, who push it further away from general comprehension and the general good. Tariffs, currencies, finances, freight-rate sheets, the laws, become instruments of privilege, and just in proportion become puzzles no people can decipher. "I have a right to buy my labor where I can buy it cheapest"—beginning as a protest against the selfish exclusions of antiquated trade guilds outgrown by the new times—has at last come to mean, "I have a right to do anything to cheapen the labor I want to buy, even to destroying the family life of the people." . . .

If our civilization is destroyed, as Macaulay predicted, it will not be by his barbarians from below. Our barbarians come from above. Our great money-makers have sprung in one generation into seats of power kings do not know. The forces and the wealth are new, and have been the opportunity of new men. Without restraints of culture, experience, the pride, or even the inherited caution of class or rank, these men, intoxicated, think they are the wave instead of the float, and that they have created the business which has created them. To them science is but a never-ending repertoire of investments stored up by nature for the syndicates, government but a fountain of franchises, the nations but customers in squads, and a million the unit of a new arithmetic of wealth written for them. They claim a power without control, exercised through forms which make it secret, anonymous, and perpetual. The possibilities of its gratification have been widening before them without interruption since they began, and even at a thousand millions they will feel no satiation and will see no place to stop. They are gluttons of luxury and power, rough, unsocialized, believing that mankind must be kept terrorized. Powers of pity die out of them, because they work through agents and die in their agents, because what they do is not for themselves. . . .

By their windfall of new power they have been forced into the position of public enemies. Its new forms make them seem not to be within the jurisdiction of the social restraints which many ages of suffering have taught us to bind about the old powers of man over man. A fury of rule or ruin has always in the history of human affairs been a characteristic of the "strong men" whose fate it is to be in at the death of an expiring principle. The leaders who, two hundred years ago, would have been crazy with conquest, today are crazy with competition. . . .

Poor thinking means poor doing. In casting about for the cause of our industrial evils, public opinion has successively found it in "competition," "combination," the "corporations," "conspiracies," "trusts." But competition has ended in combination, and our new wealth takes as it chooses the form of corporation or trust, or corporation again, and with every change grows greater and worse. Under these kaleidoscopic masks we begin at last to see progressing to its terminus a steady consolidation, the end of which is one-man power. The conspiracy ends in one, and one cannot conspire with himself. When this solidification of many into one has been reached, we shall be at last face to face with the naked truth that it is not only the form but the fact of arbitrary power, of control without consent, of rule without representation that concerns us.

Business motived by the self-interest of the individual runs into monopoly at every point it touches the social life—land monopoly, transportation monopoly, trade monopoly, political monopoly in all its forms, from contraction of the currency to corruption in office. The society in which in half a lifetime a man without a penny can become a hundred times a millionaire is as overripe, industrially, as was, politically, the Rome in which the most popular bully could lift himself from the ranks of the legion onto the throne of the Caesars. Our rising issue is with business. Monopoly is business at the end of its journey. It has got there. The irrepressible conflict is now as distinctly with business as the issue so lately met was with slavery. Slavery went first only because it was the cruder form of business. . . .

It is an adjudicated fact of the business and social life of America that to receive the profits of crime and cherish the agents who commit it does not disqualify for fellowship in the most "solid" circles—financial, commercial, religious, or social. It illustrates what Ruskin calls the "morbid" character of modern business that the history of its most brilliant episodes must be studied in the vestibules of the penitentiary. The riches of the combinations are the winnings of a policy which, we have seen, has certain constant features. Property to the extent of uncounted millions has been changed from the possession of the many who owned it to the few who hold it:

1. Without the knowledge of the real owners.
2. Without their consent.
3. With no compensation to them for the value taken.
4. By falsehood, often under oath.
5. In violation of the law.

Our civilization is built on competition, and competition evolves into crime—to so acute an infatuation has the lunacy of self-interest carried our dominant opinion. We are hurried far beyond the point of not listening to the new conscience which, pioneering in moral exploration, declares that conduct we think right because called "trade" is really lying, stealing, murder. "The definite result," Ruskin preaches, "of all our modern haste to be rich is assuredly and constantly the murder of a certain number of persons by our hands every year." To be unawakened by this new voice is bad enough, but we shut our ears even against the old conscience. . . .

Our system, so fair in its theory and so fertile in its happiness and prosperity in its first century, is now, following the fate of systems, becoming artificial, technical, corrupt; and, as always happens in human institutions, after noon, power is stealing from the many to the few. Believing wealth to be good, the people believed the wealthy to be good. But, again in history, power has intoxicated and hardened its possessors, and Pharaohs are bred in counting rooms as they were in palaces. Their furniture must be banished to the world garret, where lie the outworn trappings of the guilds and slavery and other old lumber of human institutions.

HOW A WALL STREET FINANCIER BECAME A PARK BENCH STATESMAN

⤙◈⤚

BERNARD BARUCH

[Bernard M. Baruch, *Baruch—My Own Story*, Henry Holt and Co., New York, copyright © 1957 by Bernard Baruch, pp. 305-316. Reprinted by permission of Holt, Rinehart and Winston.]

Bernard Baruch started out to be a Wall Street operator, and succeeded handsomely.* But he wasn't quite satisfied; and when government called him during the emergency of World War I, he gladly responded. This account of his experiences at that time is doubly interesting because it illustrates the new trend for business leaders to serve government when needed, and because it suggests that some of the methods and approaches of private business administration can be applied to large-scale government problems—government, of course, having now become the largest business in the world. Baruch's subsequent belief in the New Deal is clearly indicated in the last paragraph.

This is how Baruch got his start at being an adviser to various Presidents, who came from the White House to consult with him as he sat on a bench in the park.

◆

SOME MEN AND WOMEN START OUT EARLY in life knowing what they want to be, and their lives become tales of how they made their ambitions come true. That, plainly, has not been true of my career. In my personal ambitions I have been constantly beset by conflicting desires. The turns my life took have been determined as much as anything by the rush of events.

Although I didn't realize it at the time, when I first came onto the Wall Street scene, it was at the end of one era in our country's history and at the beginning of a new one. The dominant financial figures of the day—Morgan, Harriman, Ryan, Hill, Duke, Rockefeller—were at the summit of their power and prestige.

Watching them and hearing of their exploits, I thought to myself, "If they can do it, why can't I?" I tried my best to emulate them, particularly Edward Harriman, who seemed to me to be the epitome of all that was dashing. The son of a minister, he had started from scratch, as I had. He bet on horses, races, prizefights, and elections—things I also liked to do.

---

* See his piece in Volume II.

In studying railroads, I had been excited by how he had taken over the Union Pacific, when it was not much more than two streaks of rust, and had transformed it into one of the finest railroads in America. My favorite Harriman story is of the time James Stillman, of the National City Bank, asked him what he most liked to do. "It's to be told that something can't be done," Harriman replied, "and jump into it with both feet and do it."

But I never was able to become a second Harriman. Perhaps I just wasn't the man. However, I think that the conditions which made possible the "robber barons," or "Lords of Creation," as they have been termed by some writers, were slipping away. That Fourth of July in 1898 when I took advantage of the imminent end of the Spanish-American War may have been more symbolic than I was aware of. For the years in which the United States emerged as a world power also climaxed the era of unrestrained individualism in American finance.

After the turn of the century, for one thing, the financial arena became too huge to be dominated by any one man or even group of men. If in 1907 a Morgan still could stem a panic, when the 1929 flood broke loose no one man could hold it back.

This change could be seen in the stock market itself. In 1898 something like 60 per cent of the securities listed on the Big Board were of railroads. This, of course, reflected the fact that the main business of America in the period after the Civil War was the physical spanning and conquest of the continent. By 1914 railroads represented less than 40 per cent of the Stock Exchange's listings, by 1925 about 17 per cent, and by 1957 only 13 per cent.

Up to World War I, almost the only financing of foreign governments done in this country had been for Britain during the Boer War and for Japan in connection with the Russo-Japanese War. Today, of course, the United States is the most important single center of foreign financing.

Another factor in the change in eras was the change in generations. Morgan and Rockefeller were more than thirty years older than I; Harriman was twenty-two years my senior, and Ryan nineteen years older. My generation was less satisfied with mere money-making. In my own case, of course, I had the example of my father constantly before me, to disturb my mind with the question, "Now that you have money, what are you going to do with it?"

But the times were also awakening a sense of social responsibility in the whole country. The titans who had made vast fortunes had begun to give their money away—something they often found more difficult to do wisely than to make it. More important were the many social changes and currents of feeling which found expression in the progressive ideas of Theodore Roosevelt and Woodrow Wilson.

As I have written, I was slow to acquire a political philosophy. My first presidential ballot was cast in 1892 for Grover Cleveland. In 1896 I was so mixed up in my thinking that I can't remember for whom I voted. I went to hear William Jennings Bryan when he came to New York and was carried away by his oratory, but when I left Madison Square Garden, the farther away I got from his voice, the more its effect wore off. Everyone I knew was against him.

I had almost made up my mind to vote for McKinley when my great-uncle Fischel Cohen, who had been on General Beauregard's staff, began talking of the Lost Cause and Reconstruction. He told me that my arm would surely wither if I marked a Republican ballot. I probably voted for John M. Palmer, the gold Democrat, whom Father was for.

When Theodore Roosevelt ran, however, I voted for him because he was against the "plunderbund." I remember how restless and discontented I often felt at the end of the day. Looking out over Wall Street and Trinity churchyard from my office window, I found myself thinking of Gray's "Elegy" and wondering whether I should not have been a doctor.

One frequent late-afternoon visitor in those days was Garet Garrett, then with the New York *Evening Post* and later to become an editor of the New York *Tribune* and the *Saturday Evening Post*. He would come in after the Exchange had closed and listen to me think aloud. When he got up to leave, he would say, "I keep telling you, B. M., you don't belong in Wall Street; you should be in Washington."

But the real turning point in my thinking—and I believe in the thinking of American businessmen generally—was World War I. The war forced a shelving of the old laissez faire tradition and thrust the government into a wholly new role. What was done in those war years was never to be completely forgotten. Afterward, whenever an emergency arose, whether it was a domestic crisis like the great depression or a Second World War, the country turned back to the pattern of action by the government which had first been developed during World War I.

I, of course, was one of the human instruments through which this revolution in national thinking and in the role of government was registered. It was not that I was particularly farsighted. When World War I broke out I certainly was no global thinker. Military strategy meant little or nothing to me; nor did I have any comprehension of what needed to be done to mobilize a nation's economy for a total war.

But as the war swept on, I did begin to think of what would have to be done if the United States was drawn into the conflict. The very first time I visited the White House was when Secretary of the Treasury William G. McAdoo arranged for me to explain to President Wilson a plan I had drawn up for mobilizing our economic resources for national defense.

When the Advisory Commission of the Council of National Defense was set up, I was made a member and was given the responsibility for seeing that the raw materials would be available for our preparedness program. Since raw materials enter into the manufacture of everything, I found myself concerned with every part of the economy. I quickly learned that the tasks given me could not be accomplished by business-as-usual methods.

A wholly new approach was needed, one which envisioned every factory and all raw materials, every business leader and worker as part of one gigantic industrial army.

What I learned I somehow had to pass on to other businessmen. It was no easy job. At some of our earlier meetings, whenever a labor leader spoke up he would be interrupted by the businessmen on the commission. I often found myself saying, "Please let Mr. Gompers finish. I would like to hear what he has to say."

In this new industrial army, men who were generals of finance or business often had to play the role of lieutenants and sergeants. Many of our business leaders had grown accustomed to thinking of themselves as virtually laws unto themselves, brooking no interference by the government or anyone else with how they ran their factories or plants. It was not easy to explain to such men why they had to shed their fiercely individualistic ways and take orders from the government or cooperate with their competitors.

I did not always succeed in making these business leaders adopt the larger view of the national interest. There was Henry Ford, for example. I went to see him at his hotel in Washington to explain why, since the steel used for automobiles was needed for war, the production of civilian cars would have to be curtailed.

Ford insisted that he could make cars and munitions at the same time. "Just tell me what you want and I'll make it," he declared.

Although I tried to explain why there just wasn't enough steel for both the war and civilian cars, he remained unconvinced.

But others, almost as intense in their individualism, did see the larger picture. One day I invited James B. Duke to lunch to discuss our plans for the tobacco industry. Duke protested that what we were doing was all wrong. I called in the man in charge of the tobacco section and said, "Mr. Duke is running things now." When Duke demurred I said, "You don't like how we're doing things. Show us what we should do. This is the problem we must meet."

Duke made some valuable suggestions. Although he was opposed to Wilson politically, he became one of my strongest supporters.

In the main, that was my approach to all of the mobilization problems which we faced. With the fighting going on there was not time enough to convert every businessman. But in every industry I could always find the man or men who could be relied on to tell us how best to meet our problem.

I already have related how Dan Guggenheim helped us cut the prevailing price of copper by more than one half. Later we were faced with the necessity of deciding what the government should pay for steel plates used in building ships. I went to H. C. Frick. He received me in his famous library. I asked him what price the government should pay.

"That's not a fair question to ask me," Frick protested. "I'm chairman of the Finance Committee of U. S. Steel."

"I haven't come to you as a steel man," I told him, "I've come to you as a patriotic citizen."

"Two and a half cents a pound," Frick snapped back.

At the time the spokesmen for some of the steel companies were asking four and a quarter cents for plates sold to government shipbuilders, while the black market price was eighteen and a half cents.

Many other businessmen—Andrew Mellon, Price McKinney, a Cleveland steel man, Clinton H. Crane of St. Joseph Lead Company, Alfred C. Bedford of Standard Oil of New Jersey, Edgar Palmer of New Jersey Zinc, and others too numerous to be cited here—responded in the same fashion as did Frick and Guggenheim.

If it had not been for my years in Wall Street I doubt that I would have been able to carry through my wartime duties. My financial dealings had given me an intimate knowledge of the personal character of many of our business leaders. I knew who would respond to a straightforward appeal to patriotism. With others I knew that, if we were to get the necessary cooperation, we would have to show them that the government was stronger than any individual.

When such a showdown came, I found myself fortunate in having made my money as a lone operator in Wall Street. Had my fortune rested on some specific industrial interest, I might have been subjected to counterpressures from business elements I was antagonizing. When the issue of setting steel prices came up, one member of our price-fixing committee remarked that the big steel companies could ruin a company he was interested in by taking away its business.

I told him that I would step out in front on the issue, explaining, "They can't hurt me."

There were numerous other ways in which my Wall Street experiences stood me well. In fact, I constantly was being surprised to find how many of the mobilization problems lent themselves to much the same approach I had used in my speculative activities.

I quickly learned, for example, that many shortages were really psychological. Frightened that they might not get what they needed, manufacturers would overbuy. Or thinking that prices were bound to skyrocket, suppliers would hold back their materials.

In the stock market I had learned how quickly a bull market could reverse itself once the continuity of thought behind the market trend was broken. In reducing the prices of key war materials as soon as we entered the war, one of my objectives was to break the prevailing expectation that prices were bound to rise and rise and rise.

Also, in Wall Street I had learned that planning a successful financial operation was much like planning a military operation. Before going into action, one had to know both the strengths and weaknesses of the opposing forces.

Often we gained the cooperation of those who were reluctant by applying pressure on their weak points. At home we used the threat of commandeering or cutting off a manufacturer's fuel or railroad transportation. With foreign countries the measures we used were different, but the principle was the same.

Once during the war, for example, the British representatives took the position that they could not control the price of jute in Calcutta because India was a separate government. I went to Secretary McAdoo and asked him to withhold further shipments of silver which were needed to stabilize India's currency. We had sent a mission to London, headed by Leland Summers, and he told the British officials there that we would hold to this position even if the Bombay and Calcutta exchanges had to be closed. The British soon found a way to control the price of jute.

Probably the most critical single problem of supply we faced in the whole war was with nitrates. The demand for nitrates, which were needed for both fertilizer and explosives, exceeded any possible production. This shortage remained acute until the very end of the war. Each time a tramp steamer carrying nitrates was sunk, it was a grievous blow.

When the United States declared war, nitrate prices jumped almost overnight by a third and then doubled within three weeks. This price rise touched off an even wilder scramble for nitrates, with speculators trying to corner much of the available nitrates to hold off the market so as to force prices even higher.

About this time President Wilson called me in and made me solely responsible for solving the problem. I racked my brain for some way out—without success. A committee of munitions manufacturers came to Washington to ask how they were going to get the nitrates which were needed to fill their contracts. I assured them the nitrates would be supplied.

When the meeting broke up, Charles MacDowell, who headed our chemical division, asked me, "Chief, what are you going to do to make good on that promise?"

"I don't know, Mac," I confessed. "But I couldn't let them go out of here thinking the government couldn't do anything."

The next few days were among the most trying I ever have experienced. I couldn't sleep or eat. Even when I drank a glass of water my throat choked up. I believe I came as close to giving way to panic as I ever have been in my life. While dressing one morning I looked at my pale, drawn face in the mirror, and said aloud, "Why, you coward. Pull yourself together and act like a man."

What happened next made me wonder whether there wasn't some special Providence looking after me. I forced myself to eat breakfast and went down to my office. I had not been there long when a Naval Intelligence officer came in with several intercepted cables which revealed that the Chilean government had its gold reserve in Germany and had been trying in vain to get the German government to release this gold reserve.

At last I had something to work on. A few days later the Chilean ambassador came in. He began complaining about the troubles his country was experiencing because of various shortages and difficulties in controlling inflation. I knew that there was in Chile something like 200,000 tons of nitrates which Germans owned but had been unable to move out of the country. If Chile would seize these German-owned nitrates, I proposed to the ambassador, I would buy it all at four and a quarter cents a pound and pay for it in gold six months after the treaty of peace was signed.

As soon as the Chilean ambassador left my office, I arranged to have the necessary ships sent down to Chile so no time would be lost in getting possession of the nitrates.

Curiously, some State Department officials objected to the deal on the ground that it violated the Trading with the Enemy Act. I was astonished by their objection. "You mean to say," I demanded, "that I can't buy German nitrates to shoot the Germans with?"

The issue was taken to President Wilson, who supported my action. The upshot of the whole affair was a satisfactory arrangement which got us desperately needed nitrates and which helped the Chilean government overcome its domestic difficulties. Yet the agreement would not have been possible if we had not known Chile's need and used that as a basis for our bargaining.

Accommodation to mutual needs remains the best basis for all agreements between nations. Although this may seem like an obvious truth, the record since the end of World War II shows that we have not yet learned how to apply this truth in our dealings with our allies. We have relied too heavily on the formal wording of treaties and have neglected to do what needs to be done to strengthen the structure of mutual interests which alone can support an enduring alliance.

One cannot buy the friendship of other nations. "Friends" acquired in such a way are quick to take offense over anything. Where there is a true basis of mutual interest, however, nations will make excuses for one another's failings and overlook one another's shortcomings.

Along with common interest, scrupulous fairness should be observed in dealing with allies. The golden rule could be paraphrased and applied to alliances—ask nothing of others that you are not prepared to do yourself.

It was Woodrow Wilson who first enunciated this principle on behalf of the United States. He insisted that whatever we bought for our own war effort should be made available to our allies at the same price that we had paid.

During a dispute over this very principle I first came to sense in Winston Churchill the qualities of greatness that were to make him so inspiring a war leader. We had proposed that England pay the same price as we did for anything bought in the United States, while Americans should pay the same price as did England for anything purchased within the Empire. Some of Britain's merchant princes opposed this arrangement. When the matter was brought up before Churchill, then Minister of Munitions, he agreed that it was the only fair way for allies to treat one another.

This identical principle was followed in allocating the nitrates being bought from Chile. I rejected all suggestions that we use our control of these nitrates for American commercial advantage. Instead we agreed to allocate them equitably among all the Allies through an International Nitrate Executive. This committee was to prove the forerunner of the Combined Boards that were used to allocate scarce supplies among the allies in World War II.

I left the naming of the chairman of this International Nitrate Executive to Churchill. Afterward he often jokingly referred to the time I made him "Nitrate King of the world."

In the more than forty years that we have been friends, I have never known Churchill to make a mean or ignoble proposal in his relations with the United States. Ever quick to defend Britain's interest, he has always accompanied it with a warm appreciation of American interests. During World War II, when the United States was faced with the need to divert supplies from Britain, I heard him protest flatly to Franklin Roosevelt, "My people are living at the limit of austerity now and their food supplies cannot be cut." I have also heard him protest as warmly against slurs made by other Englishmen upon this country and its leaders.

At one dinner he gave for me in London, a number of Tories

were present who disliked Franklin Roosevelt and the New Deal. One gentleman decided to amuse the company by asking me the riddle, why were Roosevelt and Columbus alike? His answer was that, like Columbus, Roosevelt did not know where he was going or where he was when he got there, or where he had been when he got back.

Rising, I replied, "Perhaps it is true that Roosevelt and Columbus were alike, since both explored new frontiers and new horizons and both brought a new world into existence to redress the troubles of the old world." Churchill banged the table in approval, crying, "Hear, hear!"

MEN AGAINST SILVER, AND SILVER AGAINST THE COUNTRY

JOHN F. KENNEDY

[Lucius Lamar, " 'Today I must be true or false . . .' Lucius Quintus Cincinnatus Lamar," in John F. Kennedy, *Profiles in Courage*, Harper & Brothers, New York, copyright © 1955, 1956 by John F. Kennedy, pp. 165–171 (abridged). Reprinted by permission of Harper & Brothers.]

One of the issues that beset government in the latter part of the nineteenth century was that of silver—whether silver should be a basis of currency or, down underneath, whether the country should deliberately enter on a course of inflation. It was almost as bitter an issue as slavery—which also had an economic motive.

We include the following selection for three reasons. One, it is an account of how government approached an important economic problem. Two, it describes the courageous action of a Senator, Lucius Lamar, who had to decide between the desires of his immediate constituents and what he considered to be the industrial welfare of the country as a whole; he took the risk of almost certainly ruining his political career and losing his friends—but, the sequel is, he actually weathered the storm and went on to become Secretary of the Interior in 1885 and a Justice of the Supreme Court in 1887. Three, it is told by John F. Kennedy, thirty-fifth President of the United States. It is taken from his book, *Profiles in Courage*, published in 1955.

———————◆———————

[IN] 1877, a new movement was sweeping the South and West, a movement which would plague the political parties of the nation for a generation to come—"free silver." The Moses of the silver forces,

William Jennings Bryan, had not yet appeared on the scene; but "Silver Dick" Bland, the Democratic Representative from Missouri, was leading the way with his bill for the free coinage of all silver brought to the Mint. Inasmuch as a tremendous spurt in the production of the western silver mines had caused its value in relation to gold to shrink considerably, the single purpose of the silver forces was clear, simple and appealing—easy, inflationary money.

It was a tremendously popular cause in Mississippi. The panic of 1873 had engulfed the nation into the most terrible depression it had ever suffered, and the already impoverished states of the South were particularly hard hit. Businesses failed by the thousands, unemployment increased and wages were reduced. Farm prices dropped rapidly from their high wartime levels and the farmers of Mississippi—desperate for cash—vowed support of any bill which would raise the price of their commodities, lower the value of their debts, and increase the availability of money. The South foresaw itself in a state of permanent indebtedness to the financial institutions of the East unless easy money could be made available to pay its heavy debts. . . .

Vachel Lindsay's poem expressed clearly the helplessness and bitterness with which the South and West watched the steadily increasing financial domination of the East:

> And all these in their helpless days
> By the dour East oppressed,
> Mean paternalism
> Making their mistakes for them,
> Crucifying half the West,
> Till the whole Atlantic coast
> Seemed a giant spiders' nest.

Silver suddenly acquired a political appeal as the poor man's friend—in contrast to gold, the rich man's money; silver was the money of the prairies and small towns, unlike gold, the money of Wall Street. Silver was going to provide an easy solution to everyone's problems—falling farm prices, high interest rates, heavy debts and all the rest. Although the Democratic party since the days of Jackson and Benton had been the party of hard money, it rushed to exploit this new and popular issue—and it was naturally assumed that the freshman Democratic Senator from poverty-stricken Mississippi would enthusiastically join the fight.

But Lamar, the learned scholar and professor, approached the issue somewhat differently than his colleagues. Paying but little heed to the demands of his constituents, he exhausted all available treatises on both sides of the controversy. His study convinced him—possibly wrongly—that the only sound position was in support of sound money. The payment of our government's debts—even to the "bloated bondholders" of Wall Street—in a debased, inflated currency, as the Bland Bill encouraged and the accompanying Matthews Resolution specifically provided, was an ethical wrong and a practical mistake, he felt, certain to embarrass our standing in the eyes of the world, and promoted not as a permanent financial program but as a spurious relief bill to alleviate the nation's economic distress.

On January 24, 1878, in a courageous and learned address— his first major speech on the Senate floor—Lamar rejected the pleas of Mississippi voters and assailed elaborate rationalizations behind the two silver measures as artificial and exaggerated. And the following day he voted "No" on the Matthews Resolution, in opposition to his colleague from Mississippi, a Negro Republican of exceptional talents elected several years earlier by the old "carpet-bag" Legislature.

Praise for Senator Lamar's masterly and statesmanlike analysis of the issue emanated from many parts of the country, but from Mississippi came little but condemnation. On January 30, the State Legislature adopted a memorial omitting all mention of Lamar but—in an obvious and deliberate slap—congratulating and thanking his colleague (to whom the white Democratic legislators normally were bitterly opposed) for voting the opposite way and thus reflecting "the sentiment and will of his constituents." The memorial deeply hurt Lamar, and he was little consoled by a letter from his close friend, the Speaker of the Mississippi House, who termed it "a damned outrage" but explained: "The people are under a pressure of hard times and scarcity of money, and their representatives felt bound to strike at something which might give relief, the how or wherefor very few of them could explain."

But the Legislature was not through. On February 4, a resolution was passed by both houses instructing Lamar to vote for the Bland Silver Bill, and to use his efforts as spokesman for Mississippi to secure its passage.

Lamar was deeply troubled by this action. He knew that the right of binding legislative instructions had firm roots in the South. But writing to his wife about the demands of the Legislature that had appointed him, he confided, "I cannot do it; I had rather quit politics forever." He attempted to explain at length to a friend in the Legislature that he recognized the right of that body to express its opinions upon questions of Federal policy, and the obligation of a Senator to abide by those expressions whenever he was doubtful as to what his course should be. But in this particular case, he insisted, "their wishes are directly in conflict with the convictions of my whole life; and had I voted [on the Matthews Resolution] as directed, I should have cast my first vote against my conscience."

If [a Senator] allows himself to be governed by the opinions of his friends at home, however devoted he may be to them or they to him, he throws away all the rich results of a previous preparation and study, and simply becomes a commonplace exponent of those popular sentiments which may change in a few days. . . . Such a course will dwarf any man's statesmanship and his vote would be simply considered as an echo of current opinion, not the result of mature deliberations.

Moreover, consistent with the courageous philosophy that had governed his return to public life, Lamar was determined not to back down merely because his section was contrary minded. He would not purchase the respect of the North for himself and his section by a calculated and cringing course; but having decided, on the merits, that the bill was wrong, he was anxious to demonstrate to the nation that statesmanship was not dead in the South nor was the South desirous of repudiating national obligations and honor. He felt that on this issue it was of particular importance that the South should not follow a narrow sectional course of action. For years it had been argued that Southern Democrats would seek to abrogate the obligations that the United States government had incurred during the Civil War and for which the South felt no responsibility. Lamar alone among the Southern Democrats opposed the "free silver" movement, except for Senator Ben Hill of Georgia, who said that while he had done his best during the war to make the Union bondholder who purchased a dollar bond at 60 cents lose the 60 cents he had given, he was now for repaying him the dollar he was promised.

One week later, the Bland Silver Bill came before the Senate for a final vote. As the debate neared its end, Senator Lamar rose unexpectedly to his feet. No notes were in his hand, for he was one of the most brilliant extemporaneous speakers ever to sit in the Senate. ("The pen is an extinguisher upon my mind," he said, "and a torture to my nerves.") Instead he held an official document which bore the great seal of the State of Mississippi, and this he dispatched by page to the desk. With apologies to his colleagues, Senator Lamar explained that, although he had already expressed his views on the Silver Bill, he had "one other duty to perform; a very painful one, but one which is nonetheless clear." He then asked that the resolutions which he had sent to the desk be read.

The Senate was first astonished and then attentively silent as the Clerk droned the express will of the Mississippi Legislature that its

Senators vote for the Bland Silver Bill. As the Clerk completed the instructions, all eyes turned toward Lamar, no one certain what to expect. As the reporter for the Washington *Capitol* described it: "Remembering the embarrasing position of this gentleman with respect to the pending bill, every Senator immediately gave his attention, and the Chamber became as silent as the tomb." A massive but lonely figure on the Senate floor, Lucius Lamar spoke in a quiet yet powerful voice, a voice which "grew tremulous with emotion, as his body fairly shook with agitation":

MR. PRESIDENT: Between these resolutions and my convictions there is a great gulf. I cannot pass it. . . . Upon the youth of my state whom it has been my privilege to assist in education I have always endeavored to impress the belief that truth was better than falsehood, honesty better than policy, courage better than cowardice. Today my lessons confront me. Today I must be true or false, honest or cunning, faithful or unfaithful to my people. Even in this hour of their legislative displeasure and disapprobation, I cannot vote as these resolutions direct.

My reasons for my vote shall be given to my people. Then it will be for them to determine if adherence to my honest convictions has disqualified me from representing them; whether a difference of opinion upon a difficult and complicated subject to which I have given patient, long-continued, conscientious study, to which I have brought entire honesty and singleness of purpose, and upon which I have spent whatever ability God has given me, is now to separate us; . . . but be their present decision what it may, I know that the time is not far distant when they will recognize my action today as wise and just; and, armed with honest convictions of my duty, I shall calmly await the results, believing in the utterance of a great American that "truth is omnipotent, and public justice certain."

TWILIGHT OF THE GIANTS, AND DAWN OF INDIVIDUALS

FRANKLIN D. ROOSEVELT

[Franklin D. Roosevelt, "Reappraisal of Values," in *Looking Forward*, The John Day Co., New York, 1933, pp. 17–36 (abridged).]

"The day of the great promoter or the financial titan, to whom we granted everything if only he would build or develop, is over." So proclaimed President Franklin D. Roosevelt in his book *Looking Forward* (1933). In a chapter on "Reappraisal of Values," he goes back into history to show why ambition and ruthlessness were necessary for stabilizing conditions in Europe and then for developing our pioneer country—but that those days have now passed, and government must step in to protect the individual citizen, whom elsewhere he called "the forgotten man," against the power of big business.

Notice how temperately he makes his points, in contrast to the early days of his administration.* He has established his position, and can afford to be more lenient; or perhaps it would be fairer to say that now he realizes the continuing importance of industry as a dynamic force, and seeks only to regulate its excesses, its abuses of power. Also, he explicitly recognizes his debt to the other great President Roosevelt, and recalls Teddy's famous phrase, "the malefactors of great wealth." †

◆

THE ISSUE OF GOVERNMENT has always been whether individual men and women will have to serve some system of government or economics or whether a system of government and economics exists to serve individual men and women.

This question has persistently dominated the discussions of government for many generations. On questions relating to these things men have differed, and . . . [in the future] it is probable that honest men will continue to differ.

The final word belongs to no man; yet we can still believe in change and progress. Democracy, as Meredith Nicholson has called it, is a quest, a never-ending seeking for these things and striving for them. There are many roads to follow. If we take their course we find there are only two general directions in which they lead. The first is toward government for the benefit of the few, the second is toward government for the benefit of the many.

The growth of the national governments of Europe was a struggle for the development of a centralized force in the nation, strong enough to impose peace upon ruling barons. In many instances the victory of the central government, the creation of a strong central government, was a haven of refuge to the individual. The people preferred the great master far away to the exploitation and cruelty of the smaller master near at hand.

But the creators of national government were perforce ruthless men. They were often cruel in their methods, though they did strive steadily toward something that society needed and very much wanted —a strong central state, able to keep the peace, to stamp out civil war, to put the unruly nobleman in his place, and to permit the bulk of individuals to live safely.

The man of ruthless force had his place in developing a pioneer country, just as he did in fixing the power of the central government

---
* For his inaugural address, see Volume III.
† For Theodore Roosevelt, see Volume III.

in the development of the nations. Society paid him well for his services toward its development. When the development among the nations of Europe, however, had been completed, ambition and ruthlessness, having served its term, tended to overstep the mark. There now came a growing feeling that government was conducted for the benefit of the few who thrived unduly at the expense of all. The people sought a balancing, a limiting force. Gradually there came through town councils, trade guilds, national parliaments, by constitutions and popular participation and control, limitations on arbitrary power. Another factor that tended to limit the power of those who ruled was the rise of the ethical conception that a ruler bore a responsibility for the welfare of his subjects. The American colonies were born during this struggle. The American Revolution was a turning point in it. After the Revolution the struggle continued and shaped itself into the public life of this country.

There were those who, because they had seen the confusion which attended the years of war for American independence, surrendered to the belief that popular government was essentially dangerous and essentially unworkable. These thinkers were, generally, honest and we cannot deny that their experience had warranted some measure of fear.

The most brilliant, honest and able exponent of this point of view was Hamilton. He was too impatient of slow-moving methods. Fundamentally, he believed that the safety of the republic lay in the autocratic strength of its government, that the destiny of individuals was to serve that government and that a great and strong group of central institutions, guided by a small group of able and public-spirited citizens, could best direct all government.

But Jefferson, in the summer of 1776, after drafting the Declaration of Independence, turned his mind to the same problem and took a different view. He did not deceive himself with outward forms. Government with him was a means to an end, not an end in itself; it might be either a refuge and a help or a threat and a danger, depending on the circumstances. We find him carefully analyzing the society for which he was to organize a government:

"We have no paupers—the great mass of our population is of laborers, our rich who cannot live without labor, either manual or professional, being few and of moderate wealth. Most of the laboring class possess property, cultivate their own lands, have families and from the demands for their labor are enabled to extract from the rich and the competent such prices as enable them to feed abundantly, clothe above mere decency, to labor moderately and raise their families."

These people, he considered, had two sets of rights, those of "personal competency" and those involved in acquiring and possessing property. By "personal competency" he meant the right of free thinking, freedom of forming and expressing opinions, and freedom of personal living, each man according to his own lights.

To insure the first set of rights a government must so order its functions as not to interfere with the individual. But even Jefferson realized that the exercise of the property rights must so interfere with the rights of the individual that the government, without whose assistance the property rights could not exist, must intervene, not to destroy individualism but to protect it.

We are familiar with the great political duel which followed; and how Hamilton and his friends, building toward a dominant, centralized power, were at length defeated in the great election of 1800 by Jefferson's party. Out of that duel came the two parties, Republican and Democratic, as we know them today.

So began, in American political life, the new day, the day of the individual against the system, the day in which individualism was made the great watchword in American life. The happiest of economic conditions made that day long and splendid. On the western frontier land was substantially free. No one who did not shirk the task of earning a living was entirely without opportunity to do so. Depressions could, and did, come and go; but they could not alter the fundamental fact that most of the people lived partly by selling their labor and partly by extracting their livelihood from the soil, so that starvation and dislocation was practically impossible. At the very worst there was always the possibility of climbing into a covered wagon and moving west, where the untilled prairies afforded a haven for men to whom the East did not provide a place.

So great were our natural resources that we could offer this relief not only to our own people but to the distressed of all the world. We could invite immigration from Europe and welcome it with open arms.

When a depression came a new section of land was opened in the West. This became our tradition. So even our temporary misfortune served our manifest destiny.

But a new force was released and a new dream created in the middle of the nineteenth century. The force was what is called the industrial revolution, the advance of steam and machinery and the rise of the forerunners of the modern industrial plant. The dream was that of an economic machine, able to raise the standard of living for everyone; to bring luxury within the reach of the humblest; to annihilate distance by steam power and later by electricity, and to release everyone from the drudgery of the heaviest manual toil.

It was to be expected that the force and the dream would necessarily affect government. Heretofore, government had merely been called upon to produce conditions within which people could live happily, labor peacefully and rest secure. Now it was called upon to aid in the consummation of this new dream. There was, however, a shadow over it. To make the dream real required use of the talents of men of tremendous will and tremendous ambition, since in no other way could the problems of financing and engineering and new development be met.

So manifest were the advantages of the machine age, however, that the United States fearlessly, cheerfully and, I think, rightly accepted the bitter with the sweet. It was thought that no price was too high for the advantages which we could draw from a finished industrial system.

The history of the last half century is accordingly in large measure a history of financial titans, whose methods were not scrutinized with too much care and who were honored in proportion as they produced the results, irrespective of the means they used. The financiers who pushed the railroads to the Pacific, for example, were always ruthless, often wasteful and frequently corrupt, but they did build railroads and we have them today. It has been estimated that the American investor paid for the American railway system more than three times over in the process, but despite this fact the net advantage was to the United States.

As long as we had free land, as long as population was growing by leaps and bounds, as long as our industrial plants were insufficient to supply our own needs, society chose to give the ambitious man free play and unlimited reward, provided only that he produced the economic plant so much desired.

During the period of expansion there was equal economic opportunity for all, and the business of government was not to interfere but to assist in the development of industry. This was done at the request of the businessmen themselves. The tariff was originally imposed for the purpose of "fostering our infant industry," a phrase which the older among my readers will remember as a political issue not so long ago.

The railroads were subsidized, sometimes by grants of money, oftener by grants of land. Some of the most valuable oil lands in the United States were granted to assist the financing of the railroad which pushed through the Southwest. A nascent merchant marine was assisted by grants of money or by mail subsidies, so that our steam shipping might ply the seven seas. . . .

We do not want the government in business. But we must realize the implications of the past. For while it has been American doctrine that the government must not go into business in competition with private enterprises, still it has been traditional for business to urgently ask the government to put at private disposal all kinds of government assistance.

The same man who says he does not want to see the government interfere in business—and he means it and has plenty of good reasons for saying so—is the first to go to Washington to ask the government for a prohibitory tariff on his product. When things get just bad enough—as they did in 1930—he will go with equal speed to the United States government and ask for a loan. . . .

Each group has sought protection from the government for its own special interests without realizing that the function of government must be to favor no small group at the expense of its duty to protect the rights of personal freedom and of private property of all its citizens.

In retrospect we can see now that the turn of the tide came with the turn of the century. We were reaching our last frontier then; there was no more free land and our industrial combinations had become great uncontrolled and irresponsible units of power within the state.

Clear-sighted men saw with fear the danger that opportunity would no longer be equal; that the growing corporation, like the feudal baron of old, might threaten the economic freedom of individuals to earn a living. In that hour our antitrust laws were born.

The cry was raised against the great corporations. Theodore Roosevelt, the first great Republican Progressive, fought a presidential campaign on the issues of "trust busting" and talked freely about malefactors of great wealth. If the government had a policy it was rather to turn the clock back, to destroy the large combinations and to return to the time when every man owned his individual small business. This was impossible. Theodore Roosevelt, abandoning his idea of "trust busting," was forced to work out a difference between "good" trusts and "bad" trusts. The Supreme Court set forth the famous "rule of reason" by which it seems to have meant that a concentration of industrial power was permissible if the method by which it got its power and the use it made of that power was reasonable. . . .

Our task now is not discovery or exploitation of natural resources or necessarily of producing more goods. It is the soberer, less dramatic business of administering resources and plants already in hand, of seeking to re-establish foreign markets for our surplus production, of meeting the problem of underconsumption, or adjusting production to consumption, of distributing wealth and products more equitably, of adapting existing economic organization to the service of the people.

Just as in older times the central government was first a haven of refuge and then a threat, so now, in a closer economic system the central and ambitious financial unit is no longer a servant of national desire but a danger. I would draw the parallel one step further. We do not think, because national government became a threat in the eighteenth century, that therefore we should abandon the principle of national government.

Nor today should we abandon the principle of strong economic units called corporations merely because their power is susceptible to easy abuse. In other times we dealt with the problem of an unduly ambitious central government by modifying it gradually into a constitutional democratic government. So today we are modifying and controlling our economic units.

As I see it, the task of government in its relation to business is to assist the development of an economic declaration of rights, an economic constitutional order. This is the common task of statesmen and businessmen. It is the minimum requirement of a more permanently safe order of society. Happily, the times indicate that to create such an order is not only the proper policy of government but it is the only line of safety for our economic structure as well.

We know now that these economic units cannot exist unless prosperity is uniform—that is, unless purchasing power is well distributed throughout every group in the nation. That is why even the most selfish of corporations, for its own interest, would be glad to see wages restored and unemployment aided, and to bring the farmer back to his accustomed level of prosperity, and to assure a permanent safety for both groups. That is why some enlightened industries endeavor to limit the freedom of action of each man and business group within the industry in the common interest of all. That is why businessmen everywhere are asking for a form of organization which will bring the scheme of things into balance, even though it may in some measure qualify the freedom of action of individual units within the business.

I think that everyone who has actually entered the economic struggle—which means everyone who was not born to safe wealth—knows in his own experience and his own life that we now have to apply the earlier concepts of American government to the conditions of today. The Declaration of Independence discusses the problem of government in terms of a contract. Government is a relation of give and take—a contract, perforce, if we would follow the thinking out of which it grew. Under such a contract rulers were accorded power, and the people consented to that power on consideration that they be accorded certain rights. The task of statesmanship has always been the redefinition of these rights in terms of a changing and growing social order. New conditions impose new requirements upon government and those who conduct government.

The terms of the contract are as old as the Republic and as new as the new economic order. Every man has a right to life, and this means that he has also a right to make a comfortable living. He may by sloth or crime decline to exercise that right, but it must not be denied him. Our government, formal and informal, political and economic, owes to every man an avenue to possess himself of sufficient for his needs through his own work. Every man has a right to his own property, which means a right to be assured to the fullest extent attainable, in the safety of his earnings. By no other means can men carry the burdens of those parts of life which in the nature of things afford no change of labor—childhood, sickness, old age. In all thought of property, this right is paramount; all other property rights must yield to it. If, in accordance with this principle, we must restrict the operations of the speculator, the manipulator, even the financier, I believe we must accept the restriction as needful, not to hamper individualism but to protect it. . . .

DEFENDER OF THE FAITH:
ORPHAN ANNIE

JAMES A. KEHL

[James A. Kehl, "Defender of the Faith: Orphan Annie and the Conservative Tradition," the *South Atlantic Quarterly*, spring 1960, vol. LIX, no. 2, pp. 192–203.]

Orphan Annie? Not exactly. But her creator, Harold Gray, *has* been expressing attitudes about business for lo, these many years—since 1924, to be exact. Daddy Warbucks is of course a businessman, the richest synthetic money-maker in the world, but it is not just his actions that express Harold Gray's philosophy; it is also the episodes in which the ageless Annie gets involved. And Gray can cover a wide range of issues.

Here James A. Kehl, professor of history at the University of Pittsburgh, analyzes this interesting phenomenon of American journalism under the title, "Defender of the Faith: Orphan Annie and the Conservative Tradition," in a 1960 article.

FOR MORE THAN A GENERATION the Orphan Annie comic strip has been making daily appearances in many American homes. To a majority of readers the strip is an untrue-to-life saga of a perambulating orphan who has moved from one impelling crisis to another, felling murderers, juvenile delinquents, highwaymen, Communists, and all other such culprits with uninterrupted monotony. To others

Annie is more than this modern Robin Hood with a heart of gold and a wicked left; she is an outlet for the expression of the political and economic philosophy of her creator and legal guardian, Harold Gray.

In order to seek out and chastise the depicted villains, Annie has moved from setting to setting, spreading her partisan doctrines as she goes. She first acquired her desire to see the world with dramatic suddenness in 1924. On that signal occasion our Annie tossed a bowl of steaming mush in the face of Miss Asthma, the mean old woman who operated the orphanage where she was staying. Her immediate reaction after this "demonstration of independence" was to recognize the advantages of travel, so she made a hasty and unauthorized departure from the asylum.

Thus under rather strained circumstances Annie launched her unique career, attended only by Sandy, her inseparable companion, and Methuselah of the dog world. In subsequent years her exploits centered in rural America, and her expressions such as "leapin' lizards," "hot alligator," and "clean as a snowflake's gizzard" won the plaudits of many. At that time she was the same crudely-drawn character she is today—buttoned shoes, circles for eyes, and a shock of unruly hair which on Sundays alternates rather distractingly between a peroxide blond and a burnt orange.

The vagabond orphan is not to blame for this synthetic effect. She had no parental training except the sporadic guidance of financier Oliver Warbucks, better known as "Daddy." This tycoon made many fortunes, but Gray gifted him with an equal facility to lose all that he had accumulated. The alternate booms and busts which marked Daddy's business career were not intended to ridicule his ability to manipulate securities or promote enterprises, but to emphasize and re-emphasize that America still remains a land of boundless opportunity where the "rags to riches" theme, made popular in the late nineteenth century, is still a reality.

Daddy did not become truly adroit at alternately succeeding and failing and Annie did not become a professional interpreter of the complicated problems of economics and politics until the 1932 election of F.D.R. Since that time Annie has not only extolled the virtues of private enterprise and laissez faire democracy, but has also kicked many New Deal measures in their respective backsides. Gray has excused this unladylike conduct on the basis that the American people like to read about the spirit of freedom and independence that characterized their fathers' America. Although this comment implies that these conditions no longer typify our society, Gray has not been consistent on this point. In his pessimistic sequences he definitely adopts this theme, but on his more hopeful days he admits that private enterprise capitalism is still engaged in a life-and-death struggle with the advocates of a powerful Federal government on the one hand and the labor barons on the other.

Since the emergence of industrial America, the problem of bigness has plagued the nation; big business, big government, and big labor have all asserted themselves and won loyal adherents. Over the years, however, public opinion about them has fluctuated, as the American people have attempted to promote their material aspirations while protecting their heritage of freedom. During the last three decades of the nineteenth century the entrepreneurs ranged unchecked through the economy, but then government regulation, restriction, and reform in the Progressive Era temporarily bridled business activity. The advent of World War I and the ensuing years of spotty prosperity suspended the effectiveness of such legislation, only to have the great depression reawaken interest in government controls and usher in the New Deal program which, in turn, gave encouragement to the labor movement.

To many this was all the evidence necessary to demonstrate that big business was caught in a vice between the jaws of big government and big labor. Newspaper editors and columnists who resented this threat to laissez faire capitalism thundered forth on their editorial pages, and among the fruits of their effort was the recruitment of Harold Gray. He quickly recognized that comics could be more than meaningless diversion; they could promote, defend, reform, glorify, and truly serve as misplaced editorials. For every American adult who has a favorite editorial columnist, three have favorite comic strip characters. With this in mind, Gray was determined to put his strip to work.

Since Annie's reading public numbers approximately 75,000,000, her Confuciuslike wisdom has had a better chance of molding public opinion than the daily efforts of many newspaper editorials. This does not mean that Annie's philosophy should be ranked with that of either Herbert Hoover or Franklin D. Roosevelt in explaining our history of the last generation, but neither can we ignore the fact that through the medium of this comic strip the philosophy of one of these men was advanced and that of the other condemned.

Through the benevolent exploits of Warbucks, private enterprise incarnate, Gray sought to preserve the rugged individualist ideal in the dark days of the depression. Bread lines, soup kitchens, and curbstone apple vendors caused many to question the system which had carried Carnegie, Rockefeller, and hundreds of others from obscurity to glittery success. Gray fought to keep this concept alive at a time when many people were coming to demand security in preference to the traditional unlimited opportunities. Although most Americans before the 1929 crash wished to provide more adequately for their security, they preferred to do so without placing curbs on business and capital. The average American believed it was only a matter of time until *his* chance would present itself; then he wanted nothing to interfere with his own schemes to get rich quickly. The harsh reality of the depression forced many to abandon this position and to advocate not only a floor under labor but also a ceiling over capital. They now recognized that even in a land of opportunity for all, labor must remain the backbone of society; only the exceptional worker was destined to duplicate the Horatio Alger feats of a Carnegie or Rockefeller. This reappraisal gave new meaning to security and new support to pensions, compensations, and the right of collective bargaining. The Warbuckses of the old school feared that this change of thought would destroy the incentive to pioneer new projects and over the last twenty-five years have repeatedly expressed their alarm.

During one of his more depressed moods Warbucks lamented that the spacious home of a friend, an entrepreneur, more closely resembled a monument than a palace; and rugged individualist Annie was quite willing to assume the role of straight man in order to aid his presentation:

ANNIE: This, a monument? Just how d'you mean?

DADDY: It was built years ago by a man who had made millions in business—built to boast of his success—yes—but it stands as a monument to a way of life. Those were the days when our great railroad systems were built—our vast land became rich farms and great cities—thousands of schools and fine colleges were founded— and endowed! And everywhere churches were built where our people worshiped—in peace and in prosperity—it was a golden age with equal opportunity for all, Annie.

ANNIE: But there *was* a lot of *poverty.*

DADDY: True—some men were gifted to make more than others from free opportunity—but that *chance* for great success was there for all—even for the poorest laborer—Carnegie—Ford—hundreds of 'em—men who *tried* and wouldn't quit!

ANNIE: But "Daddy"—isn't it lots better to know that you'll be cared for, no matter what, even if no one ever can get really rich? No more worries?

DADDY: . . . You've read history, Annie—there have been and *are* people who are fed and clothed and cared for all their lives— they never have to worry about a job—they never get too rich—they are buried free when they die! We call those millions of people *slaves!*

ANNIE: Gee! Slaves! Yeah! But who wants to be a slave?

DADDY: Nobody, Annie—but people have to decide for themselves—while they *still can*—be *free* or be a *slave.*

ANNIE: But that's silly! Everybody wants to be free.

DADDY: Sometimes I wonder—freedom means struggle, bitter hard work, long chances, often poverty—once in a while, great success! But always *hope,* Annie! Yes, always *hope,* and equal opportunity.

In spite of the protests of Annie and Daddy, new concepts of promoting the general welfare were incorporated into the New Deal, but these and other Gray creations have fought determinedly ever since to keep rugged individualism undefiled. One of their first opportunities came in 1933 when the Federal government hauled Samuel Insull, the utilities czar, into court on charges of income tax evasion. Gray seized this occasion to dramatize his belief that certain income taxes were wrong. He maneuvered Warbucks into a situation comparable to that of Insull and proceeded to editorialize in his comic strip against the limitations which the corporate income tax imposed on capital-plant development. The script provided that patriotic Daddy should resign himself to the payment of the required taxes and take the necessary steps to set up a separate account to meet the burden, but he wondered: "Is this the answer to ambition? The reward for giving every ounce of thought and effort for a lifetime?"

These worries were soon compounded when a trusted clerk stole the millions Daddy had funneled into his tax fund. He could not meet his tax obligations and stood helpless before the "brutal hands of the Department of Justice" and that unscrupulous district attorney, Phil O. Bluster, presumably typical of the new government officials. To his political cohorts Bluster exclaimed: "We must convict Warbucks. Think how the voters will eat that up. Warbucks is innocent, but we've faked enough evidence to convict him." Because of such diatribes by the cartoonist, sympathy for Daddy was stirred up among the readers of the 135 newspapers in which the Orphan Annie strip appeared; they knew that Daddy, and Insull by inference, was being railroaded by "scheming politicians and revolutionary malcontents."

The exoneration of Warbucks in fiction (and Insull in reality) did not terminate the controversy over the merits and limits of private enterprise. When Gray concluded his attack on the ceiling over capital, he undertook to discredit the floor that was being placed under labor. In this new conflict, paralleling the fight of the rugged individualists against the Wagner Labor Relations Act of 1935, Warbucks appeared as the owner of a model factory which produced "eonite," a product capable of revolutionizing civilization.

Out of the kindness of his heart Warbucks wanted to make eonite available to everyone through a factory which offered ideal working conditions for the employees. In spite of his efforts, discontent was

whipped up by J. Gordon Slugg, a false financier, and Claude Claptrap, a petty politician who unfortunately, according to Gray, read
Das Kapital instead of *The Wealth of Nations.* Through rabble
rousers with slouch hats and shaggy black beards, Slugg and Claptrap
incited the employees against dear old Daddy. They organized the
workers and began to collect fees, fines, and dues, supposedly under
the regulations of the Wagner Act. Their demand for ever higher
wages crippled the industry. Claptrap added to the discontent with
harangues which asserted that eonite belonged to the "pee-pul," not
to Warbucks alone. Momentarily aroused by Claptrap's protesta-
tions, the workers burned the factory only to realize that they had
been tricked into destroying "the hand that fed them." Having acted
in haste, they reflected in haste, reversed their decision, lauded
Warbucks, and smeared the agitators with a coating of tar and
feathers without even considering the need for a card in the plasterers'
union.

   This evaluation of a New Deal labor law was too much for one
of the West Virginia newspapers. Suddenly Annie was not funny
any more. On the assumption that her antics were a "vehicle for
a studied, veiled, and alarmingly vindictive propaganda," they were
dropped from the paper. The fictional triumph over Slugg and Claptrap, however, did not seem to impede the New Deal program. It
did irritate the forces of the extreme left: the *Daily Worker* retaliated
in an appropriately named comic, "Little Lefty." In this strip Lefty,
the ingenious teen-age son of "economically handicapped" parents,
attacked capitalism with the assistance of his remarkable dog,
Spunky. The relationship between these two was like that of Annie
and Sandy, but undoubtedly Spunky was the more intelligent of
the two dogs. In this battle of the ideologies Sandy's vocabulary, as
always, was limited to "arf! arf!" but Spunky, who spoke a back-alley
English, commanded a repertoire of vilifications of the private enterprise system to surpass that of many a Kremlin agent.

   Lefty attempted to resolve such national and civic problems as
racial intolerance and slum clearance, but according to the *Daily
Worker* his greatest success was against the "little fascist Orphan
Annie." Lefty frequently quipped about "the homeless orphan"
and that fairy tale, capitalism, which her strip represented. To make
his position even more explicit, Lefty sent Gray a Christmas gift in
1936—a secondhand trash barrel to throw his Orphan Annie in.

   Through such attacks, which had neither the subtlety nor the continuity of Gray's masterpiece, Lefty kept sniping at the philosophy of
private enterprise for several years. And Annie kept struggling in her
inimitable manner to advance it, but in the opinion of her creator
the coming World War II was a severe blow to her cause. The influence of the central government spread more widely than ever before,

affecting in new ways both industry and the lives of individual citizens.

To Gray the meaning of this trend was obvious; government bureaucracy was determined not only to eliminate economic competition, but to regiment the American people beyond all justifiable limits. His comic strip analysis of this regimentation was revealed in 1943 during Annie's sojourn in Gooneyville, where she uncovered a corrupt ration board official, Fred Flask. For this sequence Annie was residing with Spike Spangle, an independent grocer who had been mistreated by Flask. As punishment for driving his car twenty miles to make a sick call which Flask's ration board had declared unnecessary, poor Spike was arbitrarily ordered to forfeit his "A" ration book for gasoline. In probing the incident, our ever-alert Annie discovered that the Flasks had three cars; one for Fred, another for his wife's daily shopping sprees, and a third for junior's trip to school each day.

Not only was long-suffering Spike asked to tolerate this disparity, but in his small store he was forced to concern himself with ceiling-price inventories and OPA questionnaires, all to be filled out in triplicate. These details meant long evenings of drudgery for patriotic Spike, but the management of several metropolitan newspapers quickly demonstrated that they could muster no sympathy for him. They detected what they regarded as a sinister parody on the Roosevelt Administration's handling of wartime controls. One publisher, in dropping Annie from his comic pages, commented that he did not oppose printing opinions contrary to his own, but he would have to "insist that opinion of whatever kind be duly labeled as such and not smuggled into comic strips in the guise of entertainment." In reporting this flare-up over Annie's antics, Newsweek suggested brightly that "some (possibly OPA directors) found Flask too realistic," and a Connecticut ration board official resented Annie's parody to the point of a $10,000 libel suit (later withdrawn) against Gray.

Not until the summer of 1944 did Gray focus his attack on the wartime limitations imposed on economic competition. By that time he had temporarily abandoned hope for the future of private capitalism. It seemed most ironical. Just when the Allies were achieving a major breakthrough on the military front, private enterprise, which had built the factories that now made victory probable, was being stifled by government regulation and restriction.

To portray this tragedy Gray brought Daddy Warbucks, his symbol of private enterprise, home to die. Daddy had been away fighting the war, but unfortunately had contracted a malady which was sapping his strength just as the government was slowly but certainly paralyzing individual initiative. Even Mrs. Hephzibah Hold, who was caring for Daddy in these last days, did not understand this quirk of fate; it seemed so unfair. He had given "his plants, his business, his fortune! every dime, for what he believed in! for a way of life we *all* believe in—or *most* of us do!"

As Daddy lingered, he reminisced with Annie at his side and yearned for a return to the "good old days." He lamented the changing times, but in the spirit of a good citizen he censured Annie for having recently evaded child labor and social security laws to accept a job while he had been away at war. The independent little waif was reluctant to accept this reprimand which was even more reluctantly given and seized this opportunity to debunk legislation designed to cramp her rugged individualistic style.

ANNIE: But, I used to work for my livin' always, up to now and it was O.K.

DADDY: The rules get changed pretty fast sometimes, Annie.

ANNIE: [*sneeringly*] I guess I've been pretty bad, breakin' th' law to hold a job, and earn my way so I could stay out of the orphan's home.

DADDY: [*assuming the responsibility*] I taught you to take care of yourself, to be independent! the way I was raised!

With this comment Daddy was admitting, in a free translation of Tennyson's passing of King Arthur, that "the old order changeth," that the rules of his generation no longer applied, that it was probably time for him to pass on. And for once the all-wise urchin did not understand.

ANNIE: What do you mean, it's time for you to go?

DADDY: I've been what's called a capitalist. Some have called me me "dirty capitalist"—but I've merely used the imagination and common sense that kind Providence gave me—it made me wealthy— powerful—hated by some—admired by others—but now? Well, Annie—times have changed and I'm old and tired—I guess it's time to go!

As Warbucks continued his appraisal of the American economic scene, those two Oriental freaks, Punjab and Asp, carried his litter aboard a waiting motor launch, a modern replacement of Arthur's barge, which bore him away "forever." Annie and Mrs. Hold waved farewell from the dock, with the latter delivering the epilogue to this little chronicle: "This country made him great—but his kind made this country great! Let's never forget that! We are seeing not only the passing of a man, but . . . of an era!"

With this heart-rending incident capitalism was laid to rest, but miraculously Warbucks reappeared within a year. When questioned about this "resurrection," the cartoonist remarked that "the situation changed last April." Franklin D. Roosevelt had died at that time, and Gray then saw a possibility for at least a modified capitalism to be revived. This restricted version, interestingly enough, acknowledged the ceiling over capital and the floor under labor which the New Deal had instituted a decade earlier—to demonstrate the impact of F.D.R.'s program even on such an ardent rugged individualist as Gray, who now conceded that some wealth was harmful and in need of government supervision. At the same time he wisely insisted that a second type of wealth be respected. These contrasting types were depicted by Mr. and Mrs. Puddle, with whom our wandering orphan spent several exciting months.

Mr. Puddle, exemplifying the type to be revered, had "started at the bottom in a steel mill, and he had so much on th' ball that he got to own th' *mill*." He was always kind and helpful to those struggling for success. When Annie appeared homeless before his door, this great capitalist took her in; his wife, on the other hand, wanted to throw poor Annie out on her ear. Mrs. Puddle, the personification of "bad" capital, had come from a line of wealthy ancestors and had no respect for her husband's achievement of working himself "from rags to riches." She had never shared the lot of the common man; and, therefore, could not appreciate his problems. Her wealth had been inherited; no one in her family had worked since her "gentleman pirate" grandfather. Her background was not known to most people, but Harold Gray, with an unwitting New Deal endorsement, "uncovered" it and disapproved. *This* kind of wealth, he argued, contributed nothing to the advancement of America.

Gray further conceded that our success lay not only in weeding out "bad" capital, but also in establishing a firm foundation on which labor could build. Above all, the wave of strikes that followed World War II convinced him that a genuine discontent was prevalent, and he interpreted this unrest to mean that manual labor was losing its dignity. He attempted to dramatize this situation when Annie stopped to live with Uncle Til and Aunt Piety Tiddely.

Uncle Til, who managed a small store for Mr. Prissy, was unfortunately plagued with a contemptuous errand-boy, Julius. Julius worked only thirty-six hours a week, but demanded that his weekly salary of twenty dollars be increased by five or he would quit. Self-made Til explained that when he was Julius' age he worked twelve hours a day, six days a week, for only ten dollars, but Julius, who had drunk at the New Deal well, replied, "So you're stupid—well, I ain't—see? So it's twenty-*five* a week or I quit." When Mr. Prissy said that it was impossible to grant the raise Julius left in a huff. The owner, analyzing the situation, observed: "Plenty of young fellows around, but as Julius pointed out—work seems out of fashion lately."

Since there was no one to perform the odd jobs around the store, versatile Annie volunteered. Julius protested with such epithets as "scab" and "dirty little punk." But, to Gray's delight, nonunion Annie felt that after Julius quit his job what happened at the store was none of his business. She proceeded to shut his mouth and his eye with a few Sunday punches to win at least this bout against the "excessive" demands of labor.

Gray, of course, saw no harm in having Annie deliver a few packages, but such conduct caused labor leaders to join newspaper editors, ration board officials, social workers, and numerous others in protesting Annie's lack of appreciation for New Deal objectives. These groups could have excused Annie's humorless, sexless character if only she had developed an affinity for ray guns and space ships instead of economics and politics. Others were astonished that some of the raw material of history has been so prominently displayed on the comic pages of the daily newspapers.

Since most comic strips build their plots around crime, humor, or melodramatics, a student of the New Deal is not likely to include any of the comics in his search for criticism and evaluations. Failure to do so is a mistake, because the Orphan Annie strip has been a relentless antagonist. Instead of viewing the New Deal as a milestone along the highway of social engineering, Annie has regarded it as a detour from Americanism. She has repeatedly demonstrated that she is a firm believer in the Protestant ethic,* in the pursuit of individual salvation through thrift and hard work, and in the competitive struggle as the keystone of our past and future national achievement.

ACROSS THE WORLD THE CONSUMER IS KING—OR QUEEN

DONALD K. DAVID

[Donald K. David, speech at graduation exercises of the first International Marketing Institute held at the Harvard Graduate School of Business Administration, summer 1960 (abridged).]

We close this section as we began it: on the subject of foreign trade. But now—5,000 or more years later—government action is being used to free trade rather than to regulate it. This is a very real freedom, too,

---

* See Kenneth E. Boulding, page 2203 in this volume.

for it means more jobs, more income, more comfort, more happiness for people in the very heart of their daily lives.

The common market in Europe was prophesied by Andrew Carnegie at the turn of the century.* Now this economic union, where different—and once opposed—countries are removing the trade barriers between themselves, is a reality; it has already revitalized trade in western Europe, while other similar combinations are developing across the world, as far as South America. And already, as the following selection shows, our leaders are dreaming of business, in the form of trade, as a truly worldwide force for freedom.

This selection is taken from a speech at the graduation exercises of the first International Marketing Institute, held at the Harvard Graduate School of Business Administration in the summer of 1960. It is significant for three reasons. First, it was delivered by Donald K. David, former President of American Maize Products Company, former Dean of the Harvard Business School, now Vice-Chairman of the Ford Foundation and Chairman of the Committee for Economic Development. Second, it represented a milestone in that here for the first time marketing men from *twenty-five* different countries across the world—business executives engaged in marketing, government trade officers, and teachers of marketing—spent 14 weeks of intensive study and living together. Third, it was a call to action to bring the world closer together by the one activity that is common to all nations, business.

If it took 5,000 years (or maybe 10,000 or 100,000 if we had records back far enough) for economic freedom to break through national boundaries in parts of western Europe and South America, in the years ahead there is still farther to go. Perhaps, in the end, trade is what will knit Russia to us, as her people learn that there is more for all when the barriers are down. In this sense, business *is* the greatest civilizing force.

———◆———

LONG-RANGE PLANNING and practical action to relate our economy and the way of life it sustains to the revolutions which mark our era is an absolutely fundamental issue which we cannot ignore and survive. To say that we are living in a changing world is more than a cliché; it is a dangerous understatement. Revolutions mark this era more than any other in the history of man's upward climb from the cave.

For us, in an advanced, industrialized country there is the scientific and technological revolution which is daily changing our lives. My friend, John Gardner, the President of the Carnegie Corporation, has said that only a handful of Americans are aware of the full meaning of this revolution.

* See page 2422 in this volume.

In our generation, the distance to Paris has been shortened from seven days to seven hours. A satellite whirling above the earth looks down on clouds forming over the North Pole or the South Pole, photographs them, and sends the picture back for tomorrow's newspaper and a better prediction of next week's weather. Soon— very soon—another set of satellites will enable us to tune our television sets directly to Berlin or Bogotá, Moscow or Melbourne, as easily as you now get your local stations.

As of now, we can barely imagine what will result from this assault by science on national boundaries. The impact is certain to be profound. At the same time, beating back against this political result of scientific advance are the new nationalisms that cover the continents of Asia and Africa particularly.

The last 15 years have seen the creation of 20 new nations with a population four times our own. In just the next three years at least ten new independent nations seem destined to be born in Africa alone. Within the next ten years, this continent may see the birth of as many as 37 new nations.

Events such as these, reflected in the headlines from day to day, are what cause the experts to refer to the revolution of rising expectations; or the revolution of rising resentment against inequality, especially discrimination on the basis of color; or the revolution of rising determination to be free from ancient masters, whether these be colonial administrators, Communist, Fascist or feudal dictators; or just plain hunger, ignorance and disease.

I do not want to propagandize, and I do not want to talk politics. But I am an American, a practitioner and believer in the American way of doing things, and as such I believe with my whole heart in facing facts and being frank about them. If in the process I say anything which offends you, I ask your forgiveness. But if I say something with which you disagree, then I will defend your right to disagree with me, or with anyone else in the world. It is part of our American way both to be frank and to welcome other peoples' frankness too. This is a two-way proposition, and it just happens that, for the moment only, I have the advantage over you in having the floor.

Well, one of the facts—and here I talk in the same business terms you have been using in your work and study—is that the United States is in some tough competition. The Soviets have challenged us "in the field of peaceful production," to use one of Mr. Khrushchev's phrases from one of his more peaceful speeches. Here, particularly with you people who have been studying marketing, I should like to raise the challenge even higher by adding also *the field of marketing*. For this is not just competition to fill men's bellies or supply convenient gadgets; this is competition or a contest in civilizations, if we think of civilization as meaning that people live richer and more satisfying lives. And this is where marketing plays its big role. It is not content to see that people exist and goods get produced, and this will be enough. Marketing is also required to see that the goods get distributed to the people at the right time and in the right proportions. Even more significant, *only* marketing—in a situation where the consumer is king (or queen)—will help people to *want* a better life and to call forth the best of business's efforts to provide it.

This then is the combination of revolution and competition that confronts us—serious for us as indeed for you. On our side, forgive me for feeling strongly that we want to protect and enrich the spiritual and material values we hold dear. But please also take heart from the fact that we feel a responsibility to the world too; we are challenged also to take your wants and desires and needs into account, because this will make it a better world for us too.

The Businessman's Own Views

"He that is above informing himself when he is in danger, is above pity when he miscarries: a young Tradesman who sets up thus full of himself, and scorning advice from those who have gone before him, like a horse that rushes into the battle, is only fearless of danger because he does not understand it."

—Daniel Defoe (1660–1731)

———◆———

It is a truism that the image of any type of individual is created more by literary figures and artists than it is by the carefully documented, well-balanced estimates of scholars. And the popular portrait of the businessman is certainly no exception. If the preponderance of the evidence focuses on the misdemeanors and the warts, no one should be surprised; the unpleasant aspects of man's behavior are always more interesting than the virtuous, socially acceptable parts. Some observers lament the fact that felicity of style preserves for posterity the ill that men do and obscures their constructive achievements.

In the following section, we try to redress the balance a little by giving a few of the more articulate businessmen a chance to speak for themselves. Businessmen have spoken out at various points throughout *The World of Business*—particularly in the entrepreneurship section, and in the last part of the philosophy section. But by and large the other sections have been "written" by what businessmen have *done,* either in the form of their accomplishments or of impressions that they have made on others.

Here, then, we have gathered together in one place some of the thoughts of businessmen about their own business.

NOBLE BLOOD AND BUSINESS

WYNDHAM BEAWES

[Wyndham Beawes, *Lex Mercatoria Rediviva: or, the Merchant's Directory*, printed for Peter Wilson, in Dame-Street, Dublin, 1754, pp. 25–26. Modernized by the editors.]

Here is a short passage from a book published in Dublin in 1754, *Lex Mercatoria Rediviva: or, the Merchant's Directory*. It is described on the title page as "A compleat guide to all men of business, whether as traders, remitters, owners, freighters, captains, insurers, brokers, factors, supercargoes, agents." Note that manufacturers are still missing from the ranks of "businessmen"; they are still artisans. There is another neat distinction on the title page too: "Calculated for the Use and Service of the Merchant, Lawyer, Senator, *and Gentleman*"—the italics being ours, of course. The gentleman was the man of leisure, who followed no business or profession.

Yet, says author Wyndham Beawes, businessmen do have noble antecedents and descendants. He himself is a merchant; for, again on the title page, he mentions that he has drawn on such "justly celebrated" sources as Savary,* but "improved and corrected by the author's own observations, during his long continuance in trade."

We quote here from his chapter "Of Merchants, whether Natives or Foreigners; their Character. . . ." He opens with a few observations on the term *merchant*. Notice also his phrase, the "mystery of merchandising." Then he launches into his discussion of the relation between businessmen and the nobility. The book does focus on the legal aspects of business, but contains miscellaneous lore and opinion as well.

———◆———

THE TERM *Merchant* (in Latin *Mercator*) or *Trader,* from *Tradendo,* as Minshew derives it, is in England, according to the general acceptation of the world, now confined to him who buys and sells any commodities in gross, or deals in exchange; that traffics in the way of commerce, either by importation or exportation; or that carries on business by way of emption, vendition, barter, permutation, or exchange; and that makes a continued assiduity or frequent negotiation in the mystery of merchandising his sole business.

It is true that formerly everyone who was a buyer or seller, in the retail way, was called a merchant, and they continue to be deemed so

---

* See his selection in Volume III.

still, both in France and Holland; but here shopkeepers, or those who attend fairs and markets, have lost that appellation.

The mercantile profession is very ancient, and generally esteemed noble and independent; in France, by two arrets of Louis XIV, the one in 1669, and the other in 1701, a nobleman is allowed to trade both by land and sea, without any disparagement to his nobility; and we have frequent instances of merchants being ennobled in that country, in regard of the utility their commerce, and the manufactures they have set up, has produced to the state. In Bretagne, even a retail trader does not derogate from his nobility, which only sleeps while he continues to exercise it, or, in other words, he only ceases to enjoy the privileges of his noblesse, while he carries on commerce, and reassumes it by giving over trade, without any letter, or instrument of rehabilitation. In many other states, and more especially in the republic of Venice, Holland, and Genoa, its value increases, and I wish I could say the same regard was paid it in England, as it merits from a trading nation; but its importance is not so justly considered by us as it ought to be, more especially as we enjoy every desirable advantage for carrying it on; and could the gentlemen engaged in it be brought to this way of thinking, and be persuaded to do justice to a profession we all esteem honorable, by a stricter imitation of the above-mentioned states, and not only to study, but appropriate their assiduity and diligence (more especially that practiced by our industrious Flemish neighbors) from a sincere conviction of the excellency of the mercantile employ, we should soon outstrip every competitor, and render the British merchant as celebrated as the British valor, or the British power, which he more than others contributes to support. It is true that trade stands so fair in the esteem of an Englishman, and promises so many occasions either for raising or improving a fortune, that many younger sons and brothers of peers are frequently bred up to, and embrace it; but then they are too apt to quit it on succeeding to the dignities of their families, or to some public employment, and withdraw those funds which might otherwise be continued in it, both to their own and the nation's emolument; whereas was a contrary practice observed, and could many (whose immense riches enable them) be persuaded to pursue their first beginnings, and destine part of their great effects to run in this channel, we should see commerce yet daily improve, and many more active professors shining at the head of it than we now do, a number of important enterprises might be undertaken, and happily concluded, to the no small increase both of public and private interest. But it is an unhappiness (I mean in regard of traffic) that many gentlemen who have been enriched by it, or their inheritors, frequently withdraw from it, either to live in retirement, or by an advancement to honors and posts, change the tranquil and pleasurable mercantile employ for the more troublesome, though splendid one of grandeur and power; and notwithstanding such may, and undoubtedly often do, look down on their quondam business as derogatory and now beneath them, yet a prime minister of France, and several successive grand dukes of Tuscany (as mentioned in the preceding discourse) I should think might countenance anyone's continuance in it, as they deemed it no disparagement to their high stations, to be distinguished for their trade, as for their eminency and greatness. And to show how commerce is thought of by most foreigners, we may subjoin to the examples quoted of the regard paid it, that many of the Italian princes are the principal merchants of their states, and think it no discredit to make their palaces serve as warehouses. Many of the kings of Asia, most of those on the coast of Africa and Guinea, traffic with the Europeans, either in person or by their ministers; so that in reality, Spain is the only country I know of where the mercantile employ is in disrepute; and there it is counted less ignoble and ungenerous to beg, than solicit a support, or improve a fortune by merchandising.

GEORGE WASHINGTON, THE BUSINESSMAN

CURTIS P. NETTELS

[Curtis P. Nettels, "Washington as a Business Man and as a Public Figure," *Bulletin of The Business Historical Society Incorporated*, Baker Library, Soldiers Field, Boston, Feb. 1943, vol. XVII, no. 1, whole no. 100, pp. 6–10.]

Here we see a side of George Washington that is usually overlooked in the history books. We see why Washington took the position he did, not just as President but as a leading public figure for two decades, and why he made such a great contribution to the country. It was Washington acting like the forward-looking but moderate businessman that he was.

This interpretation, based on solid history, has been made by Curtis P. Nettles, now of the Cornell University faculty; it appeared in the February 1943 issue of the *Bulletin of The Business Historical Society,* under the title "Washington as a Business Man and as a Public Figure."

Those who think of businessmen as conservatives may be quite right . . . so long as they understand what conservatism is, particularly as practiced by businessmen. It is not resistance to change, to new things that may represent progress. Rather it is reluctance to give up established values *just* for the sake of change; or, to put it another way, it is determination to accept *only* change that is designed to bring net improvement, i.e., that will not exact a cost which is dearer than the gain. It is not refusal to take risks, either; for risk-taking is the heartbeat of business. Rather, it is the will to calculate risks, and then take those, not that are least dangerous, but that are potentially most valuable relative to the danger—and then the courage and tenacity to make them come true.

That is the way Washington acted.

———◆———

IN THE SHAPING of our institutions, no period is more important than the years 1775 to 1797. And few will discount the contributions which were then made by Washington. The stamp of his influence appears at every significant point.

His latest biographers speak of his father as "a merchant, an ironmaster, a seafaring man." It is, of course, well known that Washington was not merely a planter, in the narrow sense of the word. In some of his letters he labeled himself "merchant." He carried on manufacturing, promoted settlement, hired labor, bought, sold, and rented land, patronized projects for improving rivers and building canals, lent money, operated flour mills, and engaged in wholesale trade as an exporter. He knew at first hand all the techniques of commerce and he believed in and practiced the rules which the businessmen of his time applied in the conduct of their affairs.

It is not surprising, then, that he made a strong appeal to his fellow businessmen; that their support was one of the bulwarks of his political strength; that on central issues a large majority of them saw things as he saw them; and that they formed the backbone of the Federalist party, of which he was the founder and head.

If, therefore, one seeks an understanding of the influence of the businessman on the public policies and institutions of the nation, the career of Washington affords as much insight as is likely to be derived from any one source. In the course of his public life, the structure of the national government took form, the credit of the Federal union was established, and a basic foreign policy came into being. A series of measures, attributed commonly to Hamilton but more properly to Washington, paved the way for the later transition from an agricultural, raw-material economy to a predominantly industrial society. As commander in chief of the American army during the Revolutionary War he was in effect the Chief Executive. He led the country during sixteen most critical years; in actuality he served the equivalent of four presidential terms.

In politics he helped to establish precedents of the greatest importance. The office of the Presidency and the scheme of relations between the executive and Congress were shaped in good measure by his judgments and decisions. In his contacts with the states are to be found the practices which have guided the relations between the Federal government and the states since his day. And his conduct in dealing with other leaders established a working plan that has survived throughout the history of the republic.

As a planter and a businessman he treasured his property and cherished his personal freedom. He perceived, of course, that if his own property and freedom were to be secure, so must be those of other people. Insisting upon the right of defending his own interests, he conceded the same right to others. In his day there existed a multitude of individuals vested with private rights—individuals who cherished their own independence and yet who were often in conflict with one another. He perceived that all could not be pressed into a single mold without depriving many of their rights. He therefore put the accent upon freedom and he sought to diffuse as much of it as was consistent with the rights the existence of which made freedom imperative. He shrank from coercion and suppression, endeavoring instead by persuasion, mediation, and respectful treatment of others to gain cooperation and voluntary agreement. "It is his maxim to convert by good usage and not by severity," remarked one of his associates.

After he became commander in chief in June, 1775, he had to rely upon the more radical elements in American society during those fateful months before July 4, 1776, when he led the movement for declaring independence of Britain. Once the Declaration had been adopted, many conservative patriots, fearing that the war might unleash leveling forces, turned to him as to a savior. Congress in December 1776 conferred upon him dictatorial powers. At the close of the war he had an opportunity to establish a military dictatorship and to head an oligarchy of wealth. He refused. If men, he then wrote, "are to be precluded from offering their Sentiments on a matter, which may involve the most serious and alarming consequences that can invite the considerations of Mankind, reason is of no use to us; the freedom of speech may be taken away, and, dumb and silent, we may be led, like sheep, to the slaughter."

He strove to avoid extremes in government and to maintain a stable balance of opposing forces. He disliked both the idea of an oligarchy and the prospect of unlimited power in the hands of a hastily formed majority. The check-and-balance scheme of the Federal government owes as much to him as to any one man. He steadily submitted to the public will when it expressed convictions persistently and strongly held. He exhibited patience, restraint, and self-control in tolerating criticism of himself, without resorting to punitive measures against his critics. A three-member committee of Congress, which contained two merchants, wrote in 1776: "Happy it is for the country, that the General of its forces can safely be trusted with the most unlimited power, and neither personal security, liberty nor property in the least be endangered thereby."

As a businessman and an employer, Washington came into touch with all sorts of people. Like many other businessmen, he judged people, not by artificial standards such as rank, family, and inheritance—or by what they professed in words—but by character and ability as exhibited in conduct and performance. He preferred an obscure person who was able and honest to a prominent, well-to-do rogue. He did not indulge in abstractions about people nor become deluded by doctrinaire concepts of the nature of classes. His readiness to recognize merit in people, irrespective of their rank or circumstances, gained friends for him at all levels, and he attained a popularity such as few Americans have enjoyed. From his long association with people—and doubtless also by reason of the popular support which he received—he derived a faith in the majority of his fellow men. In the end the people will be right, he said. At the time of Shays's Rebellion he stated that a large number of people would not revolt unless they had real grievances, and he therefore called for reforms of such grievances as did exist. At the time of the Whisky Rebellion he waited long before taking decisive action. He then used a force so strong that bloodshed and injury were averted, and he pardoned the leaders who had been guilty.

In large measure the American businessman has benefited enormously by the remarkable internal stability of the country which has prevailed during most of its history. To this stability men of wealth have contributed greatly by their acceptance of the results of popular elections which have often been displeasing to them personally. In his "Farewell Address" Washington counseled against meeting adverse political trends by a forcible seizure of power. He said: ". . . let there be no change by usurpation; for though this in one instance may be the instrument of good, it is the customary weapon by which free governments are destroyed. The precedent must always greatly overbalance in permanent evil any partial or transient benefit which the use of it can at any time yield."

His financial records, relating both to his personal expenditures and to his business affairs, give evidence of his integrity. The minuteness and completeness of those records show that he felt that he had nothing to hide. The same regard for exact and open transactions marks his management of army finances during the war. He did not shrink from bringing high associates to account for irregularities. Although he esteemed Benedict Arnold as a soldier, he administered a strong rebuke to that unstable adventurer for making use of public property for his private benefit. At a later time the readiness of Hamilton to admit publicly certain moral lapses in his private life, in order to vindicate his integrity in financial matters, gives evidence of the standards of Washington's administration in the business affairs of the government.

If Washington is not a popular figure today, that fact may be explained in part by the nature of the materials with which he worked. No one gave more careful attention to details. He denied himself the luxury of advocating noble projects which could not be carried out. He did not deceive himself or others, and no one justly accused him of hypocrisy. "Hypocrisy," wrote Edmund Burke, "of course, delights in the most sublime speculations, for, never intending to go beyond speculation, it costs nothing to have it magnificent."

Washington thought in order to act, and his thinking was therefore concerned largely with concrete obstacles and the practical means of overcoming them. His business writings abound with allusions to land surveys, descriptions of goods, detailed instructions to overseers, and reports of experiments; and he pursued each topic to the last degree of minuteness and precision. As commander in chief he thought in terms of wagons, powder, horses, uniforms, roads, creeks, fortifications, army regulations, soldiers' pay, terms of enlistment, and number of troops. The Constitutional Convention over which he presided in 1787 devoted most of its labors to the discussion of specific forms and details of government. As President he prepared with exacting care each stone in the new edifice of national union. He reserved judgment until he had mastered facts and then he translated decision into action. In doing so, he displayed the fruits of the early training of a businessman who made and executed plans with the knowledge that loose thinking, a false step, or careless management might be the means of his undoing. His grasp of large issues proceeded from his mastery of the many small facts which determined them.

One is not likely to take the trouble of mastering details unless one has a definite accomplishment in mind. Mastery of detail is thus evidence of a constructive sense. Like other outstanding businessmen, Washington thought in terms of future development. In the 1760s, he gave up tobacco planting, then a declining interest, and directed his efforts toward achieving a diversified economy. Scientific farming, internal improvements, westward expansion, and manufacturing engaged his attention as he turned from the past to the future. More than any other man he helped to construct a new nation, fashioning from raw materials a new army, a new government, and a new national policy, and in the end achieving something the like of which had not existed before. To public life he applied the same spirit of improvement and construction which had distinguished his activities as a businessman.

Thus his life, both private and public, reveals no contradictions. The things he stood for and which he helped to fix in the nation's institutions and practices represent in general the American business-man at his best: respect for freedom, aversion to dictatorship, integrity in financial affairs, a practical nature, a constructive sense, a willingness to accept distasteful election returns for the sake of social stability, a capacity to judge men, and an appreciation of the rights and virtues of people in circumstances other than his own.

THIS AFFLUENT SOCIETY—1784

BENJAMIN FRANKLIN

[Benjamin Franklin, "On Luxury, Idleness, and Industry," in *The Complete Works in Philosophy, Politics, and Morals, of the Late Dr. Benjamin Franklin* . . . , printed for J. Johnson, St. Paul's Church-yard, and Longman, Hurst, Rees and Orme, Paternoster-row, London, 1806, vol. II, pp. 424–430.]

This selection is entitled "On Luxury, Idleness, and Industry" in the 1806 collection of *The Complete Works in Philosophy, Politics, and Morals, of the Late Dr. Benjamin Franklin.* . . . Originally Franklin wrote this as a letter to one Benjamin Vaughan, Esq., in 1784; and Vaughan published it in *The Repository,* a short-lived periodical of that period.

The views are very relevant today—when luxury (we now call it "affluence") and idleness (we now call it "leisure") are certainly more pronounced than they were two centuries ago. Franklin does not defend useless labor; far from it. But he does see the value to the economy that comes from some people wanting better or new things, and other people providing them. He might actually be talking back, with prophetic insight, to Kenneth Galbraith (*The Affluent Society,* 1958) and to Vance Packard (*The Waste Makers,* 1960), both of whom today decry our standard of living as too high for our own good.

———◆———

IT IS WONDERFUL how preposterously the affairs of this world are managed. Naturally one would imagine that the interest of a few individuals should give way to general interest; but individuals manage their affairs with so much more application, industry, and address than the public do theirs that general interest most commonly gives way to particular. We assemble parliaments and councils, to have the benefit of their collected wisdom; but we necessarily have, at the same time, the inconvenience of their collected passions, prejudices, and private interests. By the help of these, artful men overpower their wisdom, and dupe its possessors: and if we may judge by the acts, arrets, and edicts, all the world over, for regulating commerce, an assembly of great men is the greatest fool upon earth.

I have not yet, indeed, thought of a remedy for luxury. I am not sure that in a great state it is capable of a remedy, nor that the evil is in itself always so great as it is represented. Suppose we include in the definition of luxury all unnecessary expense, and then let us consider whether laws to prevent such expense are possible to be executed in a great country, and whether, if they could be executed, our people generally would be happier, or even richer. Is not the hope of being one day able to purchase and enjoy luxuries, a great spur to labor and industry? May not luxury therefore produce more than it consumes, if, without such a spur, people would be, as they are naturally enough inclined to be, lazy and indolent? To this purpose I remember a circumstance.

The skipper of a shallop, employed between Cape May and Philadelphia, had done us some small service, for which he refused to be paid. My wife, understanding that he had a daughter, sent her a present of a new-fashioned cap. Three years after, this skipper being at my house with an old farmer of Cape May, his passenger, he mentioned the cap, and how much his daughter had been pleased with it. "But," said he, "it proved a dear cap to our congregation." "How so?" "When my daughter appeared with it at meeting, it was so much admired that all the girls resolved to get such caps from Philadelphia; and my wife and I computed that the whole could not have cost less than a hundred pounds." "True," said the farmer, "but you do not tell all the story. I think the cap was nevertheless an advantage to us, for it was the first thing that put our girls upon knitting worsted mittens for sale at Philadelphia, that they might have wherewithal to buy caps and ribbons there, and you know that that industry has continued, and is likely to continue and increase to a much greater value, and answer better purposes."

Upon the whole, I was more reconciled to this little piece of luxury, since not only the girls were made happier by having fine caps, but the Philadelphians by the supply of warm mittens.

In our commercial towns upon the seacoast, fortunes will occasionally be made. Some of those who grow rich will be prudent, live within bounds, and preserve what they have gained for their posterity; others, fond of showing their wealth, will be extravagant, and ruin themselves. Laws cannot prevent this: and perhaps it is not always an evil to the public. A shilling spent idly by a fool may be picked up by a wiser person, who knows better what to do with it. It is therefore not lost. A vain silly fellow builds a fine house, furnishes it richly, lives in it expensively, and in a few years ruins himself; but the masons, carpenters, smiths, and other honest tradesmen have been by his employ assisted in maintaining and raising their families; the farmer has been paid for his labor, and encouraged, and the estate is now in better hands. In some cases, indeed, certain modes of luxury may be a public evil, in the same manner as it is a private one. If there be a nation, for instance, that exports its beef and linen to pay for the importation of claret and porter, while a great part of its people live upon potatoes, and wear no shirts, wherein does it differ from the sot, who lets his family starve, and sells his clothes to buy drink? Our American commerce is, I confess, a little in this way. We sell our victuals to the islands for rum and sugar; the substantial necessaries of life for superfluities. But we have plenty, and live well nevertheless, though by being soberer we might be richer.

The vast quantity of forest land we have yet to clear, and put in order for cultivation, will for a long time keep the body of our nation laborious and frugal. Forming an opinion of our people and their manners by what is seen among the inhabitants of the seaports is judging from an improper sample. The people of the trading towns may be rich and luxurious, while the country possesses all the virtues that tend to promote happiness and public prosperity. Those towns are not much regarded by the country; they are hardly considered as an essential part of the states, and the experience of the last war has shown that their being in the possession of the enemy did not necessarily draw on the subjection of the country, which bravely continued to maintain its freedom and independence notwithstanding.

It has been computed by some political arithmetician that if every man and woman would work for four hours each day on something useful, that labor would produce sufficient to procure all the necessaries and comforts of life, want and misery would be banished out of the world, and the rest of the twenty-four hours might be leisure and pleasure.

What occasions then so much want and misery? It is the employment of men and women in works that produce neither the necessaries nor conveniences of life, who, with those who do nothing, consume necessaries raised by the laborious. To explain this:

The first elements of wealth are obtained by labor, from the earth and waters. I have land, and raise corn. With this, if I feed a family that does nothing, my corn will be consumed, and at the end of the year I shall be no richer than I was at the beginning. But if, while I feed them, I employ them, some in spinning, others in making bricks &c. for building, the value of my corn will be arrested and remain with me, and at the end of the year we may all be better clothed and better lodged. And if, instead of employing a man I feed in making bricks, I employ him in fiddling for me, the corn he eats is gone, and no part of his manufacture remains to augment the wealth and convenience of the family; I shall therefore be the poorer for this fiddling man, unless the rest of my family work more, or eat less, to make up the deficiency he occasions.

Look round the world, and see the millions employed in doing nothing, or in something that amounts to nothing, when the necessaries and conveniences of life are in question. What is the bulk of commerce, for which we fight and destroy each other, but the toil of millions for superfluities, to the great hazard and loss of many lives, by the constant dangers of the sca? How much labor is spent in building and fitting great ships, to go to China and Arabia for tea and coffee, to the West Indies for sugar, to America for tobacco? These things cannot be called the necessaries of life, for our ancestors lived very comfortably without them.

A question may be asked: Could all these people now employed in raising, making, or carrying superfluities, be subsisted by raising necessaries? I think they might. The world is large, and a great part of it still uncultivated. Many hundred millions of acres in Asia, Africa, and America are still in a forest, and a great deal even in Europe. On a hundred acres of this forest a man might become a substantial farmer, and a hundred thousand men, employed in clearing each his hundred acres, would hardly brighten a spot big enough to be visible from the moon, unless with Herschel's telescope, so vast are the regions still in wood.

It is, however, some comfort to reflect that, upon the whole, the quantity of industry and prudence among mankind exceeds the quantity of idleness and folly. Hence the increase of good buildings, farms cultivated, and populous cities filled with wealth, all over Europe, which a few ages since were only to be found on the coasts of the Mediterranean; and this notwithstanding the mad wars continually raging, by which are often destroyed in one year the works of many years' peace. So that we may hope the luxury of a few merchants on the coast will not be the ruin of America.

One reflection more, and I will end this long rambling letter. Almost all the parts of our bodies require some expense. The feet demand shoes; the legs stockings; the rest of the body clothing; and the belly a good deal of victuals. Our eyes, though exceedingly useful, ask, when reasonable, only the cheap assistance of spectacles, which could not much impair our finances. But the eyes of other people are the eyes that ruin us. If all but myself were blind, I should want neither fine clothes, fine houses, nor fine furniture.

DON'T BE AFRAID TO STOOP—AND PICK UP A PIN

~~◦◊◦~~

F R O M *Hunt's Merchants' Magazine*

["Lafitte, the French Banker; or A Fortune Made By Picking Up a Pin," *The Merchants' Magazine,* Freeman Hunt, ed., Sept. 1844, vol. 11, no. 3, pp. 289–290.]

"A fortune made by picking up a pin" is the subtitle of a little lesson on the importance of attention to details, in France apparently as well as in the United States, in the mid-1800s as well as in the mid-1900s. This is from an 1844 edition of *Hunt's Merchants' Magazine.*

———◆———

IMPORTANT RESULTS often follow from the most trifling incidents. A remarkable case of this kind is related in an English paper, respecting Lafitte, the French banker, and which was the foundation of the immense fortune he afterwards accumulated. When he came to Paris, in 1788, the extent of his ambition was to find a situation in a banking house; and to attain this object, he called on M. Perregeaux, the rich Swiss banker, to whom he had a letter of introduction. This gentleman had just taken possession of the hotel of Mademoiselle Gurmard, which had been put up in a lottery by that lady, and won by the fortunate banker. It was to this charming habitation, which has since been demolished, that M. Lafitte paid his first visit in Paris; and, as it were, took his first step in the Parisian world. The young provincial—poor and modest, timid and anxious—entered by that gateway which had witnessed so many gaieties in the last century. He was introduced into the boudoir of the danseuse, then become the cabinet of the banker, and there modestly stated the object of his visit.

"It is impossible for me to admit you into my establishment, at least for the present," replied the banker; "all my offices have their full complement. If I require anyone at a future time, I will see what can be done; but, in the meantime, I advise you to seek elsewhere, for I do not expect to have a vacancy for some time."

With a disappointed heart, the young aspirant for employment left the office; and while, with a downcast look, he traversed the courtyard, he stooped to pick up a pin which lay in his path, and which he carefully stuck in the lapel of his coat. Little did he think that this trivial action was to decide his future fate; but so it was. From the window of his cabinet, M. Perregeaux had observed the action of the young man. The Swiss banker was one of those keen observers of human actions who estimate the value of circumstances apparently trifling in themselves, and which would pass unnoticed by the majority of mankind. He was delighted with the conduct of the young stranger. In this simple action, he saw the revelation of a character. It was a guarantee of a love of order and economy, a certain pledge of all the qualities which should be possessed by a good financier. A young man who would pick up a pin could not fail to make a good clerk, merit the confidence of his employer, and obtain a high degree of prosperity. In the evening of the same day, M. Lafitte received the following note from M. Perregeaux:

"A place is made for you in my office, which you may take possession of tomorrow morning."

The anticipations of the banker were not deceived. The young Lafitte possessed every desirable quality, and even more than was at first expected. From simple clerk, he soon rose to be cashier, then partner, then head of the first banking house in Paris; and afterwards, in rapid succession, a Deputy, and President of the Council of Ministers, the highest point to which a citizen can aspire. On what a trifle does the fortune of a man sometimes depend!

THE TRUST: FEUDALISM OR CIVILIZATION?

FROM THE *U.S. Investor* AND CHARLES R. FLINT

["The new feudalism bids fair to be the dominant feature of the twentieth century—until it is overthrown, as it inevitably must be," *U.S. Investor*, May 27, 1899, pp. 1–2.]

[Charles R. Flint, "The Trust: An Alliance of Work, Brains and Money," in James H. Bridge (ed.), *The Trust: Its Book*, Doubleday, Page & Company, New York, 1902, pp. 112–123.]

The trust or "combination" was a subject of bitter disagreement in the latter part of the 1800s, and the controversy was at its height just at the turn of the century. Actually, this form of business organization was often no larger than the modern corporation, which we take for granted today. But it was a new device, really a new concept; i.e., that by combining companies, you combined people and resources on a large scale, and could do business on a large scale. (In that period it was not legally so easy to operate across state lines; hence the advantage of having a number of companies. Also, this was a quicker way to grow to national size.) So we had the birth pains of a new and exciting way of doing business.

But different attitudes toward this development prevailed among businessmen while it was taking place. Herewith we present two opposed views. One appeared as an unsigned editorial in the May 27, 1899, issue of the *U. S. Investor,* carrying this caption: "The new feudalism bids fair to be the dominant feature of the twentieth century." The other is a 1902 essay based on a speech before the Providence Commercial Club on "The Trust: An Alliance of Work, Brains and Money," by Charles R. Flint (1850–1934), a partner in the firms of Gilchrist, Flint and Company and W. R. Grace and Company (engaged in South American trade), organizer of the Coast Clipper Line, Consul of Chile in New York, and negotiator of the purchase of warships abroad for the U. S. Navy—a busy, versatile man.

It is interesting to note that the book in which Mr. Flint's essay was published, *The Trust: Its Book,* also included a rather stodgy article by James J. Hill, the daring financier who built a railroad empire. Hill says that "all progress is the development of order" and makes the point that the trust works in this direction by "the application of uniform methods to the production of what [the people] require."

The case for Standard Oil (see page 2424) of course presents, as a specific example, the most celebrated and successful trust of them all.

————◆————

I

WE ARE ON THE EVE of the twentieth century, and, according to some, are just entering the manhood of the race. The centuries that have already elapsed mark but the infantile stage in the progress of humanity. So far we have hardly got our eyes open. Hitherto, self-interest has ruled the world. The law of the survival of the fittest has been the predominating factor. We have possessed a greater elegance and more of the comforts of life than our barbarian ancestors, but at heart we have been governed by the same motives as they. Our increasing wealth has produced in us an access of good nature, the fruits of which may be witnessed in our various charities and benevolences; but our altruism is merely one way of finding an outlet for our superfluous energy without any real deprivation to ourselves. Thus it is that some people reason.

The twentieth century is to be very different, so different as to throw all preceding epochs of the world's history into the shade, and to make them appear but the "mewling and puking" time of infancy. Henceforth, everything is to be on a large scale and for the benefit of humanity. Man is to become a new order of being. He will be no longer the grasping creature of old. His sole aim in the future will be to subordinate himself to the good of the race. An era of altruism of the truest is before us. It must needs be, of course, that men will constantly be found with greater energy and ability than the general run but this energy and ability will be devoted to the supreme task of advancing the good of the race, rather than to advancing their possessors with the greatest rapidity to the position of number one. The individual is destined to become of little importance, society to become all-important. Such is the cheering prospect which, according to some excellent people, the twentieth century holds out to us.

It is far from our desire to mar such a picture. We are impelled, however, to ask one question. What evidence is there that human nature has experienced such a change in its fundamental character-istics as to make such an outlook possible? It seems to us that nothing short of a revolution in the moral nature of men is needed to bring about such a state of affairs as is predicted for the twentieth century. This paper is not devoted to discussions in ethics and we must not dwell on this phase of the situation at length. The future interests us because of its economic possibilities, but, as every thoughtful person knows, economics and ethics stand in very close relation to each other —in fact, they were in the beginning taught as one science.* So that in the course of this article we may inadvertently trespass on the grounds of the moralist.

A subject can always be much more easily understood if it is dis-cussed in the concrete. Perhaps we can get a very good idea of what the twentieth century is going to be like if we ask who are going to be its typical men. We may answer this by starting right here in Bos-ton and choosing Mr. Thomas W. Lawson. We make no mistake in this choice, because, if we are not greatly mistaken, he has already been quite a good deal talked about in this light. It only remains to ask how far Mr. Thomas W. Lawson represents the subordination of private to public interests. Does he bear any resemblance to the mil-lennial man? But as there are some who do not take this excellent personage quite seriously, let us make another choice. There is Mr. Rockefeller. We think we have heard it stated that this eminent finan-cier aims to be worth a billion before he dies; and we should say that if he keeps on as he is going, he is quite likely to attain that end. Now, of course, there is the fundamental question, Is it possible for a man who aims to be worth a billion dollars to have subordinated private interests to the good of the public? But waive that. What shall we say of the Standard Oil trust's method of killing off its competitors? Do they suggest the millennium?

We must not forget the great army of trusts. Are they not—by a sort of anticipation—the summation of all the best that is to be found in the twentieth century? What is to be the spirit of the twentieth

* The reference is to Aristotle.—EDITOR

century? The spirit of that remarkable period is to be an overwhelming eagerness on the part of everybody who has a "good thing" to share it with everybody else. That is exactly the spirit that is governing the trust movement. Every man who has an industrial plant is anxious to let the public have it. His modus operandi is to form a trust, and to let the millions buy the shares of the combine. The fact that he sells stock to several times the amount of the real value of his property, is, of course, a minor factor, and need not be dwelt upon.

Another indication that the twentieth century is going to be a great improvement on past times is to be found in the growth of luxury. Fortunes have accumulated so rapidly and have attained such enormous figures that the happy possessors thereof have great difficulty in knowing how to spend their incomes. Even after liberal donations are made to charity, more remains than can easily be devoted to the pleasures of life. We have not yet heard that any host has put pearls in his guests' wine, but that point will undoubtedly be reached before long. Life among the very wealthy in this country (and abroad, too, to a certain extent) has become a delirium, an unceasing round of excitement—in many cases not entirely devoid of the bacchanalian features which were so prominent a characteristic of the revels of the worst periods in the past. It must be admitted that it requires strong intellectual faculties to harmonize such a state of affairs with the simplicity and self-abnegation that have been predicated of the twentieth century. Probably the wisest course would be to close one's eyes to such facts as we have just alluded to, and to treat them as if they were not.

If we may be allowed to express our opinion quite frankly regarding the twentieth century, we will say that it seems to us that it is likely to equal (even if it does not surpass) any that has preceded it in avariciousness and the subordination of public interests to private greed. The event may falsify this view; but judging the future in the light of present phenomena, we are justified in speaking as we do. On May 6, 1899, there appeared in these columns an article entitled "The New Feudalism," in which a comparison (and a striking one, we think) was drawn between the industrial conditions of today and the mediaeval feudalism. Among other things, we said: "The feudal lord of today is not intent upon war. It is not by ownership of the soil that he exacts the services of his fellows. He is the same rapacious personage that he formerly was, but he has changed his complexion somewhat. He is now a lord of trade. He is gradually working the industries of the world out of the hands of the many into his own, and the many bid fair, other things being equal, to fall into a relationship with him similar to that in which the vassal of old stood to his feudal chief."

The new feudalism bids fair to be the dominant feature of the twentieth century—until it is overthrown, as it inevitably must be. When its downfall will occur is beyond the power of prophecy. Meanwhile let us trace a few of its results. One of its results is being witnessed already in an alarming degree. We refer to the subverting of the political rights of the people. That was a prime feature of the old feudalism. Either by cajolery or by force, the barons succeeded during a very large part of the time in effecting legislation favorable to their interests and detrimental to the public good. The same general policy is pursued today openly and unblushingly, in increasing measure, by trusts, corporations and wealthy individuals, in their eagerness to get laws passed in their interest. To be sure, part of the blame can be laid on the purchasable or pusillanimous legislators with which our Congress and our state legislatures are filled, but these are comparable with the venal or timid kings and emperors of old. The main fact is that there is a rapidly growing disposition, on the part of those who can wield sufficient influence, to bribe or terrorize the lawmaking powers into submitting to their will and granting them whatever privileges they may ask, even when their requests amount to a demand for the right to oppress the people most shamefully. The picture is not overdrawn. It might justly be painted in darker colors. We know of men—estimable enough in other relations of life—who think no more of buying a legislature than they do of ordering a new suit of clothes.

Another result of the new feudalism is the shameless extravagance and indulgence in luxury which characterize such a large portion of our monied class. Wealth is acquired so fast that arrogance is begotten. Class distinctions arise with fearful rapidity. The owners of millions find it hard to identify themselves with the mass of the people. Their wealth surrounds them with awe in the eyes of those who have not got beyond a moderate income; of necessity they form a class by themselves, and it requires but a short time to make them lose a large part of their sympathy with mankind in general. There are, of course, some notable exceptions to the rule, but there are to every rule. When one grows rich gradually, as the result of hard, conscientious labor, he adjusts himself naturally to his changing condition; his head is not turned; he does not become wealthy enough to find an unbridgeable gulf between himself and the rest of his kind. That is the difference between the results accomplished by the new method and by the old.

If we may be allowed to digress for a moment, we will call attention to one striking analogy. It used to be a frequent occurrence in the Middle Ages for a baron to die leaving funds to endow a monastery or some other religious institution. Such bequests were common on the part of men who had lived the most rapacious and bloodthirsty lives. After years of unbridled robbery and oppression, they would think of their souls' welfare; hence the gifts referred to above. Is not their experience paralleled in the present? It is a delicate thing to discuss the motives of others; but it is certainly proper to put the diverse acts of a man's life together and strive to ascertain their relation. We see today men who have practiced every deception in the stock market, or who have bribed legislatures and Congresses to obtain legislation whereby to oppress and defraud the public, or who have deliberately conspired to drive weak competitors out of business by the most outrageous and despicable methods, or who have taken advantage of another's misfortune or ignorance to possess themselves of his property, or who have of design wrecked enterprises committed to their trust, in order to secure the wreckage for themselves, or who have issued prospectuses and advertisements to investors full of lies. We see them thus engaged, and we read of their contributing large amounts to endow colleges, hospitals, churches and missionary societies. The parallel with the Middle Ages is complete.

This is not a bright picture. But we may ask, What is the use of deceiving ourselves? None is so blind as he who will not see. To talk about the twentieth century as if the present indications were that it would usher in the millennium is to display an egregious foolishness. Certainly there never was a time when there was more rapaciousness, more eagerness to possess oneself of one's neighbor's property by fair means or foul (but, of course, always under the guise of law) than at present. Does human nature show signs of becoming immediately transformed? Obviously, no.

We have an aim in saying all this. It is, to prevent those who are within the sphere of our influence from being misled by the current optimism. Pessimism is abhorrent, but unalloyed optimism is productive of even worse results. Good and evil, honest men and rogues, have from the start been contending for supremacy in this world, and are likely to be as deeply immersed in the struggle at the end of the twentieth century as at the end of the nineteenth. The greatest rascality masquerades in the guise of a public benefactor, and the public are most in danger when they feel most secure. Therefore, do not believe that trusts and the various other alluring financial enterprises which are now seeking the favor of investors (and which come as the alleged harbingers of the twentieth-century millennium), are what they claim to be, merely on the representation of their promoters. The presumption is that they are designed primarily to make money for the latter, rather than to serve an altruistic end. That is the safest view to take of them at the start, until they have demonstrated their honesty and their ability to succeed.

II

In studying the evolution of industrial life, we find that combination is coincident with civilization. Savages have little power to combine, because combination depends on trust in our fellow man, and in primitive life it is fear that rules. One of the first steps in industrial evolution was to subdivide production into trades. Each did what he could do best, settling accounts by an exchange of products. Later, those engaged in the same trade formed partnerships, then corporations, and finally consolidations of corporations.

Against this march of industrial progress there has always been opposition. There have always been those who, appealing to special interests, to the unsuccessful, the discontented and the misinformed, have endeavored to obtain political favor by opposing progress, by endeavoring to prevent the natural, and mutually beneficial, cooperation between capital and labor.

Today there are men of intellectual refinement and pleasing personality far removed from the centers of finance, commerce, and industrial activity, who read of industrial life, but who are not in it; who are studying the history of industrial progress, but are not making that history—and yet, as Bismarck said, "cursed with the dangerous gift of oratory," they are advocating theories in business and finance that, if adopted, would shake the very foundations of our industrial existence. They are half-thinkers, because they think without the facts. They remind one of General Grant's most amusing after-dinner speech to the newspapermen of New York. He said: "A feeling of awe comes over me when I realize that I am in the presence of men of such marvelous capacity. Your rapidity of conception, your unerring judgment, seem supernatural. When I was before Richmond, surrounded by men who had made a life study of military tactics, when, after days and nights of deliberation, a plan of campaign was finally determined upon, one of you would get down to your office late at night and in a few minutes dash off an editorial telling how we were all wrong, and pointing out what we ought to do. Your remarkable versatility was shown in formulating legislation, and you were peculiarly strong in international diplomacy where the existence of state secrets made it impossible for you to get at the facts."

In this great territory of ours we always have with us those who try to make people believe that their siding is the main track. We have had the "Know-Nothing" craze, the "Greenback" craze, the "Granger" craze, and the "Silver" craze; but they were all rejected by the good sense of the American people. Today our farmers recognize that the markets of the world have been opened to them through the great system of railways which have resulted in the heavy steel rail, the eighty-ton locomotive, and the continuous haul. Economically, the wheat fields of Dakota are nearer to London and Paris than the farms of Yorkshire and Burgundy. Thus favored, our farmers during the past few years have paid off so many mortgages that if ground into paper pulp, they would make ballots enough to elect a President.

The men of sound judgment, leaders in the industrial wars for the supremacy of the American farmer, the American manufacturer and the American wage earner, should not be disturbed by the clamor of those who, not in the struggle, cannot appreciate actual conditions, and whose leadership, if accepted, owing to their inexperience, would conduct us to inevitable disaster.

Industrial evolution, which is as inevitable and as unalterable as the law of gravitation, has attained its highest development here in the United States. Every unprejudiced man must recognize its advantages, and that it is because of them that we are taking so important a position in the world's markets, increasing our national wealth, furthering the welfare and increasing the prosperity of our people.

The great problems of the economics of production have been solved. What interests us most today is not so much the fact of our great industrial prosperity; it is, rather, the question whether the advantages of that prosperity are equitably divided among the contributors to it:

(1) Capital,
(2) Superintendence, and
(3) Labor.

(1) The share to capital takes the form either of interest or dividends.

We find that the rate of interest paid to those furnishing money to industrial enterprises is decreasing. Fifty years ago, the average rate throughout the United States was 8 per cent per annum. Now it is less than 5 per cent. This general rule can be laid down: that the greater the confidence, the higher and more perfect the industrial organization, the lower the rate of interest. During the year 1896 the stability of our currency and the fundamental conditions of our industrial development was regarded by many with doubt; and money loaned as high as 20 per cent. The investor is ever willing to take lower interest in exchange for greater security and for a steadier and less precarious demand for his funds. Thus that form of industrial organization which furthers careful financing, opens wider markets, and guarantees greater confidence and stability, is directly in the interest of capital, although the rate of return on capital is thereby steadily reduced.

The dividends received by shareholders are larger than the interest rates, because the risk is greater. Moreover, being partners and share-holders, they are entitled to a larger share in the advantages of combination. Still it is doubtful if the aggregate of dividends is as large as the aggregate of interest. Dividends are never absolutely certain, and they are never paid until labor and superintendence have first had their share.

(2) What is the position of the man of superior intelligence? For superintendence stands midway between capital and labor.

Highly developed organizations, resulting in enormous volume of business, have increased the necessity for intelligence. As the supply of brains is not equal to the demand, the price of brains is high. The turning over of individual businesses to combinations has caused the retirement of old men to the advisory board for judgment, and has made way for young men for action. You ask, "What chances have our young men?" While you are asking the question, those of ability and energy have already started on a career of successful industry. If the student will leave his books and the orator his stump and go to our factories, to our great farms, to our mines, to our lines of railways, they will find ten times as many men receiving over $3,000 per annum as there were 30 years ago.

Mr. Schwab, of Pittsburgh, is a type. He started as a stake driver of an engineering corps. Today, though under forty years of age, he is President of the largest iron company in the world. I can point out a hundred successful men today where you could not have named ten under old conditions.

But, it is said, they are dependent. Dependence upon each other is, however, the condition of civilization. The very word *civilization* implies community life, and community life means mutual dependence. Complete independence is found only in the wigwam of the Indian. There the young man builds his own house, makes his own clothes, gets his own meat, and keeps his bank account, if he has any, in his pocket. The best opportunity he has for distinction is in showing superior prowess in hunting, or superior strength in paddling his own canoe. In civilized life, interdependence is more profitable than independence. Your young man, instead of paddling his own canoe, can command one of those great combinations, which is doing so much to benefit the world—the modern steamship. Was Captain Clark less the commander or Chief Milligan less the engineer, because each was dependent on the other in making the historic run and the splendid fight of the *Oregon?* Each gave to the other his opportunity. One might just as well say that a man has no opportunity in political life because we have a police system and no man can do as he pleases. On the contrary, just as a good system of national police is a guarantee of liberty so these great organizations are guarantors of opportunities which otherwise would never exist.

Let us not waste time in considering who will take care of these young men of superior intelligence; they will take care of themselves. The Almighty has given the greater power to superior intelligence, and as Samuel J. Tilden, one of nature's great monopolists in the domain of intellect, has said: "You cannot substitute the wisdom of the Senate and Assembly for the plan of moral government ordained by Providence."

(3) Let us now consider the interests of the workingman in this economic evolution which has produced the perfect machinery and giant factories, supported by great aggregates of capital represented by shares which enable all to become investors. It is a fundamental fact that the man of superior ability cannot accumulate for himself without giving to the wage earners an opportunity to earn the larger share, and it is always an increasing share.

The tendency today is to a minimum of profits and to a maximum of wages. When profits become abnormal, they invite competition, and are immediately reduced. In which case the consumer alone is benefited. If they are not sufficiently abnormal to invite competition, then labor demands a larger share of the profits in the form of increased wages; and it is either voluntarily or necessarily agreed to. In this case, the body of wage earners reaps the advantage; and, inasmuch as the body of wage earners is the great body of the community, the community is benefited. Employees know almost as promptly as do the employers whether a mill is earning an extravagant profit. If it is, they at once demand their share, and the employer must inevitably yield. It is thus that wages always tend to a maximum, and profits to a minimum.

The maintenance of the high standard of wages now paid in the United States is absolutely dependent upon our realizing the advantages which come through superior organization. We are today shipping manufactured goods to countries where the rates of wages average 40 per cent less than our wage earners are receiving. Of our exports of manufactured goods, 80 per cent are produced by large industrial corporations. Articles of manufacture which we do not produce through consolidations are being almost entirely supplied to the neutral markets by the cheap-labor countries—Germany, Belgium, and England. The centralization of manufacture and consequent use of special machinery have emancipated the slave—have raised the American workman to the position of overseer, not of pauper labor, but of its productive equivalent, machinery. And he is receiving, and is entitled to, the wages of superintendence. The intelligent labor leaders understand this perfectly. It was my pleasure to entertain at my home some of the best known of these. Speaking of labor conditions, I asked one of them to define the difference between his organization and that of the professional agitators. He

replied: "We hope to bring about by evolution what they claim should
be accomplished by revolution." They said that they "welcomed new
machinery, because it did the work which had heretofore degraded
labor."

The wage earners of the United States are today enjoying a higher
standard of living and a larger measure of well-being than wage
earners have ever before enjoyed in the history of the world. They are
the real money power. The railroad managers have rails and rolling
stock; the miner has mines; the manufacturer has bricks, mortar and
machinery, and most of them have debts, and many are mortgaged
to the banks for savings; but the wage earners in the United States
have on deposit in cash in the savings banks, subject to call,
$2,500,000,000.

Thus through cooperation and combination every interest is being
benefited, labor most of all. As wage earners become more intelligent,
as they become overseers of machinery, they better understand these
conditions. They have the intelligence to recognize that their greatest
comfort and happiness is in furthering the industry of which they are
a part. Today one of the great advantages that the United States has
over Europe is that its laborers are the more intelligent, are the
healthier and happier. The European wage earner, instead of welcom-
ing labor-saving machinery as our workingmen in the United States
have done, has tried persistently to retard its general use. The result
has been that wages have been lower in Europe. The American workman has received more because he has produced more. This is the
great reason why, notwithstanding our high wages, we are so rapidly
extending our trade with foreign markets. The best factory inevitably
gets the most work. There is a continual struggle for existence
between good factories and poor factories, and the good factory
invariably wins.

The law of consolidation of capital and division of labor holds as
good in the field of distribution as in that of production. It is inevitable and it is profitable. The department stores and the mail order
stores sell for 10 per cent instead of 30 per cent profit, and the consumer thus saves 20 per cent. The profit obtained by the distributor of
staples, on the way from the farmer to the consumer, is less than one-
quarter what it was 30 years ago. The farmer secured a wider market, the consumer gets his staples much more cheaply, and the enterprising middleman has improved banking and transportation facilities
to do a larger business. This is why he has adopted as his motto,
"Quick sales and small profits."

The real benefits of "capitalistic production," as compared with
production on a small scale, are twofold. The first and greatest benefit
of industrial combinations goes to the whole body of the community
as consumers, through reduction in prices. The next benefit, and that

next most largely distributed, goes, as I have shown, to the workers
through increase of wages, and thus it happens that the workingman
gains simultaneously in two ways. He gets more money for his work
and more goods for his money.

A STEEL MAN PROPHESIES THE
FUTURE OF THE WORLD

ANDREW CARNEGIE

[Andrew Carnegie, "Europe Versus America" (Rectorial Address, St. Andrews
University, St. Andrews, Scotland, Oct. 22, 1902), in *The World's Work*, Nov.
1902, vol. V, pp. 2797–2810 (abridged).]

Andrew Carnegie, the great American steelmaker, a Scot by birth, was
asked to deliver the Rectorial Address at St. Andrews University, St.
Andrews, Scotland, in 1902. He spoke on "Europe Versus America" in
a way which showed so much understanding of the basic characteristics
of the new and the old worlds, and so much prophetic insight about
the future, that we have reproduced about half of it here.

We have given Carnegie the benefit of the doubt in our deletions, by
omitting misprophesies about Canada, Australia, and Japan, all of
which he considered to have slim industrial potentials. But his batting
average is still amazing; you will observe, for instance, how accurately
he foresaw the future strength of Russia and the common market in
Europe.

The text of the speech was published in *The World's Work* of November 1902—a magazine of considerable interest in its own right, since
it used a large number of pictures in a style similar to the modern *Life*.*

I THOUGHT that I might interest you by considering a subject now
attracting wide attention—the economic changes which have come
and are impending in the relative position and power of nations, since
it has been necessary for me during my business career to watch and
study these and to base action upon them. The growth of nations in
wealth and population, the social conditions and aptitudes of their
people, natural resources, prospects, ambitions, national policy, all
bore directly upon our problem.

It was upon no easy task that the American manufacturer entered
when he determined to struggle for a place for his country among manufacturing nations, and it behooved those who risked their capital, or

---

* For more of Carnegie, refer to index listing in this volume.

incurred debt in the attempt, to keep a wary eye upon the doings of
their established competitors, and weigh future probabilities of development in other lands.

In studying the manufacturing world, Britain claimed more attention than all other nations together, for here was the seat and throne
of manufactures. We examine the globe and note how much is marked
red under the Union Jack, and speculate upon what would be left if
this were obliterated.

But if in viewing the world's material development we should
consider what would be left if her inventions were deleted, a greater
void still would be found in this nobler field of conquest, for this
island has also been the seat and throne of invention, the work not of
the barbarous sword, but of the brain of civilized man. That development rests upon the steam engine of Watt, one arm of which embraced the sea through the steamship of Symington, another covered
the land through the locomotive of Stephenson. Here is the great triad
which has created the modern material world. This audience will not
fail to note with satisfaction that all of these magicians were Scotch
(the first two native-born, the last by descent)—a remarkable fact,
and not to be readily accounted for except upon a hypothesis which
national modesty prevents a born Scot from suggesting here in the
presence of so many distinguished members of other nations.

Arkwright, Hargreaves and Cartwright, through their inventions,
brought economical spinning and weaving of textiles; those of Nelson
and Cort, cheap iron; Bessemer, Siemens, Martin and Thomas, cheap
steel, the most important article of all, since it is the basis of so many
other articles. It is the inventions of these men based upon steam that
have revolutionized the conditions of human life upon the earth, and,
in passing, will you be good enough to note how many of these, and
indeed of the supremely great in other fields as well, have at first
worked with their hands? Whatever the future may have in store,
nothing can rob Britain of the credit of having given to the world the
means for its surprising development. Material progress is Britain's
child. At the time of which I speak, she was the only important manufacturing nation, for here naturally her inventions were first utilized.
The reward obtained from this monopoly—for such it was—made her
the richest of all peoples *per capita*. Her realized wealth is still unequaled. Forty-odd years ago she made more iron and steel, manufactured more machinery, mined more coal, wove more cloth, than
all the rest of the world. It was Britain in the one scale, the world
in the other, the world kicking the beam.

In the dawn of this prosperity came Cobden and Bright, who insured cheaper food for the workers, which further stimulated manufacturing and insured Britain's pre-eminence. The theories of these
great men and their school were justified in their day, one being that

the various nations of the world were created with different qualities and resources, all so beautifully arranged that one was to supplement the other. Britain's destined part clearly was to manufacture the raw materials of other lands. Interchange, of raw and finished and of different products, was evidently nature's intention, thus uniting the nations in the noble task of supplying each other's wants. Nations were destined to be cooperating parts in one grand whole, and thus commerce became the golden chain to bind the world in bonds of peace and good will.

There was only one flaw in the entrancing theory, but that was fatal—the various members were not satisfied with the parts assigned to them in the beneficent drama. On the contrary, each evinced the strongest desire to develop its resources and manufacture its own raw materials as far as possible. None relished being the mere hewers of wood and drawers of water to another nation: all wanted to play Hamlet, and as is usual in the most talented companies of performers, all believed themselves destined by nature for the great part. There came to the aid of the new ambitious lands, automatic machinery and scientific methods which largely solved the question of skilled labor. A few managing Britons, or Americans, can now readily be obtained to establish manufactures in any part of the world, and educate the natives to become satisfactory workers.

In my travels round the world I carefully noted this weighty fact. I saw the peons of Mexico weaving cloth in factories, and engaged in iron and paper works, at two and three shillings a day in silver, worth only one-half value in gold; the people of India, the Japanese, and the Chinese, all doing excellent work in cotton and jute mills; the Negroes in the United States steadily rising in the scale and becoming good workmen in mines and in iron and steel works; the Russian, Hungarian and Italian, Swede and Norwegian, all making good workmen.

Capital, management and skilled labor have become mobile in the extreme. The seat of manufacturing is now, and will continue to be, more and more simply a question where the requisite raw materials are found under suitable conditions. Capital and skilled labor have lost the power they once had to attract raw materials; these now attract labor and capital. The conditions are reversed. The cotton industry, for instance, was attracted from Old to New England, and is now attracted from it to the southern states alongside the raw material. The jute industry, once centered in Dundee, is now also established in India, near the jute supply.

Another factor is clearly seen: the most patriotic people of every land consider it a duty to develop their resources. Hence Canada today gives twelve shillings a ton bounty for every ton of pig iron produced, and Australia has a scale of bounties, and has just offered

a large one for the manufacture of steel rails. They are not content
to be dependent even upon the motherland for manufactured articles.
Germany, Russia, and America give protection, and all the colonies
tax your productions, thus giving their home producers incidental
protection.

Another element enters. Business methods have changed in the
past twenty years; manufacturing especially has been revolutionized
by new inventions, improved machinery and new and enlarged
demands. The old rule of thumb has given place to scientific precision. The technical schools furnish the young foremen and superintendents. Automatic machinery has developed a new class of workmen more intelligent than the old. The size of works has increased
tenfold, and instead of partnerships devoted to one process, all
processes, from the minerals in the mine to the finished articles, are
combined in one. Railroads are constructed and fleets of steamships
built and worked, all the needed materials are owned, the company
is its own insurer, and everything entering into the product or needed
to maintain the works is made by it. One by one subsidiary branches
or new departments are added, and from a score of small streams of
profit, unknown to the small producer of the past, the main stream is
fed.

So rapidly does one improvement follow another that some parts
of the huge concerns are constantly undergoing reconstruction. Old-
established works are seriously disadvantaged by the new order of
things, especially if under joint stock ownership, because it is difficult to get from numerous small owners the capital needed for
modern improvements. Hence the old countries, and particularly
Britain the pioneer, have been disadvantaged, and the new American
land, with a clean slate to begin upon, much favored.

The causes specified have already changed the positions of Britain
and America as industrial powers. America now makes more steel
than all the rest of the world. In iron and coal her production is the
greatest, as it is in textiles—cotton, wool, and silk. She produces
three-fourths of the cotton grown in the world. The value of her
manufactures is just about three times that of your own; her exports
are greater. The Clearing House exchanges of New York are almost
double those of London in amount. She furnishes you with most
of the necessary food products you import. She has two-fifths of
the railway mileage of the world.

Thus [America] has become the foremost nation in wealth, manufactures, and commerce, and promises soon, in some branches, to
occupy the position which Britain occupied when it was Britain
versus the world. She already does this with steel. Although no
Briton can be expected to see with satisfaction his country displaced
from first place, there is yet cause for rejoicing that supremacy

remains in the family. It is not altogether lost what the race still holds. Macbeth's fate is not Britain's. The scepter of material supremacy has been wrenched by no unlineal hand. It is her eldest son, the rightful heir, who wears the crown, and he can never forget, nor cease to be proud of, the mother to whom he owes so much. The relative position of Germany has also changed. She has forged ahead, her product of steel being now second to that of the United States. In other departments her rate of increase is also great. She promises to run Britain close, perhaps by the end of the decade, for second place as a manufacturing nation. During the ten years previous to 1900 she added 5,500,000 to her population, and almost doubled her production of iron, and increased that of iron ore from 11,000,000 to 19,000,000 tons.

In comparison with these three countries others are of trifling moment in the production of staple articles for export, always excepting that giant of the future, Russia, whose latent resources are enormous, and whose growth is so steady, not only through increase of population, but through accretions of contiguous territory. She must occupy a great position, but not in our day, nor perhaps in the next generation: if she hold together, she will be a continent under the government like the American Union, although, as far as known, not with comparable resources and conditions. She has employed more than one of my former assistants to construct and manage steel works, and is vigorously developing her resources in many lines. Her production of iron has doubled in the last 12 years. Coal mined in 1890 was 90,000,000 [metric] tons, and in 1900, ten years [later], 150,000,000 *—an extraordinary increase. The cotton industry has also developed during the ten years. It is probable that she will soon supply many of her own chief wants, great as these are to be; but as these will be largely additions to present world needs, this will not greatly lessen the trade now tributary to other nations.

Belgium, for its size, is the most wonderful of all manufacturing nations, but too small and fully developed to play a greater part than now in the world's trade. One notes with surprise the magnitude of her commerce. Exports and imports per capita much exceed those of Britain, exports being as 11.4 per head to 6.14—almost double; even her imports are greater.

France occupies a unique position. She may be said to have, in the artistic quality, substantially a monopoly most difficult to break. Till women reach the height of wisdom attained by man and establish a uniform and unvarying style of dress, and as long as articles of luxury are in demand, and till men reach the wisdom shown by women in regard to French wines, so long will France remain in the

---

* Carnegie's original figures, obviously in error, have been corrected by the editors.

first class of nations, although much further increase of her trade is not probable. I might also say that as long as the French people remain so industrious, frugal, and free from the vices of other lands, gambling and drinking, so long her position is secure. It is significant that the silk trade of Britain has passed entirely into her hands, and that in motor machinery she is pre-eminent in Europe. . . .

In the race for the world's trade between these countries several considerations are important. *First*—let this vital fact be noted—the most powerful weapon for conquering foreign markets is a profitable home market. It might also be taken as an axiom that the nation fortified by the best home demand for any article will finally conquer the world's trade in that article in neutral markets. In economic circles "the law of the surplus," as I have ventured to call it, attracts increasing attention. Manufacturing establishments are increased year by year until they become gigantic, simply because the more made, the cheaper the product, there being a score of cost accounts divisible by product. By giving men constant employment, and having a reputation for never stopping, the best men are attracted and held—an important point. The manufacturer upon a large scale can afford to make many contracts in distant parts of the world, and even some at home, at a direct loss in times of depression, knowing that, upon the whole, the result will be less unprofitable by running full than running short time or stopping. Hence, those possessing the most profitable home market can afford to supply foreign markets without direct profits, or even at a loss whenever necessary.

I speak from sad experience on this point, for during most of my life we have had to encounter Britain's surplus in our markets in times of depression here, to the great disadvantage of the home producer and advantage of the British manufacturer. This position the United States now in turn occupies toward Britain and other manufacturing countries, since it has the greatest and most profitable home market, not only for steel but for most articles. Invasions of Europe, and especially of Britain, by American manufacturers are not to be apprehended to any considerable extent, except at rare intervals. It is not the amount imported, however, that discourages the home producers; the knowledge that he is open to serious competition from abroad, a small amount of which will break his market, is what makes him loath to invest the great sums sometimes necessary to keep him in the front, and robs him of the do-or-die resolve, which often is of itself the secret of victory in the struggles for life.

Second, the question of population bears directly upon the industrial development of nations, since increased numbers expand the home market. There are today 78,000,000 of people in the American Union. More than 600,000 immigrants from Europe will have landed on her shores this year. Her rate of increase between 1880 and 1890 was just about three times that of the United Kingdom. Last decade it was not so great, although more than double, having fallen, because of five years of depression caused by an agitation upon the standard of value, the most disturbing of all economic questions. Nevertheless she added 13,500,000 to her population. This decade, even at no greater native rate of increase than the last, will add more than 15,000,000. Every morning the sun rises it greets more than 4,000 new faces added to the Union.

Germany's population is 56,000,000; she added 5,500,000 last decade. The increase of the United Kingdom was 3,600,000. It is a serious disadvantage to Britain in the contest that her home market cannot expand as rapidly as the American, or even the German. Size of productive territory, as affecting population, is a prime factor in the race for the first place among nations in material production.

Third, we see proofs of another important law. Just as raw materials now attract capital and labor to any part of the world, so untilled fertile soil increases and attracts population. We note the rapid increase in the Mississippi Valley, and that America is consuming more and more of its own food supplies. It already manufactures as much of its enormous total cotton crop as Britain imports, and not more than 10 per cent of all its field crops, except cotton, are ever exported. Wherever food products can be grown profitably people will increase until the limit of food supply is reached. Where exceptional conditions exist, such as valuable minerals, population may remain in excess of the food supply, as with this favored island; but permanently to maintain population beyond food supply, a nation must be able to supply needed articles to so much better advantage than the purchasing nations can produce or procure them as to enable it to endure the disadvantage of higher cost of food.

It seems clear that the spread of manufactures will be so general that the leading nations will finally supply most of their principal wants—at least to a much greater extent than hitherto. . . .

We hear of huge industrial combinations on land and sea, but the combination of 45 states, some of them larger than the United Kingdom, forming the American Union, which promises soon to equal Europe in the production of many of the staple articles, and is already producing more than the rest of the world of the article of prime importance, is a portent of infinitely more consequence to the world than any possible industrial combinations, the latter being trifling in comparison. At the present rate of progress America will, in the lifetime of many present, have a population equal to that of Europe today, excluding Russia.

The influence of a united continent upon the separate smaller nations of the world is already felt. Europe sees its art treasures and its shipping lines and the center of finance passing to the new land as primacy in manufacturing, in wealth, and in commerce have already done, under the law of gravitation, which operates in every field, even in that of literature. Eight copies of the *Encyclopaedia Britannica* find their home in the new land for every one in the old land of publication. The manufacturers of the new land invade the old and compete in the world's markets. These facts have not escaped the attention of the nations. Austria's Premier was among the first to direct attention to the situation, and he has been followed by others in authority. Europe is alarmed at the threatened consequences, and the search is now directed to the discovery of countervailing forces. The first necessary step in this task is to compare the two continents and note the points of difference which create the dangers feared. We have treated of the positions of different nations hitherto; now we must contrast Europe and America as units—continent against continent.

There are some portentous contrasts.

First, we find Europe an armed camp, every man's time and labor for years taken for military training, not merely unproductive labor, but labor costly to the state. Nearly 9,000,000 of men are thus called to military duty. The American Union, on the other hand, has only an army of 66,000 men, and there is no conscription. Its men are in the industrial, not in the military, army, constantly adding to the material wealth of the country. She is further enriched through the operation of conscription in Europe.

Europe has 410 battleships, cruisers and coast defense ships; America, 35.

It would be difficult to overestimate the effect of this contrast upon the industrial development of the two continents.

Second, America is one united whole at peace with itself, and enjoys immunity from attack by neighbors, or even by Europe, since she supplies so many parts of it with necessary food products that nonexportation of American products would produce not only famine prices, but actual famine itself, and compel peace. Hence industrial development has one indispensable condition—peaceful security. In Europe this is lacking, for it is divided into hostile camps. That its huge armaments cannot go on unceasingly growing is evident—an explosion must come. That this is considered imminent is evident from the measures taken by the nations to protect themselves from its consequences. If rulers and statesmen did not see the inevitable result impending over their heads—a Damocles' sword—they would strain less violently in preparation. It is impossible for industrial development to proceed satisfactorily under the shadow of this dreaded catastrophe. There is nothing so timid as capital.

Until these contrasts cease, anything approaching equality of power between the industrial armies of the old and the new worlds is unattainable.

Third, since his continent has less than thirty people per square mile, the American has a constantly expanding home demand, urging him to extensions, and justifying costly improvements and the adoption of new processes. He has also a continent under one government. He establishes his several works at the centers of the various markets. If a needed ingredient be found in one state, another somewhere else, if it be desirable to construct works for one part of a process here, or there, or ply ships, or build railroads in any part of this broad area, he proceeds without hesitation, dreading neither interference with supplies, hostile legislation, nor national antipathies. "No pent-up Utica contracts his powers": more, the boundless continent is his, as are all its markets, free from tariff. His operations are free from start to finish.

The result is that every process of manufacture in the Union flows naturally to the localities best adapted for it, there being no barriers to free selection. The best places also are selected for assembling materials, raw or partially prepared, for their final forms. In short, it is free, unrestricted trade in everything under the same conditions, same laws, same flag, and free markets everywhere over an expanding continent—advantages which only those experienced in industrial trade will estimate at their full value.

The European manufacturer finds obstacles to such varied expansion in a continent divided into hostile and warring states, with different laws and exactions and tariffs at every boundary, the fear of war overhanging all. He is almost compelled to confine his investments and works to the small area of his own country and its small home market.

One of many telling advantages which industrialism receives from political union in America is that a great home demand for any article from one united people occupying a continent evolves standard forms, the evolution of the best types, which justifies the manufacturer in erecting special machinery and running it exclusively upon each part of the type. Railway, electric, harbor, bridge—engineers in these and other branches adopt the standard forms: hence whenever a huge bridge, for instance, is needed promptly in any part of the world—Egypt or India—America is applied to; the steelmaker has his bridge construction and bridge erection departments managed by specialists who know what is best much better than any general engineer can possibly do. The proper plans for the standard bridge required are taken and the work begins instantly. Note here that the steelmaker is also the bridge contractor: a vital point. The bridge is probably open for traffic before the European engineer could have submitted plans and the bridgemaker had contracted with the steel-maker. A new bridge in Europe is a new creation in which several separate contractors have participated; in America it is from standard patterns evolved from experience and completed from start to finish by one contractor.

In greater or less degree this exists in the manufacture of the principal articles of which America is now the greatest producer. Consider agricultural machinery. One of the leading English manu-facturers once told me that he had been compelled to abandon foreign markets and finally to cease business. The American manufacturer had triumphed. While here [in Britain] three or four hundred machines were sufficient for the season's demand, his friend in America put in hand seven thousand. Megalomania again. This out-put justified the automatic machinery used in every process of manu-facture. If my memory be correct, it was 22 men in Britain for two men in America in one of these processes—that is, the machinery did 20 men's work. Why, then, not adopt it in Britain? you say. Small home demand is the adequate reply, and that demand itself open to the American competitor. . . .

More and more clearly must the truth be realized that the industrial struggle among the nations is bound up with the political, the question of magnitude being at the bottom of supremacy in both. A nation cannot be small in size and in population and remain great in material products or material power. To maintain first rank industrially, com-mercially or financially small nations must merge with others and become prosperous parts of one great federated power. Once the race was between separate nations, henceforth it is between conti-nents.

Let us therefore assume that Continental Europe will be finally compelled, after greater or less sacrifice, through ruinous wars or peaceful negotiations, if not to federalize in some form, yet to adopt means to insure peace among themselves which would lead to some form of federation under free trade. It would then be . . . Europe versus America; with the former relieved from militarism there would be equality so far and both could prosper with a large home market and participate in the ever-increasing trade of the world. There is little room today for operations upon a small scale either in industrial-ism or in nationalism—nation against nation was once well enough. Britain and France, Italy, Germany, Austria-Hungary were each once of sufficient size to rank as great powers, but the American Con-tinental Union—forty-five states in one—has changed all that. The solid mass of this great body in action will by mere momentum force its way through small industrial warring units into opposition. There is also huge Russia to be reckoned with, which likewise threatens to overshadow the small nations.

The closing paragraph of Morley's *Life of Cobden* is most pertinent to today's conditions:

"Great economic and social forces flow with a tidal sweep over communities that are only half conscious of that which is befalling them. Wise statesmen are those who foresee what time is thus bringing, and endeavor to shape institutions and to mold men's thought and purpose in accordance with the change that is silently surrounding them."

The question arises, what would Britain do if Continental Europe be thus relieved from internal dangers and under free trade possessed of the indispensable home market, and were finally to be federated into one *Zollverein* or great power? Would she remain a small separate island nation of forty-five or fifty millions, against the hundreds of millions of the Continent? Or, if invited, become a member of the European consolidation—our race submerged by Slav, Teutonic, and Latin races? Or would the mother-heart, beating fast within her, turn her gaze longingly to her children across the sea, then hundreds of millions strong, and, grasping their outstretched hand, murmur, "Whithersoever thou goest I go; thy people are *my* people": the English-speaking race thus becoming again as it was before—for offense never, for defense ever—one and inseparable.

It is for essays upon this momentous question that I shall offer the usual Rector's prizes.

Students of St. Andrews: My subject has been the industrial ascendency of the world, once yours, and now passed to your lineal descendant, who bears the industrial crown. But, gentlemen, in this audience, assembled in Scotland's oldest university, the thought that fills your heart and appeals to mine, is, of what value is material compared with moral and intellectual ascendency, supremacy not in the things of the body but in those of the spirit! What the barbarous triumphs of the sword compared with those of the pen! Peace hath her victories much more renowned than those of war: the heroes of the past have been those who most successfully injured or slew; the heroes of the future are to be those who most wisely benefit or save their fellow men. What the action of the thews and sinews against that of the Godlike reason, the murdering savage armies of brutal force against the peaceful armies of literature, poetry, art, science, law, government, medicine, and all the agencies which refine and civilize man and help him onward and upward! Shakespeare and Milton, Burns and Scott, Newton and Hume, Bacon and Locke, Cromwell, Hampden, Pym, Sidney and Russell, Burke, Gladstone, Bright, Tennyson, Browning, Arnold, Carlyle, Ruskin, Darwin, Watt, Symington, Stephenson, Bessemer, Arkwright, Hargreaves, and others of the past; and all the leaders of today who march in the train of the white-robed angel of peace and good will among men.

What matters what part of the world makes the most steel, iron, cloth or ships, if you produce the highest poets, historians, philosophers, statesmen, inventors, teachers? Let others make more of the food for the body of man, if from you come the best books for his soul, or the highest examples of lives grandly lived. Let more of the millions of the people of the world be clothed by other lands and other hands, as long as you educate and apparel the minds, leading men in the higher paths.

There is no ascendency of the world and that the highest, where neither unbounded fertile territory, immense store of minerals, nor numbers, nor aught material, are of value, where megalomania reigneth not. For the crown of this realm you have no cause to struggle; it is already yours; it has never been lost; it remains here in the old home. Nor has the blast yet blown of any challenger from either of the four winds of heaven. The crown of the material world physical reasons prevent you wearing, although man for man you may remain the equal or superior of any. There is no reason why you should lose the other. See to it that you do your best to guard it against all comers, men of St. Andrews, for precious it is beyond all others, and blessed among and beyond all other nations is she whose brow it adorns.

Let other nations therefore distribute among themselves as they may the victories of materialism. Precedence for Britain, the dear old home of our race, is the thing of the spirit, the modern Greece, and more than Greece ever was to her world, at whose shrine all that highest and best of the nations of the world will dutifully attend to testify their gratitude, admiration, reverence and love.

COMBINATIONS: THEIR USES AND ABUSES

~~✥~~

S. C. T. DODD

[Samuel Calvin Tait Dodd, *Combinations: Their Uses and Abuses, with a History of The Standard Oil Trust*, George F. Nesbitt & Co., New York, 1888, pp. 9–46 (abridged).]

As the people of the United States underwent a revolution in social organization during the last quarter of the nineteenth century, shifting from chief reliance on individual endeavor to collaborative effort, opponents of change and those hurt in the process raised their voices in protest. One manifestation of this revolution was the emergence of big business, and many were the criticisms, some justified and some quite the contrary.

Samuel C. T. Dodd (1836–1907) believed that large-scale enterprises were the prime instruments in achieving the great increases in the production of goods and services in the United States between 1870 and 1900, but he was also aware of the inequities occasioned by the change. To him the major issue, however, was how best to make the large corporation a socially beneficial instrument. While recognizing both "the uses and the abuses" of large concentrations of capital, he urged the enactment of clear and just regulatory laws as a means of effectively utilizing big business and simultaneously averting the dangers of unrestrained use of privately exercised economic power.

To be sure, this plump, learned Presbyterian was the general solicitor of the Standard Oil Trust and might be expected to defend large combinations, but he was a man of highest moral principles and enunciated them almost daily to his employers. The statement which follows is one of many by Dodd and was issued while he was a Standard Oil employee. He was one of the first to make the distinction between "uses" and "abuses" of large corporations, so effectively popularized by Theodore Roosevelt * in his differentiation of "good" and "bad" trusts and so effectively utilized by him in his successful campaign to dissolve the Standard Oil Company (New Jersey).

In reading this selection two circumstances should be kept in mind: Dodd's comments were first made before the Senate General Law Committee of the State of New York, which was considering legislation to regulate trusts; and at this time (1888), petroleum's chief use was for illumination.

———◆———

WHEN AN UNFORTUNATE ORATOR, solely for alliteration's sake, spoke of "Rum, Romanism, and Rebellion" as closely related, he made a great mistake. Just as great a mistake is made when we unite the terms *combination* and *monopoly*. There is, in fact, no necessary relation between them. The wonderful success of modern business is dependent upon combination. It is as much a necessity of trade and commerce as steam and machinery. By combination capital is obtained, enterprises of magnitude conducted, great results accomplished. By combination small capitalists can successfully compete with large capital. Every partnership is a combination. Every corporation is a combination. Destroy the right to combine and business on a large scale becomes at once impossible. Unity of action would be destroyed. Our railroads would be eaten with rust. Our ships would rot in their harbors. Our warehouses would decay. Mankind would become segregated as savages, each acting for himself alone and endeavoring to destroy others. Surely people do not stop to think what they mean when they utter their wild cries against combinations.

Possibly some combinations are monopolies, but monopoly does

* See his selection in Volume III.

not necessarily arise from combination. A monopoly can be held by a single person as well as by a combination of many persons.

A monopoly is a grant by the government for the sole buying, working, making or using of anything. Less than a century ago the right to labor was to a great extent a privilege which the sovereign might rightfully sell to his subjects. In those days, it has been said, the prying eye of the government followed the butcher to the shambles and the baker to the oven. The peasant could not grind his corn in his own mill, nor sharpen his tools on his own grindstone, nor make his oil, wine, or cider at his own press. Those natural rights and liberties which belong to every individual were taken from him and sold as exclusive privileges to favored creatures of government. No wonder that the term became one of odium, and that it still remains a term of reproach. Let it not be forgotten, however, that the struggle against monopoly ever has been, and ever will be, a struggle against interference in business by government.

But it is by no means true that every monopoly is an unmitigated evil. Many exist at this day which are admitted by jurists, statesmen, and economists to be among our greatest blessings. Every grant of a patent right is a monopoly. Every grant of an exclusive right is a monopoly. Our railroads, gas companies, and water companies, insofar as they possess exclusive privileges, are monopolies. Yet no one but a socialist or an anarchist would deprive the people of them or of the blessings they have conferred. I, however, am willing to admit that entirely too many of them exist. The greatest stride in law reform that has been made in this country in the last 20 years consists in placing in so many of our state constitutions the provision that no special or exclusive privileges shall be granted.

Combinations of capital and of persons, whether as partnerships, associations, or corporations, without any grant of exclusive privileges, are in no sense of the word monopolies.

Without combination, without partnerships, without joint stock associations, without corporations, the business of the world would stagnate. They are as indispensable to the manufactures and commerce of this nineteenth century as the air is to our existence. It may be a surprising statement, but it is true, that all the evils of the old monopolistic system that have survived to this day exist in consequence of the restrictions which have been placed by law upon freedom of combination.

The greatest step forward which has been made in jurisprudence in the last half century has been in the partial removing of restrictions upon combination. And the greatest blessing that legislation can confer upon commerce and manufactures is to leave the right of combination entirely unrestricted, while it directs careful attention to the prevention of such evils as combinations may be found to give rise to or to foster. Combination is a power for good. It may also be a power for evil. The power must not be destroyed; it must be regulated. I wish to go back a little to prove my assertion that freedom of combination renders monopoly impossible. Less than half a century ago the natural right of the British people to combine for trading in any manner except as partners was denied, and the issuing of a transferable stock without special legal authority was a criminal offense. For this reason the few corporations which were created by Parliament held exclusive franchises and were, therefore, monopolies. I go further and say that the right thus to combine was denied to the people in order that the few upon whom this privilege was conferred *should* hold a monopoly. We brought our laws and customs upon this subject from England, and until within a very few years in most of the states of this Union freedom of combination was denied, and the right was granted by special legislative acts to those who were political favorites or who were able to purchase special privileges. Those were the days of monopolies. Some of the eastern states, notably Massachusetts and Rhode Island, long ago freed themselves from this error, and allowed all persons freely to combine for manufacturing, mining, or mercantile purposes. The consequence was an era of prosperity in those states in marked contrast to the condition of the states whose laws forbade such combinations. In no state did capital reap a better profit and labor a richer reward. The laborer was thus enabled to invest his small accumulations in the business in which he was employed. . . . Today there is scarcely a state in this Union in which any three or three thousand persons may not combine their capital, be it small or great, in any lawful business enterprise. . . .

Political economists recognized this necessity long before it was adopted by our lawmakers. John Stuart Mill [1806–1873] . . . says, "when markets are large, and a large opening for exportation, large systems of business are effective. Large establishments are substituted for small ones. This change from small to large is wholly beneficial. It may have some drawbacks, but when once the system of large establishments is established, the change from large to larger systems is an unqualified benefit." Again . . . "The progress of the productive arts requiring that many sorts of industrial occupations should be carried on by larger and larger capitals the productive power of industry must suffer by whatever impedes the formation of large capitals through the aggregation of smaller ones."

He further contends that the only hope of breaking up the separation of mankind into employer and employed and giving the employed an interest in the business is in the extension of the combination or partnership principle, and urges that all legal obstacles to combination should be taken away. . . .

But is combination an unmixed blessing? No one pretends that it is. It is attended with, or may give rise to, greater or less evils, and it is the duty of legislators and judicial lawmakers to keep a watchful eye upon, and to repress the evil. Every force is a blessing, although it may be used for evil as well as for good. We do not abolish guns because they are the instruments of murder. We do not prohibit the manufacture of dynamite because it is used by anarchists. We use steam, notwithstanding its dangerous qualities. To talk of preventing combinations is childish and futile. To pass laws which will prevent them from accomplishing bad results is the most important purpose to which the legislative mind can be directed.

The usual charge against combination is that it destroys competition. "Where combination is possible competition is impossible," was once uttered by a wise man, and thousands re-utter it utterly regardless of its correct application. It was said by George Stephenson with regard to railroads which have exclusive privileges, and are, to that extent, monopolies. As competition is necessarily confined to two or three companies, combination among them certainly may destroy competition. The saying has been applied to all kinds of business, utterly forgetful of the fact that no business is carried on without combination, and the greater the business the greater necessarily the combination. Competition is not thereby destroyed. It is simply carried on on a higher plane. The man who transports on a wheelbarrow gives way, it is true, to the man who transports on a wagon. But wagoners compete. The individual with small capital gives way to aggregated capital. But the individual unites his capital with others, and the aggregations compete. The business is in consequence done better and more cheaply. The profits are possibly larger. The public, however, is benefited by a better and cheaper product.

Competition which is beneficial is not a fierce strife between persons each to undersell the other, carried to the furthest extreme without cooperation or compromise. This would be a fit mode for savages, not for civilized men.

The beneficial effect of competition is undoubtedly to furnish the public the best material at the lowest price, but that is neither accomplished by mere blind cutting under in prices, nor is it prevented by reasonable understandings, arrangements, or agreements in reference to price. The business of the world could not be carried on if producers or sellers of commodities could have no understanding between themselves as to prices. The competitor who begins by cutting prices below what his neighbor can sell at does so only to crush them out that he may afterwards sell higher. Such competition is neither honorable nor of ultimate benefit to the public. It is of public benefit that all dealers should obtain fair profits. But the public demands, and this is what a beneficial competition accomplishes, that business be so conducted that the public shall get the best products at the least cost.

This is not done by selling below cost, but by reducing the cost of producing, manufacturing and transporting in every possible way. Only the competitor who does this is a public benefactor. He is the man who buys the best tools at any cost; who advances from the old coulter and beam plow through all the improvements to the steam plow; who abandons the sickle for the cradle, and the cradle for the reaper; the man, in fact, who makes two blades of grass grow where one grew before. Such a competitor benefits the public, and the man who, unable to advance, plodding on in the ways of his forefathers, asks for legislation to protect him against his progressive neighbor whom he stigmatizes as a capitalist, is entitled to pity, but can only be helped at public expense. It seems to be a favorite modern notion that any advance in methods of business by which the poorest competitor is injured is contrary to public policy. If this were true the public would derive no advantages from competition. The foremost in the race would be forced to wait for the hindmost to catch up. The rule in business is emphatically the survival of the fittest. Only thus can the public receive benefit from superior skill and economies in business. Competition crushes out competitors, but does not destroy competition so long as all have the right to compete.

Those methods of business are correct and legal which subserve the greatest good of the greatest number. To this end unrestricted competition is absolutely necessary and so is unrestricted combination. . . .

When I speak of unrestricted combinations I do not mean that combinations should be allowed under all circumstances and for all purposes. While combination is not *per se* evil, its purpose may be. The law is possibly our best guide on this subject. It has progressed as experience and the necessities of business required it to progress, from the idea that all combinations were wrong to the idea that all persons should be left free to combine for all legitimate purposes. To this day, however, the law is properly very jealous of certain classes of combinations, such as:

1. Where the parties combining exercise a public employment, or possess exclusive privileges, and are to that extent monopolies.

2. Where the purpose and effect of the combination is to "corner" any article necessary to the public.

3. Where the purpose and effect of the combination is to limit production, and thereby to unduly enhance prices.

These things are illegal and properly so. The mistakes of writers on trusts and combinations consist in assuming that all combinations are for such purposes, whereas the purpose and effect of most combinations is just the reverse of this, namely, to lessen the cost of production, increase the amount of consumption, and outdistance competitors by selling at [lower] prices. The difference between the assumed and the real purpose and effect is as great as between using dynamite in constructing public improvements and using it in destroying property.

Time would not permit me to review the cases laying down the law on the subject of combinations for illegal purposes. Those, and they are the majority, relating to railroads and public carriers are not pertinent to the case. All the others, including the well known coal cases and the salt cases, were arrangements with the direct and avowed purpose of destroying all competition, diminishing supplies and raising prices.

These things are just as unlawful without combination as with it. In other words, the evil is not in combination but in its purposes and results.

And let it be noted here that where the law speaks of agreements destroying competition it does not refer to the fact that competition between those who associate is thereby destroyed, for if this were illegal two persons could not enter into partnership. It condemns any arrangement the purpose or *necessary* tendency of which is to destroy *all* competition and thus to prejudice the public.

So, far from condemning all combinations which may affect competition, the law favors combinations the object and tendency of which is to lessen the cost of production and prices to the public.

Judge Gibson is correctly quoted in Mr. Crain's printed brief as saying, in Com. *vs.* Carlisle: "A combination is criminal whenever the act to be done has a *necessary* tendency to prejudice the public or to oppress individuals by unjustly subjecting them to the power of the confederates, and giving effect of the purpose of the latter *whether of extortion or of mischief*." You will notice that it is not the combination, but the purpose of extortion and mischief, and the *necessary* tendency to prejudice the public, that is criminal. Judge Gibson, in the same case, also says:

"The combination of capital for purposes of commerce, or to carry on any other branch of industry, although it may in its consequences indirectly operate on third persons . . . is a common means in the ordinary course of human affairs *which stimulates to competition,* and enables men to engage in undertakings too weighty for an individual." I wish you to mark that, in the opinion of the greatest judge who ever adorned the bench of Pennsylvania, such combinations *stimulate to competition. . . .*

Less than a century ago the iron hand of the government was upon all business. Not only combination in business but a great portion of that which today constitutes business, was prohibited, unless specially allowed by the government. It was a crime for workingmen to combine to raise their wages. It was a crime to buy in one market to sell at a greater price in another. It was a crime to purchase produce on its way to market. It was a crime to export certain commodities. Some of the bills presented here, and some of the arguments in their advocacy, would have you forget all that has been learned for a century and adopt the laws of an age when business in its modern sense was unknown; when the iron hand of government not only controlled but paralyzed trade; when workingmen were slaves prohibited from acting together for their own benefit; when the leaders of political combinations which undertook to influence legislation, whether wisely or unwisely, were beheaded as traitors.

Before doing so, contemplate what such a thinker as Buckle . . . says of those old laws: "Every European government which has legislated respecting trade has acted as if its main object were to suppress the trade and ruin the traders. Instead of leaving the national industry to take its own course it has been troubled by an interminable series of regulations, all intended for its good, and all inflicting serious harm. To such a height has this been carried that the commercial reforms which have distinguished England during the last twenty years have solely consisted in undoing this mischievous and intrusive legislation. It is no exaggeration to say that the history of the commercial legislation of Europe presents every possible contrivance for hampering the energies of commerce. In every quarter and at every moment, the hand of government was felt. Bounties to raise up a losing trade, and taxes to pull down a remunerative one, this branch of industry forbidden, and that branch of industry encouraged. Laws to regulate wages; laws to regulate prices; laws to regulate profits, interference with markets, interference with manufactories, interference with machinery, interference even with shops."

Gentlemen, legislation has made some progress backwards the last few years. Is it not time to call a halt?

No legislature can interfere with freedom of combination for legitimate purposes without striking trade and commerce prostrate at its feet. If you enact, as certain bills before you would have you enact, that no two men can agree on the price at which they will sell any article, or that two individuals cannot agree to cease competing in sales, or that no combination which affects prices shall be legal, you destroy not only all partnerships, all corporations, all aggregations of capital, all unity of effort in business, all compromises by which the disasters of overcompetition are frequently averted, but you simply render business impossible. Your act should be entitled "an act to effectually prevent trade and commerce."

A word further as to associations of great magnitude. I have said the magnitude must correspond with the market. A small association may monopolize a small trade. The agreement of two grocers in a country village may fix prices for that village. Will competition be thereby destroyed? By no means, for the field is open to any comer, and if prices are fixed too high buyers will seek a new market or a third grocer will come in. In a city the rule is the same. The business must be enlarged to meet the enlarged market. Great combinations may take place. They do not, however, affect the market as much as the agreement of the two grocers in a country village affects their market. The field is open to all comers, large or small. Arbitrary prices will simply invite new capital.

When the world is the market the business must be on equal magnitude. Associated capital on a corresponding scale is required. Still the field is open to all comers. Now and again new manufactories may be drawn into the association. No monopoly is created, for new ones spring up to take their places. Prices must be kept at the lowest possible point to keep new capital from the field. Millions of dollars, with the world for a market, do not have half the effect of monopolizing that market that the formation of a partnership by two grocers has on the market of a country town.

I repeat again, because it is a principle that seems to be lost sight of, that the right of association must be free, that the magnitude of associations must correspond with the magnitude of the business to be done, that business cannot be localized, that it cannot be confined by state lines, that when the problem is to open and to keep open the markets of the world, it is sheer madness to attempt to restrict the business as that of a local manufactory may be restricted. All the wisdom learned from experience and from political economists for the last half century must be thrown to the winds at the mad bidding of socialistic enemies of capital before such a result can be accomplished. You may accomplish it but you will accomplish the destruction of trade and commerce at the same time. . . .

The sum of all that I have said is briefly this: The use and legitimate effect of industrial combinations is *to furnish the public a larger supply of commodities at a smaller price.* The illegal purpose and effect of such combinations is *to furnish the public a smaller supply with intent to unduly increase the price.*

Wise legislation will prevent the abuse without interfering with the useful results.

I now propose to review the history of the Standard combination, both prior and subsequent to the formation of the trust, and I expect to demonstrate that the necessities of the business demanded association on a large scale; that the business has always been competitive both at home and abroad; that the combination has constantly cheapened manufacture and improved the manufactured products; that it has increased the demand, and diminished prices to an extent unparalleled in any other business; that, in short, it has furnished oil at the lowest possible prices at home, and built up an American trade of fifty millions a year abroad, which it maintains against the fiercest competition. . . .

HISTORY OF THE STANDARD OIL COMBINATION

Petroleum was discovered in 1859. At first it was simply distilled, and a product obtained [that was] unsatisfactory and dangerous. Improvements were made, new products discovered, hundreds of patents taken out and hundreds of refineries erected in the oil region. They were universally small and cheap. In the principal cities more extensive refineries with more expensive and perfect machinery were established. All the refineries were competitive, and although for a time the business was prosperous, for many years the history of the refining business was mainly one of disaster, failure, and bankruptcy. Up to 1872 oil had not been sold as low as twenty-five cents per gallon; it was sold at times as high as fifty cents per gallon, and yet refiners on the whole made little money.

Now a reasonable profit is made at 7¢ per gallon and a far better product manufactured. This result has been largely accomplished by the Standard Oil Combination. . . .

Cheapening Transportation—In 1872 the pipe line system was in its infancy. A number of local lines existed. Their service was inefficient and expensive. There was no uniform rate. The united refiners undertook to unite and systematize this business. They purchased and consolidated the various little companies into what was long known as the United Pipe Line System. The first effect of this combination was a reduction of price of all local transportation to an uniform rate of at first 30¢ and soon after 20¢ per barrel. The pipes were placed at every well. A storage system was also adopted. Huge iron tanks were built in which oil could be stored awaiting a market. The cost of storage has been reduced until it is now cheaper than that of any other commodity. Oil was taken from any well, stored in these tanks, and a certificate given the producer showing the amount. These certificates ultimately became the medium of trade in oil. They were bought and sold, and when presented at any pipe line terminus at any railroad the oil was delivered on board cars. The amount of capital back of these certificates, and the uniformly careful manner in which the business was conducted, eventually created such public confidence in them that they have been dealt in by thousands of persons in this and other countries who never saw a barrel of crude oil. Exchanges for their sale exist in several of the principal cities. They are taken by banks as collateral. They are as good as money. They are now dealt in on the New York Stock Exchange. Oil is delivered on them in New York as well as in the Oil Region.

Although the business was built up and owned by those who built up and own the Standard Oil Company, the business is done for the public. Its benefit to the oil trade has been incalculable. Instead of, as is sometimes charged, the Standard being the sole buyer, the buyers are numbered by thousands. The producer not only gets the highest possible price which competition to purchase will bring, he gets also cash in hand. He never sees his oil from the moment it leaves his well. When he wants his well tank relieved, he telephones a pipe line gauger, sees his oil pumped, receives a ticket showing the amount, takes it to a pipe line office and gets a certificate which he can hold, borrow on or sell in any exchange, as he sees fit. No one can estimate this advantage to the business. Without combination, aggregated capital and public confidence in the security, it could not have been accomplished. Should you dissolve the combination and disperse the capital which makes these certificates secure, the system could no longer be maintained.

The figures will show that in one year the production of oil exceeded 31,000,000 barrels, or 9,000,000 barrels in excess of consumption. Consider for a moment what this means. Every day of that year iron tankage had to be built to accommodate 25,000 barrels of surplus oil. This meant an army of iron workers and tank builders, and a cost per day of $7,500.

This the Standard Oil Companies accomplished. How, without aggregated capital, could it have been done? It is idle to speak of the work as Herculean. In these days, by combination of money and effort, the labor of a thousand Hercules is easily accomplished.

So much for local transportation and storage. About 1879 or '80 it was discovered that railways were inadequate to the task of getting oil to the seaboard as rapidly as needed. Combined capital and energy were equal to the emergency. No need to detail how it was done. Today there reaches from the Oil Regions of Pennsylvania and New York to the principal cities iron pipes conducting oil as it comes from the wells. Two such lines reach to New York harbor with a capacity of 25,000 barrels per day. There is one such line to each of the cities of Philadelphia, Baltimore, Buffalo, Cleveland and Pittsburgh, built by the Standard Oil combination at a cost of millions and doing business for the public. . . .

Cheapening Cost of Manufacture—The Association of Refiners united the best knowledge and skill in the business. If one had a patent it was open to all. If one had a secret the others shared it. Methods were compared. New plans were tested. Results were and are carefully collated. If one establishment succeeds in saving the fraction of a cent per barrel in making oil the reason is known and the method of saving adopted. If good results are obtained in one manufactory and bad results in another, the reason is at once discovered and faults corrected. Scientific men are constantly employed who have made useful discoveries in new products and new methods of manufacture. The consequence of all this is that since 1872 the actual cost of manufacture of refined oil has been reduced 66 per cent.

The public have the advantage of this in the reduced price at which the oil is sold, which benefit amounts to millions annually.

The same cheapening of manufacture has taken place in the manufacture of barrels, tin cans, boxes for enclosing cans, paint, glue, and acid.

In 1872 barrels cost the trade $2.35 each. They are now manufactured by our own manufactories at a cost of $1.25 each. About 3,500,000 barrels are used per annum. This single item amounts to $4,000,000 per year.

In 1874 cans cost 30¢ each. They are now made by our manufactories for less than 15¢. Thirty-six million cans are used each year, and this one item of saving amounts to $5,400,000 each year.

In 1874 wooden cases cost 20¢ each. They are now manufactured by our own manufactories at a cost of about 13¢ each. The saving in this item alone amounts to $1,250,000 each year.

The same cheapening process has taken place in the manufacture of tanks, stills, pumps, and everything used in the business.

All these millions are saved by the economies which combination of persons, capital, experience and skill render possible, without reducing the wages of a single laboring man.

The Business in By-Products of Petroleum—After illuminating oil is manufactured a large residuum is left. Up to 1875 this was always used as fuel at the refineries. The Standard devoted special attention to this residuum. Experts visited the great shale works in Scotland and studied their methods. The consequence was that extensive works were erected for the manufacture of products from this residuum, principally lubricating oils and paraffine wax. These works are necessarily expensive, and manufacture the residuum of a large number of refineries. Small refineries cannot advantageously engage in this branch of business and cannot afford to manufacture illuminating oils unless they can dispose of their residuum. This is one of the reasons so many small refineries prove failures. The cost of manufacture of lubricating oils and wax has been reduced by improved methods and constant attention, and the price to the consumer has been constantly reduced, averaging today 50 per cent less than in 1878.

The use of illuminating oils was introduced to the public with comparative ease, because it met an urgent need. Lubricating oils, on the contrary, met with slow recognition, having to supplant sperm, lard, and fish oils. In Europe, in addition, the products of shale had to be competed with. The work was pushed with vigor, with capital and with success. An enormous home and foreign trade has been established in these by-products.

Numerous other useful products are obtained from petroleum, and no expense has been spared to find a use and a market for them. All this results in ability to sell illuminating oil at a price but little above the cost of the crude product, and thus to make it "the poor man's light."

Markets for Products—To make the consumption as great as it is, the first essentials were good quality and cheapness. But that is not enough. Twenty-five years ago the world was just beginning to hear of petroleum. When this Standard Combination was formed, twelve years had elapsed and the world was using less than 6,000,000 barrels per annum. Of that 3,500,000 barrels were exported. In two years afterwards the exports were nearly 6,000,000 barrels. The reason for it was that no single refinery could afford to keep agents in Europe and Asia to demonstrate the advantages of this product, open means for its convenient and safe transshipment and force it upon the trade. The refiners when combined could do it, did do it and continue to do it. The consequence is that petroleum is today the light of the world. It is carried wherever a wheel can roll or a camel's hoof be planted. The caravans on the desert of Sahara go laden with Pratt's Astral, and elephants in India carry cases of Standard White. Ships are constantly loading at our wharves for Japan, Java and the most distant isles of the sea. Our country's revenues are swollen $50,000,000 per year by this trade. Think you it was built up or maintained without cause? It never could have happened without combination of persons and capital, and without the support of combination and capital the whole trade would be swept to destruction as the vanishing of a cloud on a summer's day. To illustrate, let me give the history of a small subject.

Complaints occasionally came to us from all parts of the world that oil is not proving satisfactory. An agent is sent to investigate. Sometimes the cause of the trouble is found to be Russian oil in American packages, or oil under false trade marks. Consuls, ministers and governments are besieged until a remedy is obtained. One great cause of complaint arose from bad wicks. Some years ago a manufactory was established by the Standard interests for manufacturing the best wick known. Its capital is large, but it sinks about all its capital every year. The wicks are sold at a price so low as to compel their use. Things like these cost thousands of dollars per annum, but they save our market. This is done at our expense, but our competitors reap their share of the benefit. Without combination it would not be done at all. . . .

I have dwelt . . . upon the history of the Standard because it is always referred to as embodying all the evils of combinations and trusts.

And yet the facts show that it, or some similar combination of

persons and capital, was and is essential to the building up and maintenance of the American oil trade; that its destruction would be the
destruction of that trade; that it has furnished the producer a cash
market and the best possible price for his oil, and that it is benefiting
the public by actual reduction in cost of manufacture and prices to
the extent of more than its aggregated capital each year. Let the state
or national legislature provide a better mode for carrying on this
business if they can, but let them not despoil the structure until a
better is provided to take its place.

A FAMOUS OILMAN'S CONCEPT OF
THE AMERICAN BUSINESSMAN

JOHN D. ROCKEFELLER

[John D. Rockefeller, *Random Reminiscences of Men and Events*, Doubleday,
Page & Co., New York, 1909. (First copyrighted 1908.) Pp. 71–76 (abridged).
Permission granted by the estate of John D. Rockefeller.]

After John D. Rockefeller had been under public criticism for almost a
generation, the former leader of the Standard Oil combination decided
to publish a calm rejoinder in the form of *Random Reminiscences of
Men and Events,* first in *The World's Work* and later as a book (1909).
He did so because he was convinced that many events in Standard Oil
history had not been fully understood, and he wanted to do justice
to the men with whom he had worked over the years. "If a tenth of
the things that have been said are true," he wrote, "then these dozens
of able and faithful men who have been associated with me . . . must
have been guilty of grave faults." He refused to accept such a dictum,
and in the course of his book gave the following characterization of
"The American Businessman" based on his own views, and observations of friends and competitors.

Whatever the story of Standard Oil's development, these first-hand
works of Rockefeller may serve to give some insight into his own
attitudes about his business affairs.

———◆———

YOU HEAR A GOOD MANY PEOPLE of pessimistic disposition say much
about greed in American life. One would think to hear them talk
that we were a race of misers in this country. To lay too much stress
upon the reports of greed in the newspapers would be folly, since
their function is to report the unusual and even the abnormal. When
a man goes properly about his daily affairs, the public prints say
nothing; it is only when something extraordinary happens to him

that he is discussed. But because he is thus brought into prominence occasionally, you surely would not say that these occasions represented his normal life. It is by no means for money alone that these active-minded men labor—they are engaged in a fascinating occupation. The zest of the work is maintained by something better than the mere accumulation of money, and, as I think I have said elsewhere, the standards of business are high and are getting better all the time.

I confess I have no sympathy with the idea so often advanced that our basis of all judgments in this country is founded on money. If this were true, we should be a nation of money hoarders instead of spenders. Nor do I admit that we are so small-minded a people as to be jealous of the success of others. It is the other way about: we are the most extraordinarily ambitious, and the success of one man in any walk of life spurs the others on. It does not sour them, and it is a libel even to suggest so great a meanness of spirit.

In reading the newspapers, where so much is taken for granted in considering things on a money standard, I think we need some of the sense of humor possessed by an Irish neighbor of mine who built what we regarded as an extremely ugly house which stood out in bright colors as we looked from our windows. My taste in architecture differed so widely from that affected by my Irish friend that we planted out the view of his house by moving some large trees to the end of our property. Another neighbor who watched this work going on asked Mr. Foley why Mr. Rockefeller moved all these big trees and cut off the view between the houses. Foley, with the quick wit of his country, responded instantly: "It's invy, they can't stand looking at the ividence of me prosperity."

In my early days men acted just as they do now, no doubt. When there was anything to be done for general trade betterment, almost every man had some good reason for believing that his case was a special one different from all the rest. For every foolish thing he did, or wanted to do, for every unbusinesslike plan he had, he always pleaded that it was necessary in his case. He was the one man who had to sell at less than cost, to disrupt all the business plans of others in his trade, because his individual position was so absolutely different from all the rest. It was often a heartbreaking undertaking to convince those men that the perfect occasion which would lead to the perfect opportunity would never come, even if they waited until the crack o' doom.

Then again, we had the type of man who really never knew all the facts about his own affairs. Many of the brightest kept their books in such a way that they did not actually know when they were making money on a certain operation and when they were losing. This unintelligent competition was a hard matter to contend with. Good old-fashioned common sense has always been a mighty rare commodity.

When a man's affairs are not going well, he hates to study the books and face the truth. From the first, the men who managed the Standard Oil Company kept their books intelligently as well as correctly. We knew how much we made and where we gained or lost. At least, we tried not to deceive ourselves.

My ideas of business are no doubt old-fashioned, but the fundamental principles do not change from generation to generation, and sometimes I think that our quick-witted American businessmen, whose spirit and energy are so splendid, do not always sufficiently study the real underlying foundations of business management. I have spoken of the necessity of being frank and honest with oneself about one's own affairs: many people assume that they can get away from the truth by avoiding thinking about it, but the natural law is inevitable, and the sooner it is recognized, the better.

One hears a great deal about wages and why they must be maintained at a high level, by the railroads, for example. A laborer is worthy of his hire, no less, but no more, and in the long run he must contribute an equivalent for what he is paid. If he does not do this, he is probably pauperized, and you at once throw out the balance of things. You can't hold up conditions artificially, and you can't change the underlying laws of trade. If you try, you must inevitably fail. All this may be trite and obvious, but it is remarkable how many men overlook what should be the obvious. These are facts we can't get away from—a businessman must adapt himself to the natural conditions as they exist from month to month and year to year. Sometimes I feel that we Americans think we can find a short road to success, and it may appear that often this feat is accomplished; but real efficiency in work comes from knowing your facts and building upon that sure foundation.

Many men of wealth do not retire from business even when they can. They are not willing to be idle, or they have a just pride in their work and want to perfect the plans in which they have faith, or, what is of still more consequence, they may feel the call to expand and build up for the benefit of their employees and associates, and these men are the great builders up in our country. Consider for a moment how much would have been left undone if our prosperous American businessmen had sat down with folded hands when they had acquired a competency. I have respect for all these reasons, but if a man has succeeded, he has brought upon himself corresponding responsibilities, and our institutions devoted to helping men to help themselves need the brain of the American businessman as well as part of his money.

Some of these men, however, are so absorbed in their business affairs that they hardly have time to think of anything else. If they do interest themselves in a work outside of their own office and undertake to raise money, they begin with an apology, as if they are ashamed of themselves.

"I am no beggar," I have heard many of them say, to which I could only reply: "I am sorry you feel that way about it."

I have been this sort of beggar all my life and the experiences I have had were . . . interesting and important to me. . . .

THE ROMANCE OF COMMERCE

HARRY GORDON SELFRIDGE

[Harry Gordon Seifridge, *The Romance of Commerce*, The John Lane Company, New York, 1918, pp. 1-5.]

Here the great merchant, Harry Gordon Selfridge, speaks out in protest against those who think romance is elsewhere than in commerce. Born an American in 1864, he spent his early career in Marshall Field and Company, Chicago; then in 1906 he went to London, where he organized the wholesale-retail firm of Selfridge and Company, Limited, which opened a large department store on Oxford Street, destined to become one of the world's most successful.

So when he says that "to work is elevating," he speaks with the authority of experience and accomplishment. Such a man is worth listening to just to try to understand how his mind works.

———◆———

TO WRITE on commerce or trade and to do the subject justice would require more volumes than any library could hold, and involve more detail than any mind could grasp. It would be history *in extenso* of the world's people from the beginning of time. For we are all merchants, and all races of men have been merchants in some form or another. The desire to trade seems to be inherent in man, as natural to him as the instinct of self-preservation, and from earliest recorded history we see trade and barter entering into and becoming part of the lives of men of all nations, and further, we see it as one of the most desirable objectives of the nations themselves. Ever since that moment when two individuals first lived upon this earth, one has had what the other wanted, and has been willing for a consideration to part with his possession. This is the principle underlying all trade, however primitive, and all men, except the idlers, are merchants.

We give this title exclusively to the man who buys and sells merchandise, but the artist sells the work of his brush and in this he is a merchant. The writer sells to any who will buy, let his ideas be what they will. The teacher sells his knowledge of books—often in too low a market—to those who would have this knowledge passed on to the young. The doctor must make an income to support himself and his family. He too is a merchant. His stock-in-trade is his intimate knowledge of the physical man and his skill to prevent or remove disabilities. He sells a part of his experience for a given sum to whosoever seeks his advice. The lawyer sometimes knows the laws of the land and sometimes does not, but he sells his legal language, often accompanied by common sense, to the multitude who have not yet learned that a contentious nature may squander quite as successfully as the spendthrift. The statesman sells his knowledge of men and affairs, and the spoken or written exposition of his principles of government; and he receives in return the satisfaction of doing what he can for his nation, and occasionally wins as well a niche in its temple of fame.

The man possessing many lands, he especially would be a merchant in fact, and sell, but his is a merchandise which too often nowadays waits in vain for the buyer. The preacher, the lecturer, the actor, the estate agent, the farmer, the employee, all, all are merchants, all have something to dispose of at a profit to themselves, and the dignity of the business is decided by the manner in which they conduct the sale.

To work is elevating. To accomplish is superb. To fill one's time with profitable enterprise is to leap forward in the world's race and to place beside one's name the credit mark of effort. It has always been so since civilization began, and all effort has always had for its object a gain of some kind, while the amount of effort is usually determined by the value of the hoped-for gain, plus the temperament, ambitions, and inclinations of the doer.

The first efforts were made in the direction of bodily protection. Food, clothing and shelter, these, in some degree, must be possessed by every individual. And the steps from these crudest beginnings of trade up to the science of commerce of the twentieth century are as interesting to study as the pages of the wildest romance. Wealth with its accompanying power has been since earliest time the goal that no honest effort can be too great to reach; and the goal it must always remain for the peoples who have the red blood of progress in their veins. And without commerce there is no wealth. Adam Smith wrote 150 years ago: "All original wealth comes from the soil"; but while the soil so amply repays labor expended upon it, the owner of the crops looks to the alchemist, commerce, to turn his golden harvests into golden coin.

Commerce creates wealth, and is the foundation of the great state. Armies are raised and paid for to win, or to protect the countries' trade, or commerce. Ships are constructed, colonies established, inventions encouraged, governments built up, or pulled down, for commerce. Commerce cuts the way, and all professions, all arts follow. If commerce is necessary to wealth, no commerce means no wealth, and our statesman soon finds himself out of employment. Where wealth again is greatest, everything else being fairly equal, arts thrive the most.

A thousand departments of mental and physical activity foster and in turn are fostered by its achievement. People must be governed, and there must be those who govern. Laws must be made, and there must be those who study, and those who execute these laws. People must be taught, and there must be teachers. All these and the church, the newspaper, the theater, the fine arts are essential to the completeness of the state, to the happiness and safety of its people; but commerce is the main stem, or trunk, where they are all branches, supplied with the sap of its far-reaching wealth. It is as necessary to the existence of any nation as blood to the physical man. That country in which trade flourishes is accounted happy, while that in which commerce droops provokes shaking of heads and prophecies of downfall.

Just as in a beautiful tapestry there must be the groundwork, the foundation upon which the design is woven, so has commerce acted as the underlying warp and woof in the development of civilization. It gives both strength and substance, and more than this, for it gives color as well. Its threads are so closely interwoven with the rest as to be almost indistinguishable from them. Or, to change the simile, commerce is the foundation upon which nations are built; but it is also the superstructure, and provides the bands of steel which support every part of the national edifice.

Commerce is the mother of the arts, the sciences, the professions, and in this twentieth century has itself become an art, a science, a profession. As it plays with a fine touch on the strings of human nature the world over, and makes happier by its fairness the youth of today and the man of tomorrow, it is an art.

As it strives for the new and discards the old, when the old has been superseded by the better, as it invents and thinks out methods, ideas, even fundamental principles, and as its laboratory is always occupied by men who are searching for the causes of its depression and experimenting upon its possibilities of progress, so it becomes a very catholic science.

And as it studies and digs deeper into the wishes and wants of the people; as it urges and proclaims its determination to force a higher and better standard of living throughout the realm of its activity; as it hates the wrong, the deceitful, and holds up the fair and straightforward; as it stands for greater accomplishment, greater power, greater happiness to its own workers and to the entire community as well, then it may truly be ranked as a profession, and one whose sphere of work is broader, whose almost unaccountable ramifications are infinitely more far-reaching than those of any other profession. Great is commerce, and great is its field of work, of thought, of development.

It is to the writer an almost incredible thing that any government could ever be so suicidally shortsighted as to discourage trade; yet history is full of the restrictions placed upon it by the very men who would have profited by making its path easier. Commerce has developed too often in spite of legislation rather than by its help. This has almost always been so, and is very true today, for as far as we can see there has been very little progress made by lawmakers toward encouraging commerce. How rarely indeed are laws passed to encourage anything. They restrict, they limit, they prohibit from this and that; and as regards the man of commerce their whole purpose seems to be too often to hamper and annoy.

However, it is folly to waste ink on this subject. It has always been so, and, for all that we can see, always will be. Some day, perhaps, some Solomon may rise and create a form of government which will please everyone; and if this new Solomon comes from the same race as his distinguished predecessor we may be sure he will see to it that in this government business shall find a true friend.

WHILE HE IS PILING DUNG

EDWARD C. BURSK

[Edward C. Bursk, "While He Is Piling Dung," in *Script* Magazine, 1939.]

Must workaday labor be basically irreconcilable with idealism? If so, must the compromise we resort to be always mean and dirty? Here is a poem written by a businessman (later a business editor) when he had not yet had enough experience to realize that work itself, well performed, can be beautiful. Or maybe he did have a hunch about it; else why, having brought his character, John Bartlett, to the age of 41, would he try to bring "dung" into poetry? (This is the same man who sold his canned peas too cheap; see his piece on Low-Pressure Selling in Volume I.)

The poem was published in a 1939 issue of *Script*, a magazine from California so short-lived that it was out of existence by the time "John Bartlett" had reached the age portrayed by the last stanza.

I

John Bartlett, one and twenty,
Would hold his head so high
He could not see the hilltop;
He only saw the sky.
He thought that he could reach it.
He thought that he could stand
Upon a piled-up hayrick
And touch it with his hand. . . .
John Bartlett kept on working
And cursed his body's needs,
Not seeing he was pulling
The corn out for the weeds.

II

Ten years were not sufficient
To bow John Bartlett's head;
He looked out toward the meadow,
And saw the hill instead.
He figured if he hurried,
He had enough of light
To climb up to its summit
And down before the night. . . .
The hill on the horizon
Was far, the planting late;
John Bartlett kept on ploughing
A furrow not too straight.

III

Ten more years teach John Bartlett
What he calls common sense;
His glance is on the meadow,
No higher than a fence.
His corn grows up the cleanest
For many miles around.
It is the talk of neighbors
How straight he ploughs the ground. . . .
Sometimes, just for a minute,
While he is piling dung,
John Bartlett stops from working,
And wishes he were young.

A CREED FOR FREE ENTERPRISE

CLARENCE B. RANDALL

[Clarence B. Randall, *A Creed for Free Enterprise*, Little, Brown & Co., Boston, 1952, pp. 3–4, 18–20, 24–27 (abridged). An Atlantic Monthly Press Book. Copyright 1952 by the author. Reprinted by permission of the publisher.]

Clarence Randall, President of Inland Steel Company from 1949 to 1953 and then Chairman of the Board, is the author of "A Creed for Free Enterprise," published first as a series of articles in *The Atlantic Monthly* and in 1952 as a book. The following selection begins with Randall's own explanation of why he, a businessman, wrote a book, and then gives a taste of his liberal thinking.

I AM AS MUCH SURPRISED as my friends will be to find that I have written a book. Until now my hallmark has been an off-the-cuff talk at a businessmen's luncheon or dinner, done in the spirit of the occasion and without manuscript. It has been my habit merely to stand up and say what I think, as though I were talking to a group of associates in my office, letting the words come as best they might. In so doing, I have tried to demonstrate by example that businessmen can and should stand up and say what they think whenever people will listen.

I now try to carry that one step further. I believe that we should also address ourselves to the reading public, that vast company of thoughtful citizens who are not invited to our luncheons, and who do not know us. I am convinced that businessmen must write as well as speak, in order that we may bring to people everywhere the exciting and confident message of our faith in the free-enterprise way of life.

We are not doing that now. We have learned how to use every modern tool except language, yet that is the tool our enemies use best. We believe in our hearts that the individualistic philosophy of social organization brings greater happiness to more people than the collectivist, but we seldom say so, and when we do, we say it only to ourselves.

This is the age of ideas. Facts and machines are still wondrously important, but it is what men believe that controls the world we live in, and what men think that threatens our way of life. The battle of ideologies is on, and we could lose it by default. If a great fire were raging in one of our plants, every man who could get there would drop whatever he was doing, no matter how important it seemed, and rush to lend a hand. Anything to save the plant! That sort of emergency compels action because you can see it; fire crackles, walls tumble in, and smoke chokes your throat.

But the glibness of the socialist planner, which rings so falsely in our ears, is a new phenomenon for which we are not psychologically prepared, and we wait timidly for others to provide the answers instead of vigorously proclaiming the truth as we ourselves see it. . . .

Most of the occasional nonsense written in this country to decry the profit motive is either ignorance or hypocrisy: it either is failure to understand the importance of self-interest in increasing the total wealth of all of the people, or just plain shutting of the eyes to the truth. For myself, I have never known a man who did not at times seek to advance his own self-interest. Professors, even those who attack our business system, vie keenly for better and bigger salaries, and clergymen want larger churches and better pay, all of which I consider to be normal and proper. Even a repulsively selfish man who knows no god but money may make tremendous contributions to society if his avarice causes him to bring into being a new or better product or produce an old one at a lower price. Just as many a necessary and useful structure may lack beauty, so may an unlovely person be useful to society. A horse with a very evil disposition can nevertheless pull the farmer's plow. So the secret of free enterprise is that we harness the natural instinct of each man to serve himself, and rely on other natural forces to see that as he serves himself he serves society.

Foremost among these forces is competition. In the management of a business the sharp bite of honest, aggressive competition is the automatic corrective that safeguards the public from extortion. No man can be said to be making too much profit if many others are trying to beat him at his own game and none can succeed. The larger his profit, the greater will be the number of those who will try and the greater the chance that they will succeed. Those who pursue him hotly have many points of attack—quality, design, service, and above all price—and he redoubles his effort as they approach because he knows that today's profit may be tomorrow's loss. He is spurred both by hope of gain and fear of loss, and never for a moment can he relax his effort. He spends his life actually producing the most that he can for the common good. How could there be a better formula than that for bringing about continuously the maximum of effort by all of the people? How can it be possible that in the long run the collective effort of nations ruled by force, where each member of society goes to his task reluctantly and without hope, will match that of free men going joyously about their tasks because they are permitted to help themselves as they add to the total wealth? . . .

But the businessman who is earnestly seeking to think through his own personal philosophy about free enterprise must go one step further and reflect upon the nature of freedom itself. I have always been unhappy at the suggestion that freedom can be expressed in the plural. Rather it seems to me it is a concept that is indivisible and sole. There are no "freedoms": there is simply freedom, and it runs as the breath of life through every phase of the American tradition. In fact, it is America.

Those daring spirits who conquered our wilderness and founded our cities and wrote our laws and began our businesses were men who broke away. No man would turn his back on the land of his fathers and the place of his birth unless he felt within himself a desire so great that it was simply irresistible. That common desire which our successive waves of immigrants from the older countries all felt was simply to live their own lives. They asked no security, and looked only to the strength of their arms and the keenness of their minds to meet their needs. But they had deep respect for each other, and assumed that their neighbors would behave as they did.

It was of such forebears that American free enterprise was born, and such is its spirit. We propose to drive as hard as we can toward our own ends but we know that we must stop short of injuring others or the whole scheme will have to be abandoned. We rely on the conscience of the individual to guide business conduct toward the general welfare. This is the responsibility side of freedom that distinguishes it from license. It is the democratic tradition because it is a self-imposed restraint instead of one that is external, as in the totalitarian states. But it is obviously subject to abuse by those who do not understand, or worse still, by that small but evil minority of men who understand and consciously ignore conscience. And in any state, when men abuse freedom there has to be law. Society has no other way of preserving itself from those who will not play the game. The proliferation of laws restricting freedom of action may be taken as an indication that more and more people either do not understand the social obligations of freedom, or lack the moral courage to do what they know is right. And when it is the business community at which the laws are aimed, it may be a sign that free enterprise is dying because it is not understood by those who practice it.

Whether or not this is a correct analysis of our business system is of little moment. But that each American businessman owes it to himself and to the system of which he is a part to make his own analysis would seem to be clear. It is a time for heart-searching and action. The march toward socialism and nationalization is on. We who would reverse that trend must recognize that this is so, and then accept day-to-day responsibility for doing something about it. But for our acts to be effective, we must first have understanding.

CHOOSING A CHIEF EXECUTIVE

CAMERON HAWLEY

[Cameron Hawley, *Executive Suite,* Houghton Mifflin Company, The Riverside Press, Cambridge, 1952, pp. 320–337. Reprinted by permission of and arrangement with Houghton Mifflin Company.]

Avery Bullard, the dynamic President of the Tredway Corporation, had suddenly dropped dead. Who was to be his successor? The issue was to be decided at an informal meeting in a private library of a leading stockholder, Julia Tredway Prince, the sole remaining representative of the founding family. Present at the meeting, in addition to Julia, were her husband Dwight Prince; George Caswell, another large stockholder; Erica Martin, the confidential secretary of Avery Bullard; J. Walter Dudley, Vice-President for Sales; Loren P. Shaw, Vice-President and Controller; MacDonald Walling, Vice-President for Design and Development; and Walling's wife Mary, from whose angle of vision the author reports this scene from *Executive Suite.*

MacDonald Walling's statement of the requisites for leadership of a modern corporation in the United States in the 1950s is remarkably significant. Or is it? Both Julia Prince and Mary Walling thought so, and they had never met prior to that fateful speech. (For another contest for the presidency of a company, see Abram T. Collier's "Debate at Wickersham Mills" page 2473 in this volume.)

Cameron Hawley was a successful businessman before he turned to full-time writing. As advertising manager for Armstrong Cork Company he had good opportunity to develop his own ideas about business, as well as to learn how other businessmen felt. So, even if this is fiction (and as such may be more sharply drawn than in real life), we have true businessmen speaking. Further, the occasion is one of the most crucial for a business organization—the choice of a new President.

—————◆—————

MARY WALLING was acutely conscious of the atmosphere of hair-trigger apprehension that hung over the stiffly seated group in the library of the old Tredway mansion. The conversation that had filled these first few minutes was forced and aimless, without point or purpose. There had been, of course, no open acknowledgment by anyone of what would be decided here this afternoon—and she sensed that there would be no such acknowledgment, even after the decision was made —yet she was sure that all of the others secretly shared her awareness that, before they left this room, the new President of the Tredway Corporation would be selected.

There had been no lessening of Mary Walling's earlier fear that her own happiness would be jeopardized if her husband moved up to the presidency, but that threat had been overbalanced by the later-rising and even more terrifying fear of what the effect on Don might be if he were to lose what he now so clearly regarded as the fulfillment of his own destiny. She knew that he could never be happy now without it—and his happiness was a prerequisite of her own.

The moment she and Don had entered the room, Mary Walling's apprehension had been aroused by the way that Loren Shaw had already pre-empted a seat beside the desk, as close to Julia Tredway Prince as it was possible for anyone to be. When, a moment later, George Caswell had come in with Erica Martin, Shaw had adroitly maneuvered Caswell into a chair between his own and Dudley's. Thus —partly by accident and partly, she was sure, by Shaw's design— Don now sat alone facing the shoulder-to-shoulder solidarity of Shaw, Caswell and Dudley. She knew that the three had lunched together and it was only too clear that the addition of Julia Tredway Prince's vote was all they needed to make Loren Shaw President. Don had said he was sure of Mrs. Prince's support, but Mary Walling found it difficult to share her husband's certainty. There had been nothing beyond simple courtesy in the way that Mrs. Prince had greeted Don when they arrived and, during these past few minutes, Loren Shaw had been making the most of his strategic position at Julia Tredway Prince's side.

Feeling herself an outsider—almost an observer with no right of participation—Mary Walling had slipped back into the corner behind her husband. She realized too late that his face was hidden from her view—by then Erica Martin had already taken the chair in the opposite corner—but there was the compensating advantage of being able to watch the room from his viewpoint and to see every glance that was sent in his direction by any of the others.

Of one thing she was now certain—Loren Shaw wasn't thinking of Don as his competitor in the battle for the presidency. The way that Shaw's eyes stabbed toward her husband when Alderson's name had been mentioned by George Caswell made it clear that Shaw regarded Don as only the lieutenant of his real adversary.

"I, too, am sorry that Mr. Alderson isn't here," Julia Tredway Prince said. "You weren't able to locate him, were you, Mr. Walling?"

Don shook his head in silence and Mary Walling wished that she could see his eyes, wondering whether he was aware as she was that Julia Tredway Prince's remark had been the first admission, even by indirection, that there was a purpose behind the invitation that had brought them together—and aware, too, of the implications of Shaw's glance.

If Julia Tredway Prince's remark had really been purposeful, the

purpose was quickly abandoned. She turned to George Caswell and
again asked a question that seemingly had no point except to force
conversation. "I understand that you flew over, Mr. Caswell?"

"Yes—and quite luxuriously. A friend of mine was good enough
to give me the use of his company's plane for the day."

"You know, that's getting to be quite a thing," Dudley burst out
as if he had withstood the restraint of silence as long as possible
"—all these Presidents of big companies having their own private
planes. I was on this NAM committee last year—had a meeting down
at New Orleans—and three of the big boys came down in their own
planes. Man, that would really be the life, having your own plane!"

Shaw cleared his throat. "I should think it might be an extravagance that would be a little difficult to justify to the stockholders."

"Oh, I don't know," Caswell said in mild rebuttal. "There has to
be some way to compensate a corporation President adequately these
days. It's hardly possible to do it with salary alone, income taxes
being what they are."

Julia Tredway Prince looked up at her husband who was lounging
against the doorframe. "Dwight and I met a man in Jamaica last
winter who had flown down in his own plane. He was the President
of some steel company—remember, Dwight?"

Dwight Prince's long face contorted in a forced grin. "Yes, he'd
traded a duodenal ulcer for a DC 3—which hardly makes me think
he'd gotten the best of it. As a matter of fact—" he hesitated as if he
were enjoying the attention he was receiving "—it's a little difficult
for me to understand why any man would want to be the President
of a large corporation these days. As far as I'm concerned it's one
of the least rewarding forms of suicide."

Mary Walling was not surprised to see Shaw's head snap up and
her husband's shoulders square, but she was puzzled by George Caswell's squinting frown.

"Oh, hardly as bad as that," Caswell said, his poise quickly recov-
ered. "In a properly organized corporation, with adequate delegation
of authority, there's no reason why the right man should be under
too great a strain."

"The right man," Shaw repeated as if it were a point to be driven
home. "And it does take the right man these days—a very different
type of man than was required in the past."

There was a warning in Shaw's purposeful tone and Mary Walling
glanced anxiously at the back of her husband's head. His shoulders
were hunched and he seemed to have no interest in anything except
his clasped hands.

"I'm not certain that I understand you, Mr. Shaw," Julia Tredway
Prince said.

Shaw seemed surprised. "It's the point that I made last evening."

There was something close to shock in Caswell's quick side glance, but Shaw was looking at Mrs. Prince and didn't see it.

"Oh, yes," Mrs. Prince said. "It's quite an interesting theory. You see—well, suppose you explain it to the others, Mr. Shaw."

There was the stillness of tense expectancy and Mary Walling saw Loren Shaw shake out a fresh handkerchief. It was the second time that she had seen him do the same thing during the bare five minutes they had been in the room.

"Well, it's a bit more than a theory," Shaw said. "The point I was making was that—well, there was a time, of course, when most of our company Presidents came up on the manufacturing side of the business. In those days that was excellent preparation for general executive responsibility, because most of the problems that came to the president's desk were concerned with manufacturing. Later, as distribution problems became more important, we sometimes saw a President rise from the sales organization—and again that was quite appropriate. Today, however, we have a very different situation. The problems that come to the President's office are predominantly *financial* in character. Matters concerning manufacturing and distribution are largely handled at lower levels in the organization. The President —who we must always remember is the agent of the stockholders— must now concern himself largely with the primary interest of the stockholders."

"And the typical stockholder isn't interested in anything but dividends?" Julia Tredway Prince asked, more as a prompt than a question.

"Exactly," Shaw said. "Of course you're an exception, Mrs. Prince. You still have what we might call a sense of *ownership*. The average stockholder doesn't think of his stockholdings as ownership—any more than he thinks of himself as the part owner of the bank where he has a savings account—or the part owner of the government because he has some defense bonds. When he buys Tredway stock he makes an *investment*. The only reason he makes it is to get a return. Thus, at the top level, the corporation must now be governed to be what its owners want it to be—a *financial institution* in which they can invest their money and receive a safe return with the emphasis on *safety*. As a matter of fact—well, you know this, Mr. Caswell—there isn't one stockholder out of ten who could even name the cities where we have our principal factories."

"You're absolutely right," George Caswell said—and the strength of the support that he offered Shaw made Mary Walling feel the hard clutch of despair. "There's no doubt that the emphasis in corporation management has gone over on the financial side. I'm sure that's why it has become so common during these last few years for men to step from investment or banking into corporation management."

Loren Shaw hesitated as if his caution had been aroused, but then quickly went ahead. "Yes, there have been cases like that—where a corporation was so unfortunate as to find itself without a major executive who was trained in financial control and modern management methods. More typically, of course, there's such a man available right within the organization."

It was a direct bid, a challenge, a throwing down of the gauntlet, and Mary Walling's heart sank as she saw that her husband wasn't going to respond. She leaned far forward attempting to see the expression on his face and, looking up, her eyes met Julia Tredway Prince's.

"Oh, Mrs. Walling, you aren't very comfortable there, are you?" Mrs. Prince said quickly. "Won't you come up here?"

It was an invitation that could not be denied and as Mary Walling moved forward Julia Tredway Prince rose from the chair behind the desk and she sat down beside her on the sofa in front of the window.

"I don't know that I get you completely, Loren," Walt Dudley said in a petulant grumble. "I can see that we have to keep the stockholders happy—got to earn a profit—but I don't see how you can say that selling isn't important—or manufacturing either."

"Of course they're important," Shaw said, his voice tinged with the forbearance of a teacher for a not-so-bright pupil. "But don't you see, Walt, they're not ends in themselves, only the means to the end. Then, too, it's a matter of management levels. As I said a moment ago, by the time you get to the presidential level, the emphasis must be predominantly financial. Take income tax as only one example. To a far greater degree than most people realize, income tax has become a primary governing factor in corporation management. In our own case—well, over the past year I've devoted a substantial amount of time to the development of a new relationship between the parent company and some of our wholly owned subsidiaries in order to give us a more favorable tax situation. Here's the point—that one piece of work, all purely financial in character, will contribute more to our net earnings than the total profit we'll make from one of our smaller factories.

"Take another example—one that I'm sure will interest Mr. Walling. Don and his associates have done a very capable job of reducing cost on our finishing operation at Water Street—producing some very nice savings—but, unfortunately, it will add little to our net earnings, less than a quarter as much as we will gain from a new accounting procedure that I was fortunate enough to get the government to approve in connection with the depreciation of the assets of our lumber company. Do you see what I mean, Walt—that top management has to be largely financial these days?"

Dudley said something and Shaw went on talking, but Mary Walling's ears were blocked with the realization that Don's hopes were blasted. What Shaw said was true. The world was changing. The Bullards were defeated and the Shaws were inheriting the earth. The accountants and the calculators had risen to power. The slide rule had become the scepter. The world was being overrun with the ever-spawning swarm of figure-jugglers who were fly-specking the earth with their decimal points, proving over and over again that nothing mattered except what could be proved true by a clerk with a comptometer.

Julia Tredway Prince cleared her throat. "Are you suggesting, Mr. Shaw, that there's no place any more for corporation Presidents of Mr. Bullard's type?"

It was the first mention of Avery Bullard's name and it came like an unexpected clap of thunder. Every eye in the room was on Loren Shaw. Even Don Walling, as Mary noticed gratefully, was watching him sharply.

Shaw was balling his handkerchief in the palm of his right hand but his voice, when he spoke after a moment's hesitation, carried no trace of the nervous tension that his fingers betrayed. "I was speaking in general terms, of course—not specifically about the Tredway Corporation."

"I'd still be interested in having your viewpoint," Julia Tredway Prince said pleasantly. "I'm sure the others would, too."

The handkerchief was a hard ball, tight-clutched in Shaw's hand, but his voice was still carefully casual. "No one can deny that men of Mr. Bullard's type played a great part in our industrial past. They belonged to an important phase of our commercial history. I would be the first to acknowledge the great debt that we owe Mr. Bullard for his leadership in the initial formation and early development of the Tredway Corporation."

The way in which Shaw had relegated Avery Bullard to the distant past was so purposeful that Mary Walling was certain that Don couldn't have missed it. She glanced at him and caught the fading of an odd half-smile that seemed to recall some memory in her mind, yet despite the quick frantic racking of her brain she could not remember when she had seen it before, nor what special meaning it had in the lexicon of their intimacy. Then, suddenly, she forgot everything else in the realization that Don was about to speak, that he was going to fight back. Hopeless or not, he would make the try! She knew that the effort might make his defeat all the more bitter, but that realization could not dim the elation that made her heart pound wildly as she waited for his first words.

"As I get your point, Loren," Don said, "you're maintaining that Avery Bullard was the right man to build the company, but now that the company has been built we need a different type of management in order to make the company produce the maximum amount of profit for the stockholders."

Mary Walling watched her husband intently, surprised at his composure. She had been expecting the flare of half-anger but his voice was cleanly dispassionate.

Shaw, too, seemed surprised, his hesitance betraying his search for a hidden trap. "I don't know that I'd express it in exactly those terms —but, yes, that's substantially what I mean."

An expectant hush had fallen over the room and George Caswell broke it by saying nervously, an undertone of near-embarrassment shading his voice. "I don't know that this is anything we have to thresh out here today—too soon for any of us to see the situation clearly. After all——" He had glanced at his wrist watch and suddenly stiffened, his eyes fixed and staring, and there was a long pause before he said in a low voice, "Coincidence, of course—happened to look at my watch—exactly two-thirty."

Mary saw other blank looks that matched her own.

"Just twenty-four hours," Caswell said in whispered explanation. "He died yesterday at two-thirty."

Mary Walling's heart sank—afraid that Don had lost his chance, afraid that the cloud of grief that now shadowed the room could not be broken. Then she heard Julia Tredway Prince say, "Avery Bullard is dead. Nothing can change that, no matter how long we wait to talk about it."

There was strength in her voice but when she turned Mary saw, in puzzling contrast, that there was a mist of tears in her eyes. She knew now what Julia had done—that she had purposefully saved the situation for Don—and she felt the warmth of a gratitude that was chilled only by the sensing of her own failure in not having been able to do for her husband what another woman had done.

But one thing was now clear. Don had been right about Julia Tredway Prince's support. With her vote and Alderson's, he needed only one more. Where would it come from? Her eyes polled the faces of the three men who sat facing him . . . Shaw, Caswell, and Dudley . . . close-shouldered and resolute. What could Don possibly do to break through the barrier of their tight-woven opposition?

Unexpectedly, it was Dwight Prince who spoke. "I've often wondered about men like Mr. Bullard. He was a great deal like my father, you know—willing to give his whole life to a company—lay everything on the altar like a sacrifice to the god of business. I've often asked myself what drives them to do it—whether they ever stop to ask themselves if what they get is worth the price. I don't suppose they do."

"It's accomplishment that keeps a man going," Dudley said in his sales-meeting voice. "That's what I always tell my boys—it isn't the money that counts, it's that old feeling of accomplishment."

An enigmatic smile narrowed Don Walling's eyes as he looked intently at Loren Shaw. "Going back to this question of the kind of a management that you think the company ought to have from here on out, Loren—the kind of a management that measures its accomplishment entirely in terms of return to the stockholders. We'd need a strong man to head up that kind of a management, wouldn't we?"

A faint flush warmed Loren Shaw's neck. "Of course."

"And it would be a big job, even for an able man? He'd have to throw himself into it—make a good many personal sacrifices in order to do a job?"

Shaw hesitated, wary and unblinking. "If he were the right man there'd be no worry on that score."

"What incentive would he have?" Don Walling demanded, and for the first time there was the sharp crackle of attack in his voice. "You will grant that there'd have to be an incentive?"

Loren Shaw forced a cold smile. "I'd say that sixty thousand a year might be considered something of an incentive."

"You would?" Don Walling's voice was whiplashed with astonishment. "Do you really think a man of that caliber would be willing to sell his life for money—for what would be left out of sixty thousand a year after tax?"

Dwight Prince's tongue-in-cheek voice cut in unexpectedly. "You could always give him his own plane as a bonus."

The flush on Shaw's neck spread like a seeping stain. "Of course there's more than money involved."

"What?" Don Walling demanded. "What Walt just called a sense of accomplishment? Would that satisfy you, Loren? Just suppose that you were the man—that you were the President of the Tredway Corporation."

Mary Walling's heart stood still as her body stiffened to the shock-wave of what Don had said. She had not expected this . . . that it would be brought out in the open . . . and the taut silence made it plain that the others hadn't expected it either.

Don Walling leaned forward. "Suppose that you were to spend the next twenty years—all the rest of your working life—in doing what you say needs to be done. Would you be satisfied to measure your life's work by how much you had raised the dividend? Would you regard your life as a success if you'd managed to get the dividend up to three dollars—or four—or five or six or seven? Is that what you want engraved on your tombstone when you die—the dividend record of the Tredway Corporation?"

The blood-color had crept out over the mask of Shaw's face, but

Mary Walling saw that it was not the flush of an embarrassment that
acknowledged defeat, but the stain of an anger born out of desperation.
Like a fighter at bay, Shaw tried to escape the attack with a diversion. "That's all very well, Mr. Walling—to take the high-minded
attitude that money isn't important—but how far do you think you'd
get next month if you offered the union negotiators a sense of accomplishment instead of the six cents an hour they're demanding?"

George Caswell grimaced, shifting uneasily in his chair. Mary Walling could sense his disappointment at Shaw's weak evasion of the
issue. Had Don seen it, too? Did he realize that Caswell might be split
away from Shaw—that Caswell might give him the one vote that was
all he needed?

Don Walling's eyes were still on Shaw. "What sense of accomplishment would you offer them—the wonderful hope that if they passed
up a raise and sweated their guts out to make that production line
run a little faster, that we might be able to raise the dividend from
two dollars to two dollars and ten cents?"

There had been a smile in his voice, dulling the edge of his sarcasm,
but now as his eyes left Shaw and fanned the whole room his words
were soberly measured. "I don't want to be facetious about this—it's
too serious for that. Loren's right when he says that we have an obligation to our stockholders—but it's a bigger obligation than just paying
dividends. We have to keep this company *alive*. That's the important
thing—and a company is like a man. No man can work for money
alone. It isn't enough. You starve his soul when you try it—and you
can starve a company to death in the same way. Yes, I know—sometimes our men in the factories give us the impression that all they
want is another raise in wages—and then another and another and
another. They make us think that getting more money is all that
matters to them. But can we blame them for that? God knows, we've
done our best to try to make them believe that money is the only
measure of accomplishment that matters to us.

"Look at what we did this last year with what we called a 'communications program.' We put out a movie that analyzed our financial
report and had meetings in all the plants. The men weren't much
interested in our financial report—we knew that to begin with, it was
·the premise we started from—so what did we do? We tried to *force*
them into being interested. We disguised the dollars as cartoons—
little cartoon dollars that jumped into workers' pocketbooks—other
little cartoon dollars that dragged in piles of lumber and built factories
—and a big fat dollar that took a trip to Washington and was gobbled
up by Uncle Sam. Oh, it was all very clever—even won some kind of
an award as an outstanding example of how to promote industrial
understanding. Understanding? Do you know what it forced our men
to understand? Only one thing—the terrible, soul-killing fact that

dollars were all that mattered to the management of this company—dollars—dollars—and nothing else."

"But that program was Mr. Bullard's own idea," Shaw cut in like a quick knife thrust.

Mary Walling had been so completely swept along that her guard had dropped and Shaw's interruption came as a shocking surprise. Her eyes flashed to her husband. Had he been caught off guard, too?

"No, I don't think we can call that Mr. Bullard's idea alone," Don Walling said. "It's something that's in the air today—the groping of a lot of men at the top of industry who know they've lost something, but aren't quite sure what it is—nor exactly how they happened to lose it. Mr. Bullard was one of those men. He'd been so busy building a great production machine that he'd lost sight of why he was building it—if he ever really knew. Perhaps he didn't."

Julia Tredway Prince's voice, so close to Mary Walling's ears that even a whisper seemed like an explosion in the silence, asked, "Do *you* know, Mr. Walling?"

Mary Walling held her breath through the moment of silence. Could he answer that question? A smile flickered on his face . . . that same tantalizing familiar smile that she hadn't been able to identify before. Now, suddenly, she remembered when she had seen it before . . . that night when he had finally designed their house . . . when, after all of his groping and fumbling had frightened her almost to the point of losing faith in him, he had suddenly made everything come right and clear.

"Yes, I think I do," he said. "You see, to Mr. Bullard, business was a game—a very serious game, but still a game—the way war is a game to a soldier. He was never much concerned about money for its own sake. I remember his saying once that dollars were just a way of keeping score. I don't think he was too much concerned about personal power, either—just power for power's sake. I know that's the easy way to explain the drive that any great man has—the lust for power—but I don't think that was true of Avery Bullard. The thing that kept him going was his terrific pride in himself—the driving urge to do things that no other man on earth could do. He saved the company when everyone else had given up. He built a big corporation in an industry where everyone said that only small companies could succeed. He was only happy when he was doing the impossible—and he did that only to satisfy his own pride. He never asked for applause and appreciation—or even for understanding. He was a lonely man but I don't think his loneliness ever bothered him very much. He was the man at the top of the tower—figuratively as well as literally. That's what he wanted. That's what it took to satisfy his pride. That was his strength—but of course that was his weakness, too."

Mary Walling listened in amazement. Where were those words coming from . . . those words that he could never have said before but were now falling so easily from his lips? Was that actually Don who was talking . . . the same man who had never been able to answer those dark-of-night questions before?

She watched him as he rose from his chair and in the act of standing he seemed a giant breaking shackles that had held him to the earth . . . shaking loose the ties that had bound him to the blind worship of Avery Bullard. He stood alone now . . . free.

"There was one thing that Avery Bullard never understood," Don Walling went on. "He never realized that other men had to be proud, too—that the force behind a great company had to be more than the pride of one man—that it had to be the pride of thousands of men. A company is like an army—it fights on its pride. You can't win wars with paychecks. In all the history of the world there's never been a great army of mercenaries. You can't pay a man enough to make him lay down his life. He wants more than money. Maybe Avery Bullard knew that once—maybe he'd just forgotten it—but that's where he made his mistake. He was a little lost these last few years. He'd won his fight to build a great company. The building was over—at least for the time being. There had to be something else to satisfy his pride— bigger sales—more profit—something. That's when we started doing things like making the sixteen-hundred series."

He turned and confronted Dudley. "Are your boys proud when they sell the sixteen-hundred series—when they know that the finish is going to crack and the veneer split off and the legs come loose?"

"But that's price merchandise," Dudley said in fumbling defense. "There's a need for it. We're not cheating anyone. At that price the customers know that they can't get—"

"How do you suppose the men in the factory feel when they make it?" Don Walling demanded. His eyes shifted from Dudley to Shaw. "What do you imagine they think of a management that's willing to stoop to selling that kind of junk in order to add a penny a year to the dividend? Do you know that there are men at Pike Street who have refused to work on the sixteen-hundred line—that there are men who have taken a cut of four cents an hour to get transferred to something else?"

"No, I wasn't aware of that," Shaw said—and the weakness of his voice signaled the first thin crack in his armor. "I don't suppose it would hurt too much if we dropped that line. After all, it's a small part of our business."

A voice in Mary Walling's mind wanted to shout out at her husband, urging him to drive in for the kill that would clinch his victory. Couldn't he see that Shaw was defeated . . . that Caswell was nodding his approval . . . that Walt Dudley was waiting only to be commanded?

But Don Walling turned, looking out of the window, and his voice seemed faraway as if it were coming from the top of the distant white shaft of the Tredway Tower. "Yes, we'll drop that line. We'll never again ask a man to do anything that will poison his pride in himself. We'll have a new line of low-priced furniture someday—a different kind of furniture—as different from anything we're making now as a modern automobile is different from an old Mills wagon. When we get it, then we'll really start to grow."

His voice came back into the room. "We talk about Tredway being a big company now. It isn't. We're kidding ourselves. Yes, we're one of the biggest furniture manufacturers but what does it mean? Nothing! Furniture is close to a two-billion-dollar industry but it's all split up among thirty-six hundred manufacturers. We have about three per cent of the total—that's all, just three per cent. Look at other industries—the percentage that the top manufacurer has. What if General Motors had sat back and stopped growing when it had three per cent of the automobile industry? We haven't even started to grow! Suppose we get fifteen per cent of the total—and why not, it's been done in a dozen industries? Fifteen per cent and the Tredway Corporation will be five times as big as it is today. All right, I know it hasn't been done before in the furniture business, but does that mean we can't do it? No—because that's exactly what we *are* going to do!"

His voice had built up to a crescendo, to the moment that demanded the shout of an answering chorus—and then in the instant before the sound could have broken through the shock of silence, Mary Walling saw a tension-breaking smile on her husband's face. In the split second that it took her eyes to sweep the room, she saw that the smile was mirrored in all the faces that looked up at him . . . even in the face of Loren Shaw.

She had sensed, a few minutes before, that Shaw was defeated, but she had expected a last struggle, a final flare of resistance. It had not come. Instinctively, she understood what had happened. In that last moment, Loren Shaw had suddenly become aware that his brain had been set aflame by a spark from Don Walling's mind—a spark that he himself could never have supplied. Now he was fired to accomplishments that had been far beyond the limits of his imagination. Mary Walling understood the faintly bewildered quality of Shaw's smile, because she, too—long ago—had found it mysteriously strange that Don's mind was so unlike her own.

George Caswell was standing, extending his hand. "We're all behind you, Don. I can promise you that."

"Yes sir, Don, you bet we are!" Walt Dudley boomed.

Shaw shook hands silently but it was a gesture that needed no words to make it a pledge of loyalty.

And now Julia Tredway Prince was standing, too. "I think the occasion calls for a toast. Dwight, would you mind—yes, Nina, what it is?"

Nina was standing in the doorway. "There's a telephone call for Mr. Walling. The gentleman says it's very urgent."

Dwight Prince stepped forward. "There's an extension in the back hall. Come and I'll show you."

Mary saw that Julia was about to speak to her but George Caswell stepped up as an interruption.

"I'm afraid I'll have to run along. The plane's waiting and I—well, I have to be back in New York for a wedding at six. I'll be down on Monday, of course."

"And you'll stay over for the board meeting on Tuesday," Julia said.

"As far as I'm concerned, it's all settled now," George Caswell said. "But you're quite right—we do need the formal action of the board."

Mary realized that at some missed moment Julia's hand had found her own and that the world had become an out-of-focus haze filled with drifting faces and floating words . . . Shaw . . . Dudley . . . Erica Martin . . . all saying the same unsaid thing in a different way . . . and then, slowly, the consciousness dawned that there was another voice saying something else and the voice seemed to come from the warm, tight-holding grip that held her hand. She was alone with Julia Tredway Prince.

"You should be very proud, Mary."

"I am—but frightened, too."

"Because you don't understand him?"

She felt her mind go blank with amazement. How could Julia Tredway Prince know . . . how could anyone know?

"Don't worry about it, my dear," Julia said. "You'll never understand him completely. Don't try. You'll be happier if you don't. He'll be happier, too. Not understanding will make you very lonely sometimes, Mary—when he shuts you away behind a closed door—when you think he's forgotten you—but then the door will open and he'll come back and you'll know how fortunate you were to have been his wife."

"I know, I know," she murmured, making no move to wipe away the tears in her own eyes because she saw that there were untouched tears in the eyes of Julia Tredway Prince. It was only after her memory echoed what Julia had said that she realized those last words had been in the past tense. Was it possible that Julia had . . . ?

There was the interruption of a sound like distant wind chimes.

Nina stood before them, uncertainly, holding a tray filled with glasses and an opened bottle of champagne. "Mr. Prince said to bring eight glasses, but——"

"Thank you, Nina." Julia took the tray from her hands and put it gently on the desk.

As her hand touched the offered glass, Mary Walling understood, for one fleeting instant, the miracle of her husband's mind. Now it had happened to her! She knew without knowing why she knew . . . and as if it were something done in a dream she was raising her glass and saying, "To Avery Bullard."

There was a long moment, a moment that could not be filled with old tears or old wine, but only with the silence of two women who shared a secret that bridged the ending of one world and the beginning of another.

"Thank you," Julia said.

When Don Walling came back into the room they were standing at the window that looked out on the Tredway Tower. It had been a long time since there had been a word between them. There had been no need for words.

They turned together.

"Sorry it took so long," he said. "There was some trouble about the connection. The others go?"

Julia nodded. "Is Dwight coming back?"

"I believe he's still talking to Walt Dudley. I heard their voices in the garden. Loren Shaw is driving George Caswell out to the airport."

"That was Fred Alderson on the phone," Don Walling said. "You know, he did the darndest thing—drove all the way down to Maryland to see Jesse Grimm. Good thing he did—cleared up a misunderstanding—but I can't imagine why he'd go to all that trouble for me."

Julia's eyes twinkled with taunting amusement. "Of course it's possible that he didn't do it for you—he might have done it for the company."

His face slowly softened into a boyish grin and, even without understanding, Mary Walling's heart raced exultantly when she heard him laugh and say, "All right, I'll learn. Just give me a little time."

He hadn't changed! He would never change . . . she must never think that he would. Julia was right . . . don't try to understand him . . . yes, that had always been her trouble. It was only when she had tried to understand him that she had been afraid. She would never be afraid again . . . never!

WHAT CORPORATION PRESIDENTS
THINK ABOUT AT NIGHT

∽◑◠

JOHN L. MC CAFFREY

[John L. McCaffrey, "What Corporation Presidents Think About at Night," in
Fortune, Sept. 1953, pp. 128–129, 140, 142.]

This selection is a speech originally delivered by John L. McCaffrey,
President of the International Harvester Company, on June 10, 1953,
before the ninth group of business executives to complete the University
of Chicago's two-year Executive Program. It was subsequently reprinted
in *Fortune,* because, according to that celebrated magazine of American
business, "it sets forth, with rare humor and candor, one company
president's insomnious experiences," and therefore should be of interest
to "all executives brash enough to aspire to the top management job."
McCaffrey, according to the same source, is "a tough, towering operations
man, who has worked for International Harvester ever since graduating
from high school in 1909. When Harvester's directors named him Chief
Executive Officer in 1951, Fowler McCormick, of the Harvester dynasty,
resigned as board chairman, leaving McCaffrey with both policy and
operations to worry about." Harvester's annual sales are over a billion
dollars.

◆———

THE MECHANICS of running a business are really not very complicated,
when you get down to essentials. You have to make some stuff and
sell it to somebody for more than it cost you. That's about all there
is to it, except for a few million details. I saw a play recently in
which one of the characters summed up the fundamental problem of
business pretty well. He said he'd been trying for two years to think
of something that would cost a dime, sell for a dollar—and be
habit-forming.

So it isn't hard to run a business, from the standpoint of business
operations. And a President doesn't usually worry too much about
the things that most people expect to bother him. For example,
he seldon lies awake very long thinking about finances or lawsuits
or sales or production or engineering or accounting problems. He is
pretty well able to take care of those during regular business hours.

Furthermore, when he approaches such problems the President
can bring to bear on them all the energy and the trained judgment
and past experience of his whole organization. He has a lot of help
with problems of that kind.

There are other problems, however, that he has to sweat and struggle with, largely by himself. They are the problems he thinks about at night. They all arise out of one simple fact. I can sum up this situation in one sentence: .

The biggest trouble with industry is that it is full of human beings.

The longer you are a President, the more firmly that fact will be riveted in your mind. That is why you will lose sleep. That is why your hair will first turn gray, then get thin, and then fall out altogether, unless you are lucky.

You will learn to your sorrow that, while a drill press never sulks and a drop hammer never gets jealous of other drop hammers, the same cannot be said for people. You will learn that a turret lathe may run one part for ten years without affecting its ability or its willingness to be switched at any time to another part. But men are not that way. They develop habits and likes and dislikes.

You will learn that you have with people the same general problems of preventive maintenance, premature obsolescence, or complete operational failure that you have with machines. Only they are much harder to solve.

You will discover that problems change rapidly, techniques change rapidly, products can be transformed in a period of months; but, unfortunately, people change slowly if at all. And you cannot rearrange or retool the human organization of your business with the same ease and frequency as you rearrange or retool the plant.

We have constructed in this country an economic system which is marvelously complicated. In the last forty years or so, this system has developed from what the football coaches call in their trade a one-platoon system to something that approximates a thirty- or forty-platoon system in industry.

All this is because we have applied to its uttermost limits the principle of the division of labor which was first described by the classical economists. We have come from the age when a product was made in its entirety by one craftsman, performing all operations, to the present age where nearly every small operation on every part of every product is performed by different men. We have reached a form of production so specialized that frequently the machine does all the work and the man merely nurses and feeds it, as in the case of the boltmaker or the automatic screw machine. The division of labor has gone so far, here in America, as it affects the factory worker, that labor has been atomized rather than just divided.

The sociologists and psychologists, as well as the practical operating men in industry, have recognized some of the problems this extreme specialization creates. There is the problem of loss of versatility. There is the problem of loss of pride in personal accomplishment and skill. There is the problem of boredom from repetitive operations, and many others, as they affect the worker at the machine or on the assembly line.

The thing I want to point out to you is this: We are only now beginning to understand that the effects of this atomizing of labor are not limited to production employees. As management, too, has become extremely specialized, these same problems have spread over into the management group, and even into the executive group. The specialization of management at all levels, including the executive, has lagged somewhat behind the specialization of equipment and employees, but it is following exactly the same course, and giving rise to the same problems.

"A GOOD OLD-FASHIONED JACKKNIFE"

The President of a modern company often seems to me like the ringmaster of a thirty-ring circus. We sit at our desks all day, while around us whiz and gyrate a vast number of special activities, some of which we only dimly understand. And for each of these activities there is a specialist.

We have engineers of assorted kinds. We have lawyers of many breeds, from patents to admiralty. We have market analysts and sales engineers and industrial-relations experts and credit men and research metallurgists and time-study engineers. We have accountants and economists and statisticians, purchasing agents and traffic men and chemists.

All of them, no doubt, are good to have. All seem to be necessary. All are useful on frequent occasions. But it has reached the point where the greatest task of the President is to understand enough of all these specialties so that when a problem comes up he can assign the right team of experts to work on it. We have a lot of people like Ed Wynn's famous painter who only painted boats and not horses, and when a customer insisted that he do a picture of his horse, the painter said: "Well, all right. But it's gonna look like a boat."

The President is like a man confronted by an enormous tool bench, who only hopes that he can pick the right screw driver for a particular special job. There must be others like me, who sometimes wish for a good old-fashioned jackknife, with twelve blades and a corkscrew, that could handle almost any job in passable fashion.

Because business has wanted these specialists, the colleges and universities have produced them by the thousands. If we need a good cost accountant, one is available. If we want an industrial psychologist, he can be had. If a man is needed to estimate a market potential with the latest scientific methods, he will be on tap.

And that's fine, as far as it goes, but it still doesn't let the President sleep at night. The President has no great problem in finding men to run a section or a department, where one line of work is followed. But he tosses plenty over the problem of finding executives who have wider knowledge, more general savvy, and enough background of the right kind to run a whole group of things.

What are the plus and minus factors in specialization, as it applies to management men? On the plus side, the great advantage is that by limiting his work to a relatively small area, the man becomes a genuine expert in that area. Many detailed improvements are possible as a result. By specializing from the start, in education and in work, he greatly reduces the time and expense which his employer would otherwise have to devote to his training. By coming as a ready-made specialist he is more useful at an earlier time, and this tends to give him a larger income at a younger age than the average man. That's an attraction to him, and is one of the reasons why he specializes.

What are the disadvantages? The great disadvantage, of course, is that specialization produces a man with limited knowledge and limited interests and experience, except in rare instances. The world of the specialist is a narrow one and it tends to produce narrow human beings. The specialist usually does not see overall effects on the business. And so he tends to judge good and evil, right and wrong, by the sole standard of his own specialty.

We have all seen the credit man whose big interest in life is not the making of good sales under variable conditions, but simply the ratio of past-due paper, and the possibility that at some future time, on a particular deal, he might be criticized.

We have seen the time-study man who clings so firmly to what he regards as a principle that he just doesn't care whether it meets ordinary human standards of fairness, or whether his actions shut down a 3,000-man plant.

We have seen the salesman who expects complicated machines to be redesigned in a week whenever one of his customers has a whim, and who bitterly blames engineering if it doesn't happen that way. Or the engineer who knows what is good for the customer, even if the customer doesn't like it. Or the manufacturing man who can't see why we won't pour more millions into his plant, even though the product is already losing money.

We have seen the industrial-relations man for whom life begins and ends with a legalistic interpretation of the union contract, and who never looks past the grievance committee, gathered around his desk, to catch a glimpse of the human individuals who work in his plant.

MIDDLE-MANAGEMENT MORALE

This narrowness of view, this judgment of all events by the peculiar standards of his own specialty, is the curse of the specialist from the standpoint of top-management consideration for advancement. Except in unusual cases, it tends to put a road block ahead of him after he reaches a certain level.

This presents a problem to the President in building his top organization. Because of the trend of the times, he finds that he has more and more specialists and fewer and fewer general executives just below the top level. Some of these specialists he simply cannot promote. And even with the others, if he does promote them, he has to ask them to make a sudden and radical change in the thinking and acting habits of a lifetime.

This may or may not present a problem to the specialist himself. In most cases I believe it does. There are men, of course, who, after achieving reasonable eminence in their specialty, ask nothing more of life. But among men of real ability, specialists or no, we usually find ambition to advance. And in such cases, specialization can produce a considerable degree of frustration.

So we have a two-horned problem. There are many specialists whom the President simply cannot promote. And because they are not promoted there is a natural tendency for the mature specialist to become somewhat sour.

There is another fact about the specialist which is a problem to him and therefore to the organization. It arises from the very fact that he knows more about his specialty than his superiors or anyone else in the business. This situation frequently arises: a problem comes up related to his special field. He produces a solution which is entirely satisfactory from the standpoint of good practice in his specialty. But then the higher management won't buy it. They do something else instead.

This can happen either because the specialist has failed to explain and sell his solution adequately, or because he did not take into account other factors of the problem which might lie outside his special field. To put it bluntly, such a situation can occur either because top management knows more than he does or because it knows less. In either case, the result for him is the same. His advice has been disregarded and his judgment overruled. That will seldom make him happy.

HIGH-PRICED OFFICE BOYS

In this area probably lies a good part of the cause for a new note which has begun to creep into some of the studies of corporate management—the beginning of concern about the morale of what is called "middle management," which includes nearly all the specialists and is largely composed of them.

The top men operate high, wide, and handsome. The decisions are theirs, so their attitudes are usually good. In spite of frequently expressed concern about attitudes of foremen and other first-line management men, it is a fact that the first-line men have specific duties and responsibilities, and they are at the point where things happen. In spite of their normal griping, they have the relief of taking personal part in action.

The man in the middle of the management pyramid, however, neither makes the decisions nor carries them out. He finds it easy to feel that his judgment is neither sought nor honored, that his training and experience are ignored, and that he does not participate to any real degree in the management of the corporation. He often feels, and he frequently says, that he is just a high-priced office boy.

Now, those are some of the reasons why many a President lies awake at night. How can he maintain the interest of and get full advantage from the specialists who are too specialized to be promoted? On the one hand, the company absolutely requires the skills of the specialists in order to carry on its complicated operations. On the other hand, he has to get future top management from somewhere. And that somewhere has to be largely within the existing company, if he is to have any management morale at all.

SHEEP WITH GOAT'S BLOOD

The problems are easy to describe. But the ground becomes uncertain and the atmosphere cloudy when someone raises the simple question: What will we do about it?

One answer that has been offered is to start with the educational processes that take place before the man goes to work. Recently we have seen, as an example, some attempts made by engineering and other technical schools to give a larger part in their courses to the liberal-arts subjects, to try to produce an educated man as well as a trained engineer or doctor or what not. I think that is a hopeful trend.

We have also seen in recent months a number of speeches by corporation officials, pointing out the necessity for rounded education and underlining the importance of the liberal-arts college for the future, not only for the future of business but also of this country. The nation, like the corporation, suffers from this problem of too much specialization.

Unhappily, it appears that we company Presidents are not practicing what we preach in this regard. True, some of us have been giving money to support liberal-arts colleges, but we have not been offering jobs to such graduates.

Fortune Magazine [in April 1953] recounted some of the actual experiences of educational institutions with business recruiters who came to the campus looking for talent. At Yale University, for example, in 1950, only 18 out of 66 corporation talent scouts were willing to talk to arts college graduates. In 1951 it was 15 out of 91. And in 1952 it was 16 out of 117. At Johns Hopkins University this year only 16 out of 200 scouts had any interest in the liberal-arts man as compared with the engineer, the chemist, or other specialists.

So we are obviously not making progress in that field and will have to change our approach before we do. These graduates are bright young men with a natural desire to eat. They see what is happening. And however much we may cry about overspecialization, we'll get more and more of it so long as our hiring policies are not in tune with top management's thinking and talking.

Another answer which has been proposed is to catch the specialist after he is in industry but while he is still young enough to respond and try to give him a wider training, a broader outlook—to take him away from his tree and show him the forest.

This has sometimes been attempted by means of coaching, as it is called. Coaching consists basically of selecting promising young men and moving them around through different functions of a business, letting them stay long enough in each to get a real feel of it. Its advantage is that it teaches through experience and not just through precept.

One of the difficulties, however, is that it soon becomes obvious to everyone that certain people are on the coaching list while others are not. You create a sheep-and-goat division among your younger men and the goats don't like it a bit. Mistakes are also made, of course, and sometimes a sheep turns out to have goat's blood in him.

BACK TO COLLEGE

Still another answer to the same problem has been the training of executives at a university. The theory is something like this. The employer says: "Here's a younger man who has a record of accomplishment up to now. There may be something wrong with him that we don't yet know, but, as matters stand, he looks as if he had the possibility for future development. Maybe he has. Maybe he hasn't. Training can't hurt and it may help a lot. So we'll give him the training, give him the chance to grow, and then wait and see what happens."

My personal view happens to be that this is the most promising of the approaches to the problem and that results so far have justified it in the case of my own company.

By one means or another, we need to produce a type of business executive who, after carefully learning that all balls are round, will not be completely flabbergasted the first time he meets one that has a square side. And he will meet them, for we live in a complicated world—a world that has spiritual and moral problems even greater than its economic and technical problems. If the kind of business system we now have is to survive, it must be staffed by men who can deal with problems of both kinds.

Businessmen today and in the visible tomorrows will need to know how to earn a profit and why it is good for everyone that a profit should be earned. That's obvious. They also need to know how to get along with, and direct the efforts of, other human beings, both individuals and groups. And, finally, every businessman needs to know enough about the society in which he lives and operates so that he can follow its changes intelligently, adjusting himself and his enterprise to changing conditions, and making sure that his business serves its most useful purpose for society.

Those are some of the problems you will think about at night, when you are President. I sincerely hope you will find better answers —and get more sleep—than I have.

DU PONT'S PRESIDENT—THE
UNCOMMON MAN

CRAWFORD H. GREENEWALT

[Crawford H. Greenewalt, *The Uncommon Man: The Individual in the Organization,* McGraw-Hill Book Company, Inc., New York, copyright © 1959, pp. x, 16–17, 25–28, 40–42. Reprinted by permission.]

Crawford H. Greenewalt is an "uncommon man"—even more than by his own definition, which is included in the selection below. President of one of the country's great corporations, E. I. du Pont de Nemours & Company, he is also one of those modern business leaders who are thoughtful about their problems, their responsibilities, as well as being men of action. (Perhaps the form of organization used by Du Pont may encourage the development of such leaders as Greenewalt.*) These excerpts are from Greenewalt's book, *The Uncommon Man: The Individual in the Organization,* which is based on the McKinsey Foundation lectures that he delivered at the Graduate School of Business, Columbia University.

---

* See the piece by Mylander in Volume III.

IT HAS ALWAYS SEEMED TO ME that shamefaced attitudes about money are uncalled for. I see nothing unworthy in the financial motive, nor do I see anything vulgar in its free exercise. I doubt, in fact, that anyone has ever devised a cleaner or more honest basis for rewarding high performance.

Is a thirst for power more acceptable? I think not; history's darkest pages seem to be those devoted to power seekers and I cannot find the ordering of other people's lives an admirable goal. Nor can I believe that there is much to be said for efforts to win the cheers of the crowd, or for mere social preening. Titles and academic honors, while gratifying to the recipient, have little value beyond the immediate person. Only vicariously may the families of the knighted Briton or the beribboned warrior share his distinctions; the reflected glow may be warm, but it cannot shine far afield.

Financial gain is, in fact, the only form of incentive fully subject to sharing with others. As such, it seems to me that it is probably the least selfish inducement of all. Whatever the scale of income, the material rewards which come the way of the individual are shared with those around him; as an incentive, they often are important only to the extent that they *can* be shared.

At lower incomes, for example, there is a sharing in the form of family comforts and conveniences, an education for the children, a small luxury for a loved one. At the upper level, the circle widens to include, through gifts and benefactions, entire communities. Our universities, our libraries, our art galleries, our churches are testimonials to the sharing process.

Money is not, in other words, a static and lifeless accumulation hoarded in miserly fashion by those who treasure it for its own sake; such legends persist largely as a remnant of the Midas story and seldom exist in fact. Like water seeking its own level, fortunes in one way or another find their way back to the general benefit.

This is not to say that money cannot and is not expended foolishly, or that its pursuit has not sometimes been accompanied by actions venal and detrimental to society. But human capacity for foolishness can by no means be confined to the fiscal area, while both venality and antisocial behavior can stem from many causes. Institutions, like vineyards, should be judged by the quality of their vintages, not by the follies of the few who misuse them.

Any corporation, it seems to me, has its own system of checks and balances and is probably more sensitively responsive to public will than is government itself. The reason is that the business organization, in addition to its internal controls, is subject to the sovereignty of the market place, a force which can express itself more rapidly and with greater effect than a thoroughly aroused and indignant electorate. I know of no corporate therapy which can immunize against customer sanctions. Certainly size is of small avail in dealing with the angry lady at the store counter once she has her dander up and her umbrella swinging.

Organizations, corporate or otherwise, are not inanimate objects, composed of steel or brick or equipment, but living mechanisms made up of human beings. In whatever field a given organization operates, it is nothing more than the sum total of the talents, the aspirations, and the characters of the human building blocks of which it is made, mellowed perhaps by the traditions and collective experience left behind by other human beings who have gone before. To speak of "humanizing" by force of law would seem to me to place a low premium indeed upon the integrity and sincerity of the human race itself.

The essential characteristics of an organization do not change with growth. What was a small body of men and women becomes a larger group. And whether it is large or small, or whether commercial, spiritual, or cultural in purpose, it represents a segment of humanity. As institutions, all organizations recruit their people from the same melting pot, the same source which supplies the human raw material for all other trades or vocations. Thus, they represent a cross section of society—the brilliant and the dull, the generous and the grasping, the expansive and the petty, the good and the bad. Grouped together, the weakness in one is compensated by strength in another, the exuberance of the young is tempered with the steadiness and wisdom of the mature.

Hence, the organization is nothing more than a slice of life. Whatever individual dispositions may be present, it is the average, the composite which must prevail. Decisions made in the name of the organization are still human decisions, and, as organizations, we are still subject only to the human will. If we can concede that people in the main have decent and honorable instincts, it must necessarily follow that, when they join together, the character of the organization will average out at about the same moral level.

In any organization, too, there will be an added pressure for conformity to the public interest arising simply out of the sheer numbers of people involved in any given decision—the larger the organization, the larger this number becomes. Thus, organizational conduct will in itself reflect the public interest as it may exist in a particular setting and at a particular time.

A disposition on the part of a single individual within the organization to be a scoundrel would encounter tough going. The number of people he would have to persuade to join him on the primrose path would, I think, dishearten the most determined. Anyone seriously committed to a life of crime could certainly find far more fruitful opportunities than exist in the field of business management.

No, the danger does not lie with any inherent evil on the part of the organization, but in quite another direction—one to which no law or legislation can apply. The hazard is that the very pressures within the group which hold the scoundrel in check will impose upon the individual restrictions which stifle the creative urge and the zeal for personal achievement.

If I were faced with a choice between a society which sublimated the good with the bad, I think I would rather take my chances with the scoundrels than risk losing the creative force unleashed by a free rein on individual effort. I am sure the country's long-term interest would sustain me here. To play Mark Antony in reverse, it seems to me that the evil which men do survives them only a short time, whereas the good, far from being interred with their bones, goes on and on forever. And the good which all men accomplish can be no more than the sum of their individual accomplishments.

Some of the critics of modern society apparently see the human race today as becoming more and more like a housing development with each member as the serial expression of a master plan. I am not convinced that the conclusion is wholly valid, and I am not at all sure that the concept can be termed modern in any respect. Original thinking has never found a ready-made acceptance, as men have learned through many generations.

Back in 1902, a very wise administrator in the Du Pont Company wrote into our first incentive plan a provision which perhaps anticipated this trait of human nature. It is part of that plan today. It provides that, in setting awards, special consideration be given to individuals who achieved a goal "in the face of objection, from within or without." It has always seemed to me that this provision characterizes the spirit of individual effort. Perhaps "conformity" represented a clear danger as far back as that day when the architects of the plan with their swirling mustaches, stiff collars, and high-button shoes saw the need of goading the timid and diffident and offered special rewards to those who would break through the barriers. The offer is still open and, as long as its spirit is maintained, we face the future with high confidence.

Some men are uncommon to extraordinary degree, others to lesser. And perhaps most uncommon of all is the common man whose achievements are exalted beyond the expectation of his circumstances.

DEBATE AT WICKERSHAM MILLS

ABRAM T. COLLIER

[Abram T. Collier, "Debate at Wickersham Mills," *Harvard Business Review,*
May–June 1960, vol. 38, no. 3, pp. 49–63.]

Here Abram T. Collier, Vice-President and General Counsel, formerly
Vice-President for Personnel, of John Hancock Mutual Life Insurance
Company, presents the management approaches of four men who are
candidates for the position of President of a textile mill. They set.forth
their "platforms" in the dramatic form of a debate. Then comes the
time for voting. (You can compare your vote with that of over 3,000
business executives who sent in ballots when the play was published in
a 1960 issue of *Harvard Business Review;* turn to page 2620 for the
results.)

---◆---

*As intruders we often feel a sense of guilt, even though our intrusion
is fully authorized. Entering an office when its usual occupant is
absent, we are uneasy and tense. Such conduct is the more remarkable
when we know full well that the occupant will not return—that he
is dead.*

*It is with such a sense of intrusion that we watch the curtain
rise on the office of David Wickersham, until recently President of
Wickersham Mills. But we see now that we are not alone as intruders.
Present with us are the eight members of the Wickersham family,
and a guest who will play an important role in the special meeting
of stockholders which is about to begin. The purpose of this meeting
is to elect a new President and thus determine the future of the
organization.*

*Visible are many relics of the past—both inanimate and otherwise.
In one corner stands a roll-top, doubtless used by some executive
a half century ago. Behind the large teakwood flat-top stands a high-
backed chair, carefully avoided, out of mute respect for the recently
deceased. On the walls are portraits of four former executives, members of as many generations. From a window is seen the dam and
waterfall on the Nobscott River and a corner of the spinning mill.*

In the cast are the stockholders:

Alfred Wickersham (elder son of the late President)
David Wickersham, Jr. (younger son of the late President)

FIG. 300. From left to right: Alfred Wickersham; Benjamin Hall; Charles Hall; David Wickersham, Jr.; Professor Morgan.

Benjamin Hall (cousin of the Wickershams)
Charles Hall (Benjamin's younger brother)
Mrs. Sarah Wickersham (the late President's widow)
Mrs. Alice Martin (an aunt of the Halls)
Samuel Weber (cousin of both the Wickershams and the Halls)
Miss Elizabeth Weber (Samuel's sister)

Also present is Dr. Willis B. Morgan, a professor from a nearby school of business administration, who has been asked to preside over the special meeting. The professor, having now been introduced and welcomed by David, Jr., rises to begin the proceedings.

PROFESSOR MORGAN: Thank you, ladies and gentlemen. Needless to say, I am very glad to be here and to give you any help I can. I became acquainted with David when he was one of my students, and I have learned from him something about the history and the problems of your company. Let me make it clear right away, though, that I am not here as an expert in the textile business, but as a moderator of this election.

You have met in this office to decide what to do with the Wickersham Mills. The understanding is that each of the principal stockholders—Alfred, Benjamin, Charles, and David—will have an opportunity to express his views on this basic problem. From this group, I expect that today you will elect the new President of the company to succeed the fine man whom you so recently lost—a difficult task.

Therefore, let me take the liberty of requesting each of you young men to be quite frank in expressing your philosophy of business. What is Wickersham Mills in business for? If you were President, what would the aims of the company be? All stockholders clearly have a right to know what goals and objectives will be sought by the man who will be almost solely responsible for protecting their inheritance.

Before we get to our discussion, however, it might be a sound idea for me to review briefly what I know about these mills and the men who have run them. I hope you will fill in any important facts that I have missed.

MRS. SARAH WICKERSHAM: Will you speak louder, sir? (*looking around for support*) Why don't people speak up any more?

PROF. MORGAN (*smiling*): I'd be glad to, Mrs. Wickersham.

Now, as I understand the story, the first mill was established here about 1848. The capital was supplied by a group of Boston financiers; however, the real start came from the imagination and drive of Alfred Wickersham. "Old Alfred," as you call him, came to this country from Manchester, England, as a small boy. Fascinated by the textile business, he determined that someday he would build, own, and operate his own concern. Starting with a small plant, he made high-grade cotton goods, prospered enormously during the Civil War, quickly paid off his loans, and found himself a man of substance, not only locally, but in the state. When he was elected governor in 1870, his son, Benjamin, became the acting manager of the mills; but until his death a decade later, Old Alfred was always a dynamic force in the business.

I am sure I have missed some of the ladies, but I have set down on the blackboard here the names and dates of the members of the family who have had most to do with the history of Wickersham Mills. (*He refers to the genealogical chart reproduced below*).

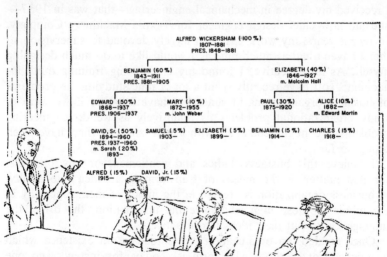

FIG. 301. Wickersham Family Tree.

As you see, the figures after each name represent the percentage of common stock owned by the individual.

Control of the business has stayed in the family for over 100 years. As a result of the death of David, Sr., earlier this month, each of you young men has an equal interest in the business; yet each of you has an independent position and an outside income. This gives you considerable freedom in deciding what to do with the business. You can keep your company going or you can sell it to any one of a number of other concerns; the price you get will not make or break any one of you. If you decide to keep it going, your purposes and objectives should be defined for the stockholders' consideration. They will also want to know what broad policies you will follow to obtain your objectives. It would be helpful for this purpose, also, if you would fill us in on your own careers just to bring all of us up to date.

(*He pauses for a moment.*)

Since David, Sr.'s, heart attack in 1956, you have seen this problem coming, and I feel sure that you have realized such an election as today's was inevitable. So let us go about our task with sincerity and good spirits. (*briskly*) Alfred, would you like to lead off?

ALFRED WICKERSHAM: Gladly, Professor. Let me say, before I begin, how pleased I am that you could join us today. Although I realize you cannot make this decision for us, your comments will certainly be a big help.

About my background—there isn't too much to say, except that I received my degree in mechanical engineering—that was in 1937— and am now chief design engineer for Textile Machinery Company. In recent years, my work has been largely devoted to supervision so that I haven't had as much time as I would like to do much designing myself. As an executive, I found my engineering training quite inadequate, so I have recently spent a lot of time studying the problems of business organizations in general. I have felt that if we were to study organizational problems as intensively as we do engineering problems, we might come up with better answers than have been found so far.

I believe this business, ladies and gentlemen, or any business, for that matter, is the means of transforming an idea into reality. A business organization is created in the minds of men, especially in the minds of those men who have the imagination, the drive, the intelligence, to put their ideas into practice.

Once created, an organization seems to have an existence which is independent of those who form it. Today, for instance, no one working for Wickersham Mills was part of the organization 50 years ago; yet the business is *essentially* the same organization. Ever since its founding, individual managers and men have come and gone, buildings have been put up and torn down, new spindles and looms have been installed and old ones thrown out. Throughout all the change, the essence of the organization has not altered; miraculously, it seems to have retained the identity which Old Alfred gave it.

In this sense, a business organization is no different from a regiment in battle. A third of a regiment may be wiped out on each of six days of fighting so that the entire body of personnel turns over 200%, but the regiment, with its sense of identity, remains. Its history, its traditions, its determination to be itself, not only live on in many different minds, but are impressed on and *change* the minds of the men who from time to time become a part of it.

SAMUEL WEBER (*raising his hand*): Can anyone get in this?

ALFRED: Certainly, Sam.

PROF. MORGAN: Of course. This is to be quite informal, and if there is a point that seems unclear to any of you, ask away. I know how important this decision is.

SARAH WICKERSHAM: Will you all *please* speak louder?

ALFRED: Yes, Mother. What's the question, Sam?

SAMUEL: I just don't get it when you say an organization doesn't really change. I may not be Einstein, but this mill sure isn't the same organization now that it was in Old Alfred's day!

ALFRED: You're right, Sam, of course. But that's not precisely what I mean. I don't mean to say that an organization does not change. It changes, naturally, much as an individual changes. Its experience, its successes, and its failures, all have an effect on the essence of the organization. They are remembered; they serve as ideals to be sought or mistakes to be shunned. But Wickersham Mills, although changed, has also survived, Sam, and survival has not been due to some star in the sky, but to the courage, the imagination, the will, and, above all, the effort of the men who have made up the company. These men never forgot the ideals Old Alfred implanted. Other mills fled to other places; many failed; many avoided flight and failure by merging with larger and more dominant organizations. Yet Wickersham, throughout the years, has never quit or lost its identity.

I guess you know as well as anyone, Sam, that when Old Alfred came to the shores of the Nobscott, he had only enough credit to buy equipment, an option on the old grist mill, and a vision. I'm told he was a self-willed old codger. He would listen to a man from the mill, ask him a question or two, and then issue a curt order. He never changed his mind. Stubborn, hard, unfeeling—that's what many people called him. But they also called him fair and just, for he was never known to go back on his word. He wanted a mill that turned out top-quality products. He demanded good work from his workers and a high price from his customers. The impact of his vision and his personality still exists.

I don't say Old Alfred had it easy. He made a pile during the Civil War, but he lost a lot of it in the panic that followed. He faced receivership so many times that he would easily understand our problems during the past few years. Maybe he never heard of synthetic fibers, but he would understand the troubles we've had in blending polyester with cotton. Five years ago, following the 1955 hurricane, when the Nobscott overflowed and ruined 40% of our spindle capacity and most of the electric power plant, $250,000 went down the drain. This would have reminded Old Alfred of the fire in the winter of 1879 which gutted the north building. Although he was 74 then, he did not hesitate to rebuild; and I am glad to say that Dad did not hesitate in 1955.

It seems to me that every organization worthy of the name *is*, and *must* be, founded on imagination and courage—the essential qualities of the human spirit. A great many companies are set up with only a clever brain behind them, sometimes even with a patent on the cleverness. But unless they also have character—by character I mean the capacity to make wise choices based on imagination and courage—they do not last.

SAMUEL (*agitatedly*): Hold on there, Alfred!

ALFRED (*calmly*): All right.

SAMUEL: This history and philosophy may be fine for eggheads, but what's it got to do with the price of cloth?

ALFRED: You may well ask where all these ideas fit into the picture at our mills. We have been spinning and weaving fine cotton textiles for four generations, and I personally do not see why we cannot continue, if—note the if—we install a new management which has not only the character, in the sense I mean, but also the authority and capacity to make important decisions concerning the very essence of the company. This business cannot continue if it has an absentee ownership or committee management. The man who runs our company, like Old Alfred, must have a free hand, a personal stake in the profits, and a right to change the policies of the company to whatever extent he may believe is necessary to make the company stronger and more effective.

SAMUEL: But, Alfred!

ALFRED (*ignoring Samuel*): Strength and effectiveness are not to be measured by production, profits, or employment. Figures may be impressive, but they are often misleading. No, the real strength of a company is to be found in its inner spirit, its *élan*, its essential morale, and its moral fiber. With these basic qualities any business can set a true course and can change course when the need arises. If it has these things, it is likely also to have a skipper who knows his business, who distinguishes between the sheer and the shoddy, and who takes full responsibility for his leg of the voyage.

I wish I had a new vision or technique to describe today, but I don't. Nevertheless, I am willing to take on the task of re-creating the Wickersham Mills, if you agree. I would bring to my job no cure-all formulas but, instead, an experienced and vigorous leadership.

If you decide you want me, I would require a clear understanding that each of you would give me an option to buy your stock at a price equal to twice its present book value—at any time within the next ten years. Meanwhile, I must be free to pledge the credit of the company to whatever extent I think necessary, to determine its dividend policy, to sell the plant and move elsewhere, to change our products here—even to change the type of business.

These terms may sound steep. I intend them to be. This business will not run itself nor will the answers be found in a calculating machine. It involves human evaluations and decisions about problems. You can never be sure you are right, but you must make the decisions quickly and have confidence that what you are doing is right. I can supply this leadership, but not if we have to hold a town meeting every time a decision has to be made. Ladies and gentlemen, there it is.

MORGAN: Thank you, Alfred. Are there any questions? (*He pauses.*) No? Well, Benjamin, will you speak next?

BENJAMIN HALL (*rising*): Okay, Professor, thank you. I feel a bit strange speaking after Alfred. I didn't know he was so damned eloquent. A couple of times there I almost wanted to applaud, but I was afraid he might lose his footing on that soap box. (*He smiles wryly.*)

Actually, I agree with a lot of what Alfred said, especially that part about Old Alfred. He really was an old S.O.B., wasn't he? He may have been *wrong,* but he was never in *doubt.* But you don't really believe all that stuff about captains and kings, do you? I remember that Emerson is supposed to have said something about an organization being the shadow of a great man; however, Emerson went out of vogue 50 years ago. But now to business.

As you requested, Professor, I will express my own thoughts on the company's future, and let you know a bit more about my background. Charles and I belong to the Hall—the non-Wickersham—side of the family. Our father was an artist; both he and Mother died when we were young, and our grandmother brought us up on heroic stories about Old Alfred and her brother, Benjamin, for whom I was named. We were led to feel a strong kinship and pride, both for the Wickershams and the mills they ran. Although Charles and I have held 30% of the stock since 1927, when Grandma died, David, Sr., always made it clear—*quite* clear, I might add—that our stock ownership was *not* to be equated with his full responsibility.

So, as a college boy, I worked at the mill summers; then after I got my M.S. in economics in 1935, I worked full time for just over three years. I enjoyed those years and I learned a lot. But, in the summer of 1938, I got restless and went off to New York, obtained a job with one of the early management consulting firms, and I have stayed in consulting work ever since.

Over the past 22 years, I have known intimately more than 100 businesses and have done work for at least as many more. The more I see of them, the less sure I am when it comes to generalizations. I am reminded of the old saw: all generalizations are false, including this one. But there is one thing I do feel fairly sure about: the days when a business could be run by one man, or even a few men. have gone—if, in fact, they were ever here.

I, for one, question whether Old Alfred was really the great man that we talk about now. I suspect that if we ever knew the facts, we would find that the mill was really run by a smart superintendent, a few good foremen, and some fairly conscientious workers —not too much different from now. Some of these people were doubtless afraid of the old man; others ignored his bluff and bluster. The mill ran in spite of him, not because of him. He was in politics most of the latter part of his life, and I seem to remember there was even some talk of a lady friend in Boston.

MRS. ALICE MARTIN (*irritably*): Benjamin, I am surprised that you should mention such a thing. There was never a word of truth in it.

BENJAMIN: Okay, Aunt Alice, have it your way. Well, I ought to take my turn at saying what I really think a business is.

In my book, a business is not the "means of transforming an idea into reality." A business is a process, a living organism. Like individual living organisms, it has many parts and a good many functions.

Management in a business organism corresponds crudely to the brain in the individual. It is a clearing house for information—the source of most, but not all, instructions sent to the acting members. It is an important part of the organism, maybe even the most important part, but the other parts are also essential. The eye that sees does, in essence, as important a job as the brain that records what the eye sees. There is no point in debating relative importance of the parts, for whether the business organism does well or poorly depends on all parts functioning together effectively. Training, discipline, incentives—these are the ingredients that enable a business to function effectively, to survive, and to grow.

Once you accept this basic premise, a great many conclusions follow as a matter of course. This mill is in the business of converting cotton and synthetic fibers into cloth. We make voile, crepe, batiste, oxford, and broadcloth. The cloth is sold then to converters who use it for dress goods and shirtings. And our problem is to put raw cotton and synthetics together with machines and labor for the purpose of producing salable cloth.

If you will review the procedures here, as I have for the last few days, you will see that the problem is basically one of scheduling. You cannot have expensive machines and expensive labor work like crazy one minute on a few small orders of broadcloth, and then loaf along until the next orders come in to cause another crisis. Right now we are weaving 70 different fabrics on 405 looms, but we have no orders beyond three months and no assurance of volume business after that.

In addition to achieving a correct mill balance, all internal procedures should be reviewed carefully. In the carding department, the breakers and pickers operate one shift daily, while the cards run three. The box looms tend to be used to capacity, but the plain looms are rarely all in use. All this just emphasizes our problem: to improve the basic process of the business.

This requires other improvements as well. My great uncle, Benjamin, was one of the first men to study the incentive system and to appreciate its impact on production. He anticipated Frederick W. Taylor and other exponents of scientific management by quite a few years. One of the reasons this mill has survived, especially after the stormy and erratic days of Old Alfred, was that the first Benjamin spent a lifetime cutting out every needless expense, finding more efficient ways for doing things, installing incentive pay, and giving everyone a feeling that he, too, was identified with the mill just as intimately as the old gentleman himself.

To work at the Wickersham Mills was something to be proud of in those days; and it was Old Ben who, in his careful, unexcited fashion, gave the organization its strong feeling of closeness and its unquenchable desire to do good work. These people took pride in doing good work, *not* because anyone told them they should, but because their work *was* good. It was as simple as that. When they played, they played hard, too. Old Ben was right there with them when they organized the first baseball team for the Nobscott River League in 1908.

ALICE: I remember that well, Benjamin, and I can't be contradicted here. I was just a girl, but Paul, your father, came home from a trip to Italy and insisted on playing with the men in the mill. He sprained his ankle and Old Ben, as referee or umpire, or whatever they call it, ran all around the field and ended up in bed for a week! I remember too . . .

BENJAMIN (*smiling, but irritated at being interrupted*): That's very interesting, Aunt Alice. Hmm, where was I? Well, anyway, I made a crack about Emerson when I started, that I remember, but I shouldn't condemn him entirely, because I think that his mousetrap theory comes closest perhaps to what I have in mind. I am not interested in a better mousetrap as a substitute for marketing; I think you have to market your product with the same efficiency you use in making it. What I mean is that an organization is a machine, or as I said before, a process. If, like the superior mouse-trap, it works better than others, it will outproduce its competitors both in quantity and quality, and success will automatically follow. It will achieve its basic purpose: to survive and grow.

I guess that's about it from me. Frankly, I am 46, and I am happy where I am. I don't even know whether I would want to take on a permanent operating job anywhere; but, if I should be called upon to do so, I'll bet I could save $100,000 the first year! This would be enough to get the company into the black, and we could go on from there.

MORGAN: Thank you, Benjamin. Are there any questions?

MISS ELIZABETH WEBER (*timidly*): Yes, I'd like to ask Benjamin a question—that is, if nobody minds.

BENJAMIN (*rising again*): Of course, Elizabeth, go ahead.

ELIZABETH: Well, you all know I'm just a librarian, and I don't know anything about business, but I like what you said about saving the mills $100,000 the first year. My, that seems to be almost all the money in the world to me! Well, what I want to ask is this: You say you aren't sure whether or not you'd want to take on the respon-sibilities of managing Wickersham Mills. Does this mean that if I vote for you and others do too, you would not be happy and perhaps could not do your best work?

MORGAN: What about that, Benjamin?

BENJAMIN: I'm awfully glad you asked, Elizabeth, for I do *not* want to leave the impression that I would take on this work, and fail to give it the benefit of my experience and—to be frank—my love for making an organization hum. Yes, Elizabeth, I would do my very best.

MORGAN: Thank you, Benjamin. Are there any further questions? No? Well then, Charles, will you tell us your views next?

CHARLES HALL (*rising*): Thank you, Professor. Just so I won't mislead you, let me say at the beginning, I think both Alfred's and Benjamin's views are straight from never-never land. This may sound harsh, but they have both taken such limited, parochial points of view that I have had trouble keeping quiet. They have looked at this business only from the point of view of those who are working in it. Don't they realize that no business lives alone—even in the field of textiles? This business, and every business, lives in the big, wide world, a world full of other businesses, governments, and nations. A business, gentlemen, is nothing more than what the big world requires it to be. But that's getting ahead of myself.

I guess I likewise owe the Professor a short *apologia pro vita mea.* I also grew up here as part of the Wickersham family, and until I went to the university in the fall of 1935, I thought the world stopped right on the edge of town. I suppose it did then, at least for all practical purposes. When I got my A.B. in the spring of 1939, I was drawn by the glitter of high finance to work for one of the big stock brokers. I served five years in the Navy during the war, ending up as a Lieutenant Commander. After the war, I shifted to the Massachusetts Bay Bank, and I have been with them ever since. Primarily, my job is to make loans to industrial borrowers. This work has enabled me to know what goes on in a lot of other businesses, and it has taught me not to make loans based on sentiments or clichés.

As a result, I must say I have difficulty in understanding what you people think a business is. It is nonsense to call it a creative transformation, or a living process. So there may be no more doubt about it, let me review the ABCs of commerce as much for your benefit, Al and Ben, as for the benefit of the ladies.

ALFRED (*sarcastically*): Thank you, Cousin Charles.

CHARLES (*amused*): You are most welcome, my dear Alfred. Now for that recap of the ABCs of business:

A. Businesses are legal entities, generally in the form of sole proprietorships, partnerships, or corporations. Now that should not be too difficult to understand, Alfred. A business is owned by the proprietor, the partners, or the stockholders, just as we own Wickersham Mills. It exists under the laws of the commonwealth; the laws of the commonwealth devolve from the authority given by the Constitution. The Constitution in turn is derived from the will of the sovereign people.

B. There are many, many businesses in operation today. This was not always so. At one time, it was difficut to get one started. Now, almost anyone who has the price of a lawyer's fee and a little credit can establish a corporation. The result, ladies and gentlemen, is competition.

C. Here I specifically refer to our business. Once the patents expired on the "water frame" that Richard Arkwright invented, there were no real limits on the number of persons who were free as birds to go into the textile business. That is, there were no limits except those imposed by the rigors of competition. My cousin Edward was a better student of the history of the textile industry than I, but I think it's fair to say that there never has been a time when competition was absent. I even include the years when our country was fighting a war and clothing a few million soldiers and sailors—although, of course, the competition was lighter then and the profits higher.

Now, I hate to be a spoilsport and mention unpleasant things, but I must point out that the earned surplus of our mills has dropped from a high of $721,000 at the end of 1951—thanks to Korea—to less than $200,000 right now. In other words, we have lost a half million dollars in the space of just nine years! Much as I liked David, Sr., he failed to reckon with the market. You cannot fight the market.

MRS. SARAH WICKERSHAM (*quite beside herself*): Wait a minute, Charles, I hear *you* quite clearly. Just because you have always been excused for your atrocious manners, I do *not* think that excuses your talking ill of your Uncle David! Don't forget he took care of you for years after your mother and father died! Why, he's barely cold in the ground, and here you stand . . .

CHARLES (*placatingly*): I'm sorry, Aunt Sarah. I guess I *was* speaking rather rudely, but I meant no disrespect. What I meant to say was that the losses our company has suffered are not the fault of any man so much as the result of adverse market conditions.

But when I say "market," I suppose I should explain what I mean. A business like ours is in many markets. When we want to buy raw cotton or synthetic fibers, we have to pay the going price unless we want to speculate in futures, and that is another business. When we need new machines, we have to pay the going price or do without the machines. When we need money to finance inventory or to expand plant, we have to pay the going price or cut down on the amount of business we can do. And, gentlemen, when we need labor, we pay what the union says we must or suspend operations. And we will need labor until the day when Alfred or some other *creative* genius invents a fully automated textile mill.

You and I may think the union leaders are stupid or arrogant, that they have put the industry in a strait jacket, and that, on balance, they may have hurt their members more than they have helped. But what we think is of little consequence. These are the hard cruel facts of the market. This is the way it works.

SAMUEL WEBER: Where does the customer come in, Charles?

CHARLES: Ah, Samuel, there's the rub; the customer's desires are the most difficult aspect of the market to predict. Yet we can never forget him, can we? If, when we buy, we must pay what the market requires, it follows that when we sell, we must accept what the market is willing to pay. Not only is this the inexorable law, but in this business, where the ultimate consumer is the buyer of dresses and shirts, we are faced with a market uncertainty that is especially difficult, in fact, almost impossible to predict. Oh fashion, thy name is woman!

But a successful management must do its best to understand its markets. You will remember that when Cousin Edward was running the mills from World War I to the 1930's, he lived through two booms and as many busts. His realistic, hardnosed approach to marketing saved the company repeatedly. He didn't sound like the economists I knew in college, if you will pardon me, Professor; but he had a good economist's ability to get above the battle, to see what was going on, to predict what was going to happen. When he saw the first war coming, he expanded in order to be ready. When he saw the postwar panic ahead, he canceled orders for new machines, laid off workers, refused orders he knew would be canceled, and prepared to sit it out.

The union also came in Cousin Edward's time. He saw that coming, too, but I must admit it was one time when he was not quite as dispassionate as he liked to be. He fought it for awhile, but he was one of the first men in the valley to acknowledge that, with government support, the union was inevitable. He signed one of the first textile contracts without wailing, or gnashing his teeth.

Gentlemen, any sentimental attachments we may have had for the business should not blind us to the facts. This is a dying industry. No sane investor will put equity into a textile plant in this part of the country, unless he wants to buy property for its liquidation value.

I am ready to do what may be necessary to keep the plant going, and to protect your investment until such time as we can dispose of it at the best price we can obtain. I will arrange whatever loans may be needed for *this* purpose, but only on a secured basis. I have a good deal of respect for the ability of both Alfred and Ben, but I plead with you—look at the situation objectively. Look at yourselves, and the rest of you look at our powers objectively. If you do, I think you will know what you should do. That's all I have to say.

MORGAN: Thank you, Charles. Are there any questions?

SAMUEL: Yes, I've got one. Do I understand you correctly, Charles, that you want to unload this white elephant as soon as you can? We'd get our cash out right away? That sounds good to me.

CHARLES: If you had listened, Sam, you'd know I didn't say precisely that.

SAMUEL: Now, just a minute, Mr. High-and-Mighty; maybe I only have 5% of the stock in this broken-down outfit, but I've got a right to ask questions just as much as the rest of you.

MORGAN (*keeping peace*): Of course, you do, Mr. Weber, of course you do. Charles said that he would keep the business going until such time as he could get a reasonable price for it. Any other questions? All right, then, David, will you please speak now?

DAVID WICKERSHAM, JR.: Thanks, I wondered if my time would ever come. I believe all of you know that I first met Professor Morgan in 1939 when I was working toward my master's degree in business administration, a degree I received the following year. After this, I accepted an Army commission and spent the subsequent years in the service. After the war, I joined the training program of the American

THE WORLD OF BUSINESS

Electric Company. After a series of jobs with that company, I am
again in New England as sales manager for the appliance division in
Springfield.

Now Dad has died, and you are here listening to us discourse on
what we think Wickersham Mills is in business for. But in all the
debate I have listened to so far, I have heard no mention of one
important word. I have not heard it, and yet, if you ask me what
the Wickersham Mills was founded for, why it has stayed in business,
and how it ever hopes to continue, I come back to a single answer—
summed up in that single word, *service*.

SAMUEL: Oh, I knew somebody would have to get noble on us!

ELIZABETH: Now, see here, Sam. I happen to think David has
something there, and I wish you wouldn't interrupt.

MORGAN: All right, David, go on.

DAVID: Thanks. I bring this up only because I see a business as a
service for somebody else. The service may be shirtings or ships;
it does not matter too much so long as it fills some reasonably decent
human need. Every business I ever heard of was started as a response
to a need of somebody outside of the business. I do not care whether
a business is the transformation of somebody's vision, a complicated
living organism, or the product of the economic and political environment in which it happens to find itself. What I do say is that
it is *nothing*—nothing *except* the service it renders to others.

To imagine a business existing without other organizations is just
as impossible as to imagine a person living all alone in an empty
world. An individual life has meaning only in relation to others. To
describe a man in a meaningful way is always to show the relation.
I may say of you, Alfred, that you are a father, a husband, a son, an
engineer, a supervisor, a golfer, an Episcopalian, and a graduate
of M.I.T. However I describe you, I do so in relation to some other
person or group of persons. If your children die, if your wife leaves
you, if arthritis prevents your playing golf, a part of your life is
taken away. And so it is with a business organization. It loses something when it loses a customer; it loses everything when it loses them
all. The business organization is the *sum* of all the people and the
other organizations with which it serves.

Another way of looking at this matter is to note that the service
we render is chosen, not by us, but by others. Of their needs, for
the most part, only a few have anything to do with physical survival.
Most of them are concerned with the *way* people want to live that
life. Some want big cars; others want to save on the expense of
gasoline. Some want comfort without regard to appearance; others,
especially the women, want appearance without regard to comfort!

CHARLES (*interrupting*): Careful now, David—you're getting to
sound like me! (*laughter*)

DAVID: Sorry, Charles, I certainly didn't mean to steal *your* thunder! But what I have said so far just begins to suggest the dimensions of the problem which, I believe, is basic to this mill. If this business is to continue, it has got to provide the individuals that make up the clothes-buying public—or some part of it—with the kind of cloth they want. At the same time, it must provide the people in the organization with the compensation and the sense of accomplishment *they* want.

In a country that makes jet airplanes and atomic submarines, we cannot expect the public to be satisfied with plain, solid-color fabrics in all the textiles it uses, no matter how convenient or how easy they are to manufacture. The public wants and we have the technical skill to make fabrics in almost an infinite variety. In any event, we cannot compete for the plain fabric business with the big companies in the South; so, as a practical matter, if we continue in business, we are confined to making specialty products and fine goods.

Ben, you mentioned that one of the key problems in operating the mill was scheduling work that would keep all our equipment in use. I agree this is a problem, but it is not going to be solved here at the mill. The only place that this will be solved is where our customers are. If our customers are to be served, we must develop some way to anticipate their needs or to influence them. What we must do, in short, is re-evaluate the total relationship of the company to those it serves.

Up to now, we have been relying almost exclusively on two commission houses in New York to take orders and sell our merchandise. I suggest that we work closer to those who use our product. There is no reason why we cannot do creative design work ourselves and keep in close touch with all the changes and trends in the market. We need to sell service as well as cloth. If a customer likes one of our designs, we can work out agreements giving him exclusive use of that design. We might even get a small premium. With enough of these arrangements set up, we may have a good chance of obtaining a substantial volume of steady repeat business. In any event, we must try to serve our customers, perhaps even persuade them to want what we are able to provide.

I claim no patent on this approach. You may remember that my father believed most of what I have tried to put in words. He was extremely aware of the needs of the men in the plant, so much so that we never had any real union trouble during the time he was at the helm.

He was also concerned about the needs of our customers. I think it was in 1946, right after the war, that he saw the possibilities of specialized fabrics made of rayon and worsted. He tried to adapt our equipment and to develop a whole line of new patterns in this field. It looked as though it would be extremely successful, and in 1948 we booked a substantial volume of business.

The problem, you may recall, was that the British devalued the pound in 1949; as a result English viyella came in at prices substantially below ours, and we were almost ruined by the inventory losses we were forced to take. Charles, you will say that Dad should have foreseen the devaluation; that Grandfather *would* have. You may be right, but that does not in any way detract from my thesis. Wickersham Mills has a right to survive only to the extent that it can continue to serve the needs of others.

MORGAN: Thank you, David. Any questions?

ELIZABETH: Yes, I think I have a most important one. It's like the one I asked Ben. David, you never mentioned whether or not you really want to be president of Wickersham Mills. Do you?

DAVID: I'm not sure I'm glad you asked that question, Elizabeth. It is difficult for me to answer clearly. Since I feel that my job is to respond to the needs of others, it would be wrong for me to push myself forward. Basically I don't want power; I simply want to *serve*. But if all of you here call on me to serve you, I will, cheerfully, and to the best of my ability.

MORGAN: Any other questions? (*pausing*) No? (*He waits another moment.*) Then permit me to make a few remarks.

Gentlemen, if I had not just heard your comments, I would not have believed that it was possible for four men who grew up more or less together, at about the same time, in the same town, and in the same kind of families, to have such different views. Each of you has expressed, most admirably, a managerial viewpoint that will inspire adherents to each of your positions. But, alas, all of you cannot be president of this company at the same time.

Before you begin your voting, let me earn my keep by being useful. Professors, you know, are supposed to be full of answers, but I assure you that most professors are, in reality, merely full of questions. However, from the right questions sometimes flow the right answers.

Before I raise these questions, though, perhaps I should sketch out the main points made by each of these young men, so that the remarks of those who spoke first will not be unfairly overshadowed by those who spoke later. If I may, I'd like to use the other side of the blackboard here to summarize, or epitomize, the goals and methods favored by each speaker.

(*He goes to the blackboard and draws the diagram reproduced on page 2489.*)

David, you were surprised when the other speakers did not mention service as an objective. But I was surprised when none of you men mentioned a word dear to the hearts of all heirs—and stockholders—

OWN ORGANIZATION

ALFRED
GOAL- Self-Realization
METHOD- Imagination
Rational Choice, Will

BENJAMIN
GOAL- Survival
& Growth
METHOD- Training,
Discipline, Skill

VIEWED
SUBJECTIVELY

VIEWED
OBJECTIVELY

DAVID
GOAL- Service
METHOD- Responsiveness
Self-Transcendence

CHARLES
GOAL- Power to Predict
and Control
METHOD- Dispassionate
Inquiry, Scientific
Knowledge

OTHER ORGANIZATION

FIG. 302. Goals of Business Advanced by Candidates.

profits. The most common answer to the question, "What are we in business for?" would, I think, be just that—*profits.* The fact that all of you have assumed this, but no one has mentioned it explicitly, indicates, perhaps, that profit is not an end in itself.

When we talk of profits being a means rather than an end, we highlight one of the great difficulties in any discussion of purpose. Almost nothing that is commonly thought to be a valid objective for a business is an ultimate. Sure, you want profits; sure, you *need* profits. But the real question is, profits for what purpose? To grow? To undertake new ventures? To provide more service? Do we all really agree that for a business organization—as for an individual—seeking profit as an end in itself is a difficult position to defend?

ELIZABETH (*raising her hand impatiently*): It may be easy for all of you up there to question profits, but if you had to watch every penny as I do, you'd know how it feels to miss even the little dividend checks I was used to getting every year. For the last few years, I've found it very difficult—very difficult. (*She takes out her handkerchief.*)

MORGAN: Yes, I know what you mean, Miss Weber, and we do lose sight, occasionally, of what profits, even of the largest corporations, mean to the small stockholder.

Perhaps, however, you will concede that profits are wanted for *some* purpose. And let me begin my summary with Ben's views. What he described as the purpose of a business is probably acknowledged by more businessmen than any other. He said a business organization is like a living organism; its purpose is to survive and grow. Like an individual with a temperature of 105°, the business teetering on the brink of insolvency knows that survival at times must take priority over everything else. But, for the reasonably healthy organization, doesn't "survival," as a goal, result in a policy of playing it safe—doesn't it develop in management a kind of Maginot-Line mentality? Without some more stirring goal, may not the quest for survival alone lead to decisions and actions that eventually result, not in survival, but in an early demise?

How about *growth,* another popularly acknowledged goal? Thousands of businessmen at regular intervals point with pride to increases in sales, in assets, and in net profits. Some even tie growth and survival together, by saying, "We can't stand still: either we grow bigger or smaller—and if smaller, we may not last at all." But whether growth is sought in its own right or as the alternative to bankruptcy, hasn't it often proved illusory?

When growth or size becomes important for itself, several unfortunate things can happen. When it takes the form of acquiring, by merger or otherwise, a larger part of a given market, but not a more economical operation or enlarged service, no public good results. When growth occurs through increased sales that do not fill a bona fide consumer need, isn't it merely illusory and short-lived?

Every businessman knows that if he wants to join in the "mad race for volume," he may well succeed in increasing it. But he may do so at an excessive price in terms of his own production costs, his organization's morale, and his customers' satisfaction. Thus he favors *sound* growth, but when he introduces the qualifying adjective "sound," isn't he in effect denying that he is seeking growth for its own sake?

But let me say this, to be fair to Ben's advocacy of survival and growth, Wickersham Mills *is* on the brink of insolvency. And you, as owners of the company, should bear that in mind as you weigh his remarks.

ALICE: Wickersham Mills has been on the brink of insolvency in the past, Professor. It has come back before, and it can again. I remember many times before the First World War . . .

MORGAN: Yes, Mrs. Martin, Wickersham Mills may come back again. I'm sure each of you hopes it will; for not only do you have a sentimental attachment to the business, but you also have an investment that must be protected. Now, what should we say about a view that regards *power* as the key to protecting your investment? Charles argued for knowledge about the world in which a business lives so that it could obtain some power with respect to that world. In this belief, he follows a long tradition that defines the ultimate goal of an organization as power to control or adjust to the environment in which it exists.

Just as nations have often sought to place themselves in a position of power over their neighbors, so have businesses sought to attain those positions where they can greatly influence—if not fully control—the activities of other businesses, of labor unions, of purchasers, even of the government to which they are presumably subservient. This view of business sees it as a vast game of wits, where the objective is for each company to acquire as much power as it can, and, if possible, more power than most. In playing this game, however, it is not anticipated that any one business—or even that any group of businesses—will succeed. Heaven forbid—that would be tyranny—or at least a violation of the Sherman Act. Charles's view expects, rather, that with everyone seeking power, the power will be countervailing and that a tolerable stalemate will result.

Let us be fair to Charles's position, however, and point out that he is not advocating power as an end in itself, but as a means of vigorously putting Wickersham Mills on its feet. He is, as he claims to be, a realist, a practical, blunt man, who is not concerned with anything purely speculative, but only with what we know, and what we can reasonably predict.

But what *is* is not necessarily what *ought to be*. Realists and practical men who look only to the goal of knowledge of what *is* or what they believe *will be* ignore one of the greatest capacities inherent in man: his ability to conceive of things as they *ought to be* and to move consciously and deliberately toward re-creating things in the light of that conception.

This brings me to Alfred's statement of business purposes as the transformation of an idea into reality. He sounds a little like Kahlil Gibran, who, you may remember, said, "Work is love made visible." He uses "love" in the sense of man's capacity for imagination and choice. And when we think of a man's power to choose, we begin to consider the possibility of moral values, to see that we have choices as to these values. Such values, many believe, are essential if we are to find the goals of a human organization. To work, they say, whether alone or in concert with others, has no significance, no human purpose, unless a man can look at the results of that work and can call them "good."

According to this view, Old Alfred and all the others in this business spent their lifetimes making cloth because they thought it was good. In so doing, they engaged in the process that nowadays is called "self-actualization." Seen from this viewpoint, they, as individuals, made actual or real what they believed, deep within themselves, *ought* to be done. And the business organization of which they were an essential part, also acquired purpose and significance because it was engaged in making actual or real an idea or vision of something which did not then exist, but which by reason of their imagination and effort came to exist. I think it is fair to call this *creative* work, for it brought into being that which did not exist before the work was performed.

Now, doesn't this type of creative or self-actualizing work come closer to providing us with a defensible business goal? But is that enough? Isn't it also limited as an *ultimate* goal or purpose? Merely to make real what we conceive to be good, no matter how lofty the conception or how difficult its execution, is to neglect another important circumstance. No one lives in the world alone, nor does any organization exist alone. And while each individual and each organization may live to make real its own inner vision, it must also recognize the visions that others likewise are pursuing.

Isn't all this simply another way of asking you to consider whether David's goal of service to others, laudable as it is ethically, also offers a management viewpoint suitable to Wickersham Mills in its present straits. Can a business be complete—and successful—if it does not emphasize service? For service enables a company to transcend itself; it enables the company to make love visible.

ALICE (*musing*): I can remember—oh, it must have been almost a half century ago—it's odd to be so old—I can remember old Benjamin saying some of the same things. Even some of the same words. It's strange.

MORGAN: It *is* strange to grow old. I, too, feel it. But time has passed, and we now face the problems of a troublesome present.

You have heard several points of view expressed by men who are young enough to have the capacity for vigorous leadership, and by men who are old enough to have acquired the wisdom of experience. Each has stressed a different point of view, but I feel sure that none of them believes his approach to management excludes the consideration of opposing views and, when the occasion demands, changing his approach temporarily. In short, I don't think a businessman with common sense ever lets his thinking get completely locked into any one point of view.

Now, with your permission, I will review briefly the rules for this election. The ballots will be sealed. After the first round, the man receiving the fewest votes will drop out. This will continue for the next round, until, finally, the man who receives a majority will be elected to the presidency. By your selection, you will have indicated your readiness to accept him on the terms which he has already suggested.

Your choice is not an easy one. Why you vote as you do is your concern. You may vote according to the closeness of your family ties, according to the dictates of your heart, or according to what you conceive to be in your own selfish interests. Whatever motives enter into your vote, you will also want to consider the philosophies these men have expressed.

Will you vote for Alfred, who feels management's function is to bring about self-realization for those associated with the business? Or will you vote for David, whose goal is service to society? Or Benjamin, who points toward survival and growth through internal discipline? Or will it be Charles that you favor for his interest in business control through greater knowledge and objective inquiry?

(Professor Morgan presses a buzzer on the table. An expectant murmur of voices is heard as a secretary enters and crisply passes out ballots. The curtain falls.)

IF in this play, as we hope, you have found some of the ideas to be as real as the characters and places are fictional, we should like to have your vote on which man should be President of Wickersham Mills.

VOTE NOW, so you can compare your vote with the votes of fellow executives. Results will be reported in the next issue of HBR.

THE personal information is requested so we can analyze the votes by position, age, and size of company.

VOTE! VOTE!
For President of Wickersham Mills
(Vote for one)

☐ ALFRED
☐ BENJAMIN
☐ CHARLES
☐ DAVID

[Listed in the order in which they spoke at the meeting.]

For statistical analysis:

Your position ....

Your age .... Years

Number of employees in your company ....

FIG. 303. The Ballot.

Fun and Satire

"I would live all my life in nonchalance
and insouciance
Were it not for making a living, which
is rather a nouciance."

—Ogden Nash (1902–   )

———◆———

This section needs no introduction, just as any one of us needs no instruction or injunction to get ready to laugh. We Americans are great laughers, and one of our most saving traits is the ability to poke fun at ourselves. Businessmen included.

The pieces which follow are gathered together here just to enjoy, to have a place to turn to for humor—with or without a bite. But there are plenty of other fun pieces, also, in other sections, where they serve to make a point.

POVERTY PLEADS THAT SHE IS THE
MOTHER OF INDUSTRY

ARISTOPHANES

[Aristophanes, *The Plutus*, in *Aristophanes in English Verse*, trans. by Arthur
S. Way, Macmillan and Company, Ltd., London, 1934, vol. II, pp. 243-250.
Permission granted by Macmillan and Co., Ltd., and Barnicotts, Ltd.]

Even in the fifth century B.C. there was some recognition of the dynamic
effect of the profit motive—although it must be admitted that in this
selection from Aristophanes the drive for financial gain is not presented
very directly or very seriously. And with good reason: Aristophanes is
our earliest master of comedy, and still one of the greatest. He also
happens to have been one of Socrates' favorite students and companions;
as such he should be expected to have some of the same classic disregard for pecuniary affairs. Why not, since as Greeks of that golden
intellectual age they had the silver mines of Athens for revenue, and for
labor the slaves from across the purple sea.

In the following scene from Aristophanes' *Plutus,* there are three
characters: Chremylus, an Athenian yeoman; Blepsidemus, a friend of
Chremylus; and Poverty, disguised as a haggard old woman. Chremylus,
a poor man but a just one, has gone to the Delphic Oracle to inquire
whether his son

> had best
> Change all his principles, and, like the rest,
> Turn swindler, rogue, one mass of villainy,
> As being the royal road to prosperity.

The oracle answers,

> On whomsoever first you light
> After you've left the temple, stick to him tight
> Until you get him to come home with you.

The first person whom he sees is a ragged, blind old man who turn out
to be Plutus, god of wealth. Plutus has been robbed of his eyesight by
Zeus so that he will be unable to distinguish between the just and unjust.
Chremylus immediately makes plans to have his eyesight restored. In
this scene, Poverty intervenes to speak on her own behalf, but despite

her eloquence, she is forced to troop off. Chremylus then leads Plutus to the Temple of Asklepius, whereupon Plutus regains his eyesight, which then enables him to reward the just with riches and the unjust with poverty.

The idea that poverty—or, rather, the fear of poverty—is the reason why men work so hard has been echoed many times since Aristophanes. We have a version of it in the old proverb, "Necessity is the mother of invention." And even today we worry about the dulling effect of security, the implication being that the modern generation will not undergo the toil and risk of individual enterprise when they can get a guarantee of comfort for life as a cog in the wheels of a large company—which is the original incentive idea in reverse.

◆

(*Chremylus and Blepsidemus move quickly toward the house. Enter Poverty, who hurries after them.*)

POVERTY: Oh what a rash and wicked deed! You'll rue it.
You pitiful mannikins, who dare to do it!
Whither away? Why run? Stop! Stop!
BLEPSIDEMUS: Oh my!
POVERTY: I will destroy you wretches wretchedly!
You essay a deed of impudence past bearing,
Such as nor god nor man has had the daring
Ever to do! For this you die, you die!
CHREMYLUS: Pray who are you? You seem pale, to my eye.
BLEPSIDEMUS: Perhaps a Fury from some tragedy scene.
She glares as madly as any tragedy queen.
CHREMYLUS: A Fury?—she's no torches.
BLEPSIDEMUS: I'll *torch* her!
POVERTY: And who, think you, am I?
CHREMYLUS: Some innkeeper
Or fishwife; else you'd not begin to bawl
At us who've done to you no wrong at all.
POVERTY: Indeed? And haven't you wronged me horribly
Trying from this whole land to banish me?
CHREMYLUS: The whole land?—surely there's the cemetery!
Come, tell us, and look sharp, who you may be.
POVERTY: Oh, but I'll make you smart this very day
For trying to thrust me from the land away!
BLEPSIDEMUS: Some neighboring pothouse-keeper isn't she
Who with short measure cheats me constantly?
POVERTY: I'll live with you for years. I'm Poverty.
BLEPSIDEMUS: Lord Phoebus! Heavens! Whither can we fly?
(*Begins to run. Chremylus catches hold of him.*)

CHREMYLUS: Here, what are you doing? O you cowardly dog!
Hi! Can't you stop?

BLEPSIDEMUS: Not I!—must really jog!

CHREMYLUS: Stop! From one woman shall we two men flee?

BLEPSIDEMUS: She's Poverty, you fool! A beast more fell
Never to earth has risen out of hell!

CHREMYLUS: Stop! I entreat you, stop!

BLEPSIDEMUS: Not I, by Jove!

CHREMYLUS: Oh come, I say, 'twill be the maddest move
Of ours, most awful, if in sheer affright
At this here creature we shall take to flight,
Leaving the god alone, and don't show fight!

BLEPSIDEMUS: Fight?—"with what weapons or what mailèd might,"
When every blessed shield and corslet stout
Of ours this vile beast has put up the spout?

CHREMYLUS (*aside*): Fear not! We've got the god: I'm sure that he
Will o'er this vixen give us victory.

POVERTY: You scum o' the earth, and dare you mutter at me,
Caught in the act of downright felony?

CHREMYLUS: You blasted beast, why do you come along
And rail at us who've never done you wrong?

POVERTY: No wrong? By heaven, d'you think it no wrong, when
You're trying to make that Plutus see again?

CHREMYLUS: Pray where's the wrong to you, if we've designed
A plan for benefiting all mankind?

POVERTY: What benefit in *your* plan would they find?

CHREMYLUS: What? Banishment from Greece of you, its curse!

POVERTY: My banishment! And pray what mischief worse
Do you think you could do to all men?

CHREMYLUS: What?
By putting this thing off till we forgot!

POVERTY: Look here—this very point I'll argue out
With you first. If I show beyond a doubt
That I'm your source of all good 'neath the sun,
And that through me you live, my case is won.
If I fail—then go on as you've begun.

CHREMYLUS: You most disgusting beast, you dare talk so?

POVERTY: You listen to reason: it strikes me I'll show
Quite easily that it's all wrong, this itch
Of yours for making all the good men rich.

CHREMYLUS: Come to our aid, O cudgel and pillory!

POVERTY: Don't make a fuss and howl till you've heard me.

CHREMYLUS: Who, when he hears such horrors, could refrain
From howling "Ow—ow"?

POVERTY: Every man who's sane.

CHREMYLUS: What penalty on your brief-sheet shall I write
Suppose you lose your case?
POVERTY: What you please!
CHREMYLUS: Right!
POVERTY: But—if you lose, the same must fall on you!
CHREMYLUS (*to Blepsidemus*): H'm—d'you think suffering twenty
deaths will do?
BLEPSIDEMUS: For *her,* yes. Two are plenty for us two.
POVERTY: You'd best die then right off! In equity
How can you possibly rebut my plea?
CHORUS: Come, you must invent some argument both cunning and
full of discretion,
That will put her force to the rout; and, of course, don't make any
weak concession.
CHREMYLUS: The first point that I take I think I can make quite
clear to the Court, that in verity
It is righteous and fair that the good have their share of the *crème de
la crème* of prosperity,
But that downright rascality—doubtful morality too—should have
sternest correction.
And so, to make real our exalted ideal, we have, after earnest reflection,
Hit at last on a scheme which is really a dream of beauty, nobility,
kindness;
This—if Plutus recover his vision, and over the earth never more stray
in blindness,
But shall go the best of mankind, and shall rest at their side, and
shall never forsake them,
While unprincipled ones and the godless he shuns, it will follow in
time that he'll make them
Turn pious, and pray to the gods, until they too to share in our wealth
are admitted.
Now, who could devise revolution more wise, for the good of the race
better fitted?
BLEPSIDEMUS: Not a soul, I aver! You needn't ask her, for *she* is
a prejudiced witness.
CHREMYLUS: But to think how unpleasant are all things at present
—a miracle, sure, of unfitness!
Who would not regard it as madness—not hard enough; raving in-
sanity, rather!—
That rogues by the score have a good time, and store of riches they
constantly gather,
Yes, rake the gold in by unscrupulous sin, while many in goodness
excelling

Are wretchedly off, ay, don't have enough to eat, and with you have their dwelling?
I therefore maintain that, if Plutus regain his sight, and give *her* her quietus,
Then a highway for men has been found, where again shall the bliss of the Golden Age meet us.
POVERTY: Well, of all men that ever I met with, I never found any that swallowed delusions
Like these two old loons, who dance to the tunes of drivel and brain-confusions!
No good would come of it, this scheme which its prophet anticipates so eager-hearted;
For, if Plutus again got his eyesight, and then among all men were equally parted,
In the usefullest art would no man do his part, scientific research would be banished;
And so when these two, all owing to you, from the face of the earth had vanished,
Who would ply the smith's craft, or make galley or raft, turn wheels, or sew garments together,
Or make shoes at all, or mold bricks for a wall, take in washing, or tan any leather,
Or cleave with the share earth's surface, and there reap harvests, or do any threshing,
If people could give up all labor, and live on your dream-fruit so "rare and refreshing"?
CHREMYLUS: All rubbish and rot! You have reeled off a lot of essentials—of course we'll obtain them,
With all that man craves, by the labor of slaves.
POVERTY: Slaves, is it?—pray, whence will you gain them?
CHREMYLUS: Why, buy them, you fool, with our money.
POVERTY: And who'll be the seller? Who'll care for the bother,
When his own pockets burst with his gold?
CHREMYLUS: Oh, athirst for gain there'll be someone or other
Who'll bring supplies forth from the lands to the north, where the man-stealing trade is so thriving.
POVERTY: But, if you reflect, you cannot expect there'll be any man-stealers surviving:
The conclusion is plain from your premises: vain is your hope that a soul will be going
To risk his own skin more money to win for a purse even now over-flowing.
No! it's *you'll* have—and how will you like it?—to plough, and to dig, and to slave—with full purses!

So that harder than ever will life be, you clever reformer!

   CHREMYLUS: On you be your curses!

   POVERTY: And you never will snore on a bed any more—for there won't be a bed in existence—

Nor on rugs, who will care, when he's gold and to spare, to weave such a thing for subsistence?

When you bring home a bride, don't think to provide her with bottles of sweet-smelling essence,

Nor in glory and pride of robes splendidly dyed to deck her desirable presence!

Wealth?—where is the profit, if still, in spite of it, you starve amid fancied abundance?

When with me you reside, all things are supplied that you need, yes, in fullest redundance.

By the craftsman I take my seat, and I make him provide whatsoever is wanted:

Like a queen I constrain him a living to gain by the specter of poverty haunted.

   CHREMYLUS: You?—pray, what on earth do you furnish that's worth the obtaining—save burns from bath-boilers,*

And a swarm of old crones who are mere skin and bones, and famine-pinched children of toilers,

And millions of lice and of fleas, and supplies of mosquitoes that no man could number

For multitude, coming round poor heads, and humming to make a nightmare of their slumber,

Screaming "Open your eyes! It's high time that you rise, unless you prefer to be starving!"

For a mantle a shred of old rag, for a bed all adorned with elaborate carving

A rush mattress with bugs crammed, bloodthirsty thugs—it's like sleeping on tossing sea-billows—

For a carpet a mat (and rotten at that), and instead of soft eiderdown pillows

A stone for your head (a fine big one); for bread, when with hunger your belly feels baddish,

Nice succulent shoots of coarse mallow, and roots and leaves of the stringiest radish.

If for sofas we ask, there's the end of a cask (of course broken); our trough for dough-kneading

Is the side of a jar (and cracked badly)—Oh, are not the blessings set forth in our pleading

Of Poverty's case a rich boon for our race? Of fine benefits, Madam, you're bouncing!

---

* In cold weather the poor used to huddle in their rags round the boilers in the basement of the public baths.

POVERTY: Your plea don't apply to true poverty; why, it's mere beggary which you're denouncing!

CHREMYLUS: Well, and are not the two blood-sisters?—weren't you and Beggary born of one mother?

POVERTY: The tyrant of Sicily thus you'd prove easily our tyrant-banisher's brother!

For in truth no such thing is the life that I bring to mankind. You have erred in confusion

Of terms; for the state of whose hardships you prate is Beggary—sheer destitution.

But what's Poverty?—life that's victorious strife with the wolf at the door, self-denial;

There's nothing left over, but earnings still cover expenses—not failure, but trial.

CHREMYLUS: What a life of high bliss, by our Lady, is this that you launch earth's voyagers off in,

If their toil and their trial and stern self-denial won't pay at the end for a coffin!

POVERTY: You turn all to grotesque and silly burlesque, with truth and sincerity tampering!

It's beyond your dull ken that my training makes men far better than Plutus's pampering,

Both in body and mind. Those to whom he is kind receive gout with its terminal tortures;

They're pot-bellied withal, thick-ankled, and all too disgustingly fleshy debauchers;

But with me they grow wiry, wasp-waisted, and fiery, a terror to foes of our nation.

CHREMYLUS: Quite so; how they grow so wasp-waisted we know—your prescription is semistarvation.

POVERTY: Well, temperance next I will take for my text: I will prove to the Court's satisfaction

That with me is residing the life law-abiding; with Plutus dwells riotous action.

CHREMYLUS: I see—she believes that poor burglars and thieves are most law-abiding and quiet!

BLEPSIDEMUS: "If they're never found out," the lady no doubt means to add—and then, who can deny it?

POVERTY: And consider the case of the demagogue-race, who "champion the cause of the toiler":

They are honest while poor; you may rest very sure that not one shows the claws of the spoiler.

But the mask is soon stripped off when fingers are dipped in the national purse, and their purity

Lies in cheating wage earners: they turn overturners of commercial and social security.

CHREMYLUS: To be sure there's some truth in your words, though the tooth of mere malice shows through your denouncing;
But all that doesn't matter—so pray never flatter yourself that you'll so escape trouncing——
To your futile endeavor to show us that ever the poor are in better condition
Than rich folk.

POVERTY: And never will you be so clever as to drive me from this my position.

BUSINESS IS A LITTLE DULL IN HELL

LUCIAN

[Lucian, *Dialogues of the Dead*, iv, trans. by F. G. Fowler, in *The Works of Lucian of Samosata*, Clarendon Press, Oxford, 1905, vol. I, pp. 111–112.]

Here is a satiric dialogue, by the man who invented this literary form, Lucian (A.D. 125 to 192). His chief target is religious superstition. In this neat tour de force he obviously is making fun of the messenger god Hermes, who is also the conductor of the dead to Hades, the ferryman Charon, who took dead souls over the river Styx, and of course all hell itself. Incidentally, Hermes also came to be considered the guardian of commerce—and the protector of thieves!

HERMES: Ferryman, what do you say to settling up accounts? It will prevent any unpleasantness later on.

CHARON: Very good. It does save trouble to get these things straight.

HERMES: One anchor, to your order, five shillings.

CHARON: That is a lot of money.

HERMES: So help me Pluto, it is what I had to pay. One row-lock strap, fourpence.

CHARON: Five and four; put that down.

HERMES: Then there was a needle, for mending the sail; tenpence.

CHARON: Put that down, too.

HERMES: Caulking wax, nails, and cord for the brace. Two shillings the lot.

CHARON: They were worth the money.

HERMES: That's all, unless I have forgotten anything. When will you pay it?

CHARON: I can't just now, Hermes; we shall have a war or a plague presently, and then the passengers will come shoaling in, and I shall be able to make a little by jobbing the fares.

HERMES: So for the present I have nothing to do but sit down, and pray for the worst, as my only chance of getting paid?

CHARON: There is nothing else for it; very little business doing now, as you see, owing to the peace.

HERMES: That is just as well, though it does keep me waiting for my money. After all, though, Charon, in old days men were men; you remember the state they used to come down in—all blood and wounds generally. Nowadays a man is poisoned by his slave or his wife; or gets dropsy from overfeeding; a pale, spiritless lot, nothing like the men of old. Most of them seem to meet their end in some plot that has money for its object.

CHARON: Ah, money is in great request.

HERMES: Yes; you can't blame me if I am somewhat urgent for payment.

AN ECONOMICAL PROJECT

~~~✺~~~

BENJAMIN FRANKLIN

[Benjamin Franklin, "An Economical Project" (apparently written March 20, 1784), in John Bigelow (ed.), *The Complete Works of Benjamin Franklin*, G. P. Putnam's Sons, New York, 1888, vol. VI, pp. 277–283.]

Ben Franklin, most American of Americans over the whole period from 1492 (or earlier) to 1962 (or later), here mixes a little business with a little fun. Ben, so sober historians tell us, in his own life was a pretty good mixer of work and play—but in his case a *lot* of work and a *lot* of play. Why, for example, did he—in the fourth paragraph of this selection—go to bed three or four hours after midnight? (For some of his more serious accomplishments, see the selection from his autobiography in Volume III.)

———◆———

TO THE AUTHORS OF THE JOURNAL OF PARIS

MESSIEURS,

You often entertain us with accounts of new discoveries. Permit me to communicate to the public, through your paper, one that has lately been made by myself, and which I conceive may be of great utility.

I was the other evening in a grand company, where the new lamp of Messrs. Quinquet and Lange was introduced, and much admired for its splendor; but a general inquiry was made, whether the oil it consumed was not in proportion to the light it afforded, in which case there would be no saving in the use of it. No one present could satisfy us in that point, which all agreed ought to be shown, it being a very desirable thing to lessen, if possible, the expense of lighting our apartments, when every other article of family expense was so much augmented.

I was pleased to see this general concern for economy, for I love economy exceedingly.

I went home, and to bed, three or four hours after midnight, with my head full of the subject. An accidental sudden noise waked me about six in the morning, when I was surprised to find my room filled with light; and I imagined at first that a number of those lamps had been brought into it; but, rubbing my eyes, I perceived the light came in at the windows. I got up and looked out to see what might be the occasion of it, when I saw the sun just rising above the horizon, from whence he poured his rays plentifully into my chamber, my domestic having negligently omitted, the preceding evening, to close the shutters.

I looked at my watch, which goes very well, and found that it was but six o'clock; and still thinking it something extraordinary that the sun should rise so early, I looked into the almanac, where I found it to be the hour given for his rising on that day. I looked forward, too, and found he was to rise still earlier every day till towards the end of June; and that at no time in the year he retarded his rising so long as till eight o'clock. Your readers, who with me have never seen any signs of sunshine before noon, and seldom regard the astronomical part of the almanac, will be as much astonished as I was when they hear of his rising so early; and especially when I assure them *that he gives light as soon as he rises.* I am convinced of this. I am certain of my fact. One cannot be more certain of any fact. I saw it with my own eyes. And, having repeated this observation the three following mornings, I found always precisely the same result.

Yet it so happens that when I speak of this discovery to others, I can easily perceive by their countenances, though they forbear expressing it in words, that they do not quite believe me. One, indeed, who is a learned natural philosopher, has assured me that I must certainly be mistaken as to the circumstance of the light coming into my room; for it being well known, as he says, that there could be no light abroad at that hour, it follows that none could enter from without; and that of consequence, my windows being accidentally left open, instead of letting in the light, had only served to let out the darkness; and he used many ingenious arguments to show me how I might, by that means, have been deceived. I owned that he puzzled me a little, but he did not satisfy me; and the subsequent observations I made, as above mentioned, confirmed me in my first opinion.

This event has given rise in my mind to several serious and important reflections. I considered that, if I had not been awakened so early in the morning, I should have slept six hours longer by the light of the sun, and in exchange have lived six hours the following night by candlelight; and, the latter being as much more expensive light than the former, my love of economy induced me to muster up what little arithmetic I was master of, and to make some calculations, which I shall give you, after observing that utility is, in my opinion, the test of value in matters of invention, and that a discovery which can be applied to no use, or is not good for something, is good for nothing.

I took for the basis of my calculation the supposition that there are one hundred thousand families in Paris, and that these families consume in the night half a pound of bougies, or candles, per hour. I think this is a moderate allowance, taking one family with another; for though I believe some consume less, I know that many consume a great deal more. Then estimating seven hours per day as the medium quantity between the time of the sun's rising and ours, he rising during the six following months from six to eight hours before noon, and there being seven hours of course per night in which we burn candles, the account will stand thus:

In the six months between the 20th of March and the 20th of September, there are

Nights	183
Hours of each night in which we burn candles	7
Multiplication gives for the total number of hours	1,281
These 1,281 hours multiplied by 100,000, the number of inhabitants, give	128,100,000
One hundred twenty-eight millions and one hundred thousand hours, spent at Paris by candlelight, which, at half a pound of wax and tallow per hour, gives the weight of	64,050,000
Sixty-four millions and fifty thousand of pounds, which, estimating the whole at the medium price of thirty sols the pound, makes the sum of ninety-six millions and seventy-five thousand *livres tournois*	96,075,000

An immense sum! that the city of Paris might save every year, by the economy of using sunshine instead of candles.

If it should be said that people are apt to be obstinately attached to old customs, and that it will be difficult to induce them to rise before noon, consequently my discovery can be of little use; I answer, *Nil desperandum*. I believe all who have common sense, as soon as they have learned from this paper that it is daylight when the sun rises, will contrive to rise with him; and, to compel the rest, I would propose the following regulations:

First. Let a tax be laid of a louis per window, on every window that is provided with shutters to keep out the light of the sun.

Second. Let the same salutary operation of police be made use of, to prevent our burning candles, that inclined us last winter to be more economical in burning wood; that is, let guards be placed in the shops of the wax and tallow chandlers, and no family be permitted to be supplied with more than one pound of candles per week.

Third. Let guards also be posted to stop all coaches, &c., that would pass the streets after sunset, except those of physicians, surgeons, and midwives.

Fourth. Every morning, as soon as the sun rises, let all the bells in every church be set ringing; and if that is not sufficient, let cannon be fired in every street, to wake the sluggards effectually, and make them open their eyes to see their true interest.

All the difficulty will be in the first two or three days; after which the reformation will be as natural and easy as the present irregularity; for, *ce n'est que le premier pas qui coute.* Oblige a man to rise at four in the morning, and it is more than probable he will go willingly to bed at eight in the evening; and, having had eight hours of sleep, he will rise more willingly at four in the morning following. But this sum of 96,075,000 *livres* is not the whole of what may be saved by my economical project. You may observe that I have calculated upon only one half of the year, and much may be saved in the other, though the days are shorter. Besides, the immense stock of wax and tallow left unconsumed during the summer will probably make candles much cheaper for the ensuing winter, and continue them cheaper as long as the proposed reformation shall be supported.

For the great benefit of this discovery, thus freely communicated and bestowed by me on the public, I demand neither place, pension, exclusive privilege, nor any other reward whatever. I expect only to have the honor of it. And yet I know there are little, envious minds, who will, as usual, deny me this, and say that my invention was known to the ancients, and perhaps they may bring passages out of the old books in proof of it. I will not dispute with these people that the ancients knew not the sun would rise at certain hours; they possibly had, as we have, almanacs that predicted it; but it does not follow thence, that they knew *he gave light as soon as he rose*. This is what I claim as my discovery. If the ancients knew it, it might have been long since forgotten; for it certainly was unknown to the moderns, at least to the Parisians, which to prove I need use but one plain simple argument. They are as well instructed, judicious, and prudent a people as exist anywhere in the world, all professing, like myself, to be lovers of economy; and, from the many heavy taxes required from them by the necessities of the state, have surely an abundant reason to be economical. I say it is impossible that so sensible a people, under such circumstances, should have lived so long by the smoky, unwholesome, and enormously expensive light of candles, if they had really known that they might have had as much pure light of the sun for nothing.

I am, &c.

A SUBSCRIBER

COMPLAINT OF A MERCHANT'S WIFE

FROM *Hunt's Merchants' Magazine*

["Complaint of a Merchant's Wife," in *The Merchants' Magazine,* ed. by Freeman Hunt, Jan. 1845, vol. 12, no. 1, p. 105.]

Even a hundred or more years ago, wives of businessmen complained about their husband's preoccupation with his work in a modern (no doubt because it is eternal) manner. The following is a letter to the Editors of the *Evening Mirror* in 1845:

"MESSRS. EDITORS—

Allow me, through your agreeable columns, to protest most heartily and fervently against a crying evil in this community, and one which preys upon the spirits and undermines the happiness of too many of us poor women. I mean that terrible, unnatural, slavish devotion which our lords and masters pay to their business; thereby at the same time destroying their own health and comfort, and poisoning the fountain of all our enjoyments. I hear nothing, from morning to night, but discussions of the tariff, or controveries about stocks, state loans, railroads, steamboats, and suchlike subjects— all which are well enough at the exchange or the countinghouse, but which should never be allowed to profane the sacredness of the fireside. Even young bachelors are often guilty of these enormities. It seems to me, at times, as if there were no more *men* left in the world —they have all become *citizens.* Their humanity seems merged in some presidency or secretaryship. They are good trustees, directors, cashiers, bankers; but they are very indifferent husbands and fathers. They are utterly without social chat—they read no pleasant books— they hate the sound of music—they visit nobody—they scarcely deign to look at the face of nature; and, as for their unhappy wives, they must put with cold looks and cold words. This is all wrong, gentlemen. It is a sad perversion of life—it is cruelly unjust to us and our daughters; and it is the too certain source of deep and lasting misery to those who indulge in it. Home is no longer the garden of the heart, watched over by love, its roses kept in perennial bloom—but thorns and briers cumber its beauty. But I feel this matter too deeply to speak in metaphors. My own domestic circle is fast losing its charms, and becoming more dismal and formal than a hotel. I am beginning to lose all pride in my household. I am growing daily more unsociable. My health and temper are both giving way. In a word, I bitterly feel and lament the want of that sympathy and communion of heart which are so liberally promised us in the marriage vow. Come, then, gentlemen, like good chevaliers, to our relief. Here is a cause worthy of your active and sprightly pens. Exhort, frighten, ridicule, if you can, our erring husbands into a return to their allegiance, and to a more rational and happy life, and you will ever oblige

Your sincere friend,

AMANDA SMITH

THE ROMANCE OF THE MARKETS

FROM *Punch*

["The Romance of the Markets," *Punch*, 1851, vol. XXI, p. 169 (abridged).]

["Protection Against the Electric Telegraph," *Punch*, July–Dec. 1852, vol. XXIII, p. 85.]

The next two selections are from the famed English humorous magazine *Punch* in the mid-1800s—1851 and 1852, to be exact. The one makes fun of the lugubrious reporting about commodity markets in the newspapers. The other satirizes businessmen clamoring for the government to protect them against the effect of new inventions, like the electric telegraph. (For a French satire on protectionism, see Bastiat's piece, page 2296, in this volume.)

Punch's fun-making is of course English, but not so slow-paced or subtle as you might expect; it has, in fact, punch.

◆

I

WE KNOW OF NOTHING so sentimental in the columns of a daily newspaper as the article devoted to the state of the markets. We seldom peruse it without a tendency to tears, which are only checked by the recollection that it is only on bags of coffee, bales of cotton, parcels of pepper, and sacks of flour, that we are exhausting our useless sympathy.

We, however, defy anyone to be otherwise than moved by the description of the markets, which is evidently the production of a writer who luxuriates in a strain of melancholy tenderness, that is excluded by universal consent from every other portion of the newspaper. The literary sentimentalist finding no market among the booksellers for his goods, has gone to the very markets themselves, and has secured a corner in the journals, where he may indulge without restraint his tendency to pathos.

Let us take a specimen of that affecting style of writing, which has found its way, appropriately enough, to Mincing Lane, ever since the mincing manner has been banished from the publications put forth by the West End publishers:

> An improved feeling had again begun to show itself in the coffee market, where dullness had until lately prevailed, and sugars began to assume a livelier aspect.

Surely this must be written by some fashionable novelist "out of luck," [who] once used to cloy the circulating libraries [and now has] rushed to the sugar cask as the only alternative to avoid the butter-shop. Substitute *Augustus Danvers* for the "coffee market," insert *Rosalie* in the place of *sugars,* and we get a sentence that would seem to form part of a sentimental novel of ten years back, when the writers of the same sort of stuff could command their £300 or £500 for an adequate lot of it. The paragraph, as amended, will stand thus:

> An improved feeling had again begun to show itself in Augustus Danvers, where dullness had until lately prevailed, and Rosalie began to assume a livelier aspect.

We know nothing of the mysteries of what is termed the "staff" of a daily paper; but we certainly picture to ourselves the writer of the markets as a pale gentleman, with a forehead shaved up to its highest, a Byron tie, a turned-down shirt collar, and a melancholy cast of countenance. We can imagine him walking moodily about the markets, looking out anxiously for a glimpse of gloom in sugars, and feeling an indescribable satisfaction in the dullness of peppers. Why is it necessary that wool should be "flat," Bengal figs "low," indigo "dull," rice "depressed," and everything that seems nice and eatable so wretchedly low-spirited? It is seldom we meet with a bit of sensible "firmness" in something or other; but, even if we do, we are told of a "tendency to give way," before we get to the end of the article.

We earnestly entreat our daily contemporaries to get rid of the dull sentimental dogs, who howl and moan over the markets, and put them into the hands of some of the more lively writers, of whom there is no lack on all the newspaper establishments. . . .

II

PROTECTION AGAINST THE ELECTRIC TELEGRAPH

Certain gentlemen, practicing as conveyancers in a peculiar line at races, public meetings, reviews, exhibitions, sights, and theaters, or otherwise interested in the irregular and clandestine transfer of property, many of whom were attired in the extreme style of fashion, assembled yesterday evening in a private room of the Old Shop, to consider what steps to take in consequence of the arrangements now in course of being made to connect all the police offices with the electric telegraph.

The worthy host, Mr. Ikey Slomans, who occupied the chair, said he felt himself much honored by the werry respectable body as had come forrads in defense of their common interests on that occasion, and begged to express his sympathy with them as a landlord. (*Hear, hear.*)

Mr. Montgomery Mortimer said that they had a new and terrible foe to contend with. To the beak—to the claw of the lobster—the law had now added the lightning. (*Oh!*) They were to be nabbed through electricity; they were to be collared by the agency of magnetism. Science had enlisted the Levin Brand as a crusher. (*Shame!*) In the exercise of the arduous profession in which they (himself, and his friends now present) were engaged, the climate of this country often became too warm for their health. (*Hear.*) A brief retirement to Boulogne, or tour on the Continent—perhaps a trip to America—was then necessary. The connection of the police offices with the electric telegraph would operate as a most injurious check upon that temporary emigration which was an essential refuge to gentlemen who followed an avocation so extremely trying. (*Hear, hear.*)

Mr. Bob Smithers, *alias* Jones, understood the gen'lm'n as had just spoke, to mean that this here 'lectric telegraph bisnis would hinder hisself and his pals from cuttin' and runnin', by makin' of 'em safe to be lagged.

Mr. Mortimer said the drift of his observations had been correctly appreciated by his honorable friend.

Mr. Bob Smithers continued. There was no chance for a cove now. The detectives was bad enough; but this here scientific dodge would be a reglar flabbergaster. (*Hear.*) Your mechanical inwentions was spifflicatin' manival dexterity. (*Hear.*) They had long hindered a poor feller from turnin' an honest penny (*Oh!*); and now they wouldn't let him turn a penny nohow. (*Hear, hear.*) He agreed with them werry respeckble old gen'lm'n as held that machinery and all that sort o' thing was the cuss o' the country. (*Cheers*)

The Reverend Mr. Cavendish Belgrave, from his observation of fashionable society, and especially from what he had heard at genteel places of worship (*ironical cheers*)—he might, perhaps, be better understood if he said swell churches—(*laughter*)—was happy in being enabled to state, for the comfort of the assembly, that there was a clerical party—not a party in an individual sense, but a party of clerical gents—in fact, of parsons—highly influential in the Legislature, who were all for going back to the Middle Ages—the good old times—when no electric telegraphs, or police offices either, existed to restrict ingenuity and limit enterprise. (*Loud cheers*)

Mr. Bill Snigg, surnamed The Downy, asked vos there no 'ope in a appeal to guv'ment? In connection with ministers he had heerd mention of Thimblerig. (*Hear.*) Was there no sitch a thing as feller feelin'? Wasn't there no sort of honor, accordin' to the sayin', among certain persons? Wouldn't the Protectionists 'old out to 'em no 'elpin' 'and, and, that 'and as they had often met in the pocket o' the people. (*Hear, hear.*) They might at all events try it on; and he proposed that a petition should be sent to the Earl of Derby, prayin' for protection agin competition with the 'lectric telegraph on be-arf of that important branch of British industry—

Mr. Belgrave.—Of which, in point of fact, we are the *Chevaliers*. The honorable gentleman added that he should have much pleasure in seconding Mr. Snigg's suggestion; but he was afraid the hope of sympathy in the ministerial quarter was a dream of a too confiding mind. The Cabinet would never legislate against electric wires, unless those wires were used to catch hares. (*Hear.*) All the government could do for them, he had reason to apprehend, would be to substitute for that temporary emigration alluded to by Mr. Mortimer, an emigration that would afford them an asylum more or less permanent (*Oh!*), but also more or less disagreeable (*Ah!*) and inconvenient (*Hisses*): a sort of emigration, in short, of which the only advantage was that of being gratuitous. (*Loud groans*)

Mr. Chizzell said he feared they must trust to their personal resources. For his own part, if science was sharp, he hoped to prove sharper. (*Hear.*) In the meantime, he would propose "Down with the Electric Telegraph!" (*Cheers*)

The toast having been drunk with acclamation, three groans were given for Professor Wheatstone; and the time of opening the theaters approaching, the assembly dispersed itself.

THE HODJA'S DONKEY GOES TO MARKET

⌒◍⌒

ALICE GEER KELSEY

[Alice Geer Kelsey, "The Donkey Goes to Market," in *Once the Hodja*, Longmans, Green & Co., New York, Toronto, 1943, pp. 63–70.]

This selection is a traditional Turkish "Hodja" story. Any Turk, and particularly a Turkish businessman wishing to make his point, can always find a Hodja story to illustrate what he means. This one gives us, as well as humor, a glimpse of action in the market place of another country. It is taken from Alice Geer Kelsey's collection *Once the Hodja*. The explanation which follows is from her foreword.

Five centuries ago, so runs the tale, a Turkish schoolmaster was berating a group of his pupils for a prank. One by one he called them to him to ask what part each had had in the mischief. Solemnly he pronounced a punishment to fit each crime.

At last came the turn of a particularly lively pupil, Nasr-ed-Din.

"And what did you do?" demanded the schoolmaster.

"Nothing." Nasr-ed-Din shrugged. "All I did was to watch and laugh."

The schoolmaster pondered a moment and hit upon the perfect punishment for one who merely watched and laughed.

"*As long as the world lasts, people will laugh at you!*"

For five centuries the people of Turkey, and of all the Near East, have been laughing at Nasr-ed-Din—and still they laugh. The humorous folklore of the nation has been hung upon the name of Nasr-ed-Din, who, on becoming a teacher-priest, added the honorary title of Hodja to his name. Young and old, rich and poor, ignorant and learned, break into a grin of anticipation whenever they hear, "That reminds me of a Nasr-ed-Din Hodja story!" There are hundreds of these stories. In many of them the Hodja's patient, long-eared donkey has a part, for the Hodja, like the Turkish villager of today, has one friend upon whom he can depend—his donkey. In most of them, too, his wife Fatima plays a part—a minor but persistent part.

———◆———

"I TELL YOU, NO! I will not keep this miserable donkey another day!" Nasr-ed-Din Hodja glared at the little gray donkey that was patiently switching off the myriad flies as it waited for the Hodja to fasten on the piece of old rug that served as a saddle.

"A new donkey might be just as stubborn," suggested Fatima.

"This wretch is more than stubborn!" stormed the Hodja. "It eats like an elephant but grows skinnier every day. It is slow as a tortoise, lazy as a pig, mean as a fox, stupid as a fish, and stubborn as a—as a—as a donkey!"

Fatima patted the little donkey, who rubbed its head affectionately against her striped sleeve. Fatima said nothing. She had argued with her husband enough times to know that it was like throwing dry leaves on a fire.

"Say your goodbyes to the creature!" Nasr-ed-Din Hodja threw one long leg over the little animal. He made the low throaty "Ughr-r-r-r," which is marching orders to a Turkish donkey. "Next time you see it, someone else will be riding it. You shall see what a fine donkey I shall ride home from the animal market. You know how good I am at buying and selling. I can sell this wretched donkey for enough to buy a fine one, and still have a gold piece left over for you to sew in your headdress."

"Ughr-r-r-r," he whirred to the donkey again. The little animal reluctantly shook its long ears, picked up one tiny hoof, and was off. Gloating over the great bargain he was to strike in the market that day, the Hodja patted the coarse hair of his donkey's neck.

Through the street gate rode the Hodja, and on toward the market place. His long legs dangled at the donkey's sides, his feet sometimes touching the cobblestones of the narrow street. It was hard to pass by the charms of market day, but the Hodja had important business on hand. He nodded to right and to left at his many friends in the market place, but kept straight on until he reached the animal market.

"Here is a donkey that will make some man proud of his bargain," said the Hodja as he handed the donkey over to the auctioneer.

"Such a good donkey should bring a good price," said the auctioneer. He poked the donkey, pinched its legs, and looked at its teeth. Like the Hodja, he spoke loudly for the benefit of anyone who might be listening.

One after another, the auctioneer led the animals up for sale but not a bid did the Hodja make. His eyes were fixed on one donkey that was bigger, sleeker, and plumper than the others. Surely that was the donkey for him. Finally, all the donkeys were sold but two—the one Nasr-ed-Din Hodja had brought and the one he had resolved to ride away. He was relieved to see that the auctioneer led up his old donkey first. It would be good to have the money for his sale jingling in his belt with what money he already had before he started bidding for the beautiful dark donkey on which he had set his heart.

"Here is a donkey worth buying!" The auctioneer rubbed his hands gloatingly as he set the Hodja's old donkey before the little group of buyers. "I have watched this donkey many a time and wished it was mine. See that wise look in its eyes! See the gentle way it holds its head! One look at this donkey shows that it would obey your orders before you gave them!"

Nasr-ed-Din Hodja looked at the donkey's eyes. There was a wise look he had never noticed.

"And look at the muscles," the auctioneer droned on. "What loads it could carry! What hills it could climb! Those slim legs mean speed. I wager this donkey could run faster than any donkey in Ak Shehir!"

The Hodja looked at the donkey's legs. He had never noticed how strong and slim they were.

"See how smooth this donkey's coat is!" said the auctioneer. "That shows good care. What a pretty shade of gray! What perfectly matching white boots on its feet!"

The Hodja squinted thoughtfully at the donkey. It was prettily marked. Strange he had never noticed.

"How much am I offered for the handsomest, strongest, wisest, gentlest, most industrious donkey in all Ak Shehir?"

"Fifty ghurush," offered a villager.

Nasr-ed-Din Hodja glared at him. Fifty ghurush for the finest donkey in Ak Shehir, indeed!

"Two liras," called the Hodja.

"Two and a half liras," called a villager.

"Three!" The Hodja held up three fingers.

"Four!"

"Five!"

"Six!"

Up and up went the price until a villager bid ten liras.

"Wait a minute!" called the excited Hodja. He grabbed his money bag from his belt and counted his money. Just what he thought! Ten liras and eleven ghurush.

"Ten liras and five ghurush," called a villager.

"Ten liras and eleven ghurush," shouted the Hodja.

He waited. Silence!

"Only ten liras and eleven ghurush for this wonderful donkey!" exclaimed the auctioneer, who knew perfectly well that was a good price. "Come, someone! Make it eleven liras."

Everyone waited. Silence!

The auctioneer handed the bridle to Nasr-ed-Din Hodja. The Hodja emptied his money bag into the auctioneer's hand. He threw his long legs over the donkey's back and settled into the familiar saddle.

"Ughr-r-r," he whirred to the donkey and off they trotted toward home. How proud of his bargaining Fatima would be!

Halfway home he began wondering why he had an empty money

bag. He had planned, by good bargaining, to bring home a donkey and more money than he carried away. It was puzzling. Perhaps Fatima could explain.

And perhaps she did.

THE SHREWD TIN PEDDLER WHO WOULDN'T BE OUTSMARTED

HUGH PETERS

[Hugh Peters, "A Yankee Lyric," in Richardson Wright, *Hawkers & Walkers in Early America*, J. B. Lippincott Co., Philadelphia, 1927, pp. 75–76.]

Here is a Connecticut poem, from the mid-1800s, ascribed to a poet by the name of Hugh Peters. In this colorful period the peddlers followed the march of population and kept it supplied with merchandise. They were far from always being scrupulous, but apparently people looked on them with indulgence, for they made fun of them with a sort of grudging affection.*

There is, in famous Yankee-land
A class of men ycleped tin-peddlers,
A shrewd, sarcastic band
Of busy meddlers;
They scour the country through and through,
Vending their wares, tin pots, tin pans,
Tin ovens, dippers, wash-bowls, cans,
Tin whistles, kettles, or to boil or stew,
Tin dullenders, tin nutmeg graters,
Tin warming-platters for your fish and 'taters!
In short,
If you will look within
His cart,
And gaze upon the tin
Which glitters there,
So bright and fair,
There is no danger in defying
You to go off without buying.

One of these cunning, keen-eyed gentry
Stopped at a tavern in the country

_____

* For more about peddlers, refer to index listing in this volume.

Just before night,
And called for bitters for himself, of course,
And fodder for his horse;
This done, our worthy wight
Informed the landlord that his purse was low,
"Quite empty, I assure you, sir, and so
I wish you'd take your pay
In something in my way."

Now Boniface supposed himself a wag—
And when he saw that he was sucked,
Was not dispirited, but plucked
Up courage and his trousers too!
Quoth he t'himself, I am not apt to brag,
'Tis true,
But I can stick a feather in my cap
By making fun of this same Yankee chap.
"Well, my good friend,
That we may end
This troublesome affair,
I'll take my pay in ware,
Provided that you've got what suits
My inclination."
"No doubt of that," the peddler cried,
Sans hesitation:
"Well, bring us in a pair of good tin boots!"
"Tin boots," our Jonathan espied
His landlord's spindle shanks,
And giving his good Genius thanks
For the suggestion,
Ran out, returned, and then—"By goles!
Yes, here's a pair of candle-molds!
They'll fit you without question!"

LAUGHING AT BUSINESSMEN IN THE 1880s

BROWN AND METCALFE

[Brown, "Another Lie Nailed Up," in *The Judge,* Dec. 20, 1884, vol. 7, no. 166, p. 12.]

[Metcalfe, "The Customary Christmas Story," in *Life,* Dec. 1889 (Christmas number), pp. 13–14.]

Here are two pieces from American humorous magazines, one from the old *Life,* one from the deceased *Judge.* Some of us remember when these two publications were vigorous rivals for our laughs. In "Another Lie Nailed Up," *Judge* makes fun of the idea that work is noble (1884); and in "The Customary Christmas Story," *Life* satirizes Dickens' story of Scrooge, and all its imitators (1889).

---◆---

ANOTHER LIE NAILED UP

IT IS SLYLY WHISPERED AROUND the globe that I am lazy. Bless your soul, I haven't got a lazy bone in my umbrella. I have no distaste for work; it is one of my delights to sit and read about all kinds of work, and you have no idea how much exercise it is and what an appetite it gives me for dinner; and if you would see me eat you would not think there was any laziness about me. My landlady says I work harder at the table than any of the rest of the boarders. There is not a minute in the twenty-four hours that I am not doing something, breathing or something else. You never catch me sitting down and quitting breathing for an hour or two like some people want to. I am too industrious for that.

I maintain that work is the most ennobling of all avocations, and always keep telling them so. When I have a man working for me it never makes me tired, no matter how hard he works; he might work himself to death and you never hear me complaining. Why, when I was young and followed a trade for exercise, my boss used to say that I could put off more work than any other hand he had; he said I was always putting it off, and yet it never seemed to exhaust me much. No matter how hot it is, I can roll up my sleeves and pitch in and rest harder than almost anybody else, and you don't hear me grunting, like some.

Talk about me doing no work! Look at a single instance. Is it not the very hardest work in this world for me to pay my bills? Don't it make me sweat? You have no idea how much I weigh when I get set down in a chair, and I rather like these avocations which require sitting down to do. I have sat half the night working at whist, and I have always thought that, above all other trades, I would like to be a shoemaker or a tailor, especially in dull times. I could accomplish the sitting part and not half try. If I had to work every week from Saturday night till Sunday morning, I would not run around making a fuss about it and acting ridiculous.

I was never tired to death in all my life, and I have witnesses to prove it. Ever since I started out for myself, I have been most industriously engaged in growing, and very few men have made a better job of it. I always get up when the sun is up and go to bed when it is down, and am dreadfully opposed to sleeping all the time. I never run away from work. You ought to see me sitting around where the carpenters are putting up a new building; and they say I seem to know more about the work than they do themselves, and they are good workmen. I firmly believe most everybody ought to do something, or see that it is done; and toil is honest and honorable for some people.

My father never had any trouble about getting me to work, like some fathers have, because whenever he wanted me to do anything right quick he always asked my brother John to do it, and I saw that it was done. Some boys would go howling around about it, but I never did; and especially when there was wood to saw I always was there with a bacon rind to grease John's saw, and my father used to say that he never saw a boy who could swing a scythe farther away than I could. I was raised on a farm, and certainly that is a place where laziness can never thrive. I left home without a cent in my pocket, and made my own way, though I was born without an education. My teacher always said that I worked hard over my studies; if I would only get down *to* the studies; and no scholars ever got ahead of me without they got above me.

Work! why, I like even to labor under a mistake or a hallucination. I love the very money that a workingman gets. I have not hesitated to seize the plebeian handles of a wheelbarrow and go along the streets with Simpson in it, just after election. I even work like smoke to get out of work. My mother used to think I was of such prominence in the household that she used to point to me and say, "There is the *rest* of the family." Of course she meant that I was the balance of it.

I never run after a railroad train or a street car. There are lots of things I don't do. My neighbors say too many. But I love to be quiet. If I intend to do any work I thoroughly consider it in all its bearings to be sure of it. This only takes a few days. I would make a good plumber if it wasn't for the plumbing. I take no part in walking matches, and avoid overheating myself at anything, as it is not healthy.

Some people think that work is a terrible thing, but, la me, I don't think anything at all of it. The intervals between work I always did enjoy, and I don't care how hard I am expected to rest, I can always accomplish it satisfactorily.

However, I never did quite get it down so fine as to look on labor as a recreation, but as a necessity when all things else fail us, and the man who won't work like a Turk will get no sympathy or job of me.

I cannot see how the report got out that I was lazy. It astonishes me. Why, I have been lately thinking of coming out next year as a workingman's candidate for governor. This report may injure my cause.

THE CUSTOMARY CHRISTMAS STORY

ROBERT SMITH was the customary Christmas millionaire. That is to say, he had a hard heart, a great deal of money, and no chickens nor children of his own. He could draw his check for thousands, and, what is more to the point, it would be cashed upon presentation at the bank, if properly indorsed. Mr. Smith had in his employ the customary Christmas clerk, with the customary half-starved appearance, the customary large family, and the customary small salary.

As he left his customarily-dingy office on the evening before Christmas the customary snowstorm was in progress and the shop windows were lighted up with their customary brilliancy, sending out the customary gleams of light, brightening up in their customary way the usual cheerless scene without. The regular Christmas chimes were ringing out their customary gladsome peal, announcing, as is customary at this time of year, "Peace on earth, good will toward men." But there was the customary absence of response in the hard heart of Robert Smith. He was thinking the customary Christmas thought of the customary Christmas millionaire—that is, whether it would not be wise to go around to his bookkeeper's the next day, and, as is usual, announce that, beginning with the first of January, his salary would be cut down 25 per cent. This would mean an annual saving of $36.67, and it seemed quite worth the while.

Robert Smith went to bed on Christmas Eve with the intention customary to Christmas millionaires of getting up next morning to make somebody else uncomfortable.

But the customary Spirit of Christmas came during the night and sat on Robert Smith's digestive appurtenances, causing him to see the customary visions intended to show Christmas millionaires the error of their ways.

It was Christmas morning. As Robert Smith buttoned the custom-

ary overcoat about him and stepped out into the customary bracing
Christmas air, his eyes beamed with the customary new light, and his
features bore the customary benevolent smile of the Christmas millionaire who has been interviewed all night by the Spirit of Christmas.

At last he reached the humble home of his bookkeeper. To the door
came the wife of that individual, with the customary wan look and the
customary number of children clinging to her skirts and staring at the
millionaire with the customary half-scared eyes.

"Oh, Mr. Smith!" she said, with the customary tremor in her voice.
"Come in!" and going through the customary act of wiping off a chair
seat with her apron, she invited the millionaire to be seated.

"Is your husband here?" asked Robert Smith.

"No, sir——"

"Well, it makes no difference," replied the Christmas millionaire,
trying to hide the real feeling of his heart, which made the customary
effort to show itself in his face. "Yesterday I had made up my mind
to reduce his salary twenty-five per cent, beginning with the first of
January. But I have changed my mind."

The usual surprised look crept into the face of the bookkeeper's
wife.

"I find that a twenty-five-per-cent reduction figures out $36.67. I
dislike odd figures, so we'll call it an even forty."

"My husband expected you would be here this morning and left
this note for you," said the bookkeeper's wife, producing a letter from
beneath her apron.

Robert Smith brought out his penknife, and, with the customary
deliberation of the Christmas millionaire, cut open the envelope. This
was what he read:

CHRISTMAS EVE

MY DEAR MR. SMITH:

I sail for Spain tomorrow morning to find out why there is
no extradition law between that country and the United States. My
wife and children follow later. I do not lock the safe tonight, as it
contains no negotiable securities or money. I also leave on my desk
the power of attorney to sign checks on your account at the bank.
The account is thirty-six cents overdrawn, and I have no further
use for the power. Goodbye, Smith! Merry Christmas, and many
of 'em!

Robert Smith gasped the customary gasp, and then proceeded to
kick himself down to his lawyer's. He wanted to get out an attachment
on the grand piano on which the bookkeeper's eldest daughter had
been artistically playing with one finger:

Christmas comes but once a year,
And when it comes it brings good cheer.

THE BUSINESSMAN IN AMERICAN FOLKLORE

~~◦~~

KENNETH WIGGINS PORTER

[Kenneth Wiggins Porter, "The Business Man in American Folklore," in *Bulletin of the Business Historical Society*, Nov. 1944, vol. XVIII, no. 5, pp. 113–130.]

Has the businessman ever been a hero in American folklore? This author of the only article on the subject says "No." Furthermore, "hostility toward the businessman is dominant almost always where he appears in folklore." Minds nurtured on such attitudes welcomed the attacks of the muckrakers as just so much more proof of the validity of their beliefs. Of course, there were some exceptions to the prevailing concepts—but see them for yourself.

———◆———

PERHAPS the most significant thing about the businessman in folklore is that he is far from an important figure in it. From this we may deduce that among those people who have created what we call folklore the businessman has either not played an important role or his function and contribution have not been understood. He is not, however, altogether missing; we might not recognize him, since he is a remote and shadowy figure compared with the businessman as we think of him today. But he is there, and the very form and circumstances in which he appears have meaning.

What is folklore? It is the most elemental, the least intellectualized evidence among civilized people of thought about aspects of life and society as they have been observed and experienced. Perhaps what is registered in folklore is not so much thought as a crystallization of folk attitudes, impressions, or convictions as expressed very largely in relation to concrete experience. Its full psychological significance is impossible to estimate. But folklore is obviously of importance as one of those major streams of influence which are basic elements in the formation of popular opinion.

Students have given little attention to the place of the business man in folklore. What follows here is by way of an exploratory journey. Examples will be given of how the businessman appears in folklore and an attempt will be made to show the significance of his appearance.

The media in which folklore exists are the ballad, the story, the saying—verbal material which characteristically and primarily originates among the masses of the population and is circulated and molded by and among them through oral communication, instead of being produced and disseminated through the professional channels of publication, the stage, and, more recently, the screen and radio. The seed of a folklore item, to be sure, may be found in a medieval Latin manuscript, an eighteenth-century chapbook, a newspaper item, but it enters into the folklore world through oral transmissions, achieving thereby appearance in a variety of versions. Indeed, fluidity, changes, additions, and shifts of emphasis produced by the varied interests, tastes, and needs of the countless oral communicators and modifiers are salient characteristics of folklore.

Since folklore is dependent for its vitality and to a large extent for its existence upon oral communication, it is obvious that it will flourish best in a society and environment which is separated either physically or intellectually, or both, from the flow of ideas, thought, or factual information through the medium of the printed page or such commercialized media of professional communication as the radio, movie, and theatre. Folklore has, therefore, displayed its greatest vitality among the residents of remote rural regions in which standards of literacy, perhaps, have not been high, the condition of most of our ancestors a century or so ago.

The great figures in American folklore, consequently, have characteristically been projections of the interests, abilities, and aspirations of the "folk" themselves—the illiterate and semiliterate population, particularly of the remoter rural areas, whose culture is traditional and is disseminated by oral communication. Davy Crockett's bear hunting, John Henry's and Casey Jones's steel-driving and locomotive engineering, even the ruthlessly murderous activities of Franky (of "Franky and Johnny") or of Stagolee and Mike Fink, were qualities and achievements which the folk, who lived and chafed under hard labor and looked upon outsiders with suspicion and resentment, could understand and admire.

The businessman has been far from the center of such occupations and interests, though he cannot be divorced from them entirely. By the businessman I mean the man who furnishes capital and direction for the processes of production and distribution. Historically, I should include the master weaver or shoemaker, on the one hand, as well as the factory owner or manager, on the other; the peddler or retail storekeeper as well as the proprietor of the department store or mail order house. I should also include the responsible salaried executive of a mercantile or industrial firm who is psychologically a businessman even though he may furnish little or no capital to the enterprise in which he participates.

I should exclude, however, from the category of businessman those who are not actually or psychologically businessmen. Among them are the journeyman-craftsman, working for wages, even though he might labor at loom or bench next to the master work-man who employed him, and similarly his modern descendant, the wage laborer. In this class is also the farmer—even the land owner —so long as his principal function is to participate in the processes of plowing and sowing, reaping and mowing, rather than ownership or management of a commercial farm or ranch. From the point of view of economic reality, this may be inconsistent, but psychologically and socially it is essential, for the reason, if for no other, that such a farmer does not think of himself as a businessman.

The more highly developed businessman, particularly the sedentary businessman in his office or counting room, participated in activities and performed functions which the folk could not understand and of which they were suspicious; banking and stockbroking were outside the limits of their experience, and the retail merchant they felt they could understand only too well—he was a man who bought cheap and sold dear, who could not be trusted, and who made money with little or no exertion. The larger the businessman's operations and the farther divorced, therefore, from the primary processes of economic life—the more typical of twentieth century "big business," in other words—the more remote he becomes from the core of the folklore kingdom.

Remote though the businessman may have been from the folk, he has not been invisible or unimportant to them. Indeed, the territory of the businessman and that of the folk have intersected in greater or less degree. Often the point of contact has been one where friction might develop. This friction has tended to change into actual hostility the suspicion which came from lack of understanding, or the vague resentment which has been kindled by the greater wealth or power of the businessman.

Hostility toward the businessman is dominant almost always where he appears in folklore. The exceptional cases are rare and significant. That hostility has a long history behind it. For instance, the medieval miller—who came nearer to being a businessman in the modern sense than anyone else with whom the medieval peasant had much experience—established the tradition of the businessman's acquisitiveness and was immortalized, frequently in association with other suspect occupations, in a series of songs and sayings, some of which survived the voyage across the Atlantic.

The most significant illustration is a ballad describing the deathbed of an old miller who, in endeavoring to determine to which of his three sons he shall leave the mill, asks each in turn how much he would take out of a bushel of corn brought to him for grinding. The mill finally goes to the youngest because of his forthright declaration: [1]

> Father, dear father, my name is Jack
> And rather than I for corn should lack
> I'd take the whole and swear to the sack,
> And whip the mill-boy when he comes back!

It was evidently considered dangerous to place material of any sort in the hands of the businessmen-craftsmen of early days to be "worked up," for we have the record: [2]

> The miller he stole corn,
> The weaver he stole yarn,
> The little tailor he stole broadcloth
> For to keep these three rogues warm.

It is significant that the one businessman, so far as I know, who is a life-sized, or rather larger than life-sized, character in American folklore, is not banker, broker, or merchant, but an entrepreneur in an extractive industry—the Brobdingnagian lumberman, Paul Bunyan. Some may be surprised at this classification of Paul Bunyan as a businessman rather than as a working man (John Dos Passos makes him a symbol of the I.W.W. lumberjacks [3]), but even a casual investigation of the canon will reveal that, though he may have started out as a lumber*jack,* he soon developed into a lumber*man.* He has a logging crew, including Johnny Inkslinger, the accountant. His income is derived from the profit he gains from the tremendous amount of timber he succeeds in getting off the logging tract he has purchased from the government.

Paul Bunyan, though a businessman, is a figure in American folklore partly because of his type of business—lumbering on at least a small scale was a part of the everyday life of every frontiersman or rural dweller in a timbered region and an activity which he understood—and partly because Paul, besides managing his business, did not disdain to work side by side with his men, and was himself capable of accomplishing as much as a whole gang. He thus performed a function which the folk could understand and appreciate.

---

[1] Cf. Mary O. Eddy, *Ballads and Songs from Ohio* (N. Y., 1939), pp. 167–170; Emelyn Elizabeth Gardner and Geraldine Jenks Chickering, *Ballads and Songs of Southern Michigan* (Ann Arbor, 1939), pp. 247–249; and many others.

[2] Eloise Hubbard Linscott, *Folk Songs of Old New England* (N. Y., 1939), p. 214. Charles Kingsley, *Westward Ho!* (1st edition, 1855), vol. i, chap. v. Cf. "When a miller's knocked on the head, the less of flour makes the more of bread."

[3] "Paul Bunyan," *1919,* the second volume in the trilogy, *U. S. A.*

He was an outdoor, democratic, American frontier manifestation of the "master workman" of the guild period.

Paul Bunyan was also in the folk tradition not merely of giant size and strength but also of gigantic capacity for and generosity with food and drink—as indicated by his pea-soup lake and skating-rink-sized griddle-cakes. A stingy man's very stinginess may be recorded in folklore, but not with admiration. And yet the Paul Bunyan legend includes some tales which suggest that he was not free from some of the faults traditionally ascribed to businessmen. He is, for example, credited with an unethical device for cutting down his payroll—frightening his men into the woods on payday with the word that government agents are coming to arrest them for logging on government land! Paul Bunyan is thus revealed in a role unusual in folklore, that of a businessman "with a payroll to meet"—in some way or other.[4]

There is a class of businessmen, petty though their operations be, who are generally treated in American folklore in a friendly if sometimes amusedly condescending fashion. These are the small traveling merchants, the peddlers, whose good nature, shrewdness, and smoothness of tongue are described in such folk-songs as "Wizard Oil" and "The Connecticut Peddler."[5] It is not surprising that the peddler is an exception to the general rule of folk-hostility to the merchant. He performed an indispensable economic function, bringing to the doors of isolated farmhouses the small but important items which made the difference between sheer barren inconvenience and squalor and some slight touch of comfort or luxury. He brought a flash of color and romance into the barren lives of his customers and fulfilled the social, recreational, and educational function of the village gossip and daily newspaper. (He has been immortalized in this role in *Oklahoma!*, the . . . popular musical show. . . .) He usually was willing to accept payment "in kind"—furs, beeswax, a ham, anything portable and nonperishable on hand—and did not insist on "hard money." Perhaps even more important, since he might never come that way again he obviously could not be expected to grant credit and therefore was not asked to do so; he consequently could not later offend by dunning his customers, as the local merchant, who supplied staples in considerable amounts on credit, was frequently forced to do, to his consequent unpopularity. Perhaps the mail order house has now taken the place of the peddler and inherited his popularity. As much is suggested in the assurance to his constituents, ascribed to

<hr>

[4] The best source of information on Paul Bunyan is Esther Shephard, *Paul Bunyan* (Seattle, 1924). See also K. Bernice Stewart and Homer A. Watt, "Legends of Paul Bunyan, Lumberjack," *Transactions of the Wisconsin Academy of Arts and Letters,* vol. xviii (1916), pp. 639–651.

[5] Carl Sandburg, *The American Songbag* (N. Y., 1927), pp. 52–53; John A. and Alan Lomax, *American Ballads and Folk Songs* (N.Y., 1934), pp. 317–320.

a red-gallused late governor of a southern state, that they "had no friends except Jesus Christ, Sears, Roebuck, and Gene Talmadge."

But the peddler in general did not become a heroic figure, though occasionally one proved to be a "man of his hands," capable of protecting his wares and his takings. Such a one was a peddler who, because of his audacity and courage in robbing highwayman Brennan, who had earlier robbed the peddler, was rewarded by his being offered the highwayman's comradeship; when the peddler cast aside his pack and took to the road as Brennan's partner, this was evidently, to the folk mind, a step up in the social scale.[6] The mingling of condescension and sympathy toward the peddler when he appears in folklore is indicated by the fact that his most frequent appearance is as the "murderee" of a ghost story.[7]

It may be more than a coincidence that a businessman who served his apprenticeship as a tin peddler, and in that capacity may have learned the trick of pleasing the populace, should be the only American businessman I know of to be the hero of a popular song. Jim Fisk, however, was celebrated therein not for his thoroughly pernicious operations as a speculator—his business activities are not even mentioned—but because of his lavish way of life, his spectacular generosity, and his death at the hands of a society man who was his rival for the affections of a gay lady. The ballad is a street song, revealing the rather low tastes and aspirations of the *Lumpenproletariat* of the Gilded Age: [8]

> I'll sing of a man who's now dead in his grave,
> A good man as ever was born.
> Jim Fisk was his name, and his money he gave
> To the outcast, the poor, and forlorn.
> We all know that he loved both women and wine,
> But his heart it was right, I am sure;
> Though he lived like a prince in his palace so fine,
> Yet he never went back on the poor.

Although Jim Fisk was a businessman (of a peculiarly predatory type), it was not as such that he won folk immortality.

It would be too much to say that Jim Fisk's associate, Jay Gould, was as much loathed by the folk as his partner was loved; on most of the population Jay Gould simply did not register. As retiring and shy as Jim Fisk was flamboyant, he was as cold and correct in his private life as he was unscrupulous in the business world; had he confined himself to stock speculation, he would probably never

[6] John and Alan Lomax, *Our Singing Country* (N. Y., 1941), pp. 317–319.
[7] For a few examples, see Charles M. Skinner, *Myths and Legends of Our Own Land* (Philadelphia, 1896), vol. i, p. 64, and vol. ii, pp. 36, 182–183.
[8] Sandburg, *op. cit.*, p. 419.

have attained even the obscure niche in folk tradition that actually
is his, but when he invaded the field of railroad operation he became
involved in strikes. He was awarded a bitter side-reference in a
railroad song, possibly composed by a former employee, riding
beneath one of the cars which he had formerly ridden as engineer
or brakeman: [9]

> Jay Gould's daughter said before she died,
> "Father, fix the 'blinds' so the bums can't ride.
> If ride they must let them ride the rod,
> Let them put their trust in the hands of God."

The implication, of course, is that the father was the sort of man
who *would* have a daughter who would make this her dying request,
and the sort of man also who would eagerly accede thereto. It is
interesting, therefore, to note that there is a diametrically opposite
version of this stanza which introduces the name of still another
railroad king, one of Jay Gould's old rivals: [10]

> Said Vanderbilt's daughter just before she died,
> "Father, fix the 'blinds' so the bums can ride. . . ."

Perhaps here was an expression of a vague pervasive feeling
that the old Commodore—tyrannical, violent, and profane though
he might be—was at least a practical railroad man, who had come
up through all the stages in the various fields of transportation from
pilot of a "periauger" to the owner of steamship and railroad lines,
and whose mythical daughter, therefore, might be expected to
show sympathy for the railroad men whom ill fortune had forced
to "ride the rods" instead of the cushions. It was perhaps a manifestation of the folk attitude to be found in the Paul Bunyan legend,
that the businessman who as a businessman deserved respect
was he who maintained the tradition of the "master workman."

No railroad man except the wastrel Jim Fisk was ever treated
with real affection in song or story. The period of the railroad
"kings" was also that of labor discontent and agrarian hostility
with the railroads as a chief object of their unfriendly attention.
James J. Hill, who belonged rather to the Vanderbilt than to the
Gould tradition, received ironical and impersonal mention in the
I.W.W. song, "Hallelujah, I'm a bum!": [11]

---

[9] Lomax, *American Ballads and Folk Songs*, p. 41; Sandburg, *op. cit.*, pp. 304–305.
[10] From memory. The contrast between the Gould and Vanderbilt versions occurred to me when I encountered them in the course of a study (1927–28) of the
railroad administrators of the nineteenth century.
[11] Phonograph record, Victor 21343-B (42137).

> Oh I like Jim Hill, he's a good friend of mine—
> That's why I am hiking down Jim Hill's main line!—

a couplet which during a period of severe depression was revised in the direction of greater bitterness, to become: [12]

> Oh I like my boss, he's a good friend of mine—
> That's why I am starving on this here bread line!

The above are all—with the exception of the last—expressive primarily of general attitudes. Since Paul Bunyan was a fictitious character, none of those who told admiring tales about his prowess could have actually known and worked for him. Those who intoned the elegy to Jim Fisk had in the great majority of cases not personally known his generosity. The references to Gould and Vanderbilt and Hill do not necessarily imply that the composers and singers had personal—they certainly had no direct—relationship with the individuals mentioned.

There is a category of songs, however, in which the singers allegedly express their opinions of the character and conduct of their own, usually unnamed, employers. The railroad worker speaks —in an Irish accent: [13]

> Our contractor's name it was Tom King;
> He kept a store to rob the min.

The cowboy: [14]

> I went to the boss to draw my roll;
> He figgered me out nine dollars in the hole.

The casual laborer, warned in time, escapes exploitation only by refusing, in I.W.W. phrase, "to take a master:" [15]

> I met a man the other day I never had met before;
> He asked me if I wanted a job shoveling iron ore.
> I asked him what the wages were; he said, "Ten cents a ton."
> I said, "Old fellow, go chase yourself! I'd rather be on the bum!"

Even the buffalo skinner of the 1870s begins to tell the same story— but concludes with a stripped and primitive violence: [16]

---

[12] Samuel H. Friedman, compiler and editor, *Rebel Song Book* (N. Y.: Rand School Press, 1935), p. 55.
[13] Lomax, *American Ballads and Folk Songs*, p. 21.
[14] This couplet from "The Old Chisholm Trail" appears in many variations; see Sandburg, *op. cit.*, p. 267.
[15] Phonograph record. A coal-mining song contains almost identical stanzas (George Korson, *Coal Dust on the Fiddle*, Philadelphia, 1943, p. 319).
[16] Lomax, *American Ballads and Folk Songs*, p. 391.

The season being over, old Crego he did say
The crowd had been extravagant, we're in debt to him that day.
We coaxed him and we begged him, but still it was no go—
We left his damned old bones to bleach on the range of buffalo.

Recently a veteran appeared who claimed to be the author of "The Buffalo Skinner." Asked about the couplets above, he laughed and said that he and his comrades had been well treated by their employer—he had written the lines "for a joke." [17] But it is obvious that here is more than a joke; here is a folk convention—that the employer *must* be described as "grinding the faces of the poor," his employees. Not that this convention lacked historical basis, but that it came to be applied conventionally, whether there was justification or not. It goes back at least as far as the border ballad, "Lamkin": [18]

> Lamkin was as good a mason
> As ever bigged in stane;
> He built Lord Wearie's castle,
> But payment gat he nane.

In the standard text Lamkin's ghastly vengeance was rewarded by ghastly retribution—but perhaps the version sung in the hall was not always that sung in the kitchen.

It is rather surprising that industry and industrial conflicts have produced so comparatively few references to employers, named or nameless. One reason, no doubt, was that in large-scale industry the discontented worker tended rather to concentrate his attention upon an individual foreman, or in time of strife on the "scabs," or vaguely to denounce the "comp'ny" in general, or capitalism, than to feel a personal concern for any individual capitalist. A railroad contractor, a cattle rancher, a buffalo-hunting entrepreneur, on the other hand, was close enough to his employees to be an object of personal dislike or denunciation if he deserved it—or even, sometimes, as we have seen, if he didn't.

One of the few songs of industrial conflict in which a specific businessman is mentioned, though not named except by inference, is hardly a folk song in its origin, though it was no doubt in its time popular among the folk: [19]

> 'Twas in a Pennsylvania town not very long ago
> Men struck against reduction of their pay.

[17] J. Frank Dobie, "A Buffalo Hunter and His Song," *Backwoods to Border*, in Texas Folk-Lore Society Publications, vol. xviii (Austin, 1943), pp. 1–6.
[18] Francis James Childs, editor, *The English and Scottish Popular Ballads* (Boston, 1886), vol. ii, pp. 320–342.
[19] Sigmund Spaeth, *Weep Some More, My Lady* (Garden City, N.Y., 1927), pp. 235–236.

Their millionaire employer with philanthropic show
   Had closed the works till starved they would obey. . . .
God help them tonight in their hour of affliction
   Praying for him whom they'll never see again.
Hear the poor orphans tell their sad story,
   "Father was killed by the Pinkerton men."

Coal mining undoubtedly produced more folksongs than any other industry. The coal town, with its company store, payment in scrip, rigid control by company-paid law officers, was a society nearer to that of a village of medieval serfs or the slave quarters of a southern plantation than to the fluid individualism we usually regard as characteristic of the United States in the nineteenth century. The sense of oppression, and of community solidarity nurtured by this rigid self-contained environment, was prolific of songs of protest, stimulated by the unusually musical temperament of the Welsh, Irish, and Negroes who were the dominant English-speaking elements in the coal camps. Coal-mining songs probably express attitudes which were also common to workers in other heavy industries, but who were not so advantageously situated for self-expression.

Although every aspect of coal-mining life is touched upon with an accusatory finger in the industry's folklore, comparatively few items refer specifically to the businessman, the coal-mine owner; as in other industries, attention is concentrated on foremen, scabs, "the company." An exception is a pathetic ballad which, however, requires a note to explain that the "rich man" was a coal operator and the "orphan" the daughter of a miner killed in a mine disaster, for whose death the company had refused compensation: [20]

The rich man slep' on a velvet couch,
   And dreamed of his silver and gold,
While the orphan laid on a bed of snow,
   A-dying from hunger and cold.

The refrain is: "No bread, no bread [No room, no room] for the poor."

Plenty of songs, however, mention the employer in general terms and collectively, always unfavorably. Sometimes the tone is one of dull, vague, unspecific complaint, as in the epitaph:

Forty years I worked with pick and drill
Down in the mines against my will,
The Coal King's slave, but now it's passed;
Thanks be to God I am free at last.

[20] Lomax, *Our Singing Country*, pp. 276–278; Sandburg, *op. cit.*, p. 319.

Oppressive wage scales are, of course, the charge most frequently leveled: in one ballad the flooding of a mine is ascribed to God's vengeance for the coal owner's tyranny. Complaints against the operators because of low wages are frequently coupled with accusations of excessive prices at the company-store:

> What's de use of me wuken any moah, mah baby?
> What's de use of me wuken any moah, mah baby?
> What's de use of me wuken any moah,
> When I hab to take it up in de company store,
> Mah baby?

Flat dishonesty, also, is ascribed to the employers, as in the anecdote concerning the conversion at a revival of one of two brothers operating a nonunion mine. Shortly after, the convert said to his brother: "Richard, why won't you join the church like me?" "It's all very well for one of us to belong to the church," grunted Richard, "but if I should get religion, who'd weigh the coal?" Finally, after a miner had toiled through a long life of hard labor, low wages, high prices, the operators, it was asserted, would treat him worse than a decrepit slave or an old mine mule:

> When a man's toiled and labored
> Till his life is almost gone,
>   Then the operators think he's just a fool.
> They sneak around and fire him
> Just because he's growing old,
>   And swear they caught him breaking company rules.

Complaints against the operators turn to militancy in the strike songs:

> In eighteen hundred and seventy-five, our masters did conspire
> To keep men, women, and children without either food or fire.
> They thought to starve us to submit with hunger and with cold,
> But the miners did not fear them, but stood out brave and bold.

In periods of serious industrial conflict, the employers were forced to turn their personal attention to the problem of breaking the strikes and the unions, and the folk singers at such times consequently looked beyond the foremen and the mine superintendents to the mine owners themselves, who then appear in the strike songs but still in a rather impersonal though highly insulting fashion. The famous Slavic-American dialect strike song, "Me Johnny Mitchell Man," which did much to whip up enthusiasm among the Slav element in the strike of 1902, is characteristic.

The rise to power of the miners' unions in comparatively recent years produced a group of songs in which the coal operators are described as irked by having their oppressive actions checked by the union, or are adversely compared to the union leadership. Opposition to the check-off system for union dues is ironically contrasted with the operators' willingness to utilize the check-off for his own purposes to pay the employees' store bill!

The growing strength of the union, in comparison with that of the employer, is praised:

> Operator will forsake you, he'll drive you from his do'.
> Away from home he'll drive you to never return no mo'.
> No matter what you do, dis union gwine to stand by you
> While de union growin' strong in dis land.

A much less embittered, healthier, more of a give-and-take attitude is finally expressed in a song celebrating union recognition; with all its jaunty defiance of the employer it seems more promising for future satisfactory relations than the gloomy, defeated, but septic character of such folk-expressions as the epitaph early in this sequence: [21]

> Now when you meet your boss you don't have to bow,
> He ain't no king—never was nohow. . . .
> You can't fire him and he can't fire you
> And if he don't like our union he knows what he can do.
> Lord, Lord, we're independent now.

If one wishes to get an overall idea of the American folk attitude to the businessman, however, one must turn from railroad kings and coal-mining magnates to the businessman with whom not merely laborers in transportation, mining, and industry, but also artisans, farmers—in fact, every American of limited resources, regularly or occasionally requiring credit—come into a relationship which too often becomes mutually disagreeable, that is "the merchant." The merchant's relations with the farmer in particular are frequently unpleasant, for the wage worker, at least when employed, is paid regularly, and can pay the merchant "something on account," while the farmer has to depend on the profits, if any, of an annual crop, and if that fails, he—and his creditors as well—suffer severely. But it is the farmer who sings the song and tells the story: [22]

[21] The coal-mining material is drawn from three works edited by George G. Korson: *Songs and Ballads of the Anthracite Miner* (N. Y., 1927), pp. 90, 161, 173; *Minstrel of the Mine Patch* (Philadelphia, 1938), pp. 234–236; and *Coal Dust on the Fiddle* (Philadelphia, 1943), pp. 72, 78, 128, 175, 239, 311, 319, 321–322, 403, 423, 429, 436–437.
[22] Sandburg, *op. cit.*, pp. 282–283. Cf. Lomax, *American Ballads and Folk Songs*, p. 333, and *Our Singing Country*, p. 290.

The farmer is the man, the farmer is the man,
  Buys on credit till the fall;
Then they take him by the hand, and they lead him from the land,
And the merchant is the man who gets it all.

The merchant, however, is popular compared to that other business man, the banker—except when, as sometimes is the case, they happen to be the same person. The hostility toward Nicholas Biddle, president of the Bank of the United States in the Andrew Jackson era, is part of a long tradition—Biddle represented, in the popular mind, the banking profession in general. Indeed, the farmer, in particular, has preserved a good deal of the old medieval attitude toward moneylending; he is frequently forced to resort to the banker for a loan, he cannot get along without such occasional accommodation, but all the time he labors under an exasperated feeling that the banker is getting something for nothing.

The banker rarely, if ever, appears in the folksongs in which businessmen of various types are mentioned; perhaps he is assumed to be included with the merchant—which is certainly the case in some places. More likely the banker, like the big industrialist, is comparatively too recent an arrival, within the ken of the folk to have been as yet assimilated into balladry. The banker, like the lawyer and the preacher, is primarily a character in the less formalized medium of the anecdote.

All the banker stories I know have a Kansas setting—though they are doubtless found elsewhere. They are imbued with a tough, swaggering, sometimes ribald humor proper to a region in which there is still some survival of the spirit of agrarian revolt that prevailed in the last decade of the past century. In those with which I am familiar the banker is always portrayed as coming out second-best—if only verbally; undoubtedly this is a product of wish fulfillment. The Kansas farmer's folk-idea of the banker is that of an annoyingly indispensable fellow, who makes it a great favor to loan you someone else's money, pries into your personal affairs, insists on prompt payment, but is all the time secretly aware of what a low, despicable profession he is in.

Many expressions of folk attitudes toward the merchant and banker come from the Midwest; they certainly express resentment enough, and even bitterness, but they are flavored with a wry, resilient humor. If one turns to the semifeudal South, the utterances change—not in content but in spirit. The humor—and humor there still is—is gallows humor; the pervading spirit is sullen despair. One reason for the difference is that the South as a whole, in all classes, is nearer a marginal economy than other parts of the country; the wholesaler squeezes the merchant, and the merchant the farmer; the bank drives the branch bank, which drives the planter, who drives his tenants. All can feel disaster snapping at their heels; there is no leeway for generosity or chivalry. Another very important reason is that the hostility between employer and employee, landlord and tenant, creditor and debtor, is frequently hardened and sharpened by a race difference. For all practical purposes it could be said that the businessman in the South is a white man, and when the Negro in song and story and folk saying says "white man," he more often than not means "businessman"— the white man *par excellence*. (In other parts of the country a somewhat similar phenomenon appears; there are many stories obviously about the businessman in general in which the name of a socio-religious group is substituted.) So we have: [23]

> Well, it makes no difference how you make out your time—
> White man's bound to bring the nigger out behind.
> If you work all the day and work all the time,
> White man's sure to bring the nigger out behind.

In "The Boll Weevil Song" a transitory note of defiance creeps in—perhaps inspired by a covert and grudging admiration for the indestructibility of "de little black bug" who is responsible for the disaster: [24]

> Den de Farmer say to de Merchant:
> "We's in an awful fix;
> De Boll Weevil's et all de cotton up
> An' lef' us only sticks. . . ."
> O de Farmer say to de Merchant
> "I ain't made but only one bale
> An' befo' I bring yo' dat one
> I'll fight an' go to jail. . . ."

Negro and white farmers alike are involved in a one-crop system and a marginal economy, and in some songs it is impossible and unnecessary to identify the race of the composers and singers; as in "Po' Farmer Ain't Got No Show": [25]

> Up steps de merchant
> Wid a high-top derby on:
> "Pay me, pay me, Mister Farmer,

[23] Lomax, *American Ballads and Folk Songs*, pp. 233–234; Dorothy Scarborough, *On the Trail of Negro Folk-Song* (Cambridge, 1925), pp. 227–228; Sterling A. Brown, Arthur P. Davis, Ulysses Lee, *The Negro Caravan* (N. Y., 1941), p. 422.
[24] Lomax, *American Ballads and Folk Songs*, pp. 114–115.
[25] Lomax, *Our Singing Country*, pp. 280–281.

For you to me belong."
Up sailed another merchant
With horses and buggies fine:
"Pay me, pay me, Mister Farmer,
For your corn is shorely mine."

Another reason for the deeper, more despairing hostility toward the businessman expressed in the songs and sayings from the South is that so often one businessman occupies relationships which in the city or in the North would probably be scattered among several. The city worker in economic straits can resent the company which underpays him, the foreman who overdrives him, the local storekeeper who refuses him credit, the installment collector who badgers him for payments, the moneylender with, perhaps, a chattel mortgage on his meager possessions—and his animosity is thus diverted and directed through perhaps half a dozen channels. But in the South, the poor tenant-farmer may find that the planter who is his landlord, the merchant who in his opinion overcharges him, the banker with a chattel mortgage on his one mule, are all the same man; his animosity becomes concentrated and personalized. Something of this situation appears in the most gloomy and desperate folksong about economic conditions within my knowledge: [26]

George Penney's renters, they'll come into town,
With their hands in their pockets and their head a-hangin' down,
Go in the store and the merchant would say,
"Your mortgage is due and I'm lookin' for my pay."
Down in his pocket with a tremblin' hand,
"Can't pay you all but I'll pay you what I can";
Then to the telephone the merchant made a call,
They'll put you on the chain gang, an' you don't pay at all.

Were I a landlord-banker-merchant in the South I should much prefer that my tenant-debtors were singing the "International" than songs like those above; here is a hint not of revolution but of a Jacquerie.

The businessman as a full-length figure in American folklore is as rare as snakes in Ireland; it has been abundantly demonstrated that, when he does appear, it is generally in a role about as popular as that of such reptiles. Yet it is not impossible that an actual American businessman should become as much of a folk hero as the mythical Paul Bunyan. Some might say that the time for folk heroes has passed, that the growth of literacy, the improvement of transportation, the development of the movie and radio, the sensational newspaper, the funny paper, the comic book, the pulp magazine, have produced an environment in which folklore and folk heroes stifle. The methods of communication, to be sure, have changed from the days of the strolling minstrel, but have the concepts? Surely Charles A. Lindbergh was briefly and tragically a folk hero. And what of Franklin D. Roosevelt? To thousands and probably millions he is a folk hero as glamorous as a synthesis of Haroun-al-Raschid, the Good Shepherd, and Jesse James. But has any businessman so captured the imagination of the multitude? Is there a possibility that one ever will?

Henry Ford, about twenty years ago, was taking on legendary proportions and demonstrating such a possibility—though it never became an actuality. He was a skilled mechanic who had risen to great wealth and power through his own exertions, but who still kept his fingers on the pulse of his business and thoroughly understood its intricacies; he was, in other words, "the master workman." He was understood to be hostile to the "banking interests" —symbol of nonproductive and predatory wealth—and thus a link with the American folk mind. His product, which he turned out in awe-inspiring quantities, was capable of immensely increasing the convenience, comfort, and pleasure of the common man— even the day laborer, even the tenant farmer. He employed vast numbers of men and was reputed to pay them the highest wages. The benefit he was regarded as conferring on the working class was somewhat similar, though on an incredibly larger scale, to that ascribed to the sixteenth-century textile manufacturer, Jack of Newbury, an English businessman immortalized in ballad lore.

In 1924, during the presidential conventions, I was working in the harvest fields with migratory laborers—Arkansas hillbillies, professional hoboes, unemployed mechanics. "Why do they waste time arguing about what politician to nominate?" one of them inquired angrily. "Ford's the only man! Why? Because he believes in giving every man a job at five dollars a day. Not like that last president they elected—Harding. Know what he said? That all a workingman needed was a pair of overalls, a jumper, and a dollar a day!"—the last, of course, was itself a piece of folklore, but the attitude toward Ford was rather typical of the speaker's class than exceptional. Eventually, of course, came the depression, layoffs, and an indiscreet labor policy, which revealed that Henry Ford, whatever his other qualifications, lacked the elemental warmth necessary for permanence as a folk hero. Probably his efforts to control his employees' private lives, discouraging the use of tobacco and liquor, ordering the cultivation of vegetable gardens, caused him a more serious loss of popularity than all his troubles with the

C.I.O. Imagine Paul Bunyan issuing such orders! But Ford had shown at least the potentialities of the businessman as a folk-hero.

What is the meaning of all this? That is a question in folk history and folk psychology which calls for more study than we have yet given it. Obviously, folk thought on business is in no small measure a memory of the past. Its concept of the ideal businessman is that of the petty capitalist master-workman employer. That employer was a doer, not a specialist in planning and in administration or the trustee of a huge investment of scattered owners, large and small. Of the businessman as administrator, folklore has nothing to say. Here is an instance of cultural lag the significance of which can hardly be exaggerated.

Moreover, that memory of the past is the memory of failure and of folk trouble, of injustice and insecurity. Who ever heard of the really *good* businessman in American folklore, other than in Jim Fisk's Robin Hood rôle? The evil that men do, or seem to do, in business lives on in folklore. Perhaps one of the most significant characteristics of the ballad which deals with the businessman is that it is in so large a measure an expression of protest against injustice and insecurity. The alleged injustice may or may not be real; the sense of insecurity probably is. What proportion of the responsibility for that insecurity should be ascribed to the folk's own shortcomings and how much to the system under which they have lived, it is obviously beyond the scope of this paper to discuss. It is enough here to point to the fact that folklore is a medium through which the past is reflected, and by which its impressions, attitudes, and convictions live on in the present.

JOHN HENRY

ANONYMOUS

["John Henry," in *American Ballads and Folk Songs,* collected and compiled by John A. Lomax and Alan Lomax, The Macmillan Company, New York, 1934, pp. 5–9. Copyright © 1934 by John A. Lomax and Alan Lomax, assigned 1958 to Ludlow Music, Inc., N.Y. Used by permission.]

Every locomotive come roarin' by,
Says, "Dere lays a steel-drivin' man, . . ."

One of the greatest epics of American industrial history is that of the network of railroads—and the men who built it.

So perhaps it is with good reason that America's best-known ballad, and her greatest work song, tells the story of a railroad worker, a gigantic Negro—John Henry.

John Henry, as the legend tells us, died while working as a "spiker" on a construction gang in the Big Bend Tunnel. The tunnel was being built by the C&O railroad about the year 1873. The job of the spiker was to hammer drills into the rock to make holes for blasting charges. It is said that John Henry's hammer weighed ten pounds, and had a handle four feet long. This is part of the legend.

But the conditions under which men worked on the Big Bend Tunnel are facts, unpleasant but true. The heat was intense; there was smoke and suffocation, falling rock and cave-ins. The Big Bend was one of the most difficult tunnels that workers had ever hacked and hammered through a mountain. It took two and a half years to do it, and in that time over a hundred men may have died. No one knows for sure; the personnel files concerning that job were destroyed by a fire.

And here the John Henry legend was born. The boss decided to bring in a steam drill, thereby saving money on manpower, and saving time through automation. Whether John Henry volunteered to match his skill against the drill, or whether he was asked to do so as a test of efficiency has not been clarified. But that day, it was man against machine. In the time allotted, John Henry drove fifteen feet into the mountain, the steam drill nine.

The ballad of John Henry has grown and has varied almost as many times as it has been sung. But the essence of the song always remains. It stands as the finest of protest songs; a protest against unemployment through technology. And it stands as the most beloved hero ballad in America's heritage of folk music. John Henry really lived. And the legend that has grown around him is a monument to man in industry.

———◆———

John Henry was a li'l baby, uh-huh,*
Sittin' on his mama's knee, oh, yeah,*
Said: "De Big Bend Tunnel on de C.&O. road
Gonna cause de death of me,
Lawd, Lawd, gonna cause de death of me."

John Henry, he had a woman,
Her name was Mary Magdalene,
She would go to de tunnel and sing for John,
Jes' to hear John Henry's hammer ring.
Lawd, Lawd, jes' to hear John Henry's hammer ring.

John Henry had a li'l woman,
Her name was Lucy Ann,

_____

* The syllables "uh-huh" and "oh, yeah" are to be repeated in each stanza.

John Henry took sick an' had to go to bed,
Lucy Ann drove steel like a man,
Lawd, Lawd, Lucy Ann drove steel like a man.

Cap'n says to John Henry,
"Gonna bring me a steam drill 'round,
Gonna take dat steam drill out on de job,
Gonna whop dat steel on down,
Lawd, Lawd, gonna whop dat steel on down."

John Henry tol' his cap'n,
Lightnin' was in his eye:
"Cap'n, bet yo' las' red cent on me,
Fo' I'll beat it to de bottom or I'll die,
Lawd, Lawd, I'll beat it to de bottom or I'll die."

Sun shine hot an' burnin',
Were'n't no breeze a-tall,
Sweat ran down like water down a hill,
Dat day John Henry let his hammer fall,
Lawd, Lawd, dat day John Henry let his hammer fall.

John Henry went to de tunnel,
An' dey put him in de lead to drive;
De rock so tall an' John Henry so small,
Dat he lied down his hammer an' he cried,
Lawd, Lawd, dat he lied down his hammer an' he cried.

John Henry started on de right hand,
De steam drill started on de lef'—
"Before I'd let dis steam drill beat me down,
I'd hammer my fool self to death,
Lawd, Lawd, I'd hammer my fool self to death."

White man tol' John Henry,
"Nigger, damn yo' soul,
You might beat dis steam an' drill of mine,
When de rocks in dis mountain turn to gol',
Lawd, Lawd, when de rocks in dis mountain turn to gol'."

John Henry said to his shaker,
"Nigger, why don' you sing?
I'm thowin' twelve poun's from my hips on down,
Jes' listen to de col' steel ring,
Lawd, Lawd, jes' listen to de col' steel ring."

Oh, de captain said to John Henry,
"I b'lieve this mountain's sinkin' in."
John Henry said to his captain, oh my!
"Ain' nothin' but my hammer suckin' win',
Lawd, Lawd, ain' nothin' but my hammer suckin' win'."

John Henry tol' his shaker,
"Shaker, you better pray,
For, if I miss dis six-foot steel,
Tomorrow'll be yo' buryin' day,
Lawd, Lawd, tomorrow'll be yo' buryin' day."

John Henry tol' his captain,
"Looka yonder what I see—
Yo' drill's done broke an' yo' hole's done choke,
An' you cain' drive steel like me,
Lawd, Lawd, an' you cain' drive steel like me."

De man dat invented de steam drill,
Thought he was mighty fine.
John Henry drove his fifteen feet,
An' de steam drill only made nine,
Lawd, Lawd, an' de steam drill only made nine.

De hammer dat John Henry swung,
It weighed over nine pound;
He broke a rib in his lef'-han' side,
An' his intrels fell on de groun',
Lawd, Lawd, an' his intrels fell on de groun'.

John Henry was hammerin' on de mountain,
An' his hammer was strikin' fire,
He drove so hard till he broke his pore heart,
An' he lied down his hammer an' he died.
Lawd, Lawd, he lied down his hammer an' he died.

All de womens in de Wes',
When dey heared of John Henry's death,
Stood in de rain, flagged de eas'-boun' train,
Goin' where John Henry fell dead,
Lawd, Lawd, goin' where John Henry fell dead.

John Henry's lil mother,
She was all dressed in red,
She jumped in bed, covered up her head,

Said she didn' know her son was dead.
Lawd, Lawd, didn' know her son was dead.

John Henry had a pretty lil woman,
An' de dress she wo' was blue,
An' de las' words she said to him:
"John Henry, I've been true to you,
Lawd, Lawd, John Henry, I've been true to you."

"Oh, who's gonna shoe yo' lil feetses,
An' who's gonna glub yo' han's,
An' who's gonna kiss yo' rosy, rosy lips,
An' who's gonna be yo' man,
Lawd, Lawd, an' who's gonna be yo' man?"

"Oh, my mamma's gonna shoe my lil feetses,
An' my papa's gonna glub my lil han's,
An' my sister's gonna kiss my rosy, rosy lips,
An' I don' need no man,
Lawd, Lawd, an' I don' need no man."

Dey took John Henry to de graveyard,
An' dey buried him in de san',
An' every locomotive come roarin' by,
Says, "Dere lays a steel-drivin' man,
Lawd, Lawd, dere lays a steel-drivin' man." *

A HORSE-TRADING COUNTRY
BANKER

EDWARD NOYES WESTCOTT

[Edward Noyes Westcott, *David Harum*, D. Appleton & Co., New York, 1898, pp. 4–21.]

Shortly after Howells had written about Silas Lapham, [†] E. N. Westcott, a businessman of Syracuse, New York, was giving the reading public a remarkably apt portrait of a small-town banker and, incidentally, a horse trader. Note the attitudes expressed toward *Caveat emptor;* the buyer knew he should be wary of the seller, but at least David Harum accepted being outwitted occasionally as a part of the game. Here

---

* This stanza and the two preceding are quoted from Odum and Johnson's *Negro Workaday Songs.*

† See the Entrepreneurship section in Volume III.

David Harum is talking with his sister, Mrs. Bixbee ("Aunt Polly" to most people).

———◆———

MRS. BIXBEE went on with her needlework, with an occasional side glance at her brother, who was immersed in the gospel of his politics. Twice or thrice she opened her lips as if to address him, but apparently some restraining thought interposed. Finally, the impulse to utter her mind culminated. "Dave," she said, "d' you know what Deakin Perkins is sayin' about ye?"

David opened his paper so as to hide his face, and the corners of his mouth twitched as he asked in return, "Wa'al, what's the deakin sayin' now?"

"He's sayin'," she replied, in a voice mixed with indignation and apprehension, "thet you sold him a balky horse, an' he's goin' to hev the law on ye." David's shoulders shook behind the sheltering page, and his mouth expanded in a grin.

"Wa'al," he replied after a moment, lowering the paper and looking gravely at his companion over his glasses, "next to the deakin's religious experience, them of lawin' an' horse-tradin' air his strongest p'ints, an' he works the hull on 'em to once sometimes."

The evasiveness of this generality was not lost on Mrs. Bixbee, and she pressed the point with, "Did ye? an' will he?"

"Yes, an' no, an' mebbe, an' mebbe not," was the categorical reply.

"Wa'al," she answered with a snap, "mebbe you call that an answer. I s'pose if you don't want to let on you won't, but I do believe you've ben playin' some trick on the deakin, an' won't own up. I do wish," she added, "that if you hed to git rid of a balky horse onto somebody you'd hev picked out somebody else."

"When you got a balker to dispose of," said David gravely, "you can't alwus pick an' choose. Fust come, fust served." Then he went on more seriously: "Now I'll tell ye. Quite a while ago—in fact, not long after I come to enjoy the priv'lidge of the deakin's acquaintance—we hed a deal. I wasn't jest on my guard, knowin' him to be a deakin an' all that, an' he lied to me so splendid that I was took in, clean over my head. He done me so brown I was burnt in places, an' you c'd smell smoke 'round me fer some time."

"Was it a horse?" asked Mrs. Bixbee gratuitously.

"Wa'al," David replied, "mebbe it had ben some time, but at that partic'lar time the only thing to determine that fact was that it wa'n't nothin' else."

"Wa'al, I declare!" exclaimed Mrs. Bixbee, wondering not more at the deacon's turpitude than at the lapse in David's acuteness, of which she had an immense opinion, but commenting only on the former. "I'm 'mazed at the deakin."

"Yes'm," said David with a grin, "I'm quite a liar myself when it comes right down to the hoss bus'nis, but the deakin c'n give me both bowers ev'ry hand. He done it so slick that I had to laugh when I come to think it over—an' I had witnesses to the hull confab, too, that he didn't know of, an' I c'd've showed him up in great shape if I'd had a mind to."

"Why didn't ye?" said Aunt Polly, whose feelings about the deacon were undergoing a revulsion.

"Wa'al, to tell ye the truth, I was so completely skunked that I hadn't a word to say. I got rid o' the thing fer what it was wuth fer hide an' taller, an' stid of squealin' 'round the way you say he's doin', like a stuck pig, I kep' my tongue between my teeth an' laid to git even some time."

"You ort to 've hed the law on him," declared Mrs. Bixbee, now fully converted. "The old scamp!"

"Wa'al," was the reply, "I gen'all prefer to settle out of court, an' in this partic'lar case, while I might 'a' ben willin' t' admit that I hed ben did up, I didn't feel much like swearin' to it. I reckoned the time 'd come when mebbe I'd git the laugh on the deakin, an' it did, an' we're putty well settled now in full."

"You mean this last pufformance?" asked Mrs. Bixbee. "I wish you'd quit beatin' about the bush, an' tell me the hull story."

"Wa'al, it's like this, then, if you *will* hev it. I was over to White-boro a while ago on a little matter of worldly bus'nis, an' I seen a couple of fellers halter-exercisin' a hoss in the tavern yard. I stood 'round a spell watchin' 'em, an' when he come to a standstill I went an' looked him over, an' I liked his looks fust rate.

" 'Fer sale?' I says.

" 'Wa'al,' says the chap that was leadin' him, 'I never see the hoss that wa'n't if the price was right.'

" 'Your'n?' I says.

" 'Mine an' his'n,' he says, noddin' his head at the other feller.

" 'What ye askin' fer him?' I says.

" 'One-fifty,' he says.

"I looked him all over agin putty careful, an' once or twice I kind o' shook my head 's if I didn't quite like what I seen, an' when I got through I sort o' half turned away without sayin' anythin', 's if I'd seen enough.

" 'The' ain't a scratch ner a pimple on him,' says the feller, kind o' resentin' my looks. 'He's sound an' kind, an' 'll stand without hitchin', an' a lady c'n drive him 's well 's a man.'

" 'I ain't got anythin' agin him,' I says, 'an' prob'ly that's all true, ev'ry word on't; but one-fifty's a consid'able price fer a hoss these days. I hain't no pressin' use fer another hoss, an', in fact,' I says, 'I've got one or two fer sale myself.'

" 'He's wuth two hunderd just as he stands,' the feller says. 'He hain't had no trainin', an' he c'n draw two men in a road-wagin better'n fifty.'

"Wa'al, the more I looked at him the better I liked him, but I only says, 'Jes' so, jes' so, he may be wuth the money, but jest as I'm fixed now he ain't wuth it to *me,* an' I hain't got that much money with me if he was,' I says. The other feller hadn't said nothin' up to that time, an' he broke in now. 'I s'pose you'd take him fer a gift, wouldn't ye?' he says, kind o' sneerin'.

" 'Wa'al, yes,' I says, 'I dunno but I would if you'd throw in a pound of tea an' a halter.'

"He kind o' laughed an' says, 'Wa'al, this ain't no gift enterprise, an' I guess we ain't goin' to trade, but I'd like to know,' he says, 'jest as a matter of curios'ty, what you'd say he *was* wuth to ye?'

" 'Wa'al,' I says, 'I come over this mornin' to see a feller that owed me a trifle o' money. Exceptin' of some loose change, what he paid me 's all I got with me,' I says, takin' out my wallet. 'That wad's got a hunderd an' twenty-five into it, an' if you'd sooner have your hoss an' halter than the wad,' I says, 'why, I'll bid ye good-day.'

" 'You're offerin' one-twenty-five fer the hoss an' halter?' he says.

" 'That's what I'm doin',' I says.

" 'You've made a trade,' he says, puttin' out his hand fer the money an' handin' the halter over to me."

"An' didn't ye suspicion nuthin' when he took ye up like that?" asked Mrs. Bixbee.

"I did smell woolen some," said David, "but I had the *hoss* an' they had the *money,* an', as fur 's I c'd see, the critter was all right. Howsomever, I says to 'em: 'This here's all right, fur 's it's gone, but you've talked putty strong 'bout this hoss. I don't know who you fellers be, but I c'n find out,' I says. Then the fust feller that done the talkin' 'bout the hoss put in an' says, 'The' hain't ben one word said to you about this hoss that wa'n't gospel truth, not one word.' An' when I come to think on't afterward," said David with a half laugh, "it mebbe wa'n't *gospel* truth, but it was good enough *jury* truth. I guess this ain't over 'n' above interestin' to ye, is it?" he asked after a pause, looking doubtfully at his sister.

"Yes, 'tis," she asserted. "I'm lookin' forrered to where the deakin comes in, but you jest tell it your own way."

"I'll get there all in good time," said David, "but some of the point of the story'll be lost if I don't tell ye what come fust."

"I allow to stan' it 's long 's you can," she said encouragingly, "seein' what work I had gettin' ye started. Did ye find out anythin' 'bout them fellers?"

"I ast the barn man if he knowed who they was, an' he said he never seen 'em till the yestiddy before, an' didn't know 'em f'm Adam. They come along with a couple of hosses, one drivin' an' t'other leadin'—the one I bought. I ast him if they knowed who I was, an' he said one on 'em ast him, an' he told him. The feller said to him, seein' me drive up: 'That's a putty likely-lookin' hoss. Who's drivin' him?' An' he says to the feller. "That's Dave Harum, f'm over to Homeville. He's a great feller fer hosses,' he says."

"Dave," said Mrs. Bixbee, "them chaps jest laid fer ye, didn't they?"

"I reckon they did," he admitted; "an' they was as slick a pair as was ever drawed to," which expression was lost upon his sister. David rubbed the fringe of yellowish-gray hair which encircled his bald pate for a moment.

"Wa'al," he resumed, "after the talk with the barn man, I smelt woolen stronger'n ever, but I didn't say nothin', an' had the mare hitched an' started back. Old Jinny drives with one hand, an' I c'd watch the new one all right, an' as we come along I begun to think I wa'n't stuck after all. I never see a hoss travel evener an' nicer, an' when we come to a good level place I sent the old mare along the best she knew, an' the new one never broke his gait, an' kep' right up 'ithout 'par'ntly half tryin'; an' Jinny don't take most folks' dust neither. I swan! 'fore I got home I reckoned I'd jest as good as made seventy-five anyway."

"Then the' wa'n't nothin' the matter with him, after all," commented Mrs. Bixbee in rather a disappointed tone.

"The meanest thing top of the earth was the matter with him," declared David, "but I didn't find it out till the next afternoon, an' then I found it out good. I hitched him to the open buggy an' went 'round by the East Road, 'cause that ain't so much traveled. He went along all right till we got a mile or so out of the village, an' then I slowed him down to a walk. Wa'al, sir, scat my——! He hadn't walked more'n a rod 'fore he come to a dead stan'still. I clucked an' gitapp'd, an' finely took the gad to him a little; but he only jest kind o' humped up a little, an' stood like he'd took root."

"Wa'al, now!" exclaimed Mrs. Bixbee.

"Yes'm," said David; "I was stuck in ev'ry sense of the word."

"What d'ye do?"

"Wa'al, I tried all the tricks I knowed—an' I could lead him—but when I was in the buggy he wouldn't stir till he got good an' ready; 'n' then he'd start of his own accord an' go on a spell, an'——"

"Did he keep it up?" Mrs. Bixbee interrupted.

"Wa'al, I s'd say he did. I finely got home with the critter, but I thought one time I'd either hev to lead him or spend the night on the East Road. He balked five sep'rate times, varyin' in length, an' it was dark when we struck the barn."

"I should hev thought you'd a wanted to kill him," said Mrs. Bixbee; "an' the fellers that sold him to ye, too."

"The' *was* times," David replied, with a nod of his head, "when if he'd a fell down dead I wouldn't hev figgered on puttin' a band on my hat, but it don't never pay to git mad with a hoss; an' as fur 's the feller I bought him of, when I remembered how he told me he'd stand without hitchin', I swan! I had to laugh. I did, fer a fact. 'Stand without hitchin'!' He, he, he!"

"I guess you wouldn't think it was so awful funny if you hadn't gone an' stuck that horse onto Deakin Perkins—an' I don't see how you done it."

"Mebbe that *is* part of the joke," David allowed, "an' I'll tell ye th' rest on't. Th' next day I hitched the new one to th' dem'crat wagin an' put in a lot of straps an' rope, an' started off fer the East Road agin. He went fust rate till we come to about the place where we had the fust trouble, an', sure enough, he balked agin. I leaned over an' hit him a smart cut on the off shoulder, but he only humped a little, an' never lifted a foot. I hit him another lick, with the selfsame result. Then I got down an' I strapped that animal so't he couldn't move nothin' but his head an' tail, an' got back into the buggy. Wa'al, bomby, it may 'a' ben ten minutes, or it may 'a' ben more or less—it's slow work settin' still behind a balkin' hoss—he was ready to go on his own account, but he couldn't budge. He kind o' looked around, much as to say, 'What on earth's the matter?' an' then he tried another move, an' then another, but no go. Then I got down an' took the hopples off an' then climbed back into the buggy, an' says 'Cluck,' to him, an' off he stepped as chipper as could be, an' we went joggin' along all right mebbe two mile, an' when I slowed up, up he come agin. I gin him another clip in the same place on the shoulder, an' I got down an' tied him up agin, an' the same thing happened as before, on'y it didn't take him quite so long to make up his mind about startin', an' we went some further without a hitch. But I had to go through the pufformance the third time before he got it into his head that if he didn't go when *I* wanted he couldn't go when *he* wanted, an' that didn't suit him; an' when he felt the whip on his shoulder it meant bus'nis."

"Was that the end of his balkin'?" asked Mrs. Bixbee.

"I had to give him one more go-round," said David, "an' after that I didn't have no more trouble with him. He showed symptoms at times, but a touch of the whip on the shoulder alwus fetched him. I alwus carried them straps, though, till the last two or three times."

"Wa'al, what's the deakin kickin' about, then?" asked Aunt Polly. "You're jest sayin' you broke him of balkin'."

"Wa'al," said David slowly, "some hosses will balk with some folks an' not with others. You can't most alwus gen'ally tell."

"Didn't the deakin have a chance to try him?"

"He had all the chance he ast fer," replied David. "Fact is, he done most of the sellin', as well 's the buyin', himself."

"How's that?"

"Wa'al," said David, "it come about like this: After I'd got the hoss where I c'd handle him I begun to think I'd had some int'restin' an' valu'ble experience, an' it wa'n't scurcely fair to keep it all to myself. I didn't want no patent on't, an' I was willin' to let some other feller git a piece. So one mornin', week before last—let's see, week ago Tuesday it was, an' a mighty nice mornin' it was, too— one o' them days that kind o' lib'ral up your mind—I allowed to hitch an' drive up past the deakin's an' back, an' mebbe git somethin' to strengthen my faith, et cetery, in case I run acrost him. Wa'al, 's I come along I seen the deakin putterin' 'round, an' I waved my hand to him an' went by a-kitin'. I went up the road a ways an' killed a little time, an' when I come back there was the deakin, as I expected. He was leanin' over the fence, an' as I jogged up he hailed me, an' I pulled up.

" 'Mornin', Mr. Harum,' he says.

" 'Mornin', deakin,' I says. 'How are ye? an' how's Mis' Perkins these days?'

" 'I'm fair,' he says; 'fair to middlin', but Mis' Perkins is ailin' same *as usyul*,' he says."

"They do say," put in Mrs. Bixbee, "thet Mis' Perkins don't hev much of a time herself."

"Guess she hez all the time the' is," answered David. "Wa'al," he went on, "we passed the time o'day, an' talked a spell about the weather an' all that, an' finely I straightend up the lines as if I was goin' on, an' then I says: 'Oh, by the way,' I says, 'I jest thought on't. I heard Dominie White was lookin' fer a hoss that 'd suit him.' 'I hain't heard,' he says; but I see in a minute he had—an' it really was a fact—an' I says: 'I've got a roan colt risin' five, that I took on a debt a spell ago, that I'll sell reasonable, that's as likely an' nice ev'ry way a young hoss as ever I owned. I don't need him,' I says, 'an' didn't want to take him, but it was that or nothin' at the time an' glad to git it, an' I'll sell him a barg'in. Now what I want to say to you, deakin, is this: That hoss'd suit the dominie to a tee in my opinion, but the dominie won't come to me. Now if *you* was to say to him—bein' in his church an' all thet,' I says, 'that you c'd get him the right kind of a hoss, he'd believe you, an' you an' me 'd be doin' a little stroke of bus'nis, an' a favor to the dominie into the bargain. The dominie's well off,' I says, 'an' c'n afford to drive a good hoss.' "

"What did the deakin say?" asked Aunt Polly as David stopped for breath.

"I didn't expect him to jump down my throat," he answered; "but

I seen him prick up his ears, an' all the time I was talkin' I noticed him lookin' my hoss over, head an' foot. 'Now I 'member,' he says, 'hearin' sunthin' 'bout Mr. White's lookin' fer a hoss, though when you fust spoke on't it had slipped my mind. Of course,' he says, 'the' ain't any real reason why Mr. White shouldn't deal with you direct, an' yit mebbe I *could* do more with him 'n you could. But,' he says, 'I wa'n't cal'latin' to go t' the village this mornin', an' I sent my hired man off with my drivin' hoss. Mebbe I'll drop 'round in a day or two,' he says, 'an' look at the roan.'

" 'You mightn't ketch me,' I says, 'an' I want to show him myself; an' more'n that,' I says, 'Dug Robinson's after the dominie. I'll tell ye,' I says, 'you jest git in 'ith me an' go down an' look at him, an' I'll send ye back or drive ye back, an' if you've got anythin' special on hand you needn't be gone three quarters of an hour,' I says."

"He come, did he?" inquired Mrs. Bixbee.

"He done *so*," said David sententiously. "Jest as I knowed he would, after he'd hem'd an' haw'd about so much, an' he rode a mile an' a half livelier 'n he done in a good while, I reckon. He had to pull that old broadbrim of his'n down to his ears, an' don't you fergit it. He, he, he, he! The road was jest *full* o' hosses. Wa'al, we drove into the yard, an' I told the hired man to unhitch the bay hoss an' fetch out the roan, an' while he was bein' unhitched the deakin stood 'round an' never took his eyes off'n him, an' I knowed I wouldn't sell the deakin no roan hoss *that* day, even if I wanted to. But when he come out I begun to crack him up, an' I talked hoss fer all I was wuth. The deakin looked him over in a don't-care kind of a way, an' didn't 'parently give much heed to what I was sayin'. Finely I says, 'Wa'al, what do you think of him?' 'Wa'al,' he says, 'he seems to be a likely enough critter, but I don't believe he'd suit Mr. White— 'fraid not,' he says. 'What you askin' fer him?' he says. 'One-fifty,' I says, 'an' he's a cheap hoss at the money'; but," added the speaker with a laugh, "I knowed I might 's well of said a thousan'. The deakin wa'n't buyin' no roan colts that mornin'."

"What did he say?" asked Mrs. Bixbee.

" 'Wa'al,' he says, 'wa'al, I guess you ought to git that much fer him, but I'm 'fraid he ain't what Mr. White wants.' An' then, 'That's quite a hoss we come down with,' he says. 'Had him long?' 'Jest long 'nough to git 'quainted with him,' I says. 'Don't you want the roan fer your own use?' I says. 'Mebbe we c'd shade the price a little.' 'No,' he says, 'I guess not. I don't need another hoss jest now.' An' then, after a minute he says: 'Say, mebbe the bay hoss we drove 'd come nearer the mark fer White, if he's all right. Jest as soon I'd look at him?' he says. 'Wa'al, I hain't no objections, but I guess he's more of a hoss than the dominie 'd care for, but I'll go an' fetch him out,' I says. So I brought him out, an' the deakin looked him all over. I see it was a case of love at fust sight, as the storybooks says. 'Looks all right,' he says. 'I'll tell ye,' I says, 'what the feller I bought him of told me.' 'What's that?' says the deakin. 'He said to me,' I says, ' "that hoss hain't got a scratch ner a pimple on him. He's sound an' kind, an' 'll stand without hitchin', an' a lady c'd drive him as well 's a man." '

" 'That's what he said to me,' I says, 'an' it's every word on't true. You've seen whether or not he c'n travel,' I says, 'an', so fur 's I've seen, he ain't 'fraid of nothin'.' 'D'ye want to sell him?' the deakin says. 'Wa'al,' I says, 'I ain't offerin' him fer sale. You'll go a good ways,' I says, ' 'fore you'll strike such another; but, of course, he ain't the only hoss in the world, an' I never had anythin' in the hoss line I wouldn't sell at *some* price.' 'Wa'al,' he says, 'what d' ye ask fer him?' 'Wa'al,' I says, 'if my own brother was to ask me that question I'd say to him two hunderd dollars, cash down, an' I wouldn't hold the offer open an hour,' I says."

"My!" ejaculated Aunt Polly. "Did he take you up?"

" 'That's more'n I give fer a hoss 'n a good while,' he says, shakin' his head, 'an more'n I c'n afford, I'm 'fraid.' 'All right,' I says; 'I c'n afford to keep him'; but I knew I had the deakin same as the woodchuck had Skip. 'Hitch up the roan,' I says to Mike; 'the deakin want to be took up to his house.' 'Is that your last word?' he says. 'That's what it is,' I says. 'Two hunderd, cash down.' "

"Didn't ye dast to trust the deakin?" asked Mrs. Bixbee.

"Polly," said David, "the's a number of holes in a ten-foot ladder." Mrs. Bixbee seemed to understand this rather ambiguous rejoinder.

"He must 'a' squirmed some," she remarked. David laughed.

"The deakin ain't much used to payin' the other feller's price," he said, "an' it was like pullin' teeth; but he wanted that hoss more'n a cow wants a calf, an' after a little more squimmidgin' he hauled out his wallet an' forked over. Mike come out with the roan, an' off the deakin went, leadin' the bay hoss."

"I don't see," said Mrs. Bixbee, looking up at her brother, "thet after all the' was anythin' you said to the deakin thet he could ketch holt on."

"The' wa'n't nothin'," he replied. "The only thing he c'n complain about's what I *didn't* say to him."

"Hain't he said anythin' to ye?" Mrs. Bixbee inquired.

"He, he, he, he! He hain't but once, an' the' wa'n't but little of it then."

"How?"

"Wa'al, the day but one after the deakin sold himself Mr. Stickin'-Plaster I had an arrant three four mile or so up past his place, an' when I was comin' back, along 'bout four or half past, it come on to rain like all possessed. I had my old umbrel'—though it didn't hender

me f'm gettin' more or less wet—an' I sent the old mare along fer
all she knew. As I come along to within a mile f'm the deakin's
house I seen somebody in the road, an' when I come up closter
I see it was the deakin himself, in trouble, an' I kind o' slowed up
to see what was goin' on. There he was, settin' all humped up with
his ole broad-brim hat slopin' down his back, a-sheddin' water like
a roof. Then I seen him lean over an' larrup the hoss with the ends
of the lines fer all he was wuth. It appeared he hadn't no whip,
an' it wouldn't done him no good if he'd had. Wa'al, sir, rain or no
rain, I jest pulled up to watch him. He'd larrup a spell, an' then he'd
set back; an' then he'd lean over an' try it agin, harder'n ever.
Scat my——! I thought I'd die a-laughin'. I couldn't hardly cluck
to the mare when I got ready to move on. I drove alongside an'
pulled up. 'Hullo, deakin,' I says, 'what's the matter?' He looked up
at me, an' I won't say he was the maddest man I ever see, but he
was long ways the maddest-*lookin'* man, an' he shook his fist at me
jest like one o' the unregen'rit. 'Consarn ye, Dave Harum!' he says,
'I'll hev the law on ye fer this.' 'What fer?' I says. 'I didn't make
it come on to rain, did I?' I says. 'You know mighty well what fer,'
he says. 'You sold me this *damned beast,*' he says, 'an' he's balked
with me *nine* times this afternoon, an' I'll fix ye for 't,' he says.
'Wa'al, deakin,' I says, 'I'm 'fraid the squire's office 'll be shut up 'fore
you *git* there, but I'll take any word you'd like to send. You know I
told ye,' I says, 'that he'd stand 'ithout hitchin'.' An' at that he only
jest kind o' choked an' sputtered. He was so mad he couldn't say
nothin', an' on I drove, an' when I got about forty rod or so I looked
back, an' there was the deakin a-comin' along the road with as much
of his shoulders as he could git under his hat an' *leadin'* his new
hoss. He, he, he, he! Oh, my stars an' garters! Say, Polly, it paid
me fer bein' born into this vale o' tears. It did, I declare for't!"
Aunt Polly wiped her eyes on her apron.

   "But, Dave," she said, "did the deakin really say—*that word?*"
   "Wa'al," he replied, "if 'twain't that it was puttiest imitation on't
that ever I heard."
   "David," she continued, "don't you think it putty mean to badger
the deakin so't he swore, an' then laugh 'bout it? An' I s'pose you've
told the story all over."
   "Mis' Bixbee," said David emphatically, "if I'd paid good money
to see a funny show I'd be a blamed fool if I didn't laugh, wouldn't
I? That spectacle of the deakin cost me consid'able, but it was more'n
wuth it. But," he added, "I guess, the way the thing stands now,
I ain't so much out on the hull."
   Mrs. Bixbee looked at him inquiringly.
   "Of course, you know Dick Larrabee?" he asked.
   She nodded.

"Wa'al, three four days after the shower, an' the story 'd got aroun' some—as *you* say, the deakin *is* consid'able of a talker—I got holt of Dick—I've done him some favors an' he natur'ly expects more—an' I says to him: 'Dick,' I says, 'I hear 't Deakin Perkins has got a hoss that don't jest suit him—hain't got knee-action enough at times,' I says, 'an' mebbe he'll sell him reasonable.' 'I've heerd somethin' about it,' says Dick, laughin'. 'One of them kind o' hosses 't you don't like to git ketched out in the rain with,' he says. 'Jes' so,' I says, 'Now,' I says, 'I've got a notion 't I'd like to own that hoss at a price, an' that mebbe *I* c'd git him home even if it did rain. Here's a hunderd an' ten,' I says, 'an' I want you to see how fur it'll go to buvin' him. If you git me the hoss you needn't bring none on't back. Want to try?' I says. 'All right,' he says, an' took the money. 'But,' he says, 'won't the deakin suspicion that it comes from you?' 'Wa'al,' I says, 'my portrit ain't on none o' the bills, an' I reckon *you* won't tell him so, out an' out,' an' off he went. Yistidy he come in, an' I says, 'Wa'al, done anythin'?' 'The hoss is in your barn,' he says. 'Good fer you!' I says. 'Did you make anythin'?' 'I'm satisfied,' he says. 'I made a ten-dollar note.' An' that's the net results on't," concluded David, "that I've got the hoss, an' he's cost me jest thirty-five dollars."

THE ROMANCE OF THE BUSY BROKER

O. HENRY

[O. Henry, "The Romance of the Busy Broker," in *The Four Million*, Doubleday, Page & Co., New York, 1906, pp. 208-214. Reprinted by permission of Doubleday & Co.]

One of the great short-story writers of all time, O. Henry (1862–1910), is the author of this selection. His real name was William Sydney Porter. Born a Southerner, he was a drugstore clerk a bookkeeper, a bank teller, and a publisher—all unsuccessfully—and then a contract writer, doing a short story a week for the New York *World* at $100 each. He had eight years of this extraordinary productivity in New York. Sympathy with the unlucky, narrative skill, imagination, mark his stories; and ever so often a high sense of humor shows through, as in this one. How busy can a busy broker get?

PITCHER, confidential clerk in the office of Harvey Maxwell, broker, allowed a look of mild interest and surprise to visit his usually expressionless countenance when his employer briskly entered at half past nine in company with his young lady stenographer. With a snappy "Good-morning, Pitcher," Maxwell dashed at his desk as though he were intending to leap over it, and then plunged into the great heap of letters and telegrams waiting there for him.

The young lady had been Maxwell's stenographer for a year. She was beautiful in a way that was decidedly unstenographic. She forewent the pomp of the alluring pompadour. She wore no chains, bracelets, or lockets. She had not the air of being about to accept an invitation to luncheon. Her dress was gray and plain, but it fitted her figure with fidelity and discretion. In her neat black turban hat was the gold-green wing of a macaw. On this morning she was softly and shyly radiant. Her eyes were dreamily bright, her cheeks genuine peachblow, her expression a happy one, tinged with reminiscence.

Pitcher, still mildly curious, noticed a difference in her ways this morning. Instead of going straight into the adjoining room, where her desk was, she lingered, slightly irresolute, in the outer office. Once she moved over by Maxwell's desk, near enough for him to be aware of her presence.

The machine sitting at that desk was no longer a man; it was a busy New York broker, moved by buzzing wheels and uncoiling springs.

"Well—what is it? Anything?" asked Maxwell sharply. His opened mail lay like a bank of stage snow on his crowded desk. His keen gray eye, impersonal and brusque, flashed upon her half impatiently.

"Nothing," answered the stenographer, moving away with a little smile.

"Mr. Pitcher," she said to the confidential clerk, "did Mr. Maxwell say anything yesterday about engaging another stenographer?"

"He did," answered Pitcher. "He told me to get another one. I notified the agency yesterday afternoon to send over a few samples this morning. It's nine forty-five o'clock, and not a single picture hat or piece of pineapple chewing gum has showed up yet."

"I will do the work as usual, then," said the young lady, "until someone comes to fill the place." And she went to her desk at once and hung the black turban hat with the gold-green macaw wing in its accustomed place.

He who has been denied the spectacle of a busy Manhattan broker during a rush of business is handicapped for the profession of anthropology. The poet sings of the "crowded hour of glorious life." The broker's hour is not only crowded, but the minutes and seconds are hanging to all the straps and packing both front and rear platforms.

And this day was Harvey Maxwell's busy day. The ticker began to reel out jerkily its fitful coils of tape, the desk telephone had a chronic attack of buzzing. Men began to throng into the office and call at him over the railing, jovially, sharply, viciously, excitedly. Messenger boys ran in and out with messages and telegrams. The clerks in the office jumped about like sailors during a storm. Even Pitcher's face relaxed into something resembling animation.

On the Exchange there were hurricanes and landslides and snow-storms and glaciers and volcanoes, and those elemental disturbances were reproduced in miniature in the broker's offices. Maxwell shoved his chair against the wall and transacted business after the manner of a toe dancer. He jumped from ticker to phone, from desk to door with the trained agility of a harlequin.

In the midst of this growing and important stress the broker became suddenly aware of a high-rolled fringe of golden hair under a nodding canopy of velvet and ostrich tips, an imitation sealskin sacque and a string of beads as large as hickory nuts, ending near the floor with a silver heart. There was a self-possessed young lady connected with these accessories; and Pitcher was there to construe her.

"Lady from the Stenographer's Agency to see about the position," said Pitcher.

Maxwell turned half around, with his hands full of papers and ticker tape.

"What position?" he asked, with a frown.

"Position of stenographer," said Pitcher. "You told me yesterday to call them up and have one sent over this morning."

"You are losing your mind, Pitcher," said Maxwell. "Why should I have given you any such instructions? Miss Leslie has given perfect satisfaction during the year she has been here. The place is hers as long as she chooses to retain it. There's no place open here, madam. Countermand that order with the agency, Pitcher, and don't bring any more of 'em in here."

The silver heart left the office, swinging and banging itself independently against the office furniture as it indignantly departed. Pitcher seized a moment to remark to the bookkeeper that the "old man" seemed to get more absent-minded and forgetful every day of the world.

The rush and pace of business grew fiercer and faster. On the floor they were pounding half a dozen stocks in which Maxwell's customers were heavy investors. Orders to buy and sell were coming and going as swift as the flight of swallows. Some of his own holdings were imperiled, and the man was working like some high-geared, delicate, strong machine—strung to full tension, going at full speed, accurate, never hesitating, with the proper word and decision and act ready and prompt as clockwork. Stocks and bonds, loans and mortgages, margins and securities—here was a world of finance, and there was no room in it for the human world or the world of nature.

When the luncheon hour drew near there came a slight lull in the uproar.

Maxwell stood by his desk with his hands full of telegrams and memoranda, with a fountain pen over his right ear and his hair hanging in disorderly strings over his forehead. His window was open, for the beloved janitress spring had turned on a little warmth through the waking registers of the earth.

And through the window came a wandering—perhaps a lost—odor—a delicate, sweet odor of lilac that fixed the broker for a moment immovable. For this odor belonged to Miss Leslie; it was her own, and hers only.

The odor brought her vividly, almost tangibly before him. The world of finance dwindled suddenly to a speck. And she was in the next room—twenty steps away.

"By George, I'll do it now," said Maxwell, half aloud. "I'll ask her now. I wonder I didn't do it long ago."

He dashed into the inner office with the haste of a short trying to cover. He charged upon the desk of the stenographer.

She looked up at him with a smile. A soft pink crept over her cheek, and her eyes were kind and frank. Maxwell leaned one elbow on her desk. He still clutched fluttering papers with both hands and the pen was above his ear.

"Miss Leslie," he began hurriedly, "I have but a moment to spare. I want to say something in that moment. Will you be my wife? I haven't had time to make love to you in the ordinary way, but I really do love you. Talk quick, please—those fellows are clubbing the stuffing out of Union Pacific."

"Oh, what are you talking about?" exclaimed the young lady. She rose to her feet and gazed upon him, round-eyed.

"Don't you understand?" said Maxwell, restively. "I want you to marry me. I love you, Miss Leslie. I wanted to tell you, and I snatched a minute when things had slackened up a bit. They're calling me for the phone now. Tell 'em to wait a minute, Pitcher. Won't you, Miss Leslie?"

The stenographer acted very queerly. At first she seemed overcome with amazement; then tears flowed from her wondering eyes; and then she smiled sunnily through them, and one of her arms slid tenderly about the broker's neck.

"I know now," she said, softly. "It's this old business that has driven everything else out of your head for the time. I was frightened at first. Don't you remember, Harvey? We were married last evening at eight o'clock in the Little Church Around the Corner."

BABBITT

SINCLAIR LEWIS

[Sinclair Lewis, *Babbitt*, copyright 1922 by Harcourt, Brace & Co., New York, and renewed in 1950 by Sinclair Lewis, pp. 138–146. Reprinted by permission of Harcourt, Brace and World Inc., and Jonathan Cape, Ltd.]

It is surprising, considering the pervasive and crucial role which businessmen have played in developing and sustaining civilization, that they have had such a poor part in contemporary novels. Even where an industrialist or banker or tradesman has been one of the main characters in the plot, he is usually shown outside his factory, or office, or store—he is a businessman only by name, not by action. And, more often than not, he does not show up in a very favorable light; either he does not think or, if he does think, he is frustrated.

What is the explanation? Is it that most novelists just are not equipped to understand the complex motivations that enable an individual to be a hard-driving competitor eight or ten hours a day yet still be a sensitive human being during the rest of his waking hours, and at his work too? Is it failure to understand that a soft bed can be as honorable as a hard one, perhaps aggravated by a tinge of jealousy? Is success in the production and distribution of material goods inherently less worth while than, say, success in keeping quarreling clients safe from the law or sniffling patients able to go out on the town? Is it that, as Miriam Beard points out, "through the stormiest ages," businessmen were "the representatives of thrift, temperance, reticence, hard work, domesticity and other qualities which wearied, instead of thrilling readers" (see her piece, "The Businessman—Villain or Lost Hero," in the Perspective section, in Volume I)? Or is it merely that, with businessmen as with Julius Caesar,

> The evil that men do lives after them,
> The good is oft interred with their bones.

Or is all this simply a literary tradition, to the effect that *good* businessmen are not interesting subjects for dissection?

To take a specific case, in the 1920s, one of the high points of business influence in American life, Sinclair Lewis turned his gifted pen to a word-portrait of all that was shallow and vapid in what was presumably a representative businessman. This satire gave a word to the language—Babbittry—and fastened an image on the American mind. It also contributed to the selection of Sinclair Lewis for the Nobel award in literature. (For another, somewhat different, view on the part of Lewis, see his piece in Volume I.)

Here are a few pages from that famous novel.

———◆———

THEY WERE ON THE NEW YORK EXPRESS, incredibly bound for Maine, incredibly without their families. They were free, in a man's world, in the smoking compartment of the Pullman.

Outside the car window was a glaze of darkness stippled with the gold of infrequent mysterious lights. Babbitt was immensely conscious, in the sway and authoritative clatter of the train, of going, of going on. Leaning toward Paul he grunted, "Gosh, pretty nice to be hiking, eh?"

The small room, with its walls of ocher-colored steel, was filled mostly with the sort of men he classified as the Best Fellows You'll Ever Meet—Real Good Mixers. There were four of them on the long seat; a fat man with a shrewd fat face, a knife-edged man in a green velour hat, a very young man with an imitation amber cigarette-holder, and Babbitt. Facing them, on two movable leather chairs, were Paul and a lanky, old-fashioned man, very cunning, with wrinkles bracketing his mouth. They all read newspapers or trade journals, boot-and-shoe journals, crockery journals, and waited for the joys of conversation. It was the very young man, now making his first journey by Pullman, who began it.

"Say, gee, I had a wild old time in Zenith!" he gloried. "Say, if a fellow knows the ropes there he can have as wild a time as he can in New York!"

"Yuh, I bet you simply raised the old Ned. I figured you were a bad man when I saw you get on the train!" chuckled the fat one.

The others delightedly laid down their papers.

"Well, that's all right now! I guess I seen some things in the Arbor you never seen!" complained the boy.

"Oh, I'll bet you did! I bet you lapped up the malted milk like a reg'lar little devil!"

Then, the boy having served as introduction, they ignored him and charged into real talk. Only Paul, sitting by himself, reading at a serial story in a newspaper, failed to join them, and all but Babbitt regarded him as a snob, an eccentric, a person of no spirit.

Which of them said which has never been determined, and does not matter, since they all had the same ideas and expressed them always with the same ponderous and brassy assurance. If it was not Babbitt who was delivering any given verdict, at least he was beaming on the chancellor who did deliver it.

"At that, though," announced the first, "they're selling quite some booze in Zenith. Guess they are everywhere. I don't know how you fellows feel about prohibition, but the way it strikes me is that it's a mighty beneficial thing for the poor zob that hasn't got any will power but for fellows like us, it's an infringement of personal liberty."

"That's a fact. Congress has got no right to interfere with a fellow's personal liberty," contended the second.

A man came in from the car, but as all the seats were full he stood up while he smoked his cigarette. He was an Outsider; he was not one of the Old Families of the smoking compartment. They looked upon him bleakly and, after trying to appear at ease by examining his chin in the mirror, he gave it up and went out in silence.

"Just been making a trip through the South. Business conditions not very good down there," said one of the council.

"Is that a fact! Not very good, eh?"

"No, didn't strike me they were up to normal."

"Not up to normal, eh?"

"No, I wouldn't hardly say they were."

The whole council nodded sagely and decided, "Yump, not hardly up to snuff."

"Well, business conditions ain't what they ought to be out West, neither, not by a long shot."

"That's a fact. And I guess the hotel business feels it. That's one good thing, though: these hotels that've been charging five bucks a day—yes, and maybe six-seven!—for a rotten room are going to be darn glad to get four, and maybe give you a little service."

"That's a fact. Say, uh, speaknubout hotels, I hit the St. Francis at San Francisco for the first time, the other day, and, say, it certainly is a first-class place."

"You're right, brother! The St. Francis is a swell place—absolutely A1."

"That's a fact. I'm right with you. It's a first-class place."

"Yuh, but say, any of you fellows ever stay at the Rippleton, in Chicago? I don't want to knock—I believe in boosting wherever you can—but say, of all the rotten dumps that pass 'emselves off as first-class hotels, that's the worst. I'm going to *get* those guys, one of these days, and I told 'em so. You know how I am—well, maybe you don't know, but I'm accustomed to first-class accommodations, and I'm perfectly willing to pay a reasonable price. I got into Chicago late the other night, and the Rippleton's near the station—I'd never been there before, but I says to the taxi driver—I always believe in taking a taxi when you get in late; may cost a little more money, but, gosh, it's worth it when you got to be up early next morning and out selling a lot of crabs—and I said to him, 'Oh, just drive me over to the Rippleton.'

"Well, we got there, and I breezed up to the desk and said to the clerk, 'Well, brother, got a nice room with bath for Cousin Bill?'

Saaaay! You'd 'a' thought I'd sold him a second, or asked him to work on Yom Kippur! He hands me the cold-boiled stare and yaps, 'I dunno, friend, I'll see,' and he ducks behind the rigamajig they keep track of the rooms on. Well, I guess he called up the Credit Association and the American Security League to see if I was all right —he certainly took long enough—or maybe he just went to sleep; but finally he comes out and looks at me like it hurts him, and croaks, 'I think I can let you have a room with bath.' 'Well, that's awful nice of you—sorry to trouble you—how much'll it set me back?' I says, real sweet. 'It'll cost you seven buck a day, friend,' he says.

"Well, it was late, and anyway, it went down on my expense account—gosh, if I'd been paying it instead of the firm, I'd 'a' tramped the streets all night before I'd 'a' let any hick tavern stick me seven great big round dollars, believe me! So I lets it go at that. Well, the clerk wakes a nice young bellhop—fine lad—not a day over seventy-nine years old—fought at the Battle of Gettysburg and doesn't know it's over yet—thought I was one of the Confederates, I guess, from the way he looked at me—and Rip van Winkle took me up to something—I found out afterwards they called it a room, but first I thought there'd been some mistake—I thought they were putting me in the Salvation Army collection box! At seven *per* each and every *diem!* Gosh!"

"Yuh, I've heard the Rippleton was pretty cheesy. Now, when I go to Chicago I always stay at the Blackstone or the La Salle—first-class places."

"Say, any of you fellows ever stay at the Birchdale at Terre Haute? How is it?"

"Oh, the Birchdale is a first-class hotel."

(Twelve minutes of conference on the state of hotels in South Bend, Flint, Dayton, Tulsa, Wichita, Fort Worth, Winona, Erie, Fargo, and Moose Jaw.)

"Speaknubout prices," the man in the velour hat observed, fingering the elk tooth on his heavy watch chain, "I'd like to know where they get this stuff about clothes coming down. Now, you take this suit I got on." He pinched his trousers-leg. "Four years ago I paid forty-two fifty for it, and it was real sure-'nough value. Well, here the other day I went into a store back home and asked to see a suit, and the fellow yanks out some hand-me-downs that, honest, I wouldn't put on a hired man. Just out of curiosity I asks him, 'What you charging for that junk?' 'Junk,' he says, 'what d' you mean junk? That's a swell piece of goods, all wool—' Like hell! It was nice vegetable wool, right off the Ole Plantation! 'It's all wool,' he says, 'and we get sixty-seven ninety for it.' 'Oh, you do, do you!' I says. 'Not from me you don't,' I says, and I walks right out on him. You bet! I says to the wife, 'Well,' I said, 'as long as your strength holds out and you can go on putting a few more patches on papa's pants, we'll just pass up buying clothes.' "

"That's right, brother. And just look at collars, frinstance——"

"Hey! Wait!" the fat man protested. "What's the matter with collars? I'm selling collars! D' you realize the cost of labor on collars is still two hundred and seven per cent above—"

They voted that if their old friend the fat man sold collars, then the price of collars was exactly what it should be; but all other clothing was tragically too expensive. They admired and loved one another now. They went profoundly into the science of business, and indicated that the purpose of manufacturing a plow or a brick was so that it might be sold. To them, the Romantic Hero was no longer the knight, the wandering poet, the cowpuncher, the aviator, nor the brave young district attorney, but the great sales manager, who had an *Analysis of Merchandising Problems* on his glass-topped desk, whose title of nobility was "Go-getter," and who devoted himself and all his young samurai to the cosmic purpose of Selling—not of selling anything in particular, for or to anybody in particular, but pure Selling.

The shop talk roused Paul Riesling. Though he was a player of violins and an interestingly unhappy husband, he was also a very able salesman of tar roofing. He listened to the fat man's remarks on "the value of house organs and bulletins as a method of jazzing up the Boys out on the road"; and he himself offered one or two excellent thoughts on the use of two-cent stamps on circulars. Then he committed an offense against the holy law of the Clan of Good Fellows. He became highbrow.

They were entering a city. On the outskirts they passed a steel mill which flared in scarlet and orange flame that licked at the cadaverous stacks, at the iron-sheathed walls and sullen converters.

"My lord, look at that—beautiful!" said Paul.

"You bet it's beautiful, friend. That's the Shelling-Horton Steel Plant, and they tell me old John Shelling made a good three million bones out of munitions during the war!" the man with the velour hat said reverently.

"I didn't mean—I mean it's lovely the way the light pulls that picturesque yard, all littered with junk, right out of the darkness," said Paul.

They stared at him, while Babbitt crowed, "Paul there has certainly got one great little eye for picturesque places and quaint sights and all that stuff. 'D of been an author or something if he hadn't gone into the roofing line."

Paul looked annoyed. (Babbitt sometimes wondered if Paul appreciated his loyal boosting.) The man in the velour hat grunted, "Well, personally, I think Shelling-Horton keep their works awful dirty. Bum

routing. But I don't suppose there's any law against calling 'em 'picturesque' if it gets you that way!"

Paul sulkily returned to his newspaper and the conversation logically moved on to trains.

"What time do we get into Pittsburgh?" asked Babbitt.

"Pittsburgh? I think we get in at—no, that was last year's schedule
—wait a minute—let's see—got a timetable right here."

"I wonder if we're on time?"

"Yuh, sure, we must be just about on time."

"No, we aren't—we were seven minutes late, last station."

"Were we? Straight? Why, gosh, I thought we were right on time."

"No, we're about seven minutes late."

"Yuh, that's right; seven minutes late."

The porter entered—a Negro in white jacket with brass buttons.

"How late are we, George?" growled the fat man.

" 'Deed, I don't know sir. I think we're about on time," said the
porter, folding towels and deftly tossing them up on the rack above
the washbowls. The council stared at him gloomily and when he was
gone they wailed:

"I don't know what's come over these niggers, nowadays. They
never give you a civil answer."

"That's a fact. They're getting so they don't have a single bit of
respect for you. The old-fashioned coon was a fine old cuss—he knew
his place—but these young dinges don't want to be porters or cotton-
pickers. Oh, no! They got to be lawyers and professors and Lord
knows what all! I tell you, it's becoming a pretty serious problem. We
ought to get together and show the black man, yes, and the yellow
man, his place. Now, I haven't got one particle of race prejudice. I'm
the first to be glad when a nigger succeeds—so long as he stays where
he belongs and doesn't try to usurp the rightful authority and business
ability of the white man."

"That's the i.! And another thing we got to do," said the man with
the velour hat (whose name was Koplinsky), "is to keep these damn
foreigners out of the country. Thank the Lord, we're putting a limit
on immigration. These Dagoes and Hunkies have got to learn that this
is a white man's country, and they ain't wanted here. When we've
assimilated the foreigners we got here now and learned 'em the principles of Americanism and turned 'em into regular folks, why then
maybe we'll let in a few more."

"You bet. That's a fact," they observed, and passed on to lighter
topics. They rapidly reviewed motor-car prices, tire mileage, oil
stocks, fishing, and the prospects for the wheat crop in Dakota.

But the fat man was impatient at this waste of time. He was a
veteran traveler and free of illusions. Already he had asserted that
he was "an old he-one." He leaned forward, gathered in their atten-

tion by his expression of sly humor, and grumbled, "Oh, hell, boys, let's cut out the formality and get down to the stories!"

They became very lively and intimate.

Paul and the boy vanished. The others slid forward on the long seat, unbuttoned their vests, thrust their feet up on the chairs, pulled the stately brass cuspidors nearer, and ran the green window-shade down on its little trolley, to shut them in from the uncomfortable strangeness of night. After each bark of laughter, they cried, "Say, jever hear the one about——" Babbitt was expansive and virile. When the train stopped at an important station, the four men walked up and down the cement platform, under the vast smoky train-shed roof, like a stormy sky, under the elevated footways, beside crates of ducks and sides of beef, in the mystery of an unknown city. They strolled abreast, old friends and well content. At the long-drawn "Alllll aboarrrrrd"—like a mountain call at dusk—they hastened back into the smoking compartment, and till two of the morning continued the droll tales, their eyes damp with cigar smoke and laughter. When they parted they shook hands, and chuckled, "Well, sir, it's been a great session. Sorry to bust it up. Mighty glad to meet you."

Babbitt lay awake in the close hot tomb of his Pullman berth, shaking with remembrance of the fat man's limerick about the lady who wished to be wild. He raised the shade; he lay with a puffy arm tucked between his head and the skimpy pillow, looking out on the sliding silhouettes of trees, and village lamps like exclamation points. He was very happy.

TOM LACHFORD, PROMOTER

STEPHEN LEACOCK

[Stephen Leacock, "Tom Lachford, Promoter," in *The Garden of Folly*, Dodd, Mead and Co., New York, 1924, pp. 145–161. Permission granted by Dodd, Mead and Co. and The Bodley Head, Ltd.]

"A half truth, like half a brick, is always more forcible as an argument than a whole one. It carries further." This debatable but undoubtedly forceful observation was made by Stephen Leacock, the Canadian essayist and humorist (1869–1944), who was also an economist. He himself was a skillful user of the half-plus truth—of satire which had more truth than nontruth in it, as all good satire must if it is to hit home. The following selection, which appeared in 1924, is offered in evidence.*

* For more 99.9 per cent truth by the same author, refer to index listing in this volume.

A Story which carries with it what is called an Atmosphere of Business and which may safely be read without loss of efficiency.

IN THE LITTLE FACTORY TOWN of Smudgeville the five o'clock whistle blew. The machines stopped. The steam died. The hands quit. The doors closed. The factories shut. Work was over.

Seth Lachford shut the door of the tumbledown place that was called Lachford's Works, and went and sat on a pile of shingles, thinking of his overhead costs. The Lachford business was so undermined by overhead that with any further depression it would go up altogether.

All around Seth as he sat were the great piles of crumbled gray dust that represented his five years' efforts to make cement. The old Lachford farm on the outskirts of the factory town had been all torn up and scarred with the fruitless attempt.

As Seth sat there, one might have looked twice, or even three times, at the man without noticing anything especial about him. But if one looked four times one observed more than one had remarked in three times. The face and the attitude were those of a man who had failed. But there was something, too, in the hard-bitten, tight-lipped, close-nipped, short-necked appearance of the man that showed that in his case failure, after all, meant little more than lack of success.

Seth Lachford rose, painfully, from the bunch of shingles, locked the door of the mean place that he called his Works, and walked across the lot to the house he called his home, where the woman he called his wife was cooking supper for the things he called his children.

"Things any better today?" she queried.

Seth head-shook dejectedly.

"Are your overhead expenses per unit of output still disproportionate to the selling cost of the product?" asked the sad-eyed woman as she helped her husband to the fried potatoes.

"Yes, Min," desponded Seth. "The capital cost of operation shows an ascending curve right along."

"I see," said Min, thoughtfully, as she poured out molasses for the children, "and each further increment of outlay merely agglomerates your differential."

"It does," said Seth.

There was a silence and Seth rose.

"Where y' going?" throbbed his wife.

"Out to sit on the shingles," Seth glumped, "and think about my overhead and my differential cost."

"All right," said Min; then, suddenly, her face sanguinated, "Oh Seth," she said, "I forgot, there's a letter from brother Tom. He'll be here in the morning, and he says he can straighten everything out."

II

Next morning Tom Lachford, promoter, blew into Smudgeville, and together Tom and Seth walked round the "plant" and looked at the crumbling piles of gray dust.

The brothers were a contrast—Seth bent and hesitant, Tom square-built, bull-chested, ox-necked, box-jawed, pop-eyed, in short, a hundred and fifty per cent American all through.

"See here, Seth," said Tom, "you've tried five years to make cement and you've failed?"

Seth desponded assent.

"You've crushed up all the rocks on the old place, and you've nothing for it but these piles of dirt?"

Seth ingurgitated but without speaking.

"Well, look here," Tom went on, "I've got an idea and it's a big thing. If we can pull it off and bring it down, I believe we can put it over."

"What y' going to do?" asked Seth.

"Going to make a fortune out of this dirt. But, first of all, I want a thousand dollars cash."

"I haven't got it," exhaled Seth, "and the bank won't lend it. I've tried them."

"Pshaw!" said Tom, "show me the way to that bank. I'll get it."

Tom Lachford walked straight to the Smudgeville First National Bank, straight into it, and straight through it to the manager's room. There was something dynamic in the way he sat down, and something almost titanic or teutonic in the way he laid his hat on the table.

"See here, Mr. Beanhead," he said. "I want the loan of a thousand dollars."

The manager spasmed. "On what security?" he winced.

"None," said Lachford.

The manager brightened.

"You offer no collateral at all?" he said.

"Not a cent," said Tom, "except my personality."

"Good!" said the banker, delighted. "You shall have it. The personal element, Mr. Lachford, has become the ne plus ultra of business. I recognize in you one of those full-blooded, high-pepped, long-sighted, wide-eyed men who are entitled to bank loans. This bank will back you."

III

That night Seth and Min and Tom sat in consultation over their buttermilk and pancakes at the supper table.

"What do you mean to do with the money, Tom?" asked Min.

Tom buttermilked a minute, and then, "Going to get a gang of men and treat that dirt."

"Treat it?"

"Yes, treat it; run it into vats and out again, sluice it, pulverize it, sling it round—anything——"

Seth stopped pancaking and earlifted.

"What's that for?" he exuded.

"I'll tell you," said Tom, "I'm going to raise bonds on it and float a company and make a clean-up."

"But it's only dirt!" said Seth. "Somehow we failed every time to make it harden into cement."

"I don't want cement," said the promoter. "Dirt'll do. Here's the idea, I'm going to give it a name—something high-sounding, see! Something that seems to mean value. Did you ever hear of molybdenum? Well, what is it? You don't know. Or carborundum or tellurium—you don't know what they are. The public don't know what they are. But they mean money. Find a deposit of any of them and your fortune's made."

Seth head-nodded silent.

"I'll have an assayer come," Tom went on, "and make an assay of all that dirt and crushed rock. That's only for appearance, of course; I don't care what he calls it. I'll give it a name that sounds good and announce it as a big discovery. See? The name I've settled on is palladium. We'll announce a find of palladium, and form a company to work it."

Min looked up from the little pile of children's clothing that she was sewing. "Issuing common stock," she said, as she bit off a piece of thread, "on a basis of prospective earnings capitalized."

"But what then?" said Seth. "If we sell the stock and it's no good?"

"We don't need to worry. We sell it and then we clear out."

"Where to?"

The sad-eyed woman looked up from the little garment in her lap. "Havana," she said.

IV

Within a week it was known all over Smudgeville that heavy deposits of palladium had been found on the old Lachford place. Gangs of men were at work. Derricks, cranes, vats, and sluices rose all over the place. Little crowds of people stood round to watch. The palladium was put into a converter and carried from there to a container from which it passed to a disturber. It was then put into a hopper. "What is it?" asked the people. "Palladium," was the answer. The Smudgeville *Intelligence* explained that palladium was a graminiferous amygdaloid and that its calcereous properties rendered it of great commercial value. It was practically impervious to collusion, which made it a high soporific.

An assayer was brought, a real one, and he walked round over the Lachford place and carried off samples. The promoter let all the town know that the assayer had been on the property. But the report of the analysis of the dirt Tom Lachford showed to no one. He shoved it into the drawer of the kitchen dresser unopened. It was the assayer he wanted, not the report.

Then Tom Lachford called again upon the banker.

"Mr. Beanhead," he said, "my brother and I have made a find of igniferous palladium. It runs at least forty-eight per cent to the kilowatt and we want to raise money for incorporation and material."

"Mr. Lachford," said the banker, "I congratulate you on your discovery. I recognize in you one of those wide-visioned, broad-sighted, frog-eyed men that make this country what it is. How much money do you want?"

"Ten thousand dollars," said Tom.

V

That evening when Tom came home he told Seth and Min that he had arranged the incorporation at thirty thousand dollars and was going to order ten thousand dollars' worth of machinery.

"What machinery?" asked his brother.

"Any machinery," said the promoter, "it doesn't matter; as long as it's bulky."

"The mere assemblage and erection of machinery," added Min thoughtfully as she helped the brothers to fried eggplant, "conveys to the investor a guarantee of bona fides."

But after supper Seth Lachford went to the kitchen dresser and took out of it the assayer's report upon the dirt, that lay in an envelope unopened. He ripped open the envelope and for a long while stood looking at the document with a frown upon his face. "I'll not sell stuff like that," he muttered. "No, sir, I'll go broke before I'll sell it." Then he went out in the gathering dusk and walked among the piles of dirt, kicking it with his feet and picking it up in his hands.

When Seth Lachford came back to the kitchen where Tom and Min sat shucking butternuts there was resolution in his face.

"Tom," he said, "when you sell out this company what do you expect to get?"

Tom looked up, stopped shucking. "Thirty thousand dollars at par," he said. "Ten thousand each for you and me and Min; perhaps a lot more."

"You'll sell it to people here in town?"

"Easy," said Tom. "There are enough suckers right here to buy it all."

"And what do they get?"

"That's their lookout," shrugged Tom. "They can sell again if they're quick enough."

"But sooner or later?"

"Oh, sooner or later someone gets stung. But it's not going to be us."

Seth sat silent a while.

"And if we let go of it now," he asked, "where are we?"

"We owe the bank $15,000, and we're ruined."

Seth looked Tom right in the face. Dynamic as he was, the younger Lachford's face fell.

"See here, Tom," evolved Seth slowly, "I'll not sell those shares."

The brothers sat looking at each other, their faces working.

"If you don't," said Tom, "it's ruin."

"I'll meet it," said Seth, his face still working.

"If you do," said Tom, his face stopping working, "you'll meet it in the penitentiary."

"Tom," said Seth, "there's been Lachfords on this place for four generations, and never a thief among them."

VI

For two weeks after that the work at the palladium deposits went on, and the Lachfords walked around the plant, avoiding each other—Tom keen and restless, Seth moody. his eyes ever on the dirt.

Only once Tom spoke to Seth. "The brokers have placed the first lot of my shares at par," he said, "and they can sell more, they say. They can't list them but they'll sell them on the curb. Give me your shares now and Min's and we'll sell them and get out."

Seth turned on his heel and, without a word, went to the house.

He called his wife aside. He took out the assayer's paper, opened it, and spread it out before her. "Tom says he'll sell your shares for ten thousand dollars, Min. Are you going to sell off that stuff," and he tapped the paper fiercely, "to your friends and neighbors, people of your own town?"

Min looked at the document. The chemical analysis was beyond her grasp, but the single item at the bottom, "estimated commercial value," was plain enough even for a child.

"No, Seth!" she said, "I can't do it. It ain't right."

"Look, Min," Seth went on, "I want my name to stand right in this town. If Tom tries to sell out those shares, could you get ten thousand dollars from your folks and buy them?"

"I might," said Min, "I doubt Pa could raise it, but if you want it, Seth, I'll try."

VII

The next day Min started off to her folks in Pennsylvania to raise ten thousand dollars, and on the same morning the shares of Amalgamated Palladium Limited went on the local exchange as a curb security, and there was great excitement in financial circles in Smudgeville. The shares opened at eighty, rose straight to par, reacted to fifty, sank down to twenty, lay there gasping and then jumped to par again in four hops. At 2:00 P.M. they were reported as restless; at three buoyant, and at closing time strong with an undercurrent of weakness.

That night Tom Lachford packed his grip to leave by the midnight express, bound toward Havana.

"I'm off, Seth," he said; "say goodbye to Min when she comes back. If you're wise you'll get, quick. The shares will break tomorrow and then——"

"I'm not quitting, Tom," said Seth; "goodbye."

VIII

Min came back two days later.

"I got the money, Seth," she said. "Pa raised it partly on the steers and the rest on a mortgage."

"Too late, I guess, Min," said Seth. "The shares went to five hundred yesterday, and this morning they're holding out for a thousand dollars a share."

IX

It was a week later that Tom Lachford sat in the Colorado Claro Hotel at Havana with a cocktail in front of him, and $4,000 in Cuban money to his credit. And it was there he got a copy of a home paper sent him by mail. He opened it with trembling hands, looking for Seth's ruin. And instead of it he saw a big headline saying that Amalgamated Palladium was selling at two thousand a share, and his hands trembled more. Last of all he read a two-column account of the discovery of graphite on the Lachford place, and he shook like a leaf all over.

Meantime Min and Seth were sitting over their buttermilk in the kitchen living room, adding up figures.

"I can't cipher it out," said Seth, "but it's millions all right."

"And what is the stuff anyways," asked Min, "if it ain't palladium?"

"Graphite, it's called," said Seth. "Always noticed those black streaks in the crushings. I guess that's it. I'm glad I didn't sell. If I could have bought back those shares I meant to give them to Tom, didn't I, Min?"

"Oh, certainly," said Min, "so did I: and I'm glad too we didn't sell. I felt bad about it all along, Seth, and when I saw that assayer's paper where it said 'commercial value ten thousand dollars a ton' a light broke in on me and I saw it wasn't right. But I still don't see why those shares jumped up that way."

"The damn fool assayer. He must have put some New York guys wise to it. They were just waiting for us, likely. I doubt, Min, whether those New York financiers are quite as easy as they make out in the story papers."

"That's so," subsided Min. "And where Tom was a bum promoter, Seth was wrong in underestimating the commercial value of scientific analysis applied to the basic data of modern business."

MARCO MILLIONS

~~⌒⌒◗◜⌒~~

EUGENE O'NEILL

[Eugene O'Neill, *Marco Millions,* Horace Liveright, New York, copyright 1927, pp. 95–104. Copyright © renewed in 1955 by Carlotta Monterey O'Neill; reprinted from *Nine Plays of Eugene O'Neill* by permission of Random House, Inc.; permission also granted by Jonathan Cape, Ltd.]

In 1927, Eugene O'Neill wrote a play that made a fool of Marco Polo,* the almost legendary world-traveling merchant of the late 1200s, and manipulated the facts about who invented paper money and cannon as well. We can only hope that the real Marco Polo was as much more noble than this picture of him as the real Kublai Khan was most certainly less noble than O'Neill has made him here for purposes of contrast.

It must also be remembered that there have been some businessmen who have allowed the profit motive to lead them into courses detrimental to society. But maybe we can take comfort from the fact that O'Neill apparently felt he had to go so far into the past, and so far across the world, to find a fictional model that was picturesque and dramatic.

The Princess Kukachin is Kublai Khan's daughter. The sage, Chu-Yin, is the emperor's adviser.

————◆————

KUBLAI KHAN: Rise (*Marco Polo does so. Kublai continues dryly.*) To what do I owe the honor of this unexpected visit?

MARCO (*hastily, but with full confidence*): Well, I was sending in to your treasury the taxes of Yang-Chau for the fiscal year, and I knew you'd be so astonished at the unprecedented amount I had sweated out of them that you'd want to know how I did it—so here I am. (*An awkward pause. Marco is disconcerted at the Khan's steady impersonal stare. He glances about—sees the Princess—welcomes this opportunity for diverting attention. Bowing with humble respect*) Pardon me, Princess. I didn't recognize you before, you've gotten so grown up. (*flatteringly*) You look like a queen.

KUKACHIN (*falteringly*): I bid you welcome, Your Honor.

KUBLAI (*as a warning to Kukachin to control her emotion*): The Princess will soon be Queen of Persia.

MARCO (*flustered and awed, bowing to her again—flatteringly*): Then—Your Majesty—if I may be humbly permitted (*bowing to Kublai*)—to offer my congratulations—and before I settle down to discussing business—if her Highness—Majesty—will accept a small

————————

* Marco Polo's own story is in Volume I.

token of my esteem——(*Here he stamps his foot. An African slave, dressed in a pink livery with green hat and shoes and stockings and carrying a golden wicker basket, enters. He kneels, presents the basket to Marco, who lifts the cover and pulls out a small chow puppy with a pink ribbon tied around its neck. He steps forward and offers this to the Princess, with a boyish grin.*) A contribution to your zoo—from your most humble servant!

KUKACHIN (*taking it—flushing with pleasure*): Oh, what a little darling! (*She cuddles the puppy in her arms.*)

MARCO (*boastfully*): He's a genuine, pedigreed pup. I procured him at great cost—I mean he's extra well-bred.

KUKACHIN: Oh, thank you so much, Marco Polo (*stammering*) I mean, Your Honor.

KUBLAI (*warningly*): His Honor wishes to talk business, Princess.

KUKACHIN (*controlling herself*): I ask pardon. (*She bows and retires to left, rear, where she stands fondling the puppy and watching Marco.*)

MARCO (*plunging confidently on what he thinks is a sure point of attack*): My tax scheme, Your Majesty, that got such wonderful results is simplicity itself. I simply reversed the old system. For one thing I found they had a high tax on excess profits. Imagine a profit being excess! Why, it isn't humanly possible! I repealed it. And I repealed the tax on luxuries. I found out the great majority in Yang-Chau couldn't afford luxuries. The tax wasn't democratic enough to make it pay! I crossed it off and I wrote on the statute books a law that taxes every necessity in life, a law that hits every man's pocket equally, be he beggar or banker! And I got results!

CHU-YIN (*gravely*): In beggars?

KUBLAI (*with a chilling air*): I have received a petition from the inhabitants of Yang-Chau enumerating over three thousand cases of your gross abuse of power!

MARCO (*abashed only for a moment*): Oh, so they've sent that vile slander to you, have they? That's the work of a mere handful of radicals——

KUBLAI (*dryly*): Five hundred thousand names are signed to it. (*still more dryly*) Half a million citizens accuse you of endeavoring to stamp out their ancient culture!

MARCO: What! Why, I even had a law passed that anyone caught interfering with culture would be subject to a fine! It was Section One of a blanket statute that every citizen must be happy or go to jail. I found it was the unhappy ones who were always making trouble and getting discontented. You see, here's the way I figure it; if a man's good, he's happy—and if he isn't happy, it's a sure sign he's no good to himself or anyone else and he better be put where he can't do harm.

KUBLAI (*a bit helplessly now*): They complain that you have entirely prohibited all free expression of opinion.

MARCO (*feelingly*): Well, when they go to the extreme of circulating such treasonable opinions against me, isn't it time to protect your sovereignty by strong measures? (*Kublai stares at this effrontery with amazement. Marco watches this impression and hurries on with an injured dignity.*) I can't believe, Your Majesty, that this minority of malcontents can have alienated your long-standing high regard for me!

KUBLAI (*conquered—suddenly overpowered by a great smile*): Not so! You are the marvel of mankind! And I would be lost without you!

MARCO (*flattered but at the same time nonplused*): I thank you! (*hesitatingly*) But, to tell the truth, I want to resign, anyhow. I've done all I could. I've appointed five hundred committees to carry on my work and I retire confident that with the system I've instituted everything will go on automatically and brains are no longer needed. (*He adds as a bitter afterthought.*) And it's lucky they're not or Yang-Chau would soon be a ruin!

KUBLAI (*with mock seriousness*): In behalf of the population of Yang-Chau I accept your resignation, with deep regret for the loss of your unique and extraordinary services. (*then suddenly in a strange voice*) Do you still possess your immortal soul, Marco Polo?

MARCO (*flustered*): Ha-ha! Yes, of course—at least I hope so. But I see the joke. You mean that Yang-Chau used to be a good place to lose one. Well, you wouldn't know the old town now. Sin is practically unseen. (*hurrying on to another subject—boisterously*) But however much I may have accomplished there, it's nothing to the big surprise I've got in reserve for you. May I demonstrate? (*Without waiting for permission, takes a piece of printed paper like a dollar bill from his pocket.*) What is it? Paper. Correct! What is it worth? Nothing. That's where you're mistaken. It's worth ten yen. No, I'm not a liar! See "ten yen" written on it, don't you? Well, I'll tell you the secret. This is money, legally valued at ten yens' worth of anything you wish to buy, by order of His Imperial Majesty, the Great Khan! Do you see my point? Its advantages over gold and silver coin are obvious. It's light, easy to carry—(*Here he gives a prodigious wink.*) wears out quickly, can be made at very slight expense and yields enormous profit. Think of getting ten yen for this piece of paper. Yet it can be done. If you make the people believe it's worth it, it is! After all, when you stop to think, who was it first told them gold was money? I'll bet anything it was some quick thinker who'd just discovered a gold mine! (*Kublai and Chu-Yin stare at him in petrified incredulity. He mistakes it for admiration and is flattered. Bows and lays his paper money on the*

Khan's knee.) You're stunned, I can see that. It's so simple—and yet, who ever thought of it before me? I was amazed myself. Think it over, Your Majesty, and let the endless possibilities dawn on you! And now I want to show another little aid to government that I thought out. (*He makes a sign to his uncle and father. The former takes a mechanical contrivance out of a box and sets it up on the floor. It is a working model of a clumsy cannon. Nicolo, meanwhile, takes children's blocks out of his box and builds them into a fortress wall. Marco is talking. His manner and voice have become grave and portentous.*) It all came to me, like an inspiration, last Easter Sunday when Father and Uncle and I were holding a little service. Uncle read a prayer which spoke of Our Lord as the Prince of Peace. Somehow, that took hold of me. I thought to myself, Well, it's funny, there always have been wars and there always will be, I suppose, because I've never read much in any history about heroes who waged peace. Still, that's wrong. War is a waste of money which eats into the profits of life like thunder! Then why war, I asked myself? But how are you going to end it? Then the flash came! There's only one workable way and that's to conquer everybody else in the world so they'll never dare fight you again! An impossible task, you object? Not any more! This invention you see before you makes conquering easy. Let me demonstrate with these models. On our right, you see the fortress wall of a hostile capital. Under your present system with battering rams, to make an effective breach in this wall would cost you the lives of ten thousand men. Valuing each life conservatively at ten yen, this amounts to one hundred thousand yen! This makes the cost of breaching prohibitive. But all of this waste can be saved. How? Just keep your eyes on your right and permit my exclusive invention to solve this problem. (*He addresses the fortress in a matter-of-fact tone.*) So you won't surrender, eh? (*then in a mock-heroic falsetto, answering himself like a ventriloquist*) We die but we never surrender! (*then matter-of-factly*) Well, brother, those heroic sentiments do you a lot of credit, but this is war and not a tragedy. You're up against new methods this time, and you better give in and avoid wasteful bloodshed. (*answering himself*) No! Victory or Death! (*then again*) All right, brother, don't blame me. Fire! (*His uncle fires the gun. There is a bang, and a leaden ball is shot out which knocks a big breach in the wall of blocks. Marco beams. Kukachin gives a scream of fright, then a gasp of delight, and claps her hands. Marco bows to her the more gratefully as Kublai and Chu-Yin are staring at him with a queer appalled wonder that puzzles him although he cannot imagine it is not admiration.*) I see you are stunned again. What made it do that, you're wondering? This! (*He takes a little package out of his pocket and pours some black powder out of it on his palm.*) It's the same powder they've been using here in children's fireworks. They've had it under their noses for years without a single soul ever having creative imagination enough to visualize the enormous possibilities. But you can bet I did! It was a lad crying with a finger half blown off where he held a firecracker too long that first opened my eyes. I learned the formula, improved on it, experimented in secret, and here's the gratifying result! (*He takes the cannon ball from his father, who has retrieved it.*) You see? Now just picture this little ball magnified into one weighing twenty pounds or so and then you'll really grasp my idea. The destruction of property and loss of life would be tremendous! No one could resist you!

KUBLAI (*after a pause—musingly*): I am interested in the hero of that city who preferred death to defeat. Did you conquer his immortal soul?

MARCO (*with frankness*): Well, you can't consider souls when you're dealing with soldiers, can you? (*He takes his model and places it on the Khan's knee with the paper money.*) When you have time, I wish you'd look this over. In fact—and this is the big idea I've been saving for the last—consider these two inventions of mine in combination. You conquer the world with this—(*He pats the cannon model.*) and you pay for it with this. (*He pats the paper money—rhetorically.*) You become the bringer of peace on earth and good will to men, and it doesn't cost you a yen hardly. Your initial expense—my price—is as low as I can possibly make it out of my deep affection for your Majesty—only a million yen.

KUBLAI (*quickly*): In paper?

MARCO (*with a grin and a wink*): No, I'd prefer gold, if you don't mind.

I'M A NATURAL-BORN SALESMAN

WILLIAM HAZLETT UPSON

[William Hazlett Upson, "I'm a Natural Born Salesman," *The Saturday Evening Post,* April 16, 1927, vol. 199, no. 42, pp. 10–11, 149–150. Copyright 1927 by the Curtis Publishing Co.; reprinted by permission of David McKay Co., N.Y., from *The Best of Botts,* copyright © 1961 by the author.]

This is the first of a long series of stories in which Alexander Botts bumbles and stumbles—but *sells*—Earthworm tractors. What happens is related through pieces of correspondence between Botts and the home office. We never see him or his bosses, but we do get to know him. He is a favorite of two generations of Americans who have followed him since the time William Hazlett Upson introduced him in *The Saturday Evening Post* in 1927.

Here is the antithesis of the slick or tricky salesman. Perhaps Botts is too naive to be altogether human, but certainly he is closer than the usual stereotype to the real life of thousands of men who devote their lives to selling products that they believe in, without any of the benefit either of superhuman intelligence or of subhuman venality. Because we sympathize with his mistakes, they are comic but not ridiculous; and we rejoice with his ultimate triumph . . . until the next time, when we must repeat the enjoyable process.

Interestingly enough, most of Upson's life has been spent as a writer and lecturer, but he did spend five early years (1919–1924) in the service department of Holt Manufacturing Company, now taken over by the Caterpillar Tractor Company.

———◆———

STONEWALL JACKSON HOTEL
MEMPHIS, TENNESSEE

March 15, 1920

The Farmers' Friend Tractor Company,
Earthworm City, Ill.

GENTLEMEN:

I have decided you are the best tractor company in the country, and consequently I am giving you first chance to hire me as your salesman to sell tractors in this region.

I'm a natural-born salesman, have a very quick mind, am twenty-eight years old, am honest and reliable, and can give references if required. I have already had considerable experience as a machinery salesman, and I became familiar with your Earthworm tractors as a member of the motorized field artillery in France. I can demonstrate tractors as well as sell them.

When do I start work?

Very truly yours,
ALEXANDER BOTTS

———◆———

FARMERS' FRIEND TRACTOR COMPANY
MAKERS OF EARTHWORM TRACTORS
EARTHWORM CITY, ILLINOIS

March 17, 1920

Mr. Alexander Botts,
Stonewall Jackson Hotel,
Memphis, Tenn.

DEAR MR. BOTTS:
Your letter is received. We have no opening for a salesman at present, but we are badly in need of a service mechanic. As you say you are familiar with our tractors, we will try you out on this job, at $100 per month plus traveling expenses.

You will report at once to our Mr. George Healy, salesman for Tennessee and Mississippi, who is now at the Dartmouth Hotel, Memphis. You will go with him to Cyprus City, Mississippi, to demonstrate a ten-ton Earthworm tractor for Mr. Jackson, a lumber operator of that place. Mr. Healy will tell you just what you are to do.

We enclose check for $100 advance expense money.

Very truly,
GILBERT HENDERSON,
Sales Manager

———◆———

STONEWALL JACKSON HOTEL
MEMPHIS, TENNESSEE

March 19, 1920

The Farmers' Friend Tractor Company,
Earthworm City, Ill.

GENTLEMEN:
As soon as your letter came, I went around to see Mr. Healy, and it is lucky for you that you hired me, because Mr. Healy has just been taken sick with appendicitis. They were getting ready to take him to the hospital, and he was pretty weak, but he managed to tell me that the tractor for the demonstration had already arrived at the freight station in Cyprus City.

He also explained that this Mr. Jackson down there owns about a million feet of cyprus timber which he wants to get out and sell right away before the present high price of lumber goes down. It seems the ground is so swampy and soft from the winter rains that with his present equipment of mules and wagons he won't be able to move any of his timber until summer.

But Mr. Healy was down there a couple of weeks ago, and he arranged to put on a demonstration to show Mr. Jackson that an Earthworm tractor can go into those swamps and drag out the timber right away. Mr. Jackson said he would buy the tractor if it did the work, and Mr. Healy was feeling very low because he was sick and couldn't go down to hold the demonstration.

"You can rest easy, Mr. Healy," I said. "When you look at me you're gazing on a natural-born salesman. I will go down there and do your work as well as mine. I will put on a swell demonstration, and then I will sell the goods."

As Mr. Healy did not seem to know just what to say to this, I gathered up all his order blanks, selling literature, price lists, etc., and also the bill of lading and the check to pay the freight on the tractor. Then I wished him good luck, and left.

From this you can see that I am quick to grasp an opportunity, and that you made no mistake in hiring me. I am leaving for Cyprus City tonight.

Cordially yours,
ALEXANDER BOTTS

———◆———

FARMERS' FRIEND TRACTOR COMPANY
SALESMAN'S DAILY REPORT

Date: March 20, 1920
Written from: Delta Hotel, Cyprus City, Miss.
Written by: Alexander Botts, Service Mechanic and Pinch-Hitter Salesman

I found this pad of salesman's report blanks among the stuff I got from Mr. Healy. I see by the instructions on the cover that each salesman is supposed to send in a full and complete report of everything he does, so I will give you all particulars of a very busy day.

I arrived at 7:51 this morning at Cyprus City—which turns out to be pretty much of a hick town in what they call the Yazoo Delta. The whole country here is nothing but a swamp, and the main street of the town ends in a high bank that they call a levee, on the other side of which is the Mississippi River flowing along about twenty feet higher than the town.

After alighting from the train, and after noting that it was a cloudy day and looked like rain, I engaged a room at the Delta Hotel. I then hurried over to the freight station where I found the big ten-ton Earthworm tractor on the unloading platform. They had dragged it off the car with a block and tackle. And when I saw that beautiful machine standing there so big and powerful, with its fine wide tracks like an army tank, with its elegant new shiny paint, and with its stylish cab for the driver, I will admit that I felt a glow of pride to think that I was the salesman and service mechanic for such a splendid piece of machinery.

(Note: Of course, as I said in my letter, I am an old machinery salesman. But the largest thing I ever sold before was the Excelsior Peerless Self-adjusting Automatic Safety Razor Blade Sharpener. I did very well with this machine, but I could not take the pride in it that I feel I am going to have in this wonderful ten-ton Earthworm tractor.)

After paying the freight, I hired several guys from the town garage to put gas and oil in the tractor, and then I started them bolting the little cleats onto the tracks. You see, I am right up on my toes all the time. I think of everything. And I figured that if we were going through the mud we would need these cleats to prevent slipping. While they were being put on, I stepped over to the office of Mr. Johnson, the lumber man.

(Note: This bird's name is Johnson—not Jackson, as you and Mr. Healy told me. Also it strikes me that Mr. Healy may have been fairly sick even as long as two weeks ago when he was down here. In addition to getting the name wrong, he did very poor work in preparing this prospect. He did not seem to be in a buying mood at all.)

As soon as I had explained my errand to this Mr. Johnson—who is a very large, hard-boiled bozo—he gave me what you might call a horse laugh. "You are wasting your time" he said. "I told that fool salesman who was here before that tractors would be no good to me. All my timber is four miles away on the other side of the Great Gumbo Swamp, which means that it would have to be brought through mud that is deeper and stickier than anything you ever seen, young feller."

"You would like to get it out, wouldn't you?" I asked.

"I sure would," he said, "but it's impossible. You don't understand conditions down here. Right on the roads the mules and horses sink in up to their bellies; and when you get off the roads, even ducks and turtles can hardly navigate."

"The Earthworm tractor," I said, "has more power than any duck or turtle. And if you'll come out with me, I'll show you that I can pull your logs through that swamp."

"I can't afford to waste my time with such crazy ideas," he said. "I've tried motor equipment. I have a motor truck now that is stuck three feet deep right on the main road at the edge of town."

"All right," I said, always quick to grasp an opportunity, "how about coming along with me while I pull out your truck?"

"Well," said Mr. Johnson, "I can spare about an hour this morning. If you'll go right now, I'll go with you—although I doubt if you can even pull out the truck. And even if you do, I won't buy your tractor."

"How about going this afternoon?" I asked.

"I'll be busy this afternoon. It's now or never."

"Come on!" I said.

We went over to the freight platform, and as the cleats were now all bolted on we both climbed into the cab.

(Note: I will explain that I was sorry that Mr. Johnson had been unable to wait until afternoon, as I had intended to use the morning in practicing up on driving the machine. It is true, as I said in my letter, that I became familiar with Earthworm tractors when I was a member of a motorized artillery outfit in France, but as my job in the artillery was that of cook, and as I had never before sat in the seat of one of these tractors, I was not as familiar with the details of driving as I might have wished. However, I was pleased to see that the tractor seemed to have a clutch and gear shift like the automobiles I have often driven, and a pair of handle bars for steering very much like those of a tricycle I had operated in my early boyhood.)

I sat down on the driver's seat with reasonable confidence; Mr. Johnson sat down beside me; and one of the garage men cranked up the motor. It started at once, and when I heard the splendid roar of the powerful exhaust, and saw that thirty or forty of the inhabitants, both white and otherwise, were standing around with wondering and admiring faces, I can tell you I felt proud of myself. I put the gear in low, opened the throttle, and let in the clutch.

(Note: I would suggest that you tell your chief engineer, or whoever it is that designs your tractors, that he ought to put in a standard gear shift. You can understand that it is very annoying—after you have pulled the gear shift lever to the left and then back—to find that instead of being in low you are really in reverse.)

As I said, I opened the throttle, let in the clutch, and started forward. But I found that when I started forward, I was really—on account of the funny gear shift—moving backwards. And instead of going down the gentle slope of the ramp in front, the whole works backed off the rear edge of the platform, dropping at least four feet into a pile of crates with such a sickening crash that I thought the machine was wrecked and both of us killed.

But it soon appeared that, although we were both very much shaken up, we were still alive—especially Mr. Johnson, who began talking so loud and vigorously that I saw I need have no worry about his health. After I had got Mr. Johnson quieted down a bit, I inspected the machine and found that it was not hurt at all. As I am always alert to seize an opportunity, I told Mr. Johnson that I had run off the platform on purpose to show him how strongly built the tractor was. Then, after I had promised I would not make any more of these jumps, he consented to remain in the tractor, and we started off again.

(Note: Kindly tell your chief engineer that Alexander Botts congratulates him on producing a practically unbreakable tractor. But tell him that I wish he would design some thicker and softer seat cushions. If the base of the chief engineer's spine was as sore as mine still is, he would realize that there are times when good thick seat cushions are highly desirable.)

As we drove up the main street of Cyprus City, with a large crowd of admiring natives following after, I seemed to smell something burning. At once I stopped, opened up the hood, and discovered that the paint on the cylinders was crackling and smoking like bacon frying in a pan.

"Perhaps," suggested Mr. Johnson, "there is no water in the radiator."

I promptly inspected the radiator, and, sure enough, that was the trouble.

(Note: I would suggest that if your chief engineer would design an air-cooled motor for the tractor, such incidents as the above would be avoided.)

I borrowed a pail from a store, and filled the radiator. Apparently, owing to my alertness in this emergency, no damage had been done.

When we started up again, we had not gone more than a few yards before I felt the tractor give a little lurch. After we had got a little farther along I looked back, and right at the side of the street I saw one of the biggest fountains I have even seen in all my life. A solid column of water about eight inches thick was spouting high in the air, spreading out at the top like a mushroom, and raining down all around like Niagara Falls.

I heard somebody yell something about a fire plug; and, as I have a quick mind, I saw right away what had happened. The hood of the tractor is so big that it had prevented me from seeing a fire plug right in front of me. I had unfortunately run right into it, and as it was of very cheap, inferior construction, it had broken right off.

For a while there was great excitement, with people running here and there, hollering and yelling. The sheriff came up and took my name, as he seemed to think I was to blame—in spite of the fact that the fire plug was in such an exposed position. I was a bit worried at the way the water was accumulating in the street, and consequently I was much relieved when they finally got hold of the water works authorities and got the water turned off. You see the fire mains here are connected to the Mississippi River, and if they had not turned the water off the whole river would have flowed into the business district of Cyprus City.

(Note: I would suggest that your chief engineer design these tractor hoods a little lower so as to avoid such accidents in the future.)

After the water had been turned off, we got under way again, clanking along the main street in high gear, and then driving out of town to the eastward over one of the muddiest roads I ever saw. The tractor, on account of its wide tracks, stayed right up on top of the mud, and rolled along as easy and smooth as a Pullman car. Behind us a large crowd of local sightseers floundered along as best they could—some of them wading through the mud and slop, and others riding in buggies pulled by horses or mules.

Mr. Johnson acted as if he was pretty sore—and I did not blame him. Although the various mishaps and accidents we had been through were unavoidable and not my fault at all, I could understand that they might have been very annoying to my passenger. Perhaps that is one reason I am sure a good salesman; I can always get the other fellow's point of view. I livened up the journey a bit by telling Mr. Johnson a number of Irish jokes, but I did not seem to get any laughs—possibly because the motor made so much noise Mr. Johnson couldn't hear me.

By this time I had got the hang of driving the machine very well, and I was going along like a veteran. When we reached Mr. Johnson's truck—which was deep in the mud at the side of the road about a half mile from town—I swung around and backed up in front of it in great style.

The road, as I have said, was soft and muddy enough; but off to the right was a low, flat stretch of swamp land that looked much muddier, and a whole lot softer. There were patches of standing water here and there, and most of it was covered with canebrake—which is a growth of tall canes that look like bamboo fishing poles.

Mr. Johnson pointed out over this mass of canebrake and mud. "That is an arm of the Great Gumbo Swamp," he yelled very loud so I could hear him above the noise of the motor. "Your machine may be able to navigate these roads, but it would never pull a load through a slough like that."

I rather doubted it myself, but I didn't admit it. "First of all," I said, "we'll pull out this truck."

We both got out of the tractor, and right away we sank up to our knees in the soft sticky mud. The truck was a big one, loaded with lumber, and it was mired down so deep that the wheels were practically out of sight, and the body seemed to be resting on the ground. Mr. Johnson didn't think the tractor could budge it, but I told him to get into the driver's seat of the truck so he could steer it when it got going.

By this time a gentle rain had started up, and Mr. Johnson told me to hurry up as the truck had no cab and he was getting wet. I grabbed a big chain out of the truck tool box, and told Mr. Johnson to get out his watch. He did so.

"In just thirty seconds," I said, "things are going to start moving around here."

I then rapidly hooked one end of the chain to the back of the tractor, fastened the other end to the truck, sprang into the tractor seat, and started the splendid machine moving forward. As the tractor rolled steadily and powerfully down the road, I could hear the shouting of the crowd even above the noise of the motor. Looking around, however, I saw that something was wrong. The truck—or rather, the major portion of it—was still in the same place, and I was pulling only the radiator. As I had a quick mind, I saw at once what had happened. Quite naturally, I had slung the chain around the handiest thing on the front of the truck—which happened to be the radiator cap. And as the truck was of a cheap make, with the radiator not properly anchored, it had come off.

I stopped at once, and then I had to spend about ten minutes calming down Mr. Johnson by assuring him that the Farmers' Friend Tractor Company would pay for a new radiator. I backed up to the truck again, and Mr. Johnson took the chain himself, and by burrowing down in the mud managed to get it fastened around the front axle. Then he climbed back into the seat of the truck and scowled at me very disagreeably. By this time the rain was falling fairly briskly, and this may have had something to do with his ill humor.

When I started up again, everything went well. The motor roared, the cleats on the tracks dug into the mud, and slowly and majestically the tractor moved down the road, dragging the heavy truck through the mud behind it.

At this point I stuck my head out of the tractor cab to acknowledge the cheers of the bystanders, and in so doing I unfortunately knocked off my hat, which was caught by the wind and blown some distance away. At once I jumped out and began chasing it through the mud. The crowd began to shout and yell, but I paid no attention to this noise until I had reached my hat and picked it up—which took me some time, as the hat had blown a good ways, and I could not make any speed through the mud. When at last I looked around, I saw that a very curious thing had happened.

In getting out of the tractor I had accidentally pulled on one of the handle bars enough to turn the tractor sidewise. And in my natural excitement—the hat having cost me $8.98 last week in Memphis—I had forgotten to pull out the clutch. So when I looked up, I saw that the tractor, with Mr. Johnson and his truck in tow, was headed right out into the Great Gumbo Swamp. It had already got a good start, and it was going strong. As Mr. Johnson seemed to be waving and yelling for help, I ran after him. But as soon as I got off the road the mud was so deep and soft that I could make no headway at all. Several of the bystanders also attempted to follow, but had to give it up as a bad job. There was nothing to do but let poor Mr. Johnson go dragging off through the swamp.

And, although I was really sorry to see Mr. Johnson going off all by himself this way, with no protection from the pouring rain, I could not help feeling a thrill of pride when I saw how the great ten-ton Earthworm tractor was eating up that terrible soft mud. The wide tracks kept it from sinking in more than a few inches; the cleats gave it good traction; and the motor was so powerful that it pulled that big truck like it was a mere matchbox—and this in spite of the fact that the truck sank in so deep that it plowed a regular ditch as it went along.

As I am a natural-born salesman, and quick to grasp every opportunity, I yelled a little sales talk after Mr. Johnson. "It's all right," I hollered; "I'm doing this on purpose to show you that the Earthworm can go through any swamp you got." But I doubt if he heard me; the roar of the motor was too loud. And a moment later the tractor, the truck, and Mr. Johnson had disappeared in the canebrake.

While I was considering what to do next, a nice looking man in a corduroy suit came over to me from one of the groups of bystanders. "This is only an arm of the Great Gumbo Swamp," he said. "If that tractor doesn't mire down, and if it goes straight, it will come out on the levee on the other side about a mile from here."

"An Earthworm tractor never mires down," I said. "And as long as there is nobody there to pull on the handlebars, it can't help going straight."

"All right," said the man, "if you want to hop in my buggy, I'll drive you back to town and out the levee so we can meet it when it gets there."

"Fine!" I said. "Let's go." I have always been noted for my quick decisions, being similar to Napoleon in this particular. I at once climbed in the buggy with the man in the corduroy suit, and he drove the horse as fast as possible into town and then out the levee, with all the sightseers plowing along behind—both on foot and in buggies.

When we reached the place where the tractor ought to come out, we stopped and listened. Far out in the swamp we could hear the roar of the tractor motor. It got gradually louder and louder. We waited. It was still raining hard. Suddenly there was a shout from the crowd. The tractor came nosing out of the canebrake, and a moment later it had reached the bottom of the levee, with the big truck and Mr. Johnson dragging along behind. As the tractor was in low gear, I had no trouble in jumping aboard and stopping it—and it is just as well I was there to do this. If I had not stopped it, it would have shot right on over the levee and into the Mississippi River, probably drowning poor Mr. Johnson.

As it was, Mr. Johnson was as wet as a sponge, on account of the heavy rain, and because he had been too cheap to get himself a truck with a cab on it. But he was a long way from being drowned. In fact, he seemed very lively; and as I got down from the tractor he jumped out of the truck and came running at me, waving his arms around, and shouting and yelling, and with a very dirty look on his face. What he had to say to me would fill a small book; in fact, he said so much that I'm afraid I will have to put off telling you about it until my report tomorrow.

It is now midnight and I am very tired, so I will merely enclose my expense account for the day and wish you a pleasant good night. Kindly send check to cover expenses as soon as possible. As you will see, my $100 advance is already gone, and I have had to pay money out of my own pocket.

Cordially yours,
ALEXANDER BOTTS

EXPENSE ACCOUNT

Railroad fare (Memphis to Cyprus City)	$ 6.10
Pullman ticket	3.20
Gas and oil for tractor	8.50
Labor (putting on cleats, etc.)	9.00
36 doz. eggs at 50 cents per doz.	18.00

(Note: It seems the crates we landed on when we dropped off the freight platform were full of eggs.)

1 plate glass window	80.00

(Note: I forgot to say in my report that in the confusion following the breaking of the fire plug I accidentally side-swiped a drug store with the tractor.)

Radiator for truck, and labor to install	46.75
Cleaning hat and pressing trousers	3.50
Total	$175.05

(Note: I will list the hotel bill, the bill for the fire plug, and other expenses when I pay them.)

FARMERS' FRIEND TRACTOR COMPANY
SALESMAN'S DAILY REPORT

Date: March 21, 1920
Written from: Delta Hotel, Cyprus City, Miss.
Written by: Alexander Botts

I will take up the report of my activities at the point where I
stopped yesterday when Mr. Johnson had just gotten out of the truck
and was coming in my direction. As I stated, he had a great deal to
say. Instead of being grateful to me for having given him such a
splendid demonstration of the ability of the Earthworm tractor to go
through a swamp, and instead of thanking me for saving his life by
stopping him just as he was about to shoot over the levee into the
Mississippi River, he began using very abusive language which I will
not repeat except to say that he told me he would not buy my tractor,
and that he never wanted to see me or my damn machinery again. He
also said he was going to slam me down in the mud and jump on my
face, and it took six of the bystanders to hold him and prevent him
from doing this. And although there were six of them, they had a lot
of trouble holding him, owing to the fact that he was so wet and
slippery from the rain.

As I am a natural-born salesman, I saw right away that this was not
an auspicious time to give Mr. Johnson any sales talk about tractors.
I decided to wait until later, and I walked back to the tractor in a
dignified manner, looking back over my shoulder, however, to make
sure Mr. Johnson was not getting away from the guys that were
holding him.

After they had led Mr. Johnson back to town, I made up my mind
to be a good sport, and I hauled his truck into town and left it at the
garage to be repaired. The rest of the day I spent settling up various
expense items—which appeared on my yesterday's expense account—
and in writing up my report. When I finally went to bed at midnight,
it was with a glow of pride that I thought of the splendid work I had
done on the first day of my employment with the great Farmers'
Friend Tractor Company, Makers of Earthworm Tractors. Although
I had not as yet made any sales, I could congratulate myself on having
put on the best tractor demonstration ever seen in Cyprus City,
Mississippi.

This morning, after breakfast, I had a visit from the nice-looking
man in the corduroy suit who gave me the buggy ride yesterday.

"I am a lumber operator," he said, "and I have a lot of cyprus back
in the swamps that I have been wanting to get out. I haven't been able
to move it because the ground has been so soft. However, since I saw
your tractor drag that big heavy truck through the swamp yesterday,

I know that it is just what I want. I understand the price is $6000, and if you will let me have the machine right away I will take you over to the bank and give you a certified check for that amount."

"Well," I said, "I was supposed to sell this machine to Mr. Johnson, but as he has had a chance at it and hasn't taken it, I suppose I might as well let you have it."

"I don't see why you gave him first chance," said the man in the corduroy suit. "When your other salesman, Mr. Healy, was down here, I gave him more encouragement than anybody else he talked to. And he said he would ship a tractor down here and put on a demonstration for me."

"By the way," I said, "what is your name?"

"William Jackson," he said.

As I have a quick mind, I saw at once what had happened. This was the guy I had been supposed to give the demonstration for in the first place, but I had very naturally confused his name with that of Mr. Johnson. There ought to be a law against two men with such similar names being in the same kind of business in the same town.

However, it had come out all right. And, as I am a natural-born salesman, I decided that the thing to do was to take Mr. Jackson over to the bank right away—which I did. And now the tractor is his.

I enclose the certified check. And I have decided to remain in town several days more on the chance of selling some more machines.

Cordially yours,
ALEXANDER BOTTS

———◆———

TELEGRAM

EARTHWORM CITY ILLS 1015A MAR 22 1920

ALEXANDER BOTTS
DELTA HOTEL
CYPRUS CITY MISS

YOUR FIRST REPORT AND EXPENSE ACCOUNT RECEIVED STOP YOU ARE FIRED STOP WILL DISCUSS THAT EXPENSE ACCOUNT BY LETTER STOP IF YOU SO MUCH AS TOUCH THAT TRACTOR AGAIN WE WILL PROSECUTE YOU TO THE FULLEST EXTENT OF THE LAW

FARMERS FRIEND TRACTOR COMPANY
GILBERT HENDERSON SALES MANAGER

———◆———

NIGHT LETTER

CYPRUS CITY MISS 510P MAR 22 1920

FARMERS FRIEND TRACTOR CO
EARTHWORM CITY ILLS

YOUR TELEGRAM HERE STOP WAIT TILL YOU GET MY SECOND REPORT
STOP AND THAT IS NOT ALL STOP THE WHOLE TOWN IS TALKING ABOUT
MY WONDERFUL TRACTOR DEMONSTRATION STOP JOHNSON HAS COME
AROUND AND ORDERED TWO TRACTORS STOP THE LEVEE CONSTRUC-
TION COMPANY OF THIS PLACE HAS ORDERED ONE STOP NEXT WEEK
IS TO BE QUOTE USE MORE TRACTORS WEEK UNQUOTE IN CYPRUS CITY
STOP MASS MEETING MONDAY TO DECIDE HOW MANY EARTHWORMS
THE CITY WILL BUY FOR GRADING ROADS STOP LUMBERMENS MASS
MEETING TUESDAY AT WHICH I WILL URGE THEM TO BUY TRACTORS
AND JACKSON AND JOHNSON WILL BACK ME UP STOP WEDNESDAY
THURSDAY FRIDAY AND SATURDAY RESERVED FOR WRITING UP ORDERS
FROM LUMBERMEN CONTRACTORS AND OTHERS STOP TELL YOUR
CHIEF ENGINEER TO GET READY TO INCREASE PRODUCTION STOP YOU
BETTER RECONSIDER YOUR WIRE OF THIS MORNING

ALEXANDER BOTTS

———◆———

TELEGRAM

EARTHWORM CITY ILLS 945A MAR 23 1920

ALEXANDER BOTTS
DELTA HOTEL
CYPRUS CITY MISS

OUR WIRE OF YESTERDAY STANDS STOP YOUR JOB AS SERVICE ME-
CHANIC WITH THIS COMPANY IS GONE FOREVER STOP WE ARE PUTTING
YOU ON PAYROLL AS SALESMAN STOP TWO HUNDRED PER WEEK PLUS
EXPENSES PLUS FIVE PER CENT COMMISSION ON ALL SALES

FARMERS FRIEND TRACTOR COMPANY
GILBERT HENDERSON SALES MANAGER

THE LITTLE PRINCE FROM ASTEROID B-612 INTERVIEWS THE BUSINESSMAN

⤔⟡⤙

ANTOINE DE SAINT-EXUPÉRY

[Antoine de Saint-Exupéry, *The Little Prince*, trans. from the French by Katherine Woods; Reynal & Hitchcock, New York, copyright 1943, pp. 43–47. Reprinted by permission of Harcourt Brace & World, Inc., William Heinemann, Ltd., and Librairie Gallimard.]

There is a businessman in the story of *The Little Prince* by Antoine de Saint-Exupéry—and, it must be admitted at once, not a very attractive one. Here the great French airman with the soul of a poet tells a children's story, but a children's story which is somewhat subtle in its reflections on life. He tells of coming down in the desert with engine failure, alone, and with just a week's ration of water to last him out while he makes repairs. We never do learn how—or whether—he managed to survive; that becomes secondary to the adventures of the little prince who had just arrived at that spot from Asteroid B-612, also a poet at heart, in love with a lovely rose back home.

The little boy is going from planet to planet. He has been to visit a king who thinks he rules the stars, a conceited man who wears a hat just so he can raise it in the event of applause, and a tippler who drinks because he is ashamed that he drinks. Now he meets the businessman—but remember he is a businessman as seen by a child, who somehow doesn't understand grown-ups or appreciate the fact that businessmen do have to create some product or service before they can count the profits . . . or the stars.

———◆———

THE FOURTH PLANET BELONGED TO A BUSINESSMAN. This man was so much occupied that he did not even raise his head at the little prince's arrival.

"Good morning," the little prince said to him. "Your cigarette has gone out."

"Three and two make five. Five and seven make twelve. Twelve and three make fifteen. Good morning. Fifteen and seven make twenty-two. Twenty-two and six make twenty-eight. I haven't time to light it again. Twenty-six and five make thirty-one. Phew! Then that makes five-hundred-and-one million, six-hundred-twenty-two thousand, seven-hundred-thirty-one."

"Five hundred million what?" asked the little prince.

"Eh? Are you still there? Five-hundred-and-one million—I can't stop . . . I have so much to do! I am concerned with matters of consequence. I don't amuse myself with balderdash. Two and five make seven . . ."

"Five-hundred-and-one million what?" repeated the little prince, who never in his life had let go of a question once he had asked it.

The businessman raised his head.

"During the fifty-four years that I have inhabited this planet, I have been disturbed only three times. The first time was twenty-two years ago, when some giddy goose fell from goodness knows where. He made the most frightful noise that resounded all over the place, and I made four mistakes in my addition. The second time, eleven years ago, I was disturbed by an attack of rheumatism. I don't get enough exercise. I have no time for loafing. The third time—well, this is it! I was saying, then, five-hundred-and-one millions——"

"Millions of what?"

The businessman suddenly realized that there was no hope of being left in peace until he answered this question.

"Millions of those little objects," he said, "which one sometimes sees in the sky."

"Flies?"

"Oh, no. Little glittering objects."

"Bees?"

"Oh, no. Little golden objects that set lazy men to idle dreaming. As for me, I am concerned with matters of consequence. There is no time for idle dreaming in my life."

"Ah! You mean the stars?"

"Yes, that's it. The stars."

"And what do you do with five-hundred millions of stars?"

"Five-hundred-and-one million, six-hundred-twenty-two thousand, seven-hundred-thirty-one. I am concerned with matters of consequence; I am accurate."

"And what do you do with these stars?"

"What do I do with them?"

"Yes."   •

"Nothing. I own them."

"You own the stars?"

"Yes."

"But I have already seen a king who——"

"Kings do not *own*, they *reign over*. It is a very different matter."

"And what good does it do you to own the stars?"

"It does me the good of making me rich."

"And what good does it do you to be rich?"

"It makes it possible for me to buy more stars, if any are discovered."

"This man," the little prince said to himself, "reasons a little like my poor tippler. . . ."

Nevertheless, he still had some more questions.

"How is it possible for one to own the stars?"

"To whom do they belong?" the businessman retorted, peevishly.

"I don't know. To nobody."

"Then they belong to me, because I was the first person to think of it."

"Is that all that is necessary?"

"Certainly. When you find a diamond that belongs to nobody, it is yours. When you discover an island that belongs to nobody, it is yours. When you get an idea before any one else, you take out a patent on it; it is yours. So with me: I own the stars, because nobody else before me ever thought of owning them."

"Yes, that is true," said the little prince. "And what do you do with them?"

"I administer them," replied the businessman. "I count them and recount them. It is difficult. But I am a man who is naturally interested in matters of consequence."

The little prince was still not satisfied.

"If I owned a silk scarf," he said, "I could put it around my neck and take it away with me. If I owned a flower, I could pluck that flower and take it away with me. But you cannot pluck the stars from heaven. . . ."

"No. But I can put them in the bank."

"Whatever does that mean?"

"That means that I write the number of my stars on a little paper. And then I put this paper in a drawer and lock it with a key."

"And that is all?"

"That is enough," said the businessman.

"It is entertaining," thought the little prince. "It is rather poetic. But it is of no great consequence."

On matters of consequence, the little prince had ideas which were very different from those of the grown-ups.

"I myself own a flower," he continued his conversation with the businessman, "which I water every day. I own three volcanoes, which I clean out every week (for I also clean out the one that is extinct; one never knows). It is of some use to my volcanoes, and it is of some use to my flower, that I own them. But you are of no use to the stars. . . ."

The businessman opened his mouth, but he found nothing to say in answer. And the little prince went away.

"The grown-ups are certainly altogether extraordinary," he said simply, talking to himself as he continued on his journey.

BUSINESS IN IRELAND—OR IS IT LEPRECHAUNS?

LORD DUNSANY

[Lord Dunsany, "Business," from *My Ireland*, Funk & Wagnalls Co., New York, 1937, pp. 108–120. Reprinted by permission of the author, Funk & Wagnalls Co., and Jarrolds Publishers, Inc.]

It's a little unfair to the Irish—though, as long as it's from an Irishman himself, Lord Dunsany, none other, it must be all right. And it is fun.

The plain fact is there have been plenty of good Irish businessmen, in Ireland and out of it, and maybe especially in America. But the Irish have a way of taking serious things lightly and light things seriously—and making the rest of us envy that gift. Here it is at its best. Maybe business ought to be the way it appears (or doesn't appear) in this story; it wouldn't interfere so much with fishing!

"ARE YOU COMING OUT TOMORROW?" said a friend to me, for the hounds were to be within five miles of me.

"No," I said. "I am writing a book about Ireland, and want to get on with it."

"About Ireland," he said. "What are you telling them?"

"Oh, sport," I said, "and poetry and history, and of course politics. But not much history, for the book is to be in one volume and that volume is to be lifted with one hand."

"Another reason why much history would be out of place in a book about Ireland," he said, "is that they none of them know any of it."

"I thought it was one of the things the people are fondest of," I said.

"They are," said he, "but in the schools, where they learn it, it is only used as missiles to throw at England, so that it gets rather tattered. It is very exciting of course, but you couldn't any longer call it history, after it has been the round of a few schools."

"Well, I don't know very much about it myself," I said.

"No, nobody does," he replied. "But you're right to give them sport; and I think there's some poetry in all of them."

"Their talk is full of it," I answered, "and all their legends."

"Yes," he said. "But what are you doing about politics?"

And then I told him about Old Mickey, and how there was one thing that everybody would want to know and Old Mickey was going to tell it me.

"Yes, you'll have to tell them that," he said. "But what about business? You should say something of that."

"Oh, yes," I said, "I suppose I should."

But the remark rather bothered me; we haven't very much business in County Meath. We used to sell fat cattle before the treaty and got £35 a head. We still sell fat cattle; but, as we only get from £12 to £14 a head for them, one can hardly call that business.

"What business is there?" I asked.

"Well, there's Guinness," he said. "And there's bound to be some more somewhere, if only you look for it. Anyway you'll have to have something about it in your book."

We were both agreed about that. And I decided to make further inquiries, and with the help of them to study the matter locally.

And by good luck I met next day just the kind of man that I wanted, a man whose kindness had helped me to get many a teal; for he had not only showed me a reedy pond to which the teal came, but many a time he had driven them for me, telling me just where to hide myself and seeming to know exactly the line that the teal would fly. He was an old friend of mine, who had known a good deal of prison in his youth; and the imprisonment, while gaining him the respect of all his neighbors, had never impaired his cheerfulness. Now that the words will soon be in cold print I begin to realize that to know the flight of teal is not in itself sufficient qualification for knowledge about business, and that there may even be amongst my readers some that will hold that before venturing to address them upon this matter I should have found an adviser with better qualifications. That may be so; indeed it is incontrovertible; and I should certainly have done so. On the other hand I was not at once able to find a man with the better qualifications, and I was undoubtedly hindered in my search for one by a certain charm that there was in Stephen O'Lara, who now stood before me, and who would, I believe, have exerted the same misleading charm on the most critical of my readers; but that, of course, I cannot prove. I had found him a good deal occupied watching a river. It was a bright morning, and he was leaning over a bridge and did not recognize me till I spoke to him. Then he jumped up, all smiles.

"I was watching the river," he said, "and didn't see you."

"It's a fine day to be doing it," said I.

"Begob," he said, "it must take a long time to get to the sea, the pace it's going now."

"It gets there all right," I said.

"I was wondering did it ever get there," he answered.

"How is the country doing?" I asked.

"Sure, it's doing grand," he said.

"And how is business doing?" I asked.

"Business is it?" said he.

"Well, yes," I said. "I rather wanted to make a study of it."

"Sure it's doing grand too," said O'Lara. "They are after opening a great new bank over at Bohermeen."

"At Bohermeen?" I said.

"Aye," he said, "to the west of the road."

It was the kind of thing that I wanted to know.

"That's the road to Fahan," I asked, so as to make no mistake.

"Aye, three or four hundred yards from the crossroads," he said.

"When did they build it?" I asked.

"They're just after finishing it," he said.

"Who is the manager?"

"The honestest man in all Ireland," he said.

And then he told me this rather interesting story.

"Pat had a bit of an army of young lads down in the West, no more nor about half a dozen. He wasn't the general himself, but there was another lad over him. And one day he went into the big bank that there is down there, and asked to see the manager. And the manager came out of his office, all business and buttons, and said: 'What can I do for you?'

"And the young lads put up their pistols, and Pat said: 'I want £4000.'

"And the manager said: 'I haven't got it.'

"And Pat said: 'Then you've not long to live.'

"And the manager said: 'I might scrape it together.'

"And he did.

" 'Can I put it into some bags for you?' said the manager.

" 'You need not,' said Pat. 'Do you think I am going about with all that money on me? Sure, I wouldn't be able to walk.'

" 'I thought you wanted to take it away,' said the manager.

" 'Have more sense,' said Pat.

" 'Then what do you want to do with it?' he asked.

" 'Sure, I'll bank it,' said Pat.

" 'Where?' said the manager.

" 'With you. Why not?' said Pat. 'You can put it to my account.'

" 'I'll want a specimen of your signature,' said the manager.

" 'There'll be no difficulty about that,' said Pat. For they had learned him to write. So he wrote down his signature, and they all walked away; and Pat turned his head round, as he was going out, in the doorway, and said: 'Is there a priest handy?'

"And the manager said: 'There is.'

" 'Because,' said Pat, 'if ever I come here for the money and don't find it, you'll want him in a great hurry.'

"With that he went away, and there was £4000 to his credit in the bank. Am I tiring you?"

"You are not," I said. "What happened?"

"Well, a few weeks went by and then the general that I told you about, who was over Pat, died one night from the prod of a cow's horn. I knew the doctor who attended him, and he told me that that was what he died of. It went through the whole length of his body. 'It must have been a very long horn,' said the doctor to me, 'and a very thin one. But that was not my affair.' Well, when Pat heard the general was dead, and being a queer fellow and the honestest man in Ireland, what's he do but go back to the manager of the bank and give him back his £4000. Yes, he done that. He did indeed. And when they wanted an honest man to run a bank, what did they do only get Pat? And where could they have got a better? For he knew a little about banking, through having had an account of his own, and he was dead honest. And it's a true story I'm telling you."

"I want nothing but the truth," I said, "for I'm writing a book about Ireland."

"It's God's truth," he said.

And then I left him to look at the river, while I went home to write about business.

But when I got home I decided that I had best first go and see Bohermeen, and have a talk with the manager of the new bank.

So when my gamekeeper came to see me next morning to ask me where I would shoot, I told him that I couldn't shoot that day, as I had some business to attend to and wanted to see the manager of the bank at Bohermeen.

"I never heard of a bank at Bohermeen," he said.

"No. It's a new one," said I.

"But it would be a grand place for snipe," he said, "and there's none of the men with rights in the bog who will object to your going there."

"Well, I'll take my gun," I said, "and we'll bring the dog, and I might get some shooting when I've finished the business I have to do."

But I said no more of the bank; for, though I valued his opinion on sport, I did not think that he had sufficiently accurate knowledge of business to justify me in basing upon his opinion on banking the information about business in Ireland that I desire to give to my reader. And soon we were off, with dog and gun in the car, to Bohermeen, which lies northwest from Tara. One cannot see from the famous hill the low levels to which I went, but very clearly one can see the Hill of Fahan, against whose feet laps the heather of Bohermeen. I have seen the Hill of Fahan from Tara at evening, with its wood on top turning ruby, till the gap that there is in the wood becomes like a gateway of Fairyland. The low steep hill in the plain is one of the principal landmarks of the country. We came to Klimessan hill, where the land dips to the west, and we saw Meath and Westmeath lying blue before us. We crossed the Boyne, and went through lands of green pastures, till we came to little fields of coarser grass, which very soon ceased altogether, and we came to the lower levels of the bog, that men have plundered but not yet tamed. A few young birches stood there, that men had planted in rows along ditches that they had dug, and some turfstacks stood there drying; but there was nothing else on those levels that told of the work of man. A road ran very lonely over the bog, looking almost shy of its own sophistication amongst ancient primitive nature. And then another road ran away to the right. So narrow was this one that it seemed almost to slink over the bog, like a man in patent-leather boots, tall hat and frock coat going on tiptoe through an encampment of gypsies, knowing he had no business there. This was the road we followed, till I came to the exact spot of which O'Lara had told me. The low levels of the cut-away bog had ended before I came there and the long black cliff lay before us at the edge of the high bog, its outline jagged by the turf cutters. It was two hundred yards past this that O'Lara had told me I should come on the new bank. I stopped the car, and the distance seemed about right and I should have been standing just about at the doorway. But no bank was there, nothing but pale brown grasses, with patches of heather amongst them, and a view over bog unbroken but for one dark row of pines to the left hand side of the view and a small wood to the right, and some mountains that are in Westmeath rising beyond it. Behind me on the other side of the road lay the lower levels with patches of whitish grass and patches of moss, and square pools shining; I saw a loose donkey there, and one in a cart, and two men standing by turf stacks. I looked again over the bog, and away to those mountains in Westmeath, but the only sign of sophistication I saw was one broken bottle, that had been thrown to the bog from the road; but certainly no bank. Had I been content to write about the Ireland I know, instead of wishing to instruct my reader about whatever business may be done in the country, I should not have been out on this wild goose chase. Let the metaphor pass: I know of no more unsuitable one by which to describe a search for a bank; but let it pass.

"We'd better shoot snipe," I said to my keeper. And that is what we did.

I was rather annoyed with O'Lara for sending me off on this absurd quest, when it was solid information I wanted; so I went a little out of my way, coming back, so as to find O'Lara. And I found him, where I usually find him, not far from the Boyne; and he seemed as pleased as ever to see me, and seemed to know, too, where I was coming from, and looked as though he were happy to have provided me with just the information I wanted. I seemed to see all that in his smile. But all I said to him by way of greeting was:

"There is no bank at Bohermeen."

"Ah," he replied, "perhaps it was a turf bank I meant."

"You told me," I said, though my annoyance was melting before his smiling face as I spoke, "that there was a particularly honest man as manager there, and I went all the way to have a talk with him."

"Sure, everything I told you about him was true," said O'Lara. "Doesn't the whole country know it? And what for do you want his right address? Wouldn't the story about him be just as true whatever address I gave you? Begob, it would. And maybe the wrong address might be better. But, sure, I'll find him for you and bring him to see you."

"It doesn't matter," I said.

"What was it you wanted him for?" said O'Lara.

"I wanted to have a talk with him about business," I said. "I'm writing a book about Ireland, and they'll want to know what business the country does."

"Haven't we Guinness?" said he. "And what do we want with any more business than that? Don't they pay millions in taxes?"

And then a troubled look came over his face.

"Begob," he said, "I've nearly given up drinking it."

"Why's that?" I gasped.

"Because of a dream I had," said O'Lara, "after drinking no more nor a bottle. And then I went to bed and I had the dream."

"What was the dream?" I asked.

"Begob," said he, "it was terrible. I dreamed that I walked down to the shore of the sea one evening; I don't know what I was doing there, but I walked down to the shore; and it was somewhere near Dublin, for I could see the Wicklow mountains. And it wasn't night, for there was still some light in the sky; but it was getting late. And the shore was crowded with people all looking out to the sea. And I said, 'What's the matter, boys?' And one or two of them answered, 'It is the end,' and went on looking out to sea. So I looked too, in my dream. And I saw the horizon all dark with the smoke of ships, and the people staring at them as though the end of the world were there. Begob, I said to myself, it's the English fleet, and those great big shells will be coming soon.

"For the smoke was tearing up and the sky was black as thunder.

" 'Is it the English fleet?' I said.

"But they had all gone silent, and wouldn't speak any more.

"And then I saw that the ships were nearer than they looked in the evening. They weren't far away at all, and were quite small. And I took a man by the arm who was standing quite near me and I shook him, and said, 'Those little boats can't hurt us; sure, they're no bigger than Guinness' boats that do be on the Liffy.'

"And the man gave a great sigh and said, 'It is what they are.'

"And I cried out then, 'Ah, boys, is it Guinness's going?'

"And I knew from the awful stillness that this was so.

"And I daren't have a sup of porter before going to bed any more, for fear would I get that dream."

"Oh, I wouldn't bother," I said. "It was only a dream."

For he looked so doleful, I had to say something to try to cheer him.

"It isn't the dream I mind," he said, "but all the truth that there is in it."

ONE MINUTE PLEASE!

ROBERT BENCHLEY

[Robert Benchley, "One Minute Please!" in *The Treasurer's Report*, Harper and Brothers, New York, copyright 1930 by Robert C. Benchley, pp. 191-201 (abridged). Reprinted by permission of the publisher.]

Robert Benchley was funny from 1915 to 1945. And as a purveyor of humor—about a thousand published pieces like the selection which follows—he was a pretty good businessman. Which makes this piece, wherein he joshes his more conventional brothers of the more conventional business world, all the more interesting. The date is 1930, just after the great crash of the stock market in late 1929.

I AM KNOWN as a bad businessman from one end of the country to just a little beyond the same end. Practically everyone in my class in kindergarten went into business after graduation, and when I say business I mean business. Whenever I see them now they are always dressed up in stiff shirts and are making marks on the backs of envelopes. Get me a hundred of my old schoolmates together and let them talk from 9 A.M. until almost dinner time and I won't understand a word they are saying. It is only around dinner time that I begin to catch a glimmer of sense and then they have to come right out and say "Martini" or "Green turtle soup." At this point I join the party.

But not until I have had it said to me eight or a dozen times that I ought to be more businesslike. "Good old Bob," they say (those of them who remember that my name is "Bob"), "you are just a sucker to be so impractical. Why don't you let us take some of your money and triple it for you?"

Leaving aside the question "What money?" I am frankly at a loss for something to say. Here I am, just a dreamer, and there they are, captains of industry, or, at any rate, second lieutenants. They have the advantage of me.

Of course, if I wanted to, I might point out that out of a possible $5000 which I have made since I left school I have had $3000 worth of good food (all of which has gone into making bone and muscle and some nice fat), $1500 worth of theatre tickets, and $500 worth of candy; whereas many of my business friends have simply had $5000 worth of whatever that stock was which got so yellow along about last November.

I was sympathetic with all the boys at that time and even advanced a little cash in a sparing manner, but I couldn't help remembering the days during the summer when I had to sit and listen to them say, "Well, I made $650,000 over the week end. What will you have, Bob, old man?" And all the time I was, in my old impractical way, sinking my money into silk neckties (which I still have) and throwing it away on life-giving beefsteaks.

I do not intend to dwell on this phase of life's whirligig, however. Who can tell, perhaps some day even we spendthrifts may find ourselves short of cash. In the meantime, those of us who have nothing but fripperies to show for our money have had a good laugh. At least we've got the fripperies.

What I do want to dwell on is the point that there are still a great many practices which are considered businesslike and efficient and which any one of us old dreamers could improve upon and speed up. Now you sit still and read this. I have sat still and listened to you long enough.

First, there is the question of business telephoning. During the last five or six years there has spread throughout the business world a method of telephoning which, so far as I am concerned, bids fair to destroy all channels of business communication. If it keeps up, I, for one, will go back to the old Indian runner and carrier pigeon methods. I won't stand for this another day. In fact, I stopped standing for it a year ago.

I refer to the delayed-pass play, so popular among busy executives. In this play your busy executive, when he wants to get me on the telephone (why he should want to get me on the telephone is a mystery), says to his secretary, "Get me Mr. Benchley on the wire, Miss Whatney." You see, he hasn't got the time to get me himself, what with all those stocks he has to tend to; so he has Miss Whatney do it for him. So far, pretty good. Miss Whatney looks up my number in the book and gives it to the operator at the switchboard, thereby releasing the busy executive for other duties, such as biting off the end of a cigar or drawing circles on his scratch pad.

The scene now changes and we see me, the impractical dreamer, sitting at an old typewriter with nothing to do but finish an article which was due the day before. My telephone rings and I, in my slipshod, impractical way, answer it. And what do I get for my pains?

"Is this Vanderbilt 0647? Is Mr. Benchley there? Just a minute, please!"

Having nothing to do but wool-gather, I wait. In about two minutes I hear another female voice saying, "Is this Mr. Benchley? Just a minute please, Mr. Kleek wants to speak to you."

Remember, it is Mr. Kleek who is calling *me* up. I don't want to speak to Mr. Kleek. I wouldn't care if I never spoke to him. In fact. I am not sure that I know who Mr. Kleek is.

"Just a minute, please," comes the voice again. "Mr. Kleek is talking on another wire."

Now, fascinating as this information is, it really wasn't worth getting up out of my chair for. Mr. Kleek could be busy on eight other wires and my life would go on just about the same. Am I to be called away from my work to be told that a Mr. Kleek is talking on another wire? I think this out as I stand there waiting.

Finally, after several minutes, I hear a man's voice.

"Hello," it says gruffly, "who is this?" I am not only to be told to wait until Mr. Kleek is ready to speak to me, but I am to be treated by Mr. Kleek as if I had infringed on his time. At this point I frankly flare up.

"Who is this yourself?" I snarl. "This was your idea, not mine!"

Then evidently Miss Whatney tells Mr. Kleek that she has got Mr. Benchley on the wire, and he is somewhat mollified. But I want to tell you, Mr. Kleek, that by that time I am not on the wire any longer and you can stick that telephone earpiece into the side of your head. Furthermore, from now on, the minute I am called to the telephone and told to wait a minute, that Mr. Anybody wants to speak to me, I hang up so quickly that the hook drops off. If Mr. Kleek or any other busy executive wants to speak to me, he can be there within four seconds after I answer or he can put in the call again. I may be just an old wool-gatherer, but I want to gather my wool somewhere else than at a telephone receiver. And that goes for you, too, Mr. Andrew Mellon! [Secretary of the Treasury]

It is possible that the telephone has been responsible for more business inefficiency than any other agency except laudanum. It has such an air of pseudo-efficiency about it that people feel efficient the minute they take the receiver off the hook. A businessman could be talking with Ajax, the mechanical chess player, on the other end of the wire and still feel he was getting somewhere, simply because to anyone passing the door he looks as if he were very busy. There is something about saying "O.K." and hanging up the receiver with a bang that kids a man into feeling that he has just pulled off a big deal, even if he has only called up Central to find out the correct time. For this reason businessmen use the telephone exclusively when almost any other form of communication would be quicker.

In the old days when you wanted to get in touch with a man you wrote a note, sprinkled it with sand, and gave it to a man on horseback. It probably was delivered within half an hour, depending on how big a lunch the horse had had. But in these busy days of rush-rush-rush, it sometimes is a week before you can catch your man on the telephone. The call is put in, but he is out. You tell your secretary to keep calling, but, if the man takes any kind of care of himself at all, he is out most all day in the fresh air. So day after day the secretary keeps calling and, in this way, autumn turns into winter and winter to spring. Perhaps you never get him.

A busy executive said to me the other day in an exasperated tone, "Aren't you ever in? I have been trying to get you on the telephone for five days. What do you do with your time, cut lawns?" You see, I am the one who was in the wrong. I was the impractical one.

I might have told him about that new invention called the "typewriter," whereby, if you can't get a man on the telephone, you can drop him a note which will reach him the next morning. Or I also might have told him that I was in my office all the time, but was so busy working that I had left word with the telephone operator not to bother me with time-wasting calls from businessmen. . . .

And so it goes through life. There are the doers and the dreamers, the men who make every second count and the men who waste their time with nothing to show for it. The first are the businessmen of the country, the others are the impractical fellows who write and draw pictures. Or perhaps it is just the other way 'round. I always get these things mixed.

AS OTHERS HAVE SEEN US

GEORGE S. GIBB

[George S. Gibb, "As Others Have Seen Us," *Harvard Business School Bulletin,* Aug. 1958, vol. 34, no. 4, pp. 28–35.]

In these volumes we have given some illustrations to illumine the text. George S. Gibb has published some other views which show how much we could have done had we had more space and more money. At the same time his article provides perspective for those trying to evaluate the growing role of the historians of business and businessmen. Perhaps we shall contribute a bit to knowledge along that very line in *The World of Business!*

WHAT DOES THE AVERAGE AMERICAN think of the businessman? Does he respect him, fear him, envy him, distrust him? In more sophisticated language, what image does the public have of the business executive today—and what has it been in the past?

To get a fix on these questions from a somewhat new angle, let us look at the business manager as the cartoonist has seen him down through the years. Since the caricaturist speaks out so boldly and simply—he has to work in the blackest of blacks and the whitest of whites if he is to get across his message—and talks to and for many people, what he has to say about us should be especially revealing.

Society has the habit of classifying the various members of the community and stamping them into stereotypes. The businessman is not exempted from this general rule; he gets typed, too. These images may or may not be close to the truth, and they are never clear cut. But they do mirror the events and trends of the time, and even influence those trends and events. So the effort to see ourselves as others see us—and have seen us—is more than an exercise in curiosity or hilarity.

Scholars have tried to describe the businessman stereotype as it existed at various times and places and as it was forged into new shapes in the furnace of history. These studies have run into trouble because of the vagueness of the data, the size of the field, and the conflicts of evidence. Consequently, right at the start, let me sharpen my focus.

Who, we should first ask, are these "others" who have seen us, and who is the "us" they have seen? . . . The "us" . . . is the American business leader, whatever his origins, and the "others," as I have said, are that indefinite segment of public opinion represented in the cartoons and caricatures of the newspaper and periodical press.

Business historians have occasionally singled out cartoons to illustrate specific points, but they have not studied the medium in chronological depth to see what it can tell about the evolving public image of the businessman. Of course we do run the risk of overestimating the accuracy of the cartoon as a clue to general public opinion. As a matter of fact, at least one specialist [1] has raised real questions about the value of even the press itself as a gauge of popular sentiment. But keeping in mind all the proper reservations, it still seems clear that over the course of three-quarters of a century American cartoonists have recorded some weighty messages. In fact, the cartoon may have been a better means of mass communication, and hence a more accurate indicator of mass sentiment, than the articles and editorials that surrounded it. Unquestionably, more people saw and understood the cartoons than read and digested the printed pages upon which they appeared.

---

[1] Sigmund Diamond, *The Reputation of the American Businessman,* Harvard University Press, 1955, p. 3.

FIG. 304. Classic Stereotypes Appeared Early. Cartoonists early conjured up the classic images of corpulent creditor and emaciated debtor. Down through the years the garb changed but not the types.

We may go one step further and presumptuously ask whether the caricaturist has not done more to shape the popular image of the American businessman than has the novelist or playwright. The book and the play reach, after all, a small percentage of the public. One wonders whether, even over a period of many years, Norris and Dreiser and Lewis appreciably influenced the *mass* impression of the American businessman. It is true that the situation is being dramatically altered today by the motion picture and television script writer. On the basis of mass exposure alone, it seems entirely likely that movies and TV will take over the place of importance that the cartoonist has held in the past. The process, in fact, seems to be well under way already.

But circulation and exposure are not the whole story. While novelists and playwrights deal with individuals, whom they seek to identify as representative of a broad or intense segment of the human community, the cartoonist works almost by definition with types. His is a one-punch message. He must create a businessman who is immediately recognizable as such. What emerges is a prototype, not an individual who happens, incidentally, to be a businessman. It is this essential simplicity that gives cartoons some measure of value as a clue to the basic public attitude of the time.

A major research job would be needed to answer all the questions raised or to look at the pile of cartoons that have been produced. Has there ever been at any one time a reasonably consistent business-man prototype? How and why has the public image, if any, changed? If recognizable changes have occurred, what do they tell us about business? And finally, what conclusions, if any, can be drawn about the future relationship of business to American society? Since defini-tive answers are beyond the reach of this article, we will have to content ourselves with a probe of the subject and some tentative findings that might serve as the basis for further inquiry.

While we are primarily interested in the American businessman of relatively recent times, it is worth while to glance briefly at the European artist of the eighteenth century. Business was a far less conspicuous part of that era, and communication media were rela-tively restricted, so the caricatures of the early businessman are few in number and concentrated in kind. At one level we find drawings of the noble and diligent man of business, pursuing his calling with

FIG. 305. Dutch Stock Jobber, or Night Singer of Shares, with His Magic Lantern. Before the nineteenth century, caricatures of businessmen tended toward extremes of satire (such as this monstrous eighteenth-century Dutch stock jobber) and sanctimony (see Hogarth's "Idle and Industrious 'Prentice" in Volume III).

all the Christian virtues. This, it seems likely, was supposed to picture the ideal rather than the typical example. The famous seventeenth-century Hogarth drawings of "The Industrious 'Prentice" are good illustrations.*

By and large, however, it was not the routine, constructive efforts of the men of commerce that attracted attention. Instead, the cartoonist's ire was roused by the wild ventures in speculation that periodically shook up the commercial centers of the Western world. It seems unlikely that there was anything remotely approaching a consistent image of a typical businessman in the public mind in those days, though the most common pictures showed avaricious, coarse, unscrupulous stock speculators. Sketches of this type, inspired by financial orgies like the South Sea Bubble, were savage and often obscene. Never since that day has the man of business been so monstrously caricatured, like the old Dutch picture of a stock jobber.

In all fairness, it should be noted that other segments of society were depicted with equally wild satire. Cynicism and revolt were everywhere. The early caricaturists ignored the constructive aspects of business, concentrated their attack on the big operator, focused on the spectacular aberrations, and displayed a consistent contempt for and ignorance of institutions like the stock exchange. They also conjured up the classic images of the corpulent creditor and the emaciated debtor.

Pictorial evidence of how Americans of the early nineteenth century felt about business is scanty. We cannot infer anything from this fact about the popular status of the businessman, for the cartoon had yet to become a common means of communication. It was only after inexpensive techniques of woodcut reproduction had been worked out in the years following the Civil War that mass media began to carry extensive illustrative material. As soon as this happened the businessman became a favorite subject for portraiture.

Artists immediately identified businessmen with the Republican party and high tariffs. In a few instances, like the heart-rending "Workingman's Plight," the picture was favorable, but the overwhelming balance of presentation was bitterly critical. A spate of brilliantly executed, demolishingly satirical tariff cartoons depicted "Capital" as the exploiter of "Labor." The infant-industries argument was a subject for infinite derision. It is hard to believe that this inspired graphic attack did not have great influence upon the public, but there is no real way of telling whether or not this was the case. The important point is that a businessman prototype was emerging, and the image was anything but flattering.

The tariff attack was a pin-prick compared to what followed. The period from about 1890 to 1907 was one of unmitigated castigation.

* See the Hogarth piece in Volume II.

FIG. 306. Tariff Protection Issues Passionately Drawn. Cartoonists, reflecting the spirit of the period, aligned Republicans, big business and protectionism on one side, and Democrats (or Populists), farmers and workers and free trade on the other.

THE FREE-TRADE BUGABOO.

FIG. 307. The Presentation Was Bitterly Critical. Big Business, or the "protection" monopolist, is saying: "Come here, my poor friends—I'll protect you from the monster." (Aside to his Congressional Allies): "Whoop it up, boys; make the jaws go—we've got to keep the workingmen frightened."

FIG. 308. A Peculiar Case of Protracted Infancy.

FIG. 309. The Trusts. A favorite target. In this cartoon by W. A. Rogers, farmer Jonathan, who has just been rooting out foreign thistles, is saying, "I guess this new breed of cattle has got to go next."

"If Willie is a good boy, and minds Papa and Nursie, they w
try to let him keep the pretty house until he is eight years old

FIG. 310. McKinley attacked as a tool of big business by cartoonist
Opper.

FIG. 311. Roped. To the cartoonists in the Age of Rage, Teddy Roosevelt was a sheer delight. His appearance and actions made perfect copy and a splendid vehicle for attacking business.

"WILL YOU PLEASE HUSH?"
From the *Herald* (New York).

FIG. 312. T.R. Has the Answer. Another cartoon by W. A. Rogers.

These were spectacular years in the evolution of American business and they have been intensively studied. The historical explanation is well summarized by Morrell Heald in his article "Management's Responsibility to Society." [2]

It was, Heald says, the "emergence of an economic order based increasingly upon large-scale enterprise with interests which affected an ever-widening circle of citizens." The reaction to this blossoming of big business was profound because neither the nation's legal system, the disposition of the citizenry, nor the ethical code of business leaders themselves were appropriate to the new situation. All the maladjustments of the changing times were echoed in a concerted attack upon the trusts. The awesome product of W. A. Rogers' pen, appearing in *Harpers Weekly* in 1887, is an early example. It was followed by many more.

Then came the climax: Teddy Roosevelt appeared on the scene. Rarely have two such susceptible cartoon subjects as T.R. and "the trusts" appeared simultaneously on the national stage, and the ink-slingers made the most of this heaven-sent opportunity. The result was a caricature that survives in places to this day—the bloated, leering figure of big business, towering above labor, government, small businessmen, and the public and grasping his prizes in omnipotent selfishness. The cartoonists derived inspiration from the muckraking journalists of the Progressive Era and joined hands with their literary brethren to create the popular image of the Robber Barons —"avaricious rascals who habitually cheated . . . robbed . . . corrupted . . . fought." [3]

This graphic attack upon the businessman was somewhat less bawdy than that by the eighteenth-century European caricaturists, but we may hazard a guess that it was infinitely more clever and devastating because of the plausibility of the prototypes and the greater interest of the audience in the message. There were, however, some striking similarities between the earlier attacks and the later. The small businessman once again escaped unscathed. Big Business was the target, and again it was the spectacular episodes and figures that were featured. Again the same prejudice against certain business institutions and functions appeared. In cartoons, as in the literature of the day, stock markets were pictured as scarcely more respectable gambling places than race tracks. Even bull operators, marvelously characterized as "the pied pipers of prosperity," and hence supposedly dear to the expansionist American heart, received harsh treatment. In periods of sharply rising prices the middleman was

[2] Morrell Heald, "Management's Responsibility to Society—the Growth of an Idea," *Business History Review* (Harvard Business School), winter 1957, vol. XXXI, no. 4.

[3] See Hal Bridges, "The Robber Baron Concept in American History," *Business History Review*, spring 1958, vol. XXXII, no. 1.

OLD MEN'S PARADISE

FIG. 313. Rockefeller and Carnegie. By cartoonist Halladay in the *Providence Journal*, December 1914.

" THE AMERICAN BEAUTY ROSE CAN BE PRODUCED IN ALL ITS SPLENDOR ONLY BY SACRIFICING THE EARLY BUDS THAT GROW UP AROUND IT." — John D. Rockefeller, Jr.

FIG. 314. Father's Picture; Son's Words. At a time when the monopolistic practices of Standard Oil Company were being violently attacked, John D. Rockefeller, *Jr.*, casually—but unfortunately—drew an analogy, in a speech before the Brown University YMCA, between business consolidation and the process of developing a rose by pruning. The press lost no time in lifting this figure of speech from its context. Cartoon by Spencer, 1905.

SANCTUS JAY-GOULDUS.

Fɪɢ. 315. The Caricaturist and . . . Jay Gould.

THE ELEVATED CYRUS FIELD.

FIG. 316. . . . Cyrus Field.

bitterly assailed, with characteristic disregard for the constructive services he performed. The government and its pertinent agencies were attacked when they failed to oppose business interests and lauded when they did so.

Yet, as might be expected, the excesses of this period of deprecation began to invoke reactions. Some of these were negative, apparently inspired more by dislike for Teddy Roosevelt than by sympathy for the businessman. In other instances, the leaders of business were characterized as hapless, cringing victims of the Federal

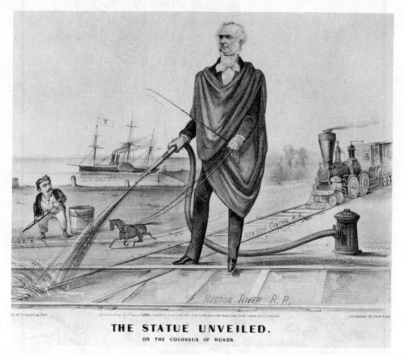

THE STATUE UNVEILED.
OR THE COLOSSUS OF ROADS.

FIG. 317. . . . Cornelius Vanderbilt and James Fiske Watering Stock.

Trade Commission monster. These exceptions to the popular prototype were not numerous, but they may have foreshadowed a softening of attitude that became noticeable here and there in the cartoonery of the second decade of the new century.

It was, however, the extracurricular activities of America's business elite that attracted the first favorable notices. Carnegie and Hill were both pictured in a favorable light as a result of their benefactions and social dogmas. Even Rockefeller, enjoying the worst press of any businessman since the days of Jim Fisk and Daniel Drew, received a congenial nod or two. The Supreme Court's decision upholding the

"PIGS IS PIGS"

FIG. 318. The whimsical "Pigs Is Pigs" cartoon (1911). This was generated by the Supreme Court's decision upholding the dissolution of Standard Oil.

dissolution of Standard Oil inspired pictures of a dismembered octopus that were reminiscent, in tone, of the preceding decade, but this same event also generated whimsical and not entirely unfavorable reactions like the famous "Pigs Is Pigs" cartoon of 1911.

More interesting still, the caricaturists gave evidence of a deeper insight into significant operational issues. A case in point is the "Better Management" cartoon inspired by the railroad rate case hearings of 1911 that first focused wide public attention on Frederick Taylor and scientific management. Indignation, it appears, was beginning to be tempered by understanding and even by sporadic sympathy. The unflattering popular image persisted, but it was no longer as clear cut as it had been in the early years of the century. Effective government control of the abuses of big business was making the old prototype increasingly implausible. It remained to be seen whether and when a new popular image would emerge.

FIG. 319. Uncle Sam's Dictum to the Railroads: "If you'll properly utilize the better management fuel, you'll not need to ask for the other." The Interstate Commerce Commission decided against an increase of freight rates by the railroads.

In the months following America's entry into World War I, the American businessman abandoned his role of public villain. He never quite became a hero, however. The caricaturists accorded him nominal recognition as a constructive part of the war effort and occasionally chided him for profiteering, but for the most part the phenomenally productive American business system seems to have been regarded as poor copy. Ironically enough, the achievements themselves elicited an inspired reaction, but they were commonly ascribed to a comparatively new symbol, "Uncle Sam," or to an older one, "Labor."

In the Republican, pro-business decade of the 1920s the earlier popular visualization of the typical businessman disintegrated still further. There was no single popular prototype. The businessman was on occasion a "good guy," credited with giving America a new way of life, or a "bad guy," charged with manipulating high prices. The basic normalcy of the times discouraged excessive reactions and promoted neglect. From the viewpoint of the businessman, still entertaining the illusion that his business was a private affair, this undoubtedly was a relief. Intermittently, of course, he was stung by the savage attacks of left-wing spokesmen like Robert Minor of the New York *Call*.

FIG. 320. Radicalism Was Never Absent. The occasion of the Bayonne Refinery strike in 1915 brought this response—probably one of the most vicious cartoons ever printed—in the capitalist-baiting *New York Call*.

Minor's cartoon, inspired by the 1915 strike at Jersey Standard's Bayonne refinery, must be ranked among the most vicious ever drawn. Such malicious and palpably false representations probably had a restricted impact and certainly failed to create a new businessman prototype. It remained for larger events to put an end to the hazy interlude of broad neglect, grudging approbation, and sporadic censure. That event was the '29 crash and the ensuing great depression.

Historical precedent indicated that after October 29, 1929, the American businessman should once again be cast in his familiar role of villain. Historians of the period, utilizing personal observation and voluminous printed evidence, tell us that this was indeed the case. Strangely enough, the cartoons of the day seemingly fail to confirm this contention in any decisive way. We should like to inquire why this was so, but for present purposes just raising the question is enough.

The businessman was commonly depicted as a bewildered victim of cosmic forces, rather than as an engineer of destruction. Soglow's cryptic picture is typical. There was, in addition, an inspirational flurry, occasioned by the N.R.A., that placed the businessman (still, let it be noted, corpulent and silk-hatted) at Uncle Sam's shoulder. Aside from this, the 1930s elicited mild pity, pronounced despair, grim humor, and an element of wry cynicism. Had the caricaturists of the age, sensitive to the marketability of their art, sensed that Americans no longer feared their business leaders? Or were the artists, like the businessmen themselves, simply bewildered?

Any attempt to set precise chronological brackets around historical epochs is bound to create trouble. Actually, there are no clear-cut division points between the phases of cartoon representation we have described. The era of the Big Spoof was foreshadowed in the 1920s —Gluyas Williams' classic masterpiece in a 1928 *New Yorker* being representative of what was to come. World War II interjected a temporary distraction, but even at the height of the war fever American caricaturists were handling the businessman with a lighter touch than ever before. After the war, the businessman prototype disintegrated completely into a series of impressions, mostly touched with humor. Displaying a perceptiveness that had been totally lacking a generation earlier, cartoonists ranged the field of business operations. Nothing was sacred. Gluyas Williams and P. Barlow created types that made businessmen wince, but not from fear. Automation, data processing, and communications became the objects of cheerful derision. The Boston *Herald*'s Dahl delightfully focused attention upon regional variances in businessman types.

Behind the hilarity lay some significant facts and issues. For the first time in the nation's history, the small businessman became topical. Invariably, as with Denys Wortman's sharp-trading but philo-

INDUSTRIAL CRISES

The day a cake of soap sank at Procter & Gamble's

FIG. 321. Gluyas Williams and the Glorious Spoof. From *The New Yorker*. Drawing by Gluyas Williams; copyright © 1928 by The New Yorker Magazine, Inc.

sophical garment district character, the treatment was sympathetic. The real point is not, however, the attitude but the fact that caricaturists had at last discovered that all business was not big business.

They also discovered the Harvard Business School, and pinpointed, with heavy-handed humor, the issues of industrial influence upon the educational system and the difficulties of academic preparation for the world of business. But, whether the issues were great or small, the treatment was most often light. Serious censure was not lacking, but it was balanced by considered approbation. This is where we are today, and we may well ask how we got here and where we may be tomorrow.

In the cartoon cavalcade of American history one can see a long-term trend from a stiff, clear-cut, and decidedly unfavorable image of the businessman to a flexible, many-faceted, discriminating, and basically sympathetic picture. The historian might well explain this trend as a manifestation of a social and economic maturity that brought with it effective curbs upon flagrant abuses of all kinds and has taught every class in society not only the necessity for getting along with the others, but also a great deal about how to do so. Certainly, as business came under regulation and learned that it must adopt new criteria of social responsibility, the public fear of business abated and the old avaricious stereotype became obsolete.

There is, however, more to the explanation than this. Kenneth Lynn, reporting on the businessman in fiction, tells us that "no writer has ever succeeded in conveying in a literary work of art what goes on in the daily lives of millions of Americans." [4] Similarly, Glover in *The Attack on Big Business* states that "Our libraries contain more concrete, clinical detail on distant primitive tribes . . . than on the corporations in our midst." [5] No historian can quarrel with these contentions. At the same time, however, noteworthy progress along these lines has been made. The "discontented professoriat" typified by Vernon Parrington and Charles A. Beard knew little of business except what was disclosed by government investigations of the more sensational and sordid events.[6] This is no longer the case. The archives of American business have been opened to scholars. The results of their investigations are spreading throughout the academic and literary world. This is a crucial area for business to be known, because it is here that the great attacks of the past have had their origins.

Notwithstanding the deficiencies of such studies, we may hazard a guess that the efforts of historians have already contributed to better understanding of the business community and will continue to do so at an accelerating pace. Understanding of the businessman and his methods and motives is also growing at the public level. The additional efforts of business itself to present its case have been noteworthy. The old defensive attitude has been entirely superseded by a constructive, aggressive program of merchandising the American business system. Despite many errors and setbacks, public relations activities and institutional advertising have unquestionably had a major impact upon the public climate. This movement has been supported by relatively few companies, but the entire business world has benefited.

[4] Kenneth S. Lynn, "Authors in Search of the Businessman," *Harvard Business Review*, Sept.–Oct. 1956, vol. 34, no. 5, p. 124.

[5] John D. Glover, "The Attack on Big Business" (Division of Research, Harvard Business School, 1954), p. 290.

[6] Bridges, *op. cit.*, pp. 3 and 4.

The great fear is that somewhere in the not-too-distant future lies a major depression and a new era of hostility that will recreate the old unhappy villain prototype. This is unlikely. To anyone who has surveyed the course of history it becomes obvious that the American businessman has become identified with the well-being of American society as a whole. This circumstance is not a product of transient prosperity, but has its origins in a better understanding of the role of business in the world in which we live. Serious students of the economy should find no cause for mirth or censure in Charles E. Wilson's famous contention that what is good for General Motors is good for the country. We cannot be far wrong in concluding, with Glover, that business, big or small, is not "necessarily at odds with democracy or with a society which is *tolerably good,* even if it is far from perfect." [7]

[7] Glover, *op. cit.,* p. 287.

RESULTS OF THE VOTE BY BUSINESS EXECUTIVES ON THE SELECTION OF A CANDIDATE TO BECOME PRESIDENT OF WICKERSHAM MILLS, AS DESCRIBED BY ABRAM COLLIER, PAGE 2473 IN THIS VOLUME.

Alfred Wickersham	20%
Benjamin Hall	22%
Charles Hall	10%
David Wickersham, Jr.	48%

Epilogue

THE MANAGERS

W. H. AUDEN

[W. H. Auden, "The Managers," *The Reporter*, May 10, 1949, vol. I, no. 2, p. 18. Copyright 1949 by W. H. Auden. Reprinted from *Nones* by W. H. Auden, by permission of Random House, Inc.]

In this probing and somehow disturbing poem—disturbing because of its sense of uneasy change, of loss of connection with the simple basics of life—W. H. Auden describes the new breed of managers. They are more dedicated, more impersonal, more powerful, than the old, as he sees them.

Of course, it is not altogether clear whether he is talking about the managers of business or the managers of government. But it hardly matters, since today government itself is big business and must be run that way; whereas business has become so important, in contract work for the government as well as in so many other activities, that it affects the lives of all peoples across the world.

Written in 1949, this is a challenge for the second half of our twentieth century and for the rest of the years that lie ahead waiting for man to fill them with his busy dreaming and his busy doing.

In the bad old days it was not so bad:
    The top of the ladder
Was an amusing place to sit; success
    Meant quite a lot—leisure
And huge meals, more palaces filled with more
    Objects, girls and horses
Than one would ever get round to, and to be
    Carried uphill while seeing
Others walk. To rule was a pleasure when
    One wrote a death-sentence
On the back of the Ace of Spades and played on
    With a new deck. Honors
Are not so physical or jolly now,

For the sort of Powers
We are used to are not like that. Could one of them
    Be said to resemble
The Tragic Hero, the Platonic Saint,
    Or would any painter
Portray one rising triumphant from a lake
    On a dolphin, naked,
Protected by an umbrella of cherubs? Can
    They so much as manage
To behave like genuine Caesars when alone
    Or drinking with cronies,
To let their hair down and be frank about
    The world? It is doubtful.
The last word on how we may live or die
    Rests today with quiet
Men, working too hard in rooms that are too big,
    Reducing to figures
What is the matter, what is to be done.
    A neat little luncheon
Of sandwiches is brought to each on a tray,
    Nourishment they are able
To take with one hand without looking up
    From papers; a couple
Of secretaries are needed to file,
    From problems no smiling
Can dismiss; the typewriters never stop
    But whirr like grasshoppers
In the silent siesta heat as, frivolous
    Across their discussions,
Out of woods unaltered by our wars and vows
    Drift the scents of flowers
And the songs of birds who will never vote
    Or bother to notice
Those distinguishing marks a lover sees
    By instinct, and policemen
Can be trained to observe; far into the night
    Their windows burn brightly,
And behind, their backs bent over some report
    On every quarter
For ever like a god or a disease
    There on the earth, the reason
In all its aspects why they are tired, the weak,
    The inattentive, seeking
Someone to blame; then if, to recuperate,
    They go a-playing, their greatness

Encounters the bow of the chef or the glance
    Of the ballet-dancer
Who cannot be ruined by any master's fall.
    To rule must be a calling,
It seems, like surgery or sculpture, the fun
    Neither love nor money
But taking a necessary risk, the test
    Of one's skill, the question,
If difficult, their own reward. But then
    Perhaps one should mention
Also what must be a comfort as they guess
    In times like the present
When guesses can prove so fatally wrong,
    The fact of belonging
To the very select indeed, to those
    For whom, just supposing
They do, there will be places on the last
    Plane out of disaster.
No; no one is really sorry for their
    Heavy gait and careworn
Look, nor would they thank you if you said you were.

SOURCES OF ILLUSTRATIONS
Volume IV

~⚬~

275–291. Photographs of Jost Amman's print, *"Aigentliche Abbildung dess Gantzen Gewerbs der Kaufmannschaft."* Gift of Philip Hofer to the Kress Library, Harvard University, Graduate School of Business Administration.

292. Photograph of the broadside, "A Proclamation Concernynge Bouchers," 1535. Kress Library.

293. Title page, N. H., *The Pleasant Art of Money-Catching.* J. Dunton, London, 1684. Kress Library.

294. Frontispiece, *The Pleasant Art of Money Catching . . . To Which Is Added, The Way How to Turn a Penny: or, The Art of Thriving,* 3rd edition. J. Lever, London, 1782. Kress Library.

295. From *Old Colony Newsletter,* April 1929 (Vol. XIII, No. 3, p. 14), which credits *Gleason's Pictorial.* Except for the picture of Franklin, this illustration has a striking resemblance to a double-paneled N. Currier print, the left panel of which is the source for the "interpretation" of the rebus.

296. From an 1875 Currier and Ives print reproduced in *American Heritage,* June 1957, p. 53.

297. From *Harper's Weekly,* July 3, 1869, p. 249. Harvard College Library.

298. Frontispiece, Charles Babbage, *Passages from the Life of a Philosopher,* Longman, Green, Longman, Roberts, & Green, London, 1864.

299. J. Keppler, "The Bosses of the Senate," *Puck,* Keppler & Schwarzmann, Publishers, N.Y., Jan. 23, 1889. Vol. XXIV, No. 620, pp. 362–363. Courtesy of the Boston Public Library.

300–303. Abram T. Collier, "Debate at Wickersham Mills," *Harvard Business Review,* May–June 1960.

304. An undated print by W. W. Chenery, published by M. I. Sheahan, Boston. Picture Collection, Manuscript Division, Baker Library, Harvard Graduate School of Business Administration.

305. From a plate in *Het Groote Tafereel der Dwaasheid,* Amsterdam, 1722. Kress Library.

306. An 1884 campaign poster. Picture Collection, Manuscript Division, Baker Library.

307. From a cartoon by C. Jay Taylor in *Puck,* May 5, 1886, reprinted in *The Tariff? Cartoons and Comments from Puck,* Keppler

& Schwarzmann, New York, 1888. Aldrich Collection, Baker Library.

308. Same as 307.

309. A cartoon by W. A. Rogers in *Harper's Weekly,* December 3, 1887. Harvard College Library.

310. A cartoon by F. Opper. New York *Evening Journal,* 1901.

311. A cartoon by Morris in the Spokane *Spokesman-Review,* 1908.

312. By W. A. Rogers, from the New York *Herald,* 1908.

313. By Halladay, from the Providence *Journal,* December 1914.

314. From *Literary Digest,* May 6, 1905, p. 654, credited to Spencer in *The Commoner.*

315. From the Picture Collection, Manuscript Division, Baker Library.

316. From *The Hour* (Cartoon Supplement), New York, June 5, 1880.

317. A copy of "The Statue Unveiled, or the Colossus of Roads," a lithograph published by Currier and Ives, 1869. William B. Osgood Field Collection, Houghton Library, Harvard University.

318. From a cartoon in the St. Louis *Post-Dispatch,* September 1911.

319. From a cartoon in the Utica *Saturday Globe,* 1911.

320. From a cartoon in the New York *Call,* July 24, 1915.

321. From a cartoon in *The New Yorker,* August 18, 1928. With permission of Gluyas Williams and *The New Yorker.*

INDEX

⌒⌒

NOTE TO INDEX: A word of explanation is in order. The first three volumes of *The World of Business* have, each, their individual indexes; the index here presented is the comprehensive one for all four volumes. Page numbers in *italics* following an author's name indicate a selection by which he is represented in the book. All other page references are in roman type. For the reader's convenience, the page numbers for each volume are listed at the bottom of each index page.

Abdera, Greece, 678
Acamapichtli, King, 194
Accounting Principles—Cases and Reports (Hosmer), 69
Adams, John, 725–26
Adams, William T., 1857
Adding Machine, The (Rice), 1500–05
Addison, Joseph, 25, *378–81*, 1603; *quoted, 3*
Adlum, Mr., 1115, 1116
"Administrator's Prayer, An" (Katz), 2255–56
Advertising Age, 495
Advertising Guide, The (Sears, Roebuck), 325–27
A.E.F.G. Consortium, 40
Aeschylus, 167
Aetna Insurance Company, 1004, 1005
Affluent Society, The (Galbraith), 633–36
After All (Day), 1493
Age of Fable or Beauties of Mythology (Bulfinch), 181
Age of Jackson (Schlesinger), 732
Age of Revolution, The (Churchill), 1529
Ahuítzotl, King, 202, 207, 208, 211
Airplane flight, the first, 1281–85
Aislabie, Mr., 824, 825, 968
Albertson, Dean, 457
Alcantara, Jacinto, 562–63
Alcinous, King, 165

Alden, Robert, 433
Aldworth, Robert, 1294, 1295, 1297
Aldworth, Thomas, 1294, 1297
Alexander III, of Scotland, 2282
Alexander III, Pope, 687, 688
Alexander, William, *1014–15*
Alexanderson, Ernst F. W., 38
Alexander the Great, 14, 581
Alexandria, Egypt, 171, 180, 581, 679, 686, 688
"Alfred of the Advertisements" (Leacock), 466–69
Alger, Horatio, Jr., 1855–62, *1862–73*
Allen, Frederick Lewis, 890, *895–933, 1855–62*
Almy, William, 1082
America as a Civilization (Lerner), 2099
American advertisements (*illus.*), 400–17
"American Advertising" (Boyce), 381–82, 384
American Austin Company, 1574
American Ballads and Folk Songs (Lomax and Lomax), 2537
"American Capitalism: Trial Balance" (Lerner), 2099–2107
American Collins Line, 1243–44
American Commonwealth, The (Bryce), 867–74
"American Constitution, The" (Churchill), 1529–33
"American Economic System, The" (Potter), 2033–45

VOL. I, pp. 1–674; VOL. II, pp. 675–1286; VOL. III, pp. 1287–1934; VOL. IV, pp. 1935–2624.

[2627]

American Federation of Labor, 1373, 1572
American Heritage, 418, 456, 732, 1070, 1076, 1105, 1132, 1144, 1235, 1554, 1819
American Individualism (Hoover), 1565
American Life Insurance and Trust Company, 1006
American Museum, 389, 390, 392, 393, 394
American Railways (Pratt), 1247–60
American Social Science Association, 2327
American Stock Exchange (Curb Exchange), 941, 942–43
American Telephone & Telegraph Co., 39
American Tobacco Company, 459–66
America's Next Twenty Years (Drucker), 1513
Ames, Fisher, 25, 723, 724, 727
Amman, Jost, 1954–72
Amsterdam, Holland, 689, 709, 794–95, 797
Amsterdam Stock Exchange (*illus.*), 795
Anasuyabai, Shrimati, 1439, 1441, 1442
Anaxagoras, 171
Anaximander of Miletus, 171
Ancient Double-Entry Bookkeeping (Pacioli), 89–115
Anderson, Adam, 1960
And Mark an Era (Copeland), 1555–57
Angier, J. D., 1120, 1122
Angle, Paul M., 1156n.
Anglia Judaica, 1034
Annals of Tacitus, The, 2273–75
"Another Lie Nailed Up" (Brown), 2517–19
Another Time (Auden), 1743
Aphrodite, 172
Apology for the Business of Pawn-Broking, 1058–67
Appel, Joseph H., *1884–93*
"Application of Thomas Marshall to Hamilton . . ." (Marshall), 1095–97
Aquinas, St. Thomas, 6, 14, 2114, *2119–25,* 2127–28, 2132
Archimedes, 583
Aristophanes, *2495–2502*
Aristophanes in English Verse (Way, tr.), 2495

Aristotle, 6, *14–21,* 121, 176, 1026, 1506, *1944–48,* 2120–21; *quoted,* 1937
Arkwright, Sir Richard, 1076, 1077, 1078, 1096, 1539
Armenian merchant, 17th century (*illus.*), 244
Armour, Philip D., 1875, 1876–83
Armour & Company, 33, 1879
Arnold, Benedict, 2395
Arnold, Horace Lucien, 1201n.
Arnold, Julian, 1507n.
Arnold, S. G., *2293–96*
Arsinoë, Egypt, 679
Artaxerxes I, 70
Artzybasheff, Boris, *painting by,* 1443
Asgill, John, 699
Ashurbânapal, 70
"As Others Have Seen Us" (Gibb), 2599–2620
Aspasia, 170
Aspinwall, William H., 1008
Assur, 162
Astor, John Jacob, 735
Athenaeus, 169
Athens and the Athenians, 168, 179, 353
Atkinson, Fred, 609
Atlantic Monthly, The, 1545, 2445
Atwood, Luther, 1123
Auden, W. H., *1743–44, 2621–23*
Augustine, St., 2120
Augustus, Emperor, 2266–73
Aunoy, Countess d', *quoted,* 5
Aurelius, Marcus, *quoted,* 566
Autobiography (Barnum), 579–80
Autobiography of Andrew Carnegie, 1182–85
Autobiography of Benjamin Franklin, 1802–18, 2173–74
Automation and Management, 1199–1207
Ayer Advertising, 491
Ayers, Leonard P., 920
Ayres, Thomas N., 1011
Aziere, Charles B., *2249–51*
Azpilcueta, Martin, 2132

Babbage, Charles, *2301–12*
"Babbage's Calculating Engine" (*illus.*), 2307
Babbitt (Lewis), *2555–61*
Babson, Roger W., 919
Babylon and the Babylonians, 9, 64–66, 67, 69–74, 75, 161, 164, 351–52, 677–78, 685

Babylonian Talmud, The, 2114, 2116

Bachelder, J., 1825

Backwell, Edward, 793

Bacon, Francis, 517–18, 1052–55; *quoted,* 4, 1599, 2257

Bacon, Robert, 1265, 1268

Bacon's Essays, 517–18, 1052

Bagehot, Walter, *749–56,* 767; *quoted,* 1289

Bainbridge, John, *528–38, 977–90*

Baker, George F., 863, 910, 1263, 1624

Baker, George F., Jr., 924

"Baker's Portrait, The," 360–62

Balchin, Nigel, *1400–02, 1719–22; quoted,* 6

Baltimore Evening Sun, 1920

Baltimore Life Insurance Company, 1004, 1006

Bank Act (1717), 809

"Bank Advertisements: Ancient and Modern," 681–82

"Bankers Are Just Like Anybody Else, Except Richer" (Nash), 765–66

Bankers' Magazine and State Financial Register, 745

Bankers' Magazine and Statistical Register, 1541, 1600

"Banking in Antiquity," 677–80

Banking Through the Ages (Hoggson), 787

Bank loan, oldest recorded, 677–80

Bank notes, 794

Banko, John, 2283

Bank of Amsterdam, 690, 696

Bank of England, 691, 712, 719, 721, 725, 729, 730–31, 749, 756, 772, 776–77, 809, 810, 820, 821; founding of, 694–708

Bank of England, 1694–1797 (Clapham), 694–708

Bank of England Act, 730–31

Bank of Genoa, 688, 700

Bank of Gloucester (Mass.), 731

Bank of Hamburg, 696

Bank of Ireland, 730

Bank of Maryland, 730

Bank of Massachusetts, 729, 730

Bank of North America, 716, 719, 722, 724, 730, 731

Bank of St. George, 688

Bank of Scotland, 699, 730

Bank of Sweden, 696

Bankrupt, meaning of, 692

Banks and Politics in America (Hammond), 711, 730–32

Barbon, Nicholas, 699, 700, 978–81

Barclays Bank, 705

"Bargaining by Pantomime—Trade in Camels," 310–11

Barker, J. M., *2251–52*

Barlow, P., 2617

Barnard, Chester I., *2068–74,* 2075

Barnard, Henry, 1607–08

Barnum, Phineas Taylor, 292, 311, 386–95, *579–80*

Barnum & Bailey's Circus, 393

"Barriers and Gateways to Communication" (Rogers and Roethlisberger), 1402–13

Barron, W. G., 772

Bart, Jean, 647

Barton, Bernard, 1603

Baruch, Bernard M., 807–08, *884–90, 2357–65*

Baruch: My Own Story (Baruch), 884–90, 2357–65

Barzun, Jacques, *652–73*

Bassus, Ventidius, 174–75

Bastiat, Frédéric, *2296–2301*

Bates, Charles Austin, 458

Bates & Company, Ted, 487, 491, 496

Bathe, Greville and Dorothy, 1098n., 1988

Batten, Barton, Durstine & Osborn, 487, 491

Battle Creek (Mich.) Sanitarium, 420, 421

Bauer, Raymond A., *642–52, 1185–99*

Baxter, Richard, 2133

Beadle, Walter J., 1731, 1732

Beard, Charles A., and Mary, *quoted,* 32

Beard, Miriam, *159–80; quoted,* 21–28

Beaton, Donald, 947

Beaumont, Texas, 1133, 1136, 1137, 1139, 1140, 1142, 1144

Beauties of Commerce, The (ibn 'Ali al-Dimishqi), 184

Beawes, Wyndham, *2390–92*

Bechtel, W. A., 1926

Beck, Theodore, *quoted,* 1199

Bedford, Alfred C., 2361

Belden, Nick, 1155

Bell, G. M., *1600–04*

Bell, J. S., 608, 617

Bell, James Ford, 609, 617

Belmont, August, 866, 885, 887–88
"Belongingness" (Whyte), 1756–66
Bemelmans, Ludwig, 1873–74
Benchley, Robert, 2596–99
Benedict XIV, Pope, 1057
Benjamin of Tudela, 1649
Bentley, John, 1150
Benton & Bowles, 487, 491
Berle, Adolph A., Jr., 1773–76, 2255
Berliner, Joseph S., 1766–72, 1930–32
Bernard, John, 284
Bernardino of Siena, San, 2128, 2132
Bethlehem Steel Company, 1384
"Better Reports for Better Control" (McLean), 136–54
Bevan, Aneurin, 2089
Bible, the, quoted, 4, 5, 157–59, 680–81, 1023, 1223, 1643–44, 1938, 2108, 2113, 2263–66
Biddle, Nicholas, 739–41, 745–46, 2036
Big Business, A New Era (Lilienthal), 502
Billings, Josh, 288
"Billsticker, The" (Sampson), 382–83
Biography of an Idea (Bainbridge), 977–90
Birdseye, Clarence, 508
Birth of the Oil Industry, The (Giddens), 119–32, 1271–80
Bissell, George H., 1121, 1122–23, 1124, 1125, 1126, 1128, 1129, 1131–32
Bissell, M. R., 435
Bissell Carpet Sweeper Company, 435–40
Black Friday (1869), 859
Blackstone, William, 1033
Blackwell, Alderman, 698, 699, 704
Blake, William, 1447, 1512n.
Bliss, C. N., 889
Blot, M. Pierre, 419
Blunt, Sir John, 812, 816, 823, 825
Blunt, Joseph, 1008, 1010
Body and Raiment (Tietjens), 1485–87
Boileau, Étienne, 1660
Bolin, Charles D., 429
Bonneville Dam, 1927
"Book of the Machine" (Butler), 1450–55
"Books for Businessmen" (Campbell), 2160–62
Boorman, James, 1008
Borgia, Caesar, 1649
Bosanquet, Bernard, 1603

"Bosses of the Senate, The" (illus.), 2350
Boston Conference on Distribution, 1574
Boston News-Letter, 1803
Boston Sunday Herald, 1374
Botsford, Harry, 1271
Boulder Dam, 1925, 1926–27
Boulding, Kenneth E., 2085, 2200–12
Bowden, Muriel, 230–36
Bowditch, E. B., 1131, 1132
Bowes, Sir Martin, 793
Boyce, Howard H., 381–82, 384
Boyce, L. Fred, Jr., 116–19
Boyer, Isabella, 1834, 1836
Bracken, H., quoted, 5
Bradford, Andrew, 1806, 1807, 1817
Brady, Anthony N., 889, 890
Bramah, Joseph, 1112
Brandeis, Louis D., 1559, 1611–16, 1775; quoted, 1599–1600
Brandini, Ciuto, 2137
Bransby, Edward, 974
Brave New World (Huxley), 1214–23
Breasted, James H., 2252
Brevoort, Henry, 1008
Brewer, Ebenezer, 1126
Brewer, Francis Beattie, 1120, 1121, 1122–23, 1124, 1126, 1127
Bright, James R., 154n., 1199–1207
Brinner, Caspar, 1955
Briscoe, John, 699
Bristol, Lee H., 2240
British East India Company, 821, 838
British Linen Company, 730
Broadway Stages (illus.), 1227
Brooks, John, 766–77
Brown, 2517–19
Brown, Moses, 1079–82, 1084–85, 1087; (illus.), 1081
Brown, Smith, 1082
Browne, John, 1293–1311
Browne, Waldo R., 386
Brunel, Marc, 1112, 1200
Bryan, William Jennings, 2037, 2359
Bryce, James, 867–74
Bryson, Lyman, 1445–46
Buderus, 834
Budge, Henry, 861
"Budget Comes of Age, The" (Peirce), 122–36
Bulfinch, Thomas, 181–82
Bull, Benjamin, 608–09
Bullard, William H. G., 38, 39, 40
Bulletin of the Business Historical Society Incorporated, 522–24, 682,

992, 1790, 1800, 1884, 2392, 2521
Bullion, introduction of, 745
Bullis, Harry A., 2240
Bull market, the big, 895–933
Bullock, Charles J., 681
Bunyan, John, *quoted,* 5
Bunzaemon, Kinokuni, 1799
Burgers, Abraham, 522–24
Burke, Edmund, 1539, 2396
Burlingame, Roger, *1679–83*
Burn, James Dawson, *397–98*
Burnett, Leo, 491
Burnham, James, *1712–19*
Bursk, Edward C., *541–61, 2443–44*
"Business" (Dunsany), 2590–96
Business Adrift (Donham), 2045
"Business—a Profession" (Brandeis), 1611–16
"Business Career of Jay Cooke" (Larson and Gras), 851–66
Business definitions, 3–8
Business Documents of Murashû Sons of Nippur Dated in the Reign of Artaxerxes I (464–424 B.C.), 69
Business Documents of Murashû Sons of Nippur Dated in the Reign of Darius II (424–404 B.C.), 69
Business History Foundation, 1683
Business History Review, 499, 711
"Business Leadership and a Creative Society" (Collier), 2074–90
"Business Man in American Folklore, The" (Porter), 2521–37
"Businessmen as Legislators," 2341–45
"Business of Business, The" (Ruml), 7–8
Business Week, 1570–74
Business without Boundary—The Story of General Mills (Gray), 607
Butcher's shop *(illus.),* 246
Butler, Samuel, *1450–55*
Butterfield, Roger, 2350
Byrd, Will "Peck," 1133, 1137, 1138

Caesar, Julius, 165, 174
Caesar, M. Philip, *quoted,* 1023
Cajetan, Cardinal, 2128
Calkins, Earnest Elmo, *quoted,* 30
Calls, Sounds and Merchandise of the Peking Street Peddlers, 366–68
Calvin, John, *2138–39*
Cambio, Domenico di, 85, 86, 88
Cambreleng, Churchill C., 735
Cambria Iron Company, 1384

"Campers at Kitty Hawk, The" (Dos Passos), 1281–85
Campbell, Donald B., *2160–62*
Candler, Asa Griggs, 346–48
Candler, Asa Griggs, Jr., 347
Candler, Charles Howard, 347, 348
Canterbury Tales (Chaucer), 230–36, 1778
Cantillon, Richard, 1056
Čapek, Karel, 1208, *1455–85*
"Capitalism" (Mencken), 2065–68
Carey, Cornthwait, 997
Carey, Ernestine Gilbreth, *1180–82*
"Cargoes" (Masefield), 180–81
Carlova, John, *1144–55*
Carlsbad, *2185*
Carnegie, Andrew, *1182–85,* 1370, *1375–90,* 1559, *2413–24; (illus.),* 2609
Carnegie Steel Company, 1381, 1383
Carlyle, Thomas, *quoted,* 5
Carpenter, Ruth Haynes, 614
Carpenter, Walter S., Jr., 1726
Carson, Gerald, *277–96, 311–15, 418–33*
Carter, Henry W., 299–300
Carthage and the Carthaginians, 166, 176–78, 179, 180, 353
Cary, Charles A., 1731, 1732
Casebook in American Business History (Larson and Gras), 851–66, 1363, 1884, 2162
Catchings, Waddill, 910
Catherine II, of Russia, *2183–84*
Cato the Elder, 180, 2261
Caxton, William, *363–64*
Century of American Life Insurance (Clough), 1001–13
Chadwick, Florence, 337
Chaloner, Sir Thomas, 1648
Chamberlen, Hugh, 699, 700
Chandler, Lester V., 733
Chapman, E. G., 773–74
Charlemagne, 1032
Charles I, of England, 690
Charles II, of England, 690, 699
Charles V, Emperor, 1680
Charles IX, of France, 2263
Chase, Salmon P., 853
Chase, Stuart, *2055–65,* 2084
Chastellux, François Jean de, 1108
Chaucer, Geoffrey, *230–36,* 1778–84
Chaucer, John, 1779, 1781, 1782, 1783
Chaucer, Richard, 1779

"Chaucer's Shipman and the Wine" (Stobie), 1290–92
Cheaper by the Dozen (Gilbreth and Carey), 1180
Cheney, O. H., 1574
Chen Huan-chang, 1448–52, 1953
Chesterton, Gilbert K., 1562–64
Cheuo-Ly, 62
"Chicago" (Sandburg), 28–29
Chicago, Burlington & Quincy Railroad, 1262, 1263, 1264, 1270
Chicago, Illinois, 28–29, 33–34
Chicago, Milwaukee & St. Paul Railroad, 1263
China and the Chinese, 221–22, 366–68, 1448–52, 1933–54, 2279–80
Chin-gui, China, 226
"Choice Russian Proverbs" (Catherine II and Prutkov), 2183–84
Chronicle of Joceline de Brakelond, 1031, 1033
Chrysostom, St., 2121
Churchill, Winston, 1529–33, 1594, 2075, 2364–65
Chute, Marchette, 1778–84
Cicero, Marcus Tullius, 78–80, 171, 686, 1526, 1527–28, 2262
Cigarmakers' Local Union No. 15, 1372
Cigarmakers' Society of England, 1368, 1371
Cincinnatus, 180
"Civilizations of the East and the West" (Hu Shih), 1505–10
Civil Law, The (Scott, ed.), 2277
Clapham, Sir John, 694–708
Clark, Donald T., 1954–72
Clark, E. C., 1277
Clark, Edward, 1819–21, 1828–37
Clark, George A., 397
Clark, John M., 2134
Clark & Company, Enos W., 852, 853
"Clark's Spool Cotton" (Munson), 395–97
Classic Stereotypes Appeared Early (illus.), 2601
Clay, A. T., 69
Clerk, Thomas, 1313–37
Clipper ships, 1235–44
Cloth merchant (illus.), 243
Clough, Shepard B., 1001–13
"Clovis on the Alleged Romance of Business" (Saki), 1921–22
Coates, James, 985
"Cobbler, The" (Herondas), 514–17
Cobbler's shop (illus.), 246

Coca-Cola, 334–48
Cochran-Patrick, R. W., 2280–85
Code Napoléon, 1057
Code of Hammurabi, 9–10, 64
Code of Justinian, The, 2277–79
Code of Maimonides, The, 1029–30, 2114–16
Coeur, Jacques, 23
Cohen, Fischel, 2359
Cohn, David L., 315–33
Cole, Arthur H., 1642
Coleman, William, 987, 1183, 1185, 1814
Collier, Abram T., 2074–90, 2473–93
Collins, Joseph B., 1008
Colturi, Philip, 534
Columbia Broadcasting Company, 504, 615
Columbia College, 1606–07, 1611
Columbia Oil Company, 1183
Columbus, Christopher, 218, 1978
Combinations: Their Uses and Abuses, with a History of the Standard Oil Trust (Dodd), 2424–37
Comedies of Plautus, The (Plautus),
Comic Almanach, The, 574–79
"Commerce, Debts, Money" (LeTourneau), 2258–63
"Commerce and the Commercial Character" (Hone), 1989–92
"Commerce as a Liberal Pursuit" (King), 580–85
Commercial and Financial Chronicle, The, 1031
Commercial Review, The, 680
Commercial Review of the South and West, 1115
Commission merchants, 709–10
"Committee System, The" (Hidy and Hidy), 1683–85
Communism, 1993–2004
Communist Manifesto (Marx and Engels), 1993
"Complaint of a Merchant's Wife," 2507–08
Complete English Tradesman, The (Defoe), 261–71
Complete Poems of Robert Frost, 1491, 1704
Complete Works in Philosophy, Politics, and Morals, of the Late Dr. Benjamin Franklin . . . , 2397
Complete Works of Abraham Lincoln, 1352
Complete Works of Benjamin Franklin (Bigelow, ed.), 2503

"Concept of the Just Price: Theory and Economic Policy" (De Roover), 2125–38

Conceptual Foundations of Business (Eells and Walton), 190–212

Condillac, Abbé de, 1056

"Conditions of the Working Class" (Leo XIII), 2186–96

Conestoga wagon, 1230–31, 1234

Confectioner's shop (*illus.*), 251

Confucius, 6, *571*, 1506, 1543, 1948–52

Confusion de Confusiones (de la Vega), 794–807

Congress of the United States, 718, 720–23

Connell-Smith, Gordon, 1294

"Consequences of Power, The" (Bryson), 1445–46

Consobrinus, Johannes, 2129

Constable, Arnold, 305

Constant, Samuel Victor, *366–68*

Constantine Porphyrogenitus, Emperor, 1032

Continental Can Company, 137

Continental Congress, 715

"Continuous Production Line in the Eighteenth Century" (Giedion), 1097–1105

Cook, William, 292–94

Cook, Zebedee, Jr., 1008

Cooke, Jay, 851–66; (*illus.*), 786

Cooke & Company, Jay, 851–66

Coolidge, Calvin, 1565; *quoted*, 1524

Cooper, Sir Astley, 300

Cooper, James Fenimore, 419

Cooper, Peter, 1554–55

Corinth, 166, 172, 179

"Cornflake Crusade" (Carson), 418–33

Corning, New York, 34, 37

Corporation in Modern Society, The (Berle, ed.), 1773–76

Corpus Juris Civilis, 2277

Corvinus, Matthias, 1786

Costain, Thomas B., *842–50*

Cotton, John, 2134

Counting house, 1968; (*illus.*), 249, 1969

Coutant, George E., 1279

Cowper, Earl, 812

Cowper, William, *1933–34*

Covey, Elizabeth, 292

Cox, Jacob D., Jr., 2239

Craggs, Secretary, 822, 823

Crane, Clinton H., 2361

Cravath, Paul D., *quoted*, 32

Creed for Free Enterprise, A (Randall) 2233, 2445–47

Crisis of Our Age, The (Sorokin), 1581–84

Crocker, George, 886

Crocker, William G., 611

Croesus, King, 170

Cromwell, Oliver, 690

Crosby, Albert H., 1121, 1122

Crosby, Dixi, 1120

Cudahy Packing Company, 33

Cullinan, J. S., 1142

Curb Exchange, *see* American Stock Exchange

Curtis, Cyrus, 1875, 1876

"Customary Christmas Story, The" (Metcalfe), 2519–21

Cutten, Arthur, 899, 921

Cybernetics (*illus.*), 1443

Cybernetics (Wiener), 1510–13

Cyclopaedia of Commercial and Business Anecdotes, 310–11, 745

Cyzicus, Greece, 678

Da Chivasso, Angelo Carletti, 2133

Damascus, 184–90

Dannenbaum, Walter, 1731, 1732

Darius II, King, 70

Darius the Persian, 179

Dark Ages, the, 167

Darwin, Charles, *quoted*, 1224

Datini, Francesco di Marco, 81–88

Daumier, Honoré, *painting by*, 782

David I, of Scotland, 2282

David, Donald K., 190, *2385–88*

David, Edward E., Jr., 1211

David Harum (Westcott), 2541–51

Davidson, James, 997

Da Vinci, Leonardo, 89

Davis, T. C., 1731

Day, Angel, 1296

Day, Clarence, 1444, *1493–1500*

Deal in Wheat and Other Stories of the New and Old West (Norris), 874–83

Death of a Salesman (Miller), 621–32

"Debate at Wickersham Mills" (Collier), 2473–93

DeBow's Review, 566

"Defender of the Faith: Orphan Annie and the Conservative Tradition" (Kehl), 2376–85

Defoe, Daniel, 261–71, 695, 978, *2171–73; quoted*, 6, 58, 2389

Dekker, Thomas, 571–72

De la Vega, Joseph, 794–807
Delos, 171
Democracy in America (de Tocqueville), 1534–37
Demosthenes, 2261
Delphi, 167
De Luna, Juan Manuel, 564–65
"Departmental, or, The End of My Ant Jerry" (Frost), 1704–05
De Roover, Florence Edler, *682–84*
De Roover, Raymond, *81–88, 1055–57, 2125–38*
"Development of Accounting Prior to Luca Pacioli . . ." (De Roover), 81–88
Devens, Richard Miller, *310–11*
Dewey, John, 1763; *quoted,* 30, 32
De Wit, John, 970
Dexter, Samuel, 1112
Dialogues of the Dead (Lucian), 2502–03
Diamond, Edwin, *1207–14*
Díaz del Castillo, Bernal, 191–92, 205
Dice, Charles Amos, 910
Dick Company, A. B., 122
Dickens, Charles, *1353–62*
Dickinson, General, 720
"Dick Whittington and His Cat" (Larson), 1790
Dictionary of the English Language (Johnson), 3
"Difference Engine No. 2" (Babbage), 2301–12
Dighton, Richard, *cartoon by,* 835
"Dinner Given by the Economic Club of New York for N. S. Khrushchev," 2091–99
Diodorus of Sicily, 163
Dionysias, Egypt, 679
"Disappointed Director, The," 1245–46
Diverse et Artificiose Machine, La (Ramelli), 1102
Dodd, Samuel Calvin Tait, *2424–37*
Dollar sign, origin of, 682–84
Dombey and Son (Dickens), 1353–62
Donham, Wallace B., *1624–30,* 2046; *quoted,* 32
"Donkey Goes to Market, The" (Kelsey), 2512–15
Donne, John, *quoted,* 3
Dos Passos, John, *890–94, 1281–85*
Dowie, John Alexander, 422

Downing, Zek, *lithographs by,* 737, 740
Drake, Edwin L., 1119–20, 1129–32, 1276
Drake, Sir Francis, 1649, 1979
Drake well, the, 1128–32, 1182; (*illus.*), 1130
Drapers' Guide, 574
Dreiser, Theodore, *1893–1904*
Dribben, Saul, 2240
Drift and Mastery (Lippmann), 1559
Drepperd, Carl W., *1070–75*
"Drive for Speed at Sea, The" (Villiers), 1235–44
Drucker, Peter F., *1513–23*
Drugstore, 16th-century (*illus.*), 248
Dryden, John, *quoted,* 3
Duff, Edward, 2224
Duisberg, Carl, 1639
Duke, Henry K., *957–58*
Duke, James B., 884, 2360
Dumnorix, 165
Du Moulin, Charles, 1056
Dunbar, Seymour, *1224–34*
Duncan, Isadora, 1838
Duncombe, Charles, 704
Dunsany, Lord, *2590–96*
Duns Scotus, John, 2128, 2129, 2132
Du Pont, Henry B., 1731, 1732
Du Pont, Irénée, 1725
Du Pont de Nemours & Co., E. I., 1722–36, 2469
Durant, W. C., 899
Dürer, Albrecht, *painting by,* 781
Dutch East India Company, 689, 795, 796
Dutch Stock Jobber (*illus.*), 2602
Dutch West India Company, 796
Dwight, Timothy, 284
Dyer, General George R., 909

Earle, Pliny, 1083
Early Bolshevik Poems, 1557
Eaton's (of Toronto), 306
Eckener, Dr. Hugo, 1571
"Economical Project, An" (Franklin), 2503–07
Economic Club of New York, 2091
"Economic Decline of the Netherlands," 709–10
Economic History Review, 709
Economic Interpretation of History, 685–91
"Economic Milieu, The" (Berliner), 1766–72

"Economic Phases" (Hoover), 1565–70

Economic Principles of Confucius and His School (Chen Huan-chang), 1948, 1953, 2279

"Economic Revolution, The" (Heilbroner), 1973–81

Economic Sophisms, 2296

Economist, The, 1538

Economist, The (Xenophon), 1526–27

"Economy of Abundance" (Chase), 2055–65

"Edible Workers" (Day), 1493–1500

Edinburgh Review, 744

Edward I, of England, 792

Edward II, of England, 791, 792

Edward III, of England, 234, 791, 792

Eells, Richard, *190–212*

"Effects of Ostentation Upon Credit," 744

Egypt and the Egyptians, 66–68, 75, 168, 351, 352, 679

"Eight Rules for Office Workers in 1872," 1374–75

Eisenhower, Dwight D., 2091

Eldon, Lord, 1602

Elements of Book-keeping (Kelly), 116

"Elephant Cutlet, The" (Bemelmans), 1873–74

Eliot, Charles W., *quoted,* 1525

"Eli Whitney—Nemesis of the South" (Whitridge), 1105–14

Elizabeth I, of England, 1294, 1976, 1979

Ellis, Fred, 291

Emancipation Proclamation, 1370

"Emerging Profession of Business" (Donham), 1624–30

Emerson, Ralph Waldo, 742, 1526, *1542–45*

Encyclopaedia Britannica, 677–80

Encyclopedia Americana, 9

Encyclopedia of the Social Sciences, 48–57

Endless Frontiers—The Story of McGraw-Hill (Burlingame), 1679–83

Engels, Friedrich, 1993

Engineers and the Price System, The (Veblen), 2005

England and the English, 163–64, 272–74, 358, 689–91, 693, 790–94

"Englishman Looks at American Marketing and Distribution Policies" (Waterhouse), 538–41

Ente Nazionale Idrocarburi, 1706

Erewhon (Butler), 1450–55

Errand Boy, The (Alger), 1862–73

Essay of Drapery (Scott), 2139–60

Essays of Elia (Lamb), 827, 1338

Estrange, L', *quoted,* 4

Etruria and the Etruscans, 171, 172–76, 179

"Europe Versus America" (Carnegie), 2413–24

Evans, Oliver, 1097–105, 1200, *1988*

Eveleth, Jonathan G., 1121, 1122, 1123–24, 1125, 1126, 1127, 1128, 1129, 1131–32

Everett, Edward, 391

Everybody's Political What's What, 1015

"Everything But the Squeal" (Swift), 1179–80

"Evolutionary Nature of Mechanization in Manufacturing" (Bright), 1199–1207

"Excellent Rules of Thriving, in Verse," 2170

"Excerpts From the Will of Keayne, 1653," 2162–69

Executive Suite (Hawley), 2448–61

Extracts from the Works of Dr. Franklin on Population, Commerce, &., 2285–86

Extraordinary Popular Delusions and Madness of Crowds (Mackay), 807–25

Ezekiel the Prophet, 156–59

Factory and Manager in the USSR (Berliner), 1766, 1930

"Factory Director, The" (Bauer), 1185–99

"Factory Sirens, The" (Gastev), 1558–59

Fahnestock, 856, 860, 863, 864

Fairfield Inn *(illus.),* 1228

Faith and Freedom (Ward), 2227

Farouk, King, of Egypt, 344

Farrington, Benjamin, *1069–70*

Fascism—Doctrine and Instructions (Mussolini), 1705–09

"Father of Our Factory System" (Welles), 1076–87

Faurote, Fay Leone, 1201n.

Fayol, Henri, *1685–1704*

Feather, William, *quoted,* 1444

Feder, Gottfried, 2011, 2012
Federal Reserve Act, 907
Federal Reserve Banks, 737, 906–07, 933, 952, 1011
Federal Reserve Board, 906–07, 908, 909
Federal Trade Commission, 40–41
Federation of Trades and Labor Unions, 1373
Feigin, S. I., 9–10
Feisal, King, of Iraq, 340
Fellowes, Sir John, 816, 825
"Fellow 'Prentices at Their Looms" (illus.), 1315
Fermant, Philip, 2283
Ferris, Paul, 773
Field, Cyrus (illus.), 2612
Field, Jake, 885–86
Field, Marshall, 28, 301, 306
Field & Leiter, 306
Filene's of Boston, 1615–16
Filer, Schmidt & Company, 950
Fire Office, 979–81
"First American Business Man, The" (Gras), 1800–02
First Bank of the United States, establishment of, 711–32; (illus.), 788
First Boston Corporation, 947
"First Inquiry, The" (Mayo), 1617–24
"First Lady of Food—The Life and Times of Betty Crocker" (Gray), 607–21
First Report on Public Credit (Hamilton), 1530
Fischer, Kermit, 2249
Fisher, Irving, 920
Fiske, James, 285; (illus.), 2613
Fitzpatrick, W. H., 953–55
Fitzsimmons, Thomas, 716
Flaccus, 686
Flagler, Henry, 1263
Fletcher, R. D., 1123
Flint, Charles R., 2402–13
Flint, Timothy, 283
Florence, Italy, 174
Florentine merchant, 14th-century (illus.), 247
Florentine Merchants in the Age of the Medici (Richards), 257–60
Flynn, John T., 834–41
Foes of Our Own Household (Roosevelt), 1560–62
Follett, Mary Parker, 2013–27, 2080, 2084
Fontana, Domenico, 1103

Foote, Cone & Belding, 490, 491
Ford, Henry, 1156–61, 1514, 1517, 1518, 1891, 2040, 2360; quoted, 1068
Ford Methods and the Ford Shops (Arnold and Faurote), 1201
Fortuna, 172–74, 1959, 1970; (illus.), 1962, 1972
Fortune magazine, 30–48, 328, 1179, 2076, 2462
Foster, William T., 910
Four Million, The (O. Henry), 2551
Four Thousand Years in the Office (Nyströmer), 61–64, 64–68
Fowler, J. A., 191–92
Fox, Joseph, 987
"Fox Who Lost His Tail" (Alexander), 1014–15
France and the French, 1528–29
Franco-Prussian War, 861
Franklin, Benjamin, 984–87, 988, 990, 1070–75, 1103, 1777, 1802–18, 2173–84, 2285–86, 2397–2400, 2503–07; quoted, 155
Franklin, James, 1803–04
Franklin stove (illus.), 1074, 1075
"Franklin Stove, The" (Drepperd), 1070–75
Frazier's Magazine, 399
"Freebooter, The" (Sombart), 1646–51
Freeman, Payton R., 997
"Free Trade" (Greeley and Arnold), 2293–96
French, Colonel, 1808
Fresneda, Sears store manager, 1592
Frey, Charles Daniel, 44
Frick, H. C., 2361
Friendly Society, 980–81, 985
Frobisher, Sir Martin, 1649
Froissant, Jean, 1783, 1784
"From the Thoughtful Businessman: Letter" (Duke), 957–58
Frost, Robert, 121–22, 1491–93, 1704–05
Fugger, Anna, 1786
Fugger, Anton, 1788, 1789
Fugger, Jacob, 23, 781, 1680–82, 1784–90, 1967; (illus.), 781, 1965
Fugger, Raimund, 1787
Fugger, Ulrich, 1787
Fugger-Thurzo Company, 1787–88
Fuller, Alfred C., 528–38
Fuller, Howard, 536
Fuller Brush Company, 528–38
Fulton, Robert, 583, 1109

Functions of the Executive, The (Barnard), 2068
Funston, G. Keith, 953
Furrier's shop (*illus.*), 246
Further Range, A (Frost), 121–22
Future of American Prosperity, The (Wernette), 761–64

Galamb, Joe, 1156, 1157, 1159
Galbraith, John Kenneth, *633–36*, 1775, 2397
Gale, Sam, 609–11, 615
Galey, John H., 1136, 1137, 1138, 1140, 1141–42
Gandhi, Maganlal, 1441
Gandhi, Mahatma, 6, *1439–42*
Garden of Folly (Leacock), 466–69, 524–28, 2561
Gardin, John, 2283
Gardner, John, 2386
Garibay, K., Dr. Angel Ma., 209
Garrett, Garet, 2359
Gastev, A. K., *1557–59*
Gates, John, 885, 886, 887, 888, 889
Gauger, Sieur, 1071–72
Geijsbeek, John B., 89, 90
General and Industrial Management (Fayol), 1685–1704
General Electric Company, 38–39
General Fund Act (1717), 809, 810
General Mills, 607, 615, 618, 619, 621
Geoffrey Chaucer of England (Chute), 1778–84
George, David Lloyd, 837
George I, of England, 821
Gerard, Ralph, 1209
Gerson, Jean, 2129
Ghibelline, the, 687, 791
Giannini, A. P., 902
"Giants Fight for the Northern Pacific" (Josephson), 1260–71
Gibb, George S., 2599–2620
Gibbon, Edward, 823, 825
Gibran, Kahlil, *606–07*
Giddens, Paul H., *1119–32, 1271–80*
Giedion, Siegfried, *1097–105*
Gilbert and Sullivan, *quoted*, 956
Gilbreth, Frank Bunker, 1181–82
Gilbreth, Frank Bunker, Jr., *1180–82*
Gilbreth, Lillian Moller, 1181
Gimbel Brothers, 306
Girard, Stephen, 788
Girard Life Insurance, Annuity, and Trust Company, 1004, 1007

Girard Trust Corn Exchange Bank (*illus.*), 787
Glaser, E. L. (Ted), 1209–10
Glass, Carter, 908
Glover, John D., 2619
"Glut in the Market," 300
Godfrey, Sir Edmund Berry, 700
Godfrey, Michael, 700
Godfrey, Thomas, 1813, 1817
God's Country and Mine (Barzun), 652–73
Goethe, 167
Golden Book of the Wanamaker Stores, Jubilee Year, 1861–1911, 1363–65, 1884–93
Goldman Sachs, 949
Gold Medal Flour, 607, 609–21
Goldsmith-bankers, 697–98, 704–06, 790–94
"Goldsmiths' Notes," 794
Gompers, Samuel, *1367–74*, 2360
"Good Clerk, a Character, The" (Lamb), 271–76
Good Old Days, The (Cohn), 315–33
Goodyear-Zeppelin Company, 1571
Gordon Riots of 1780, 776
Gorer, Geoffrey, *quoted*, 633
Gorgas, General Josiah, 1113–14
Gould, Jay (*illus.*), 2611
Grace, Robert, 1814
Gracián, Baltasar, 2161
Graf Zeppelin, airship, 1570, 1571
Gragg, Charles I., 2085
Graham, Sylvester, 418, 433
Grand Coulee Dam, 1927
Grant, Ulysses S., 2408
Grant Advertising, 491
Gras, N. S. B., *851–66, 1800–02*
Gray, Harold, 2376–85
Gray, James, *607–21*
Great Depression of 1929–1934, 1570
"Great Fire of London" (Bainbridge), 977–84
Great Fire of London (1666), 791, 792, 794, 977–84
Great Northern Railroad, 1262, 1264, 1270, 1271
Great Pierpont Morgan, The (Allen), 890
"Great Wealth a Misfortune" (Mann), 1541–42
Greece and the Greeks, 74–77, 164, 165, 168–69, 170–71, 176, 179, 353, 514–17, 567–70, 678, 681–82, 685–86, 1525, 1526, 1939–44, 1944–48
"Greek and Roman Accounting" (Ste Croix), 74–77

Greek merchant, 17th-century (*illus.*), 244
Greek Science (Farrington), 1069–70
Greeley, Horace, 391, *2293–96*
Green, William, 1572
Greene, Mrs. Nathanael, 1105–06
Greenewalt, Crawford H., 1723, 1728, 1731, *2469–72*
Gregory, Attorney General, 1372
Grenville, Sir Richard, 1649
Gresham, Sir Thomas, 792, 793
Grevenbroch, Jan, *painting by,* 780
Grey, Henry M., *973–77*
Grey, Lord, 812
Grey Advertising, 487
Griffith, Thomas, *1593–99*
Griffits, William, 987
Grout, John, 724
Guadalajara, Mexico, 1586, 1588–89, 1593
Guatemala, 193
Guelph, the, 687, 791
Guffey, J. M., 1136
Guggenheim, Daniel, 2361
Guild, James, 288–89, 294
Guild of Mercers, 233
Guilds in the Middle Ages (Renard, ed.), 1658–78
Gunther, John, *456–66*
Gurney, Baron, 1602
"Gusher at Spindletop" (Owens), 1132–44

Hackett, Walter, *444–55*
Hadrian, Emperor, 2275–76
Hadrian's Memoirs (Yourcenar), 2275–76
Haile Selassie, of Ethiopia, 340
Hales, John, 1976
Haley, Catharine Maria, 1822, 1828, 1833, 1837
Haliburton, Thomas Chandler, 288, *518–21*
Halkett, Samuel, 1602
Hall, James, 997
Halladay, *cartoon by,* 2609
Hallam, Henry, 1033
Halsey, Stuart & Company, 946
Hamburg, Germany, 689
Hamilcar, 178
Hamill, Allen W., 1133–44
Hamill, Curt, 1133–44; (*illus.*), 1135
Hamill, Jim, 1133, 1141, 1142
Hamilton, Alexander, 711–12, 714–15, 716–17, 718–19, 723, 726, 727–28, 729, 730, 986, 1084–85, *1087–95,*

1095–97, 1110, 1237, 1530–33, 2036, *2286–92,* 2371–72
Hammond, Bray, 711, *730–32, 732–43*
Hammurabi, 9–10, 60, 64, 959
Hand, Learned, 2081
Hand-in-Hand, the, 982–84
Hanes, Robert M., 1632
Hankey, Henry, 705
Hannay, Samuel, 1010
Hannibal, 178
Hanseatic League, 359
Harbin, Manchuria, 1508
Harder, Del, 1514
Harding, Warren G., 1565
"Hardship of Accounting, The" (Frost), 121–22
Hardy, George Sherburne, 1875
Harley, Earl of Oxford, 808, 809
Harley, Henry, 1280
Harper, William Rainey, 28
Harper's Monthly Magazine, 590, 1399, 2312
Harriman, Edward H., 885, 887, 1260–71, 2357–58
Harry, David, 1811, 1817
Hartman, Lou, 460–61
Harvard Bureau of Business Research, 1574
Harvard Business Review, 122, 136, 541, 642, 957, 1402, 1624, 1631, 1722, 2074, 2200, 2225, 2239, 2255, 2266, 2473
Harvard Business School Bulletin, 2599
Harvard College, 729
Harvard Graduate School of Business Administration, 1555, 1624
Harvey, Robert, 1294
Haven & Wiley, 291
Havens, Rensselaer H., 1128, 1131
Hawkers and Walkers in Early America (Wright), 288, 298–300, 2515
Hawkins, John and William, 1650
Hawley, Cameron, *2448–61*
Hawley, Edwin C., 885, 886, 887, 888, 889
Hawthorne, Nathaniel, 287, 291, 742
Hayakawa, Dr. S. I., 1406
"Heard by Telephone" (Metcalfe), 1365–67
Heathcote, Sir Gilbert, 700, 708
Heilbroner, Robert L., *256–57, 1973–81*
Henderson, Carter, *561–65*
Henry, O., *2551–54*
Henry, Patrick, 1530–31

Henry II, of England, 1663
Henry IV, of England, 233
Henry V, of England, 791
Henry VIII, of England, 792
Henshaw, David, 735, 739
Heraclitus of Ephesus, 171
Herculaneum, 355
Herodotus, 76, 172, 2259; *quoted,* 956
Herondas of Syracuse, *514–17*
Heron of Alexandria, 2271
Herries, John Charles, 838–39, 840, 841
Hesse-Cassel, Landgrave of, 834
Heth, Joice, 387–88
Hewitt, Abram S., 1554, *1604–11, 2315–27*
Heyroun, Thomas, 1779, 1781
Hibbs, W. B., 886
Hidden Persuaders, The (Packard), 637–42, 645
Hidy, Ralph W., and Muriel E., 709, *1683–85*
Higgins, Pattillo, 1133, 1136, 1140
Hill, George Washington, 461–66, 470
Hill, Hamilton A., *2327–41*
Hill, James J., 1260–71, 2403
Hill, Percival, 461
Hillary, Sir Edmund, 337
Hilprecht, H. V., 69, 70
Hilton, Conrad, 2240
Himera, sea battle of, 179, 180
Hindenburg, airship, 1570
Hippodamus, 171
Hiroshige, 1800
"Historical Review of Interest, An," 1031–34
History and Development of Advertising (Presbrey), 350–60, 363–64, 399, 1890
History of Advertising, A (Sampson), 369–78, 382–83
History of Insurance in Philadelphia for Two Centuries (1683–1882), 191–92
History of Mechanical Inventions, A (Usher), 1203
History of the Business Man (Beard), 21–28, 159
History of the Principal Discoveries and Improvements, In the Several Arts and Sciences . . . (Defoe), 2171–73
History of Travel in America (Dunbar), 1224–34
Hitler, Adolf, 6, 335, 1706, *2011–12*

Hoare, Richard, 705
Hoare & Company, 772, 775–76
Hoe, Robert, 1821
Hogarth, William, *1313–37*
"Hogarth Elucidated" (Clerk), 1313
Hoggson, Noble Foster, *quoted,* 787
Holbrook, William C., 289–91
Holland, John, 700
Holland and the Dutch, 689, 709–10
Homer, *quoted,* 1, 10–14
Homeric Age, the, 165–68
Homestead Act (1863), 2038
Hommedieu, Ezra l', 684
Hone, Philip, *1989–92*
"Honest Man, The" (Lyon), 1554–55
Honest Whore, The (Dekker), 571–72
Hoover, Herbert C., 902, 904–05, 926, 1526, *1565–70; quoted,* 32
Hope, Mr., 689
Hopkins, Claude C., *434–44, 457,* 490
Horace, 175
"Horatio Alger, Jr." (Allen), 1855–62
Horch, August, 1640
Hosmer, W. A., 69
Hostiensis, Henricus, 2128
Hotchkiss, George Burton, 571
"Hot Cross Buns," 369
Houblon, Abraham, 700
Houblon, Sir James, 700
Houblon, Sir John, 700, 703, 704
House of Baring in American Trade and Finance (Hidy), 709
House of Mitsui, The (Russell), 1791
"House of Morgan, The" (Dos Passos), 890–94
Hoving, Walter, 1574
Howard, Earl, 2022
Howe, Elias, 1113
Howe, Elias, Jr., 1823, 1825, 1828, 1829
Howells, William Dean, *1839–54*
Hower, Ralph M., *301–10*
How to Run a Bassoon Factory (Spade), 1400–02, 1719–22
Hubbard, O. P., 1120
Hubbard, General Thomas Hamlin, 886
Huckabee, Weyman C., *2239–40*
Hucksters, The (Wakeman), 462, 470–80, 498
Huet, Monsieur, Bishop of Avranches, 1960
Hughes, Thomas, *quoted,* 5
Hume, David, 1033; *quoted,* 675

Hunt, Walter, 1822
Huntington, Collis P., 1261
Huntington, Mrs. Collis P., 886
Huntington, H. E., 886
Hunt's Merchants' Magazine, 296–98, 300, 305–06, 580, 744, 1031, 1115, 1554, 1989, 2293, 2401–02, 2507
Hu Shih, *1505–10*
Hussein, of Jordan, 340
Huxley, Aldous, *1214–23; quoted*, 30
Hyde, A. L., 290
Hymns of the Atharva-Veda, 2111

Ibn 'Ali al-Dimeshqi, abu Al-Fadl Ja'far, 184–90
Iceman (*illus.*), 252
Ickes, Harold, 1929
"Idle 'Prentice at Play in the Churchyard During Divine Service" (*illus.*), 1319
"Idle 'Prentice Betrayed by a Prostitute, and Taken in a Night Cellar with His Accomplice" (*illus.*), 1331
"Idle 'Prentice Executed at Tyburn" (*illus.*), 1335
"Idle 'Prentice Returned from Sea, and in a Garret with a Common Prostitute" (*illus.*), 1327
"Idle 'Prentice Turned Away and Sent to Sea" (*illus.*), 1323
Igibi bank of Babylon, 678
Iliad of Homer, 10–14, 75
"I'm a Natural Born Salesman" (Upson), 2573–86
I'm a Stranger Here Myself (Nash), 765
Importance of Living, The (Lin Yutang), 1577
Indle, S. W., 872
Industrial and Commercial Correspondence of Alexander Hamilton . . . , 1087–95, 1095–97, 2286–92
Industrial engineering, 1180–82
"Industrial Justice: the Tool-Owner and the Tool-User" (Roosevelt), 1560–62
Industrial Revolution, the, 50, 51
"Industrious 'Prentice a Favorite, and Entrusted by His Master" (*illus.*), 1321
"Industrious 'Prentice Alderman of London; The Idle One Brought Before Him and Impeached by His Accomplice" (*illus.*), 1333
"Industrious 'Prentice Grown Rich,

and Sheriff of London" (*illus.*), 1329
"Industrious 'Prentice Lord Mayor of London" (*illus.*), 1337
"Industrious . 'Prentice Out of His Time, and Married to His Master's Daughter" (*illus.*), 1325
"Industrious 'Prentice Performing the Duty of a Christian" (*illus.*), 1317
"Industry and Idleness" (Hogarth), 1313–37
Ingersoll, Blanche, 614–15
Ingham, Samuel, 735
Inquisition of Queensborough, 1290
Institutes of the Christian Religion (Calvin), 2138
Institutes of Vishnu, The, 566, 1024–26
Insull, Samuel, 934, 1706, 1708, 2380
Insurance Fables for Life Underwriters (Alexander), 1014–15
Insurance Guide and Hand-Book on Fire, Life, Marine, Tontine, and Casualty Insurance (Walford), 964–77
Integritas, 1970; (*illus.*), 1972
International Harvester Company, 2462
International Marketing Institute, 2385
"Iron Messiah, The" (Kirillov), 1557–58
"Irreplaceable Anton Fomich, The" (Berliner), 1930–32
Irving Trust Company, 1574
"Isaac Singer and His Wonderful Sewing Machine" (Lyon), 1819–39
Iselin, Adrian, Jr., 889
It Pays to Advertise (Megrue and Hackett), 444–55
Ives, William A., 1126, 1128, 1132

Jack, Andrew B., 1824–25
Jackson, Andrew, 732–43, 746, 1086, 2036
Jackson, James Caleb, 422
"Jackson's Fight with the 'Money Power,'" (Hammond), 732–43
Jacob Fugger the Rich (Strieder), 1784–90
James II, of England, 699
James VI, of Scotland, 2281, 2283
Janes, Herman, 1277
Janssen, Sir Theodore, 696, 700, 825
Jarman, Maxey, 2240
Jay Cook, Private Banker (Larson), 851–66
Jefferson, Thomas, 718, 719, 725, 727,

734, 1087, 1101–02, 1112, 1531–33, 2036, 2371–72
Jennings, William, *quoted,* 156
Jerome, St., 2120
Jerusalem, 167, 687
Jevons, W. S., *quoted,* 5
Jeweler's shop (*illus.*), 243
Jewish merchant, 17th-century (*illus.*), 244
Jews, moneylenders in England, 791
Jews and Modern Capitalism, The (Sombart), 2197
Joachimsthaler, the, 683, 684
John I, of England, 1033, 1034
John II, of France, 1666
"John Henry," 237–41
Johns, C. H. W., *959*
Johnson, Samuel, 719; *quoted,* 3, 60, 349, 514
"John Wanamaker, 1838–1922," 1363–65, 1884
"Joint Liability: The Ruin of a Great Merchant Company" (Lopez and Raymond), 1651–55
Jones, Bobby, 342
Jones, Edgar R., *400*
Jordan, Ambrose, 1828
Jordan, Marsh & Co., 306
Josephson, Matthew, *1260–71*
Journal of Accountancy, The, 116–19
Journal of Economic History, 2125
Journal of Marketing, 538
Journal of Social Science, 2327
Judd, Charles B., 436
Judge magazine, 2517
Juilliard, Augustus P., 889
Jungle, The (Sinclair),1390–99
Justinian I, Emperor, *2277–79*

Kahn, E. J., Jr., *334–48*
Kahn, Felix, 1926
Kahn, Otto, 1261
Kaiser, Henry J., 1777, 1922–30
Kami, Mike, 1209
Kanbalu, China, 219
Kant, Immanuel, 24–25
Kapital, Das (Marx), 1993–2004
Karloman, of France, 2126
Katz, Robert L., *2255–56*
KDKA radio broadcasting station, 41
Keayne, Robert, 1979, 2125, *2162–69*
Keeley, James, 44
Keen, Charles, 1155
Keene, James, 889, 1266
Keezer, Dexter M., *48–57*
Kehl, James A., *2376–85*

Keimer, Samuel, 1806–07, 1808, 1810, 1812, 1813
Keith, Sir William, 1808–09
Kelland, Clarence Budington, *1904–20*
Kellenbenz, Hermann, 794
Kellogg, Ella Eaton, 425–26
Kellogg, Emma, 423
Kellogg, J. P., 420
Kellogg, John Harvey, 420–23, 429, 430–31
Kellogg, Will K., 423, 426, 428, 429–33
Kelly, Patrick, 116
Kelsey, Alice Geer, *2512–15*
Kendall, Amos, 735, 736, 739
Kennedy, John E., 490
Kennedy, John F., *2365–69*
Kenyon & Eckhardt, 491
Kerr, Clark, 1765–66
Kett, Robert, 1977
Keyser, Virginia, *1585–93*
Khrushchev, Nikita, 2091, *2094–99*, 2387
King, Charles, *580–85*
King, Rufus, 1607
Kingsley, Darwin P., *quoted,* 31
Kin-sai, China, 226–29
Kinsman, J. Warren, 1731, 1732
Kirillov, V., *1557–58*
Kitchener, General, 837
Kitty Hawk, North Carolina, 1281–84
Klein, George, 649
Klein, Julius, 930; *quoted,* 31
Knickerbocker Magazine, 119–21
Knowlton, Dexter, 295
Koran, the, 2117
Kreisler, Ed, 561–65
Kreuger, Ivar, 934–38, 1706, 1708
Krokodil, 1930–32
Kuan Chung, 1509
Kublai Khan, 218
Kuhn, Loeb & Company, 885, 947, 1264, 1265–66, 1267, 1271

Lady Chatterley's Lover (Lawrence), 2027–33
Lafargue, Paul, 1638
"Lafitte, the French Banker: or A Fortune Made by Picking Up a Pin," 2401–02
Lake, Moses, 384
Lalique, René, 34, 37–38
Lamar, Lucius Quintus Cincinnatus, 2365–69
Lamb, Charles, 116–19, 262, *271–76, 827–34, 1338–45*

"Lamb Among the Ledgers" (Boyce), 116–19
Lambe, Samuel, 696
Lambert, Sir John, 825
Lamont, Thomas W., 924–25
Lann, Joe, 948
Larson, Henrietta M., *182–84, 851–66, 1790*
Lasker, Albert D., 435, 456–66, 490
"Latest Quotation, The" (Carlsbad), 2185
Law, John, 719, 810, 1981
Lawrence, D. H., *2027–33*
Laws of Plato, The, 567–70
Lawson, Thomas W., 2404
Lazarus, F. & R., 306
Leacock, Stephen, *466–69, 524–28, 757–59, 2561–68*
Leaves of Grass (Whitman), 1449
LeBlanc, M., 1112
Lee, Irving, 1409n.
Lefèvre, Edwin, 912
Lehman Brothers, 949
Leisure Hour magazine, 399
Leisure hours of bankers, 745–48
Le Maire, Isaac, 796
Lenox, James, 1606n.
Leo XIII, Pope, 6, *2186–96*
Lerner, Max, *2099–2107*
Lessius, Leonardus, 2133
Le Tourneau, Bob, 1925–26
Le Tourneau, Charles, *2258–63*
Letters and Social Aims (Emerson), 1542
Let Us Live in Peace and Friendship, 2091
Lewis, John L., 1439
Lewis, Sinclair, *590–606, 2555–61*
Lewis, William B., 734
Lex Mercatoria Rediviva: or, the Merchant's Directory (Beawes), 2390–92
Libbey, William, 1889
Libel of English Policy, 233
Libertas, 1970; (*illus.*), 1966
"Liberty, Learning, and Property" (Hewitt), 1604–11
Life and Death of Ivar Kreuger (Stoneman), 934–38
Life magazine, 1013, 1365, 1922, 2184, 2185, 2517
Life of Robert Owen . . . , 1350–52
"Life Without Principle" (Thoreau), 1545–54
Lilienthal, David E., 502

"Limits of Persuasion" (Bauer), 642–52
Lincoln, Abraham, 6, 294, 734, 855, *1352–53,* 1371, 2036–37
Lincoln, General Benjamin, 991–92
Lind, Jenny, 391–92, 394
Lindeberg, Florence, 612
Lindsay, Alexander, 2228
Lindsay, Vachel, *quoted,* 2366
Linguarum Peritia, 1970; (*illus.*), 1972
Lintner, John. V., 1773
Lin Yutang, *1577–80*
Literary Lapses (Leacock), 757
Little Prince, The (Saint-Exupéry), 2587–89
Livingston, Mortimer, 1008
Lloyd, Edward, 974
Lloyd, Henry Demarest, 1839, *2346–56*
Lloyd, Samuel Jones, 1603
Lloyd's of London, 772, 773–74, 973–77
Lloyd's Yesterday and Today (Grey), 973–77
Locke, John, *quoted,* 3
Lodge, Henry Cabot, 2091, *2092–93*
Loftingh, John, 701
Logan, James, 987, 1648
Lombards (Longobards), 791–92
Lombard Street, A Description of the Money Market (Bagehot), 749–56
London, England, 690; Lombard Street in, 749–56, 791–94
London Corporation, 690
London Joint Stock Banks, 756
"London Lackpenny," 364
London Stock Exchange, 769–72, 1447
London *Times,* 693, 935
Lonely Crowd, The (Riesman), 2229
Lone Striker, or, Without Prejudice to Industry, The (Frost), 1491–93
Longworth, Nicholas, 1115, 1116–17
Looking Forward (Roosevelt), 2369
Lopez, Robert S., 184, *959–64, 1651–55*
Lord & Taylor, 302, 305, 306, 307
Lord & Thomas, 440, 456–66, 490
"Lord Macaulay on American Institutions" (Macaulay), 2312–14
Lorimer, George Horace, 759, *1875–83*
Louis VII, of France, 359
Louis IX, of France, 1660
Louis XIV, of France, 1528
Louis XVIII, of France, 841

Louis Philippe, of France, 1706
Louisville & Nashville Railroad, 885–90
"Love Letter to a Factory" (McGinley), 1414–15
Love Letters of Phyllis McGinley, The (McGinley), 1414
Lowell, A. Lawrence, *1555–57; quoted,* 31
"Low-Pressure Selling" (Bursk), 541–61
Lübeck market (*illus.*), 241
Lucas, A. F., 1136, 1137, 1139–40, 1142
Lucas well at Beaumont, Texas, 1132–44
Luce, Henry, 1875
Lucian, 2502–03
Lucky Strike, 459–66
Ludlum, Dr. S. D., 1618
Luttrell, Temple, 163
Lu Yu, *1777–78*
Lydgate, John, *364–65,* 1783
Lydia and the Lydians, 76, 170, 176, 179
Lynn, Kenneth, 2619
Lyon, Peter, *1554–55, 1819–39*
Lyrics of Trade for the Christmas and New Year's Holidays, 1865–66, 395–97

Macaulay, Thomas Babington, 700, 703, *2312–14*
Macculloch, J. R., 754
MacDowell, Charles, 2363
MacDuffie, Marshall, 2094
MacEcelsalach, Amargin, 2281
MacGercin, Munremur, 2281
Machaut, Guillaume de, 1783–84
Machiavelli, Niccolo, 174, 1715
"Machines Are *This* Smart" (Diamond and Simmons), 1207–14
Mack, Charles E., 41
Mackay, Charles, *807–25*
Maclay, William, 718–19, 720, 721, 725
MacNessa, Conchobar, 2281
MacOllaig, Tigherumas, 2281
MacPherson, Crison, *painting by,* 1274
Macy, R. H., 304, 305, 306, 307, 309
Macy Company, R. H., 1574
Madison, James, 719, 721–23, 725, 726–27
Madison Avenue, U.S.A. (Mayer), 483–99
Maecenas, 175

Maffei, Marquess Scipione, 1057
Maghfeld, Gilbert, 235–36
Magna Charta, the, 212, 1033, *1034–35*
Magnus, Albertus, 2126, 2127
Maimonides, 2114
"Management by Executive Committee" (Mylander), 1722–36
Managerial Revolution—What Is Happening in the World (Burnham), 1712–19
"Managers, The" (Auden), 2621–23
Man in the Gray Flannel Suit, The (Wilson), 1744–56
Mann, Horace, 1526, *1541–42*
Mantz, Elmer, 677
Manufacturers Trust Company (*illus.*), 789
"Man Who Could Not Be Cornered, The" (Lorimer), 1875–83
Marchal, J. F., 1132
Marchants Avizo, The (Browne), 1293–1311
Marco Millions (O'Neill), 2569–73
Marconi, Guglielmo, 38
Marconi Wireless Co. of America, 38, 39
Marconi Wireless Telegraph Co., Ltd., 38, 40
Maringhi, Giovanni, *257–60*
Maritain, Jacques, 1774
Market woman (*illus.*), 252
Marks, Carl, 949
Marriott, Fred, 1153–54
Marshall, Thomas, *1095–97*
Marx, Joseph and George, 997
Marx, Karl, 1594–95, *1993–2004,* 2037, 2085, 2127
Masefield, John, *180–81, 1399*
Mason, Edward S., 1773
Massachusetts Hospital Life Insurance Company, 1004
Mattei, Enrico, 1706
"Matter of Business, A" (Lewis), 590–606
Maximilian, Emperor, 1786
Maxwell, Clerk, 1511
Mayer, Martin, *483–99, 938–53*
Mayes, Herbert R., 1857
"May I Just Step Inside?" (Bainbridge), 528–38
Mayo, Elton, *1617–24, 1757, 1758–65*
McAdoo, William Gibbs, 2360, 2362
McCaffrey, John L., *2462–69*
McCann-Erickson, 487, 491
McClellan, General George B., 855

McCollom, E. V., 619
McCormick, Cyrus, 1113
McCormick, Edward, 952
McCormick, Fowler, 2462
McElwain, William H., 1613–15, 1616
McFaddin, Perry, 1135
McGinley, Phyllis, *1414–15*
McGrath, Patrick, *1293–97*
McKay, George C., 426
McKinley, William (*illus.*), 2606
McKinney, Price, 2361
McLean, John G., *136–54*
McMein, Neysa M., 613–14
McNeel, R. H., 920
Means, Gardiner C., 1774
Mécanique de Feu, La (Gauger), 1072; (*illus.*), 1072, 1073
Mechanization Takes Command (Giedion), 1097–1105
Mediaeval Scotland (Cochran-Patrick), 2280–85
Medici, Lorenzo de', 175; (*illus.*), 781
Medieval Trade in the Mediterranean World (Lopez and Raymond), 959–64, 1651
Medina, Harold, 946
Megrue, Roi Cooper, *444–55*
Mein Kampf (Hitler), 2011–12
Mellon, Andrew, 2361
Memphis, Egypt, 679
Mencken, H. L., *1490–91, 1920–21, 2065–68; quoted,* 676
Mencius, 1949–52
Mendel, Lafayette, 619
Men of Wealth (Flynn), 834–41
"Mercantile Transactions in Scotland," 296–98
Merchant, N. H., *quoted,* 676
"Merchant, The" (Plautus), 182–84
Merchant bankers, 709–10
Merchant of Prato: Francesco di Marco Datini (Origo), 81–85
Merchant of Venice, The (Shakespeare), 1037–52
Merchants, miscellany of (*illus.*), 237–55
Merchants' Magazine, see *Hunt's Merchants' Magazine*
"Merchant's Prayer, A," 2111–12
Mercury, 1959; (*illus.*), 1958
Meredith, Hugh, 1810, 1811, 1812, 1814–15
Mérida, Mexico, 1586, 1589
Merrill Lynch, Pierce, Fenner and Smith, 944–45, 953

Merry Adventures of Robin Hood, The (Pyle), 213–17
Mesopotamia, 160–63
Metcalfe, *1365–67, 2519–21*
Metropolitan Life Insurance Company, 956
Metternich, Count, 839
Mexican American Review, 2160
Mexico, ancient, Aztec civilization in, 190–212
Mexico City, 1586, 1587, 1589, 1593
Michels, Robert, *quoted,* 26
Mickle, Samuel, 1814
Midas, King, 170
Mien, Kingdom of, 225–26
Mifflin, John, 987
Miletus, 170–71, 176
Mill, John Stuart, 1540, 2427
Miller, Arthur, *621–32*
Milligan, Patrick Ward, 774
Millinery shop (*illus.*), 255
Milton, A Poem in Two Books (Blake), 1447
Minor, Robert, 2616–17
Minos, King, 165
Minturn, Robert B., 1008
Mississippi Bubble, 810
Mississippi Company, 1981
Mitchell, Charles E., 908, 920–21, 924
Mitchell, Sidney Z., 911
Mitsui, Hachirobei, 1794, 1796–1800
Mitsui, Ju-san, 1797
Mitsui, Saburozaemon, 1795, 1796
Mitsui, Sokubei, 1791, 1792–95
Mitsui shop interior (*illus.*), 1797
Mizner, Addison, 1838
Model T Ford, 1156–61; (*illus.*), 1160
Modern Corporation and Private Property (Means), 1774
Mohammed the Prophet, 2117
Molina, Luis de, 2129
"Money" (Stein), 759–61
Monroe, Harriet, 1485, *1488–90*
Monroe, James, 1085–86
Monselet, Elise, 1856
Montagu, Charles, 691, 695
Monterrey, Mexico, 1586, 1589
Montgomery-Ward, 315
Moorhead, William G., 851, 858–59
"Morals of Trade, The" (Spencer), 585–90
Morgan, H. Wayne, *711–30*
Morgan, J. Pierpont, 749, 866, 885, 888, 889, 890–94, 1260–71; (*illus.*), 786

Morgan & Company, J. P., 888–89, 924
Morris, Arthur J., 2240
Morris, Gouverneur, 716
Morris, Joseph, 987
Morris, Lewis, Jr., 284
Morris, Robert, 712, 715, 717–18, 719, 986–87
Morrison, Harry, 1926
Morse, Samuel F. B., *painting by*, 1109
Morton, John, 986
Mother Goose's Nursery Rhymes, 369
Mount Stephen, Lord, 1262
Mulock, Charles, 1125
Munro, H. H., *see* Saki
Munson, Alexander D., 395
Murashû Sons of Nippur, 69–74
Mussolini, Benito, 174, *1705–09*
Mutual Life Insurance Co. of New York, 1007–11
Mutual Safety Insurance Company, 1007
Muys van Holy, Nicolaas, 796–97
"My Financial Career" (Leacock), 757–59
My Forty Years with Ford (Sorensen and Williamson), 1156–61
My Ireland (Dunsany), 2590
Mylander, William H., *1722–36*
My Life in Advertising (Hopkins), 434–44
Mystery of the New-Fashioned Goldsmiths or Bankers Discovered, 793–94

N. H., Merchant, *2170–71*
Napoleon I, of France, 836–37, 838–39, 841
Nash, Ogden, *765–66, 2494*
Nast, Thomas, *cartoon by*, 865 2226
Nation, The, 2341
National Broadcasting Company, 42, 360, 504, 615
National Corporative Council, 1706
National Gazette, 725
National Intelligencer, 995
National Land Bank of England, 695
National Petroleum Company, 1706
National Planning Association, 1585
National Retail Credit Association, 1574
National Road, 1227–34
Nation's Business, 2228
"Nature of Executive Responsibility" (Barnard), 2068–74

Nelson, Donald, 1928, 1929
Nettels, Curtis P., *2392–97*
Neudörfer, Johann, 1954, 1955
Nevill, Sir Hugo de, 1034
Nevins, Allan, 457, *2315–16*
New England Courant, 1803
New England Mutual Life Insurance Company, 1006
Newenton, Thomas, 236
"New feudalism bids fair to be the dominant feature of the twentieth century . . . ," 2402–13
Newman, James R., 1015
"New Methods of Work, New Methods of Management" (Stalin), 1709–11
Newsweek, 1207
New View of Society or Essays on the Principle of the Formation of the Human Character . . . " (Owen), 1345
New Voices: An Introduction to Contemporary Poetry, 1485
New Yorker, The, 334, 528–38, 766–77
New York Life Insurance and Trust Company, 1004, 1005, 1006, 1010
New York Stock Exchange, 866, 926, 931, 940–42
Nezahualcóyotl, King, 204
"Nicely Nicely's Broker's Tip" (Fitzpatrick), 953–55
Nicholas Biddle (Govan), 732
Nine Plays of Eugene O'Neill, 2569
Nine Soviet Portraits (Bauer), 1185–99
Nippur, 69–74, 162
Norman, Craig & Kummel, 487
Norris, Frank, *874–83*
North, Lord, 812
Northern Pacific Railroad, 857, 858–64, 866, 885, 1260–71
Northern Securities Corporation, 1260, 1269–71
Northrop, F. C. S., 2081
"Note on Our Dollar Sign," 682–84
"Novel Enterprise, A," 1013–14
Noyes, Morillo, 289, 290, 292, 294
"No. 1 Shipbuilder" (Piel), 1922–30
Nyströmer, C. Bertil, *61–64, 64–68*

Obligatio, 1970; (*illus.*), 1965
Ockerfo, or the Preachers Oration— A Discourse Upon Usury (Wilson), 1035–37
O'Connor, Charles, 1856

Octavian, Emperor, 175
Odyssey of Homer, 10
"Of Cheating Which Is Committed in Buying and Selling" (Aquinas), 2119–22
Official System of Chou, 2279–80
"Of Negociating" (Bacon), 517–18
"Of the Sin of Usury" (Aquinas), 2122–25
"Of Usury" (Bacon), 1052–55
Ogden, Robert, 1887
Ohmann, O. A., 2109, *2225–55*
Oil, transportation of (*illus.*), 1272, 1273, 1276
Oil Creek Transportation Company, 1277
O'Keefe, *quoted,* 1338
Olcott, Frederic P., 889
Old Country Store, The (Carson), 277–96, 311–15
"Oldest American Business Firm, The" (Gras), 1800
Oldest Code of Laws in the World (Hammurabi), 9
Oldest Code of Laws in the World, The (Johns), 959
Old Lombard Street, 790–94
Olds, R. E., 440–42
"Old Self-Interest, The" (Lloyd), 2346–56
Old-time Steam Cars (Bentley), 1150
Oléron, Laws of, 1290
Oliver Evans (Bathe and Bathe), 1098n., 1988
"On Buying and Selling" (Gibran), 606–07
Once a Week magazine, 399
Once the Hodja (Kelsey), 2512
One Hundred Poems from the Chinese (Rexroth, ed.), 1777
O'Neill, Eugene, 218, *2569–73*
"One Minute Please!" (Benchley), 2596–99
"On Foresight" (Whitehead), 2045–55
"On Luxury, Idleness, and Industry" (Franklin), 2397–2400
Only Yesterday (Allen), 895–933
"On Machinery" (Ricardo), 1447–49
On Our Way (Roosevelt), 1575–77
"On the Compatibility of Intellectual Improvement With the Successful Prosecution of Business" (Bell), 1600–04
On the Principles of Political Economy and Taxation (Ricardo), 1447–48
Opper, *cartoon by,* 2606
Optical shop (*illus.*), 248
Orations of Marcus Tullius Cicero, 78–80
Organization Man, The (Whyte), 1756
"Origins and Establishment of the First Bank of the United States" (Morgan), 711–30
Origo, Iris, *81–88*
Otis & Company, 946
Outline of Man's Knowledge of the Modern World (Bryson, ed.) 1445, 2033
Ouvard, Gabriel Julien, 23
Ovid, *quoted,* 379
Owen, R. S., *2240–41*
Owen, Robert, 23, *1345–49, 1350–52*
Owens, William A., *1132–44*
Owens-Illinois Glass Company, 36
Oyster stand (*illus.*), 253

Pacioli, Luca, *89–115*
Packard, Vance, *637–42,* 645, 2397
Palmer, Edgar, 2361
Palmer, John Horsley, 1603
Palmer, John M., 2359
Palmer, Potter, 28
Palmyra, 180
Papal Encyclicals in Their Historical Context (Fremantle, ed.), 2186
Paris, Mathew, 1033
Parkinson, C. Northcote, *1737–43*
"Parkinson's Law, or the Rising Pyramid" (Parkinson), 1737–43
Parliament, British, 699, 714, 809, 810–11, 821
Parton, James, 433
Pascal, Blaise, 970, 1056
Pasion, the banker, 169
Passage from the Life of a Philosopher (Babbage), 2301
Paterson, William, 23
Path to Riches, The (Sullivan), 692
Patterns (Serling), 1416–38
Peabody, George, 892
Peculiar Case of Protracted Infancy (*illus.*), 2605
Peddlers, 2515–16; (*illus.*), 238, 245, 254
Peirce, James L., *122–36*
Pell, Alfred S., 1007–08, 1009, 1010
Pemberton, Israel, Jr., 987
Pemberton, John Styth, 345–46

Penney, J. C., 2240
Penney Company, J. C., 1574
Pennsylvania Company for Insurances on Lives and Granting Annuities, 993–1001, 1003
Pennsylvania Rock Oil Company of Connecticut, 1127, 1128, 1129, 1130, 1132
Pennsylvania Rock Oil Company of New York, 1124, 1126
Pennsylvania Steel Company, 1384
Pepsi-Cola, 334, 343–44
Pepys, Samuel, 698, 699, 794, 978
Perfect Merchant, The (Savary), 1311–12, 1528–29
"Perfect Salesman—A Complete Guide to Business" (Leacock), 524–28
Perfume merchant (*illus.*), 242
Perkins, George W., 888–89
Perkins, Ruby, 535
Perkins, Thomas Nelson, 40
Permanente Cement Mill, 1928
Perot's Sons Malting Company, 1802
Perregeaux, M., 2401–02
"Personal Note, A" (Mencken), 1920–21
Perssen, Esther, 2245–47
Peters, Hugh, 2515–16
"Petition" (Bastiat), 2296–2301
Petrarch, Francis, 1783
Petty, Sir William, 697
Phelps, Orson, 1822, 1823, 1825, 1837
Philadelphia Contributionship for the Insurance of Houses from Loss by Fire, 987–90
Philadelphia *Public Ledger & Transcript*, 860, 861
Philadelphia waterfront (*illus.*), 1805
Philip II, of Portugal, 689
Philip V, of Spain, 809
Philip Augustus, of France, 359, 1664
Philippa, Queen, of England, 1784
Philip the Fair, of France, 2263
"Philosophy for Advertisers," 455–56
Philosophy of Civilization, The (Schweitzer), 2220–23
Philosophy of Labor (Tannenbaum), 1762–63
Philpot, B., 1280
Phoenicia and the Phoenicians, 163, 164, 165, 178, 179, 581
Physiocrats, 1532
Pickett, H. E., 1280

Piece-of-Eight, 682–83, 684
Piel, Gerard, *1922–30*
Pierpont, Asabel, 1126, 1127, 1128
"Pigs Is Pigs" (*cartoon*), 2614
"Pioneer In American Life Insurance Marketing, The" (Stalson), 992–1001
Pioneering in Big Business 1882–1911 (Hidy and Hidy), 1683
Pipe lines, 1271–80
Piraeus, 168
Pitt, William, 1539, 1540
Plato, 169, *567–70*, 1026, 1506, *1939–44*
Plautus, Titus Maccius, *182–84;* quoted, 790
Pleasant Art of Money-Catching, 2170
Pliny, 1069
Plutarch, *1026–29*
Plutarch's Morals (Plutarch), 1026–29
Plutus, The (Aristophanes), 2495–2502
Pocock, Lewis, 965, 971, 972
Poe, Edgar Allan, *quoted,* 1776
Polignac, Prince Edmond de, 1831
Politics and Economics of Aristotle, The, 14–21
Politics of Aristotle, The (Aristotle), 1944
Polk, James K., 734
Pollock, David, 1602
Pollock, Sir Frederick, 1602
Polo, Marco, 218–30
Polybius, 2108
Pompeii, 354–56, 357, 361–62
Poor Richard's Almanac, 2173
Pope, Alexander, *quoted,* 808
Portable Russian Reader, The (Guerney, ed.), 2183
Portable Voltaire, The, 572–74
Porter, Kenneth Wiggins, *2521–37*
Porter, William Sydney, *see* Henry, O.
Portland, Duke of, 818
Post, C. W., 428–29
Post, Minturn, 1010
Potato standard, putting money on, 761–64
Potter, David M., *2033–45*
Potter, William, 924
Potts, Stephen, 1811
"Power: Liberator or Enslaver?" (Selekman and Selekman), 2213–20

Power and Morality in a Business Society (Selekman and Selekman), 2213
Powers, John E., 436
Pratt, Edwin A., *1247–60*
Pravda, 1210, 1709
Prejudices (Mencken), 1490–91
Presbrey, Frank, *350–60, 363–64,* 399, 1890
Presbyterian Ministers' Fund, 1002, 1005
Presentation Was Bitterly Critical (*illus.*), 2604
Preston, Simon, 771–72
Principles of Scientific Management (Taylor), 1161–79
"Principles of the Former Essays applied to a Particular Situation" (Owen), 1345–49
Prior, Matthew, *quoted,* 3
"Production of Iron and Steel in Its Economic and Social Relations" (Hewitt), 2315–27
Profiles in Courage (Kennedy), 2365
"Progress of Wealth and the Preservation of Order," 1538–41
"Promise of Automation, The" (Drucker), 1513–23
Property: Its Origin and Development (Le Tourneau), 2258
Prophet, The (Gibran), 606–07
"Prospectus of the Society for Establishing Useful Manufactures" (Hamilton), 1095
"Protection Against the Electric Telegraph," 2510–11
Proust, Marcel, 1838
Prutkov, Kosma Petrovich, *2183–84*
Pruyn, John V. L., 1008
"Psychological Foundations: Constructive Conflicts" (Follett), 2013–27
Ptolemy Epiphanes, 351
Publications of the Modern Language Association of America, 1290
Puebla, Mexico, 1586, 1589
Pujol, Araceli, 563, 564, 565
Pullman, George M., 1366–67
Punch, 384–85, 455, *1245–46,* 2508
"Punch's Money Vagaries," 745
Purdy, Ken, 1155
Puritanism, 2138
Pyle, Howard, *213–17*
Pyle, J. G., *quoted,* 1264–65, 1269

Quarterly Journal of Economics, 1055

Quintessence of Capitalism (Epstein, ed.), 1646
Quirin, E. L., *2247–48*
Quo Vadimus? (White), 480–83

R.U.R (*Rossum's Universal Robots*) (Čapek), 1455–85
R-100 and R-101, airships, 1571–72
"Rabbit and the Goat," 2184–85
Rabinowitz, Jacob J., *1029–30*
Radicalism Was Never Absent (*cartoon*), 2616
Radio Corporation of America, 38–42
Radio-Keith-Orpheum Corporation, 42
Railways, American, 1247–60
Raleigh, Sir Walter, 1649, 2141
Ramelli, Agostino, 1102
Ramey, Robert, 1208
Randall, Clarence B., 2233, *2445–47*
Randall, Henry S., 2312
Randolph, Edmund, 727
Random Reminiscences of Men and Events (Rockefeller), 2437–40
Ransom, Barzillan, 1828, 1837
Raskob, John J., 899, 904, 910, 930
Ratner, Victor, 498
Raymond, Irving W., 184, *959–64, 1651–55*
Raymond of Pennaforte, 2126
RCA Photophone, Inc., 42
RCA-Victor Company, Inc., 42
Read, Mr., 1806, 1807
Read, Thomas T., 1507n.
Reading I've Liked (Fadiman, ed.), 1873
"Reappraisal of Values" (Roosevelt), 2369–76
Redlich, Fritz, 1631
Reed, James, 1277
"Relations of the Businessmen of the United States to the National Legislation" (Hill), 2327–41
"Religious Foundations of Economic Progress" (Boulding), 2200–12
Rembrandt, *painting by,* 785
"Reminiscences in Retailing" (Appel), 1884
Renard, Georges, *1656–78*
Reporter, The, 2621
"Reporter at Large—Thaw on Threadneedle Street" (Brooks), 766–77
Report of the Record Commissioners of the City of Boston, 2162
"Report on the Subject of Manufac-

tures" (Hamilton), 1088–94, 1110, 1531
Republic, The (Plato), 567, 1939
"Rerum Novarum," 2186
"Retirement" (Cowper), 1933–34
Reuther, Walter, 1513–14, 1515, 1518
Rexroth, Kenneth, 1777
Rhodes, 171, 180, 183
Rhodes, Ida, 1210, 1212, 1214
Rhodes, John, *2241–43*
Rhodes, Samuel, 987
Ricardo, David, 754, *1447–49*, 2039, 2133
Rice, Elmer, 1444, *1500–05*
Richard II, of England, 236
Richards, Gertrude R. B., 257
Richards, Robert L., 1731
"Rich Merchant by Bookkeeping, The," 119–21
Richmond, Charles, Jr., 1126
Riesman, David, 2229
Risaliti, Bernardo, 257
Rise of Silas Lapham, The (Howells), 1839–54
Roach, John, 1371
Robber Barons, The (Josephson), 1260
Roberts, Hugh, 985, 986, 987
Robinson, Claude, *2247*
Robinson, E. S. G., 76
Robinson, Frank M., 345, 346
Robinson, George Buchan, 912
Robinson, Morris, 1007–08, 1009, 1010
Rockefeller, John D., 28, 930, 1266, 1267, 1516, 1683–84, 2404, *2437–40*; (*illus.*), 2609
Rockefeller, John D., Jr. (*cartoon*), 2610
Rockefeller, William, 1263, 1268, 1271
Roethlisberger, F. J., *1402–13*, 2083
Rogers, *quoted*, 3–4
Rogers, Carl R., *1402–13*, 2083, 2084
Rogers, James E. Thorold, *685–91*
Rogers, Samuel, 1603
Rogers, W. A., 2608; *cartoon by*, 2605, 2607
Romance of Commerce, The (Selfridge), *2440–43*
"Romance of the Busy Broker, The" (O. Henry), 2551–54
"Romance of the Markets, The," 2508–10
Rome and the Romans, 75, 78–80, 166, 168, 172, 174, 176–77, 179–80, 354–57, 678–79, 686, 1525, 1527–

28, 2261–62, 2266–73, 2273–75, 2275–76, 2276–79
Romulo, General Carlos, 340–41
Roosevelt, Franklin D., 1526, 1560, *1575–77*, 2040, *2369–76*
Roosevelt, Theodore, *1560–62*, 2037, 2359, 2374; (*illus.*), 2607; *quoted*, 1642
Root-beer seller (*illus.*), 253
Rosenblueth, Arturo, 1510
Rosetta stone, the, 351
Ross, Douglas, 1211
Rothschild, Carl de, 828
Rothschild, Evelyn de, 773
Rothschild, House of, 858, 885, 886
Rothschild, James de, 838, 841
Rothschild, Nathan de, 836, 838–39, 840, 842; (*illus.*), 835
Rothschild, Solomon de, 838, 841
Rothschild & Son, N. M., 772, 773
Rothschild family, 834–41; (*illus.*), 783
Rotterdam, Holland, 709
Rowe, Ina, 609
Royal Bank of England, 730
Royal Exchange of London, 790, 793
Royal Insurance Company, The, 790
Royal-Liverpool Insurance Group, 791
Royal Society, British, 2301
Rucellai, the, 23
Ruml, Beardsley, *7–8*
Runyan, Damon, 953–54
Rupp, Walter H., *2244–45*
Ruskin, John, 1598–99
Russell, Bertrand, *quoted*, 30
Russell, Oland D., *1791–1800*
Russia and the Russians, 1766–72, 1930–32, 2091, 2094–99, 2387
Rusticiano of Pisa, 218
Ryan, Tom, 884
Ryff, Andreas, 256–57, 1978

Sadymatte, the banker, 170
"Saga of a Salesman" (Henderson), 561–65
Sahagún, Fray Bernardino de, 209
Saint-Exupéry, Antoine de, 1444, *2587–89*
Saki (H. H. Munro), *1921–22*
Salamis, battle of, 179
Sampson, Henry, *369–78*, *382–83*
Sams, Earl C., 1574
"Sam Slick, the Clockmaker" (Haliburton), 518–21
Samson, James, 285

Samuel, Arthur L., 1208, 1212
Sandburg, Carl, 28; *quoted,* 29
San Francisco-to-Oakland Bay Bridge, 1927
San Luis Potosí, Mexico, 1586, 1589
Sarabhai, Sjt. Ambalal, 1439, 1441
Sardis, 170
Sargent, George B., 861
Sarnoff, David, 1777
Saturday Evening Post, The, 759, 1875, 1904, 2573
Saturday Review of Literature, 1855
Savary, Jacques, *1311–12, 1528–29*
"Scattergood Baines—Invader" (Kelland), 1904–20
Scawen, Sir William, 700
Schiff, Jacob H., 861, 887, 1263, 1265–66, 1268, 1271
Schiff, John, 947
Schliemann, Heinrich, 23
Schmeling, Max, 342
Schmidt, Muhlenberg, 997
"Scholastic Economics" (De Roover), 1055–57
Schopenhauer, Arthur, 1103
Schwab, Charles M., 2410
Schwab, David, 1368
Schwarz, Matthäus (*illus.*), 781
Schweitzer, Albert, *2220–23*
Scientific Foundations of Business Administration (Metcalf, ed.), 2013
Scientific management, 1161–79
Scotland, mercantile transactions in, 296–98
Scott, William, *2139–60*
Scovil Manufacturing Company, 291
Script Magazine, 2443
Sears, Roebuck & Company, 315–33
Sears, Roebuck de Mexico, S.A. (Wood and Keyser), 1585–93
Second Bank of the United States, 732–43, 746; (*illus.*), 788
Second Punic War, 176
"Secret of Business Is the Management of Men, The" (Carnegie), 1375–90
Securities and Exchange Commission, 951
Securities Exchange Act (1934), 934
Select Collection of Scarce and Valuable Economical Tracts (McCullough, ed.), 2285
Selected Writings of Abram S. Hewitt (Nevins, ed.), 2315
Selekman, Benjamin M., *2213–20*
Selekman, Sylvia Kopald, *2213–20*

Selfridge, Harry Gordon, *2440–43*
Selfridge, Oliver, 1212
Sell, Henry, 433
Seneca, 797
Seneca Oil Company of Connecticut, 1132
Serling, Rod, *1416–38*
Seventy Years of Life and Labor (Gompers), 1367–74
Sforza, Francesco, 1649
Sforza, Louis, 89
Shakespeare, William, 6, 366, 1037–52; *quoted,* 1, 3, 5, 156, 349, 566, 1720, 1776
Shannon, Claude, 1208, 1213
Sharp, James, 1074
Shasta Dam, 1927–28
Shaw, George Bernard, *1015–22*
Shea, Charlie, 1926
Sheldon, Anson, 1123, 1124, 1126, 1127
Sheperd, Howard, 2240
Sherman, George J., 1280
Sherman, William T., 1114
Sherman & Co., William, 302
Shipman, George P., 1011
Shocking History of Advertising (Turner), 433
Shoemaker, Jacob, 994, 999, 1000
Shoe shop (*illus.*), 243
"Shopping Tour, Early 15th Century, A," 364–65
Sidon, 179
"Significance of Business History, The" (Wohl), 499–502
"Significance of the Jewish Religion in Economic Life" (Sombart), 2197–99
Silliman, Benjamin, Jr., 1123, 1124, 1125
Simmons, George, 305
Simmons, Henry, *1207–14*
Sinclair, Upton, *1390–99*
Singer, Isaac Merritt, 1113, 1819–37, 1838–39
Singer, Mortimer, Jr., 1838
Singer, Paris, 1838
Singer Manufacturing Company, 1835
Sinope, Greece, 678
Six Companies, Inc., The, 1926–27
Sixtus V, Pope, 1103
Slater, Hannah, 1082
Slater, Samuel, 1076–87
Smiley, A. W., 1279
Smith, Adam, 689, 1977, *1981–87,* 1994, 2441

Smith, Alfred E., 902–03, 905
Smith, J. Gregory, 857, 859, 862
Smith, John, 987
Smith, Captain John, 1649
Smith, L. R., 1201n.
Smith, Seba, 288
Smith, Winthrop, 943–44
Smith Corporation, A. O., 1200
Smollett, Tobias, 719
"Social Aims" (Emerson), 1542–45
Social and Cultural Dynamics (Sorokin), 1581
Social Problems of an Industrial Civilization, 1617
Social Thought of the World Council of Churches (Duff), 2224
Society for Establishing Useful Manufactures, 1095–96
Society of Merchant Adventurers of Bristol, 1294
Society of Merchant Adventurers of England, 1295, 1296
Socrates, 1644–46, 1939, 2495
Solomon, 2113
Solon, 179, 2261
Sombart, Werner, 25, *1646–51,* 1886, *2197–99*
"Some Events at the Widow Pratt's" (Bainbridge), 984–90
Sorensen, Charles E., *1156–61*
Soroban, the, 62
Sorokin, Pitirim A., *1581–84*
South Atlantic Quarterly, 2376
Southern Pacific Railroad, 1261
South Sea Act (1717), 809, 823
South Sea Bubble, 719, 807–25, 981, 1774; footnote to, 827–34
South Sea Company, 808–25
"South-Sea House, The" (Lamb), 827–34
Soviet Union, 1185–99; *see also* Russia and the Russians
Spade, Mark (Nigel Balchin), *1400–02, 1719–22; quoted,* 6
Spanish Company, 1294, 1297
Spartan and the Spartans, 168, 176, 179
Spectorsky, A. C., 489
Speers, Wallace C., *2243–44*
Spencer, *cartoon by,* 2610
Spencer, Herbert, *585–90*
Spengler, Oswald, *quoted,* 1444
Speyer, James, 889
Spindletop, 1132–44; (*illus.*), 1134, 1143
Spinola, Ambrogio de, 689

Sponsler, Mary Ann, 1822, 1832, 1833, 1834, 1837, 1839
Square Egg, The (Saki), 1921
Ssŭ-ma Chien, *1953–54*
Stachelberg, Mr., 1373
Stagecoach (*illus.*), 1230
Stagecoach travel, 1225–34
Stalin, Joseph, 6, 1709–11
Stalson, J. Owen, *992–1001*
Standard Oil Trust, 1683–84, 2433–37
Stanhope, Charles, 823, 824
Stanley, Francis E., and Freeland O., 1146–54
Stanley Motor Carriage Company, 1148, 1154
"Stanleys and Their Steamer, The" (Carlova), 1144–55
Staplers, *see* Merchants of the Staple
"Steam Shovel, The" (Tietjens), 1485–87
Ste Croix, G. E. M. de, *74–77*
Steele, Richard, 378; *quoted,* 4
Stein, Gertrude, *759–61*
Steinkraus, Herman, 2240
Stephenson, George, 2428
Stewart, A. T., 301, 304, 305, 306, 307
Stiles, Ezra, 1106
Stinnes, Hugo, 23
Stires, Patience, 1856
Stobie, Margaret R., *1290–92*
Stock exchanges, 794–807, 842–50
Stock market crash of 1929, 918–33
Stoneman, William H., *934–38*
Story of Advertising, The (Wood), 386–95, 502–14
Story of a Stanley Steamer (Woodbury), 1149
Story of My Experiments with Truth (Gandhi), 1439–42
Stowell, Lord, 1602
Strabo, 2262
Stratton, Charles S. (Tom Thumb), 391, 392, 394
Straus & Company, S. W., 1572
Strettel, Amos, 987
Strickland, William, 788
Strieder, Jacob, *1784–90*
Struthers, Thomas, 1276
Strutt, Jedediah, 1076, 1077
Studies in the History of Accounting, 74, 81
Studley, Thomas, 1801–02
Sullivan, James, *692*
Sullivan, John, 716

Sullivan, Stauffer, Colwell & Bayles, 487

Summa de Arithmetica, Geometria, Proporcioni et Proporcionalità (Pacioli), 89–115

Summa Theologica, 2119

Summers, Leland, 2362

Sumner, William G., 733, 2232

Sunderland, Earl of, 812, 823

"Superannuated Man, The" (Lamb), 1338–45

Superior Iron Company, 1384

Swedish Match Company, 935, 936

Swift, Jonathan, *quoted*, 815

Swift, L. F., *1179–80*

Swift & Company, 32–34

Sword-blade Company, 820, 823

"Swordsman and Salesman in the Homeric Age" (Beard), 159–80

Sybaris and the Sybarites, 169–70, 175–76

Syng, Philip, 985, 986, 987, 988

Taciturnitas, 1970; (*illus.*), 1972

Tacitus, *2273–75*

Taft, William Howard, 1891

Taishi, Shuho, 1795–96, 1797

Taken at the Flood (Gunther), 456–66

Talfourd, Serjeant, 1602

Talley, Lee, 343

Talmud, the, 2114–16; *quoted,* 21

Tampico, Mexico, 1586, 1589

Taney, Roger, 732, 735, 739

Tannenbaum, Frank, 1762–63, 1765

Tariff Protection Issues Passionately Drawn (*illus.*), 2604

Tarquin the Proud, 179

Tatler, The, 378–81

Taussig, Frank W., 1555

Tawney, R. H., 1035

Taylor, Frederick W., *1161–79*, 1758, 2225

Taylor, John, 719, 725

Taylor, Myron C., *quoted,* 30

Taylor, N., *quoted,* 6

Taylor, Talbot, 888

Tebbel, John, 759

Temple, Sir William, 696

Tempter, The (Wiener), 1442

Tennyson, Alfred Lord, *quoted,* 1224

Tenterden, Lord, 1602

Teotihuacan, Mexico, 192, 193

Terence, 1527

Texcoco, Mexico, 196

Thackeray, William Makepeace, 574

Thaler, the, 683, 684

Thales of Miletus, 170, 171, 179

Thebes, 168

Thebes, Egypt, 679

Thebeth, Province of, China, 223–25

Theocritus, 681–82

Theory of Business Enterprise, The (Veblen), 2005

Theory of the Leisure Class, The (Veblen), 2005

"Thinking Ahead—Will Businessmen Be Civil Servants?" (Toynbee), 2266–73

Thirty Years' War, 796

This Is My Best (Burnett, ed.), 2055

Thomas, Haab & Botts, 950

Thomas, Norman, 903

Thompson, J. Walter, 487, 489, 491

Thoreau, Henry David, 743, 1526, *1545–54*

Those Were the Good Old Days—A Happy Look at American Advertising, 1880–1930 (Jones), 400–17

"Three American Vices" (Lin Yutang), 1577–80

"Thrivingest People in the World" (Carson), 277–96

Thrupp, Sylvia L., 2139–60

Thurzo, George, 1786

Thurzo, Johann, 1785–88

Tietjens, Eunice, *1485–87*

Tilden, Samuel J., 2411

Tin-gui, China, 226

Titan, The (Dreiser), 1893–1904

Titusville, Pennsylvania, 1120, 1123, 1124, 1127, 1129, 1131, 1132, 1279, 1280

Titusville Pipe Company, 1280

Tlacopan, Mexico, 196

"To a Locomotive in Winter" (Whitman), 1449–50

Tocqueville, Alexis de, 754, *1534–37,* 1594, 1597

" 'Today I must be true or false . . .' Lucius Quintus Cincinnatus Lamar" (Kennedy), 2365–69

"Tom Lachford, Promoter" (Leacock), 2561–68

Tomorrow's Business (Ruml), 7–8

Tom Thumb, General, 391, 392, 394

Tontine, The (Costain), 842–50

Tonto, Lorenzo, 969

Towle, H. Ledyard, 46

Townsend, James M., 1123, 1129, 1130, 1131, 1132

Toynbee, Arnold J., *2266–73*

Travels of Marco Polo, The, 218–30

Treasure Room, 1969; (*illus.*), 1970

Treasurer's Report, The (Benchley), 2596

Treasury of Russian Life and Humor (Cournos, ed.), 1557

Treatise of Cicero, De Officiis (Cicero), 1527–28

Troy Iron and Steel Company, 1384

"True Secret of American Wine Making" (Weller), 1115–19

"Trust, The: An Alliance of Work, Brains and Money" (Flint), 2402–13

Trust, The: Its Book (Bridge, ed.), 2402

Trusts, The (*illus.*), 2605

Truxal, John G., 1209

Tuck School, Dartmouth College, 1555

Tugman, J. C., 2253–55

Tula, Mexico, 193

"Turbine, The" (Monroe), 1488–90

Turgot, A. R. J., 1056

Turner, E. S., *433–34*

Twain, Mark, 2089

"Two Strong-Willed Women" (Russell), 1791–1800

Tyre, 157–59, 178, 179, 581

Ulysses as a merchant, 181–82

"Unbusinesslike Business" (Chesterton), 1562–64

Uncle Sam's Dictum to the Railroads (*cartoon*), 2615

Uncommon Man, The: The Individual in the Organization (Greenwalt), 2469–72

Union Fire Company, 985

Union Pacific Railroad, 863, 1261, 1263, 1271

United Fruit Company, 39

U.S. Investor, 2402–13

United States Steel Corporation, 1385–88

"Universal Drink, The" (Kahn), 334–48

"Unknown Citizen, The" (Auden), 1743–44

Upson, William Hazlett, *2573–86*

"Urban Retailing 100 Years Ago" (Hower), 301–10

Usher, Abbott Payson, 1203, 1204–05, 1206–07

Utopia of Usurers and Other Essays (Chesterton), 1562–64

Van Buren, Martin, 735, 740

Vanderbilt, Cornelius, 2036; (*illus.*), 2613

Vandergrift, Jacob Jay, 1275

Van Mierop, M. K., 975

Van Rensselaer, Philip S., 1008

Van der Rohe, Mies, 487

Van Syckel, Samuel, 1278–79, 1280

Van Werveke, Hans, 2134

Vaughan, Benjamin, 2397

Vduart, Nicolas, 2283

Veblen, Thorstein, 500–01, *2005–10,* 2199–2200

Venetian merchant, 17th-century (*illus.*), 244

Venice and the Venetians, 357, 687–88

Vermont Central Railroad, 853, 858

"Vice of Gambling and the Virtue of Insurance" (Shaw), 1015–22

Victoria, of England, 391

Victor Talking Machine Company, 42

Villard, Henry, 866, 1261, 1264

Villiers, Alan, *1235–44*

Villiers, George, *quoted,* 6

Virgil, *quoted,* 1338

Virginia Company, 1801–02

Vitoria, Francisco de, 2129, 2133

Vladislaw, of Hungary, 1786

Voltaire, *572–74*

Von Neumann, John, 1213

Von Oldenburgh, Count Anthony, 971, 972

Vrable, Edward G., 337

Vyner, Sir Robert, 793

Wakeman, Frederic, 462, *470–80,* 498

Walford, Cornelius, *964–77*

Wallace, DeWitt, 1875

Wallace, Henry A., 2263

Wallace, James N., 889

Wall Street, 867–74, 885

"Wall Street: Men and Money" (Mayer), 938–53

Wall Street Journal, 561, 953

Walpole, Robert, 811–12, 819, 821

Walter, W. Grey, 1208

Walters, Henry, 884–85

Walton, Clarence, *190–212*

Walton, Izaak, *quoted,* 5

Wanamaker, John, 301, 305, 307, 436, 574, 1363–65, 1884–93; *quoted,* 349

Wanamaker, Rodman, 1887

Wanamaker, Thomas B., 1887

Wanamaker's new establishment (1876), (illus.), 1889
Warburg, Paul M., 191
Ward, Barbara, 2227
Ward, William H., 1731
Warner, Jared, 294
Warner, Lloyd, 1761–62, 1763, 1765
Washburn Crosby Company, 607, 608–21
Washington, George, 381–82, 720, 724, 726–27, 728, 1531, 2392–97; quoted, 1642
"Washington as a Business Man and as a Public Figure" (Nettels), 2392–97
Washington Market (N.Y.C.) (illus.), 254
Waist-High Culture, The (Griffith), 1593–99
Waterhouse, Stuart G., 538–41
Waterloo, battle of, 842–50
Watson, Thomas J., 2240
Watt, James, 583, 1539
Wattis, W. H., 1926
"Way to Wealth, The" (Franklin), 2173–84
Wealth Against Commonwealth (Lloyd), 2346
Wealth of Nations, The (Smith), 689, 1981–87
Webb, George, 1811
Weber, Max, 24, 2133
Webster, Daniel, 740, 1108
Webster, Noah, quoted, 4
Weighing House (illus.), 1968
Weir, L. C., 886
Weller, Sidney, 115–19
Welles, Arnold, 1076–87
Wellington, Duke of, 837, 838, 839
Wernette, Philip, 761–64
Wertheim & Company, 949
Westcott, Edward Noyes, 2541–51
Western Health Reform Institute, 422
Westinghouse Electric & Manufacturing Co., 39
Westminster Review, The, 585
Wharton, Duke of, 812
Wharton School, University of Pennsylvania, 1555, 1624
"What Corporation Presidents Think About at Night" (McCaffrey), 2462–69
Wheeler, Albert, 418
Wheeler, John, 1295
Whelen, Israel, 993–94

"While He Is Piling Dung" (Bursk), 2443–44
"Whistles and Shaving Bristles" (Gilbreth and Carey), 1180–82
White, Agnes, 609
White, E. B., 480–83
White, Ellen G. (sister), 419, 420, 422
White, R. H., 306
White, William Allen, 336
Whitehead, Alfred North, 2045–55
Whither Mankind (Beard, ed.), 1505
Whitman, Walt, 1449–50
Whitney, Eli, 1087, 1105–14; (illus.), 1109; first milling machine of (illus.), 1111
Whitney, Richard, 925, 927–30, 931
Whitridge, Arnold, 1105–14
Whyte, William H., Jr., 1756–66
Wiener, Norbert, 1208, 1214, 1442, 1510–13, 1519
Wiggin, Albert H., 924
"Wild Flower Man, The" (Lu Yu), 1777–78
Wiley, Oren, 288, 291
Wilkeson, Samuel, 854
Wilkinson, David, 1083
Wilkinson, Marguerite, 1485–86
Wilkinson, Oziel, 1082
William III, of England, 691, 712
Williams, Calvin and Charles, 1155
Williams, Gluyas, 2617; cartoon by, 2618
Williams, Sir John, 1602
Williams, Roger, 1731, 1732
Williamson, Samuel T., 1156–61
William the Lion, of Scotland, 2281, 2282
Willys, John E., 440
Wilson, A. B., 1825
Wilson, C. H., 709–10
Wilson, Charles E., 2620
Wilson, James, 716
Wilson, Sloan, 489, 1744–56
Wilson, Thomas, 1035–37
Wilson, Woodrow, 38, 39, 40, 41, 1532, 1559, 2360, 2362, 2363, 2364; quoted, 1524
Wilson & Company, 33
Winder, R. McD., 775–76
Wine merchant (illus.), 242
Winkler, John, 1264
Winkler, Max, 906
Winschuh, Josef, 1631–41
Winter's Tale, The (Shakespeare), 366

Winthrop, John, *2162–69*
Wisdom of Confucius, The, 571
Wit and Wisdom of the Talmud (Peters, ed.), 2114
Wohl, Richard, *499–502*
Wolcott, Oliver, 1110, 1112
Wood, James Playsted, *386–95, 502–14*
Wood, Richardson, *1585–93*
Wood, Robert E., *quoted*, 1067
Woodbury, George, 1149
Woodlock, David J., 1574
Woodman, Herbert, 2091, 2094
Woodruff, Robert W., 342
Wool market merchants (*illus.*), 237
"Workers, The" (Masefield), 1399
Works of Lucian of Samosata, The (Fowler, tr.), 2502
Works of William Hogarth, The, 1313
World Council of Churches, 2224
Worldly Philosophers, The (Heilbroner), 256, 1973
World of Mathematics, The (Newman), 1015
World's Work, The, 1375, 2413, 2437
World War I, 1583–84
Wortman, Denys, 2617
Wright, Chester W., 499
Wright, David McCord, 2080

Wright, Richardson, 288, *298–300*
Wright, Wilbur and Orville, 1281–85
Wycliffe, John, 2136
Wynne, R., *quoted*, 379

Xenophanes, 76
Xenophon, *1526–27, 1644–66*
Xenophon's Memorabilia of Socrates, 1644–46

"Yankee Lyric, A" (Peters), 2515–16
Yonge, Charles Duke, 78
Yorke, Samuel, 999
You and I (Monroe), 1485
Young, Loretta, 338
Young, Owen D., 38, 39, 40, 1624–25
Young & Rubicam, 487, 491
"Young Businessmen and Germany's Future" (Winschuh), 1631–41
Young Millwright and Miller's Guide (Evans), 1101
Yourcenar, Marguerite, *2275–76*
Yucatan, 193

Zai-tun, China, 229–30
Zama, battle of, 180
Zane, Jonathan, 987
Zieber, George, 1822, 1823–25, 1828, 1829